The Pacific is an HBO Miniseries presentation of a Playtone and DreamWorks Production Executive Produced by Tom Hanks, Steven Spielberg, and Gary Goetzman, the producing team behind the Emmy® Award–winning and Golden Globe®–winning 2001 HBO miniseries *Band of Brothers*. The epic ten-part miniseries tracks the intertwined journeys of three U.S. Marines—Robert Leckie (James Badge Dale), Eugene Sledge (Joe Mazzello), and John Basilone (Jon Seda)—across the vast canvas of the Pacific during World War II. *The Pacific* follows these men and their fellow marines from their first battle with the Japanese on Guadalcanal, through the rain forests of Cape Gloucester and the strongholds of Peleliu, across the bloody sands of Iwo Jima and through the horror of Okinawa, and finally to their triumphant but uneasy return home after V-J Day.

D0034376

THE
PACIFIC

HUGH AMBROSE

NAL
CALIBER

NAL CALIBER
Published by New American Library, a division of
Penguin Group (USA) Inc., 375 Hudson Street,
New York, New York 10014, USA
Penguin Group (Canada), 90 Eglinton Avenue East, Suite 700, Toronto,
Ontario M4P 2Y3, Canada (a division of Pearson Penguin Canada Inc.)
Penguin Books Ltd., 80 Strand, London WC2R 0RL, England
Penguin Ireland, 25 St. Stephen's Green, Dublin 2,
Ireland (a division of Penguin Books Ltd.)
Penguin Group (Australia), 250 Camberwell Road, Camberwell, Victoria 3124,
Australia (a division of Pearson Australia Group Pty. Ltd.)
Penguin Books India Pvt. Ltd., 11 Community Centre, Panchsheel Park,
New Delhi - 110 017, India
Penguin Group (NZ), 67 Apollo Drive, Rosedale, Auckland 0632,
New Zealand (a division of Pearson New Zealand Ltd.)
Penguin Books (South Africa) (Pty.) Ltd., 24 Sturdee Avenue,
Rosebank, Johannesburg 2196, South Africa

Penguin Books Ltd., Registered Offices:
80 Strand, London WC2R 0RL, England

Published by NAL Caliber, an imprint of New American Library, a division of Penguin Group (USA) Inc.
Previously published in an NAL Caliber Hardcover edition.

First NAL Caliber Trade Paperback Printing, September 2011
10 9 8 7 6 5 4 3

NAL CALIBER and the "C" logo are trademarks of Penguin Group (USA) Inc.

NAL CALIBER TRADE PAPERBACK ISBN: 978-0-451-23225-0

THE LIBRARY OF CONGRESS HAS CATALOGED THE HARDCOVER EDITION OF THIS TITLE AS FOLLOWS:

Ambrose, Hugh.
The Pacific/Hugh Ambrose.
p. cm.
Companion book to the television miniseries.
ISBN 978-0-451-23023-2
1. World War, 1939–1945—Campaigns—Pacific Area. 2. Marines—United States—Biography. 3. United States. Marine
Corps—Biography. 4. United States. Marine Corps—History—World War, 1939–1945. I. Pacific (Television program)
II. Title.
D767.9.A46 2010
940.54'59730922—dc22 2009041530

Set in Adobe Jansen
Designed by Patrice Sheridan

Printed in the United States of America

THE PACIFIC

STEPHEN E. AMBROSE

IN MEMORIAM

1936–2002

Hey Dad,

I was lucky

to be your son

and proud

to be your partner.

Acknowledgments

THE STORY OF HOW THIS BOOK CAME TO BE WRITTEN BEGINS WITH MY FATHER, the historian Steve Ambrose. He called me in 1992, as I completed the course work for my master's degree in American history, asked if I "could do some research for him," then said the magic words "I'll pay you." In the course of that research, for a book entitled *Undaunted Courage*, we were both surprised and delighted to find we enjoyed working together. As the years passed and the number and variety of projects increased, my father generously allowed me a greater role as his researcher, agent, and fund-raiser for nonprofits. We had a ball.

After we completed his book on America's first transcontinental railroad, I suggested a book on the D-days of the Pacific War. It was hardly an original idea, given the enormous success of his book on D-day in Normandy. He said, "Let's do it." In the course of developing a new collection of original stories, our work came to the attention of my father's friend the director Steven Spielberg. Steven was also interested in developing a story on the Pacific War. Working in tandem with this great filmmaker led to a number of exciting and unanticipated developments, chief of which was the documentary *Price for Peace*. Dad and I were both so proud of our involvement in this film, directed by James Moll.

When my father became ill, he decided he could not finish a book on the war against Japan. "It's just too big," he said. He asked me to finish it. After he passed away in 2002, I was not sure how I would accomplish such a feat until I received a call from Steven Spielberg in early 2003. Steven and his friends Tom Hanks and Gary Goetzman had decided that the Pacific War needed to be told in a manner similar to their miniseries with HBO, *Band of Brothers*. It needed to be representative of the entire experience and it needed to connect the greatest battles. Steven (through his company DreamWorks) and Tom and Gary (through theirs, Playtone) had engaged the screenwriter Bruce McKenna to develop the story of the war in Japan. I was hired to help Bruce, who had written episodes of *Band of Brothers*, and his team of writers find the stories for the miniseries. Once again, great good fortune had called me, and I gratefully accepted, with alacrity. We faced a big challenge. The war against Japan was more complex than the one in Europe. All of America's military services played key roles in many different battles in different countries. Finding a narrative thread to connect a representative sampling of those battles was not easy.

Bruce already had begun to do some reading and spoke to me about two books that he loved: E. B. Sledge's *With the Old Breed* and Robert Leckie's *Helmet for My Pillow*. I took this as a good sign. He had identified two of the most important memoirs about the Pacific War. They differed not only in where and when the authors had served, but also in how the men had responded to their experiences. Upon request, I put him in touch with the Sledge family. The Sledges expressed interest in the project and put Bruce in touch with Dr. Sidney Phillips. By the time Bruce called me back, he was ecstatic. Dr. Sidney Phillips had served in the same company with Robert Leckie and was one of Eugene's best friends. Bruce had found a way to connect the first battle in the war with the last battle. Dr. Phillips had already written a splendid memoir of his service entitled *You'll Be Sor-ree!* The story of John Basilone was added to the mix later, when we found the moment of happenstance that connected John Basilone to Phillips and Leckie. That connection allowed the miniseries to include "Manila John," a unique individual with a different set of important experiences.

DreamWorks and Playtone brought their vision of a miniseries, covering a vast sweep of the war as seen through the eyes of a few fascinating men, to the only place to realize their vision, HBO. With HBO on board, "the stars had aligned," so far as Bruce and I were concerned. While the show's producers supervised Bruce and his team as they developed the miniseries, I continued to conduct original research on those aspects that needed further illumination. Many other stories were explored during the course of several years as we strove to leave no stone unturned. Working for the writers and producers of *The Pacific* has been a fabulous experience for me. Their love for the men and women who served America so magnificently was apparent from the first day. One part of a huge process, I learned so much about storytelling from Steven, Tom, Gary, and Bruce, as well as from other key figures of the project, like Tony To and Tim Van Patten.

The stories for the miniseries were eventually chosen by the producers. I had, in the meantime, become excited about two other characters, Austin "Shifty" Shofner and Vernon "Mike" Micheel. Although E. B. Sledge mentioned Austin Shofner in his book, I paid Shofner little attention until I came in contact with Colonel Otto Melsa, a veteran himself and a big fan of Shofner. His enthusiasm encouraged me to learn more. Similarly, I wish to thank Arnold Olson, a veteran of USS *Enterprise* and one of the founders of the Web site www.cv6.org. Olson did not know me from Adam, but he kindly gave me contact information for a number of fascinating navy pilots, including Vernon "Mike" Micheel. The more I learned about Mike and Shifty, the more I felt that their stories fit perfectly with the others. An idea for a companion book began to take shape.

As a huge fan of Dr. Sidney Phillips, I felt privileged to spend a weekend with him (those of us who are truly blessed get to drink a beer and smoke a cigar with him). At one point in our interview, he mentioned that his friend John Wesley "Deacon" Tatum had kept a daily diary. Mr. Tatum allowed me to use his diary, which is a truly amazing document. It allowed us to tell the story of the Battle of Guadalcanal at a new level of intimacy. For the Basilone story, his niece Diane Hawkins allowed us full access to the Basilone Family Collection of material relating to her uncle. This treasure trove of untapped information, along with the material gathered in the Basilone Reading Room of the Raritan Public Library and the support of Basilone's friends (Richard Greer, Clinton Watters, Chuck Tatum, Barbara Garner, and others), helped us find the real John Basilone. The final pieces of the puzzle came when I visited the Special Collections and Archives of Auburn University. Dwayne Cox and his assistant John Varner were both generous and efficient. The papers of Eugene Sledge revealed more about him and about King Company.

After all the pieces came together, I saw a new vision for this book. Originally, I had envisioned the companion book to be written similar to the way my father wrote his book *D-Day*. I would weave together the stories of hundreds of veterans into an organic whole. I had amassed a collection of new research capable of sustaining such a book. In light of the amazing history assembled by the producers and writers of *The Pacific*, and armed with new research, I decided to try something else. I would use the connections between the veterans to relate key parts of the war not found in the miniseries. For instance, the war could not have been won without the U.S. carrier fleet and its naval aviators. Seeing something of the type of empire that Japan's leadership strove to create was also important. While a book can explore a much larger territory than a ten-hour miniseries, there is still a limit to the number of stories a reader can be expected to track through the vast conflict. To add the battles of Bataan and Midway, therefore, I needed to cut one of the characters depicted in the miniseries. It was a difficult choice. Ultimately I decided that there was relatively little I could add to Leckie's own extraordinary firsthand account and that the loss of Leckie's voice, while unfortunate, would allow the book to remain an effective companion to the miniseries as well as encompass more of the ocean of enmity we call the Pacific War. The vision for this book is more properly described in the following introduction. I would like to thank Steven Spielberg and my friends at Playtone, as well as Kary Antholis and James Costos of HBO for allowing me to deepen *The Pacific.*

In all the years of research, I have had so many kind people help me. Time and space, alas, prevent me from mentioning them all. Here is the short version. The families of the four men who had passed away by the time my work began (Basilone, Sledge, Leckie, and Shofner) have helped me immeasurably. I was lucky to interview Phillips and Micheel at length and to have the full cooperation of the Shofner family, particularly Stewart, Alyssa, and William "Wes" Shofner. I would like to express my gratitude to Vera Leckie, Joan Salvas, and the other members of the family of Robert Leckie. They all went to great lengths to help us tell the story of Lucky Leckie in the miniseries. The family of Dr. Eugene Sledge—Mrs. Jeanne Sledge and her sons, John and Henry—extended to Bruce, me, and the rest of the crew every kindness and gave of themselves to help us understand him. I have so enjoyed the time I spent with all of them. I hope that what the veterans and their families read below justifies their faith in me.

The 1st Marine Division Association provided me with the opportunity to find the men who had served with the five individuals in this book, and the interviews with these men have made all the difference. The United States Marine Corps, whether through its Historical Division or its Motion Picture & TV Liaison Office, has answered many an odd question from me. The Battle of Midway Roundtable (BOMRT), an online conversation between the veterans of Midway, the historians and experts on the battle, and hundreds of fans, taught me a great deal about it. The roundtable continues to extend our knowledge of this critical event in a spirit of cooperation. To me, the BOMRT represents the promise of the Internet fulfilled. I also gratefully acknowledge the help of Judy Johnson, who leads the team of archivists at Georgia Tech; of Hill Goodspeed, a historian with the National Museum of Naval Aviation; and of my good friend Tom Czekanski of the National WWII Museum.

I would like to thank the President and CEO of The National WWII Museum, Dr. Gordon H. "Nick" Mueller, for allowing me to continue on with the museum on a part-time basis these past few years. I have been the beneficiary of a positive synergy.

As I have been able, I have hired people for short periods of time to help with some of the legwork of research: transcribing interviews, scanning documents and the like. I would like to thank: Julie Mitchell, Kirt Garcia, Rob Lynn, Beth Crumley, Robert Carr, Kristin Paridon, Seth Paridon, Dustin Spence (who found Barbara Garner), David Zeiler, Lacey Middlestead, Jonathan Wlasiuk, Warren Hower, and Kevin Morrow. Dick Beilen of the U.S. Locator Service provided the copies of the military records I needed and is a great guy to work with. I also thank my team of experts: attorney Mike McMahon, accountant Mike Lopach, and agent Brian Lipson, who stuck with me through a lot of lean years.

The team at Penguin/NAL immediately grasped my idea for the book and supported it enthusiastically. In particular, I offer my thanks to Natalee Rosenstein and Michelle Vega for making every effort to help me succeed.

A number of friends and acquaintances have helped me in a variety of ways in the long process of writing the book. I would like to thank James Moll for his sage advice. I am grateful to Kristie Macosko for the many kindnesses she has extended to me. I wish to thank my graduate advisor, Dr. Michael Mayer of the University of Montana, who has been such a great teacher and mentor to me. His review of the first half of the manuscript meant a great deal to me. I'd like to thank the historians Colonel Joseph Alexander, Colonel Jon T. Hoffman, Dr. Donald Miller, Augustine Meaher IV, Alf Batchelder, Eric Hammel, Dr. Allan Millett, and Barrett Tillman for allowing me to gain from their knowledge. I would like to thank Barry Zerby of the National Archives and John Heldt, reference librarian for the Lewis and Clark County Library, for speeding me on my way toward the documents. My friend Martin K. A. Morgan, a talented military historian, has helped me in numerous ways, including drawing the small map inserts. My friends John Schuttler and Kate Cholewa each read an early draft of the first section; their advice and encouragement were appreciated. John also did some research for me. Lou Reda of Lou Reda Productions, assisted by Greg Miller, provided me with transcripts of interviews with Eugene Sledge. The volunteers at the National WWII Museum alerted me whenever a veteran of Iwo Jima passed through the door. John Innes, nicknamed "Our Man in Honiara" by Bruce McKenna, has twice taken me across the battlefields of Guadalcanal, which he knows by heart. Tangie Hesus has twice toured me around Peleliu. Chris Majewski is the "tunnel rat" par excellence who has twice driven me around Okinawa. I also need to thank Commander Jack Hanzlik of the United States Navy, who arranged for Bruce and me to "catch a hook" aboard USS *Ronald Reagan*, spend an evening with her impressive crew, and catapult off her flight deck the next day. Wow.

The experiences we had retracing the battles and the research we conducted have left an indelible mark upon all of us involved. The war against Japan, although part of World War II, was distinct from that waged against Germany. America's victory changed the world. It enabled human civilization to advance. Combat in the Pacific exacted a high price from the men who won it. That cost startled us at every turn. We are grateful to all of the men and women who paid it. We endeavor to honor them by presenting as much of their story as we could, as honestly as we could.

My mother, Moira Buckley Ambrose, read the first draft of the first section of this work. Her encouragement and suggestions meant everything to me. Had she lived to read the full draft, this would be a better book. I treasure my memories of her. May she rest in peace with her beloved husband, Steve.

I conclude this acknowledgment of my gratitude with the most important person of all, Andrea Ambrose. My beautiful and talented wife is my partner in all things. We made the long journey we call *The Pacific* together. I am a lucky guy.

Introduction

HUNDREDS OF GREAT BOOKS HAVE BEEN WRITTEN ABOUT THE PACIFIC WAR. THE majority of these volumes fall into one of three categories: a book about the war in general; a book that illuminates every detail of a single battle or important aspect; or a book by a veteran about his experiences. While all of these have their place in the historiography of such an important event, there is room for one more.

The goal of *The Pacific* is to take the reader through the Pacific War, from first to last, through the eyes of a select few of the men who fought it. In this way, the reader enjoys the immediacy of the individual narrative, but sees the war as a whole. To achieve this goal, the five stories included here were chosen because they are representative of the experience. Between these men, they fought many of the great battles of the Pacific War. The coincidences and relationships that connect the five men allow their experiences to arrive in the context within which they occurred. The historical perspective emerges in a variety of ways. After carefully choosing the right stories, and developing them to their fullest, the author has chosen to provide only a thin skein of omniscience. Given its goal, this work is self-evidently not a definitive history of the entire war or even of the battles that it covers.

Attempting to tell the story of individuals is fraught with perils. Sources contradict one another. The fog of war leaves mistaken impressions. The fog of time increases these misapprehensions. The documents are incomplete, sometimes inaccurate, and always more revealing of the aggregate experience than that of the individual. Relying on the letters, reports, and journals written during the war, though, solves most of these problems.

History books relate what happened. This work focuses on what the men thought was going to happen, what they endured or witnessed, and what they believed had happened. Determining what someone thought at a particular time, before their understanding was shaped later by new information, is highly problematical. Contemporaneous accounts remain the best source. These accounts form the basis of this book. For reasons that will become obvious, I chose not to distinguish between remarks made at the time and those made many years later. Instead, I took great care to prevent the rosy glow of memory from obscuring the facts.

The diaries, letters, and reports of Austin Shofner, Sid's friend John "Deacon" Tatum, John Basilone, and Eugene Sledge are new to the war's scholarship. They are rare and extremely valuable documents. They have made possible the vivid and unrelenting stories told herein. They also offer new insights and new information on key events and important individuals, as the avid military historians will discern.

The basis of research for four of the individuals whose lives appear in this book (Sidney Phillips, Austin Shofner, Vernon Micheel, and Eugene Sledge) amounts to a core group of documents: their respective military records, letters, journals, memoirs, memoirs of friends, photos, and interviews. Since this book intends to tell the story of these men in their words as much as possible, these sources are quoted and paraphrased liberally (except in the case of Eugene Sledge's memoir). In order to make the endnotes of this book less cumbersome, these sources will be cited in the first endnote of each story, in a "super endnote." The additional material used will be cited in the text as necessary. The story of the fifth veteran, on the other hand, could not be handled in this manner. John Basilone's story was pulled together from a hundred different sources, none of which offers more than a piece of the whole.

The Cast

The vast and complex war against Japan can be understood by following five individuals through it. On the day the Pacific War began, they were (in order of appearance):

Lieutenant Austin C. "Shifty" Shofner—the scion of a prominent family with a long record of military service, he considered himself a professional marine. He had seen the barbarity of Japanese occupation up close and looked forward to leading men in combat.

Ensign Vernon "Mike" Micheel—the prospect of being drafted had forced him to leave the family farm and complete the navy's flight school in the fall of 1941. The challenge of being a naval aviator deepened at every turn.

Sidney C. Phillips—the easygoing teenager went down to enlist when the war started because his buddy William "W. O." Brown said they should do it. They thought they would join the navy because Mobile, Alabama, was a navy town.

Sergeant "Manila John" Basilone—the son of immigrants had found happiness in the rough-and-ready life of a marine. Having previously served overseas, John had already experienced America's postcolonial foreign policy. He thought it was worth fighting for.

Eugene B. Sledge—the serious, intelligent son of a famous doctor, he watched as his best friend, Sidney Phillips, enlisted without him. The sight mortified him. For a year he deferred to his parents, who insisted that his elder brother Edward's service would represent the family's contribution to the war effort.

Robert "Lucky" Leckie—viewers of the HBO miniseries *The Pacific* will note that one of the miniseries's central characters, Robert Leckie, appears briefly in this text. Viewers will also notice that this volume features two men, Austin Shofner and Vernon Micheel, who are absent from the miniseries. The explanation can be found in the imperatives of print versus those of film. While the book and the miniseries share a core story, they are different mediums. Each must do what it does best.

ACT I

"HOUSE OF CARDS"

December 1941–June 1942

As the 1930s gave way to the 1940s, the people of the United States thought little of the Empire of Japan. Americans worried about their economy, which had wallowed on the brink of collapse for a decade, and wished to stay out of the world's problems. The speed at which Nazi Germany had come to dominate Europe had, however, provided President Franklin Roosevelt with enough political capital to take a few steps toward preparing the country to defend itself. Roosevelt and his military leadership also opposed the Japanese drive to dominate vast stretches of China. The Japanese government, ruled by a military cabal that included Emperor Hirohito, had created an ideology to justify its colonial conquest and built a military to enact it. Japan obviously intended to seize other valuable areas along the Pacific Rim. The United States controlled some of these valuable areas and it expected to keep the region open to trade. Roosevelt endeavored to curb Japan's expansion by a series of economic and diplomatic measures backed up by the U.S. military—the smallest and least-equipped force of any industrialized nation in the world.

First Lieutenant Austin Shofner woke up expecting enemy bombers to arrive overhead any second. Just after three a.m. his friend Hugh had burst into the cottage where he was sleeping on the floor and said, "Shof, Shof, wake up. I just got a message in from the CinCPAC saying that war with Japan is to be declared within the hour. I've gone through all the Officer of the Day's instructions, and there isn't a thing in there about what to do when war is declared."[1] With the enemy's strike imminent, Lieutenant Shofner took the next logical step. "Go wake up the old man."

"Oh," Hugh replied, "I couldn't do that." Even groggy with sleep, Shofner understood his reluctance. The chain of command dictated that Lieutenant Hugh Nutter report to his battalion commander, not directly to the regimental commander. Speaking to a colonel in the Marine Corps was like speaking to God. The situation required it though. "You damn fool, get going, pass the buck up." At this Hugh took off running into the darkness surrounding the navy base on the Bataan Peninsula in the Philippines.

Shofner followed quickly, running down to the docks, where the enlisted men were billeted in an old warehouse. He saw Hugh stumble into a hole and fall, but he didn't stop to help. The whistle on the power station sounded. The sentry at the main gate began ringing the old ship's bell. The men were already awake and shouting when Shofner ran into the barracks and ordered them to fall out. The bugler sounded the call to arms. Someone ordered the lights kept off, so as not to give the enemy's planes a target.

His men needed a few minutes to get dressed and assembled. Shofner ran to find the cooks and get them preparing chow. Then he went to find his battalion commander. Beyond the run-down warehouse where his men bunked, away from the rows of tents pitched on the rifle range where others were billeted, stood the handsome fort built by the Spanish. Its graceful arches had long since been landscaped, so Shofner darted up the road lined by acacia trees to a pathway bordered by brilliant red hibiscus and gardenias.[2] He found some of the senior officers of the Fourth Marine Regiment sitting together.* They had received word from Admiral Hart's headquarters sixty miles away in Manila that the Japanese had bombed Pearl Harbor. Their calmness surprised him.

Shofner should not have been taken aback. Every man in the room had been expecting war with the Empire of Japan. They had thought the war would start somewhere else, most likely in China. Up until a week ago, their regiment had been based in Shanghai. They had watched the emperor's troops steadily advance in China over the past few years as more and more divisions of the Imperial Japanese Army landed. The Japanese government had established a puppet government to rule a vast area in northern China it had renamed Manchukuo.

The Fourth Marines, well short of full strength at about eight hundred men, had been in no position to defend its quarter of Shanghai, much less protect U.S. interests in China. The situation had become so tense the marine officers concocted a plan in case of a sudden attack. They would fight their way toward an area of China not conquered by Japan. If the regiment was stopped, its men would be told essentially to "run for your life."[3] The officers around the table this morning were thankful the U.S. government finally had yielded to the empire's dominance and pulled them out in late November 1941, at what now looked like the last possible moment.

Upon their arrival at Olongapo Naval Base on December 1, the Fourth Marines became part of Admiral Hart's Asiatic Fleet, whose cruisers and destroyers were anchored in Manila Harbor, on the other side of the peninsula from where they were sitting. Along with the fleet, U.S. forces included General Douglas MacArthur's 31,000 U.S. Army troops as well as the 120,000 officers and men of the Philippine National Army. Hart and MacArthur had been preparing for war with the Empire of Japan for years. The emperor must have been nuts to attack the U.S. Pacific Fleet in Pearl Harbor. Now that he had, his ships and planes were sure to be on their way here, to the island of Luzon, which held the capital of the Philippine government

---

*The reader's convenience, not military practice, guides the nomenclature used here to identify military units.

CABANATUAN ⊙

□CAMP O'DONNELL

N

Philippine Sea

⊙OLONGAPO

B
A
T
A
A
N

Manila Bay

⊙MANILA

South China Sea

CORREGIDOR

20 miles

★ LUZON ★

Martin K. A. Morgan

and the headquarters of the U.S. forces. The enemy's first strike against them, the officers agreed, would likely be by bombers flying off Formosa.*

With all this strategic talk, Shofner could see that no orders were in the offing, so he went back to his men. His headquarters company had assembled on the parade ground along with the men from the infantry companies. The word being passed around was succinct: "japs blew the hell out of Pearl Harbor." He confirmed the news not with fear, but with some relish. Lieutenant Austin "Shifty" Shofner of Shelbyville, Tennessee, had always loved a good fight. Of medium height but robust of build, he loved football, wrestling, and gambling of any kind. He did not think much of the Japanese. He told his men that an attack was expected any moment. Live ammunition would be issued immediately. Next came a sly grin. "Our play days are now over and we can start earning our money."[4]

The marines waited on the parade ground until the battalion commander arrived to address them. All liberties were canceled. The regimental band was being dissolved, as was the small detachment of marines that manned the naval station

---

*Formosa is now known as Taiwan.

when the Fourth Marines arrived. These men would be formed into rifle platoons, which would then be divided among the rifle companies.[5] Every man was needed because they had to defend not only Olongapo Naval Station, but another, smaller one at Mariveles, on the tip of the Bataan Peninsula. The 1st Battalion drew the job of protecting Mariveles. It would depart immediately.

The departure decreased the regiment by not quite half, leaving it the 2nd Battalion, Shofner's headquarters and service company, and a unit of navy medical personnel. The riflemen got to work creating defensive positions. They dug foxholes, emplaced their cannons, and strung barbed wire to stop a beach assault. They located caches of ammunition in handy places and surrounded them with sandbags. Defending Olongapo also meant protecting the navy's squadron of long-range scout planes, the PBYs. When not on patrol these flying boats swung at their anchors just off the dock. The marines positioned their machine guns to fire at attacking planes. Roadblocks were established around the base, although this was not much of a job since the only civilization nearby was the small town of Olongapo.

The men put their backs into the work. Every marine had seen the Japanese soldiers in action on the other side of street barricades in Shanghai. They had witnessed how brutal and violent they were to unarmed civilians. Most of them had heard what the Japanese had done to the people of Nanking. So they knew what to expect from a Japanese invasion. Shofner felt a twinge of embarrassment that these preparations had waited until now. The biggest exercise undertaken since their arrival had been a hike to a swimming beach. Shofner thought back to the day before, December 7, when he had spent the entire day looking for a spot to show movies. He let those thoughts go. His assignment was to create a bivouac for the battalion away from the naval station. The enemy's bombers were sure to aim for the warehouses and the fort. As noon on the eighth approached, he moved with the alacrity for which he was known. He took his company across the golf course, forded a creek, and began setting up camp in a mangrove swamp.

ON THE OTHER SIDE OF THE INTERNATIONAL DATE LINE, THE AFTERNOON OF December 7 found Ensign Vernon "Mike" Micheel of the United States Navy preparing to do battle with the Imperial Japanese Navy. He carried a sheaf of papers in his hands as he walked around the navy's air station in San Diego, known as North Island. Despite the frenzy around him, Mike moved with deliberate haste. He stopped at the different departments on the base: the Time Keeper, the Storeroom Keeper, the Chief Flight Instructor, and so forth, endeavoring to get his paperwork in order.

A few hours before he and the other pilots of his training group, officially known as the Advanced Carrier Training Unit (ACTU), had been told that the Japanese bombed Pearl Harbor. Their pilot training was being cut short. They would board USS *Saratoga* immediately and go to war.

The Sara, as her crew called her, could be seen from almost anywhere Mike walked. She was the navy's largest aircraft carrier and towered over North Island, the collection of landing strips and aircraft hangars on the isthmus that formed San Diego Harbor. She was the center of attention, surrounded by cranes and gangways. Several squadrons, which included maintenance personnel as well as the pilots, gunners, and airplanes, were being loaded aboard. Most of these crews had been scheduled to board the Sara today. The big fleet carrier had been refitted in a shipyard up the coast and, strangely, arrived a few minutes before the declaration of war.[6] But new guys like Mike had had no such expectation.

Micheel prepared himself for active duty without the burning desire for revenge on the sneaky enemy to which most everyone around him pledged themselves. He knew he wasn't ready. He had not landed a plane on a carrier. Most of his flight time had been logged in biplanes. He had flown some hours in single-wing metal planes, but he had only just begun to fly the navy's new combat aircraft. Even when the Sara's torpedo defense alarm sounded and an attack appeared imminent, it was not in Mike's nature to let anger or ego overwhelm his assessment.[7]

Mike did not consider himself a natural pilot. He had not grown up making paper planes and following the exploits of pioneers like Charles Lindbergh. In 1940, the twenty-four-year-old dairy farmer went down to the draft board and discovered that he would be drafted in early 1941. If he enlisted, he could choose his service. His experiences in the ROTC, which had helped pay for college, had instilled in him a strong desire to avoid sleeping in a pup tent and eating cold rations. On a tip from a friend, he sought out a navy recruiter. The recruiter assured him that life in the navy was a whole lot better than in the infantry, but then he noticed Mike's college degree. "You know, we've got another place that you would fit, and that would be in the navy air corps. . . . It's the same thing as being on the ship with the regular navy people, but you get paid more."

"Well, that sounds good," Mike replied without enthusiasm. He had ridden on a plane once. "It was all right. But I wasn't thrilled about it." The recruiter, like all good recruiters, promised, "Well, you can get a chance to try it. If you don't like it, you can always switch back to the regular navy."

More than a year later, Mike arrived at North Island with a mission that placed him at the forefront of modern naval warfare. When civilians noticed the gold wings on his dress uniform, they usually assumed that he was a fighter pilot. The nation's memories of World War I were laced with the stories of fighter pilots dueling with the enemy across the heavens at hundreds of miles an hour. That heady mix of glamour and prestige also had fired the imaginations of the men with whom Mike had gone through flight training. Each cadet strove to be the best because only the best pilots became fighter pilots. When they graduated from the Naval Flight School at Pensacola, the new ensigns listed their preferred duty.

Though he had graduated in the top quarter of his class, and been offered the chance to become an instructor, Ensign Micheel listed dive-bomber as his top choice. While few had heard of it before their training, the dive-bomber was also a carrier-based plane. It served on the front line of America's armed forces. Instead of knocking down the enemy's planes, its mission was to find the enemy's ships and sink them. Mike wanted to fly from a carrier. In his usual quiet way he figured out that the surest way for him to become a carrier pilot was to become a dive-bomber. Many of his fellow classmates had listed fighter pilot as their first choice. Most of them would later find themselves behind the yoke of a four-engine bomber. Although officially ordered to a scouting squadron, he essentially received his first choice. Scouts and bombers flew the same plane and shared the same mission. Mike came to North Island to improve his navigation enough to be a great scout, but also to learn the art of destroying ships, especially enemy carriers.

Now he filed his paperwork and walked to the Bachelor Officers' Quarters to pack his bags without once having attempted the difficult maneuver of dive-bombing. As the sun set, a blackout order added to the confusion and tension. Men who had been on liberty or on leave continued to arrive, full of questions. Micheel and the other new pilots headed for the Sara and the moment they had been working toward. They boarded an aircraft carrier for the first time. Every space was being crammed with every pilot, mechanic, airplane, bullet, and bomb that could be had. Rumors ran wild. The new pilots found their way to officer country, the deck where officers' staterooms were located.

The loading went on through the night, without outside lights. Then dawn broke. The Sara stood out from North Island just before ten a.m. on December 8. The clang of the ship's general quarters alarm sounded minutes later. Before she departed, however, calmer heads had prevailed. Micheel and the other trainees had been ordered off. As the great ship headed for open sea, those watching her from the dock would have assumed the Sara and her escort of three destroyers were headed straight into combat.

Monday's newspapers carried the story of the "Jap attack on Pearl Harbor" as well as warnings from military and civilian leaders that an attack on the West Coast was likely. It fell to the servicemen of North Island to defend San Diego. The detachment of marines on the base began digging foxholes, setting up their guns, and protecting key buildings with stacks of sandbags. The airmen hardly knew how to prepare. The Sara had taken all of the combat planes assigned to Mike's training unit. All they had to fly were the ancient "Brewster Buffalo" and the SNJ, nicknamed the "Yellow Peril" because of its bright color and the inexperienced students who flew it.

FIRST THING MONDAY MORNING, DECEMBER 8, SIDNEY PHILLIPS RODE HIS BIKE down to Bienville Square in the center of town and met his pal William Oliver Brown, as agreed. They walked over to the Federal Building, which housed the re-cruiting offices of all the service branches. The line of men waiting to enlist in the navy stretched from the navy recruiting office, through the lobby, out the door, down the steps, down St. Georgia Street to the corner, and down St. Louis Street for half a block.[8] Mobile, Alabama, was a navy town. The angry men in the line would have spat out the word "japs" frequently. Not the types to simply take their places behind this crowd, Sid and William, whom everybody called "W.O.," walked up to the head of the line to see what was going on. A Marine Corps recruiter spied the two teen-agers, walked over, and asked, "You boys want to kill Japs?"

"Yeah," Sidney said, "that's the idea."

"Well, all you'll do in the navy is swab decks." The recruiter explained that if they wanted to kill "japs" they had to join the marines. "I guarantee you the Marine Corps will put you eyeball to eyeball with them." Neither Sid nor W.O. had ever heard about the marines beyond the name. They were not alone, which explained why the recruiter worked the crowd. The recruiter told them that the marines were part of the navy, in fact "the best part." Then he tried a different tack: mischief. "You can't get in the navy anyway. Your parents are married." Sid laughed out loud. He looked at W.O. and could see he was thinking the same thing. The marines might be their kind of outfit. But neither could sign up on the spot; as seventeen-year-olds, they had to bring the papers home and get their parents' signatures. A cursory fit-ness test also revealed that Sidney's color perception was impaired. Not to worry, the recruiter said, the color test will likely be changed soon. He told Sid to come back after Christmas. W.O. said he was willing to wait.

Sid went home and found that getting his parents' permission was a bit tougher than he had anticipated. His mother had two brothers in the navy—Joe Tucker was a pilot stationed in Pearl Harbor—and she felt that was enough. His father, the principal of Murphy High School, expected his son to be drafted soon, however. Young men were already being drafted and on this day President Roosevelt had declared war on Japan officially. But there was something else. The threat was real. Sid's father had served in World War I. He had raised his two children to love their country enough to protect it. When his only son stepped forward, he could not say no.

While his parents' discussion had only just begun, Sid figured his father would bring his mom around in time for him to go with W.O. However, it did not look like Sid's other best friend would be joining them. Eugene Sledge wanted to sign up, too, but his parents forbade him. Eugene had to finish high school. Eugene had a heart murmur. His brother had joined the army. Eugene's dad had lots of reasons. None satisfied his youngest son. Like Sid, Eugene felt a duty to serve. It came in part because of the sneak attack. His sense of duty also came from his family's long tradition of serving in the military. His dad, a doctor, had served in World War I. Both of his grandfathers had fought in the Civil War.

While Eugene and Sidney shared many interests, their passion for Civil War history bonded them. Most weekends found them at one of the battlefields just outside Mobile. Eugene's parents had a car for him, an almost unheard-of luxury, so they could drive over to Fort Blakeley or Spanish Fort. In part, the trips represented an escape from the structured lives they led. The ruins of the forts lay abandoned and ignored, so Sid and his buddy "Ugin" could do as they pleased. They loved to dig in the earthen breastworks for artifacts like minié balls and Confederate belt buckles. Eugene often brought his guns with them and they held target practice. They also read widely about the war and the battle fought there. The Army of the Confederacy had held Fort Blakeley even after the Yankees closed the port of Mobile and conquered Spanish Fort. On the same day General Lee signed the surrender at Appomattox, some twenty thousand men fought the last major battle of the Civil War at Blakeley. The Eighty-second Ohio led the Yankees' charge, which at last flushed the outnumbered and outgunned Confederates from their positions. Sid and Eugene loved tracing each unit's actions, refighting the battle from the mortar pits, rifle pits, and the great redoubts of the artillery.

The war against Japan undoubtedly would become as important as the Civil War. "The dirty japs," as most Americans referred to them, had launched a sneak attack while their ambassadors in D.C. spoke of peace. It was treachery. The desire to be a part of their country's glorious victory burned inside of Sid and Eugene. Like the Rebels at Fort Blakeley, who fought to the death long after the war was lost, they longed to prove their courage for all time. Now, if only they could get their parents' permission.

*   *   *

WHILE EVERYONE SPOKE ENDLESSLY ABOUT PEARL HARBOR, CORPORAL JOHN Basilone was incensed by the Japanese attack on the Philippines. His reaction surprised no one in his company. Although a corporal in the marines, Basilone had served a two-year hitch with the army, most of it in Manila, years ago. He had told so many stories about Manila that his friends had long ago nicknamed him "Manila John."[9] Every marine told sea stories. Stationed in a tent camp on the coast of North Carolina, they had little recreation aside from shooting the breeze. The tattoo on John's right biceps of a beautiful woman elicited comments and questions. He told them that her name was Lolita and he had met her in Manila "quite by chance, during one of those storms which blew up so suddenly."[10] To escape the driving rain he stepped into a small club and there she was.

John had known neither the Filipinos nor their country until Lolita had introduced him. Though poor, the Filipinos—who pronounced the word Pill-ee-peenos—worked hard and took pride in their identity. They had fought a protracted war for their independence and forced the U.S. government to establish a timetable for its withdrawal. With the issue of independence settled before his arrival, John had come to know a woman and a people who loved America. They looked to America for help. The first president of the Philippines had asked General Douglas MacArthur to build the country's army and command it as field marshal. To protect the fledgling democracy until it could defend itself, the U.S. Army maintained a large force there. Even as a lowly private, Basilone understood the biggest threat came from Japan.[11] They had been trying to push America out of the Far East for years.

December 9 brought news of Japanese attacks on other countries and islands in the Pacific. As the scale of their conquest in the Pacific shocked the nation, John told everyone that Manila would not fall.[12] General MacArthur commanded a powerful force from his suite atop the Manila Hotel, where he could look out at the bay on one side and over the city's main thoroughfare, Dewey Boulevard, on the other. Northern Luzon had impressive defenses, the most important of which John had seen one evening on a boat trip with Lolita.[13] She directed their boat out of Manila Bay and around the tip of the Bataan Peninsula into Subic Bay. They motored up along the northern coast of Bataan, in the direction of Olongapo, for dinner at a special restaurant. It had been a memorable night in a lot of ways, but John also recalled passing the island fortress guarding the entrance to Manila Bay: Corregidor, known as "the Rock." Its ancient rock walls, topped by giant coastal artillery, towered above the greatest warships ever built.

By the time his hitch with the army expired, John had decided to go home a single man. Lolita came looking for him right before he shipped out. He had been lucky to miss her, he liked to joke. She brought a machete and cut his seabag in half.[14] Being marines, his friends believed about half of what he told them.[15] But the point of John's stories was never to make himself look good. He liked to laugh and swap stories. A careful listener would have, however, deduced something else. John loved Manila because it had been there that he had come into his own. The adventurous and physically demanding life of a professional soldier had quelled a deep-seated restlessness. Unlike his struggles in civilian life, John had discovered a knack for soldiering.

Manila John's path from the army to the Marine Corps had been neither straight nor easy, but he eventually had made it from Manila to the machine-gun section of Dog Company, 1st Battalion, Seventh Marine Regiment (D/1/7). He faced the war secure in his place in the world. He loved being a marine. He knew his job. Instead of being a cause of concern for his parents, he was sending home $40 a month to his mother.[16] That peace brought out his natural disposition: a cheerful, fun-loving, easygoing spirit that drew others to him.[17] He had his feelings inscribed on his left shoulder. It bore a sword slashing down through a banner proclaiming "Death Before Dishonor."

LIEUTENANT SHOFNER'S WAR GREW SLOWLY. THE ENEMY BOMBED THE U.S. bases around Luzon for a few days before they began landing troops on December 10. They chose isolated areas and their troops walked ashore. Reports of their movements reached the Fourth Marines almost hourly as the top brass in Manila struggled to devise plans and their various units strove to carry them out. The Fourth continued to man its post at Olongapo despite rumors of other assignments. During the day, the marines prepared to defend the beaches. The air raid alarm sounded often but, so far, nothing. At night, the marines marched back to their camp in the swamp. The blackout was enforced. Food had to be rationed. They ate twice a day or, as the saying went, "breakfast before daylight and dinner after dark."[18] Inside of two weeks, someone surely noted, they had gone from Peking duck to cold C rations. A few days of foul weather made camp miserable, but the storm did bring a respite from reports of fresh attacks.

The twelfth dawned clear, so the marines watched as a few of the PBYs of Navy Patrol Wing Ten landed in the bay. The morning's patrol was over and the seamen had secured their planes when five enemy fighter planes fell upon them. With their heavy machine guns and 20mm cannons, the Japanese planes quickly destroyed seven flying boats, the entire squadron. Two or three attackers made a run at the marines' base, guns blazing. About forty .30-caliber machine guns returned their fire. No one hit a plane. The .30 caliber had not been designed as an antiaircraft gun, but the marines pulled their triggers anyway. One gunner swung hard to track his target and shot holes in the water tower.

The next day the alarm sounded at ten thirty a.m. for what Shofner thought must be the fiftieth time. As the commanding officer (the CO) of the Headquarters Company, he led it once again across the golf course and into the swamp. He looked up, counted twenty-seven Japanese bombers above him, and heard a noise he had never heard before. The sound of bombs falling toward him was unforgettable. Explosions erupted as the planes disappeared. Shofner returned to the base. A sudden gust of wind, he learned, had driven the bombs past the base and into the town. The village was on fire and the marines went to assist. They found a dozen had been killed and many more wounded. Bombs landed near the regiment's field hospital, although its tents, emblazoned with large red crosses on fields of white, had been set up a mile out of town. The marines decided the emperor's air force had aimed for the hospital and it made them angry.

The attack prompted Shofner's CO to reassess the situation. The regimental commander could not allow his men to be killed before the land campaign began. If the assault came at Olongapo, the defenses were as ready as they could be. But his unit was not going to sit on a target. The Fourth Marines moved their camp a few miles into the hills, where the jungle hid them from bombers. A skeleton crew manned the naval base during the day, but the rest prepared for a battle they knew was coming somewhere, soon. The enemy was on the move. As the battalion's supply officer, Shofner concentrated on moving necessary supplies to the new bivouac. As an officer he did not lift boxes, of course, but he had to decide what could fit on their limited supply of trucks. Marines from the rifle companies, meantime, rounded up all Japanese civilians in Olongapo and turned them over to the army's police force.[19]

When the communication lines to Manila went dead, it was assumed this was the work of saboteurs. News of other enemy landings on Luzon continued to get through to them by runner and radio. The enemy's bombers paid another visit to Olongapo before the night of December 22, when the regiment went on high alert at about one thirty a.m. The first report stated that fifteen transports had landed enemy troops on Lingayen Gulf. Top U.S. commanders always had expected the main assault to cross the beaches of Lingayen. The Fourth Marines were ordered to prepare to move out to repulse it. The next communication reported "87 jap transports." A long, anxious night passed. The regiment stayed put. Shofner assumed it was because they were only five hundred men. Later he found out the regiment had been put under MacArthur's command. While the Fourth awaited its orders, the enemy's troop transports were spotted in Subic Bay. The marines charged down to defend Olongapo but found an empty ocean.

The Fourth's CO drove to Manila to assess the situation. At six p.m. on December 24, Shofner watched the colonel's car return to their camp at high speed. A battalion officers' conference followed. Colonel Howard told them he had been ordered to withdraw immediately to the small base at Mariveles, on the tip of the Bataan Peninsula. Units of the Imperial Japanese Army had overwhelmed all opposition easily and had advanced to within forty miles of their position. To his officers, he likely also admitted the full scope of the situation. From his conversations with Admiral Hart and later with General MacArthur and his staff, it was clear that the U.S. forces were in disarray. MacArthur's chief of staff, General Richard Sutherland, had told Howard the Japanese "were converging on Manila from three directions."[20] The enemy air force had destroyed most of the thirty-seven new B-17 bombers and the remainder had flown south to Mindanao. Admiral Hart was departing by submarine and taking his remaining fleet south. General MacArthur was abandoning Manila and ordering all of his troops to prepare for a defensive stand on the Bataan Peninsula. MacArthur's headquarters was moving to the island of Corregidor. He ordered the Fourth Marines, after picking up its 1st Battalion in Mariveles, to Corregidor to protect his headquarters. Colonel Howard told his officers to begin packing immediately.

Lieutenant Shofner's job as the battalion's logistics officer demanded his best efforts to get all of the equipment and supplies on the trucks and headed south on the dirt road. The first convoy of trucks left about noon on Christmas Day. Shofner and his friend Lieutenant Nutter led some men back to the naval station. They had a few hours to get the necessities. So far as their personal gear, each marine had a backpack. Beyond that, the colonel had allowed one footlocker for officers. Everything else had to be left behind.

Shofner hated to leave behind the large and diverse collection of personal effects he had stored in the warehouse at the dock. It caught him off guard. As the scion of a well-to-do family, he had become an officer and a gentleman after serving as president of his fraternity (Kappa Alpha), lettering on the varsity football team of the University of Tennessee, and earning a scholarship from the "T" Club as "the athlete with the highest grades." His mountain of baggage included not only an array of military uniforms and sporting equipment of all types, but also a few dozen suits for every occasion—from black tie, to silk, to sharkskin. In Shanghai he had amassed an impressive array of exquisite Chinese furniture, furnishings, art, and apparel. Some of the silken damasks and jade carvings doubtless were intended as gifts for his girlfriend, his mother, or others in his large family. When he had been posted to Shanghai six months earlier and learned war was imminent, he had been pleased. Shofners had fought in every American war. The idea of retreating, however, had never occurred to him.

He packed his footlocker with necessities, including just one small memorial: a plaque bearing the insignia of the Marine Corps from the Fourth Marine Regiment's Club. As he sped away, he hoped his oriental rugs and ivory statuettes would be found by some local Filipino.

Shofner arrived at Camp Carefree, an army rest camp at the tip of Bataan, that evening and enjoyed a turkey sandwich for his Christmas Day dinner. So far as he could tell, Bataan had not been prepared for a defensive stand. He found an open bunk in the officers' quarters and let exhaustion overtake him. The air raid siren woke him at midnight. Everyone ran outside and lay down in an open field, as ordered. From where he lay, Shofner could see a freighter burning just offshore, and beyond it, the city of Manila lit by a hundred raging fires. MacArthur had ordered the city, known as the Pearl of the Orient, abandoned by his forces. He informed the Imperial Japanese Army it was open to them. They bombed it anyway.

The enemy had gotten the drop on the United States. That much was obvious on Christmas Day. The officers and men of the Fourth Marines committed themselves to hanging on until the United States Navy showed up with reinforcements. Then the bastards would catch hell.

THE DAY AFTER CHRISTMAS, SID, W.O., AND SOME OTHERS WERE SWORN IN. JUST like that they were marines. People had heard about the marines now. The marines who defended Wake Island had repulsed the first attempt by Japan to invade the island a few days after the attack on Pearl Harbor. When asked later to detail his supply needs, the officer in charge had radioed "send us more japs!"* Wake had been overrun on Christmas Eve, but not without the kind of fight Americans had seen lacking elsewhere. Preparing to depart, Sid got together with Eugene. Eugene gave Sid a copy of *Barrack-Room Ballads*, by Rudyard Kipling, as a going-away present. The

---

*The officer in command of the USMC defense battalion and the USMC fighter squadron, Commander Winfield S. Cunningham, sent a list of his supply and reinforcement needs. Most historians believe the quote above was "padding" added to the message to make it more difficult for the enemy to decode.

book contained a favorite poem, "Gunga Din." Both of them could quote passages from memory, such as the opening stanza:

> You may talk o' gin and beer
> When you're quartered safe out 'ere . . .
> But if it comes to slaughter
> You will do your work on water,
> An' you'll lick the bloomin' boots of 'im that's got it.
> Now in Injia's sunny clime,
> Where I used to spend my time
> A-servin' of 'Er Majesty the Queen,
> Of all them black-faced crew
> The finest man I knew
> Was our regimental bhisti, Gunga Din.
> It was "Din! Din! Din!
> You limpin' lump o' brick-dust, Gunga Din! . . ."

Sid did not open the book on the steam train to Parris Island, South Carolina. The new life intoxicated him. He and W.O. and a carload of new best friends sang songs. Upon arrival, Sid learned he was not a marine. He was a shitbird. In the estimation of his drill instructor (DI), who delivered his opinion at high volume and at close range, Sid Phillips was not going to ever reach the exalted position of marine. He was his mother's mistake. Then it was time to run: run to get their gear, run to their barracks, run to the parade ground, run, run, run! To Sid's complete surprise, his training focused on earning the privilege of being a United States Marine. Only occasionally did he dig a foxhole, stab a dummy with a bayonet, or learn something related to killing Japanese soldiers. The Marine Corps set a high standard with the rigors of boot camp. The humiliation and the profanity heaped upon all the boots (recruits), as well as the all-encompassing demands placed upon them, went well beyond the other services. Every action would be performed the Marine Corps way using Marine Corps terminology, or else.

Sidney and W.O. and their new friend John Tatum, also from Alabama, had been raised to respect and obey authority. They adjusted to boot camp rather easily. Shorn not just of hair but also of all personal privacy, Sid disliked using the head (toilet) in front of sixty others and lining up to have his penis inspected for gonorrhea. The prospect held out by his instructors, that of becoming the world's best fighting man, seemed worth the punishment. On the first day, each boot had been issued a rifle, a 1903 bolt-action Springfield, so Sid looked forward to the day when he would be taught to use it. Rifle instruction came last. In the meantime he and his fellow boots drilled ceaselessly, learning to march in lockstep. To survive, they learned their instructor's personal marching cadence. No drill instructors yelled, "March, one, two, three." It demanded too much from the vocal cords. Besides, a DI could really vent his disgust of the shitbirds by shouting something like "HAWrsh! AWN! UP! REEP!"[21]

CORREGIDOR INSPIRED CONFIDENCE IN THE MEN OF THE FOURTH MARINES. After arriving by ferry on North Dock, they put their gear on a trolley and began the climb up the steep hill. They had all heard the Rock was an impregnable fortress. Their escort described the great tunnels carved in the rock below them and the huge coastal gun emplacements on the hills above them. The island was shaped like a tadpole; its tail stuck into Manila Harbor, its round head facing the South China Sea. The narrow tail was mostly rocks and beaches. Dominated by Malinta Hill, the tadpole's tail held the docks, power station, and warehouses; this area was called Bottomside. Beyond Malinta Hill, they came to the high hill known as Middleside, where their barracks were located, as well as a hospital and a recreational club. Beyond Middleside was another, steeper hill, called Topside, encompassing most of the wide area of the tadpole's head. On Topside, the lush forest gave way to manicured lawns surrounding stately mansions for officers, a golf course, and a profusion of casemates holding the giant coastal artillery. More than fifty big guns, from three inches to twelve inches in diameter, had been emplaced. The Rock, kept cooler than the mainland by an ocean breeze, had it all.

Having arrived at Middleside Barracks on the evening of December 27, the marines spent two quiet days getting squared away. Organizing the supplies kept Shofner busy. His regiment, which now included its 1st Battalion as well as a detachment of four hundred marines from another base, brought rations to feed its twelve hundred men for at least six months, ammunition for ten days of heavy combat, khaki uniforms to last for two years, and medicine and equipment for a one-hundred-bed hospital. Of course Corregidor had mountains of munitions already stockpiled.

When the air raid sirens went off about noon on December 29, no one paid much attention. The Japanese had never bombed Corregidor. Shofner was standing near the barracks when he saw the formation of planes. The antiaircraft guns began firing. The sun glinted off the metal shapes falling toward him. He ran into the bombproof barracks. He joined the rest of the regiment, every last man of whom was splayed out on his belly. One bomb came through the roof but exploded on an upper floor; another could be heard crashing through but did not detonate; many others went off nearby. "And thus began," Shofner wrote in his diary, "the worst day I have ever spent."

A bomb had wounded one marine. He was taken to the hospital as everyone else abandoned Middleside Barracks. It had become a giant target and more air-planes were overhead. Shofner met some nurses looking for a doctor; bombs had hit the rear of their barracks. All Shofner could find was a dentist, but he sent him. Another squadron of bombers came over, then another and another. He lost count after a dozen formations had each released a vast amount of high explosives. Most of the time he lay on his back, watching the Rock's antiaircraft (ack-ack) shells explode well short of their targets. He wondered whether the planes were too high, if the aim was off or the proper fuses were missing, or if perhaps the poor shooting was the fault of untrained personnel. He could not tell. The bombs fell without a discern-ible pattern so one could only hope, intensely. The last echo faded four hours later. The marines sustained four casualties, one of whom later died. The buildings of Middleside, including his barracks, lost the capacity to provide much shelter, much less a sense of security.

Irritated by doubt for the first time, Shofner got to work. His company was ordered to set up camp in James Ravine. That meant setting up a galley to feed the men, laying communications wire, and other preparations. He worked all night. The other units of the regiment moved to their sectors and prepared to defend the beaches of Corregidor. The 1st Battalion took the most vulnerable sector, en-compassing Malinta Hill and Bottomside. Shofner's battalion had the easier job of securing Middleside, where he was, and Topside. Since it was unlikely the enemy would try to land anywhere but Bottomside, Shofner's position was considered a reserve one. Still, all hands fell to, spending the balance of each day stringing barbed wire, placing land mines, and digging trenches, antitank traps, and caves for shelter. The air alarm occasionally failed to go off and bombs detonated close to him a few times. As battalion mess officer, he saw to it that each man received two rations per day. Thankfully there was plenty of drinking water and they could bathe in the sea. Learning to keep oneself near shelter and to run for it at the first hint of an aircraft engine took time. In the course of the next ten days, 36 marines were killed and another 140 were wounded.[22]

*   *   *

THE MONTH OF DECEMBER HAD PASSED AT NORTH ISLAND WITH ALMOST NO flight training. Mike had flown once. The regime of daily instruction had resumed in January. The pilots in the Advanced Carrier Training Unit had promptly made a mess of it. Every day for a week, one of Mike's colleagues had landed without first lowering the plane's wheels, or tipped the plane over on the ground. The mistakes could have resulted from the pause in training, or perhaps the ensigns had war jitters. When it happened again on January 12, their CO lined up the ensigns in the hangar at four thirty p.m. "I don't want any more accidents," Commander Moebus bellowed. "The first guy that has an accident, he'll find out what I mean by having no more accidents!"

After the meeting, Micheel took off in a bright yellow SNJ to practice flying at night by flying at dusk. He flew for over an hour and approached the landing field before full dark. Just as his wheels began to touch pavement, the control tower radioed to him, "Abort your landing! Take off! Plane on the runway!" Mike pulled the plane up. As he flew along the expanse of runway, he looked down and saw only one other plane, well out of his way. Ticked off, he decided he would not make a complete new approach through the traffic pattern. He kept the aircraft prepared for landing: prop in a low pitch, a rich mixture in the manifold, flaps down. He came around quickly and began to land again, nose into the wind. The tower came on the radio again and said he was cleared. Just before touchdown, the Klaxon on the control tower began to screech, indicating his wheels were up. Mike had brought them up after the first attempt. He shoved the throttle forward but it was too late. The Yellow Peril slid on its underbelly. Screeching down the center of the main runway left him flushed with embarrassment.

The plane's wooden propeller was a goner and the engine needed some maintenance due to the abrupt stop. The mechanics would have to change the flaps and bend the metal fuselage in places. The SNJ was not irreparably damaged, but now he had to go face Commander Moebus. Ensign Micheel reported to his CO and admitted he had been distracted and had not run through his landing checklist a second time. Just as Mike feared, the commander was hot. He charged Mike with "direct disobedience of orders" and grounded him immediately. Moebus decided to make an example of Mike to all of his students. He wrote the navy's Bureau of Navigation, the governing body of naval aviation. After explaining the chronic problems he was having with his students as well as the warning he had given Micheel just before he took off, Moebus requested that Ensign Vernon Micheel be "ordered to duty not involving flying." Only such drastic action would get his students' attention.

Moebus's letter betrayed more than just the exasperation of a commander, though. He attributed the problems in his ACTU to "inaptitude incidental to entry of large numbers of cadets and the forced draft method of training in large training centers which does not entirely eliminate mediocre material." Put another way, the navy's new flight training program was failing. Commander L. A. Moebus expressed the frustration many graduates of the Naval Academy at Annapolis felt toward the hordes of civilians now coming through the Naval Aviation program. Men like Vernon Micheel, who had attended college to become a dairy farmer, could never be a professional on par with an Annapolis man.

While waiting for a reply from the bureau, Moebus ordered his wayward ensign to stay with the wounded SNJ. Beginning the next day, as the mechanics repaired it, Ensign Micheel prepared a report listing the cost of each new part and of each hour of labor expended. The roar of aircraft engines echoed through the big hangar constantly. Mike tried not to think about where he would wind up if he was expelled from the ACTU.

THE JAPANESE STOPPED BOMBING THE ROCK IN MID-JANUARY, MUCH TO LIEU-tenant Shofner's relief. The pause gave the Americans time to prepare. General MacArthur issued a statement to all his unit commanders. He ordered each company commander to deliver this message to his men: "Help is on the way from the United States. Thousands of troops and hundreds of planes are being dispatched. The exact time of arrival of reinforcements is unknown . . . it is imperative that our troops hold out until these reinforcements arrive. No further retreat is possible. We have more troops in Bataan than the Japanese have thrown against us; our supplies are ample; a determined defense will defeat the enemys' attack. It is a question now of courage and determination. If we fight, we will win; if we retreat, we will be destroyed."[23] The message improved morale on the island, even as the sounds of the battle on Bataan reached them.

In early February, the enemy began shelling Corregidor with their artillery. It became clear to all immediately that shells fired from big guns hurt a lot more than bombs dropped from twenty thousand feet. The whistle of incoming rounds lasted only a few seconds, as opposed to the long, monotonous hum of an approaching bomber squadron. The whistle came on rainy days and at night. It made walking aboveground hazardous. The marines, who lived on top of the island, began to envy the army, most of whom had crowded into Malinta Tunnel, deep under the Rock.

Shofner was promoted to captain on January 5 and took command of the 2nd Battalion's reserve company. His two rifle platoons and one machine-gun platoon stood ready to answer a call from any unit on the beaches. The shelling usually cut the communications wires, however, so there were more and more periods of time when he only knew what he could see. He had his men shovel several feet of dirt into the walls of Middleside Barracks to create a final defensive line. He had them dig caves to give them shelter from the barrages.

Shofner, nicknamed "Shifty" by his friends because he always had an eye for tricks and shortcuts, would have certainly begun to notice the problems with the island's renowned defenses. Some of the great ten-inch guns could not be turned to engage the enemy's artillery because they had been built to face ships at sea. A few of the other main gun batteries already had been destroyed because their concrete barbettes left them open to the sky. The island's power plant had been built in an exposed position. The Fourth Marines learned quickly how to keep low. They suffered fewer casualties in February than they had in January, although they received more gunfire. At night they stood their posts, watching for landing boats and hoping for their navy. If an electrical storm brought flashes of light, one of Shofner's guards was sure to report, "that's our fleet coming in."

The departure of the president of the Philippines, Manuel Quezon, could not be hidden from the men. The gold and silver of his treasury had departed already. These troubling signs put the same questions to everyone's lips: "Where the hell's the navy?" and "What's the matter back home?"[24]

ENSIGN MICHEEL TRACKED THE COST OF REPAIRING THE AIRPLANE WITHOUT complaint. While his colleagues roared aloft, he spent his days watching the mechanics work. He enjoyed learning the intricacies of engines and ailerons. Three weeks passed before the CO called him into the office to inform him he had been reinstated. Commander Moebus did not elaborate, but Mike could guess the truth. The chief of the Bureau of Naval Aviation had reviewed his file, concluded that the wheels-up landing had been an isolated lapse, and sent a reply to Moebus that fell just short of saying, "Hey, there's a war on, you know."

Mike had missed out on advanced instruction in tactical flying, navigation, and scouting. He took his first flight in the backseat of an SNJ, watching one of his peers work through a navigation problem. A schedule of classroom instruction mixed with flight time followed. Ten days later, on February 19, the ACTU received the navy's modern combat aircraft. For some of his classmates, this meant climbing into an F4F Wildcat, the navy's best fighter. For Mike, it meant climbing into the SBD Dauntless, the navy's scouting and dive-bombing aircraft. His squadron had received SBD-3s, the latest version. He began flying an hour or so most every day. Sometimes an instructor flew in the plane, with Micheel riding in the rear seat gunner's position, but usually Mike flew himself as part of a group led by an instructor. Although his daily instruction varied somewhat, two advanced maneuvers came to the fore.

Micheel made his first attempts at dive-bombing. Putting a plane into a seventy-degree dive from twelve thousand feet and dropping like a stone took a young man's courage. By deploying special flaps on the SBD's wings, called dive brakes, the pilot could hold the plane under 245 knots. But the steep angle lifted him off his seat and had him hanging in his harness, with one hand on the control stick and one eye stuck on the telescope set into the windshield of the Dauntless. Through the bombsight, he watched the target grow in size rapidly. At about two thousand feet above the target, he toggled the bomb release and pulled out of the dive. The force of gravity squished him into the bottom of his seat.

Part of every day had to be spent on the other great challenge of naval aviation, landing his Dauntless on the deck of an aircraft carrier. The difficulty of a carrier landing had loomed on the horizon since flight school. Pilots practiced it, logically enough, by landing on a strip of the runway that bore the outline of a carrier deck.

It began with a specific approach pattern. The pilot approached the ship from behind. He flew past the carrier on its starboard (right-hand) side at about one thousand feet. The pilot was now "in the groove." Once he passed the carrier by a half mile (depending on how many planes were also in the groove), he would make a left-hand turn and come back toward it. Lowering his elevation, his landing flaps, his wheels, and most important, his "tail hook," the pilot made his final preparations for landing. Looking to his left as he approached the ship's bow, he had an unobstructed view of any other planes landing on the deck ahead of him. Spotters on the carrier deck would signal him if they saw a problem with his plane or on the deck.

As the pilot reached the stern of the ship, he began a hard left-hand turn that would bring him around 180 degrees and just over the stern of the ship. At this point the pilot could look down and see a man standing on the stern port corner of the carrier with large paddles in his hands. Usually dressed in a suit of yellow to make him clearly visible, the Landing Signal Officer (LSO) gave the pilot directions by waving his big paddles and tilting his body. If the pilot followed those commands exactly, the LSO slashed one paddle across his neck. The pilot cut the engine and his plane dropped onto the deck, its tail hook caught a wire, and he was home free. It was a controlled crash landing onto a moving target.

Mike and his classmates spent many hours mastering the fundamentals of carrier landings on a remote section of runway. A pilot could not come in too fast, nor too slow, or too high or too low. His plane also had to be in the proper "attitude" in the air, with its nose up and hook down, in order to make a perfect three-point (one for each wheel) landing. In a few hours of flying time, the ensigns simulated as many landings as they could: circle the deck, get the slash (or "cut"), crash, power up and away. Then they met back in their classrooms with the LSO, who reviewed each of their techniques in detail.

None of their practice took place on a carrier. The navy, as the ensigns likely found out through scuttlebutt, was running short on those. *Saratoga* had been torpedoed in January and had sailed to Bremerton, Washington, for repairs. To keep the enemy guessing about whether the Sara had survived, her status had not been made public. Instead, the newspapers carried stories of Admiral Halsey using *Enterprise* to strike Japanese strongholds in the Marshall Islands, in the central Pacific. "Pearl Harbor Avenged" read one headline, but about then the British fortress on Singapore fell.[25] The enemy now controlled half of the Pacific Ocean. In the bull sessions held at the officers' club, the ensigns would have discussed the futures of the four remaining fleet carriers in the Pacific: *Yorktown*, *Lexington*, *Enterprise*, and *Hornet*. Each pilot already had been assigned to serve on one of them. Ensign Micheel knew he would be joining USS *Enterprise*. As a dive-bomber pilot, Mike likely wondered just how many big carriers the enemy had, exactly, since he had to go sink them.

PRIVATES SIDNEY PHILLIPS, W. O. BROWN, AND JOHN TATUM, WHOM THEY HAD taken to calling "Deacon" because of his penchant for quoting scripture, departed Parris Island wearing the emblems of the United States Marine Corps: an eagle, globe, and fouled anchor. While few of their cohorts had failed to make the grade, each of them came away with a few firm beliefs. The USMC was the world's best combat unit. The marines were the first to fight. Their mission, amphibious assault, was the most difficult feat of arms. Once marines seized the beachhead, the army "doggies" would come in and hold it. These beliefs had been burned into them while they had learned to perform the manual of arms with precision, slapping their rifles so hard the sound carried a hundred yards. Being one small part of this great team gave Sidney a feeling of strength and comfort unlike anything he had ever experienced.

After arriving by train at New River, North Carolina, one afternoon in mid-February, they formed into ranks on a great muddy field. Ahead of them stood a large tent, its open flaps revealing bright lights and busy activity. One by one, each man was called forward. Inside, NCOs (noncommissioned officers, such as corporals and sergeants) met and interviewed him. Sid walked through the mud, answered the NCOs' questions, and was assigned to How Company, 2nd Battalion, First Marines

(H/2/1). So was W.O. The Deacon received the same assignment. What luck, they thought. After a time Sidney realized everyone in their group had been assigned to the 2nd Battalion, First Marines.

The three friends stuck together and were assigned the same hut. The next morning they found three inches of snow on the ground and no orders to follow. For the next few days they just had to keep the stove in their hut hot. More men arrived, as did the USMC's newest uniform, the dungarees. The two-piece uniform of heavy woven fabric, intended for use in the field and in combat, was the first piece of equipment issued that had been designed for the new war instead of the last Great War. Sidney preferred it to his khaki uniform because it had large pockets and a stencil of the corps' emblem on the breast. The helmet he wore was the same kind his father had worn in France.

Instruction began on February 18, when the NCOs introduced them to some of the weapons used by their company: the .30-caliber Browning Machine Gun and the 81mm mortar. These and the other heavy weapons of How Company, they were told, would support the assault by the riflemen of the other companies of their battalion (Easy, Fox, and George). The 81mm mortar captured the attention of Sid and Deacon. Big guns had always fascinated them and they made sure their NCO knew it. W.O. was happy enough to stay with them. Other men disparaged the 81mm as "the stovepipe" and tried to get assigned something else. The self-selection worked. After a few weeks, the NCOs assigned the three friends to the same mortar squad, #4 gun, of the 81mm mortar platoon. All six members of #4 gun squad were Southerners except for Carl Ransom from Vermont. Ransom, hearing the others naming themselves the Rebel Squad, quickly asserted that he had grown up in the southern bedroom of a house on the south side of the street.

Although they occasionally had an afternoon of instruction on something else, the #4 squad quickly became focused on their weapon. Sid repeated sections of its manual over and over, chanting it like a rhyme. The 81mm mortar was "a smooth bore, muzzle loading, hand fed, high angle type of fire . . ." Corporal Benson, who commanded #4 gun, had them begin mastering the precise movements for assembling and firing the weapons by repetition. At Benson's command, one man set down the base plate, another the bipod, and a third the tube. The job of clamping the three parts together naturally fell to Deacon. A bit taller and a bit older, John Tatum took it all more seriously than Sidney and W.O. Corporal Benson took the mortar sights from the case and attached and adjusted them.

The endless repetition and chanting quickly led to competition between the gun squads. Deacon wanted to be the fastest. He studied *The Marine's Handbook*, the red book issued to all privates. By early March Deacon became acting corporal even before he had earned his stripe as a private first class. Sid and W.O. had no wish for promotion. They enjoyed the rivalry, though, and #4 squad assembled their mortar in the respectable time of fifty-five seconds. Corporal Benson never praised them.

Like most NCOs, Benson regarded them as too soft to be good marines. When the new men complained about the cold, they were told to wait until summer, when the chiggers and mosquitoes returned. Any new marines who rejoiced at receiving steel bunks on March 9 were told they were babies who had it too easy. Benson had lived in a tent on some island called Culebra for months, and that, he assured them, had been much worse. Sometimes, when his squad beat the squads of the mortar platoon, Benson might be inspired to tell them a few sea stories of a marine's life in Puerto Rico or Guantánamo Bay, Cuba. The First Marines had spent much of the past three years in the Caribbean, working out the techniques of amphibious landings. They had been in the boonies so long they had taken to calling themselves "the Raggedy-Assed Marines." Benson had learned to curse in Spanish, and when he started in, it brought a slow, mischievous smile to Sid's face. Deacon might be horrified, but Sidney Phillips loved a good laugh.

THE GREAT INFLUX OF NEW MARINES WAS LEADING TO PROMOTIONS FOR THE old hands. A few weeks earlier, Manila John had made sergeant.[26] His company not only received new marines, but also a number of experienced men who had asked to be transferred. John's regiment, the Seventh, was considered good duty because by early March it was clear the Seventh would lead the attack against the enemy. It had the highest percentage of experienced marines and it was receiving all the new equipment first. As they prepared for the first amphibious assault—which, for all the talk, the USMC had never once performed against a hostile foe—the men in John's machine-gun section were realizing they had an unusual sergeant. It wasn't his sea stories about life as a soldier, or even his insistence that he was going to "land on Dewey Boulevard and liberate Manila."[27] All sergeants had sea stories and some of those wanted to liberate Shanghai. Sergeant Basilone, with his prizefighter's physique and dark complexion, made a big impression, but his relaxed manner said he was just one of the guys.

Most NCOs liked to make their men hop. Manila John regarded his men, new or old, as part of the fraternity.[28] He did not struggle to enforce discipline. John set the standard.[29] He loved being a marine and he expected the others to feel the same. He expected them to obey his orders because that's what marines did. He expected them to train hard during the week and then go into Wilmington or Jacksonville with their buddies and drink beer. That's what he did. Manila's best friend was another sergeant named J. P. Morgan. Morgan, known for being difficult, had a tattoo like John, only his was on the base of his thumb. When he had had it inked years previously, the tattoo had symbolized his Native American heritage. When anyone looked at it in 1941, though, they saw a swastika, the symbol of Hitler's Nazi Party.[30] The identification did little to improve J.P.'s demeanor.

John and J.P. each commanded one section of .30-caliber machine guns in Dog Company. At the moment, Manila spent most days instructing the men of his company, and to a certain extent the men of his battalion, on the operation of the Browning .30-caliber water-cooled machine gun. The machine gun's reputation of immense power drew lots of enthusiastic young men. They did not get lectures from their sergeant; they got hands-on demonstrations. The grace and ease with which he handled the weapon belied the short, choppy sentences he used to describe it.[31] Despite popular perceptions, the machine gun was not like a hose that sprayed out an endless stream. Holding the trigger down would burn out the barrel. Replacing a barrel took time. Spraying it all around might work for an enemy at close range, but it would prevent the gunner from dominating parts of the battlefield in the way it was designed to do.

Dominating the field meant preventing the enemy from ever getting close. Fire short bursts, John would have cautioned. That kept the gun cool. To make those bursts effective, don't free-hand the aim. Use the traverse and elevation mechanism (T&E). Slight turns of these dials made minute adjustments to the aim, which produced significant changes at two hundred yards. Good gunners did not aim for individuals. They created kill zones way out there on the battlefield. They killed the enemy in big groups or forced them to keep their heads down long enough to allow marines to attack them. A good gunner also knew his machine intimately. It began with being able to break the gun into its main components, or fieldstrip it, to clean them. Like any machine, however, the machine gun could be tuned. The rate of fire could be adjusted and, like all sergeants in all machine-gun sections, John had his guns set to his preferred cyclical rate, the one that he felt balanced the needs of endurance and killing power.

Manila John's battalion also spent a lot of March in remote areas of the base, living in their pup tents. The CO of 1/7, Major Lewis Puller, pushed them hard. Unlike some other officers, the major went with them on their six a.m. hikes, matching them step for step. He liked to have them work on their field problems near where the artillery units fired their 75mm and 105mm cannons.[32]

The word on Major Puller was that he had proven his mettle in the guerrilla wars in South America. Puller's nickname, "Chesty," came not because he had a muscular chest, but a misshapen one. Nothing about the major's physique reminded anyone of the marines on the recruiting posters. His direct and aggressive manner, however, shone through. Old hands in 1/7 liked to tell the story of the afternoon Major Puller had marched his battalion off to the boondocks. A loudmouth from another outfit had heckled them about the camouflage they wore. As his companies marched past, Puller had spied Private Murphy in Charlie Company. "Old Man," Puller had asked Murphy, "are you going to let him say those things about your company?" Murphy had stepped out of formation, punched the heckler in the kisser, and stepped back into formation. No one missed a step.[33] The new men had been around just long enough not to believe everything they heard, but they also knew the story epitomized the Marine Corps spirit being imbued in them.

IN THE PAST FEW WEEKS, SHOFNER HAD FOUND PILES OF SILVER COINS LEFT abandoned. Marines who had swiped them while helping to load the Philippine treasury on barges had realized that money had no value. Three hundred silver dollars, once a princely sum, was now regarded as deadweight. His marines expected their future to resemble the unmerciful pounding that was destroying their comrades on Bataan. The abandoned money, while remarkable, made more sense to Shifty than the radio broadcasts he heard. A radio station in San Francisco regularly broadcast General MacArthur's communiqués, which had been issued from the tunnels beneath the Fourth Marines.

In his pronouncements to the American people, MacArthur had described a different war, a war that he was winning. His headquarters had reported that "Lt. General Masaharu Homma, Commander-in-Chief of the Japanese forces in the Philippines, committed hara-kiri." General Homma had been disgraced by his defeats to MacArthur. "An interesting and ironic detail of the story," the communiqué had continued, "is that the suicide and funeral rites occurred in the suite at the Manila Hotel occupied by General MacArthur prior to the invasion in Manila."[34] Three nights after issuing this empty bluster, MacArthur and his key staff had boarded torpedo boats and fled to Australia.

The departure of General Douglas MacArthur had signified defeat, a defeat rapidly approaching in the last week of March. The enemy's heavy artillery began to swing away from Bataan and toward Corregidor, while their heavy bombers resumed their deliveries. U.S. forces on the Rock denied the Imperial Japanese Navy

(IJN) the use of Manila Harbor and therefore resistance had to be eliminated as quickly as possible.

The destruction placed great demands on all of them. A flight of bombers started fires in the houses around Shofner's barracks on March 24. He organized some firefighters. As they fought the flames, a giant explosion rocked the area. A bomb had hit a store of forty thousand 75mm shells. The shells began exploding, sending shrapnel flying. Shofner and his men prevented the blaze from spreading, then pulled a wounded man away from the conflagration. The next night he led a party to save a radio station from the flames. Two nights later, incendiary bombs ignited buildings next to Middleside Barracks and it looked like a whole line of buildings would go up in flames until Captain Shofner led the team to contain it. It seemed to him that some of the enemy's phosphorus shells had delayed-action fuses; they seemed intended to kill any would-be rescuers. The next night he had to put out a fire in his supply of .50-caliber ammunition, an exceedingly dangerous effort. Without that ammo they could not stop an invasion. On the way back to cover, Shofner heard cries for help. A cave had collapsed. He found a few men and a doctor to help him. They rescued two wounded men and pulled out two corpses. His superior officers told him later they were writing letters of commendation for his actions.

Even as the bombing built toward a crescendo on Corregidor, Shofner learned the truth about Bataan. For weeks, Americans and Filipinos from all service branches had been coming over from the embattled peninsula. These men arrived in need of food and clothing as well as weapons. Some of them had no military training. They had been divided up among all the military units on the island anyway. The Fourth Marines, like the other units, were attempting to train them. Some of what these refugees said he already knew, but much of the story emerged bit by bit, over time.

From the outset, the U.S. and Philippine army forces on Bataan had lacked food and medicine, and had quickly run short on ammunition, artillery support and air cover, and everything else. Worse, this disaster should never have happened. Bataan was supposed to have been prepared for exactly this type of defensive stand. For decades the United States had recognized that in the event of a war with Japan, its forces on Luzon would have to retreat to the Bataan Peninsula and await reinforcements. General Douglas MacArthur had decided in the late 1930s, however, to abandon this plan. The Philippine army, which he had created, and the U.S. Army, which he now commanded, would beat the emperor's troops at the beachhead. His decision meant that Bataan had not been prepared with caches of supplies or by military engineers to a significant degree.

MacArthur's performance had not improved following the news of Pearl Harbor. Many hours after the war began, the enemy's airplanes had found the army's fleet of brand-new "Flying Fortresses" on the ground, parked wingtip to wingtip. The few planes not destroyed had had to flee. Once the Imperial Japanese Army entered the game, it had put MacArthur's armies to rout. Americans and Filipinos had fought to the extent of their training, equipment, and experience. Bravery alone could not stop an experienced and fully equipped foe. When MacArthur had at last issued the order to fall back to Bataan, it had been too late. While combat units fell back in good order, tons of supplies and equipment had had to be abandoned. Tens of thousands of American and Filipino soldiers and sailors, along with an assortment of national guardsmen, airmen, marines, nurses, and coastguardsmen, had held off the Japanese army these past few months while eating the monkeys out of the trees. MacArthur had visited Bataan only once.

The more Austin Shofner learned about Douglas MacArthur, the more it produced within him and so many others a deep and abiding anger. Some debated who was responsible for what, but not him. Captain Shofner insisted that the field marshal, hired to protect the Philippines, alone was responsible for this debacle. Many others agreed. They hung a nickname on him: "Dugout Doug."

On April 6, the word went around that Bataan would fall at any moment. Shofner was trying to get some of the new men squared away in a barracks when a shell struck the far end of the building. The concussion split the door he was leaning against, sending him reeling and knocking out a man next to him. Recovering, Shofner went to the blast site. The grisly scene shocked him. Five men had been killed and twenty-five had been wounded. He and others loaded the wounded into a truck and Shofner drove it through the artillery barrage to the hospital. The empire had endless amounts of shells to fire. Later, one wounded army corpsman screamed, "Let me die! Let me die!" as Shofner put him on a stretcher. In the hours that followed, he had more and more close calls. The concussions gave him and his men blackouts. They spent much of their time in their caves and tunnels, where the throbbing and shaking earth tortured them.

On the day Bataan surrendered, April 9, small boats filled with desperate men tried to make it to Corregidor. The marines could see them. The first shots by the enemy's artillery sent great geysers of water into the air. Slowly, though, the Japanese got the range. A few shells got close enough to damage one or two of the boats. The passengers jumped in the water and tried to swim. It was about two and a half miles from shore to shore. Not many of them made it. The Fourth Marines spent that night on alert, expecting an invasion at any moment. They did not expect, however, to receive any help from their countrymen. General Wainwright, who had taken command after MacArthur had departed, had told them the truth: they were being sacrificed.

THE EVENING OF APRIL 10 FOUND MANILA JOHN IN THE ATLANTIC OCEAN, aboard USS *Heywood*. The scuttlebutt had been right. The Seventh Marines were leading the counterattack. Along with their trucks, machine shops, tanks, water purification units, and antiaircraft guns, the Seventh had been joined by batteries of artillerymen and companies of engineers.[35] The 1st Raider Battalion, a new unit in the corps designed to operate behind enemy lines, also had joined them. Standing out on the weather deck, Manila John and his buddy, Sergeant J. P. Morgan, would have seen the dark shapes of the other troopships and of the destroyers guarding them. No lights issued from the flotilla. The question was, where were they going? In the past month speculation had run from Iceland, where the Second Marines were, to Alaska. Although they had not been told, the marines could tell they were sailing south. This course would probably not lead them to Europe. The likelihood of service in the Pacific became a certainty when they reached the Panama Canal. The question then became, where did one start fighting the Japanese? Manila had fallen, as had Guam and Wake; only the men on Corregidor yet held their ground.

THERE HAD BEEN NO FINAL EXAM. TEN DAYS EARLIER MIKE HAD LISTENED TO some of the other pilots talking about boarding a ship. Minutes later the CO had walked up to him and said, "You're on it, go to Pearl." In the early afternoon of April 16, he stood topside and watched his ship enter Pearl Harbor. It looked like the bombs had just exploded. Six inches of oil covered the water. It stank. It stuck to everything. Micheel saw men working in that awful soup, slowly righting the wrecked ships. Other crews looked like they were trying to recover the bodies of sailors. Four months ago right there, he thought, men had drowned inside their ships; others had been trapped without food, water, oxygen. A wave of sadness at the loss of life broke quickly, leaving a new desire. Mike wanted to exact revenge. He was here to get them. He set off down the gangway to find the Administrative Office of the U.S. Pacific Fleet's Commander Carriers at Ford Island, in the middle of Pearl Harbor. He reported for duty, only to be told USS *Enterprise* had left on a mission and would return in a week or so. His squadron, Scouting Six, had an office at the Naval Air Station (NAS) on the other side of the island, on Kaneohe Bay.

Two days later, Mike took his first flight from NAS Kaneohe Bay to familiarize himself with the area. An experienced pilot from his squadron rode in the rear seat. Mike, the pilot behind him, and the whole island of Oahu were buzzing with the news making headlines that day. The United States had bombed four industrial areas in Japan, including one in Tokyo. The news story had come from the Japanese government, which had condemned "the inhuman attack" on schools and hospitals.[36] The Americans cheering "Yippee" and "Hooray" replied to the Japanese government's indictment with a countercharge. "They bombed our hospital on Bataan. Give it to them now!"[37] For Micheel, an Iowan not given to cheering, the bombs had put the Japanese on notice. Americans weren't going to give up.

In the days that followed, Mike helped to prepare for the return of his squadron by ferrying in new planes. The newspapers continued with the big news. Tokyo asserted that the bombing strike had been carried out by B-25s, a two-engine bomber used by the U.S. Army. The B-25s, they continued, had been launched from three U.S. carriers, flown over Japan, and landed in China. British journalists confirmed the arrival of U.S. planes in China, but the local reporters examined all the possible angles. The *Honolulu Star-Bulletin* reminded readers the navy had a carrier-based bomber, the Dauntless, and doubted that a plane of the size and weight of the B-25 could be flown onto a carrier.[38] Neither the navy nor the War Department offered any comment. The information was classified. When a reporter asked President Roosevelt from whence those American planes had come, he smiled and said, "Shangri La."

The return of USS *Enterprise* also was classified. Hours before it arrived, Scouting Six flew off its deck and landed at Kaneohe Bay. Micheel's introduction to his new squadron was cool; they were not welcoming and he was not one to break the ice. Thankfully a number of new pilots were joining it, including Ensign John Lough.[39] John and Mike had gone through flight training together, starting all the way back in Iowa with preflight. On the weekends, they had shared car rides home together, so they knew each other's families. John had gone to the ACTU in Norfolk, but somehow they had wound up together for the big day. April 29 passed in a whirlwind of preparations, culminating with Scouting Six landing on the deck of the carrier affectionately known as the Big E. Mike and John landed riding in the rear seats, not the cockpits. Tomorrow the Big E would sail into the combat zone. Tomorrow, Mike and John and other new pilots would have to make their first landings on the flight deck, then do it twice more to qualify as carrier pilots.

That challenge would wait until tomorrow. One of Mike's first tasks was to stow his gear in his room. Pilots received some of the best rooms on a carrier, even junior officers like Ensign Micheel, although the staterooms of senior pilots had portals. He shared a room with Bill Pittman. Bill had been on board since December, but he had just been switched from Bombing Six to Scouting Six.[40] Pittman showed Mike the way through the great maze that is a fleet carrier. Located on the hangar deck, near the bow, their stateroom was not too hard to find. Standing in the doorway, Bill said, "Well, I guess we have to make a decision here. Who's going to get the upper or lower bunk?"

"I don't know. How are we going to make the decision?"

"What's your service number?" Bill asked. "The guy with the lower serial number will get the lower bunk."

"Mine," said Mike, reciting from memory, "is 99986."

"Mine is 99984."

"Okay," Mike conceded, "you get the lower bunk." He did not care much, so it never occurred to him to ask to see Bill's service number.

The next stop was his squadron's ready room. Scouting Six's was located in "the island," the carrier's command center, which rose above the flight deck.[41] The ready room was where the men spent most of their time. Large comfortable chairs, each with its own folding desk, faced a bulkhead loaded with charts, a blackboard, and a large Teletype display. This is where Bill Pittman and Mike split up. The veterans, men who had flown against the enemy's bases on a series of raids, stuck to themselves. They tended to stay in the front of the room, so the new guys gathered in back, near the coffeepot. Before dinner, the squadron commander would have reviewed the next day's assignments. Some of the veterans would fly scouting missions, while others would assist in the carrier qualifications of the new pilots.

In the officers' mess, where black stewards placed silver tureens on tables covered in white linens, Mike would have heard more about the bombing of Tokyo from his new comrades. They called it the Doolittle Raid, after the man who had led it. *Hornet* had carried the army's B-25s, which only just managed to fly off the deck, while *Enterprise*'s planes served as guardians. Colonel Jimmy Doolittle's planes had been forced to launch early because they had been spotted by Japanese fishing boats. The boats meant the army pilots could expect to meet fighter aircraft over Tokyo. If that prospect was not bad enough, the B-25s had had their guns removed because they were so close to being too heavy to handle this mission. The Doolittle mission had been damn near suicidal. Along with giving Mike the straight dope on it, the pilots would have shared another part of the story not found in the press.

The B-25s had not been flown onto *Hornet*—just as the newspapers had speculated, that was impossible; they had been loaded aboard in Alameda. Since it had been impossible to keep this loading a secret, the navy had simply issued a statement that the planes were being shipped to Hawaii. The problem started when word got around the San Francisco Bay Area that *Hornet* was headed to Pearl. Hundreds of defense contractors had demanded to be taken aboard. Each had asserted that his business in Pearl was vital to the nation's war effort and he could get there no other way. The navy's efforts to put them off had almost worked. One contractor had come, as the story went, "thundering down to the dock and insisted on a ride to Honolulu," or he would "go to Washington."[42] Rather than attract any more attention, and thereby arouse the suspicion of enemy spies, the navy had decided to let this particularly vocal businessman catch his ride to Honolulu by way of Japan's territorial waters.

As they dined, the Big E's task force steamed south toward the equator. Accompanied by *Hornet*, she was ferrying a squadron of Marine Corps fighter planes to Efate, an island in the New Hebrides, south of the equator. No part of the journey could be regarded as safe. All operations, including flight operations, would be conducted in radio silence.

The next morning, April 30, began as always with the ship going to general quarters, or battle stations, about daybreak. The pilots hustled to their ready room to receive briefings on their mission, the launch sequence, the weather, and more. The CO of the squadron, known as the skipper, gave each man the number of the plane he would fly. When Mike walked out on the great wooden flight deck that morning, the wind greeted him. A wind of about twenty-five knots, blowing from bow to stern, made it possible for a plane to take off from a carrier. What the Big E could not get by pointing herself directly into the wind, she created with her great turbines churning eighty feet below.

A few Wildcats took off to provide the ship and her escorts with protection from enemy planes. A few scouts went looking for ships or submarines of the Imperial Japanese Navy (IJN). Then it was time for the new guys from all four squadrons to qualify. The Big E, known officially as CV-6 in navy terminology, embarked four squadrons: Fighting Six, who flew the Wildcats; Torpedo Six, who flew the TDB torpedo planes; and two squadrons that flew the SBD Dauntless. Although identified as Bombing Six and Scouting Six, the two shared the same duties. All the airplanes shared the same color scheme, two tones of pale blue, marked by white stars.

Mike met the captain of the plane to which he had been assigned, number 4563. The plane's captain regarded the Dauntless 4563 as his plane. He made sure it was ready for any pilot who was assigned to it. A good plane captain also helped the pilot, encumbered by his parachute and chart board, get strapped into the cockpit. Even with Mike's average build, he just fit. A sandbag had been placed in his rear seat;

no one was going to risk his life with an untried ensign. Outside, the plane captain turned the starter crank handle faster and faster until he felt that the flywheel inside had reached the right speed. He yelled, "Clear!" as a warning to other deckhands. Mike toggled the starter and watched his gauges as the engine came to life. When his turn came, he gave his Dauntless a touch of power and taxied to the center of the deck.

Off to his right the carrier's island rose several levels above him, with the ship's battle pennants and great antennae soaring high above. Spectators usually filled the catwalks (balconies) on each level of the island. With a perfect view of any crashes, these catwalks were known as Vulture's Row, except for a spot where the airmen stood. Known as PriFly (for Primary Flight Control), this spot was reserved for the air group commander. No one down on the busy flight deck, however, paid the gawkers any mind. The settings of his flaps, his propeller, and other items on his checklist demanded a pilot's full attention.

As the plane ahead of him roared off, Mike eased forward till the tip of his starboard (right) wing came level to the launch officer, dressed in white. To stop, he pushed down hard on the wheel brakes. The launch officer gave his arm a crazy swirl, and in response Mike ran up his engine to full power. The noise and vibrations, by now old friends, became tremendous. Mike looked down at his instrument panel, paying particular attention to the magnetos. Satisfied, he looked back at the launch officer. Both men listened carefully to the roar of the engine for any errant pops or pings. A second passed. When the launch officer determined the plane was ready and the flight deck was clear, he gave Mike a thumbs-up sign. It was a question. "Ready?"

"Ready," he signaled, fist clenched, thumb up. The launch officer kneeled down and pointed toward the bow of the ship. Mike released the brakes and the Dauntless gathered speed. The deck length of *Enterprise* was 802 feet, but he didn't get to use it all. Depending on where he was spotted for takeoff, he might have had six hundred feet. It did not seem long enough at that moment. His plane dropped a little when it rolled off the bow before starting its slow climb.

Mike flew a standard training flight of over an hour, watching the flight operations on the decks of both *Hornet* and *Enterprise*. A few destroyers and cruisers, small compared to a fleet carrier, were escorting them. A hand signal from his flight leader told him to get into the groove. As he had done since his first solo flight, Mike concentrated on the mechanics. He went down the checklist: "You're going to be this far out from the ship, at this position; you're going to make your turn at this time when you're at the stern. If . . . there's a lot of wind, you've got to turn early so you don't get blown back here." In his final turn, he could see the Landing Signal Officer down below his port wing. His paddles said "looking good." Mike came out of the turn and the LSO gave him the cut. He cut the throttle, the plane dropped to the deck, and the tail hook caught a wire. Carrier landing number one was followed quickly by landings number two and number three, although in a different plane with a different sandbag. He happily noted them later in his flight logbook. These flights were his last for the month, April 1942. His skipper, Lieutenant W. E. Gallaher, signed his logbook and Mike became a carrier pilot. The logbook showed Mike had flown a total of 371.9 hours in his naval career.

The first few days in May brought a bombardment of apocalyptic proportions, including a twenty-four-hour period when something like sixteen thousand shells of all calibers detonated.[43] The emperor's army had ringed the bay with some thirty-seven batteries of artillery, all pointed at the Rock. The enemy no longer smothered it indiscriminately. A few weeks earlier two hot air balloons had risen off the peninsula, their baskets providing a perfect vantage point for artillery spotters.[44] They aimed some of the cannons at specific targets. Buildings, trees, birds, deer—everything was disappearing. The encompassing malevolence could make breathing hard, not to mention sleep. Shofner, who began to suffer dysentery (diarrhea), likened it to "life in the bull's eye."

Few men were not cowed, especially those who had come from Bataan. They had seen this before. During the hours of abuse, the marines often wondered about the thousands of soldiers who lived deep down in the Malinta Tunnels; few of these units had been seen aboveground recently. A rumor passed that the officers in the tunnels still had houseboys laundering their uniforms.[45] To Shofner and the Fourth Marines, who were expected to maintain an ability to hold off an invasion, their disappearance amounted to cowardice. They made up a name for the condition: "tunnel-itus." The marines dug tunnels, of course, to the extent possible, but they had to put themselves at risk each day. The marines, as well as the army's coastal artillery units, had to repair damage to their trenches and firing positions for the day when the invasion began, even as the landscape became blackened and denuded. On clear nights, the marines could see that the lights had come back on in Manila. The Japanese were probably living it up.

On May 2, the enemy spotters located one of the last great batteries still firing on the Rock, Battery Geary. It took three hours, but one of their shells penetrated Geary's magazine. The detonation of that much ordnance rocked Shofner's tunnel back in Middleside. He went to help. Only a few shards of the eight twelve-inch mortars remained. Chunks of concrete and metal littered the west end of the island. All the trees within a hundred yards had been cut to stumps. He and some others eventually rescued five men from an adjacent magazine.

A few nights later Shofner happened to catch the English broadcast of Tokyo radio. It predicted "the war in the Philippines would soon be over." Only a few hours passed before he heard a report of small-arms fire on the beaches of Bottomside. Shifty stayed at the entrance of his tunnel in Middleside, watching. It could be another false alarm. A few weeks earlier a report of an enemy landing had turned out to be two of his platoons shooting at one another. Before midnight, however, he received confirmation of a small landing in the 1st Battalion sector. With it came the order to be ready to move out immediately. After midnight, he could see the flashes of battle down on the beaches. At dawn on May 6, he saw about forty landing boats departing. The enemy landing, he was relieved to see, had been repelled.

He wanted to get his men aboveground and to the barracks for a proper meal, but the artillery barrage had not lifted, so they ate some C rations. Echoes of machine-gun and cannon fire down on the beaches still reached him. Someone was still fighting. At about eleven thirty a.m., the phone rang. His CO ordered him to "execute Pontiac by 12 o'clock." Shofner had just been ordered to surrender.

It came as a shock. They had not fired a shot. They had not been called to help repel the landing. The CO directed him to have his men destroy their weapons. He was to prepare them to move to an assembly point, to offer no resistance, and to avoid reacting to the insults that were sure to come. Captain Shofner called his men together. Any man who had stood with him these past few months was now a member of the Fourth Marines, regardless of his original unit. Shofner was proud of all of them. "Marines," he began before emotion choked his voice. Tears came. Months of anguish had come to naught. He noticed bitter tears on others, even in the eyes of his sergeants. Their captain struggled to find the words. They heard him say, "Boys, we've lost, but we've got to survive, we are not gonna give up within ourselves."

Captain Shofner unsheathed his Mameluke, the traditional sword carried by officers of the United States Marine Corps. No marine unit, so far as he knew, had ever surrendered in battle. He dashed the gilded blade into pieces. It was over. He ordered them to begin disabling their weapons, starting with the larger calibers and working down to their rifles and sidearms.

The destruction ceased at noon and white sheets were displayed on poles and on the ground. Austin Shofner encouraged his men to go to their former barracks and retrieve their packs, clothing, gear, and personal items. As his men scattered, he did the same. Shifty took great care in selecting and packing his gear. Knowing he would be searched, he found clever ways to hide small items of value, like rolling Philippine pesos into his roll of toilet paper. Always one for tradition, he took out the plaque of the Fourth Marines Club. It bore the emblem of his beloved corps and could not be discarded. He handed it to his runner, Private First Class Arthur Jones, reasoning that a private would not be as thoroughly searched as an officer. "Hang on to that plaque."

"Yes, sir."

A few men started to shave and get cleaned up.[46] The opening salvo of artillery caught everyone off guard. The drone of oncoming bombers soon followed. The unexpected attack killed several of his men and wounded more.[47] One round knocked Shifty to the ground, again, but he made it back to the tunnel. He listened to the radio station KGEI, in San Francisco, broadcast the news of the surrender, then lay down and slept. The next morning, soon after the shelling stopped, the first Japanese troops arrived.

As soon as the enemy assured themselves of no opposition, they shouldered their rifles.[48] Looking quite pleased, the soldiers searched their prisoners for small arms, helped themselves to any items of value, then marched the group off toward the beach. The Fourth Marine Regiment no longer existed.*

AFTER WEEKS OF TRAINING IN THE FORESTS AND SWAMPS AROUND NEW RIVER, the crew of #4 gun could set up their mortar in thirty-eight seconds. The payoff came in the first week of May. They fired their first live rounds. Allotted sixteen shells, Sid and Deacon and W.O. and the other members each took a turn dropping a shell into the big mortar tube. The round launched with a dull, brassy ringing sound, arched high into the air, and exploded a few hundred yards away. Deacon, the squad's gunner, called them "beautiful."

Sid, the assistant gunner, liked the complexity of the 81mm mortar. Aiming and firing the weapon required a lot of skill. He and Deacon had to shoot azimuths and calculate both range and deflection. They consulted range cards to determine the correct amount of propulsion and the proper angle to launch a shell a specific distance. The mortar squad also began applying that knowledge to specific circumstances, or what they called field problems. Aiming at stationary targets gave way to multishell salvos, such as zone firing or sweeping fire.

---

*Of the roughly 1,200 officers and men of the Fourth Marines who fought for Luzon, 357 were listed as wounded in action and 331 either were killed in action, died of wounds, or were missing and presumed dead.

On the weekends they usually had liberty. If they went with Deacon, they would go into Wilmington, see a USO show, and maybe even meet some girls. There would be no alcohol, however. Deacon would not stand for it. His adherence to all the tenets of his Baptist faith made him an unusual marine. Sid and W.O. did not mind overly. They did not always take liberty with Deacon. One Saturday they told Deacon they were going to Wilmington, but they went to the Civil War battlefield of Bentonville, North Carolina, instead. Sidney and W.O. knew without asking that everyone in their squad would have called them stupid for wasting a liberty like that. With the recent departure of the Fifth Marines, the First Marines would be leaving for their own battlefield, somewhere, quite soon.

WITH NEW QUALIFIED PILOTS ABOARD, THE VETS IN SCOUTING SIX SEEMED only too happy to let them practice their craft by flying the scouting missions. The senior officers had had their fill of missions that were seemingly intended to improve morale rather than achieve "significant military results," and ferrying planes to some island base qualified.[49] As another vet put it, "this looks like another assault on the outhouse of Wake [Island]."[50] In the first week of May, Mike flew most every day as the task force steamed south. In four hours, he flew out two hundred miles, took a dogleg of about thirty miles, and then flew back toward the ship.

Tasked with spotting Japanese submarines, Mike worried about finding his way back to the carrier. The hours it took to fly a 430-mile dogleg search pattern created more than enough ocean to get lost in. Even as prevailing winds and cloud banks affected his course and speed, his carrier changed directions and speeds as part of its operation. Point Option, where plane and ship planned to meet four hours later, was an estimate. Before he left the ready room, Lieutenant Dickinson, the squadron's executive officer (XO), checked to make sure Micheel had all the data correctly entered into his Ouija (plotting) Board. Dickinson offered no encouragement, although the XO disliked inexperienced pilots who dropped bombs on any shapes they saw in the water and thereby killed schools of fish.[51] Mike found antisubmarine patrols a lonely business.

For all the important information measured by the aircraft's gauges, two essential pieces of information were not displayed: the speed and direction of the wind. He marked these down on the Ouija (pronounced wee-jee) Board before departing, knowing that it could change drastically during a long flight. Mike had been taught to read the surface of the ocean through his binoculars: the stronger the wind, the larger the waves. Seen from an altitude of fifteen hundred feet, the foam flying off the wave tops indicated the direction. During the course of a two-hundred-nautical-mile flight, the wind could change from ten knots out of the east to twenty knots out of the west. Such changes had drastic effects upon the plane's ground speed, fuel consumption, and direction. If the mood of the Pacific was calm and its color one limitless shade of cobalt, then his course had not been disrupted.

Along with tracking the wind, Mike had a secret weapon to help him find his way home: a navigational aid known as the YE/ZB. Toward the end of his flight on May 7, as he approached Point Option, Mike took his plane up to about five thousand feet. Disconnecting his long-distance communication radio, he plugged in the YE/ZB, which received a simple coded signal broadcast from his carrier. It provided, within a limited range, enough directional information to locate the ship. Taking his plane up to altitude was the moment of truth. If the YE/ZB wasn't working, or if he had failed to write down the day's code for its signal, or if his calculations had been off and he was out of range—he and his gunner would disappear. Two search planes had disappeared six days earlier, one flown by an experienced pilot. The doubts tugged at him until he verified his course. It came in loud and clear. He plugged his long-range radio back in and closed on the Big E.

After making carrier landing number eight, Mike went to the squadron ready room and heard the news. USS *Lexington* and USS *Yorktown*, America's other two operational carriers, had found Japanese carriers in the Coral Sea, just north of Australia. The planes of *Lexington* had sunk an enemy carrier. The commander of the Lex's scouting squadron had radioed the immortal line "Scratch one flattop!" The sinking of *Ryukaku* was news sure to put a grin on every face.* In the first battle against enemy aircraft carriers, the Dauntlesses had proven they could do the job. The radiomen in the Big E's communications center were besieged for news about the course of battle. Those who heard passed the news throughout the ship. It was all anyone could talk about.[52] The enemy task force included two of the carriers that had bombed Pearl Harbor, *Shokaku* and *Zuikaku*. Bad news followed, though, as the enemy's planes hit some of the U.S. ships in the Coral Sea before darkness fell.

Looking over their maps, the pilots of Scouting Six could see that their intended destination, Efate, would position them just two days from the battle in the Coral Sea. So they went to bed that night pondering the possibilities. Mike did not fly the next day, so he could hear the latest reports. The news was bad. By midday, Japanese pilots put two torpedoes into *Lexington* and dropped a bomb on *Yorktown*. By day's end, U.S. pilots scored some hits on *Shokaku*. The Lex, however, went down

---

*The IJN had no carrier named *Ryukaku*. The U.S. had sunk the *Shoho*.

late that night. The experienced pilots in Micheel's squadron knew many of those serving on both the Lady Lex and *Yorktown*. Naval aviation had been a small fraternity until recently. News reports the next day confused the situation.[53] The Navy Department claimed it sank nine ships and damaged three. An Australian broadcast increased the total to eighteen, while the Empire of Japan alleged its planes had sunk one battleship, the *California*, two U.S. carriers (Lex and *Yorktown*), and one British carrier, *Warspite*.* The navy officers listening to the enemy claims in the wardroom of the Big E could laugh them off—the battleship *California* was still in Pearl Harbor. Scouting Six's XO, Dickinson, asserted that the Lady Lex "had more than paid for herself in dead-jap currency."[54] Still, they had to wonder what this loss meant for them. No one knew the extent of *Yorktown*'s damage. The United States might only have two operational aircraft carriers, while the Imperial Japanese Fleet had at least eight flattops of various sizes, if not more.[55]

More experienced pilots than Ensign Micheel flew the Big E's scouting missions for the next few days. One of the scouts launched from *Hornet*, though, not only got lost, he failed to switch off his long-range radio when he spoke to his rear seat gunner on the intercom about the YE/ZB. Ships all over the fleet heard him say, "Get that receiver working. What's this little switch for? Boy, this is serious. Can't you hear anything? I can't hear anything either. What the hell do you suppose is wrong with that thing? It worked all right yesterday. What the hell good is a radio beam when you can't pick it up?"[56] No one spotted the enemy and therefore the flattops continued with their mission to deliver reinforcements. The island of Efate proved unprepared for the marine squadron, so it flew off to Noumea, the port city of New Caledonia, instead. With its mission completed the task force turned toward Hawaii. The ensigns went back to conducting antisubmarine warfare (ASW).

In addition to the routine ASW missions, the skipper assigned Mike the duty of assistant mechanical officer. As such, he started working with the plane captains and their maintenance men in the giant effort it took to keep the squadron's eighteen Dauntlesses flying. A lot could go wrong with the plane's R-1820 Cyclone radial engines. Mike had learned about radial engines and the other parts of a plane during his training, and again when he was punished on North Island, but he was no mechanic. As an officer, he supervised the work and made sure the paperwork got processed.

The men he supervised were a part of his squadron, or what was then called the "brown shoe navy." All of Scouting Six, from Skipper Gallaher to the lowliest

---

*All of these claims of ships sunk during the Battle of the Coral Sea were highly inflated.

aviation mechanic's mate third class, had boarded the carrier as one unit. As airmen, their uniform was a khaki shirt, khaki tie, khaki pants, and brown leather shoes. Their duty stations, in the air or in their squadron room, tended to separate them from the men of the ship's company. Mike's new job, however, brought him into contact with the officers, petty officers, and seamen who served on the Big E regardless of the squadrons she embarked. These men, members of the "black shoe navy," tended to refer to airmen as Airedales.

While brown shoe and black shoe served on the same team, an unseen force produced friction. A seismic change had occurred within the United States Navy. For more than a hundred years, the battleship had been the foundation of the fleet. Only the best officers had gained command of battlewagons like USS *Arizona*. In the past decade, however, naval aviators had begun to buck the traditions, the strategy, and the tactics. The aircraft carrier was the most potent naval weapon, they argued, and Japan's attack on Pearl Harbor could be seen as the final ascendancy of the carrier over the battleship.

Such seismic change met resistance from older sailors—the officers and petty officers. Younger sailors, the seamen and yeomen, tended to be less concerned about tradition and more jealous of some of the privileges of being an Airedale. For instance, every black shoe had, in addition to their normal duties, a station to take when the ship went to general quarters. Seamen also stood watch in rotation. Flight crews did not stand watch. It was easy to resent the glamorous life of a pilot while sweating through another shift down in the holds of Big E. Their tours of duty, however, entitled the black shoes to consider *Enterprise* as theirs, in a way the aviators could not.

Ensign Micheel, to be effective, had to keep these attitudes in mind. He also was coming to understand that the rift between old pilots and new in Scouting Six was not due entirely to the latter's replacement of lost friends. The older men wore the ring of Annapolis and they trusted those who wore it, the career naval officers. None of them went out of their way to train the new guys, most of whom were "ninety-day wonders." So Mike and John picked it up as they went along. When not assigned to fly, Mike liked to watch flight operations from Vulture's Row.

The intricate and dangerous work occurring below him on the flight deck took a lot of time to understand. Each man wore a specific jersey color based on his task, such as loading the plane's bombs, and he performed his job at a specific point in the process. Mike watched a Wildcat roll to the takeoff spot. The pilot gunned the engine, gave the thumbs-up, and roared down the deck, taking off for a search mission. After the fighter dropped off the bow, it did not reappear. Since the drop from the flight deck to the sea was eighty feet, even without considering the plane's forward momentum, the thought of this hapless fall was enough to cause fear to the point of physical illness. As *Enterprise* roared past the wrecked plane, unable to stop, Mike and many others looked down and saw it begin to sink. The pilot floated free. The collision with the ocean had knocked him out. The plane sank. The unconscious pilot sank. The "rescue destroyer" arrived too late.

The loss confirmed Mike's suspicion. Taking off, when a sharp wind shear or a stutter in the engine power could mean sudden death, was more dangerous than landing. By the time he got into the groove of the landing pattern, on the other hand, a pilot had been in the air for a few hours. A power failure at that moment seemed unlikely. Micheel decided to pray more often, especially during takeoffs. On the radio that night, Tokyo Rose revised her claims for the U.S. warships her airmen had sunk in the recent battle in the Coral Sea. The U.S. Navy for its part denied losing a carrier in that battle. The following day, all the aircraft in all the squadrons on *Enterprise* took off. Micheel landed on Ford Island, in the middle of Pearl Harbor, on May 26, near where his ship would dock later.

MAY 26 FOUND SHOFNER HAPPY AND RELIEVED TO BE IN THE CITY JAIL OF MANILA. The surrender had been followed by weeks of living on a beach without shelter and with very little food and water until, when their captors finally had taken them off Corregidor, seven thousand Americans and five thousand Filipinos had boarded three ships. The ships had not come, however, alongside one of Manila's docks. Instead they had dropped anchor off Parañaque. When the afternoon had grown oppressive, the POWs had been forced to climb down into Japanese landing craft, which had taken them to within a dozen feet of the shore. The order to disembark had not been understood immediately. What were the guards thinking? Enough shouting and pointing of rifles, however, had persuaded the men to jump into the chest-deep water with their packs and wade to shore. They had formed into a long column, four abreast, and marched up Dewey Boulevard through the heart of Manila.

Great throngs of Filipinos had lined their way. The import of it all had taken a while to occur to them, but slowly the POWs realized that the Japanese were staging a victory parade. They wanted the Filipinos to witness the beaten and bedraggled Americans. Struggling under their packs, the Americans had been humiliated. The locals, however, had not suddenly accepted the Japanese as the master race. The people had offered the Americans water and even tossed pieces of fruit. These acts of kindness had angered the guards and they swung their rifles at the offenders.

When prevented from helping, some of the people had cried. Through the throngs, the POWs had struggled across the city to the gates of Bilibid, Manila's jail.

Inside, the months of hardship ended. Although the jail could hold only two-thirds of the men, everyone took turns inside, escaping the elements. The guards served three meals a day, mostly rice, and there was enough clean water to bathe. Small amounts of canned food, cigarettes, and native fruits were sold. The money used was Philippine pesos that the lucky individuals had hidden from enemy looters.

With the secure incarceration, the looting subsided. Allowed to organize their men once again, the officers began to direct the work details that performed the tasks needed by their captors. After all they had endured, the hodgepodge of sailors, soldiers, marines, and men from other service branches felt safe at last. Only one point seemed out of order. Japanese soldiers, even privates, required all prisoners regardless of rank to salute or bow to them. The demand galled the officers, but any hesitancy resulted in the prisoner being severely beaten. Even a quick salute, however, did not always suffice. Japanese guards frequently punched and kicked unfortunate prisoners for no discernible reason.

THE SEVENTH MARINES HAD NOT STORMED ASHORE. ON MAY 27 THEY COMpleted unloading their gear at the town of Apia, on the island of Upolu, in Western Samoa. They were joining other U.S. forces that had landed months earlier. The Seventh, with its power generators, radar, big dozers, and heavy artillery, would prepare to defend the city's harbor and construct an airfield.[57] They set up their bivouac in the city park. They began digging trenches. As a sergeant, Manila John did not dig trenches. He and his buddy J.P. enjoyed themselves in the local establishments.[58] In the evening the marines could go buy a beer at the store or even have a meal in the town's only restaurant. The Samoans welcomed the marines. Even a private could afford to hire a local to do his laundry. They found the native girls pretty but protected. It all added up to good duty, although one glance at the map showed the entire Pacific Ocean lay between Samoa and Manila. The clang of the air raid alarm sounded a few times, falsely as it turned out, but it served to remind everyone they were still playing defense.[59]

AFTER A WEEK SPENT IN THE SURF OF ONSLOW BEACH, CARRYING THEIR HEAVY mortar through the sand as they practiced landings, the crew of #4 gun got back to their hut to find they had a seventy-two-hour pass for Memorial Day weekend. They could leave as soon as they dressed appropriately. Sidney could have worn his dress green uniform. Since everybody knew without being told that they would ship out after this break, Sid wanted to go home wearing the dark blue uniform with the red stripe down the leg and the white barracks cap. He had not been issued a dress blue uniform, so he paid $20 to rent one. He and W.O. walked out to the highway that night and started hitching rides. Even though the fancy uniform stopped a lot of cars, it was still a long way to Mobile.

Upon arrival, Sid figured he had just over twenty-four hours to say hello and good-bye to family and friends before starting back. In the afternoon, his family got out the camera and took some photos out on the lawn: Sidney with his sister Katherine, Sidney with his parents. Eugene Sledge came by, clearly impressed by the uniform and envious of Sid's experiences. Eugene's parents had not relented. Having just completed high school, Gene would be allowed to attend Marion Military Institute in the fall. Around them, everything was changing. Thousands of workers were flooding into Mobile to build ships for the navy. Out in the gulf, German submarines were sinking U.S. ships. The Nazis had taken over Europe; the Japanese, the Pacific. Eugene was still chafing under his parents' control. Sidney Phillips, on the other hand, was part of the cataclysm. In a few hours W.O. would show up, and Sid would shake his father's hand and go do something about it.

Act II

"EVEN UP AND SQUARED OFF"

May 1942–December 1942

The Empire of Japan expected its massive victory at Pearl Harbor and elsewhere to convince the Americans to cede the Pacific Rim to them. The opposite occurred. Hatred of the Japanese knew no bounds. Americans gave their government carte blanche to exact vengeance. Part of the Roosevelt administration's challenge was to funnel some of that fury toward the campaign against America's biggest threat, Nazi Germany. The strategic goal, to hold the line against the empire while defeating the Third Reich, took a sharp twist because U.S. intelligence services decoded much of Japan's communications. These intercepts revealed first an attempt to lure the United States into a decisive carrier battle, followed by an attempt to sever the supply lines between the United States and Australia. These moves required decisive action, even when the empire's forces held a significant military advantage.

When Scouting Six took off from Ford Island to meet the Big E, already sailing toward their next mission, Ensign Micheel flew with his new permanent gunner, J. W. Dance. After flying with a few different airmen, Mike had hit it off with Dance. They flew a long scouting pattern that afternoon, May 28, returning hours later to their carrier task force. Within a mile of *Enterprise* sailed *Hornet*. A phalanx of cruisers and destroyers surrounded them as they headed north from Hawaii. After catching a wire with his tail hook, Mike left the engine running for the plane pushers. He and Dance climbed out and walked down to the ready room.

The room was abuzz with news. One of the torpedo planes had crashed on landing and gone in the drink. The crew had been fished out, but even though the pilot was a lieutenant commander and the skipper of the squadron, they would not be returned to their ship this day. The Big E was in a hurry. Something big was in the wind. Mike would have had the feeling that he was the last guy to hear this. He would have been right. The Big E had been in a hurry-up, high-alert mode for more than a week now and he hadn't noticed. Seamen in the engine room had heard something was up.[1] The new ensign, however, had assumed it was always like this.

On June 1 the official word came from Admiral Spruance, the commander of the task force. Fleets of enemy battleships and enemy carriers and enemy troop transports would soon attack the island of Midway, about a thousand miles from Hawaii. Admiral Spruance planned to ambush them. The admiral did not feel the need to say much more. According to scuttlebutt in the ready room, the United States had broken the enemy's communication codes. Three different enemy task forces would hit the island on June 4. "Man," thought Mike as he heard these forces described, "they've got the whole fleet coming at Midway Island. . . ."

All the pilots kept a sharp eye on the Teletype screen at the front of the ready room. As soon as contact reports came in, the air operations office above them would receive and process information, then send it across their screen. So far, only the latest meteorological and navigational information appeared. Although the task force continued to move, it was holding station at 32 degrees north latitude, 173 degrees west longitude. This location, about 325 miles northeast of Midway Island, had been chosen by Admiral Nimitz, the commander of the Pacific Fleet. Under his direction, Admiral Spruance's forces would wait for the Japanese carriers here, an area Nimitz had named Point Luck.

The skipper of Scouting Six, Earl Gallaher, did not seem to get excited. He delivered neither a pep talk nor a long discourse on the various possible tactical situations. He stuck to what was known. The main scouting duties would be handled by the army's B-17 bombers and the navy's PBY scout planes based on Midway Island. These big four-engine planes could fly great distances. These planes would find the enemy carriers, which were expected to attack from the northwest. Marine Corps dive-bombers and army air corps bombers on Midway would meet the enemy head-on; the dive-bombers from *Enterprise*, *Yorktown*, and *Hornet* would ambush them. To pass the time, the skipper had them watch a slide show of profiles of Japanese ships and planes. He wanted his pilots to differentiate between enemy fighters and dive-bombers.

The next day, the flight officer scheduled Micheel and Dance to fly a scouting mission. The aggressive scheme of zigzagging by the task forces would make returning more difficult. He had been ordered to maintain absolute radio silence. If his motor quit, the skipper told him, he had to crash "and hope for the best in your rubber boat."[2] Mike pulled alongside the launch officer thinking the spot a bit too far forward. It would be nice to have a longer runway. He jammed the brakes, revved the engine, and began reciting lines from the 23rd Psalm, "And yea though I go through the valley of the shadow of death, thou art with me . . . ," before the launch officer pointed to the bow and ducked out of the way. The weather was terrible, though. It forced an early return. The only new ships on the horizon were USS *Yorktown* and her escorts, sailing a few miles away. The U.S. force now comprised three fleet carriers plus the squadrons on Midway. Four or five enemy carriers were expected, plus a fleet of main battleships and the invasion force. No one had ever seen a battle like this before. The key to victory over the enemy, as was self-evident, lay in finding them first. Since the Japanese could be expected to launch their attack on Midway at dawn, the dive-bombers would endeavor to hit their carriers before the enemy planes returned.

Other scouts flew on June 3, as the rest of the squadron waited, making sure the U.S. carriers were not ambushed. In the morning a Midway-based scout plane reported that the "main body" of the enemy's fleet was approaching Midway from the west. This caused a sensation for a time, but soon enough the word was delivered from the front of the room: "this task force was the landing force, not the carriers." The enemy landing forces would be ignored for the time being. Since the report included course and speed, Mike plotted it anyway. So far as he could tell, that task force was well out of range, which is what mattered to him. In the late afternoon a report came in that army aircraft had located four large enemy ships and left one "burning furiously."[3] Sketchy as they were, the reports received throughout the day served to confirm their understanding. Tomorrow was the day. The last navigational information to appear at the front of the ready room at seven forty p.m. showed a general course change toward Midway. To make itself a hard target for submarines, however, *Enterprise* would spend the night zigzagging according to plan number seven.[4] The next morning would find her and the other carriers about two hundred miles north-northeast of Midway.

Scouting Six and the other flight crews had reveille at three thirty a.m. on June 4. Tension in the ready room started out high. As time passed Mike was, in his own estimation, "starting to pucker." He sat in the back, smoking cigarettes and taking it easy on the coffee, so he wouldn't make himself uncomfortable during a long flight. Few men spoke. Just after seven thirty a.m., the Teletype punched out "carriers sighted" by a reconnaissance plane.* The "This is it" moment faded, however, as information on the Japanese carriers' position, course, and speed failed to appear. Tension and frustration spiked. Without position, speed, or direction, Micheel figured the scout's report amounted to "We've got a bunch of ships out here going someplace." Ten minutes later, another scout report came across the screen: "many enemy planes heading Midway, bearing 320, distance 150." The pilots calculated the enemy squadrons were about 230 miles southwest of them. While this news confirmed the presence of enemy carriers, Scouting Six still lacked the information needed to plot a course to intercept the flattops. Assuming the enemy aircraft were flying in a straight line, the Big E changed course to intercept. The "talker" (a yeoman with a

---

*Most histories of the Battle of Midway have used a standardized time because they are covering all aspects of a battle taking place across several time zones. The times given here were those of Ensign Micheel's ship and therefore, presumably, of his wristwatch.

telephone draped around his neck) shouted: "Pilots, man your planes!" The men of Scouting Six stood up and did something unusual. They shook one another's hands and, while walking out the door, wished one another good luck. The yeoman yelled, "Belay that. All pilots return to the ready room."[5]

"What the hell is going on?" someone asked as they filed back in. As Ensign Micheel considered the situation, it occurred to him that neither he nor, he guessed, any of the other replacement pilots had ever flown off a carrier with a 500-pound bomb under the fuselage and a 100-pound bomb under each wing. He had flown scouting missions with a 350-pound depth charge strapped to the belly, but he had never tried to take off with 700 pounds beneath him. Judging from the low wind speed displayed on the Teletype, he prepared himself to drop ten to twelve feet off the bow before his Dauntless attained flying speed.

Another ten minutes elapsed. Then definitive news came. Another PBY patrol radioed Midway Island. The report was forwarded to the Big E. "Two carriers and other ships bearing 320, distance from Midway 180 [nautical miles]." Scouting Six added this data to their plotting boards—their course and speed and that of the enemy—to produce a probable intercept point. The plot put the enemy force about two hundred miles west of Mike's task force. The aircraft carriers of the Imperial Japanese Fleet were twenty-five miles out of the Dauntless's strike range.

With the tactical situation in view, Gallaher returned from a meeting with the air operations staff to brief his squadron. While *Yorktown* awaited events, *Enterprise* and *Hornet* had been ordered to sail southwest to close with the enemy. The air group commander would order the squadrons to sortie at the first opportunity, which would be soon. With calm seas and clear skies, the weather affected the strike in one way. The direction of the wind, coming out of the southeast, meant that the carriers would steam away from Midway (and the enemy) to launch their squadrons. Upon takeoff, the four *Enterprise* squadrons would join up as a coordinated strike. The formation would fly a heading roughly southwest to intercept.

As part of their routine, the pilots noted the location of the nearest island in case of emergency. That was Midway. Instead of providing a specific Point Option, a spot to meet *Enterprise* after the mission, Gallaher told them to expect it to continue to steam toward Midway Island. Reports of Japanese planes bombing Midway began to filter in. The torpedo squadrons would fly at a low altitude of fifteen hundred feet, the dive-bombers would cruise at twenty thousand feet, while the fighter pilots in their Wildcats positioned themselves higher still. In view of the Wildcats' more limited range, Mike heard the skipper say, "the fighters are going to take us three-fourths [of] the way there and then come back." This did not make much sense to him. The communications officer told Mike not to bother turning on his YE/ZB; the ship was not going to switch the homing beacon on. Mike did not get a chance to ask why the hell not.* It was time to go.

He wrote down the ship's final course corrections and speed as Gallaher told his men to expect the enemy carriers to continue to steam toward Midway. As each pilot completed his navigation on his Ouija Board, he reached the same conclusion. "Wow," Mike said, "we're going to be pretty close to maximum range." The order to man his plane came again about nine a.m. As Mike filed out, his section leader told him, "Stay close. Don't be a straggler, stay close." Micheel walked past most of Scouting Six's planes to find his in the pack. A few fighters, the combat air patrol, were taking off.

Behind his squadron sat the Dauntlesses of Bombing Six, which carried thousand-pound bombs underneath. Rear seat gunners and plane captains waited next to each of the light blue shapes. Mike met Dance and climbed into 6-S-17, a plane he had not flown previously. She started easily. He taxied up as the others departed and eventually became number two for takeoff. Just as the pilot ahead of him began to race his engine, he noticed a new board being hung over the PriFly balcony. The air group staff was notifying those pilots still on the deck of new information about the location of the enemy carriers. This was crazy. He taxied forward. With seconds left before he made his first attempt at taking off with a full load, and perhaps midway through the 23rd Psalm, Mike did not copy any of the updated information onto his Ouija Board. He gave the high sign and released his brakes.

Circling above the carrier, the pilots of Scouting Six formed up into sections of three, into divisions of six, the three divisions at last joining their wedges into a large V of Vs. Bombing Six had to repeat the process, then the torpedo planes. Knowing that his target lay somewhere out near the edge of his plane's maximum range, it galled Micheel to burn gas circling the ship. After all the Dauntlesses on the flight deck had taken off, he watched as the Devastators and Wildcats started coming up on the elevator. Men pushed these into takeoff position. All Mike could think was, "Golly, I don't know if I'm going to have enough gas, and here they are, circling us around the aircraft carrier. . . ." *Enterprise* had pulled away from *Hornet*; each carrier was ringed by a few heavy cruisers, a number of destroyers, and a lot of airplanes. *Yorktown* steamed a little farther away. Before the squadrons of Devastators and Wildcats had formed up, though, the commander of the *Enterprise* air group and his two wingmen led both squadrons of Dauntlesses away in a southwesterly direc-

---

*The *Enterprise*'s YE/ZB transmitter was switched on and functioning.

tion at about nine forty-five a.m. The formation began its climb to twenty thousand feet at a higher speed than the usual 120 knots for a scouting mission. After all the wasted time, now they were in a hurry.

Climbing to twenty thousand feet required Micheel and Dance to put on their oxygen masks. The ocean four miles below them became a broad expanse of indigo blue under a clear sky dotted by the occasional small cumulus cloud. Mike obeyed his orders and stuck close to his section leader. He kept the tip of his wing within a few feet of his leader. Flying a tight formation required Mike's attention. He did not compare his actual heading with the one written on his board, nor did he make other notes. He kept his plane in the proper spot. He did keep an eye on the passage of time and his gas gauge; two hours in the air meant the Dauntlesses were reaching their maximum range. He saw nothing below them. He could not see any of the *Hornet*'s squadrons. The planes droned on. He started eyeing his watch more often as it edged toward noon. Scouting Six should have arrived at the intercept point but no one turned around. Every passing second made a safe return more and more improbable.

The air group commander made a sharp right turn. It did not become a 180-degree turn back to the carriers. It resembled the turn in a dogleg search. Mike could not radio for instructions. He waited. A pilot caught his eye and signaled him to look down. There was a ship. He could barely see the tiny thing, but he could clearly see a long white streak behind it. That ship must be in a hurry to churn that kind of stern water. Given its position, it could not be a U.S. ship. The squadron made a slight course correction as the skipper adopted the ship's heading. They quickly flew well ahead of the little ship and arrived at the edge of the Imperial Japanese Fleet. Screened by destroyers and flanked by battleships and cruisers, four flattops steamed northwest, well spaced from one another. Ensign Micheel had never seen that many ships.

The enemy fleet was steaming along, cutting bright swaths in the ocean.[6] No Japanese fighter planes could be seen. The air group commander did not take time to set up for a classic attack. He started a descent toward bombing altitude, twelve thousand feet, which also increased the group's speed. As they flew over the escorts ringing the fleet and approached two carriers, Mike's section leader, Lieutenant West, pointed down to one, then patted his head. Their target was the large flattop on the left, closest to them. Scouting Six's three divisions edged away from one another. Each would attack the long yellow oblong from a different angle. Mike's division turned farther to port (left). They had no time to assume the prescribed echelon (stair step) attack formation. Scouting Six flew right over the top of the carrier, one large enough to be of the Kaga class, and the first division began to disappear, followed quickly by the second division.

Ensign Micheel had a lot to do. The air at one thousand feet differed greatly from the thin air at fifteen thousand, so he dialed in a slightly different trim with his trim tabs, closed the cowling, and changed the propeller's pitch (the degree to which it catches air). He set his arming switches so his bomb fuses would arm upon their release. West saluted Mike, the signal to dive, then peeled off and dove himself. In the final seconds, Micheel put his left hand on the throttle. He looked over at his friend John Lough, flying just off his starboard wing, ready, and saluted. With his right hand on the stick and his feet on the rudder pedals, Mike pulled his nose up and cut the engine to idle, opened the dive brakes, and rolled his plane over. The nose sank and the Dauntless plunged. He put the plane into a seventy-degree dive. Gravity took hold and the harness bit into his shoulders. For the first few thousand feet, he aimed his plane with the naked eye. At about six thousand feet Mike looked into his 3X telescopic sight. Along the bottom of that sight ran a tiny ball in a semicircular track.

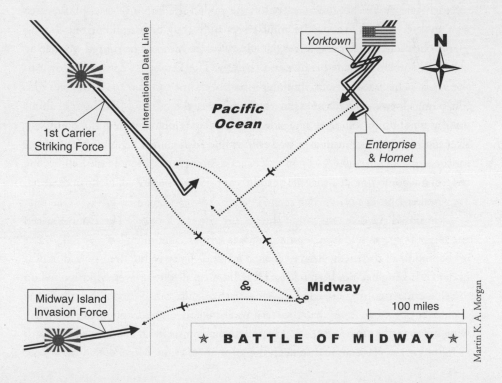

The little ball showed him whether the plane's wings were level. If the ball moved off dead center, he was skidding. Watching the ball, he continued to adjust the trim. In the center of his telescope, Mike could see the plane in front of him nearing the target. Farther below, bombs exploded on the ship's yellow deck, as it swung into a tight turn. A squadron of planes stood on her deck.

The dive felt good. "Boy, this is nice," Mike thought. "I'm just flying down. I got a nice rising sun painted on the bow of the ship for a target." And then he noticed the white specks coming off of this ship. He wondered what it was for a moment, until black puffs appeared nearby. Enemy antiaircraft gunners were shooting as he fell toward them at 240 knots (275 mph).

He aimed for the bow. The ball held in the center, but the ship seemed to be slipping away from him. He tried increasing his dive angle. A steeper dive increased the chances of hitting the ship, since it decreased the distance between the release point and the point of impact. The plane below him cleared the ship. It looked like his bomb hit. Dance was calling out the elevation into the intercom: five thousand feet, four thousand feet. Mike had a clear view of what might be *Kaga* now. She was slipping fast. With no more angle to increase, he adjusted his sights for the center of the ship. Dance called out three thousand feet. Mike tried to wait one more second, to reach twenty-five hundred feet, before he pulled the bomb release. He tried to wait another second, to allow the bomb to get fully away, before pulling out.

As he pulled back, the g-forces felt a bit weak to him and he started wondering if he had somehow made his dive too shallow. The Dauntless flew right down to the water as he eased her out, thinking it had been just too easy to have been right. His bomb's forward speed could have carried it over the carrier. Mike thought about pulling up sharply, rolling to one side, and getting a look at where his bomb hit. Everybody did it. The maneuver, however, would make him a big, slow sitting duck for the ship's antiaircraft (AA) gunners or its fighter planes. He told himself, "I can't control my bomb now. It either hit or didn't, and I'll let the guy who followed me tell me whether I hit or not."

He closed the dive brakes and shoved the throttle forward. The Dauntless did not jump as she should have. Something was wrong. Skimming low over the water in the middle of the enemy fleet, he looked around. The one-hundred-pound bombs under each wing had not been released. He hadn't pulled that lever. Mike looked up to see a cruiser cutting directly across his path. Cruisers had lots of AA guns. He decided the bow had fewer than the stern and broke that way, dropping his two small wing bombs as he crossed its path. He pulled back on the stick and headed skyward.

Jinking his plane around to keep the gunners off him, Mike looked for enemy fighters. If the cruiser's gunners shot back he didn't notice, but then Dance didn't notice any great explosions behind them, either. Up they went. Looking around, he saw a sight that amazed him: not one plane—friend or foe—in view. He didn't know how to get back to his carrier, he didn't know where the rendezvous point was, he was low on fuel, and he had the sneaking suspicion he was on the wrong side of the enemy fleet. Mike pulled out his Ouija, looked at his watch, and realized he could not navigate himself home. He put his plane on his best guess of a heading, eastward, heedless of the angry ships below. Dance, in the rear seat and facing backward, kept watch for fighters. Puckering gas, Mike leveled the plane off at about two thousand feet and slowed it down to 110 knots.

Dance saw them first: two dive-bombers closing from behind and then zooming past. They bore the markings of *Enterprise*'s bombing squadron and they looked like they knew how to fly home. Mike adjusted his heading. The urge to close up, to fly in formation, gave way to the realization that he did not have the fuel to burn. The two Dauntlesses got far ahead of him. He willed himself to remain calm. It was still a beautiful day in the Pacific. He had the right heading. More than an hour passed. Miles away on the horizon, the U.S. fleet hove into view. A wave of elation washed over him.

The two planes ahead of him, though, began to lose altitude. He caught up to them without trying. One slid into the sea, followed quickly by its partner. He guessed they had run out of fuel, although no one said anything over the radio. Seeing them go down in the open ocean scared Mike. He made a note on his plotting board as they passed overhead. His watch read a few minutes before two p.m. Dance swung his chair so he faced west and watched. A few minutes later Dance said, over the intercom, "Both crews have gotten out and they were in the raft."

The landing, his eighteenth, went easily. He taxied forward to where the plane handlers took over. He told Dance to meet him in the ready room for the debriefing and strode toward the bridge. Micheel wanted to make sure that the air group staff or the captain or someone knew about the two crews who went down. Up on the third story of the island, however, he had a hard time attracting anyone's attention. A mile or so away, great clouds of smoke engulfed *Yorktown*, rising in a column to a mushroom high above. The antiaircraft fire made the sky around it look like it was "breaking out in a rash."[7] With one of America's three carriers fighting for its life in plain view, none of the brass paid much attention to an ensign in a flight suit and Mae West (life jacket). Ensign Micheel, on his first visit to this exalted station, finally just grabbed someone, a second or third class petty officer, he couldn't even tell, and gave him what little info he had. "About ten miles astern" of their position, four men were in rubber rafts and needed to be rescued. Pointing at a map, he demanded, "Put an x there that these guys went down there." He had done what he could, but he was not sure it was enough.

Back in the ready room, it was euphoria. They and the other squadrons had left three enemy carriers burning. Everyone thought "it had been the best dive they had ever made."[8] Mike's roommate, Bill Pittman, said he had been attacked not by a Zero, but by a German Messerschmitt.* Pittman's gunner had shot it down, even though his machine gun had fallen out of its mount in the dive; the gunner had held the twin .30 caliber in his lap.[9] Other pilots attested to seeing the gunner holding the 175 pounds of machine gun in his hands and firing it. It was amazing. While everyone stood in the front of the room talking excitedly, Mike went to the back with Dance to meet the air staff's intelligence officer. The intelligence officer asked the pair for their "two bits." Beyond the positions of the two downed pilots, Ensign Micheel did not feel he had much to add to what was already obviously well known. He had dropped on the carrier on the left as ordered. It looked like *Kaga*. He had not seen any fighters and he had been lucky to make it back. The officer turned to Dance and asked if he had anything to add. "When we landed," Dance said, "we only had four gallons of gas left in our plane."

With the ship at general quarters, the officers' mess was closed. Sandwiches and lots of black coffee were there for those that wanted it. Most of the pilots were intent on figuring out "who had scored a hit and on which jap carrier." If it had not been *Akagi* or *Kaga*—both of which had participated in the sneak attack on Pearl Harbor—it had been large enough to be in their class. Gallaher noted that the *Akagi* was the only carrier to have its island on the port side; that made it easier to identify.[10] The pilots of Bombing Six claimed that Scouting Six had cut them off in their dive and they had had to fly on to the far carrier. Someone put up on the screen all the silhouettes of the carriers, as seen from above. Each pilot picked out the one they thought they hit. It was fun. Elated pilots could not share their stories without using their hands to show the relative positions and angles of their planes and their targets and anything else. They agreed their skipper, Gallaher, had planted the first hit and perhaps as many as four more hits had followed.[11] When asked, Mike said he had been told to dive on the carrier to the left, so he did. He was not sure of the name of it or the other nearby. "They were large carriers. That's all."

As time passed it became clear that no more Dauntlesses would land. By their

---

*U.S. Navy pilots reported seeing and/or dogfighting Japanese flying the Me-109 or other German-made aircraft with some regularity. These reports were inaccurate.

count, seven crews were missing at that moment, including the executive officer, Dickinson, and most of the third division.[12] The good cheer faded. Mike looked around and noticed John Lough was missing. Was John out there in a life raft?

There was hardly time to think. *Yorktown*, a sister to the Big E, might sink soon. Some of her planes had landed on the deck above them. Pilots and their crewmen also circulated word of the losses in the other *Enterprise* squadrons. The torpedo squadron in particular had lost a lot of men. Those losses left a bitter taste, since everybody knew the old torpedo planes were, as one put it, "easy prey for Jap fighters."[13] Worse, their torpedoes often failed to detonate. From the bomber squadron came rumors that there was "something screwy" with the new electrical arming system installed in their planes. The new system's malfunction had caused some bombs to be dropped prematurely.

When Gallaher came back to the ready room at about five p.m., he brought news that a second strike would be flown against another task force. Although volunteering was believed to bring bad luck in the navy, Ensign Micheel wanted to go. He did not want to sit around waiting for a torpedo to hit the hull. He went up to the skipper and told him, "I'll volunteer for the second flight." Lieutenant Gallaher did not make his decision based upon volunteers or, much to Mike's relief, upon rank. Those pilots whose planes were in flying condition would go. As determined by the planes' captains, Scouting Six had seven flyable planes. Pittman would not go: the enemy had blown a huge hole in his starboard wing before his gunner drove them off.[14]

Gallaher kept the briefing short. A scout had spotted one enemy carrier, two battleships, three cruisers, and four destroyers at latitude 31 degrees, 40 minutes, longitude 172 degrees, 10 minutes west. That placed it to their northwest and well within range. Gallaher would lead a strike comprised of what was left from Scouting Six, Bombing Six, and the squadron from the *Yorktown*, Bombing Three. It totaled twenty-four Dauntlesses armed with a roughly equal number of five-hundred- and one-thousand-pound bombs. *Hornet's* Dauntlesses would follow them. All the Wildcats would remain, protecting the carriers. Twenty minutes later, Mike and Dance walked back out on the sunny flight deck as their carrier turned into the eight-knot breeze and picked up the speed necessary for flight operations. The Big E's flight deck was not crowded. Their plane, S-6-17, had one five-hundred-pound bomb, but no wing bombs. Fewer planes meant a longer flight deck. Another quick prayer and they set off. A towering column of smoke from *Yorktown* could be seen as the ad hoc group formed up.

They found the fourth enemy flattop easily and quickly. As they approached,

Gallaher got on the radio and informed the group that his squadron and Bombing Six would dive on the carrier. He ordered the other squadron, Bombing Three, to dive on one of the escorting cruisers or destroyers. Gallaher led Scouting Six around the perimeter of the ships below. The skipper obviously wanted his team to drop with the sun at their backs and therefore make it harder for the ship's gunners and its captain. He signaled the men to move into echelon formation. From nineteen thousand feet they began to descend, gaining speed as Gallaher brought them over the target in such a way that their dives would take them from bow to stern over the ship, thus increasing their accuracy.

Micheel saw the carrier below him. Smaller than the one earlier, it churned wakes seemingly in all directions at once as it maneuvered. Gallaher's plane slid over on its back and dove away. Two followed; then the division leader saluted and dropped away. Completing his checklist, Mike rolled up and over, dropping out of the sun from fifteen thousand feet. A roll out of echelon started him in the opposite direction. He spun around bit by bit until he drew a bead on his flight leader.

In the next seventeen seconds he saw flak coming up at him. The carrier and her escorts slewed this way and that. Dance called off their altitude as they plunged. Smoke roiled up at them. The carrier swung hard into another turn in the final seconds. Mike could not get the Dauntless to track the motion and it looked like he would miss, so he threw it into a bit of a skid to the left and pulled the bomb release lever. He figured he had missed the flight deck. Perhaps he had gotten in close enough to damage the hull. Without a look back, he jinked his way around the escort ships, gained altitude, and joined up with Scouting Six. Black bursts of AA fire followed them.

They flew eastward for the second time that day, plenty of gasoline in their tanks and another successful mission under their belts. As Scouting Six and its friends arrived over the Big E and assumed a landing pattern, the late sun sent its rays horizontally across the deck.

Once more they found themselves in the ready room, debriefing, as the clock approached nine p.m. The pilots of Scouting Six planes claimed one direct hit and at least one if not two probable hits on the fourth carrier, said to be named *Hiryu*. The pilot who had dropped behind Mike told him his bomb had missed the carrier. It had exploded just off the starboard bow. That sounded right to Mike. The Dauntlesses of Bombing Three had disobeyed Gallaher's order because it looked to them like it had not been hit. After almost crashing into the leader of Bombing Six, the *Yorktown* squadron had hit the carrier hard, leaving it burning from "stem to stern."[15] That meant the enemy had lost two carriers and had two others on fire. The admiral in command of the task force and the captain of *Enterprise* both sent along their congratulations. Captain Murray included a wish "that many of our gallant and heroic shipmates in the Air Group who are now unaccounted for will be rescued."[16]

Amid the heated speculation of who had hit what came the first news of the planes from *Hornet*. Its second strike had ignored the burning carrier and had attacked one of the cruisers. *Hornet*'s losses from the first strike had not been as bad as thought: some of its planes had landed at Midway. Mike wondered aloud, "Well, what in the world would they go to Midway for?" No one responded. Their thoughts focused on the men from their own ship; *Enterprise* had lost more than half of her aircrews. Scouting Six had suffered the fewest losses. Eight of its sixteen planes were down, although one flight crew had been pulled from the ocean. Only four Devastators of the torpedo squadron had returned—some of them blamed the Wildcats for allowing ten of them to be shot down. The Japanese had bombed the hell out of *Yorktown* and she had been abandoned. Another battle like this and they'd all be dead. A lot of the talk concerned the enemy fighters, the Zeros. Someone had counted six Zeros on the second mission; others recalled a dozen. One Dauntless had been shot down during its dive; two others just after their dives. A few had landed aboard with bullet holes.

Ensign Micheel wondered how he could have missed seeing all the Zeros. Was he blocking them out somehow? He recognized that lately he had begun deliberately ignoring anything that threatened to scare him. Blocking out Zeros seemed very unhealthy. Everybody else had seen them. It gave him a peculiar feeling. After a time, he decided he would not have made a good fighter pilot after all.

Sleep must have come easily for the pilots of Scouting Six. With several enemy task forces still steaming toward Midway, including a flattop, the Klaxon for general quarters and the call to man their planes would wake them early the next morning. As they slept, the Big E, *Hornet*, and their respective flocks of support ships steamed back toward the U.S. mainland, away from the enemy and the damaged *Yorktown*. In the early hours, the task force reversed course. As the pilots came back into the ready room on June 5, they were once again headed into battle. The fighters launched first, determined to protect the remaining carriers; then the search planes took off. Most of Scouting Six sat in their ready room and waited. As the morning passed, it became clear that the enemy had given up. The task force sped up its chase westward, hunting the retreating enemy.

That day and the next, the scouts found a few stragglers, enemy surface ships that either had hung around to pluck their men from the sea or had been too damaged to move quickly. The dive-bombers went after them. Without the danger of

Zeros, these ships should have been easy marks. The results, however, were mixed. Scouts reported finding the enemy ships several times. The reports proved misleading or completely false. The remaining carrier dive-bombers did hit two enemy larger cruisers or battleships. One enemy ship not only dodged the bombs of thirty-two diving Dauntlesses, however, but also shot one plane down with its AA guns. Returning from this mission, one that certainly did not justify the loss of a crew, Micheel and a few other new pilots received credit for their first night landing.

They had seen the necessity of a night carrier landing coming from a long way off, as the water went from blue to black below them. They reached the Big E as the light failed, causing difficulties as the Dauntlesses jostled to get into the landing groove. A dim red light illuminated the dials and gauges on the planes' control panels. Below them, the flattop's landing lights came on, outlining the flight deck. Coming around the stern of the ship, Mike saw that the LSO had lighted paddles to guide him in and give him the cut. After he was aboard, he admitted to himself that getting aboard had been "another pucker job." One of his colleagues mistakenly landed on *Hornet*, while a few *Hornet* planes landed on *Enterprise*.

With the return of the sortie, the Battle of Midway ended. By the next morning, the Japanese ships would be within range of their land-based planes on Wake Island. The U.S. carrier squadrons had chased the enemy as far as was prudent and necessary. There was time to linger in the wardroom after dinner and talk. A bottle of whiskey came out and was passed among them. Though normally an illegal maneuver in Uncle Sam's navy, all of the aircrews had the opportunity to drink—if not from a personal supply, then from the ship's doctor. Mike had a shot. After much discussion, the pilots decided the ship that had eluded them had been a light cruiser, and those were just too fast and too small to hit. The disappearance of the enemy task forces, still numerically superior and suspected of including a carrier, remained a surprise to Mike. It just didn't make sense to him.

In the early hours of June 7, before he and the pilots of Scouting Six reached their ready room, USS *Yorktown* slipped beneath the waves, the victim of a Japanese submarine's torpedoes. The two remaining American flattops fueled the fleet and set sail for Alaska, which had also been attacked by aircraft of the Imperial Japanese Navy. The day marked the six-month anniversary of the attack on Pearl Harbor—June 7 even fell on a Sunday. The pilots could relax and savor the moment. The army bombers on Midway were reporting more hits on the fleeing enemy. After a few days, a storm settled in around them and canceled flight operations. The task force soon gave up Alaska, turned around, and headed south for Pearl Harbor. On the way back, the radio room picked up a broadcast from Tokyo. The empire claimed to have sunk "one aircraft carrier of the 'Enterprise type' and one of the 'Hornet type,' each of 19,900 tons."[17] The claim stood in stark contrast to Radio Tokyo's claim of June 6—that it had sunk six U.S. carriers and captured Midway Island.[18] On board *Enterprise* and the other ships that had won the battle of Midway, men estimated the Japanese losses at "four—possibly five—Japanese carriers," plus "three battleships damaged or sunk," as well as "four cruisers and four troop transports" damaged or sunk.* As many as eighteen thousand to twenty thousand Japanese had gone down with those ships.[19] Since *Yorktown* had been abandoned before she sank, her personnel taken aboard the escorts, the U.S. losses would be slight by comparison.

Ensign John Lough's best friend on *Enterprise* was eventually tasked with surveying the missing pilot's belongings. Many men had the same task at that same moment. "The thing to do," Mike was told, "is to go through everything he's got . . . if there's anything there that's questionable," anything that might upset his parents, "you don't send it to them." In John's stateroom, he found nothing the least objectionable. John had been "a straight arrow kid." In the box of personal items Mike included a letter because he had to say something. He knew them. Expressions of friendship and of loss made it past the censors, not details. Although some flight crews had been pulled from the water in the days after the battle, Mike held out little hope of John's rescue. His duty to John made thoughts of his own fate unavoidable. "You're not infallible," he told himself as he packed it all up. Nothing could protect him from a bad break in the dangerous life of a naval aviator.

On the morning of June 13, two weeks after the battle for Midway began, the carriers neared the Hawaiian Islands and the squadrons took off for Ford Island.[20] Upon arrival the pilots were granted liberty and given a room at one of the fine hotels on Waikiki Beach—the Royal Hawaiian or the Moana—reserved by the navy. Officers paid $1 per night to stay at a hotel where guests paid $70 a night in peacetime.[21] The pilots certainly recognized this as one of those times when rank had its privileges. The pampering staff and the fine cuisine had disappeared, however. Honolulu had barbed wire on its beaches, checkpoints with armed guards, and a ten p.m. curfew. Businesses downtown had limited hours of operation. The city was completely blacked out at night. The two hotels, under these conditions and filled with navy

---

*These estimates of Japanese losses were widely inflated. The Imperial Japanese Navy lost four carriers (*Kaga*, *Akagi*, *Soryu*, and *Hiryu*), as well as one cruiser, *Mikuma*. Estimates of her casualties have run as low as 2,500 men. By contrast, the United States lost two ships, *Yorktown* and *Hamman* (DD-412), and about 340 men.

officers, felt a lot like being on a carrier except everybody wore their dress uniforms. The young ladies on the beach and in the restaurants attracted a lot of attention. Mike decided not to try to elbow his way through the crowd to speak with one.

All the civilians knew about the Battle of Midway; the newspapers had carried the story since the day it began. On June 4, U.S. military leaders assured the public they had expected an enemy attack on U.S. territory as a reprisal "for the April 18 raid on Tokyo and other Jap industrial centers by Lieutenant Colonel Jimmy Doolittle and 79 intrepid companions."[22] Admiral Nimitz, commander of the Pacific Fleet, had been cautious initially about announcing the number and type of ships sunk at Midway.[23] His press releases praised the efforts of all those who had inflicted "very heavy" damage on the enemy, particularly the flight crews of the army, navy, and Marine Corps. In the days that had followed, reporters citing unnamed sources in naval intelligence leaked the fact that the U.S. forces "Knew Jap Task Force Was Coming—And Were Ready." Nimitz declared on June 6 that "Pearl Harbor has been partially avenged," and began providing details about what the reporters began calling "the greatest naval battle of the war."[24]

The day before Enterprise's squadrons arrived at their hotels in Waikiki, the newspapers had headlined interviews with the flight crews of the army air corps' big bombers. "The Army pilots who actually dropped the bombs reported personally that they made hits on three Japanese carriers . . ."[25] The dive-bomber pilots not only believed they represented a revolution in naval warfare about which the public was largely ignorant, but knew they had sunk the flattops.[26] The first night in the dining room of the Royal Hawaiian Hotel, a table full of Scouting Six pilots found themselves within earshot of a table of army pilots. The crews of the four-engine and twin-engine bombers spoke of sinking the carriers. Incensed by one army pilot's account of how he won the battle, one of the Dauntless pilots yelled, "By God, that's a damn lie!" and the fight was on.[27] Bill Pittman, Mike's roommate, took part in the melee and told him all about it the next day.

Even as some Scouting Six pilots raised a little hell, others were coming back from it. Micheel spotted Tony Schneider, one of the Big E's missing Dauntless pilots. Ensign Schneider, with Bombing Six, said he and Lieutenant Edwin Kroeger had run out of gas on the return from the first bombing run. They had landed near one another and the four men had gotten into two rafts. It had taken five days for them to be picked up, Tony said, five days in a rubber raft in an empty ocean. Mike told him his story of following two planes on his return from the first mission and something struck a chord. As they discussed the way the two planes went down, Tony and Mike came to believe they had shared that terrifying moment.

*   *   *

Sid's father had driven them out of Mobile through the new Bankhead Tunnel and let them off by the side of the highway. Sidney Phillips and William "W. O." Brown had been joined by another How Company man on his way back from Biloxi. Securing rides north proved difficult and the three arrived late into their base at New River. They walked in nervously, knowing what happened to marines found to be AWOL (absent without leave). As it turned out, most of the regiment had had the same problem to some degree, so their tardiness was ignored.

During the first week of June, they had Field Days, meaning they cleaned their camp. They also packed the battalion's equipment before moving on to their weapons, their packs, and their seabags. Orders to put their coats and their bathing suits on the top of their seabags offered no clues as to their impending destination.

On June 8, they packed all day and boarded the train. Sid and his friend John "Deacon" Tatum claimed the last two seats in the last coach. At last they were under way. The feeling of adventure gathered steam as the world they knew passed. In Chattanooga they jumped off to get candy and ice cream. When night came, the black porters made up their beds in the sleeping car with clean sheets. In a few days, the old locomotive pulled them into the vast Southwest. The vistas opening up before them were ignored by the platoon, but the cattle ranches and oil wells and herds of antelope delighted Sid and Deacon. Place-names floated past: Dodge City, Boot Hill, even a monument to Wild Bill Hickok. At one stop they bought souvenirs from some Indian woman and told themselves they were "sightseeing at government expense." They stopped for lunch at a Harvey House and one of the women asked them if they were CCC boys.* Like many civilians, she did not recognize the green USMC uniform, but the angry response her question elicited fixed that.

The thrill of the new, however, explained only part of the energy and excitement in the air. A feeling of impermanence gilded every moment.[28] Even after arriving in San Francisco on June 13 and being assigned a berth on a ship in the harbor, the feeling of a higher purpose impelling them toward an unknown destination produced a carefree exuberance. They were not allowed to leave the ship every day, or even for an entire day. How Company stood inspection one morning, just to keep discipline

---

*The Harvey House was a well-known chain of restaurants situated near railroad stations. The CCC was the Civilian Conservation Corps, which offered work for unemployed men from 1933 to 1942. It focused primarily on the conservation and improvement of natural resources.

tight. When liberty came they found many locations under guard, like the Golden Gate Bridge and the Oakland Bay Bridge. While some of How Company found their way to a bar, and others to the theater, Deacon and Sid walked to Chinatown. Signs in English gave way to exotic hieroglyphics. "Boy," Deacon declared, "those chink gals are good-looking." The wares displayed for sale included the strange and the unknown. Sid bought a newspaper and read about the navy's victory at Midway. He wondered if his uncle, a navy pilot, had been involved. The newspaper also carried a story about the big General MacArthur Day celebration held at a local stadium, when soldiers leaped from their foxholes "just as they did at Bataan."[29] At a bookstore he bought some great books on the Civil War, which he sent home.

All leaves were canceled on Sunday, June 21. Each marine aboard USS *George F. Elliott*, the entire 2nd Battalion of the First Marines (2/1), had to dump out the contents of his seabag on the pier for inspection. The word was the ship would sail at three a.m. This time, the word was close. At four a.m. it stood out from the pier and steamed past the island of Alcatraz. A marine called to a figure standing on the prison's dock, "Hey, Lucky, want to trade places?" *Elliott* passed through the submarine nets, under the Golden Gate Bridge, and into open sea. Twelve ships joined *Elliott*, which Sid noted unhappily bore the number AP 13. Towering waves and gale-force winds rocked the convoy. The vomiting began soon thereafter. Those who became seasick joined those who were hungover and soon the heads (toilets) were filled and the deck was awash with vomit. Sid and Deacon watched the coast fall away.

The next day it was announced that they were headed for New Zealand, a journey that would take nineteen days because the convoy would have to zigzag as a precaution against submarines. The groans and grimaces accompanying the news came from most of the 2/1, who had decided after twenty-four hours that no place they had ever been rivaled *Elliott* for discomfort. Overcrowding made it difficult to sleep, eat, stand, or use the head. Discomfort gave way to disgust whenever the mess served chipped beef on toast, also known as shit on a shingle. When the ventilators went off in the holds, the marines blamed malicious swabbies. At the ship's store, the swabbies served the swabbies first, leaving their guests with few leftovers. Announcements over the ship's PA system blared commands frequently; each began with a loud "Now hear this . . ." The experience left the marines sputtering words like "rust bucket" and "African slaver."

Within a few days Sid found himself on a work detail, chipping the paint off the interior surfaces of the ship. As had been discovered during the attack on Pearl Harbor, the years of accumulated paint burned very well. The paint had to be removed for the safety of the ship. To Sid and the fifty others who had to do it, however, it felt like make-work and they cursed it heartily. One morning a massive sailor, the chief bosun's mate, came up to Sid as he was chipping paint and ordered him to follow.

"I am going to give you one of the best jobs available," the chief said, leading him to a large bathroom. Sid had just become the captain of the Officers' Head. "You are going to thank me in a few days." One deck below the ship's bridge, the head held six porcelain sinks, toilets, and urinals. Six shower stalls lined one wall. As he was instructed on how to keep all of the porcelain spotless, he thought of the long troughs of running seawater the men used for toilets downstairs. Here, he would be one of the few enlisted men with access to fresh water for bathing and washing his clothes. The tall bosun had been absolutely right.

Crossing the equator offered some relief from the days of washing the head and watching the flying fish. On July 1, the ship's crew observed the navy tradition of initiating the pollywogs into shellbacks, "into the solemn mysteries of the deep." The lieutenants of the 2/1 got the worst of it, getting their hair greased with oil by the order of Neptunus Rex, Ruler of the Raging Main. The ceremony lightened the mood on a ship on which men had been ordered not to toss their cigarette butts over the side, lest they leave a trail for an enemy submarine to follow. Crossing the equator also meant sitting out on deck in the warm night air, watching *Elliott* churn a long bright ribbon of phosphorescence behind it. A stargazer, Sid was excited to at last see the famed Southern Cross, only to be disappointed when he found it so "irregular." Sid and Deacon admitted, "We really are tired of salt water."

When land hove into view ten days later, though, the warmth of the equator had fallen far astern. July was winter in the Southern Hemisphere. *Elliott* sailed into the harbor at Wellington, ringed with high mountains and busy with ships from all of the allied countries. As usual, a fair amount of waiting around preceded the moment when the enlisted men stepped off the ship into the cold and rain. Sid and Deacon went walking to take it all in—signs for Milk Bars, distinctive trams gliding by, cars with right-hand drives. Deacon observed that the city, although much larger than Mobile, looked "twenty years behind the times."

The New Zealanders welcomed the marines. At church one afternoon, Sid and Deacon met an older woman named Florence who invited them to her home for tea. Up the narrow streets they walked, wet and cold, carrying her groceries. Tall buildings had antiaircraft guns on them. All the windows were blacked out. Inside, they met Flo's invalid father and discovered her home did not have an icebox.

The escape from duty, however, ended quickly. All the privates of the 2/1 became members of working parties. *Elliott* was going to be combat-loaded imme-

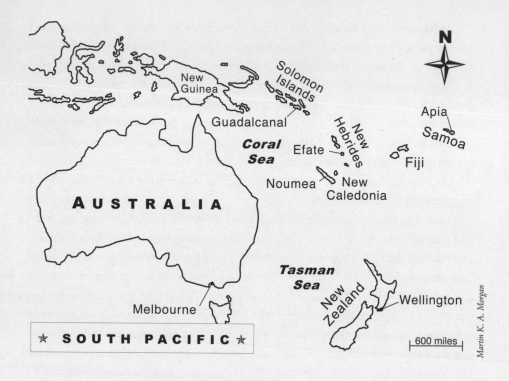

Martin K. A. Morgan

diately. In a ship loaded for combat, the equipment and supplies are organized to sustain men in combat efficiently. In other words, the equipment and supplies on the ship would now be unloaded so as to be reloaded. Although officially the word was that they were preparing for a three-month jungle training exercise, the speed and execution of the entire process made everyone aware that something big was going on. All the ships of the First Marines were unloading and loading. The Fifth Marine Regiment, which had arrived in Wellington before them, left their camps, came down to the docks, and began to load their ships. In the rain, night and day, at high speed, simultaneously, the process turned the docks into a chaotic mess.

For ten days, Sid worked four hours on and four hours off. He and the others hefted heavy boxes of ammunition from every weapon: 155mm, 105mm, 75mm, 90mm, 81mm, 37mm, 60mm, 20mm, .50 caliber, .30 cal, .45. The green boxes of .30-caliber ammunition had no handles, the mortar shells came in a peculiar cloverleaf packaging, and there were no gloves available to help with the spools of barbed wire. Cardboard boxes held all of their rations. The cardboard disintegrated in the rain, and soon the working parties stomped through a thick mush of wrappings and wasted food sprinkled with shiny tin cans.

With all of its hatches open, the ship could not be heated. The officers and NCOs observed the work; not one deigned to help. The Wellington dockworkers had gone on strike. Even some of the Yankees of How Company appeared adept at shirking. Sid cursed them all as a marine should, as his Rebel Squad of #4 gun put their backs into the job. Sailors manned the cranes and marines drove the trucks. When they loaded goodies like rations of chocolate, they stuffed some into their pockets. When they handled clothing, they stole some sweaters to keep warm and helped themselves to a clean pair of pants. A few other guys noticed and tried it, but got caught, much to the joy of Sid's squad.

Most days, Sid and the other members of #4 gun used their break to get off the dock and into the city. They bought lots of fruit, had a decent meal, or just got out of the weather by taking in a movie. *A Yank in the R.A.F.* was playing.* They met some New Zealand soldiers and compared weapons, emblems, and duties. The marines thought they learned a lot about the locals, including the use of "bloody" in most sentences, the preference for U.S. Marines over the U.S. Army, and the "heavenly ambition" of the young New Zealand women "to marry an American in the hopes of getting to the States." It surprised them to learn that the locals did not like to be called British, just as the people they met insisted on referring to Sid and Deacon as Yanks.

More ships arrived in the bay around them, including a dozen of the navy's big battleships and cruisers. When the work ended on July 20, #4 gun slipped off to have tea and meat pies at the Salvation Army. Afterwards, all of the 2/1 went on a conditioning hike in the hills. Hiking seemed like a relief after the drudgery of loading; at least it came with a view. That evening, Sid and Deacon, having heard they would be shipping out soon, bought two pounds of candy to take with them and were surprised at the glares of disgust they received from the locals. When the next morning brought no sergeants demanding work, everyone knew they were headed for "the real thing," which sounded like a destination. That evening *Elliott* got under way. The long convoy of troop transports, including the Fifth Marines and a number of battleships, sailed north. Announcements about "maneuvers" fooled few. Deacon spoke of the destiny before them being God's Will. Sid asked for his old job back, as captain of the Officers' Head. The silly title made him smile, but the rights and privileges improved life aboard the rust bucket.

*   *   *

---

*R.A.F. stands for the Royal Air Force of Great Britain. Its Spitfires had beaten the German Luftwaffe in the Battle of Britain.

THEIR LEAVES ENDED AFTER A WEEK AND THE PILOTS ALL REPORTED BACK TO
Ford Island. Ensign Micheel noticed that most of the senior pilots, the old hands like
his skipper, Gallaher, had disappeared. They had rotated home to train new squadrons and had, when they received their orders, departed before anyone changed their
mind. Their haste seemed perfectly reasonable. Micheel and some of the other ensigns of Scouting Six were told to report to the commanding officer of Bombing Six
at Naval Air Station Kaneohe. Mike's gunner, J. D. Dance, however, was not coming
with him to the new squadron. The Aviation Radioman Third Class had requested
flight training. Mike had happily written a recommendation, and Dance had been
accepted.

The new members of Bombing Six found a warm welcome at NAS Kaneohe.
A band played and cold beers were proffered to pilots and airmen as they stepped
from their planes.[30] Located on the western edge of the island of Oahu, Kaneohe
had only recently been constructed. The barracks, officers' club, and other buildings
did not have air-conditioning, so the rooms grew pretty warm until the breeze came
up in the late afternoon. A light rain usually followed. Unlike the airfields on the big
island, Kaneohe sat well out of the flight traffic patterns, so there was little in the
way of air traffic control. Life was easy.

Bombing Six had lost a lot of its veterans to reassignments. Lieutenant Ray
Davis, the new skipper, had flown with a *Hornet* squadron at Midway. None of the
dive-bombers off *Hornet* had sighted the enemy's carriers. Davis reviewed the files of
his new men before interviewing them. In Ensign Micheel's personnel file, Scouting Six's skipper, Gallaher, had described him as "an enthusiastic and industrious
young officer." For his service during the Battle of Midway, Lieutenant Gallaher had
recommended that Ensign Vernon Micheel receive the Distinguished Flying Cross.
Recommendations did not come stronger than that. When Lieutenant Davis asked
Micheel in his interview to name his preferred duty, Mike said he wanted to continue to serve aboard a carrier in the Pacific. His voice was calm, his eyes steady. Ray
saw something he liked in the blond-haired, blue-eyed ensign and designated him
the squadron's flight officer. The administrative job, to be performed in addition to
flight duties, did not mean as much to Mike as Ray's attitude. As Bombing Six began
its regime of practice at NAS Kaneohe, Ensign Micheel discovered he was "one of
the fellas."

SHIELDED FROM THE SUN AND ABLE TO GET ENOUGH CLEAN WATER, THE POWS
in Bilibid Prison stopped suffering. They noticed their prison held men who had been

incarcerated before the war as prominent Filipinos loyal to the United States. Bilibid also held anyone who was white, since the Japanese assumed Caucasians must be either American or British. One of the cells contained a German. He spoke English well enough to tell all of them of his devotion to the Nazi Party and Adolf Hitler. The Americans took to calling him Heine. For lack of something better to do, Shofner and his friends began to needle Heine, whose wonderful country had an alliance with the empire. "All you have to do is go see the Japanese commander and he would release you. After all, you are an ally of the Japs and you shouldn't be in here with us. You should be getting the royal treatment." Heine agreed and demanded to see the commandant, the prison warden, or whoever ran the prison. He came back bruised and beaten. He had no identification or proof, but that had not been the issue. The guards had not cared.

Heine could not understand why his country had allied with such an ignorant people. True Germans should have nothing to do with them. Shofner could not resist. "You saw the wrong man," he said. Heine demurred. But the prisoners had nothing but time in the jail and Captain Shofner was losing at poker, so he pressed on. "Heine, it's up to you to clear this matter up. You should go up and explain it again . . . the interpreter fouled it up some way . . ." Shifty and others amused themselves by egging him on. At last Heine's pride got the better of him and he went again. He returned bloodied once more, much to the amusement of all.

The guards came for the Filipinos first. A few days later, they selected a group of senior officers and took them away. Soon, the guards loaded a group of a few hundred men onto trucks every few days. Shofner, who was keeping a journal, knew that it was June 26 when he and about two hundred other prisoners bid Heine farewell. Many of the men were too weak to climb onto the trucks. They were driven to the Manila railroad station and loaded into steel railway boxcars. The guards crammed them in, approximately eighty men to each car, until there was not enough room for all the men to sit down. So the prisoners took turns standing and sitting. Those who sat had to sit between each other's legs. Six hours later, they arrived at a small station, where they boarded trucks. It turned out to be a short drive to Prisoner of War Camp Number One, Cabanatuan.[31]

The wall of barbed wire, interspersed with guard towers, stretched away in either direction across a great open plain. After entering the main gate, Shofner and the other new prisoners were searched. His camera and his compass were taken by the camp officials. A guard wrote down his name, as if these items would be held for him. He was assigned to one of the three sections of the camp and assigned to a ten-man squad.[32] He was told that if any one of the ten men escaped, all the others would be shot. They called this a "shooting squad."

Once inside the fence, Austin Shofner and the other new men met a few former officers, who tried to keep track of the men and were interested in any news from outside the camp. The new men, however, had the most to learn. The central fact of their new existence had been expressed many times by the guards: "No Geneva Convention!"[33]

Approaching their barracks, the recent arrivals would have noticed the neat row of dead bodies covered in flies. Those who expressed shock were told, "You'll get used to that."[34] Men were dying at the rate of forty per day and the guards made burying the bodies difficult. The odor of decay turned their stomachs. The barracks, built of nipa and bamboo, had no lights or running water or mosquito netting.

Most of the men Shofner met had been in the army, as the camp held some eight thousand soldiers and about two hundred marines and navy personnel. Shofner recoiled at the filthy, haggard men around him. Many were dressed in rags, without shoes. Wounds and infections marked their skin. The camp had a hospital, but it was not much better than the barracks and it was already full.

These men who filled the camp called themselves the Battlin' Bastards of Bataan. They spent much of their day standing in line to fill their canteens at the spigot or inside the barracks out of the sun. Though the POW camp provided very little to sustain life and almost no medical care for those in need, it was not Cabanatuan that had brought them so low. Holding off the Imperial Japanese Army (IJA) on Bataan had demanded everything from them. Four months of it had left them malnourished, diseased, weak. When the battle finally ended, seventy thousand men had been rounded up and ordered to march from the tip of Bataan, Mariveles, up the peninsula to Cabanatuan and similar camps nearby. A lot of men lacked the strength to march seventy miles. A lot of others, denied sufficient water and food along the route, gave out.

It had become a march of death. The Japanese guards beheaded some. They forced prisoners to kill weaker men and bury them. Americans died by the hundreds and Filipinos by the thousands. When at last the gates of Cabanatuan closed behind them, they soon discovered their captors wanted them to die. The lack of basic sanitation—there were open sewers on the north end of their compound because the Japanese had not built facilities—had given birth to hordes of flies carrying disease. Diarrhea had become common and many could not make it far from the barracks before their bowels released. Without toilet paper, Shofner learned, "paper, rags and leaves were at a premium."

That evening Shofner took his place in the line outside one of the six galleys serving food in the compound. He received one mess kit of steamed white rice, with about one-half a canteen cup of greenish soup with no substance in it. The rice, he noted, "looked like sweepings from the mill floor." Many of the grains were not husked and the rice "contained much foreign matter . . . like gravel, rat manure, dirt, and rice worms." There was no way for the prisoners to clean it. All a POW could do, as he sat on the bamboo floor with his mess kit, was decide how much to pick out of his food. A few finicky men picked out the rice worms, with their white bodies and black heads. Shofner decided to eat the worms, as most others did, just as he learned to be grateful that he still had a mess kit with which to eat.

Ready to go to sleep that night, Shofner found a space on the floor of barracks number two. His body touched the bodies of those on either side of him. He pulled from his pack his mosquito netting, noticing that almost half of the men lacked this protection from mosquitoes carrying malaria. Four feet above him was the next deck of sleeping men. In the morning before chow, the prisoners picked up those who had passed away during the night. As usual it took time to get the guards to allow the bodies to be buried outside the gate in a former rice paddy. When they at last granted it, no religious services were allowed, so the chaplains made sure to bless the bodies beforehand.

Shofner's compound, number two, encompassed a space of seven hundred yards by about five hundred yards. While the guards put enlisted men on work parties, officers were exempt. He played a lot of poker, playing with a wild abandon to prevent "my mind from feeling sorry for myself." He talked his way into becoming in charge of the softball team, which played three times per month. He read anything he could get his hands on. Like all prisoners, he waited for those days when the guards added a camote top, the leafy part of the Philippine sweet potato, or some hard roasting corn to their rice.

His diet, which had been limited for a long time before he became a prisoner, caught up with him. Shofner's tongue swelled up to twice its normal size. The sores on his lips could only mean one thing. He had scurvy. His mouth felt like the most sensitive part of his body. Chewing became unbearable, so he tried to slide spoonfuls of rice past his tongue—just drop it down his throat without chewing. Left unchecked, scurvy would eventually kill him, if it did not allow some other disease to take him first. During the day, he licked his lips and kept them apart. While he slept, however, the bloody sores on his lips sealed themselves together and he awakened—screaming, half suffocated. He caught his breath, then screamed again at the painful separation.

Shofner had to find a source of vegetables or fruit. He got himself assigned to working parties outside the camp. He caught sight of a wild lemon tree in the jungle.

The lemons were as big as grapefruit. When the right moment came, he grabbed some and began to eat quickly. The lemon juice touched his lips and tongue and it was as if he was sucking on a blowtorch. The acid burned everything it touched. He gobbled as many as he could and stuffed a few in his pocket before the guards noticed. Within a week, the skin began to heal.

ON JULY 15, BOMBING SIX FLEW OUT TO *ENTERPRISE*, ALREADY UNDER WAY WITH her task force and another force surrounding USS *Wasp*, sailing south.[35] Mike made his twenty-third carrier landing, a total of which he was keeping track, with his new rear seat gunner, Radio Machinist Gail W. Halterman. In the ready room, the skipper told them they were not headed for a raid against enemy bases or to a showdown with carriers. They would support a marine invasion of the Solomon Islands. The pilots of Bombing Six had received no training in how to support a ground assault. Hitting a building or a beach, they agreed, had to be easier than hitting a light cruiser turning hard to starboard at thirty knots. Now an old hand, Mike did not get saddled with many boring ASW missions, but the air group commander ordered an ambitious training schedule for all flight crews.[36]

Eleven days later the USS *Saratoga*'s task force joined up, as well as another comprised entirely of cruisers and destroyers. This great fleet, comprising three of America's four carriers, would shepherd a flock of troop transports to the islands of Guadalcanal and Tulagi, on the southeastern end of the chain of islands called the Solomons. First, however, the dive-bomber pilots would have a chance to practice their new mission, supporting a ground assault, on July 30, in the Fijis.

THE BOREDOM OF LIFE ABOARD USS *GEORGE F. ELLIOTT* FADED. THE OFFICERS ordered live ammunition issued. On the deck the machine gunners loaded their belts and the BAR men loaded their clips. The three-inch deck gun began firing and the concussions made everybody jump. Soon the 20mm AA guns fired some practice rounds at high speed. The next day a submarine was spotted and the convoy went on alert. The destroyers dropped depth charges and someone later said that an oil slick had been sighted. As the marines of the 2/1 contemplated the first action of war they had witnessed, the convoy entered another big storm that made most of them sick.

When they reached the Fiji Islands, the weather improved. Other convoys joined them and the sight of fifty ships impressed Sid until he saw "three carriers on the horizon at one time." Their great size and distinctive flat shape made them stand out. *Elliott* approached close enough to a carrier for them to watch the airplanes land on it. "Pretty dangerous," Deacon observed. The next day, July 27, the ships anchored off a small island called Koro, where a practice landing would be held. It took all day to prepare for the next morning. Deacon was appointed acting corporal for #4 gun, so he was told what their boat assignment was. From now on, he would carry a BAR and give orders. Sid took his place as gunner but, for the time being, he still had to carry the base plate.

Deacon had guard duty in the middle of the night, so he was still groggy when he met Sid and the squad. Before the sun rose, the Higgins boats swung out from their davits and the cargo nets hung over the side. Sid climbed up from the hold carrying his sixty-pound pack and the forty-five-pound base plate of the 81mm mortar. He and the machine gunners, who carried as much weight as he, brayed like mules. On the starboard side aft, the mortar section found the nets leading to their boat. Sid's base plate and other heavy parts were lowered on a line to them. A heavy roll of wire fell into their boat and broke the arm of a fellow in one of the other gun crews. Lieutenant Benson cursed loudly as poor Jontiff was hoisted back aboard.

The ride in to shore looked good: the ships were shelling the beach, and the carrier planes whizzed overhead and dropped bombs, until a coral reef stopped the Higgins boats well short of the beach. The amtracs crawled over the reef and went ashore, but the boats could not risk being damaged on the eve of the real thing. They quickly got snarled in confusion and eventually roared back out to *Elliott*. Lieutenant Benson was so angry he made his mortar section keep practicing loading and unloading well into the evening. The next few days went about the same. The marines in Higgins boats could not land, so they entertained themselves by trying to make one another seasick. The marines in the amtracs returned each day bragging about all the wonderful mangoes, coconuts, and bananas they had found onshore.

On July 30 the ships weighed anchors and got under way. Each man was given a one-page typed letter from the commanding officer of the First Marine Regiment, Colonel Clifton Cates.[37] "D-Day and Zero Hour are near," Cates wrote them, "of the first major offensive of Marine Corps units in this war." His message contained no specifics. The marines would make the Japanese pay for their "unwarranted treacherous action" so long as each man gave his utmost. "This is no ordinary war," he concluded, "it is for the right of liberty and freedom," and for the protection of their families. "We have enjoyed the many advantages given to us under our form of government, and, with the help of God, we will guarantee that same liberty and freedom for our loved ones and to the people of America for generations to come."

The task of briefing the men on the details fell to the junior officers and NCOs. "The japs," they said, had almost completed an airfield "on the Guadalcanal Island." Any planes based at the airfield would control a wide area, including the shipping lanes between the United States and Australia. The 1st Marine Division and its attached units would invade Guadalcanal and a small island twenty miles away called Tulagi. After landing on Red Beach, the First Marines would cross three rivers and hike through swamps and an old coconut plantation to reach the objective. While the First Marines secured the high ground, the Fifth would take the airfield.

During the next few days, the men prepared themselves for combat. White mosquito nets were issued, so the marines dyed them dark using cans of navy coffee. The ammo carriers for #4 gun took six shells out of their cases and put them into the six pouches of their new canvas assault ponchos. Sitting next to Sid on the forecastle, watching small islands pass, Deacon foresaw two options: death or victory.

On the afternoon of August 1, the ship went on high alert. A submarine had been spotted. It caused an uproar as the convoy maneuvered and the destroyers went slicing toward the threat. The ship's radar picked up enemy planes and an announcement beginning with the usual "Now hear this . . ." ordered all machine gunners to report with their weapons to the weather deck. As the depth charges shot geysers into the sky around them, marines held their weapons ready and scanned the horizon. The all clear sounded an hour later. The alert had not, however, made them feel heroic. It made them wonder if they were headed for another Bataan. The lush islands *Elliott* passed occasionally had once looked lonesome. Sid had joked about going ashore and finding Dorothy Lamour, the actress. Now the dots of land looked sinister. At night, the marines could see fires burning. The word was the islands were inhabited by cannibals.

One of How Company's lieutenants held jungle warfare training on deck. The company's skipper, Captain Ferguson, told his men that "five thousand japs" had dug themselves into Guadalcanal, an island about sixty miles long and twenty miles wide. He was counting on his mortar section to play a big role on Friday, when they landed. In the convoy around them, someone noticed the carriers had disappeared; the rumor was they had gone to strike Guadalcanal on August 4 to make the landing easier. Every day it got hotter and hotter, until the holds belowdecks were ovens. Deacon chewed his tobacco like it was his last day. On Thursday morning the marines noticed the ships of the convoy had increased speed. *Elliott* seemed to be making its top speed. No one would tell them why. Everyone in the mortar section acted jumpy, but only one man, Herman, seemed scared to the point of being a danger. That night the 2/1 sat on deck, unable to sleep, and unable to smoke cigarettes.

No one could light a match; once dusk had come the word passed that the "smoking lamp was out." The enemy might see it. Deacon prayed for God to be with them.

THE CAPTAIN OF USS *ENTERPRISE* DECLARED THE REHEARSALS A SUCCESS, although Ensign Micheel and the dive-bombers had not seen hordes of marines racing across Koro Island when they made their runs. One would have thought that was the point. When the convoy set sail for the targets, the troop transports forced the flattops to slow down. As they approached the Solomon Islands, the carriers got out in front of the convoy and increased both the number of scouting flights per day and the fervor with which they were conducted. Briefings in the ready room described the strategic situation.

The Japanese had built a large harbor for its navy and numerous airfields for its army on an island six hundred miles to the west of Guadalcanal at a place called Rabaul. Between Rabaul and "the Canal" ran the Solomon Islands in two irregular rows, with a channel of water between them. With a huge base at Rabaul and satellite bases on Guadalcanal and its neighbor Tulagi, the entire area had to be regarded as hostile waters. No preinvasion bombardment would be conducted because the element of surprise was essential. The flight crews and AA batteries aboard *Enterprise* expected "to defend against Jap counterattacks."[38] Good news came in the form of bad weather on August 5 and 6, making "interception by enemy aircraft most difficult."[39]

On the morning of August 7, the ship's captain announced over the ship's public address system, "this force will recapture Tulagi and Guadalcanal Islands, which are now in the hands of the enemy."[40] He was not relaying information as much as stating their goal. The day before the ship's Plan of the Day had informed all hands, "we expect tomorrow to be 'Der Tag' for our attack," a curious use of the German words for "The Day."[41] "Today's theme song for the Japs at Tulagi," the daily flyer continued, will be "There'll Be Some Changes Made." "The changing will be made by the United States Marines, aided and abetted by the *Enterprise*, *Saratoga*, and *Wasp* air groups, which will serve a 'Moonlight Cocktail' to the Nips in the form of a shower of thousand pound bombs . . ."[42] In the meantime, all hands would stow their personal gear in lockers so that if the IJN sank their ship, the crew's "boxes, books, magazines, etc" would "not get adrift."

Each of the ship's squadrons had already been briefed on its missions and had even reviewed photographs of the targets.[43] Davis and his pilots had been given the island of Tulagi, an island about twenty miles to the north of Guadalcanal. The photos showed the small harbor and a few buildings in which the British located their colonial government. Part of the marines' invasion force would seize Tulagi and a few tiny islands near it on D-day. Bombing Six would help the marines by attacking troop concentrations and AA emplacements between the village of Sasapi and the prison on the northeastern side of the island.[44]

The first planes, the Wildcat fighters, took off in the darkness to protect the fleet from enemy planes—an enemy scout was thought to have sighted the task force—and to destroy the aircraft thought to be based on the target's airfield. Dawn had not broken when Davis led Bombing Six off the deck at 0643. Twin rows of yellowish white light, just breaking the surface of the wooden flight deck and hooded, framed their launches into the sky. Forming up south of Guadalcanal became difficult because of the low visibility offered by the quarter moon and the high number of planes. All three carriers were steaming within a few miles of one another. Large attack groups were launched from each. As ordered, the airplanes showed "only a dim white light on the tail until at least 5 miles clear of the carrier, where they were permitted to turn on running lights in order to expedite the rendezvous."[45] In the darkness, pilots could see the twin blue exhausts of the plane ahead of them. The tail light was very hard to see. Sections got lost. As had happened at Midway, they wasted a fair amount of time forming up, although for a different reason. At least each squadron would work independently, though, so once Davis had his eighteen planes together, he led them around the western end of Guadalcanal, crossing the channel between Guadalcanal and Tulagi as the sun came up. Below, Mike could see all the little boats scurrying around the larger troop transports near both islands. Large cumulus clouds with their bases at about one thousand feet dotted the airspace. They passed through a rain squall or two.

Bombing Six arrived overhead of the small island in standard formation and dove in turn, as per usual, to prevent mishap. In his dive, Mike noticed very little in the way of AA fire and focused on his aiming points. The buildings of the village grew quickly inside his scope. There was the prison. With no corrections to make, he dove as deeply as he could and released his thousand-pound bomb. He climbed back into the sky. Neither he nor his gunner could see any enemy planes. Columns of smoke rose from both target islands, so it all looked good. Mike, who had flown with Davis in the first division, watched as the other divisions got redirected. The air group commander, who was circling the whole area, decided Tulagi had had enough. These remaining divisions dove on two flyspecks just to the east of Tulagi called Gavutu and Tanambogo. Before returning to the carrier, the squadron used their heavy machine guns. When his turn came, Mike made a strafing run on targets of opportunity and pushed himself to get low and make it count. Then his squadron flew back to the carrier, landing at nine thirty a.m. The deck crews were already bathed in sweat, launching and then landing flights of scouts, combat air patrols, and bombing missions at a frenetic pace.

EARLY FRIDAY MORNING, THEY RECEIVED AN APPLE, AN ORANGE, AND THREE EGGS for chow. The day started with the usual "hurry up and wait" as they got to their debarkation point. Some of the sailors found the #4 gun squad "and shook our hands like we would all be dead before the day was over, and they just wanted us to know there were no hard feelings between Swabbies and Marines." Sid had never seen the big guns of a cruiser blow smoke rings as they loosed a volley, or watched the airplanes overhead make their bombing and strafing runs. He found it fascinating. One of the shells looked like it hit a gas depot or something because it sent up a tower of black smoke. He found it neither difficult to get settled into the boats with all his heavy gear nor boring to wait while his boat found its place in the rings of boats, each ring an invasion wave. A breeze brought the smell of cordite to him and he thought briefly of dove hunting. Every man in #4 gun knew they were participating in the first amphibious assault since the Marine Corps had made it its raison d'être. Being marines, they made jokes about it.

The circle of boats broke before nine a.m., the line formed, and they ran to the beach. Sid took one last look around—across the calm sea to the great flag waving from the cruiser, to the small flags hanging from the backs of the line of Higgins boats. He noticed that the cartridge belts around his friends looked odd now that every loop held a shiny bullet. He wondered if the men who fought the Civil War had been as young as he and his friends. He chambered a round in his '03 rifle and set the safety, "determined to get at least one of the enemy before they wiped us out." The boat stopped short of the shore. The ramp dropped and out they ran.

It took a few moments to notice. The first wave of men, from the rifle platoons, sat under the trees and laughed as the mortarmen struggled out of the water. No enemy had been sighted and the assault had not continued inland. More waves arrived behind them every few minutes.

THE BIG E'S DECK CREWS RELOADED AND REFUELED ONE-THIRD OF HER BOMBING squadron in forty-five minutes.[46] Davis, Bill Pittman, Mike, and the others flew around the western end of Guadalcanal, the side closest to the enemy's base at Rabaul, and reported to the air group commander (CAG) from the carrier *Wasp* once they arrived over Tulagi. The CAG received reports from one of the ships below, which in turn was in touch with the marine commanders onshore. The process took time. Another third of the squadron showed up and began to circle with them. They saw no enemy flak at all, but heard a lot of chatter from pilots of all three carrier squadrons on the radio. Some of the talk had to do with enemy planes in the area—dogfights necessitated communications between Wildcat pilots—and some of the chatter came from excited pilots announcing their squadron's arrival, the carrier they were from, the type of bomb they carried, and requesting target assignments.[47]

The CAG eventually directed Davis's eight planes to the tiny green gumdrop of an islet east of Tulagi called Gavutu. As they neared their target, one of the gunners hollered, "Here they come! Here they come!" on the radio. Two Zeros took a bead on the section leader, in front of Mike, who pulled his plane over to block their shots. Behind him, Halterman swung around his machine gun and started firing. Other gunners in the section joined in. The Zeros fled and Mike shouted, "Success!" He had seen his first Zero. The *Wasp* air group commander, flying in circles, directed their runs until they were out of bullets and bombs.

The Dauntless pilots returned to *Enterprise* just short of six hours in the air, for the day, strapped on top of that throbbing Wright-Cyclone engine, expecting trouble. That was a lot. In the ready room, Mike found out the rear seat gunners had shot down one of the enemy fighters. Divisions of Bombing Six launched two more strikes that afternoon, without Davis, Mike, or Pittman, striking places on Guadalcanal called Kukum and Tenaru River. *Enterprise*'s flight deck continued to operate at high speed all afternoon. Later pilots spoke of being able to see Red Beach from a great distance because of the massive piles of white boxes.[48] Pilots hanging out in the ready room would have also heard, certainly from the stewards serving dinner in the officers' wardroom, that the fighter squadrons had had their hands full all day. Enemy bombers and dive-bombers, protected by Zeros, had attempted to put a few holes in the troop transports and their escort ships. The two-engine bombers flew in a big V of Vs from the direction of Rabaul. Some of the Wildcats had been so busy they had run out of gas and landed in the ocean. The deck crews had been so busy, they had set "a new record for a single day's operation in a combat area" of 236 takeoffs and 229 landings.[49]

WHILE THE OFFICERS GOT THINGS ORGANIZED, THE MARINES BROKE OPEN THE coconuts at their feet, drinking the juice and eating the meat. Then the riflemen led the way to Grassy Knoll. Hiking through the coconut plantation was not too different from the boonies of the training camp in New River. A break came early, when they reached the Ilu River in less than an hour. The Ilu proved much deeper than expected, so it could not be forded. The marines sat down in a group, like green troops will, and waited for a makeshift bridge to be built. An amtrac parked itself in the center of the river and engineers used planks to build a bridge.

Once they crossed, though, they forced their way through a dense jungle. It got hot when the hike began. Married to his forty-five-pound base plate, Sid struggled to keep up as they climbed over ridges that were not very high but were steep. The banyan trees, breadfruit trees, and the sudden clearings gave the jungle moments of beauty. He emptied his canteen quickly. They crossed the Tenaru River, but he and the others obeyed the order not to drink out of the rivers. Word came that the Fifth Marines, advancing along the coast directly to the airfield, had met some opposition. Deacon thought it "a grand war" so far. By dark, Sid dropped his gear, exhausted and dehydrated. "They told us to dig foxholes, but I don't think anybody did." He opened his can of C rations and muttered something about dog food. No one slept too well with all the bursts of small-arms fire. Each one began by signaling an enemy attack and ended by betraying another jumpy marine.[50]

THE HIGH MOUNTAIN RANGES ON THE SOLOMON ISLAND CHAIN HAD SEVERELY limited the effective range of the carrier's air search radar. The carriers could not remain south of Guadalcanal. For the second day of air support, *Enterprise* launched its squadrons from a position near the eastern end of the island, the corner farthest away from Rabaul. Fighter planes and one antisubmarine patrol comprised the first six flights of the day because the IJN knew where they were.[51] Just after nine a.m., Bombing Six flew into the channel expecting enemy fighters. Micheel had heard the enemy on Tulagi was putting up a difficult resistance against the marine assault. He focused on the job at hand, scouting for enemy submarines in the water between and around the target islands. At about ten thirty a.m. the squadron was ordered to bomb another tiny island nearby.[52] Micheel pushed over from six thousand feet and, like the day before, took his Dauntless down to engage the enemy. His skipper noted Micheel's "courage and initiative in seeking out and destroying assigned enemy antiaircraft gun emplacements and troop concentrations."[53] The incendiary bullets the Dauntlesses fired, though, did not set wooden houses or canvas tents on fire.

His squadron flew two more flights that morning. Other scouts went looking for the airmen lost the previous day. Mike missed these and ended up flying with the scouting squadron in the early afternoon. The strike flew around the area, waiting to be assigned a target, hearing the chatter on the radio of dogfights. They returned aboard with all of their bombs still attached. Landing with a bomb in the rack made pilots want to double-check their arming switches; it also meant the bombers had accomplished nothing. The pilots assumed the marines on Tulagi could use some more help. The relay of information from the marines on the ground, through radiomen on the ship, to the CAG in the air, and on to the strike leader had proven unwieldy.[54]

Without targets, the job of supporting the marine attack seemed over. The fighters had shot down thirteen enemy planes. Of the six pilots missing, three had been recovered. The Wildcat pilots had a lot of experience with the Zeros to discuss. The senior officers spent a lot of time discussing the problems of air support and of devising ways to improve communication with troops. They knew they could reduce marine casualties and speed up the seizure of objectives. Colored panels and/or smoke bombs to signal targets were suggested, as was "the issue and use of 'walkie-talkie' sets like those supplied to civil police forces in the United States for radio communications."[55] By nightfall all three carriers steamed south, exiting the area quickly. After two days of combat, the admiral in command assumed enemy submarines would arrive at any moment. The aircrews and ground crews welcomed the respite, but it begged the question: Who was going to guard the troop transports from all those enemy airplanes?

ANOTHER DAY'S FORCED MARCH THROUGH TOUGH TERRAIN BROUGHT THE 2/1 TO A grassy knoll. Was it "the" grassy knoll, the objective they were supposed to reach the day before? Deacon thought so. Sid knew it was not, knew something was wrong with the plans, and knew that every marine in the 2/1 had run out of water and was dying of thirst. Water carriers arrived at last, but there was not enough chow. They dug in. The word was that the carrier pilots had shot down nineteen enemy aircraft. One of them had crashed into *Elliott*. Somewhere in the channel of water visible from their vantage point, their ship and all of their gear had gone up in flames. After setting up a perimeter defense, they received the password "Lucky Strike." When it got dark, the smoking lamp went out and the rain began to fall. Hours later, the ships offshore began to fire. Had it not been for the reports carrying over to him, like the deep angry rumble of thunder, Sid might have thought he was watching "lightning bugs moving around." The arcs of light sometimes ended in a large explosion. Everybody cheered the U.S. Navy. Flares dropped over the scene and searchlights swept it. A plane came over and dropped a flare over the 2/1.

First thing in the morning came the announcement, "We're going back to the beach." The 2/1 trekked downhill without breakfast, lunch, or water. Eight men of the more than forty in the platoon fell out of ranks, exhausted. In the midafternoon, the battalion reached the airfield and, beyond it a half mile, the village of Kukum and finally the beach. No ships swung at anchor in the channel. The fleet had departed. The naval battle they had witnessed was the Imperial Japanese Navy (IJN) sinking four of the big cruisers. Most of the swabbies who had served on *Elliott* had made it ashore. All were shaken, some burned, and a few had been killed.

Sid and the others cheered. "We won't ever have to ride in that rusty old bastard again." Nor could they resist the chance to wonder aloud, "Where's the navy? Don't we have a navy?" Rations were distributed, but not enough to fill a belly for the evening. The ships had unloaded only about half their supplies before they departed. The members of #4 gun squad started eating coconuts, and Deacon pulled out his last package of fig bars. After dark, another unit started firing at the 2/1, but they shouted the password "Yellow!" enough times to stop it before anyone was hit.

MIKE AWAKENED TO FIND THE NEWS OF THE NAVY'S DEFEAT JUST OFF THE COAST of Guadalcanal on everybody's lips. Unlike the disaster at Pearl Harbor, the cruisers of the navy and the Royal Australian Navy had been beaten in a fight. Along with the four cruisers sunk, a fifth, USS *Chicago*, had been mauled near Savo Island. Instead of the carriers sailing north to even the score, however, the amphibious fleet was coming south toward them. In the ready room, Ray Davis told his men that the Japanese were expected to send landing forces to retake the airfield. The top brass assumed a carrier task force would accompany the enemy's invasion force. *Enterprise, Wasp,* and *Saratoga* would stay close enough to be ready to help as needed, but far enough out to make a counterattack difficult. The ambitious schedule of ASW and scouting missions would continue. The fleet remained on high alert. Dauntless scouts found and strafed an enemy submarine two days later.[56]

SOME OF THE CONFUSION SORTED ITSELF OUT ON THE FIRST FULL DAY NEAR THE airfield. The two regiments of marines began to divide up the duty of securing their hold on this large flat area, mostly open with high brush called kunai grass. The enemy counterattack was expected to come across the beach near Kukum, so rifle pits and machine gunners began to dig in there. The 81mm mortar platoon dug their positions a thousand yards or so back from the beach, so it would be in their range. Planting the base plate and connecting the tube and bipod meant not having to carry them, which was good, but now the digging began. The work did not pre-vent Sid, Deacon, W.O., and the others from shooting one of the cows meandering in the plain. Deacon guessed it weighed four hundred pounds as he dressed it out. They also fired at the three big enemy bombers that flew overhead about three p.m., but no one got a hit. While Deacon prepared the barbecue, the rest went scavenging among the buildings near the airport and in the village of Kukum. Sid cut insignia off of uniforms and pocketed two officers' belt buckles. He noticed something about the enemy's recent bivouac. "The whole camp smelled like Colgate tooth powder."

Two more air strikes hit them that day. Sid could not stop himself from watch-ing them. Deacon counted twenty-three in one flight. With the falling bombs came word that Japanese ships were on the way. That night, a lot of marines fired at trees and bushes while others yelled the password "Malaria!" The sergeant of #4 gun squad, Karp, got so scared he could hardly move. He wasn't the only one around who looked "lumber-legged."

After a difficult night, the squad relieved their hunger and their stress by going hunting and looting again. Everybody was doing it. They decided to kill another cow that day and kill the pigs they saw later. The enemy's supply dumps and build-ings yielded all sorts of interesting military souvenirs, as well as more practical items like bedrolls, cigarettes, liquor, and canned rations. The #4 gun squad stole enough food to last three days. This came in handy, as the word came that the division only had enough rations for five days. On the roads and paths connecting Kukum to the airfield, marines drove around in captured vehicles. Sid roared with laughter at the sight of one grinning marine driving a Japanese steamroller, feigning a carefree indifference, smoking a cigarette. He had painted "Under New Manage-ment" on the side.

The air raids continued to arrive a few times a day. When the Zeros came down low to strafe, Sid pulled his .45 pistol and returned fire. One night two submarines surfaced just offshore and shelled the area for half an hour. With all the flying shrap-nel, the marines decided to dig their foxholes, bomb shelters, and mortar pits deeper into the dark rich soil. Working parties brought supplies back from Red Beach, where the landing had taken place, using captured IJA trucks. Other marines dug large sup-ply and ammo dumps around the airfield. The marines' 90mm AA guns, emplaced around the airfield at last, began to return fire. The enemy's bombers flew higher. Marines on patrols began to exchange gunfire with the enemy in the jungle.

The #4 gun squad took its turn on guard the night of the sixteenth, when they patrolled along the Tenaru River in "the densest jungle ever." Sometime after mid-night, Deacon thought he heard "japs signaling with their coconut shells." He whirled around and pulled the trigger on his BAR, snapping off five rounds at an ambusher. They heard someone jump into the river; then grenades started going off. Sid and the guys spent the rest of the night standing guard, unable to see, "in terror of being bayoneted." In the morning they rewarded themselves with a breakfast of tomatoes, corn, fried potatoes, jam, quiche, butter and crackers, and great coffee. They had to enjoy it while it lasted, because the battalion HQ had placed guards around the captured stores. All men would now receive their share of food at the battalion mess. The #4 gun squad knew that meant they would surely starve.

In between the air raids, and the sickening terror they brought, and the working parties, the squad occasionally got a chance to swim in the warm ocean and throw coconuts at one another. The grueling pace allowed few such moments. A patrol on the eighteenth wiped out a reconnaissance patrol of eighteen Japanese officers and men. Well equipped, they were obviously scouts of a larger force that had just landed.[57] Another patrol brought H Company to the remains of marines whose bodies had been savaged and desecrated by the Japanese. The horror underlined a fact that the enemy had made clear several times already: no prisoners, no rules, no mercy. Hearing about other patrols, however, had made less of an impression than seeing it up close.

The sound of aircraft engines on August 20 turned out to bring joy, not pain. Two squadrons of U.S. planes circled the airfield and landed. These planes had the initials USMC on their sides, much to the delight of all hands. Bataan had never had reinforcements like these. On Guadalcanal, though, the news was never all good.

On the same day the mortar section moved closer to the Tenaru because an attack was expected. The #4 guns ran in a row parallel to the ocean, still well back from the river, and the crew of #4 spent the afternoon digging a new pit and getting the weapon sited. The move did not mean Sid and Deacon had to abandon their "honey" of a bomb shelter, which they had constructed of logs and strung with netting to be both bombproof and mosquito-proof. The mortarmen spent their time in one of three locations: their mortar pit, which had some foxholes around it; their camp, where they slept aboveground; and their bomb shelter belowground, into which they ran when they were shelled by ships or bombed by planes. No one from the squad was at camp that night, however, since Benson had alerted everyone for night action. As had become usual, many men from the mortar squad manned their rifles in foxholes along the river, buttressing the rifle companies. This night Sid, Deacon, and two others manned the mortar pit. As usual, two men slept in the pit while the other two stood watch.

At about three a.m. heavy artillery fire and MG and rifle fire woke Sid and

Deacon. The hammering of weapons firing was sustained and concentrated at the intersection of the beach and the river on their right. This was not some jittery guy firing at iguanas in the bush. The foursome jumped up to prepare to fire the mortar. They made sure their rifle or pistol was handy, too. Behind them the 75mm cannons shelled the area across the river. It seemed like hours passed as real combat was waged close by. Word came for #3 and #4 guns to move up. The squad broke down the 81mm and moved up to within a hundred yards of the river, right into the battle, stumbling and cursing in the semidarkness. The machine gunners and the riflemen lined the bank, hammering away. At the point where the river met the sea, where a sand spit made it easy to ford, the 37mm cannons methodically pumped rounds. Dawn had broken when they set up the guns and, during a pause, they heard men cheer, "Hurrah, here comes the 81s."

The #4 gun opened fire as soon as they could see the bubbles in their sights. Deacon had them fire their HE (high explosive) shells in a zone pattern on the other side of the river. The short range made for a high sharp arc before they burst amid the coconut plantation. Around Sid and Deacon, the ammo carriers broke down the cloverleaf shell containers, then opened the waterproof shell case and handed a round to the assistant gunner, Sid, who tore off excess increments and dropped the shell down the tube. W.O. cleaned up the excess increments (the small packs of gunpowder that propelled the shell) before they were ignited accidentally. The team got into a rhythm, not holding back. Their shells' launch could not be heard over the cannonading. The rending crash of their HEs' explosions marched among the rows of coconut trees, evil in its power. A few hours later, a heavy volume of fire cut into the line of marines. The enemy's mortars had found their range. Near Sid's position, a sliver of shrapnel sliced off a man's head. Another shell landed in a foxhole with four men. The smell of burned flesh and of sweet blood mixed with the cordite. The fusillade drove Sid and Deacon and others back from their guns.

The team returned to the mortar amid the pieces of bodies. They began blasting away again, starting at one position and moving left or right. The riflemen and the machine gunners began waiting while the HE marched across the battlefield. The approaching blasts drove the remaining enemy from his cover and they would fire at the targets. The sense of urgency began to wane. Colonel Pollack, the CO of the 2/1, came over and directed them to fire at an amtrac that had been abandoned in the river. A Japanese machine gunner was using it for cover. It took a few rounds before #4 gun squad dropped a round into the amtrac. A cheer went up. Late in the afternoon, word came to cease fire.

Standing next to #4 mortar and awaiting orders, Sid saw the horror of war up close in the sudden quiet. The corpsmen finished removing the wounded and started removing the bits and pieces of bodies. Beyond the marine line and to the left, on the point of the sand spit, the bodies of the enemy lay piled two and three deep. "The whole earth to our left flank," Deacon wrote in his journal, "was totally black with dead japs. The mouth of the Tenaru is nothing but a mass of bodies."

A few survivors tried to get away by swimming out to sea, but "our men picked them off like eating candy." Others lay amid the pile, waiting only for a marine to get close enough for the chance to kill him with a grenade. One of those explosions taught every man to shoot into each body or else jab a bayonet to make certain all were dead. It was easy to tell which ones needed another bullet, since so many of the enemy had been torn into pieces. They had run right into the hail of bullets and canister shot of the 37mm, which sprayed lead pellets like a giant shotgun, scything down men by the squad.

The stupidity of the attack was self-evident. Without feint or forethought, heedless of the cost, the crack troops of the Imperial Japanese Army had rushed forward. The IJA had not known that an islander had tipped off the marines, but one of the Japanese soldiers had fired a flare before their first attack.[58] Their bodies got ground into a meaty red pulp when the marines' Stuart tanks drove over the sand spit in the late afternoon as part of a pincer movement. A battalion of infantry had crossed the river well to the right and was advancing north to the ocean, flushing the remainder toward the Stuarts. Shooting the enemy across the Tenaru lost the heat of combat; it came to have the precision of the rifle range. Colonel Cates, CO of the First Marines, walked over to shake hands with the #4 gun squad and tell them they had laid down a perfect barrage. The cooks brought up hot coffee and C rations. Sid got into line. The marine next to him observed that "Marines would have to stand in line to get into hell."

The members of #4 gun who had fought as riflemen arrived with tales of killing enemy soldiers at close range. They also told of how the squad had lost their sergeant, Karp. A Japanese colonel had sliced his face open with his sword, then opened his chest and stomach, then ran him through. The colonel had wounded another marine before someone shot him. Dusk came. The mortar squad began filling sandbags and preparing to spend the night at their new position. The storytelling continued throughout H Company. Lucky Leckie, one of the machine gunners, said his friend Chuckler had seen lights across the river and had been the first to shout, "Who goes there?"[59] After the firing started, Lucky and Chuckler had had to move their weapon several times to keep from being hit. At the point where the river met the sea, Hell's Point, as the sand spit was being called, machine gunner Johnny Rivers had held fast. It was said he killed one hundred of the emperor's troops after he died. His dead fingers had frozen on the trigger.

Stories like Johnny Rivers's, who had been called Chief because of his Indian heritage, formed the core of the men's understanding of the Battle of Hell's Point.* The next day, everyone started looting the bodies, trying not to breathe through their noses, with the knowledge that the First Marines had done it. They had stood up to the vaunted Japanese army. Inside the packs they found hand grenades, American money, and lots of condoms. Estimates of the enemy dead ran from 750 to more than 1,000. Fourteen had been taken prisoner, although not by How Company marines, adding to the 300 in the stockade. Sid found USMC emblems, snapshots of marines with their girlfriends, and a wooden cigarette case with the word "Guam" printed on it; these men had looted the marine barracks on Guam.[60] The Japanese had been equipped with ten heavy machine guns, many more light machine guns, grenade throwers, and a few flamethrowers. The latter had not been used. The tally for his company's losses ran to four killed in action and eight wounded. His battalion lost thirty-four killed and seventy-five wounded. Occasional shots still rang out through the day. Some came from enemy snipers. Others came from marines finding and killing wounded enemy soldiers.

Across the river, bulldozers dug pits for mass graves. An orderly column of Korean and Japanese POWs marched past Sid's mortar squad on their way to the pits to help bury their comrades. One of the MPs guarding the work detail called out as if on parade ground, "In cadence count!"

"Roosevelt good man, Tojo eat shit!" yelled his charges. Sid fell over with laughter, in love with the magical power of humor. The men of the #4 gun squad felt a deep pride in their role in the victory. The stovepipe boys had proven themselves and their weapon. Sid and the squad collected the photos of the marines and their girlfriends taken from the dead bodies and burned them. In his evening service, Deacon prayed, "Oh God, that our own men never fall into the same trap as these japs."

ON AUGUST 22 THE THREE CARRIERS AND THEIR TASK FORCES HEADED NORTH to the Solomon Islands. The infamous Admiral Yamamoto, architect of the sneak attack on Pearl Harbor, had sent down a great fleet to wipe out the U.S. forces on Guadalcanal. *Saratoga, Enterprise,* and *Wasp* sailed throughout the night to meet it even as an enemy scout plane betrayed their location.[61] The next morning they had

---

*Historians refer to the Battle of Hell's Point as the Battle of the Tenaru.

taken station about seventy miles to the north and east of Guadalcanal when word came of enemy transport ships steaming down the channel formed by the twin lines of Solomon Islands to Guadalcanal. The Big E, as the task force's duty carrier, provided the search planes while the pilots on the other carriers stood ready. Ensign Micheel was among twenty-three scouts that took off at first light, trying to find the bad guys first. With each pilot on a separate leg, they covered 180 degrees of the ocean. Mike saw nothing and returned a few hours later. Two scouts reported submarines. Later that afternoon another Dauntless patrol found a sub and claimed hits. All three enemy subs had been headed south at high speed toward them, so the assumption was they represented the vanguard of Yamamoto's surface fleet.[62]

In the afternoon a scout reported finding an enemy flattop and her escorts. *Saratoga* launched her bombing, scouting, and torpedo squadrons against the light carrier *Ryujo*. The Sara's planes found nothing and bad weather forced them to land at Henderson Field, on Guadalcanal. Word came later that the enemy carriers were still well north of them. With that reversal, *Wasp* and her escorts sailed south out of the combat zone to refuel. Her departure left the Sara and the Big E on the front line.

THE 2/1 REMAINED AT HELL'S POINT BECAUSE ITS REGIMENTAL COMMANDER expected another attack either from across the Tenaru or on the beach near it. Sid and Deacon lived near the carcasses. The two 81mm mortar crews had been given a lot of credit for the slaughter; the obscenity of it was inescapable and soon became chilling. One corpse made them both laugh: he "was ripped wide open from his loins up to his chin and his chest laid open and his ribs broken back like a chicken, no entrails, heart, lungs or anything laying in him. He looked like a gutted possum. . . ." The radio that night carried a program from San Francisco celebrating their victory. Visions of their families hearing the news brought a moment of joy. A heavy rain fell. No one in the squad could relax enough to sleep. The prolonged tension had given them all diarrhea.

The worry that more of the enemy were coming became specific in the morning with news that four IJN transports, four destroyers, and two cruisers were sailing toward them. Sid's squad bolstered themselves with eggs, bacon, and good coffee. They watched planes from the two squadrons based on Henderson Field fly in and out. Before lunch, the First Marines buried their dead. They sang "Rock of Ages" and "America." The trumpeter played taps. Afterward they dug more holes in the ground—new positions for themselves. Word came that the navy had sent some ships, submarines, and some planes to protect them. At four p.m. Lieutenant Benson called the 81mm to alert. The #4 gun squad received fifty rounds of HE and twenty rounds of the light. The Imperial Japanese Navy would arrive in force at four a.m. Warned that this was the big one, the squad expected another sleepless night. Around them, men test-fired their weapons to set ranges and calibrations. Even the nonbelievers in the squad, Deacon noticed, joined in the nightly prayer. Ready at last, Sid's squad "lay in wait for action now. So beware Mr. jap for the U.S. Marines."

THE CLOUDY MORNING OF AUGUST 24 WIDENED INTO A BEAUTIFUL CLEAR DAY. Micheel and twenty-two other dive-bombers took off at six thirty a.m. to find the IJN fleet fanning out over the ocean in every direction but to their southeast, which the PBYs from Efate and Espiritu Santos covered. Mike's search pattern, flown through dark clouds, took him well over four hours to complete. He saw lots and lots of ocean, its waves large enough to help him navigate. When he came back aboard, there was news of an enemy carrier sighting and of IJN submarines near his task force. Yamamoto knew their location. His dive-bombers were on the way. All available Dauntlesses were prepared for another search to the north and east of their position. The two carriers churned southward, getting a good wind over the flight deck. After takeoff, the twenty-three planes swung north and fanned out.

Mike's dogleg search took almost five hours to complete. He had not been given an exact spot for Point Option; he had simply been told to expect *Enterprise* to steam due north, on a heading of 000 degrees (True), advancing about ten kilometers for each hour of flight.[63] His navigation proved adequate. He saw the *Saratoga's* massive square frame break the skyline first, steaming along about fifteen miles from his carrier. He approached the task forces from a particular heading, in order to identify himself as a friendly plane. Black puffs exploded near his plane, jarring him. The AA gunners on the Sara were shooting at him. He broke away quickly, checking to make sure his IFF system was on; the signal it transmitted identified him as a friendly. He came around again to the correct bearing. The Sara's gunners cut loose on him. "So I went back out and came in the place we weren't supposed to come in. Nobody shot at me!"

The overzealousness of the antiaircraft batteries became more understandable when he entered the Big E's landing pattern. Air ops radioed him that the ship had been hit. Plumes of smoke rose from her. More than twenty aircraft were flying circles around her, waiting. Mike found a place in the circle and waited while the crew repaired the Big E's flight deck. Once again, he found himself running out of fuel. It gave him the nagging worry he called "puckering." *Enterprise* began receiving her planes at last, though. Weary after nine hours of total flight time, he made his fiftieth carrier landing and let the plane handlers take it from him. Walking the flight deck he noticed a patch of metal boiler plating covering a large section. He walked over to where another bomb had hit, on the starboard side of the stern. The bomb had exploded next to a five-inch antiaircraft gun, setting off the gun's ammunition as well. Mike looked "in that turret and those guys were cooked right at the turret, right at their positions, just fried like an egg or like a piece of toast."

With the ship damaged and the probability of more attacks high, Mike's job was to get out of the way. Bombing Six sat in the ready room and waited. Two sailors sat up front, each with a ship's phone. One man heard reports from the air operations office. The other sailor's phone connected him to damage control. The latter had a lot of information to relay about the ship's condition. The rudder had jammed, he told them soon after Mike walked in. "We are sailing in a circle." A great shudder, felt throughout the ship, followed. The engines had been thrown into reverse in order to prevent *Enterprise* from ramming one of her escorts.[64] The sailor with the phone also yelled things like, "Hey, they've got a fire down in compartment such and such" or "They're patching the deck at frame something or the other." Mike did not pay attention to the details. The repairs were out of his hands.

News about the missions of the other pilots, however, did get his interest. Davis and his wingman had taken the most likely sector to find the enemy, 340 to 350 degrees True. They had found them all right and set up for a perfect strike on the flattop: the sun at their backs and the wind in their faces. The carrier turned so hard to starboard, though, she had spun through a 60-degree arc by the time Davis's five-hundred-pound bomb exploded, five feet off the starboard side aft. His wingman's bomb had detonated another fifteen feet away. Two other comrades had made dives that day, diving on a large cruiser. They had also come up just shy of the mark. All four pilots described blasts of AA fire, "like silver dimes" coming up "in bunches" until they exploded in red and black.[65] Davis had radioed the coordinates to the Big E twice; one had never been received, the other had arrived too late to do any good.

The loss of his transmissions must have seemed unremarkable, if unfortunate, amid the deluge of stories and information about this day. Special guest Ensign Behr had a wild story. A Sara pilot, he had landed on *Enterprise* because of a foul-up on Sara's deck. He and his strike had found the IJN carriers, too, and dove. The Zeros had chased him most of the way back, so he had no clear idea of his success, but someone's bomb had smacked it good. For the moment he attached to Bombing Six. His plane, shot through with bullet holes, had been pushed over the side. Two of Mike's other squadron mates told an even crazier story, though. They had returned from their search to find enemy dive-bombers attacking their ship and both pilots and their gunners had cut loose on them. The Aichi-type 99 dive-bombers had flown off without obvious signs of damage.

Mike had not seen the enemy planes. He would not have mentioned being shot at by the Sara's gunners, since apparently the AA gunners had shot at a lot of pilots. As the men talked, the sailor on the phone to air ops yelled that radar had picked up another flight of attackers. The Wildcats from *Saratoga* would have to handle them. *Enterprise* could not conduct flight operations; two of her elevators were out. The upshot of it all was that Yamamoto's ships had not been stopped. Most probably they were still sailing south, preparing to attack again the next day.

The Big E, meantime, had her rudder straightened, if not fully repaired. The fires still burned. She sailed south at a stately pace, listing three degrees, flanked by *Saratoga* and an array of destroyers, cruisers, and the battleship *North Carolina*. Eventually Mike started to hear about his carrier.

About thirty enemy planes had attacked *Enterprise*, their dives every bit as steep, every bit as determined, as any Dauntless. Twenty bombs exploded near her, sending geysers of water over her deck, bending her painfully at the waistline. Two of the attackers, set afire by AA guns, had attempted to crash into her. These had been driven off. Three bombs detonated on or inside of the ship. The damage-control teams, who had patched the deck so Mike could land, and who had straightened the rudder, had hours more of dangerous work. In asbestos suits and armed with hoses of water and foamite, they fought to extinguish fires in several decks, to stop leaking, and to assess the damage to two of the giant elevators used to move airplanes. The medical teams coped with dozens dead and dozens more wounded.

Doctors and repairmen worked on all night. The carrier limped south for another day, meeting up with *Wasp* on the twenty-fifth. As it became obvious that the Big E would be out of the war for a while, it became equally obvious that her squadrons could not be sidelined as well, particularly when the marines on Guadalcanal needed pilots and planes badly. A few planes would have to stay and guard the ship, which Mike heard was headed for Pearl Harbor, and some would go fight with the marines.

Those decisions, however, would have to wait. After the Big E exited the combat zone, she had to stop for a moment and, in the ancient tradition of the navy, commit the bodies of her dead to the deep. Seventy-two enlisted men and six officers of the ship's crew had been killed in what they had begun to call the Battle of the Eastern Solomons. At nine a.m. on the twenty-sixth the Stars and Stripes were lowered to half-mast and the call went out.[66] "All hands bury the dead." The ship came to a stop. The men assembled on the flight deck. Those in the Honor Platoon took their positions. When the chaplain came to the committal, the Honor Guard stepped to attention and saluted. Mike watched as the bodies, each wrapped tightly in a clean mattress cover laced with heavy weights, slid feetfirst over the side. At the benediction, the crew's heads bowed. A seven-man squad fired three volleys. The bugler sounded taps. As the last note faded, the ship resumed course and speed, as per tradition, and the men of *Enterprise* said their good-byes over the broad foaming wake. Thy will be done.

THE IMPERIAL JAPANESE NAVY AND ARMY RARELY SKIPPED A DAY. ANOTHER surprise from the Tokyo Express arrived every few hours: ships and submarines shelling them at night, bombers thundering overhead in the day. From what Sid's squad could tell, the planes on Henderson and the U.S. Navy were "mopping up with the jap navy." The mortar squad continued to scrounge eggs or flour for pancakes to supplement the two ladles of rice per man being issued at the mess. On August 28, Topside issued a postcard to each man so he could write home. The 2/1, who had lost much of their personal equipment when the *Elliott* sank, were also issued one captured IJA backpack apiece. The members of the #4 gun squad wrote "Remember Hell's Point" on their new packs. Two days later, scuttlebutt had it that the emperor had landed as many as 150,000 troops on the island, although other men passed along lower figures. Against such a force, the 1st Marine Division fielded ten battalions, now that the Raider and the Parachute battalions had come over from Tulagi. The marines "really hope it is all false, for we really are all tired of war and want to go back to good old USA." In his nightly prayer, Deacon added, "God speed the day."

The men of the mortar squad often found themselves on a working party at Lunga Point, unloading a ship as fast as possible. A lot of it was ammo, aviation gas, and C rations, but on September 1 six truckloads of mail arrived. Later, the enemy's bombs hit a few stockpiles of aviation gasoline and of aerial bombs, making for big fires. Many of the bombs that day exploded in and around the area held by the 2/1. Another shelling at three a.m. sent Sid a little crazy, and he ran around outside yelling. The next day he received some more mail, as the postmaster got it all sorted, and some newspapers from home. More bombs fell around Henderson Field. Lieutenant Benson held a rifle inspection that afternoon and, as usual, he told his #4 gun squad to expect an all-out attack when it got dark.

With hours to pass before the attack, the mortar squads held a joking contest.

Durocher, a friend in the platoon from New York, had begun to perform little skits now and again. He would hold up his bayonet like a microphone and launch into a radio show, imitating a popular news commentator of the day, H. V. Kaltenborn. Durocher began, "I have some good news tonight," just as Kaltenborn had begun his programs for decades. "Nothing is too good for the boys overseas," he continued, "and so we've decided to send the boys on Guadalcanal nothing." Snatches of songs or phony commercials might follow, but his program could also get interrupted by one of President Roosevelt's "fireside chats." The iconic voice with its distinctive accent began, "My fellow Americans. I hate war. My son James hates war. My dog Fala hates war. My wife Eleanor hates war. And I've been in war and I've been in Eleanor and I'll take war." In moments like this, Sid let the laughter well up inside him and wash away so much of the pain and the fear in his heart.

Within the tight confines of their air raid shelter, Sid burst a large boil on Deacon's buttock accidentally with a clod of dirt and now his friend could scarcely walk. "Blood and corruption" ran down his leg. Deacon would never utter a curse, but had he been able to move quickly, he would have burst Sid's head. W.O. had become so weakened by diarrhea and sleep deprivation he could not stand. Sid tended to him, bringing him food and carrying him to the slit trench when he had to relieve himself, making sure to tell W.O. at every turn "what a pain he was and how we all wished he would quit goofing off and pretending to be sick. . . ."

Ships had begun to arrive in dribs and drabs, so NCOs "volunteered" their men for working parties to unload the small lighters then sent to shore. How Company, dug in near the beach, furnished plenty of manpower. Sid's squad had loot to trade with the swabbies, though, so they could get goodies while they worked "like jackasses." Sid finagled a few cups of sugar, a cup of cream, a bit of butter, salt, and baking soda. With plenty of fresh coconut shavings for flavor, he boiled water and made pull candy in the rain. While munching the sticky treat, sitting in their "slop holes," they debated the possibility of going home soon. They heard one of the lieutenants speak "very encouragingly about us going home for the forming of the third brigade."

Later that night the squad had guard duty. Sid and Deacon traded their pistols for rifles to stand the guard. Lieutenant Benson ordered them to fall in, inspected their weapons and ammo, and marched them to their posts near the river. As they climbed into the foxholes, Benson announced, "Anyone on top of the ground was an enemy and could and should be shot." He ordered them to relieve themselves inside their foxholes by using their helmets. Benson reminded them that his foxhole was behind theirs. When the enemy troops came, Benson warned, do not "come back there looking for your mother, because there was nobody there but old Benny and he had a BAR on full automatic and you would get cut in half." Ladling in a dose of his trademark sarcasm, Benny encouraged them to "be sure and fire . . . stupidly when there was no target because that would show the Japs" where they were. With that, he left them. It got quieter. Something was always making noise in the jungle, which was unnerving. Until, as soon became common, the enemy yelled, "Marine, you die!" A pause, then, "Marine! You die!" The enemy wanted to see the flashes of their rifle fire, so they would know where to attack, only they had trouble pronouncing the letter *r*, so what the marines usually heard was "Maline! You die!"

They stood guard only every other night. The wail of the air raid siren sounded twice a day. The twenty-six bombers that arrived overhead at eleven a.m. on September 10 unloaded their ordnance on the 2/1's positions. The monstrous thunder enveloped them. In times like these, Sid found himself in his muddy earthen pit, staring into Deacon's eyes. He saw friendship there and faith in God. He could rely on John Tatum. When the all clear sounded, they came aboveground to find their tents, packs, and weapons scarred by shrapnel. Some of it was useless. Great trees had been knocked down. How Company sustained eleven casualties, three of them from its 81mm mortar platoon. Sid's wounded friends were carried out to the airfield and evacuated by a four-engine bomber later that day. "We," Deacon Tatum wrote in his journal, "are all nervous wrecks."

ON AUGUST 27, ELEVEN DAUNTLESSES OF BOMBING SIX AND THEIR CREWS received orders to report to the senior naval aviator, on the island of Efate, for "further assignment as directed by competent authority." Put another way, they were headed for a forward air base where a great deal of confusion existed. They and their planes would be used as needed. While his gunner, Halterman, jammed two seabags into the back of their plane, Mike checked his .45, which hung on a shoulder holster. It was clean, loaded, and unused. *Enterprise* turned into the wind and Bombing Six set off for the same small island in the New Hebrides that had been the carrier's goal months ago on Mike's first war cruise.

Back in May, the Big E had intended to drop off a squadron of marine pilots on Efate to protect America's supply line to Australia by building a chain of military bases beyond the reach of Japan. A link in that line, Efate clearly had been growing every day since then, developing its port facilities, supply depots, salvage capabilities, and temporary camps for troops. Mike got a quick view of the port and the base as his squadron circled and landed on the muddy field.

Lieutenant Ray Davis and his squadron reported in to Major Harold W. Bauer, who served on the staff of Admiral John McCain, the commander of the U.S. air forces in the South Pacific. Major Bauer would have been glad to see them. The mission of McCain's COMSOPAC and the air wing Bauer commanded had grown from protecting a supply chain to supporting the battle raging for control of the Canal.[67] His air wing and its service unit numbered less than a thousand men. Bauer helped give the pilots and marines on Guadalcanal whatever they needed. The demand was growing daily. The navy had sent Bauer a group of ensigns fresh from flight school in Pensacola. These men needed time to train. The veterans of Bombing Six would go to the Canal before the rookies, whenever that was. Davis, Pittman, Micheel, and the others found a rack in the tents near the airfield and waited.

As officers, they did not have to fill the fifty-gallon drum that served as their shower, although Mike learned not to take a shower in the morning, when the water was still ice-cold. The mess hall served food on tin plates, the mud on the airfield took a toll on the carrier planes, and the pilots did not have anything much to do. "We were saving those airplanes to go to Guadalcanal so we didn't fly too much." After the fast pace of life on the Big E, Efate felt like a quiet backwater. The marines guarding the base told the pilots not to stray off the base. The "aborigines in the hills . . . were cannibals." Having served in the field artillery during his ROTC training in college, Mike liked to joke that he had joined the navy specifically to avoid such a life. Lieutenant Davis spent his days writing a long report about the recent carrier battle and setting forth a list of recommendations.

In two weeks, Bombing Six got the call to fly up to the island of Espiritu Santos and report to the commander of all the aircraft in the South Pacific. Buttons, the code name for the airfields on Espiritu Santos, was a much bigger and busier base than Efate. A number of squadrons flew big multiengine patrol planes, often the navy's PBY, to provide crucial intelligence about enemy moves in the South Pacific in general and in the Solomon Islands in particular. Mike landed on Buttons on September 14, his last stop on the way to Cactus, the code name for the airfield on Guadalcanal. Among the four-engine beasts along the taxiways stood thirty carrier planes; they had come off *Saratoga*, which had been torpedoed a week after the Big E was hit.

SEPTEMBER 14 FOUND BASILONE AND THE MEN OF D/1/7 ON THE DECK OF USS *President Adams* in the harbor of Espiritu Santos, watching their convoy get under way.[68] The ships carrying the Seventh Marines had already attempted to reunite them with the rest of the 1st Marine Division, but had been turned back several times by enemy ships, enemy planes, or enemy submarines. The retreats had had little effect on the morale of his machine gunners, Sergeant John Basilone noted, because of the view from the deck. Manila John and his friends "looked in awe at the tremendous panorama spread out before us. On the horizon as far as we could see were ships, freighters, transports, heavy cruisers, sleek destroyers, [and] bulky aircraft carriers. . . ." One of his gunners had exclaimed earlier, "Jeez, we could go right into Tokyo Bay," but after days aboard *President Adams* they were ready to settle for just making it to the big show.[69]

John, his buddy J.P., and the rest of their regiment had been hearing about their division's big fight for some time now. Few of them enjoyed the irony of having sailed for Samoa months ago expecting to be the first to fight, only to guard airfields and take long conditioning hikes while the First and the Fifth took it on the chin. The news of the imperial ships sending more and more men every day to Guadalcanal, what guys called the "Tokyo Express," made no sense to John. "We could not understand where our navy was. Why couldn't they stop the jap transports?"[70] The next day they noted a large column of smoke on the horizon. Only later did they hear that an IJN submarine had slammed four torpedoes into the belly of their escort, the carrier *Wasp*. Did that mean their convoy would turn around again? None of the swabbies bothered to tell them.[71]

VERY FEW MEN IN SID'S SQUAD WOKE UP ON SEPTEMBER 14, SINCE IT HAD BEEN impossible to sleep for two nights running. On the twelfth, "an old squeaky plane" had flown over and hung two flares over Henderson Field. Everyone knew what that meant. When the shelling started, the mortar squad "lay in nervous trembles in our holes." The ships not only shelled Lunga Point and the airport; they switched on a powerful spotlight and began to search for the marines' heavy artillery. About one a.m., the ships' shells began stalking them and the mortar platoon had had to run for it, through a darkness lit by menacing red explosions, for their old positions farther back from the point.

Daybreak brought a short lull before the first Japanese fighters arrived, making pass after pass, strafing the airfield with their heavy machine guns. Sid and Deacon lay in a foxhole, the bullets ripping the ground around them, expecting to be hit at any moment. The night of the thirteenth rang with the violence of the big guns and their concussions rocked the ground under Sid's feet. The eruptions originated not from offshore, however, but from the 75mm, 90mm, and 105mm cannons of the 1st Marine Division. When Sid's squad manned their mortars at one a.m., the firing was concentrated on one location. In a phrase used by everyone (except Deacon), the shit had hit the fan south of the airport. The inferno engulfed a long ridge. The ridge, whose barren crest rose well above the jungle, started a few hundred yards from Henderson and jogged south, well back into the interior. The #4 gun squad stood by and awaited orders. "Once more we are battling life and death and japs." The battle continued the next day and the squad heard the Japanese were rushing the lines in three places, but mostly along Bloody Ridge, where they confronted the Raider and Parachute battalions. Deacon got a look at a captured officer's map, which had his platoon's position marked in red.

The continuous shelling gave way to the fits and starts of "mopping up operations," after another twenty-four hours on high alert, and the mortar squad heard some good news. Sealed orders had arrived, to be opened on September 18. The Seventh Marines were due to arrive at any moment. This surely meant they were going home. The rumors built daily, as the marines awaited the opening of the "sealed orders," and word came of a speech by FDR in which he promised "our mothers that we would be home by Xmas," and of the imminent arrival of forty thousand of "Dugout Doug's boys." A big sea battle had been fought nearby and it was said the battleship USS *North Carolina* had sunk twenty enemy ships. Sid's squad sat around their holes the next two nights singing folk songs and hymns. Deacon took off his boots for the first time in nine days.

THE SEVENTH MARINES ARRIVED OFF GUADALCANAL ON THE MORNING OF September 18, a Friday. The sun ascended into a clear sky. From the ship, this island looked like Samoa: a mountain ridge running the length of it, though well back from the palm trees near the shore. The process of climbing down into the Higgins boats and riding to shore felt a lot like another practice run except for the navy destroyer off to their right, shelling an area of beach about a mile away.[72]

They walked off the ramp and into the friendly harassment of the marines on Lunga Point. Catcalls like "Where ya' been?" and "It's about time you got here, now that the fighting's over" welcomed them.[73] John and his men dropped their packs in a heap along with the almost four thousand other members of the Seventh Marines. The word was the enemy could show up at any minute and that the only supplies the marines could count on were what they brought with them. The officers barked orders to the NCOs. John, J.P., and other NCOs yelled at the enlisted men. Confusion ensued.[74] The marines had never been trained to unload ships and most rifle company commanders had only a basic understanding of logistics. The enlisted men grabbed boxes off the small lighters and humped them onto the beach. Cursing freely, they piled the stuff wherever it was handy.

An airplane did show up overhead after a time and things got lively. The AA guns began firing and it looked like some hits had been scored. The plane came racing for the beach. The marines started "running for the trees, for we were sure we were going to get strafed."[75] Bracketed by AA fire, though, it swung around and landed in the water. A boat went out to check on it. The marines went back to their drudgery in the sand and surf. Word came later that the plane had been "one of ours"; the gunner had been killed, and the pilot was mad as hell.

The ships had not been fully unloaded when Topside realized it needed to shift the priority from unloading the boats to moving the piles of supplies off the beach and getting them organized into dispersed and covered dumps inland. That process had not been completed when it gave way to the necessity brought on by darkness. After a long day of drudgery, the eleven hundred men of the 1/7 and its attached units set up their bivouac under some coconut trees on Lunga Point, near the village of Kukum. The junior officers, despite being briefed on the situation, did not push the men to dig foxholes. Hours after sunset, an enemy ship came into the channel and shelled the area around the airfield, including Lunga Point, for two to three hours.[76]

During their first shelling, men from the 1/7 could be heard praying. The prayers "began in Polish, Italian, [or] German, and then they would switch back to English," observed one joker; "they was going to make sure old Allah understood them I guess."[77] In the morning, the men of Dog Company could see gouges in the trees cut by ragged chunks of steel bigger than a man's hand. Two men of the 1/7 had been killed; two were wounded.[78] One of the wounded men, the rumor had it, had started yelling "Help! Help! Help!" As the shells continued to fall, Lieutenant Colonel Puller walked over to him and said, "Son, try and keep quiet. The other men are going through the same thing. . . . I'll get you a corpsman to take care of you." The story of Chesty Puller under fire came with a kicker: "the poor guy had his foot blown off."[79]

The tropical heat they were used to; the destruction wrought by enemy shells they were not. The new guys noticed that men in the First Marines and Fifth Marines looked dirty, unshaven, and distinctly unimpressed by the previous night's action.

Around noon the men of the Seventh Marines were ordered to cease unloading. The 2/7 and 3/7 grabbed their gear and headed south, past the airstrip, to man a sector of the perimeter. The 1/7 was going on a patrol.[80] That afternoon, Chesty Puller led them west to the Pioneer Bridge over the Lunga. On the far side of the river, a skirmish broke out in the thick jungle. Shots were exchanged with an unknown number of enemies. One marine fell. Chesty, at the point of attack, ordered his men forward. The resistance melted away and the 1/7 pushed a bit farther through the dense vegetation before digging in for the night. The jungle closed in. A few times they were awakened by their guards who, as John said, "got a little shadow happy," and fired at branches and bushes. In the morning, 1/7 headed back to the perimeter around the airfield. Another skirmish with the enemy broke out, leaving two marines wounded, before the battalion returned to the bivouac near the airfield.

Manila John and his friends got called out of their bivouac to the sound of gunfire that night. The IJA was attacking the 2/7 and the 3/7 and the regimental commander ordered the 1/7 to reinforce. The 1/7 scurried south in the darkness and heard a lot of firing, but eventually the word passed along that this was just trigger-happy marines firing at one another.[81] Angry officers and NCOs cursed their men liberally and demanded fire discipline. Word came that General Vandegrift himself had ordered them to rely on their bayonets at night. One of the local experts, the Australian Martin Clemens, was brought in to brief the NCOs on jungle noises.

THE SEVENTH MARINES, IN THE ESTIMATION OF THE #4 GUN SQUAD, "IS A QUAKEY bunch. Too much so." It was neither a compliment nor a joke.

THE DAILY DEATH RATE IN CABANATUAN, WHICH HAD DROPPED IN AUGUST, dropped again in September to about fourteen men a day. The weaker men had died from malnutrition, diarrhea, or malaria. The stronger ones had been helped by the Red Cross, which had been allowed to send in quinine to combat malaria. Months of hunger, however, had debilitated the prisoners. Thoughts of food shut out memories of home and cut off desires for sexual intimacy. Hunger set the prisoners in competition with one another. Some men curried favor with the guards by supplying information. Some doctors sold medicines on the black market to those who had money. Whenever a prisoner became too sick to eat, the others made sure his portion did not go to waste.

By September the camp's guards had smoothed out the burial process. They allowed chaplains to hold services and grave markers to be placed. A bar of soap per man had been issued, although water remained in very short supply. The Japanese had also begun to allow prisoners, on occasion, to purchase food and medicines from them. The guards required the cash in advance. Being able to buy even small amounts of additional food meant the difference between life and death.

Austin Shofner had brought money with him. Before leaving Corregidor, he had rolled a number of $20 bills of Philippine currency into a roll of toilet paper because "I thought I might need it someday." A can of food sold for one peso from the guards, but they didn't always have anything to sell. Prisoners on working parties smuggled in cans of food, and some of these were also sold on the black market. These cans went for ten to twenty pesos apiece. In a good week, Shofner was able to buy two cans of food, usually of salmon or sardines.

Austin Shofner shared the extra food. He loaned money for food and medicine in a world where the concept of a loan made no sense. The grateful recipients in Cabanatuan POW Camp Number One did not regard the loans or the food as charity. It was heroism. He was risking his own life to save others.[82]

Of course he could not save many lives with two cans of food per week. The all-encompassing deprivation cut at their bodies. Survival required constant attention. The mental and physical demands, however, could be borne only so long as a man had hope, and hope had to be found outside the compound. The prospect of rescue receded, however, with each month of captivity. If America was more powerful than Japan, why had they been lied to on Bataan about reinforcements being on the way? How could their country forget about them? The anguish persisted day after day as they tried to keep the flies off their food, tried to conserve their strength. Although every POW by this time knew how essential hope was to survival, that knowledge alone did not protect one from succumbing. When one of Shofner's friends told him, "Death isn't hard. Death is easy," he knew it would soon be over.

Like every prisoner, Austin Shofner had to gird himself for the mental challenge as well as the physical demands. With plenty of time on his hands, he did so. He thought about his father, who had played football for the University of Tennessee, just as he had. He thought about his football coach at UT, Robert Neyland, who had had as much influence on Shofner as his own father had. Coach Neyland had taught his team how to win. "You've got to play for the breaks," Neyland had always said, "and when you get one—score!" Neyland had toughened Shofner physically, but he also taught him to size up the odds, to know when a little trickery could shift the balance. Austin Shofner had found he had a gambler's eye. He had earned the nickname "Shifty." These memories reminded him of the energy and power he received whenever he felt like playing the odds and betting it all. After more than five months of being a POW, Shofner decided to look at the war as a football game. It was halftime. The other side had run up the score. But Shifty was getting back in the game.

*   *   *

JUST SHY OF TWO MONTHS ON THE ISLAND, HOW COMPANY AND THE REST OF THE 2/1 pulled out of their positions near Hell's Point at the mouth of the Tenaru River. Of course the order to move arrived just after Sid and Deacon had built themselves a nice new hut, so they were already angry when they heard they were taking over the 3/1's positions south of the airfield because the men in the 3/1 were in bad shape. "They are cracking up!?" demanded Deacon. "What do they think we are?"

The #4 gun squad had scrounged too hard and too long to leave anything behind. Scraps of lumber to build a hut, bedding liberated from the enemy stores in the early days—it all came with them, so they "looked like a bunch of gypsies moving out." Their new position had them tied in with the Tenaru well upstream, although now it ran on their left as they faced south.* The dense jungle opened into a large field in the center of the 2/1 section of the line; beyond the field to the right, dense

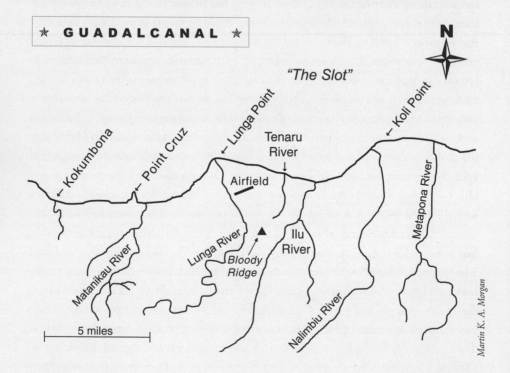

★ **GUADALCANAL** ★

N

"The Slot"

Kokumbona

Point Cruz

Lunga Point

Tenaru River

Koli Point

Airfield

Matanikau River

Lunga River

Bloody Ridge

Ilu River

Nalimbiu River

Metapona River

5 miles

Martin K. A. Morgan

---

*Later, in 1943, it was discovered that what the marines had called the Tenaru River was Alligator Creek. The Tenaru lay west of the marines' perimeter and theretofore had been referred to as the Ilu River.

jungle disconnected them from Bloody Ridge, where the Raiders and Parachute battalions had had the big battle a week earlier.

The condition of their new home outraged Sid's squad. No foxholes had been dug, no emplacements built. "We can plainly see the 3rd is a very inefficient bunch of men." Somebody else, at that very moment, was setting up shop in the "palace" left by the 2/1 on Hell's Point. Thankfully, Benson had already told them they would be moving to a new position very soon. Sid and Deacon cooked up some "Naisha Kaika" (Japanese rice cereal) and were delighted to discover that while they could hear the shelling on the airfield, the bombs didn't go off near them anymore. The snipers in the jungle around them also seemed tame by comparison. The #4 gun squad got a good night's sleep.

ON THE MORNING OF SEPTEMBER 24, THE THREE RIFLE COMPANIES OF THE 1/7 stripped themselves down to essentials and walked west for another patrol across the Lunga. The word spread across the division that Lieutenant Colonel Puller would, in the words of Charlie Company's captain, "rather fight than eat."[83] Most of Dog Company, including John's machine-gun section, stayed behind. Basilone found a piece of brown wrapping paper about this time and wrote his parents. "I have arrived safely on Guadalcanal," was all he said.[84] As for his friends on the patrol, the first report came when Able and Baker companies returned a day later with some wounded. It sounded about the same as the first patrol: a series of short, sharp firefights with the enemy with a few losses and no clear resolution. Then Able and Baker departed again. A day later Charlie Company returned, and then Able and Baker came stumbling into camp in the middle of the night. Manila's friend Richard, who had been with Able Company, told him the patrol had become "a haul-ass retreat!"[85]

In the morning no one from the patrol eagerly shared details about it. The officers in battalion headquarters were angry. Regimental HQ was said to be angry. The 1/7 patrol had grown into a complicated offensive before degenerating into a mess. Able and Baker companies had found themselves on a hill on the far side of the Matanikau River, cut off from the marine lines, surrounded by enemy forces. No one had brought a radio. With the enemy closing in, they had taken off their T-shirts and spelled H-E-L-P. A pilot happened to see the sign and radioed in. Hearing the news, Chesty jumped aboard a destroyer and went racing toward the scene. With its five-inch deck gun, the destroyer *Monssen* had cleared a path from the Alamo to the ocean, and the boys had run for their lives following the line of explosions.

With the enemy running hard to cut the marines off, John's good friend, Platoon Sergeant Anthony P. Malanowski, Jr., of Able, had picked up a BAR and covered the retreat. The marines reached the beach under heavy fire. Puller had some Higgins boats waiting for them, manned by coastguardsmen and navy coxswains brave enough to be sitting ducks. The loaded boats had only just gotten away; three coxswains had been wounded. No wonder the rifle platoons of the 1/7 had returned in a foul mood. After ten days on Guadalcanal, the battalion had suffered 10 percent casualties, including nine officers.[86] No one wanted to think about what the Japanese were doing at that moment to the marines who had been unable to make the run to the boats—men like Tony Malanowski, who had given them time to get away. So they stopped talking about the mission entirely. The battalion moved across the airfield area, south, to the jungle beyond the airport.

ISOLATED IN A THICKET SOUTH OF THE AIRFIELD, SID'S SQUAD HEARD AN ABBRE-viated report: "1st Battalion, 7th, surrounded in ambush. 2nd Battalion sent up to their aid." The mortarmen had also heard that all of the ships of the Imperial Japanese Navy were sailing toward them—nothing new there. They had managed to augment the spoonfuls of rice served at battalion with steak and beans cooked by Deacon. One of the mortarmen standing guard, Lester, heard a column marching toward them on the trail and, as ordered, Les stepped forward and challenged. A raspy voice replied: "This is Lieutenant Colonel Puller, Commanding Officer of the First Battalion, Seventh Marines: the best damn outfit in the United States Marine Corps."[87]

"Pass, friend," Lester stammered as Chesty Puller stalked past, the barest glimmer of a wink in his eye for the young marine on guard. The marines marching behind "the living legend," as Les later described the colonel, had just grinned at him.

SHIFTY KEPT HIMSELF AS CLEAN AS POSSIBLE. HE BOUGHT FOOD ON THE BLACK market as he could, but he ate the worms in his rice. He ate grass, leaves, whatever would fill the void. He told jokes, played softball, teased his friends, and kept an eye out for others, like him, who were playing to win. Shifty knew he needed a team of men whom he could trust—for survival, if not escape. Two likely fellows, Mike Dobervich and Jack Hawkins, bunked in his barracks and they were both marines, which was important. The three men had all heard a rumor that one thousand prisoners would be sent to another camp. They discussed the idea of volunteering to go. In the past each prisoner had endeavored to miss such shipments; some of those

POWs had reportedly been sent to Japan. However, they agreed no place could be worse than Cabanatuan. To stay was to die.

On the morning of September 26, the prisoners learned that the guards had foiled an escape attempt by three officers. The circumstances of the escape seemed a little odd. No trial was held. Just outside the fence in full view of all, the guards tied the wrists of each of the three escapees behind them. A rope from the post above them was tied to their wrists and suspended each body just enough so only their toes could touch the ground. Under the supervision of their officers, the guards beat them until their faces were unrecognizable. The men hung there for two days, bleeding, their shoulders wrenched by their weight. They received no food or water. The IJA medical personnel revived them so they could be beaten again. The guards required any Filipinos using the road near the men to strike them. If a Filipino did not strike the escapees severely, the Japanese struck the Filipinos.

"I had never imagined," Shofner wrote in his diary, "that such punishment could be taken by the human body, nor that man could endure such pain." At the end of the second day, the guards cut them down and compelled them to walk into the brush. One man with a broken leg could not walk, even when stabbed with a bayonet. They dragged him maybe fifty yards, until they reached three shallow graves. Two of them were shot and the third beheaded. All the men in the barracks where the escapees had lived, of which Shifty was a member, were immediately confined to barracks unless they were getting food or relieving themselves. The punishment would last for one month. Shifty wondered if he and his two friends had just missed their chance to get out of Cabanatuan POW Camp Number One.

THE 1/7 MOVED INTO A LINE OF HALF-FINISHED FOXHOLES AND BUNKERS FACING south. The 3/7 held the sector to their right, up on Bloody Ridge. On their left, the line ran into a sector held by the First Marines. Without the benefit of either a commanding height or a river, the 1/7 had a lot of work to do to create a defensible line across this area of flat, somewhat swampy jungle.

The battalion's 37mm cannons and .50-caliber machine guns went to the most vulnerable spot, the left end of the line, where it met the First Marines' sector. A flat plain opened there that stretched southward well into the jungle. From the far end of that plain came a jeep track running due north directly at their line, taking a little jog west as it crossed the 1/7's line, before heading north again to Henderson Field. Any attack would certainly come down that road. At the junction of the road and their lines, the marines built a cheval-de-frise, a three-dimensional oblong of barbed wire.

Sturdier than a double apron of barbed wire, the cheval-de-frise could be swung open with difficulty when necessary.

The cheval-de-frise was to Basilone's left. The riflemen from Charlie Company dug foxholes along a line running from it to the ridge on his right. Manila ordered his men to begin digging two machine-gun pits, each large enough for two guns, about forty yards apart. The traverse of each gun would support the riflemen between them as well as a large area to either side. Other men hacked down trees and brush to clear fire lanes or strung barbed wire. The gap between the point of John's machine gun and the wall of jungle on the far side of the barbed wire did not provide the kind of range a machine gunner craved. Behind him, the battalion headquarters dug in and ran telephone wire. After a week they learned Chesty would soon take them back across the Matanikau River and onto the offensive.

The 1/7 woke up to a big breakfast on October 7. At the battalion kitchen, they received meat and potatoes and fruit, beans, and bread in their mess kits, and cups of hot coffee to wash it down.[88] For hungry men living in the boonies, the meal went beyond being a healthy start to something more like a reassurance. Everybody knew the IJN had landed a lot of men and equipment on the other side of the Matanikau River. At the prospect of going over there again, one private wounded himself badly enough to be evacuated.[89]

The new attack included a lot of units, including most of the Seventh Regiment. The attackers would not only have air cover, but the big guns of the division's artillery would be on call as well. Topside, Manila noted, had learned "a costly lesson from our recent failure. . . ."[90] For Basilone and his friends, it boiled down to this: the 1/7 and two other battalions would cross the Matanikau well upstream, then sweep northward and hit the enemy troop concentrations from the flank. Unlike the first patrol, this time John's machine-gun section would accompany a rifle platoon of Charlie Company.[91] While carting the machine guns through the jungle was tough, the earlier patrols had shown that anything could happen. If they engaged a large enemy force, the riflemen would need the support of Manila's heavy machine guns.

As the 1/7 left the mess, every marine put some C rations in his pocket. The little gold cans contained meat with hash, meat and beans, or some other dreadful combination. The 3/2 led the way, followed by the 2/7, with the 1/7 in the rear. Chesty liked to have Fidel Hernandez, a big marine out of Dog Company, be his point man.[92] Chesty called Fidel "Hombre," but John and the others often called him "Chief" because he had some Native American ancestry as well as Spanish. Not far behind Fidel came his platoon leader, his company commander, and the battalion commander himself. Chesty had always been clear about his expectations for his platoon leaders and company commanders: "You lead your men," he insisted, "you do not lag behind."[93] Strung out single file, the three battalions made one long column snaking west from the airfield, then south into the island's interior.

In the midafternoon, they came to a stream, one of the tributaries of the Matanikau. A single coconut log crossed it, with a length of communications wire as a handrail.[94] Only a few men could cross it at a time, creating a bottleneck that made the 1/7 vulnerable. Lookouts were posted downstream and upstream and the process got under way. Charlie Company crossed, then began the ascent up the other side of the valley. Climbing the steep ridge was a backbreaker. Men slid, dropped equipment, and cursed eloquently. Those few hundred yards took an hour.[95] Charlie Company set up their bivouac on top of the ridgeline and posted the guard. Well into the evening, the other companies were still gaining the ridge and joining them.

Even before the men had risen in the morning, the first few drops of a downpour made the prospect of another day of slogging through the jungle less appealing. The rain grew into a torrent and forced a delay. On the morning of the ninth the 1/7 crossed the larger fork of the Matanikau. As it continued pushing west, the two battalions ahead of them had begun turning north. The 1/7 continued west before turning north, in order to guard the marines' left flank.

By the sound of it, the lead battalions had met a large enemy unit. Amid the bombs from U.S. planes and artillery, the sound of return fire could be heard.[96] About a thousand yards from the river, 1st Battalion gained a ridge where they could see the surrounding terrain.[97] Squad leaders like Basilone were called forward and shown the lay of the land. To the north, they could see the 2/7 firing at the enemy to their left. They could see the ocean another two thousand yards beyond the 2/7. The distances, however, could not be understood in yards. The steep hills and dense jungle imposed limits on every consideration.

Chesty gave Charlie Company a special assignment.[98] He ordered them to flank the enemy position that was exchanging fire with the 2/7. Captain Moore led his men down into a ravine, first west, then hooking around to the north. Upon gaining the high ground, they had a beautiful view. Across a narrow valley, they looked into the enemy positions on the barren ridge opposite them. The enemy's attention was focused on the 2/7.

No one fired before Captain Moore gave the order. The marines took their positions and set up their weapons. Basilone's machine guns joined in as Charlie Company began raking the enemy troops at close range. With their targets silhouetted against the sky, some marines thought it was a bit like shooting on a rifle range.[99] Over the barrel of his machine gun, Manila watched as the enemy "bodies jerked in a crazy dance."[100] The Japanese, of course, wheeled around to face this new threat, but they lacked cover. It also quickly became apparent that the main force of the IJA was congregated in the depression between the two opposing forces.

Charlie Company's 60mm mortars began dropping rounds down there while guys on the ridge fired rifle grenades at likely targets. Then the 81mm mortars, back with the rest of the 1/7 a bit south and east of Charlie, joined in. The enemy found themselves trapped in the ravine. They could not charge Charlie Company's ridge. They could not remain in the ravine. They could not survive on their ridge, much less defend themselves. Several times the enemy tried to set up a machine gun in a large tree on the edge of the ravine. Each time, Charlie Company's machine gunners and mortarmen cut them to pieces.[101]

For two hours, Charlie Company had them dead to rights. The marines kept most of the enemy soldiers trapped in the lowland. Artillery, fired from within the perimeter, began to explode in the valley.[102] The relentless killing finally caused the enemy to break and run for their lives. Hundreds had died and more had been wounded. The carnage made some of John's section puke. Return fire started to come from the position occupied by the 2/7. A few men went down before it ended suddenly.

Before all resistance had been extinguished and before Charlie Company had made sure every figure lying out there was dead, Captain Moore began ordering them to prepare to withdraw. That surely struck some of them as odd. They loaded their dead and wounded onto litters. The way led east, skirting the depression in front of them, of course. A few marines searched the dead—some for intelligence and some for souvenirs—and they found the bodies of large, well-equipped men. This IJA unit obviously had not been on Guadalcanal long. As rear guard for the entire mission, Charlie Company had to watch its back as it marched to the mouth of the river. A few shots rang out, but this harassment tapered off as they got to the beach. The other battalions had crossed. Charlie Company stood watch while the rest of the 1/7 crossed the Matanikau near its mouth.

Trucks began taking the others back to the perimeter along the coast road, so Charlie began to cross. On the other side, the marines deployed along the bank, ready for anything. The trucks drove slowly and the wounded went first, among them Steve Helstowski, one of Manila's gunners and a close friend.[103] Full dark found a dozen men still waiting for their ride, including Captain Moore and Colonel Puller.

At last a truck arrived and they loaded up. The truck broke down. The group started to hike back in the direction of the airfield. With no moonlight, it became so dark it turned black. Without flashlights, they got lost. They wandered around, in and out of the perimeter and through several company CPs.[104] Everybody knew this was a good way to get shot by one of the many trigger-happy marines out there.[105] Furious, Puller demanded guides from these other units, but the guides promptly got them turned around again. At last they stumbled into marines from the First Regiment. They knew that those men held the Seventh's left flank, so they followed the First's line to the right.

Those taking their shift on guard after midnight watched as the final Charlie men stumbled into their positions. Next they heard the voice of Chesty, who was at his battalion HQ a few hundred yards away. Though he obviously had a phone in his hands, Chesty yelled, "I and the remnants of my battalion have returned!" Evidently the person on the other end asked for a repeat, so he bellowed the same thing even louder.[106] Around him, the 1/7 shared a chuckle.

In the morning, there was time to piece together the story. Sergeants tallying the men for their muster rolls reported to the battalion HQ that the 1/7 had lost five killed and more than twenty wounded on the patrol. Charlie Company and the attached men from Dog Company had carried their dead out, but Chesty had ordered others buried where they fell, on the IJA side of the river.[107] Manila's friend Steve had been wounded in the leg bad enough to be evacuated.

The emperor's troops had paid dearly. Manila could tell his friends in Dog Company that they had gotten the Japanese dead to rights and hundreds of them had dropped and then, all of a sudden, orders came and C/1/7 had pulled out. Marines who had been up to battalion would have added the missing piece: Charlie Company's flank had been left wide open when the 2/7 had been ordered to pull out. The move had been ordered by the regimental commander, who had been well to the rear of Chesty's command post (CP). Chesty had yelled over the phone to regimental HQ something about getting off their asses and getting up to the front before issuing orders, but it had been too late to stop the pullout. No wonder Chesty had blown his stack when he finally made it back.

Manila and the rest of the returnees also got some news from the men who had stayed behind to hold the 1/7's front line: a convoy of IJN ships and transports had been spotted sailing toward the Canal.

W.O. HAD NOT ONLY RECOVERED FROM HIS DYSENTERY; HE ALSO HAD BECOME adept at theft. The rest of the #4 gun squad paid no attention when he slipped off, leaving them to dig emplacements, because he returned with goodies: four pounds of bacon on one trip, and a few days later, almost two gallons of dough. As if to put W.O.'s skill in proper perspective, that same day the battalion PX issued to each squad "one package of gum, 1 and 3/4 ounces of candy, four cans of tobacco," to complement each man's allotment of Japanese rice. Deacon happily took the dough and made biscuits; the next day he added jam to bake pies, and later slathered it in syrup for pancakes. The cook's biggest challenge was keeping W.O.'s dirty hands out of the process.

As their new positions took shape, the company commander ordered the mortars to have gun drill with live rounds. The first section of 81mms opened up and rained shells down near Fox Company. No one was hit. Deacon muttered something about Duffy in first section being a "crackpot." Second section, which included the Rebel squad, laid down a systematic barrage that earned the praise of the platoon's officers.

With their emplacements dug and their aiming stakes in, the work tapered off for the 81mms. Aside from the occasional working party down at the beach, Sid's squad waited for the next battle. Out beyond their lines, patrols from the 2/1 often ran into enemy patrols; they found two Japanese 75mm guns about eight thousand yards from the 2/1's lines, and someone said a patrol had captured two Japanese women snipers. The two or three air raid alerts a day seemed normal. Above their gun pit, "planes fought like wild men right over our heads." In one raid, they counted "17 zero fighters and 23 bombers" shot down, and they calculated the "approximate loss to the Nip was $6,770,000, the loss of the bombs not included."

Totaling up enemy losses felt good, so during one three-hour-long air raid they moved on to enemy ships. Using the best scuttlebutt available, they calculated the IJN had lost "60 ships in 60 days." Positive rumors fed their hopes. Word came that forty-five thousand of "Dugout Doug's boys" (the U.S. Army) had landed on the island of Bougainville, on the western end of the Solomon Island chain. The rumor that fresh army regiments would replace marine regiments in the next few days, allowing the marines to return to San Diego, recurred regularly, so it had some credibility. Sid's squad also continued to augment its rations. When the barley they received "smelled like japs," Deacon traded his IJA bayonet to some swabbies in Kukum for cheese, beans, Spam, and bread. Another night he managed to create holeless doughnuts before the squad began another of their sing-alongs.

Humor moved Sid more than songs, though. On the night of October 12, he heard the guns of the Seventh Marines banging away and someone say it "must be some starving japs trying to give up." The next day, the army landed at Kukum, some thirty-five hundred strong. The first air raid siren sounded at ten thirty, the second at noon. Both waves of planes dropped thousands of pounds of high explosives. Sid's squad sent W.O. and others down to Kukum to see what could be stolen or traded from the doggies and the swabbies.

The prospects for swindling and stealing also attracted Manila John. He and his friend Richard walked down, hoping to trade some "jap booty" for "torpedo juice" (grain alcohol). "Let's start a rumor," John said.

"What the hell do you want . . . ," Richard began, before the two came upon another marine. John said, "Hey, they found Amelia Earhart and her navigator and four kids on an island." The two walked on, sharing a laugh. The trip did not prove successful and they returned to camp and learned the 1/7 would go in reserve near the airport and the 3/7 would replace them. They also heard a pilot had been dispatched to the far side of the island to pick up Amelia Earhart and her family.*

The shelling began with the IJA's artillery firing from the other side of the Matanikau. It moved around methodically, saturating the marine perimeter in general and the airfield in particular. Heavy shelling cued the arrival of Jockstrap to Dog Company. A Dalmatian, Jockstrap belonged to the assistant division commander, General Rupertus, who likely had named his dog something else. Jockstrap, however, preferred to be with Dog Company, particularly Sergeant Conrad Packer, when the shit hit the fan. Each explosion caused the dog to dig deeper underneath Packer.[108] Tonight's shelling had Jockstrap digging hard when Washing Machine Charlie appeared overhead and dropped flares. Flares provided an aiming point for the enemy's ships.

It started with what sounded like a door slamming. Somewhere out in the channel, a door hanging ten thousand feet in the air had just slammed. In the moment it took to realize how preposterous the notion was, the whistling of the first shells began to grow in pitch and volume until it sounded like a subway car entering a station. The detonation thundered like nothing the marines had ever heard. Well back from the airfield and in a bunker, John felt the threat turn to panic around him as colossal eruptions wiped other thoughts and concerns from his consciousness. In an hour and a half, the ships fired about a thousand shells into the area of the airfield. "The din and concussions were unbelievable. Good brave men gave way and sobbed."[109]

In the morning of October 14 they learned the shelling had come from two enemy battleships firing fourteen-inch shells. Each shell weighed more than two thou-

---

*Amelia Earhart, a pioneer in aviation and holder of the Distinguished Flying Cross, disappeared in 1937 somewhere over the Pacific Ocean while attempting to circumnavigate the globe.

sand pounds. No one in the Fifth Marines or in the First Marines denied that what they had all endured had been the worst ever. John could only say it had been "an ordeal of torture."[110] Two Dog Company second lieutenants, Richards and Iseman, had been killed by a direct hit on their bunker.[111] Ten men from Charlie Company, who had been on a working party unloading ships, had been killed in the shelling. The 1/7 moved down to the airfield, in reserve off the front line, but in the target zone. Fires raged. The largest came from the gasoline storage areas. Great holes had been torn into the runway. In the afternoon, the enemy artillery across the Matanikau began shelling them. Dog Company and their dog Jockstrap started digging again.

ON THE MORNING OF OCTOBER 14 THE PILOTS OF BOMBING SIX LEARNED THAT the night before the Imperial Japanese Navy had shelled Henderson Field and the marine positions around it. Some forty men had been killed, most of the planes had been rendered inoperable, and a big gasoline dump had gone up in flames. The IJN had prepared the way for another push to take the island. The need was great. The eight planes of Bombing Six, along with a like number of spare Dauntlesses, were the last reinforcements immediately available in the South Pacific.[112] Bombing Six, the briefing concluded, would depart for Cactus today.

It would not have taken them long to get ready for takeoff. They had been expecting to go into action and they did not have very much with them. Micheel, who had been promoted to lieutenant junior grade two weeks earlier, took off with a new gunner in his rear seat, Aviation Machinist's Mate Second Class Herman H. Caruthers. The flight lasted more than four hours. As they neared the airfield, they would have seen plumes of smoke, some of which were rising from the airfield. From a thousand feet up, a pilot could see two airstrips. The larger one, Henderson, ran east to west in a wide plain. The western tip ended just short of a river.

Almost 4,000 feet in length, 150 feet wide, and mostly covered by a steel mat, the gravel airstrip had been created by the Japanese for their big land-based bombers. After the last month on Efate and Espiritu Santos, Mike had become accustomed to the dust and gravel kicked up during a squadron landing. Following his skipper, he would have turned off the landing strip onto the taxi strip. The ground crews directed the airplanes to parking areas, or hardstands, spaced out in intervals along the edges of the runway. Some of the coconut trees had been left in and around the hardstands in order to obscure the planes from above. It was rough terrain to move a plane around in. Mike would have seen a fair number of wrecked planes scattered about, some perhaps still smoldering.

Lieutenant Austin Shofner devoted himself to the United States Marine Corps. He arrived in Shanghai, China, on April 28, 1941, for his first posting overseas.

Courtesy of the Shofner Family

A portrait of Ensign Vernon "Mike" Micheel wearing the naval aviator's Wings of Gold, taken upon graduation from flight school on October 6, 1941.

Courtesy of Vernon Micheel

Boot camp allowed Sidney Phillips to indulge in one of his favorite hobbies— guns. Here he checks out the Browning automatic rifle, or BAR. His father, the principal of Mobile's Murphy High School, kept this photo on his desk throughout the war.

Courtesy of Dr. Sidney Phillips

While in boot camp, Sid received this photo of his friend Eugene with his favorite pistol and his dogs, Lady (*left*) and Deacon. It was signed "Your most humble and obedient servant, Gene."

Courtesy of Dr. Sidney Phillips

Eugene Sledge and Sidney Phillips, in Mobile, Alabama, in late May 1942, at the moment the two friends parted.
Courtesy of Dr. Sidney Phillips

Sidney Phillips, having just completed boot camp, spent Memorial Day with his family before heading off to war.
Courtesy of Dr. Sidney Phillips

A photo of the Sledge family shows (*from left to right*) Dr. and Mrs. Sledge; Eugene; his older brother, Edward; and his aunt, Octavia Wynn. Edward, headed off to war, always seemed to be one step ahead of Gene.
Courtesy of Jeanne Sledge

John Basilone (*left*) served in the army in the mid-1930s and was stationed in Manila, capital city of the Philippine Islands. The tales he told of his life there earned him the nickname "Manila John."

Courtesy of the Basilone Family

Taken on September 19, 1940, this photo of Private John Basilone marked the completion of the Marine Corps' boot camp.

Courtesy of the Basilone Family

Soon after John Basilone enlisted in the Marine Corps in July 1940, he knew he had found his place in the world. As seen here with a girlfriend in late 1940, his happy-go-lucky smile had returned.

Courtesy of the Basilone Family

James "J. P." Morgan, a hothead, listened to one man—John Basilone. The two friends fought the Battle of Guadalcanal together.

Courtesy of the National Records Center

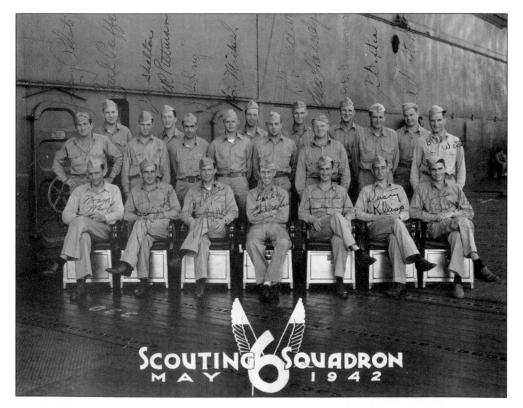

Scouting Squadron Six poses on the deck of USS *Enterprise* shortly before the Battle of Midway. Ensign John Lough stands in the top row, fifth from left; his friend Ensign Mike Micheel stands next to him, sixth from left.

Courtesy of Dennis Rodenburg

A navy pilot throttles his engine up to full power before receiving permission to launch off the deck of a carrier. *National Archives*

The Japanese aircraft carrier *Hiryu* burns during the Battle of Midway in June 1944. *Navy Historical Center*

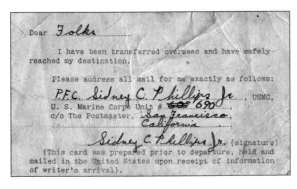

Dear Folks

I have been transferred overseas and have safely reached my destination.

Please address all mail for me exactly as follows:

PFC. Sidney C. Phillips Jr. , USMC,
U. S. Marine Corps Unit # 695 690 ,
c/o The Postmaster, San Francisco,
California

Sidney C. Phillips Jr. (signature)

(This card was prepared prior to departure, held and mailed in the United States upon receipt of information of writer's arrival).

The need for protecting the secrecy of the location of the First Marine Division with the need of the men to communicate with their families led to this card, dated July 1942.

Courtesy of Dr. Sidney Phillips

The invasion of Guadalcanal on August 7, 1942, went well. For America's amphibious assault force, the test had only begun. *National Archives*

The airstrip known as Henderson Field, code-named Cactus, became the center of the Pacific War for the latter half of 1942. *National Archives*

The wardroom of the aircraft carrier USS *Enterprise*, seen here on the day of the invasion of Guadalcanal, provided pilots with a level of luxury unknown to the troops.   *National Archives*

The Battle of Hell's Point marked the first combat on Guadalcanal. Sid Phillips helped win the battle and then had to live near the corpses for weeks.   *National Archives*

Mike found his service on Guadalcanal as difficult as any challenge he ever faced. As a member of the Cactus Air Force, he flew a Dauntless, like the one pictured here, "up the slot" of the Solomon Islands in 1942. While not the fastest aircraft, the Dauntless earned Micheel's trust for its reliability in flight and its stability. It handled a seventy-degree dive from twelve thousand feet with grace and verve.

National Archives

A Japanese plane dives through the antiaircraft fire toward USS *Enterprise* in the Battle of the Eastern Solomons, August 24, 1942. Somewhere above the enemy, Ensign Micheel circles the ship, hoping he will have a ship on which to land.   *National Archives*

The proof of John Basilone's induction into the Domain of Neptunus Rex, an old navy tradition, was signed by the legendary Major Lewis B. "Chesty" Puller, as Davey Jones.
Courtesy of the Basilone Family

John Basilone (*left*) and his friend Richard Greer share a laugh before departing from their base, located outside of Melbourne, Australia. John, doing his impression of Napoleon, has prepared for his liberty by visiting the base's enlisted men's club.
Courtesy of Richard Greer

John Basilone and his best friend, J. P. Morgan, in early 1943, at the Seventh Marine's base in Mount Martha, Australia, near Melbourne.
Courtesy of Richard Greer

Sid Phillips's regiment had the good fortune of being stationed at the Melbourne Cricket Ground, seen here in 1943, below the wings of an RAAF Beaufighter. The delights of the city were but steps away. *Courtesy of the Melbourne Cricket Ground*

The First Marine Division paraded through the streets of Melbourne, Australia, in early 1943 to accept the thanks of a grateful nation. *Courtesy of Hugh Corrigan*

John "Deacon" Tatum (*left*), Stan Bender (a new man in the squad), and Sidney Phillips (*right*) show off their makeshift uniforms in Australia in 1943.   *Courtesy of Dr. Sidney Phillips*

The recipient of the Medal of Honor for his service on Guadalcanal, Sergeant John Basilone went barnstorming with a rotating cast of well-known actors (here, John Garfield stands to the right of Virginia Grey, who holds a bouquet) and other heroes of the U.S. armed services.   *Courtesy of the Basilone Family*

When the stars of the Third War Loan Drive gathered for a group photo, actress Martha Scott's fondness for Sergeant Basilone became apparent.   *Courtesy of the Basilone Family*

Sergeant John Basilone and actor John Garfield take the stage on September 10, 1943, to ask the people of Jersey City to fund the war effort by buying bonds.

Courtesy of the Basilone Family

As a spokesman for the United States Marine Corps, Sergeant Basilone supported the induction of women into the corps.

Courtesy of the Basilone Family

John returned to his hometown as a hero, a proud day for his family and the Italian-American community. Not pictured here was his brother, George, who was with the Fourth Marine Division in September 1943, when this photo was taken.

Courtesy of the Basilone Family

On Cape Gloucester, the 81mm mortars delivered devastating fire in the few instances when they were needed. *National Archives*

The conditions on Cape Gloucester exceeded the imagination of the marines who had fought in the jungles of Guadalcanal. *National Archives*

A chow line on the island of Pavuvu, the rest camp for the First Marine Division.
National Archives

Andrew A. Haldane, who earned a promotion to captain on Guadalcanal, led King Company through the jungles of Cape Gloucester and the wasteland of Peleliu. *Courtesy of Steve Moore*

Eugene Sledge exited boot at the end of 1943. His war bore almost no relation to the one fought by his friend Sidney Phillips. *Courtesy of the National Records Center*

Merriell "Snafu" Shelton, seen here in his first photo as a marine, was the "meanest son of a gun" Eugene Sledge ever knew. "I loved him to death," Gene Sledge later wrote, "because he saved me many a time." *Courtesy of the National Records Center*

Romus Valton Burgin, Sledge's squad leader on Peleliu and Okinawa, made sergeant. *Courtesy of R. V. Burgin*

Soon after climbing out of their planes, the new pilots would have realized that they had entered a chaotic situation. Everyone there had been greatly affected by the previous night's cataclysm. Six pilots and four enlisted men had been killed. The marine general in charge of all flight operations, Roy Geiger, was busy moving the operations center. The rude wooden building left by the Japanese, called the pagoda because of its distinctive roofline, had been blown to bits. The new operations center was a tent not far away. The ground crews and veteran pilots had to shake off the effects as fast as possible because there was a lot of work to do: assess the damage, bury the dead, clean up the wreckage, and fight the oncoming enemy.

Two waves of Japanese bombers and fighters had struck the field by the time Mike arrived.[113] The first raid had dropped its bombs unchallenged; the Wildcats had not been able to get into the air in time. The U.S. fighters had been ready for the second wave, which had arrived overhead at 1:03 p.m. They had shot down fifteen bombers and three Zeros. The waves of enemy planes had been attempting to knock out the airfield in preparation for the arrival of their ships. The updated scouting report at four p.m. revealed one imperial battleship, three cruisers, and four destroyers bearing down on Guadalcanal on course 130 degrees at a speed of twenty-five knots; while this powerful force was still 180 miles out, another force of destroyers and troop transports was even closer. In the early evening, two groups of Dauntlesses rose from Henderson Field, their target the troop transports and destroyer escorts. While these thirteen dive-bomber pilots confronted the enemy, the new arrivals started getting orientated.

The Dauntless dive-bombers shared the use of the main airstrip with the torpedo planes and any PBYs or B-17s that came through. The Wildcats did not fly off of Henderson. They used the smaller airstrip, designated Fighter One but appropriately called the Cow Pasture. Today, however, the dive-bombers used the Cow Pasture because an enemy fieldpiece was shelling Henderson. As the men of Bombing Six were introduced, Mike realized "we had a mishmash of everybody." To the Marine Corps squadrons had been added pilots from each of the three U.S. carriers to have been damaged or sunk recently: *Enterprise*, *Saratoga*, and *Wasp*. Some of the men Mike had met on Espiritu Santos. Only one squadron had arrived recently as a complete unit. The others, like Mike's Bombing Six, had arrived in dribs and drabs. All told, there were about twenty-three Dauntlesses ready to fly, but there was very little gasoline.

Spread out under the coconut trees on the northern side of the field was Mosquito Gulch, as the pilots referred to their quarters. Being shown a tent with six cots for living quarters came as no surprise. The foxholes and trenches that had been dug near every tent got the new guys' attention. After a visit to the mess tent for the evening meal, it came time to hit the rack because the next day would demand just as much from them. The two Dauntless strikes had returned before dark, having scored a combined total of five possible hits on the enemy transports.[114] The screening warships had fired up a lot of flak. Everyone expected another attack soon. The unrelenting heat made a blanket unnecessary. Sleep came slowly to the guys lying in their clothes or in their skivvies. Keeping some clothes on, they had been warned, made it easier to run for the nearest bunker when the shelling started.

Lieutenant Micheel's initiation into the Cactus Air Force continued later that night, when a floatplane came over. The pilots ran for their bunkers in the light of the flares hanging above. The salvos from the enemy warships concentrated on the two airstrips, which put the new guys in the bull's-eye. Sitting in a bunker swatting mosquitoes, Mike endured the raid. After the all clear sounded, he walked back to discover what he called "the problem of living in the tent." Flying metal and exploding trees had torn great holes in it. His tent mates agreed they needed more protection. The next morning, they went to steal some sheets of steel grating, called Marston matting, used to cover some of the main runway. They had something else they needed that sheet metal to cover.

ORDERED TO HAVE 50 PERCENT OF ALL PERSONNEL ON GUARD AT ANY ONE TIME, no one in the 2/1 got much sleep the night of October 14. Another night of shelling meant the start of a ground assault. IJN convoys supposedly had been sighted eighty-five miles away. In the morning, word came that seven enemy transports were unloading at Kokumbona. Lieutenant Benson ordered his mortars to break down the guns immediately and prepare to move out. Soldiers began arriving to take the 2/1's positions. The mortarmen "wished the doggies luck as we boarded trucks," and wound their way toward the airfield.[115] The IJA artillery seemed to chase their convoy as it wound its way north, to cross the Lunga River, then southwest, to some hills facing the jungle. Twenty-six bombers came over and welcomed them to the neighborhood with a carpet bombing. The marines' AA guns plucked two of them from the sky. Looking out to the coast, Sid's squad could see the Japanese transports unloading. U.S. planes bombed and strafed them, "killing thousands," but it looked to the squad like the B-17s hit the IJN the hardest, leaving four smoking. Two of the enemy's transports got away, leaving a ghastly scene: "water full and beach lined with dead." The #4 gun squad started digging in.

*   *   *

Not scheduled to fly on his first full day on Cactus, Lieutenant Micheel walked over to the operations tent and soaked up the situation. Like the ready room on the Big E, the tents around the ops tent offered plenty of hot coffee and the latest intelligence. The uniform of the day was khaki pants, khaki short-sleeved shirt, and army boots; those not about to fly might wear only shorts and boots. In order to provide some protection from the fierce sun, the pilots were issued blue baseball caps; the mechanics wore red ones.[116] Like most of his comrades, Mike wore his pistol in its shoulder holster, even when he was not flying.

October 15 started badly for the Cactus Air Force. The holes in Henderson Field prevented its use. Ground crews were still assessing the damage to the planes and looking for supplies of aviation gasoline. Crews drained the gas tanks of wrecked airplanes. The first Wildcats took off at dawn. A single Dauntless dive-bomber followed, the first of four to make individual attacks against the five enemy troop transports and eight destroyers that were landing troops a few miles down the shoreline. At six forty a.m., a scout reported another group of heavier battlewagons a few miles out, and five destroyers twenty miles out.

The morning's all-out search for aviation gasoline uncovered five separate spots where the drums had been buried by working parties. One cache of one hundred barrels had been buried down on the beach near Kukum.[117] Lost drums of gasoline only pointed up the chaotic nature of life on the Canal. Out on the field, engineers used a combination of U.S. and Japanese heavy equipment to repair the strip. On the flight line, the ground crews had long since learned how to keep the planes flying despite chronic shortages of essential items. Spare parts often came from the wreckage of other aircraft, most of which had been collected into a boneyard just off the strip. Without carts and hoists for the bombs, the men manhandled five-hundred- and thousand-pound bombs onto and off of planes. They fueled the planes using hand pumps connected to fifty-five-gallon drums of fuel.[118] The plane captains eventually declared eleven more Dauntlesses fit to fly. The Klaxon announced the noon enemy raid at eleven a.m., which proved to include fewer bombers than usual. After the Wildcats fought the enemy planes, a number of sorties of Dauntlesses took off in the afternoon for the enemy ships. One PBY pilot took off with two torpedoes jerry-rigged to the wings; he managed to launch one of them into the side of an enemy ship. An enemy fighter chased the lumbering PBY all the way back to Henderson Field, where the six machine guns of a Wildcat turned it into a ball of fire a few hundred feet above Micheel's head.[119]

Lieutenant Commander Ray Davis led the last strike of the day. He and two others flew over the three transports burning fiercely on the shoreline to chase after the ones fleeing up the slot. Ray found his quarry about sixty-five miles away, dove through the AA fired by the destroyers. One of his wingmen scored a hit. The Cactus Air Force had savaged the enemy and sent them packing, for the moment. A lot of the emperor's ships were still steaming around the slot.

A few of the navy's transport planes, the R4D (known to the army as the C-47 and to the world as the DC-3) landed with drums of gasoline and departed with wounded marines and fifteen exhausted pilots. Six Dauntlesses arrived. The supply ships due that day, however, had been turned back. As the day ended, a few of the pilots flying the torpedo planes announced that they were going to grab rifles and go up into the hills to help the Seventh Marines.[120] Mike declined. He had been scheduled to fly the next day and it looked like there would be enough gas.

First he had to suffer through an intense barrage. Fifteen hundred of the eight-inch naval shells kept every airman and every marine cringing inside their bunkers and foxholes for more than an hour. In the morning, there were ten flyable Dauntlesses. In the ops tent, the skipper's priority of the day soon became clear: to destroy the enemy troops and matériel. Planes from the carrier USS *Hornet*, which had sailed into the area during the night, would assist. For Mike's briefing, a few marine officers came into the operations tent and joined in the briefing on enemy locations. After orientating the new guys, pointing out locations like Bloody Ridge, the Matanikau River, and the beaches of Kokumbona, one of them put his finger on a spot, looked directly at the pilots and said, "You go out there and get this place. . . ."

Mike walked to his Dauntless, parked under a coconut tree. The holes cut by shrapnel had been filed down until they were smooth. The plane captain and his team left the small holes at that. They screwed down any tears that threatened to open wider at speed. They covered the large gashes with pieces of tin cut from the fuselages of wrecked planes. In the cockpit, Mike looked down the length of his wing and noticed four or five large patches. "None of them were structural," he was assured; "they're just airfoil."

The airstrip lacked the smoothness of his carrier's flight deck. Its great length, however, offered Mike all the room in the world to gain flying speed. He hardly got his wheels up before he was over the target area. He looked down at the jungle below, back at the map on his plotting board, and then back down. Translating the poor map to the green terrain below was a difficult piece of orienteering. When the flight leader felt like he had the target, he radioed back to base. He received a curt reply,

"Clear the bomb." The planes pushed over into a short dive to get their aim and then pulled the release.

Mike dropped a depth charge, not a general-purpose bomb, in part because the Cactus Air Force happened to have a lot of them. Mike had heard depth charges "were good to drop on guys in the woods . . . the shrapnel would go out all over." The enemy fired at him, but nothing could hit him at his speed except an AA gun. He completed the mission in less than an hour, then repeated it. The Mitsubishi bombers made their run at the marines and Henderson Field about three p.m., releasing their ordnance as the Wildcats dropped down upon them.

More exhausted pilots rotated off Cactus that night. Their departure meant more work for Bombing Six. A test of endurance began. Most days included at least one hour spent in a bunker, riding out the enemy air raids. Only a few days into the campaign, his buddy Bill Pittman jumped into a hole, only to land on a shard of jagged metal. It cut him badly and he left for sick bay. The Japanese artillery across the river played havoc with them on the airfield. Named Pistol Pete, the 150mm howitzer had developed a nasty habit of shooting at planes in the final moments of their landing pattern.

Though he saw marines all around—marching in formation, guarding the aircraft—the mess hall was the only place he came into close contact with them. Getting in the chow line, he first came to the medics handing out Atabrine. Once inside, mess men ladled "chili or . . . meat loaf or something like that" onto a tin plate and he found a seat where he could. From the conversations around him, Mike would have understood that the reconstituted potatoes sticking to his plate were regarded as a major step up from K rations. Though he did not ever learn much about the specifics of the ground campaign, from what he and his fellow pilots could see, "we didn't have any problem thinking that the marines, as long as they were supplied, they would be able to hang on."

Bombing Six's tactical missions against ground troops—dropping depth charges and strafing troop concentrations—grew out of the self-evident need to help the marines. With air superiority over the island for most of each day, the navy pilots could help the infantry campaign. They had not been trained, however, to provide "close air support." Direct radio communication between pilots and commanders on the ground had not been developed. Some of the problem was technological. Navy radios were problematic; marine radios were worse. The sets in Mike's plane operated on different frequencies than the radios of the marines. While the rear seat gunner could try to dial in lower frequencies, this did not become the easy answer.

Without pilots and marines trained in common procedures, and constrained by the emerging technology of radio, the leadership groped their way toward a solution during the heat of battle. Expediency won out. Marines marked targets using white phosphorus rounds.

Supporting the ground campaign ranked a distant third in priority to finding the Tokyo Express and stopping it. Having been in this battle since D-day, Bombing Six understood the nature of the fight and the routes by which the enemy struck them. With all of the challenges of getting as many Dauntlesses as possible into the air each day, the organization of the search missions looked "kind of happenstance" to Mike. He could see why. The CO of the Cactus Air Force, General Geiger, made his decisions based on the available aircraft. He and his staff had to maintain a striking force of Dauntlesses loaded with bombs designed to sink ships at the ready, while dispatching others on scouting or infantry support missions. Four days after Bombing Six landed, the CO pointed to Mike and another guy and said, "Okay, you've got the center marker. You've got the outside slot." He gave them a takeoff time for a scouting mission.

Flying a search mission over the Solomons demanded less skill than an ASW search off *Enterprise* because the chain islands made it so easy to navigate. Up the slot he flew, aware that somewhere in those islands, hiding in nameless bays just out of range, the Tokyo Express was waiting for darkness. As directed, he paid particular attention to the island of New Georgia on this first trip. He returned home empty-handed, feeling like a failure and afraid that everyone would have to pay for his failure by spending the night in the foxhole while a cruiser or two plastered the perimeter. Men would get hurt, even die. In the afternoon he flew another mission against the ground troops, then did it all again the next day, when he arrived back at Henderson to find that most of the planes over the field belonged to the Japanese. For some reason, the Zeros allowed his Dauntless to land undisturbed. Mike attributed it to just dumb luck. The word in the ops tent was that Admiral Halsey had relieved Admiral Ghormley as the commander of the South Pacific. Having come within a hair of losing his life, the news of "some admiral relieving another admiral" made no impression on Micheel.

The next day he had better luck. He flew in a strike of twelve planes led by the skipper of another squadron. They found three enemy destroyers 175 miles out. Aiding the ships' powerful defensive weapons were a dozen floatplanes. Avoiding the enemy planes and AA guns made dive-bombing difficult and they scored one near miss. The next day, the scouts found no warships. Micheel made quick strikes against the enemy up the beach at Kokumbona.

The following day, October 21, the long-range scouting planes flying off of Espiritu Santos reported enemy ships in the slot. The strike team, including Mike, got the order to scramble. After the briefing in the ops tent, he walked out to his assigned plane to take a good, hard look at it and, once airborne, he stared at the gauges and evaluated their readings. The plane captain would not put him in a plane with a serious mechanical problem, but the Cactus crews defined the term "serious problem" differently than did the men on the hangar deck of the Big E. Along with the patches, a plane's airspeed indicator might need an adjustment, or a radio that had checked out on the ground might fail in the air. Sometimes Mike flew one plane without a gyro because "well, as long as the weather's great you don't need a gyro."

Mike flew with his friend Dick Mills. As they cleared the coastline, each pilot and his gunner fired a short burst from their guns as a test. Dick's machine guns, though, had not been properly synchronized with the propeller in front of them, and he shot his prop off. The Dauntless began to lose flying speed quickly. Mike stayed with Dick's plane as it went down in the water near Russell Island. Dick made what looked like a good landing. Mike opened the throttle to catch up with his strike. Over the target area, they saw waves breaking over a reef. Assuming that the air corps bombers at high altitude had mistaken these waves for wakes, the navy pilots called it a fake and flew home.

After reporting the loss of Dick to Ray upon his return, there was not much to do. Micheel did not get around much. He knew enough to stay away from the front lines, and on Guadalcanal the front line lay in any direction he might choose to walk. Much as he would have liked to cool off down at the Lunga River, he refrained. While the "adventurous guys in our squadron" went swimming, he had heard reports of snipers down there, and he wasn't "too anxious to meet up with one of those." A fear of snipers explained only part of his behavior. After ten days on Cactus, he felt the weight of the struggle and realized innately that he needed to conserve his energy.

DURING THE PAST FEW NIGHTS THE SOUND OF HEAVY ARTILLERY HAD CARRIED UP to Manila John and the rest of the 1/7, who had returned to the jungle south of the airfield. The enemy had continued landing forces on the other side of the Matanikau and, unsurprisingly, their attacks had come across the river's mouth. Despite all of the supposedly successful U.S. air strikes and naval battles, two nights earlier the IJA had tried to send nine tanks across the mouth of the river. The line had held. The mounting pressure, however, had Topside shifting units within the perimeter.

The day before, General Vandegrift had visited the 1/7's line, now known as Sector Three, and declared it a "machine gunner's paradise." This morning he ordered the 2/7 out of Sector Three and up to where it was needed, along the Matanikau River. A number of large holes in the marine perimeter existed over there, and even with the 2/7, the marines would only be holding the high ground. If all those Japanese landing over there crossed the river and found their way through one of the gaps, General Vandegrift ordered his men to "fight as guerrillas."[121]

The order to "fight until you are killed" reached Manila John and the 1/7 loud and clear.[122] By October 23, though, it was old news. The Japanese left no alternatives. Vandegrift's description of Sector Three as a "machine gunner's paradise," however, only applied to parts of it—like the large field in front of Able Company on his left, or the steep sides of Bloody Ridge manned by Baker Company to Basilone's right. Charlie Company, to which John's two machine-gun sections had been attached, held the center of the line in a flat, dense jungle. The hard work of creating a defensible line had been started on their first deployment here a few weeks earlier. As they turned to the task again, it escaped no one's attention that their job required the skills of a World War I infantryman, not those of an amphibious warrior. Short on food and men, facing a rising tide of the enemy, the men of the 1/7 "knew to a certain extent how the boys on . . . Bataan must have felt."[123]

Charlie Company's riflemen dug their foxholes and strung a double apron of barbed wire using metal poles. Basilone placed his two sections about forty yards apart and had his men clear more brush to lengthen their firing lanes and dig their machine-gun pits deeper. Each section, comprised of two guns and seven men, could cover the line between them as well as a similar swath to either side.[124] The enemy would surely target the water-cooled heavy machine guns, so the gunners framed their firing ports with earth and sandbags, laying coconut logs over the top. The 81mm mortars, well behind them, and the 105mm artillery a mile back, registered a few rounds along the 1/7's front.

A patrol returned in the afternoon having found some IJA equipment on some high ground about a thousand yards south of Bloody Ridge. The news, like that from others in the past few days, counted for little when measured against the infernos raging around the airfield, around the Matanikau, and out at sea. Garland, one of John's men, returned from the hospital, bringing word that Steve Helstowski, Manila's buddy who had been wounded on the last trip across the Matanikau River, had been evacuated by plane.[125]

The next day brought rain. A hard, soaking rain fell most of October 24, enough to make life in foxholes miserable.[126] Movement became difficult and work stopped.[127] In the afternoon, Sergeant Briggs from Able Company led his platoon of men to the cheval-de-frise out in front of John's section of line. Made of sharpened sticks and barbed wire on a wooden frame, the cheval acted as a gate across the trail leading south to the observation post (OP), which was on a hill fifteen hundred yards south.[128]

About four p.m., Charlie Company's skipper began to get uneasy. Captain Moore ordered his men to pull on their heavy gloves and string more barbed wire, "paying particular attention to the area behind the cheval-de-frise." He got them to wire it tight, attaching "as many trip flares as we had time for."[129]

The rain had died away, but the clouds remained, leaving the marines sitting in cold water in the dark. "At about ten p.m.," as Basilone waited to be relieved of the watch, "the telephone rang. I picked it up and listened to it." Instead of the usual news of another air raid, he heard Sergeant Briggs at the OP reporting to Puller at the CP "that there was a large concentration of japs" moving past his position and "headed our way."[130] Chesty ordered his men, particularly his 81mm platoon, to give Briggs a chance to escape by holding their fire for as long as possible.[131] Before hanging up his connection to his companies, platoon, and sections, Chesty said, "Hold!"[132]

Even as Manila put the phone down, "the Japanese were already throwing hand grenades and dynamite."[133] Hundreds of them raced up the Bowling Alley to Able Company's section, to John's immediate left. He and the other gunner yanked the ponchos off their guns, swung them hard to port, and pulled the triggers. The violence swelled quickly. The point of the attack came, as expected, where Able Company's line met that of the soldiers of the U.S. Army at the edge of the Bowling Alley. Most of the battalion's heavy weapons, including three 37mm cannons, commanded this area.[134] Charlie Company's guns could only lend support by picking off men on the flank. At long range and with a view limited by the jungle, John would have used the Browning's traverse and elevation (T&E) mechanism to control his bursts.

When finally the wave broke, the enemy soldiers fell back into the jungle. The machine gunners leaned back, unclenching themselves and catching their breaths. From the other side came shouts of "You die tonight, maline!" The low moans and painful cries of wounded would have also been heard.

The next charge, led by men holding rifles affixed with bayonets, came at Charlie Company directly.[135] A horde gathered at the cheval-de-frise, lit by trip flares. All of the extra barbed wire there paid off, though, as it delayed them. The artillery, mortars, and machine guns pounced. Basilone watched the bodies jerk and twist painfully as the stream of bullets cut into them. The rising pile of bodies seemed to have no effect on the men who followed, but eventually the charge faded. He noticed that his guns had burned through a lot of ammunition. Rather than order someone else to do it, Manila made a dash for the battalion CP, loaded bandoliers around his neck, and dashed back.[136]

The next attack came from the right and the left simultaneously. The enemy supported the attack by throwing a lot of grenades. John's machine-gun section pointed their muzzles toward the threat and fired into the mass of bodies. Private LaPointe from John's other machine-gun position appeared at his elbow and yelled in his ear, "Sarge, both right flank guns are knocked out."[137] There were dead and wounded, he continued. John figured the guns had just jammed, though "not wanting to take any chances," he picked up one of his machine guns with its tripod—all ninety-one pounds of it—yelled, "Powell, Garland, come with me," and hustled out of the back of the pit.[138] Hitting a main trail a dozen yards behind their pit, they turned left and ran for the second section.[139]

Hustling through the brush Manila "ran smack into a party of japs—about eight of them."[140] Cradling a bulky machine gun put John at a disadvantage, but he fired, Powell and Garland fired, and the enemy fell. The marines ran on. Tracers and flares and explosions flashed in the darkness.[141]

Coming upon his second section, he realized it had been hit by a grenade or a mortar round because most of the guys weren't moving. He could see Cecil Evans firing his rifle and screaming at the Japanese to come and get some more.[142] In the bunker, Billie Joe Crumpton fired his rifle as best he could, one arm wet with blood.[143] His face betrayed none of the crazy bravery of Evans, who was running around yelling, only a grim determination to hold his position against all comers.

Manila did not put his machine gun into the emplacement near the broken ones, but set it outside. "I didn't want to put it in a hole. The Japs sneak into holes."[144] He dropped behind the gun. Figures came running across the clearing. John aimed it freehand and pulled the trigger. He knew if he let his fear win, he'd burn out the gun.[145] He had to trust Crumpton, LaPointe, and Powell to handle some of them. They could not get them all, however. A few of the rushers swept past well to the left or right before the charge broke. Another pause, they noticed. After giving his gun to Powell, Manila crawled over to check on the broken machine guns.

Even in the darkness it was clear the Browning nearest Crumpton had been demolished and its crew killed. John rolled into the hole with the other gun and let his hands fall to their work. He had to forget all the din, ignore the rising number of mortar explosions that signaled the start of another charge. He had to feel it and hear it.

His fingers slipped over the heavy Browning. Beginning with the obvious, he pulled the trigger, yanked the bolt back, then opened the feed cover. By training he divided problems into several major categories: Were the rounds being fed? Yes. So were the rounds being chambered properly? Yes. There was not a broken cartridge in the chamber; both extraction and ejection seemed fine. So the failure to fire likely had something to do with the firing pin, or the sear spring, or maybe the breach lock.[146] He eliminated those possibilities. The trouble was the head spacing, or the space between the base of the cartridge and the face of the bolt.[147]

Finding and using the gun's tool kit may not have been an option. There was a quick way to set the head space. It was not precise, but then adjusting any settings on a hot gun was not recommended. John pulled the bolt back three-quarters of an inch, screwed the barrel into the barrel extension (without the gun's combination tool, he could use the tip of a bullet) until the action just closed (recoiling parts went fully forward) without being forced. He unscrewed the barrel two notches. He positioned the belt feed lever stud over the cam groove bolt. Had he had time, Basilone would have cocked the weapon and pulled the trigger to hear the firing pin engage, but it's more likely he connected the ammo belt.

The yelling became a chorus. They were coming. He snapped the cover shut. The only distinguishable words in their yelling were "Banzai!" and "You die, maliney!"[148] The enemy intended to knock out the guns by throwing grenades and firing mortars. He pulled the trigger and the Browning roared to life, its rhythmic pulse steady and reassuring. Bullets smacked around him. Basilone and his men were pinned down, taking fire from all sides now, holding on.[149] The other machine gun fell silent. Billie Joe Crumpton had been hit again, by grenade fragments in the leg, and had been overcome.[150]

John told LaPointe and Evans to guard the flanks with their rifles. They had to hit the individuals. Manila began rolling from one Browning to the other, keeping them from overheating, aiming for the groups crossing the wire. Sometimes the mud on the belts forced him to stop and clean out the receiver. Sometimes, he'd hear, "Look out!" John would grab his .45 pistol and whirl around to find Japanese sneaking up behind him. He shot them in the only area visible to him: their faces.[151] There were too many, though, and they were everywhere. When the emperor's troops yelled, he and Evans and LaPointe yelled insults back. "We thought," Basilone said, "our time had come."[152]

The big shells of the marine artillery crashed among the trees on the other side of the line, as did the 81mms, although some seemed to go too far, while others landed short amid the marines.[153] John knew the attackers would try to crawl through the grass underneath his line of fire. Only one had to get close enough to hit him. So he made sure to rake the ground regularly.[154]

The ammunition ran low as exhaustion set in. It felt to Manila "like we had fired all night."[155] Most sergeants would have sent a man to get more and thereby stayed in command at the line. The enemy had run around behind them, though, cutting the marines off.[156] He told his guys to use their rifles for as long as possible. They had to save the last belts of machine-gun ammo for the next charge.[157] John picked up his pistol and, with his men providing some covering fire, ran forward toward the enemy, then turned and ran "across the front of his own company in the face of heavy enemy fire."[158] It shocked everyone who saw him do it. As soon as he could, he cut back through the line and into the jungle toward the CP.

Near the ammo pits, several sergeants belted .30-caliber ammunition as fast as they could. Manila slung a bunch of belts over his shoulders until he staggered under the weight. He grabbed some dynamite caps because they were handy.[159] Pistol in his hand, Basilone trudged the direct route back through enemy-held territory to LaPointe and Evans.[160] The belts were heavy. Bullets sang in the air around him and he felt like an easy mark. "That lousy hundred yards," he said later, took him fifteen minutes.[161] The moon came out, providing some light, making it easier to kill. The marines' artillery pounded the enemy's rallying points, a hundred yards beyond the barbed wire.

The enemy came in another rush just as first daylight began to filter through the trees. The dead bodies covering the barbed wire made crossing it easier. John's firing lines had become blocked by the pile of bodies out there, so he shifted one of his guns to get a better angle. But he didn't fire immediately. He waited. He waited as the enemy got close enough to hurt him, waited until "the japs charged within point-blank range," until he didn't have to have an accurate aim to hit someone, and pulled the trigger.[162]

After this charge faded, Manila noticed squads of soldiers surging into the foxholes and gun pits, relieving exhausted marines.[163] He was among the last to notice the soldiers, since the 3/164 had been reinforcing the 1/7's line for hours now. Enemy troops were loose in the area. Not far from Manila's position a larger enemy force of about forty was determined to hold on to its breach in the marine line. While Evans, LaPointe, and their sergeant held their post, squads of marines and soldiers set about wiping out the salient in the lines and the individual infiltrators. The process lasted for hours, as it could only be done at close range with rifles and pistols.[164]

The soldiers could snap off a full clip of eight shots as fast as they could pull the trigger, while the marines had to slide the bolt back on their Springfields after every shot. Men armed with Springfields killed slowly: Bang! Pause. Pause. Bang! Pause. Pause. Soldiers with Garands, however, fired Bang! Bang! Bang! in groups of eight before the ammo clip was spat out. The "mopping up operations" continued on through the day, the high ping of ammo clips being spat out discernible, as the defensive position line was reestablished.

Colonel Puller came over to Sergeant Basilone and said, "Nice work."[165] By Chesty's count, "there were nearly a thousand japs—dead japs—out in front, and several hundred also dead, between our lines and the wires." Someone counted thirty-eight dead stacked up around the front of John's right gun position.[166] Many hundreds more lay dead in the jungles beyond, killed by the artillery or heavy mortars before they could join one of the six "banzai attacks." Any estimate of the enemy's wounded, using these rough estimates of the KIAs, would number in the thousands.

The colonel, assisted by the officers of the 1/7, also listened carefully to their men recount the action so as to prepare to write their reports. The number of enemy dead near John's position, while impressive, did not compare with the total in front of Able Company's position. Able Company, however, had had a lot more heavy weapons. Able Company had not been overrun.

Chesty congratulated all of the 1/7 on a job well done. The 1/7 had only been at 75 percent of its authorized strength and it had held a length of the perimeter usually defended by two battalions with some help from the soldiers.[167] As the sergeants began counting noses for their muster rolls, it looked like the night had cost the 1/7 nineteen dead, thirty wounded, and twelve missing in action. John heard the machine guns had burned out twenty-six thousand rounds of .30-caliber slugs. "After that I discovered I was hungry, so I went to the CP to see about getting chow. All we could get was crackers and jam. . . ."[168]

In the late afternoon, the 3/164 had taken responsibility for this section of line. The 1/7 may have given them a nod of appreciation before moving up into the relative safety of Bloody Ridge. Before pulling out, John went over to see some of his friends in Able Company, who had stopped the main onslaught coming out of the Bowling Alley. He pointed to one of the 37mm cannons, which had fired canister shot all night, and told his friend Manny, "God bless you guys. Thank you. That, that's the best weapon the world ever saw."[169] A few of his Charlie Company marines, their skipper noticed, walked up Bloody Ridge carrying the new Garand.[170]

The IJA attacked again that night. A few shells landed on the ridge, but this fight belonged to the army. Over the next few days Charlie Company would be drawn back into the fight for brief periods, but there would have been a lot of talk about what had happened and who got hit. The enemy's biggest salient had come near Manila's position, between Charlie Company and Baker Company. Platoon Sergeant Robert Domokos had organized a few men into an assault and wiped them out.[171] Sergeant London "Pappy" Traw, a machine-gun platoon sergeant who had been around a lot longer than Manila, had also been at the point of attack, although attached to Baker Company. He had been killed.[172] More than ten bodies had been counted in front of Private First Class Edmund Dorsorgna's position.[173] One of the gun crews on Ed's right flank had fled, leaving him exposed. He had had to fix his machine guns four times that night. John's Dog Company had lost five WIA and six KIA, including Corporal Weydandt, whose enlistment had run out two weeks before, but he had continued on, although he had decided not to reenlist. Charlie Company had lost eight KIA and nine WIA, including Anderson, who had been shot in the ass.

ON THE MORNING OF OCTOBER 25, LIEUTENANT MICHEEL WOKE UP ANGRY THAT he had had to endure another night's shelling because the day before he had failed to find the Tokyo Express. Worse, after two nights of rain, "it was just sloppy as heck" and the Wildcats were struggling to get off the ground. The fighters' Cow Pasture had not been covered in Marston matting. Although Henderson Field had been sheathed in the steel planking, the Dauntlesses and torpedo planes could not take off because the Japanese artillery kept shelling it. Gasoline had run short again. The first enemy planes arrived at eight a.m. Mike, disgusted, "sat there and watched those japs drop bombs on us. . . ." Scouts radioed reports of more enemy ships headed for them. If the Dauntlesses didn't get up to stop them, he thought, "we're never going to get off this island."

FROM THEIR HILLTOP OP WEST OF THE LUNGA RIVER, SIDNEY AND HIS SQUAD could see Henderson Field. "Everywhere you looked was jap planes." The marines watched the proceedings wearily, having been up most of the night expecting to be called to help the 1/7 at any moment. They had heard the shit hitting the fan up in Sector Three, even as it had rained so hard one had to seek shelter just to "have room to breathe." All night long the sound of the 1/7's machine guns, 37mms, and 81mm mortars had carried to them. The battle the night before had followed days of watching the infantry and the airplanes fight the IJA along the Matanikau. In the past few days U.S. planes and artillery had loosed a furious barrage beyond the river. Reports had come to Sid's squad that "the dead are hip deep high over a 5 mile area . . . [the] whole beach covered with dead japs."

The morning of the twenty-fifth, however, U.S. planes were very late taking off from Henderson. It looked like the enemy planes circling over it were waiting for permission to land. From their vantage point, Sid and Deacon watched as, at last, the dogfights finally broke out. "All over the heavens . . . plane after plane came down. Zeros burst in midair and blew up before hitting ground. The ground AA riddled the bombers and several Zeros . . . they were dropping like flies. Three Japanese destroyers entered the harbor. We watched them sink a [U.S.] transport and a gun boat." Then the three enemy warships started shelling Kukum and the airfield. "God," Deacon prayed, "please give us more victories and peace."

THE WILDCATS HAD BEEN HARD AT WORK FOR HOURS, CLEARING THE SKY OF raiders, before the first strike of dive-bombers took off at one p.m. Five dive-bombers went chasing after the three destroyers that had parked off Lunga Point earlier that morning and shelled Kukum and the airfield. They found one cruiser, one light cruiser, and two destroyers. The Dauntlesses later reported one sure hit, on the cruiser, and a couple that were at least near misses. Another strike followed. Bombing Six got its turn around three o'clock. The four planes led by Ray Davis scored two near misses. Mike flew on the fourth strike, with three other dive-bombers, a few Wildcats and four P-39s. Up the channel they went, searching for the destroyers and any other members of the Tokyo Express scurrying up the slot. They found their targets at about four thirty. The four runs of the dive-bombers resulted in one near miss on the light cruiser. The pilot of the P-39, however, upstaged them with a direct hit on the cruiser, the largest and most important warship in the group. The Japanese continued to flee, the two largest ships trailing oil. The mission took just under two hours and then they were back at the field, watching the furious fighter battles in the sky. One of the fighter pilots, Captain Joe Foss, shot down four Zeros that day.

Mike had no sense of victory, only grave doubt. The total number of flyable Dauntlesses was a dozen, with about the same number of Wildcats ready for action. The field was still in poor condition, there were shortages of everything, and the enemy's 150mm artillery fired at them at will. Just as he rarely showed his anger, though, so too did Mike keep his concern to himself. When Bombing Six's skipper, Ray Davis, evaluated the men in his command, in Lieutenant Micheel he saw a pilot who "with utter disregard for his own safety . . . carried out all missions unflinchingly."[174]

Before bed, they learned *Enterprise* and *Hornet* had steamed into the area. The appearance of U.S. task forces usually meant that the Imperial Fleet carriers had also returned. The tired Cactus pilots enjoyed a night free of the shells from Japanese ships. The next morning in the ops tent, pilots heard reports of the battle raging between the carriers just five hundred miles away. They also received reports of carriers, battleships, and every other enemy ship nearing their position. Mike and two others spent the morning bombing and strafing an area south of the fighter strip, what the marines called Sector Three. Reports of enemy warships continued to pour in. None of the strike missions, however, located these ships. By the late afternoon they heard that the Japanese dive-bombers had hit both carriers and that the U.S. pilots had gotten some hits, too. Sometime the following day the news came that the Big E was now the only U.S. carrier in the Pacific Ocean. USS *Hornet* had been sunk.*

The Cactus Air Force could expect some more relief to show up soon—whatever was left of the *Hornet*'s former planes and pilots. On occasions like this, the squadron doctor opened a big bottle of whiskey in the ops tent and allowed his pilots to take a few snorts. This wasn't the "medicinal brandy" issued by the navy. The doctor had found a Seabee who had a supply of whiskey and a crazy desire for airplane parts. The doc arranged to have instrument panels and other interesting items snapped off the scrapped planes. Asked what the guy wanted them for, the doc said that, as he understood it, the Seabee intended "to build an airplane after the war was over." A few tips of the glass ended Navy Day, 1942.

IN THE RAIN ON MONDAY, OCTOBER 26, A THOUSAND POWS PREPARED TO WALK out of Cabanatuan POW Camp Number One. First they had to say good-bye to their friends. The strong, who were leaving, would look at the weak and wonder if they would live long. Those staying behind would wonder if the group was sailing for Japan, a destination that ruled out escape, made liberation seem remote, and probably meant death. Each side, though, wanted desperately for someone to survive, for someone to tell the story of Cabanatuan to the world, and most of all for someone to tell their individual fates to their respective families back home.

On the hike to the train depot, Shifty carried a bag filled with all his equipment and the provisions he could purchase. What he jokingly called a deluxe car—eighty men to a boxcar—carried them slowly along. "At one of the frequent train halts . . . a group of Filipino children tested the jap guards on our boxcar and found out they

---

*This carrier battle came to be called the Battle of Santa Cruz.

did not understand English. The children then sung God Bless America." The train took them to Manila.

They spent only one night in Bilibid, marching down to the docks the next day and boarding a ship, formerly a U.S. ship, SS *Erie*, and now *Erie Maru*. Loading one thousand men into an eight-thousand-ton freighter already full with barrels of aviation gasoline led to the usual orders for the POWs to squeeze themselves into tight confines belowdecks. When the ship pulled away from the dock, the guards relaxed. Shifty and his friends Mike Dobervich and Jack Hawkins worked their way back on deck. They climbed onto the top of large rice sacks, with fresh air and a modicum of room. It was immediately decided that one of them would remain there at all times to protect the space from other POWs. They had found a space that improved their chances of survival ever so slightly. They would fight to keep it.

THE BATTLES RAGED DAILY AROUND THE #4 GUN SQUAD. TO THE SOUTH, THE ARMY had fought off another banzai attack and killed sixty-five, capturing one POW. To the west, at the Matanikau, the marines had killed eight hundred to nine hundred and taken no prisoners. This latest struggle for the Matanikau had, according to Deacon's calculations, nearly equaled in ferocity their Battle of Hell's Point, but it had only lasted eight hours, whereas the 2/1 had fought for sixteen hours. Shells from the big artillery guns on both sides swished over their heads by the hour.

Sid Phillips and Deacon hiked to the wreckage of a downed Zero. They "dug out part of the pilot's body." Deacon took the pilot's cigarette case. Sid found a coin in his pocket. It wasn't much of a haul, but it had been something to do other than waiting and watching. Mail call came that day. The return of a fairly regular mail service encouraged all of them to write home more. It was around this time that Sid wrote his friend Eugene Sledge back in Mobile. "Don't join anything," Sid advised him, "not even the Boy Scouts or the Salvation Army."

A working party went to the airfield and the beach and returned to the #4 gun squad with a load of chow, chocolate, and gossip. The navy boys at the field had boasted of sinking "three battlewagons, fourteen destroyers, two transports, six cruisers, two aircraft carriers and one aircraft tender." More mail was expected, more IJN ships were expected, and the First Marines were departing November 11. After reading his copies of the Mobile newspaper, Sid let the others read them. Everyone was in a good mood because they were going home soon.

*   *   *

MICHEEL RESPONDED TO THE CONSTANT TENSION BY EATING. "I MADE THE MESS hall every chance I could get because I was losing weight like mad. I had the trots. It's amazing I could make the flights and never have any problem, but the minute I get out of the airplane I had to run." He kept his strength up by eating, but the combination of physical and mental exhaustion dropped his weight to 127. He found himself hoping he'd get off Cactus soon and back on a carrier.

It was about this time that Dick Mills, who had gone down near Russell Island, returned. Mike took one look at his friend and realized Dick looked better than he did. "So I asked him how he gained so much weight. He said, 'I had chicken every day.'" Whatever concern Mike had had for him evaporated. Dick had obviously been well cared for. At the ops tent, Dick advised his friends that if they went down, not to kick off their boots as they had been told. They would need their boots to climb out of the rocky shoals. Dick said he had cut his feet. Having endured three weeks of constant strain on the Canal, Mike had lost about twenty pounds. He just could not take this advice too seriously. He started teasing Dick about his crash, telling everyone Dick had gone "cuckoo and . . . shot off all his prop."

Of all of the pressures Bombing Six faced, the enemy's artillery drove them crazy. It had become known as Pistol Pete, even though the IJA had several big 150mms. Pistol Pete could fire at them at all times, day and night. Although "he" dueled with the marine artillery and sought out troop concentrations, Pistol Pete obviously enjoyed shooting at planes during their most vulnerable moments, during takeoff and landing. The sporadic fire and excellent camouflage had so far prevented anyone from locating the gun, but a five-inch fieldpiece was too big to be ignored.

One of the Bombing Six pilots came up with an idea. "Let's see if we can get that guy to shoot at us. We'll take a plane up there and circle over the top like you're looking for him, see if he'll shoot at you, and then we'll have the attack airplanes over here watching. As soon as he fires, they've got him spotted, they'll attack him." It was worth a try. Mike agreed to be the decoy. As he had done for some time, he took whichever rear seat gunner agreed to go. Airman Spires volunteered. When the other airplanes got in position, Mike started making passes over the general area, west of the Matanikau River. It worked. "Every time I'd come at him it was okay and then as soon as I'd turn away, POW! He'd let go. My rear gunner would say, 'He's shooting at us! He's shooting at us!'" Each time, Mike got on the radio to his friends and asked, "Did you see that?" and each time came the reply: "No . . . try it again." Mike had been circling up there almost an hour when he finally heard, "We've got him." Mike cleared out and the others bombed and strafed the area. When he landed, the rear seat gunner told him he quit. "I'm not flying anymore! You're making a guinea pig out of me!" As it turned out, Spires did not mean it. He flew again. As for Pistol Pete, he was out of commission for about five days.

Bombing Six had the watch one evening in early November when word came of another ship unloading in the Japanese area. The pilots and their leaders had had it with the Tokyo Express avoiding them by sneaking in at night and getting away before dawn. Dauntlesses had begun to attack the Tokyo Express at night by glide bombing—making an approach decidedly less steep than a dive—when possible. A few days before, on November 2, three Dauntlesses had taken off at dusk to chase three enemy destroyers, which the IJN used to bring in men and supplies because of their speed. None of the aircraft had returned.[175] Ray Davis decided it looked possible on this night, and to prove it, he would make the first run.

As Mike checked out his Dauntless, preparing to make the second run, he looked into the dark sky above him. He had flown night missions before, one just a few days previously against a destroyer near Russell Island.[176] He had had some training in night flying, and had flown through plenty of bad weather. These missions depended on visibility. With a bright moon over a clear sky, he could see the horizon. Even with good light, a pilot had to rely more on the plane's instruments than on his own perception. Relying upon the altimeter, the airspeed indicator, the compass, and a few other key instruments to stay on course took concentration, experience, and steady nerves.

Flying on a night like this, though, when there was no light, scared Mike. A black sky meant no horizon, and no horizon, Mike told himself, meant "you'd get vertigo real easy. You figure you're turning, the seat of your pants tells you you're turning and you look at your gauges and you're going straight ahead." Reconciling one's senses with one's gauges often led to panic, or worse, dizziness. Lieutenant Micheel eased the plane along the taxiway and out to the end of Henderson Field. He waited for Ray to return, his engine idling.

Landing at night on a carrier demanded great skill, but glide bombing at night—on a dark night—came close to impossible. Trying to drop a bomb "on top of a black object and pull off of a black object" caused vertigo in even the most experienced pilots. Executing such a maneuver at high speed, as the pilot coped with spinning dials, sweeping needles, and the powerful impulses of his own perception, just demanded too much. In the past, men had hung flares over the target and these had made it easier to hit it, but the flares also caused the pilot to lose his sight. A flare made pulling up and flying home an even bigger challenge.

Ray's plane landed at the far end of the great runway. It rolled toward Mike, not turning onto the taxiway, until he stopped within a few feet. Ray's gunner jumped out and ran over and jumped up on Mike's wing and yelled over the idling engine, "Skipper says cancel the flight. Don't go." A wave of relief hit Mike. His guardian angel had landed on his shoulder. The two airplanes taxied back to their hardstands. Walking back to the operations tent, Ray said he had flown over the target at five thousand feet, yet "it was so dark you couldn't see the ship from the air. . . ." He concluded "it wasn't worth risking aviators. . . ." No one back at the tent questioned the decision.

ALONG WITH THEIR COMMANDING VIEW OF MUCH OF THE BATTLE, SID AND HIS friends heard all about it. The movements of units, the body count, and the number of rounds expended—a great deal of it rumor, they knew all too well. The army over in Sector Three had killed enemy troops by the thousands and had not only pulled German Lugers and Samurai swords off the bodies, but the doggies were supposedly holding fencing duels with the Japanese sabers. The marines' shortwave radio had picked up enemy transmissions and it had been deduced that the enemy planes that had flown in so low a week earlier had been sent to land on the empire's new airport—Henderson Field. The news was met with hoots and catcalls of "Too bad, Tojo." Transcripts of the interrogation of four Japanese POWs were circulating, though. These prisoners stated that they "wanted to quit the war and especially fighting the 'bloodthirsty' marines." Out in the harbor, the #4 gun squad could see increasing numbers of U.S. ships. On November 2, working parties unloaded seven 155mm guns, known as Long Toms; the word was the Long Toms could fire a shell ten miles.

All of the ships arriving off Lunga Point also meant that the Eighth and the Twenty-second marines were landing soon. "Rumors are we leave Sun or Mon for Tulagi—have a chemical bath—shots—New Zealand." They waited for the next big push by the enemy, who continued to send air strikes. Attempts by the Tokyo Express to reinforce its troops were now often turned back. So many Japanese ships had been sunk, Deacon joked, that Prime Minister Tojo needed "a diving bell to inspect his navy now." For the enemy troops already on the island, "Our planes run those japs crazy over on the other point, strafing and bombing." On November 7, a number of new squadrons landed at the field, including not just more Wildcats and dive-bombers, but also B-17s. The word was Guadalcanal would soon become the United States' biggest B-17 base in the Pacific. When the radio broadcast from San Francisco announced the plans for relieving the 1st Marine Division off of Guadalcanal, it sounded to the jaded marines of the #4 gun squad "too good to be true." Another marine told them he had heard that Admiral Nimitz had been relieved of duty. Sid's squad didn't know what to believe.

*　　*　　*

THE ORDER TO MOVE OUT CAME IN THE LATE AFTERNOON ON NOVEMBER 3. THE 2/7 had encountered a large number of enemy a few miles east of the perimeter. Sergeant Basilone distributed ammo and rations, his men grabbed their gear and heavy machine guns, and they walked down from Bloody Ridge.[177] Instead of waiting inside the perimeter for an attack, the 1/7 would help the 2/7 take the offensive.[178]

More than a dozen Higgins boats met the marines at Lunga Point just after six p.m. They motored eastward, toward Koli Point. The shore ran along to their right, monotonously dark. Hours passed. The officers obviously were having trouble locating the landing spot. They saw lights onshore but could not tell if it was the enemy or the 2/7. Chesty and his other officers knew they had to get out of the boats before they ran into an enemy sub or even one of the navy's torpedo boats. All the landing craft went back to Lunga Point to get reorganized. The officers radioed the 2/7 and agreed upon a light signal to give one another. The 1/7 motored back to Koli Point. Around midnight, the landing craft dumped the 1/7 on the beach near a river. After posting the guards, everyone slept on the beach.[179]

The landing made for an inauspicious start to what Manila later called the Seventh Marines'"jap hunt."[180] The 1/7 and 2/7, joined by battalions of the army, spent almost three weeks chasing the enemy through the swamps and across the rivers east of Koli Point. It began with destroying the abandoned weapons and equipment they found and progressed into brief, intense firefights. They chased the IJA so far east that they walked off the maps they carried. Not having a map didn't bother Chesty in the least, so it didn't bother his men. In one of the latter skirmishes, the shrapnel from the shell of an enemy field cannon cut into the indefatigable Colonel Puller, who had been up near the front as usual, and he allowed himself to be evacuated after the crisis had passed. It was not a severe wound and it did not affect the outcome. The U.S. forces slowly boxed in the enemy force. The marine artillery, miles away inside the perimeter, ignited a firestorm inside the box. Most of the enemy escaped due to the difficulties imposed by the terrain and—according to the marines—the inefficiency of the army units.

It had taken as much brute strength as bravery to make the operation a success and the marines could be happy to have destroyed the threat. A number of days passed, though, while they waited to return to the perimeter; days spent "eating cold rations out of a box," as Manila described it, dampened their spirits.[181] Although the recent foray had not caused many casualties in the 1/7, only 75 percent of its original men walked back up to Bloody Ridge upon their return to the perimeter. The battalion had begun to lose a lot of men to jungle diseases, like malaria, including the skipper of Charlie Company. Each man still standing had lost a great deal of weight since his arrival.

Good news awaited them back in Sector Three. They had missed another shellacking delivered by imperial warships on November 11–12. Chesty Puller had recovered as much as he was going to allow himself to recover and had taken back his command of the battalion. Another regiment of marines, the Eighth, had landed. Individual replacements had come ashore to bring the 1/7 back up to strength. Mail call had begun to be sounded with regularity. That meant the possibility of a letter to Manila from Stephen Helstowski's sister, Helen. John had gotten in touch with Helen because their correspondence brought a little something else into his life. Manila, however, convinced J.P. or Richard to write his letters to her for him.[182]

Best of all, the supply ships had brought in good chow. The battalion mess served pancakes, nice big pancakes with great big piles of strawberry jam on top of them. After eighteen days of cold rations, hotcakes were a wonder.[183] Sometime during the next few days, someone discovered an enemy soldier in the chow line. The marine dungarees he wore, which had allowed him to get into line, now put his life in imminent danger as men guessed how he had come to have the clothes and helmet. They brought him before Puller, who "had him on the ground and was cursing him up and down," to no effect.[184] The prisoner was taken away.

SINCE THE JAPANESE HAD NOT MARKED *ERIE MARU* AS A POW SHIP, THE POWs hoped that a U.S. submarine would slam a torpedo into her. Any alternative, even taking their chances in the ocean, seemed preferable to further incarceration. From their perch high atop a pile of rice sacks, Shifty and Dobervich and Hawkins could tell they were sailing south and took heart. They evaluated the guards to see if they could be overpowered in a coup de main, but decided against it. They debated jumping overboard when they sailed within a mile or so of an island. They watched as the ship pulled into port on November 7 and the disembarkation began about one p.m.

The guards put the POWs' baggage with the camp's stores on the trucks and they set off. They walked through the afternoon and into the evening. Men began to fall out of the column, unable to continue. No one was allowed to stop walking. The question had to come: Was this another Bataan? Hawkins and Dobervich fell out somewhere close to midnight. Shofner and the others arrived at the camp gates at three a.m., having hiked twenty-nine kilometers.

Trucks brought in the men who had quit the march, unharmed. The first morning, Sunday, the men were given a chance to rest. A former penal colony, the POW camp still held about 150 of the original 2,000 civilian prisoners. Another 900 American POWs, officers and men who had been stationed on Mindanao, were also held there. From them they learned the camp took its name, the Davao Penal Colony, from the large city about fifty kilometers away on the coast of Mindanao, the most southern of the Philippine Islands.

The barracks were large, tin-roofed buildings with solid wood floors. Each held 250 men. At night the sleeping men crowded the floor space. No decks for sleeping had been built above them, though, so Shifty found it easier to breathe than in his last barracks. Davao also had a mess hall that seated almost half the prisoners at one time. Having a place to sit for meals and, on Sundays, worship, seemed like luxuries to the men from Cabanatuan. At the noon meal and at the evening meal the rice included cassava or camotes. There was fresh water for drinking, washing, and bathing.

At the first assembly, Major Maida shouted that he had "asked for prisoners capable of doing hard labor," but he "had been sent a batch of walking corpses."[185] The major informed them that all officers were required to work. The Davao Colony produced foodstuffs for Japan on several thousand acres of rich farmland around them. "The first day of each month," he ordered, the "entire American prisoner complement had to appear in military formation and salute the Japanese flag, and salute throughout the 'Rising Sun' ceremony." Major Maida, however, had made no mention of "shooting squads." Shifty knew right away that as long as the POWs worked hard and produced the required amounts of food, they would be provided enough food to become healthy once more. He had gambled and won.

THE NEW SQUADRONS ARRIVED ON CACTUS READY FOR ACTION. RAY DAVIS offered to have them fly wing on Bombing Six until they got the lay of the land. They took one flight. In the ops tent for the debriefing, Ray warned them to stay away from the floatplane base about a hundred miles away. Bombing Six had not attempted to bomb the floatplane base because they had had other priorities and because the enemy planes could be expected to fight back. Dauntlesses had not been designed for aerial combat—they had been designed to fight off an enemy fighter, to survive an attack, but not to initiate aerial combat. The new guys dismissed the warning. Mike worried they were too "rambunctious," but Ray said, "Okay, they want to go on their own, let them go on their own." Some of the new guys did not come back from their first mission. No one knew for sure what had happened. Bombing Six assumed they had gone looking for trouble.

Even with all the reinforcements, Ray decided his squadron would not slack off. "We'll fly our flights right down to the end," he declared. On November 5, Ray asked Mike to fly his wing on search up the slot and around New Georgia. As they walked out to their planes, Ray said, "When we get up to the end of that island, there's no use . . . making that dogleg through that channel. We'll just fly over the top of the mountains." Mike nodded his assent and away they went.

After flying up the slot, they made the left-hand turn over the top of New Georgia. A cloud bank obscured their vision. So Ray led them down to drop out of the clouds. When they popped out, they saw ten ships of the Imperial Japanese Navy. Even pulling back on the sticks, their dives took them down to where Mike felt "we were right in the middle of them." Ray dodged and jinked, Mike followed, and they flew toward the open sea. Ray got on the radio and alerted the strike force. Instead of gaining altitude and arming their bombs, Ray led Mike back to Henderson Field. Mike did not ask his skipper why they had not turned around. Ray had proven his courage so many times that Mike figured it was something else. He was still wondering when, three days later on November 8, he and Ray and the remaining members of Bombing Six boarded an R4D and started the long journey back home. They flew to Efate and then to Noumea, New Caledonia. They could relax. Their only job was to await transportation home.

UP ON THEIR HILL, SID'S SQUAD WATCHED ANOTHER ENEMY AIR STRIKE COME IN on a Wednesday afternoon, only to be met by a tremendous barrage of AA guns. So many fired, it "looked like an asphalt highway across the sky." A lot of Zeros and bombers fell prey to the dark clouds bursting around them. Then the bad news came: "the biggest jap convoy in history is three hundred miles off" and due to arrive Friday, November 13, at two thirty a.m. Deacon prayed, "Please God, give us the strength to face and overcome the enemy and gain peace." His prayers seemed to be answered the next day, when three battalions of infantry landed at Lunga. Some of the marines were also replacements, and a few made their way to the #4 gun squad. They looked like Navy Yard marines, though—men more accustomed to filing papers than firing an 81mm. All hands turned to, preparing themselves, their fortifications, and their weapons for battle. That Thursday, way out to sea, the shit hit the fan. They watched the great warships fire shells and watched the shells tear through the air for miles. The next morning, Friday, the word passed that the United States had won the battle out at sea, but the emperor had landed sixty-five thousand men eleven miles from the marine perimeter.*

When Mike heard about another big navy battle raging in the waters off Cactus, he thought, "Oh God, we're going to get called back up there." Hours passed, then days, but the call did not come. One afternoon, Ray called his guys together. The skipper said a big decision had to be made, and rather than make it himself, he wanted all the guys to hear the options and take a vote. Option number one, they could take a passenger ship back to Pearl Harbor, then pick up another ship for the States. "Or," he said, "we can get on a Dutch freighter and go back straight to the States." The freighter would take a lot longer to get home and it would travel unescorted. The pilots weren't worried about enemy submarines, though. To a man they "were afraid if we got bumped off at Pearl, we'd turn around and come right back down to where we were. So we said, 'We'll go all the way to the States.' "

After the vote, Ray went down to COMSOPAC to make the arrangements. New orders arrived for each man of Bombing Six. But they all began the same. They were to report aboard the freighter *Tabinta* for transportation to the West Coast. Upon arrival, they would report to the commander of the "nearest Naval District." They set sail on the sixteenth. At four p.m. Mike heard an unfamiliar signal over the ship's PA system. It heralded, he found out, the daily liquor ration. He had his choice between a can of warm beer and a shot of spirits. This came as a happy surprise to the weary men of Bombing Six. The U.S. Navy banned alcohol on its ships, but not the Dutch.

That evening the men were seated for dinner and had an even better treat. "They gave us fresh salad. And then they gave us spaghetti and meatballs. And that was delicious. We hadn't had anything like that, so we stuffed ourselves with spaghetti and meatballs. Then the stewards came around and said, 'How would you like your steak, sir?' 'Well,' we said, 'we're too full to eat the steak. We'll get it tomorrow.' So we did."

Since *Tabinta* made only eleven knots, heading east across the great ocean all by herself, the pilots settled in for a long trip. Unlike a carrier, though, the ship did not go to general quarters every day. Day after day, Bombing Six had all the peace and quiet they could stand, and a ration of liquor every afternoon at four p.m.

*　　*　　*

---

*This battle is known as the Naval Battle of Guadalcanal.

WITHOUT WARNING, A GUARD BROUGHT SHIFTY INTO A ROOM. HE WAS GOING TO be questioned. This was always a risky situation for a POW. A Japanese naval officer asked him to be at ease, offered a cigarette, and asked if Shofner had ever known any Japanese naval officers. Shofner replied, "Sure, I have quite a few friends in the Japanese Navy and I've found them to be all gentlemen."

"Where?"

"At Shanghai." The officer admitted he had not visited Shanghai. Shofner complimented the officer on his command of English and then, sensing an opening, he started to play upon the IJN's disdain for the IJA by looking his questioner square in the eye and telling him all U.S. forces wanted to be POWs of the Imperial Japanese Navy because they knew them to be gentlemen. It worked. The interrogator agreed and soon sent him away.

The next time he went in for questioning, he had already heard from another POW that the camp's leadership wanted to know about each prisoner's skills and training. Shifty, who had seen enough of the camp to know that being a worker in the fields would allow him the chance to steal lots and lots of food, wanted no part of reassignment. By the time he walked into the room, he was ready.

"What do you do?"

"Well, I'm a Marine." The officer clarified himself. He wanted to know if the prisoner had any specialized training. Shifty knew a good liar wouldn't just say, "I have no education," nor would he provide a reason to be reassigned. He replied, "I graduated in banking. I [am] capable of operating a bank." There was little danger of the guards asking him to manage their accounts.

"What else do you do?"

"I'm a football player."

"Other qualifications?"

"That's my two qualifications."

"Get out."

Plenty of work awaited him and the others. The Davao Penal Colony ran a plantation of several thousand acres. There were about seventy-five acres of bananas, a large portion of papaya, citrus fruit, avocados, jackfruit, coconuts, and other tropical fruits. Several hundred acres grew grains. Herds of carabao and cows had to be tended, and the eggs from ten thousand chickens harvested.

MORE RUMORS ABOUT THE GREAT VICTORY OVER THE ENEMY FLEET CONTINUED filtering up the hill to Sid's squad the next day. According to the scuttlebutt, eleven imperial warships had been sunk, including three battleships. The transports had been forced to beach, whereupon the fleet and the navy planes had savaged the troops in them. By Sunday, U.S. ships in the slot were trying to pick up the survivors out of the water. This idea met with derision in the mortar platoon. If the situation was reversed, would the IJN be picking our men up? "No" was their emphatic answer.

In another surprising gesture, two enemy officers and two of their enlisted men who had been captured were released on November 19. They were asked to go negotiate the surrender of the remaining troops. Airplanes dropped messages over the enemy positions. The marines and the army now had 137 pieces of artillery, and before they laid waste to the enemy areas, they were giving the enemy a chance.

The IJA ignored the peace offering, so the fighting continued. While enemy planes and enemy snipers continued to cause casualties, the great batteries of artillery owned the area around the marine perimeter. The batteries of marine artillery made a large-scale ground offensive against them all but impossible. Sid's mortar position, being well behind the line, had grown relatively safe. So he watched and he waited. The squad sang their favorite songs most nights; they called it a "jam session."

A rumor made the rounds that two Japanese colonels, who had known Colonel Cates, the CO of the First Marines, before the war, had radioed him. "If we catch you we won't have any mercy, although we were once friends." This struck everyone as odd, since every day more men and supplies and planes and equipment were arriving, whereas the marines had known for some time that the Japanese were "on their last legs." Cates supposedly had radioed back, "Remember Hell's Point." On the same day, November 23, Cates announced that they would be leaving soon. The rumor of celebrating Christmas in Wellington, New Zealand, after a brief stop in Espiritu Santos, now seemed possible. Bottles of whiskey had been shipped in for officers, some of whom proceeded to get drunk and fight, whereas the enlisted men got better chow, including steak and eggs.

A few days later, another enemy air raid came over, killing six and wounding nineteen. The enemy infantry, however, endured a rain of artillery shells and air strikes. Seventy enemy soldiers, out of water, tried to surrender. A sergeant "shot them down like the damn dogs they are," Deacon heard. The atrocity elicited only a statement of fact. "They extend no mercy to us, so need not expect it."

UP ON BLOODY RIDGE, MANILA'S MEN HAD GOTTEN A LITTLE ORNERY. THE 1/7 HAD decided they had done their share of offensive work and would leave the chore of long patrols to the fresh army battalions. In the meantime, they manned their line and waited for the day when they left this awful place. In late November, Chesty signed Basilone's promotion to platoon sergeant.[186] Manila, who had experienced the prewar years as both a soldier and a marine, would have been delighted to see the war greatly speed up the promotions process. A few days later, an attack of malaria overcame him so badly he was sent to the hospital.

THE YEAR 1942 HAD SEEMED AN ETERNITY TO EUGENE SLEDGE.[187] MOST OF HIS friends, including his best friend, Sid Phillips, had gone off to war. The nearest he had gotten to the action was Marion Military Institute, a junior college a few hundred miles north of Mobile. Beginning in September, Cadet Sledge had chosen chemistry as his major. Although he wore a uniform and observed the forms of military organization, his enthusiasm soured. He wanted to make his career in the Marine Corps. Further study, even though it included a class in military science, seemed pointless. He needed his parents' permission to enlist and he pursued it relentlessly. During the Thanksgiving break, he at last wrung a concession from them. Dr. and Mrs. Sledge agreed to sign the consent form if Eugene agreed to attend the USMC's new V-12 program. The V-12 program would give him a college education, which they wanted, and it put him on a path to becoming an officer. His father, a leading physician known across the South, secured his son a place in the program.

After he returned to Marion Military, Eugene Sledge volunteered for the Marine Corps' reserve on December 3, 1942. The enlistment contract to "serve in the Marine Corps in time of war" required him to "solemnly swear" to "bear true allegiance to the United States of America"; to "serve them honestly and faithfully against all enemies whomsoever"; and to "obey the orders of the President of the United States, and the orders of the officers appointed over me. . . ." Being a reader, Sledge read every word with growing delight. This was exactly what he wanted. He signed his full name, Eugene Bondurant Sledge, and received a promotion to private first class. A few weeks later, he underwent the standard physical examination. In all respects, the examiner found him normal: Private First Class Sledge had 20/20 vision, brown hair and brown eyes, stood a shade under five feet eight and weighed 132 pounds. Passing the physical did not bring change, however. His course work would continue until he entered the V-12 program in the summer.

* * *

TABINTA DOCKED IN SAN FRANCISCO ON DECEMBER 6, 1942. ITS PASSENGERS disembarked the next day, December 7. Lieutenant Micheel had survived one year of war. The first thing to do was get paid. So he and the others visited the bursar of the Twelfth Naval District. Mike picked up $220, which included his $6 per day travel allowance. He and Ray and the others had a few days of fun in the city, though it was crowded. Mike preferred the quiet hotel bars and stayed away from the rowdy places. Reporting to NAS Alameda on the tenth, each pilot got in line to be processed. The first thing Mike received was his orders home on leave for thirty days. He told the navy where he'd spend it, at home, and the navy let him know what he could say and what he could not say while there.

As Mike made it down toward the end of the table, a man asked, "Where do you want to go next?"

"What's your options?"

"Well, you can go to the same squadron or you can go to another squadron; you can be a Landing Signal Officer; or you can do something else." Mike could feel the men behind him crowd him—everyone was anxious to get out of here and get home. He said, "I'll just go with the same group." His preference was duly recorded and he was informed his next assignment would be mailed to his home. As he was walking away, it irritated him that he had had no time to consider his options, much less learn anything about the other choices.

He took a train back to Davenport, Iowa, wearing his dress navy uniform. Along with the welcome from his parents and family and all the uncles and aunts came interviews with the local newspaper and an invitation to speak at the Rotary Club. It surprised and pleased him to find out he "was a big hero when I got home then because I'd been in the Battle of Midway." He accepted several invitations to speak at local clubs and answer questions about what was going on out there. His audiences would have soon understood that they were not going to get much about his role. Mike had a way of turning aside such topics. He told them the marines would win the battle for Guadalcanal if they got the support they needed. When asked if he had gotten a hit on a carrier, he'd say he didn't know, he never had turned around to look.

One afternoon he went to visit the parents of his friend John Lough. They lived across the river from his house. He had met them briefly when he and John had shared rides home during their flight training. It must have been very difficult for Mike to walk up the path to the front door, and even more difficult for John's parents to receive him. The Loughs had known of their son's disappearance for six months. They had received the telegram informing them that he went missing in action on June 4, 1942. The telegram said they would be informed as soon as more information became available.

Mike told them some of the things they needed to hear. During the launch on June 4 a malfunction in the plane ahead of John's had forced it to be struck, so by happenstance, John had flown in Mike's section that day.[188] Three planes made up a section: Lieutenant (Junior Grade) Norman West led the section. Mike flew the number-two wingman spot, and then John was the number three. They and their gunners had launched off the flight deck of USS *Enterprise* to stop a gigantic Japanese fleet from invading the island of Midway. Mike would have told them of the long flight out to maximum range, of a chance flash of white wake that had led them to the enemy. None of the enemy's carriers had been damaged when Scouting Six arrived overhead. Using his hands to illustrate how a Dauntless dove, he said, "The section leader went first, I went second; John came over here and went third." The last step Mike had made before pushing over had been to salute his friend John. "That was the last I ever saw of him."

Mike explained that the Zeros had not been a problem for him as they had for others. The big problem had been getting back to the ship. He had landed with enough gas "for one more trip around the carrier." A lot of the planes behind his had failed to return. His friend Bill Pittman had been back there and had had a large hole taken out of his wing by a Zero. "So they may have all gone down someplace. I don't really know." He assured them the navy had searched the ocean for days and days with their big PBY flying boats. And then the story came to an end. He had told them the truth. Never much of a talker anyway, Mike struggled to find the words. "John . . . had . . . the same training I had, had the same ability I did, and it just was bad luck." For their part, the Loughs refused to accept the loss. The navy had listed Ensign Lough as MIA, missing in action. They maintained their hope that their son had gone down "on one of those islands out there . . ." in the Pacific. John would make it back to them.

ONE LAST GREAT RAIN POURED DOWN UPON THEM, FLOODING THEIR BUNKERS. Water rose over their beds in their shacks, sweeping mud into their weapons and equipment. The #4 gun squad spent the morning of December 3 shoveling it all out. When the Eighth Marines arrived, though, they turned it over, grabbed their gear, and departed for Kukum. Hoping for an immediate departure, they waited a day before setting up their tents. Of course, such things rarely happened in the United States Marine Corps. For days on end, they loafed, read mail, and played cards. The news about the battle continued to reach them, and they could certainly hear the artillery and the airplanes, but they paid more attention to who had left and who was on deck to leave. Units from the Fifth Marines boarded ship and departed for Espiritu Santos and then on to Brisbane, Australia.

Deacon made sergeant and moved out of Sid's tent and in with other NCOs. Sid got put on another working party. On December 11, he and W.O. were out on a barge, unloading supplies to bring into shore, when an enemy air strike came in. The supply ship cast off the barge "and left them to their mercy." So he watched the air raid as a sitting duck in a channel of water so loaded with sunken ships it had become known as Iron Bottom Sound. After the all clear, they got a tow back to the dock and learned how funny the rest of the mortar platoon thought they were.

After two weeks, on December 17 they learned their departure was another nine days away, so they set up their tents. Two days later, the officers read off the embarkation orders. The assembled marines of the 2/1, like all the units of the 1st Marine Division, were told that no member of the First Marine Regiment, upon departure, "will have or keep in his possession any article of Army clothing or any item of Army equipment that has not been properly issued him by an authorized Marine Corps Quartermaster representative, or for which he does not hold a proper receipt of purchase."[189] Read to the men at three separate assemblies, the order made clear that all of the M1 Garand rifles marines were carrying around were not getting on the ship with them.

Sid and his friends paid a visit to the division cemetery the next day. They walked back to Hell's Point, along the banks of the Tenaru River. According to their count, in five months they had endured 257 air raids, 163 shellings, and nine banzai attacks. They watched a movie that night and boarded ship the next day, December 21.*

DEPENDING UPON THE TYPE OF WORK DETAIL, THE WORKDAY BEGAN AT EITHER six a.m. or eight a.m. at the Davao Penal Colony. Lunch break lasted for two hours. The workday ended about five p.m. Shifty's first job had been moving rock for a railroad bed. He found it curious that the Japanese not only had so little in the way

---

*The First Marine Regiment landed with 136 officers and 2,937 enlisted personnel, not counting its medical team. Three officers and 30 enlisted men were killed; 3 officers and 41 enlisted men were wounded. Like its parent division, the First lost a much greater number of men to disease, especially malaria.

of machinery that they expected to handle this problem with teams of men, but also that they were so obviously unfamiliar with machinery. When the engine of the train broke down, the guards forced the men to move it back to the station. Pushing, pulling, heaving, Shifty thought this was a stupid waste of energy.

At least he received more fuel for the hard work than the handfuls of rice at Cabanatuan. Along with pieces of a varied selection of fruit, including exotic ones like jackfruit, the POWs also enjoyed a meat stew once or twice a week. Beyond the meals served in the mess hall, many men working in the fields supplemented their diet with whatever came to hand. The prisoners still ate a lot of rice, though. A few weeks after their arrival from Cabanatuan, another group arrived. These men, both American and Filipino, had been captured on Mindanao and surrounding islands. The new guys arrived in fine condition and it made Shofner's group feel like "scarecrows."[190] As the weeks passed, though, some of the men—particularly the younger men—began to feel their strength return.

Work ceased on December 24, when the POWs received two days off. In the mess hall, a group of Americans and Filipinos provided some entertainment. The Filipinos gave all Americans a small casaba cake. The Japanese officers gave each POW a package of Southern Cross cigarettes. Not to be outdone, the U.S. officers—army, navy, and marine—pooled some of the money they had to give each man a Christmas present of one peso, enough money to buy tobacco through the black market.

During the party, Jack Hawkins told Mike Dobervich that he did not intend to spend another Christmas in prison. The subject had been discussed on and off since their first meeting with Austin Shofner in Cabanatuan, but when they told Shifty of their decision, they delivered it with a new seriousness. Escape meant survival. It meant freedom and the pride of being one's own man. After all they had been through, though, another reason was just as important. "Our mission," as Shifty stated it, "was to reach Allied territory and report the treatment of Japanese prisoners of war so that something could be done to save the lives of many American prisoners."

While the mission's objectives could be clearly stated, the method of reaching Allied territory, which meant Australia, fifteen hundred miles away, seemed irrational. They would have to steal a plane or a ship. A plane seemed preferable, since the Imperial Japanese Navy might catch up to a wayward ship. The one thing they had in their favor: they had heard from the other Americans that the Empire of Japan controlled mostly port cities. Great swaths of the wild backcountry of Mindanao remained unoccupied.

The three marines shelved the plan and focused on the team. The team would be comprised of men with requisite skills: a navigator, a mechanic, a pilot, a medic if not a doctor, and someone who knew Mindanao to serve as their guide. The three marines would be responsible for any combat. Every member needed to be in top physical condition. Supplies and equipment also had to be gathered and safely stored. The details of the actual day of escape had to be worked through with great care.

Shifty knew an army pilot who had fought with great bravery in the air war over Bataan, Captain William "Ed" Dyess, and approached him. He suggested another pilot as well as an aviation mechanic. Dyess and his two army air corps men had been in the Philippines for a month before the war began; the three marines, a week. None of them knew anything about the island of Mindanao or how to get from it to Australia. They knew they were ready to think through all of the problems, prepare themselves to the extent possible, and go.

ACT III

"THE PAUSE THAT REFRESHES"

Christmas 1942–Christmas 1943

AMERICA'S VICTORY IN THE BATTLE OF GUADALCANAL TAUGHT HER LEADERS that the war would be both long and costly. While Washington did not discern how devastating the campaign had been to the enemy's army and navy, it knew the crisis had passed. The end of the first year of conflict found the United States assured of its connection to Australia and comfortable that the Battle of Midway had blunted the offensive capability of Japan's carrier fleet.

ABOARD USS *JOHNSON* IN THE HARBOR OF ESPIRITU SANTOS, SID'S SQUAD HAD A meal of the standard shipboard fare. Each man received a box from the Red Cross. Sid opened his to find the "contents completely molded and useless except for a sewing box." The ship's store served Coca-Cola if one could get to the store in time. All in all, it was the "driest and poorest Christmas" anyone could remember. The officers, of course, were served a turkey for their Christmas dinners. When the 2/1 disembarked, they moved into a tent camp under coconut trees with lots of flies. Deacon found a PX, one run by black U.S. Army troops, which sold candy and cigarettes. Sid took some of his "jap souvenirs" and went out to some of the ships looking for trades. He also went aboard USS *Enterprise*, swinging at anchor in Segond Channel, but found it less generous than USS *Honolulu*, where he was given lots of free ice cream.

On New Year's Eve, a double ration of beer was doled out, a double feature was shown at the base theater, and the colonel announced they were departing soon for Australia. The small-arms fire that took place at midnight marked the beginning of 1943 and the fact that the veterans of Guadalcanal never went anywhere without their rifles, clean and loaded, and their helmets. After a few days, they boarded another transport and shipped out for Australia. They arrived off the coast of Brisbane and, as usual, waited a few days. The Fifth Marines had already gone ashore to a rest camp. Word came that the Fifth Marines hated the camp and had complained. General MacArthur, who commanded all U.S. forces in Australia, had replied that there was no shipping available to take them anywhere else. It took some time, but Admiral Halsey made the ships available. Sid's ship hoisted anchor and got under way; the 1st Marine Division sailed south, to Melbourne. Along the way, the heat of the tropics subsided.

Through a narrow pass, the ship steamed into a large bay and at last came to the dock on a clear summer day in mid-January 1943. Sid's squad knew something had changed when they were told to leave the heavy mortars behind; someone else would unload them. The embarkation ramps dumped them off at electric trams. The trams took them through the downtown to a station, where trucks took them on a short ride to the Melbourne Cricket Grounds, a stadium. "Women and girls lined the way, waving and blowing kisses." Sid and his squad "knew immediately we were in heaven."

A great repast awaited them inside the stadium. In the covered sections of the bleachers, the seats had been replaced by steel bunks. The PX sold milk, Coca-Cola, cigarettes, and other treats, but as soon as it got dark, marines in stained and ragged uniforms started slipping out. Thin and weak but determined to take liberty, the veterans had to walk about a mile to reach the center of the city. Although streetlights and neon signs had been dimmed, the marines saw people wearing clean clothes and living aboveground. They saw order, peace, civilization. For their part, the Australians welcomed them like old acquaintances, usually with a cheery "Good on you, Yank." Sid felt "absolute joy and ecstasy."

THE SEVENTH MARINES, THE LAST REGIMENT OF THE 1ST MARINE DIVISION TO land on Guadalcanal, was the last to leave. After spending Christmas at Lunga Point, Puller's 1/7 embarked on January 5 and sailed directly to Melbourne. It disembarked on January 13. The marines in Basilone's machine-gun platoon carried their adopted dog, Jockstrap, in a seabag. As they came down the ramp, the Australian immigration officer noticed Jockstrap's head poking out. "That dog can't come in here." The gunners stopped, angry and armed. "The hell he can't," one replied. The official decided to look away and the unloading continued.

The city of Melbourne slid past their windows as their train took them along the edge of it and then south around the bay to the village of Mornington. Waiting trucks carried them the short distance to their camp at Mount Martha. Rows of green eight-man tents surrounded a few semipermanent buildings sheathed in tin. The remoteness of the camp made it more difficult to skip out that evening. The trouble started the next morning. John's buddy J. P. Morgan went AWOL from nine thirty a.m. on the fourteenth "until apprehended by U.S. Army military police" at four thirty p.m.[1] Manila John, however, did not get caught.

*   *   *

LIEUTENANT MICHEEL MET UP AGAIN WITH RAY DAVIS AND A FEW OTHERS FROM Bombing Six at North Island in San Diego when their leaves expired in early January. Bill Pittman had recovered and showed up as well. Settling into the Bachelor Officers' Quarters, the pilots would have learned that not much had happened in the Pacific since their return. Mike heard about the medals being awarded for Midway. Pilots from other squadrons had already been awarded Navy Crosses and Distinguished Flying Crosses for their participation. Unlike Bombing Six, those pilots had not been on Guadalcanal and had therefore been available to accept them. Ray and Bill had received theirs upon their return to San Diego.

They assured him that, based on what had been awarded them and others, Mike would soon get a Navy Cross. The navy's rationale had been divined. "Everybody that flew four flights" got a Navy Cross. Although "some of the guys that didn't fly four flights got them too," depending on whether they had flown the first two missions on June 4 or the second two. "Anybody that just flew the last two, they didn't get it. They might have got a DFC but they didn't get a Navy Cross." After a few days, Bombing Six received their new planes, the Dauntless's newest version (-4) and fourteen new ensigns. Mike's first flight in more than two months came in mid-January, when his squadron flew to their new naval air station at El Centro, California. Just inland from San Diego and a hop from the Mexican border, Bombing Six's new home was in the desert.

The pace of in-flight training began slowly in late January. The training began by making sure the new pilots could fly a decent formation. As flight officer, Mike made sure the veterans showed the new guys a thing or two about gunnery, dive-bombing, and the like. He also had to spend some time in the backseat of an SNJ, as his protégés practiced "flying on instruments," or performing maneuvers without being able to see outside. "Outside of making sure that they didn't fly into us," and other aerial instruction, "I really don't remember that we made any effort to bring them into the squadron." Just as he had had to find his own way when he first went aboard the Big E, Micheel and his friends expected the new men to find theirs. The friendship and trust that existed between Mike, Ray, Bill, and the others could not be extended easily. The new pilots were expected to measure up.

The beginning of February meant that Ray Davis would begin holding a monthly inspection. The squadron assembled on the flight line, outside their hangar. Ray stepped up to his friend Lieutenant Junior Grade Vernon Micheel and presented him with a Navy Cross, the highest decoration for valor the Navy can bestow and second only to the Congressional Medal of Honor. A golden cross hung from a ribbon whose thin white stripe separated two broad stripes of navy blue. Like those awarded to others who had flown at Midway, Mike's citation concluded:"His gallant perseverance and utter disregard for his own personal safety were important contributing factors to the success achieved by our forces and were in keeping with the highest traditions of the United States Naval Service."[2] Ray pinned on the medal, stepped back, and saluted him.

ON FEBRUARY 1, SHOFNER HAD "THE HAPPIEST DAY OF PRISON LIFE." HE RECEIVED a few letters from home. To hear that his family were all well in a letter postmarked in June of 1942 was to know joy. It moved him more than the Red Cross packages the guards had distributed a week earlier, although these boxes had contained treats like chocolate, cigarettes and cookies; necessities like canned meats, sardines, and even toilet articles. Along with all the goodies there was some clothing and a small supply of quinine and sulfa drugs. Each prisoner received two boxes, although the guards had stolen from some of the boxes. Copies of the Manila newspaper were provided to each barracks. In addition, the guards gave each man fifteen cans of canned meat and vegetables. The prison officials also made sure the prisoners had blankets, mosquito nets, canteens, and mess kits.

On top of this shocking largesse, the camp commander allowed his prisoners to send a postcard home. The chance to tell their families that they were still alive, even if it was a tiny postcard on which they filled in a few blanks, brought hope. The supply of quinine came in handy almost immediately, as Shifty had his first bout with malaria. He took the pills and hoped he had averted a trip to the hospital. Going into the hospital meant a loss of privileges. It meant the loss of his spot on a work detail. It meant he might lose his chance to escape.

Even though the lives of the POWs had improved greatly in Davao from Cabanatuan, almost half of them lacked the strength for a work detail in March of 1943. Not working made recovering from dengue fever, beriberi, tropical ulcers, dysentery, and the like more difficult. The cans of food and supplies of medicines were consumed quickly. Those who could work could steal, although the guards had become more watchful. Punishment for stealing food from the emperor of Japan was meted out with fist, boot, and club immediately. Still, it had to be done.

Using the quinine worried Shifty, though. His team of would-be escapees were not indulging themselves in all of the great canned food like the other POWs. Canned food had to be saved for the escape, just like the medicine. The camp commander made the saving of food more difficult when he cut the supply of fresh vegetables. All of the prisoners needed to work in the fields in order to make up the loss. In Shifty's case, the medicine worked. It knocked down the malaria. He remained on the detail.

Shifty went looking for a navigator. Quietly, with his poker face in place, he observed and assessed the naval officers. As with most of the marine officers, disease and malnutrition had rendered most of the navy men unfit for a difficult journey. He approached Lieutenant Commander Melvyn McCoy. At an appropriate point in their conversation, Shifty asked him if he could navigate a ship from Mindanao to Australia. McCoy knew where this discussion would go. He liked how it had begun. McCoy had met Shifty in Bilibid, played poker against him in Cabanatuan, and had watched him give money to other POWs so they could buy food.[3] He knew Captain Austin Shofner had the strength and the courage to succeed. So McCoy replied that he had been a top mathematician at the United States Naval Academy. He could devise a formula for navigating the great ocean.

When at last Shifty broached the subject of escape directly, Commander McCoy let Shofner know he had already begun planning to break out with three others. He could not abandon them. This wrinkle halted the conversation. The commander and the captain returned to their respective groups. Each group had to consider if the total number of both groups—ten—would be too many. On the other hand, could the two groups afford to remain separate when they knew that whichever group went first would spoil the chances of the second? Last, they had to evaluate the men in the other group for toughness and health, if not for skill. Enough men had faltered during the many months since the surrender that having a discussion among so large a group brought great unease. The considerations created a slow dance. At length, though, they decided to go together.*

Rather than dwell too much on their chances in a small boat somewhere in the Pacific, the men focused on the specifics. Commander McCoy assumed command, as the highest-ranking officer, a command tolerated by Shifty in part because McCoy respected all of the work and planning Shofner had already performed. Circumstances also prevented McCoy from dictating each policy. Shifty involved himself in every step of the process. Lists of equipment and tools were drawn up, amounts and

---

*Listed alphabetically, the men who attempted it were: Lieutenant Leo Boelens (Army); Lieutenant Michael Dobervich (USMC); Captain William Dyess (U.S. Army Air Corps); Lieutenant Samuel Grashio (Air Corps); Lieutenant Jack Hawkins (USMC); Corporal Paul Marshall (Air Corps); Lieutenant Commander Melvyn McCoy (Navy); Major Stephen Mellnik (Army); Captain Austin Shofner (USMC); Sergeant Robert Spielman (Army).

types of food were specified in a penal colony where most men did not have enough to eat and many did not have "any footgear of any kind."[4] Along with an axe, a rope, and a tent or section of tarp to provide some protection from the strong rains, McCoy insisted he have a sextant for navigation. In case the escape succeeded but the effort to depart the island did not, they gathered the seeds of fruits and vegetables.

Shofner, Hawkins, and Dobervich were plowing the casaba field with Brahma steers in late February. They and a few others from the team used the bulls to pull their carts and plow the field. Using the draft animals required the teams to go to them on Sunday, when everyone else had the day off, and bring them to a new pasture. This got the plowers out of the gated compound. McCoy and his men worked on the coffee-bean-picking details, which also worked on Sundays as per the camp commandant's orders. With little supervision, which they handily evaded, the team hid tin cans full of their supplies in various places, including Shifty's favorite: under large anthills.

Beyond the fields in which they labored, a wall of jungle stood over a swamp. The only clear path out of the fields led down the road to the city of Davao. The IJA considered the miles of dense jungle and deep swamp to form an impenetrable barrier on three sides. The team agreed, reluctantly. Recruiting a guide would force them to extend the circle of trust beyond Americans. It had to be done. Shofner, aided by Hawkins, who spoke Spanish, oversaw the selection. He started by finding out as much as he could about the Filipinos who had been incarcerated there for civil crimes. In time, he came to know two men who had the knowledge to lead the way, but who had both been convicted of murder. They were Benigno de la Cruz and Victoriano Jumarong. Ben told them he had been convicted of murder, but he had done it in a fit of emotion. He had killed the man who was trying to steal the woman he loved. He said he regretted it. Victor proclaimed his innocence. Playing his cards close to his vest, Shifty took his time in verifying their knowledge of the area before bringing them up to speed.

NOT EVERYONE FROM HOW COMPANY OF THE 2ND BATTALION OF THE FIRST Marines made roll call on the first morning at the Melbourne Cricket Grounds. The first sergeant looked out to see maybe thirty guys in formation, somewhat less than the two hundred or so he had on his muster roll. For every name he called, though, he heard an answer. He decided to call out a few names of men who had been buried on Guadalcanal and, lo and behold, they answered aye as well. On this lovely morning First Sergeant McGrath did not care. He was drunk, too.

On the second day in Australia Sid and the other privates first class received £15, or about $48. It was a modest amount considering the United States Marine Corps owed him close to $400 after six months on the Canal, when no one had been paid. New uniforms were also issued, but because of a shortage of marine uniforms, he received an army jacket. The seabags that they had left in Wellington were supposed to be on their way, and Lieutenant Benson had his company fill out official government forms listing all of the items they had lost on USS *George F. Elliott*. Uncle Sam was going to repay them for the loss of their personal possessions.

At every opportunity, the marines headed up the street. They arrived in Melbourne with a great thirst: for milk, for steak, for beer and whiskey, for women, for ice cream, for everything they had missed. It would take some time, given the difficulty of understanding the accents of the merchants, for Sid to understand the new monetary system: pence, shillings, pounds, and a mysterious unit known as two bob. A pint of beer cost sixpence, though; a steak covered in fried eggs cost about two shillings; and a trip on a train anywhere in town was sixpence. Sid concluded that the fifteen pounds in his pocket, with no rent to pay or requirement to purchase food, made him a millionaire.

The warmth of the welcome the 1st Marine Division received from the people of Australia overwhelmed them. Australia had been bombed by Japanese planes, her ships had been attacked inside her harbors by Japanese submarines, and tens of thousands of her men were in Japanese POW camps. The rush of imperial conquest down the Pacific Rim seemed to be aimed right at them. Australia was fighting for its survival and for that of the British Empire, of which she was a part. The newspaper let the people know that the marines had just won an important victory. As he walked through the streets, Sid had adults walk up to him and say, "Good on you, Yank, you saved Australia." An invitation to their homes for dinner or to spend the weekend often followed. Sid attempted to explain that he was not a "Yank."

THE TRUCKS TOOK THEM TO THE STATION, WHERE THE 1/7 CAUGHT THE TRAIN to Melbourne. Manila John and his friends did not buy tickets for the train. Any money spent on something other than wine, women, and song was considered a waste, "and the song," Richard Greer added, "was a complete waste."[5] Basilone found a bar he liked called the Barbados. The owner, of Italian descent, gave him a little leeway. "John would make what he called the blockbuster. He'd go in the bar, and he'd put an ounce of bourbon, an ounce of scotch, an ounce of rum, and an ounce of everything he can find and make an 8 ounce glass."[6] It had the desired effect. "You start sipping it in the morning and you couldn't find your ass with both hands by dinner." Not all of the marines seen stumbling down the sidewalk were drunk, though. Malaria continued to catch up with men who had thought they had escaped its clutches. Marines filled Melbourne's new hospital.

The young women of Melbourne bewildered the marines. The girls approached the guys on the street and asked them for a date. It left the heroes of Guadalcanal with their mouths hanging open. That kind of thing didn't happen back home; but then, the dates often involved going home to her house and having dinner with her family. It involved going out with a group of new friends to see films, strolling the arcade, and the like. For more than a few, the adventures grew amorous once a few logistical problems were overcome. Women were not allowed into bars and even going into a lounge was considered risqué. The bars closed at six p.m. The deadline created the "6 o'clock Swill," with men gulping the last drops from their glasses before being shown the door. The Americans learned quickly, though, that some hotel pubs and restaurants were able to serve alcohol later than bars; it was also easier to get their dates to join them in these establishments. Where to go after the dinner and drinks posed another problem. Taking long walks in one of the city's parks was popular.

Order and discipline returned to the division. Inspections and reviews were held most mornings. Each man received a shoulder patch for his makeshift uniform. The white stars of the Southern Cross adorned a field of blue. The word "Guadalcanal" ran down the large red "1" in the center. The battle, for which the division earned the Presidential Unit Citation, had become its identity. The old salts rotated stateside to train new divisions. Others received a week's liberty and skipped town. Most, however, had to content themselves with their afternoons and evenings off. It was enough time for Manila John to blow through $100 in his first month.

On February 22, the Seventh Marines went into the city as a regiment. It formed up with the First Marines, the Fifth, and the division's artillery regiment, the Eleventh. When the breeze caught Old Glory and unfurled it, Sid's eyes moistened, and he laughed heartily when his friend observed "in a loud voice how that wind burns your eyes." At twelve noon, the 1st Marine Division marched through throngs of thousands of people for six miles. The USMC bands played "Semper Fidelis" and "The Star-Spangled Banner" and the "Marines' Hymn." Australian bands also marched. The delightful melody of one of their songs, "Waltzing Matilda," got the Americans' attention. It made a great addition to the parade. "Part of that long green machine going through the streets of Melbourne," Sid felt a great sense of power well up inside of him. The sight of "every man in step, heads up, shoulders back, many thousands of miles from home" prompted Sid's friend to mumble, "Uncle Sam's Marines are showing off."

During the afternoon it became clear that the other regiments envied the First's prime location. The rivalry and insults surprised no one. The Australian troops, though, had begun to cause real problems. Marines attributed their anger to jealousy—the marines had better uniforms, lots of money, lots of free time, and had been called the saviors of Australia by Australians. The 1st Division had arrived in a city where so many young men had been called to duty, if not in the armed services, then in some other capacity of war mobilization. The circumstances had conspired to put Sid and Manila John and their friends in the catbird seat. They set about making the most of it—but also to start watching their backs when alone.

In late February, Bombing Six received orders to report to the inspector of naval aircraft at the Curtiss-Wright Aircraft Corporation in Columbus, Ohio. The squadron would pick up new aircraft and ferry them back to their base in California. Bombing Six knew from their skipper that the new planes were the Curtiss-Wright SB2C dive-bomber, known as the Helldiver. Some pilots over in San Diego had already received some and Mike had heard that those guys "were pulling the tails off of them in dives." It did not sound like his kind of airplane. A few days later, they all climbed into the back of a transport plane for the two-day trip to Columbus.

On the first of March, Bombing Six reported in to the inspector of naval aircraft, who sent them along to the commander of the U.S. Naval Aircraft Delivery Unit. They had a few days to receive instruction on the new planes from representatives of the factory, who also assured them that the kinks had been worked out of the design.

The engineers had created the SB2C to outperform the Dauntless. Its bigger engine and four-bladed propeller produced a top speed of 286 mph. For improved speed and maneuverability, the "2C" carried its thousand-pound bomb inside a bomb bay. Its 20mm cannons provided greater protection, and a larger fuel tank added range. Mike finally got away from the company representatives and into the cockpit on March 5. He flew for about an hour in the new plane that his squadron would fly. He realized, "I was partial to the SBD [Dauntless], I didn't like that 2C. There wasn't anything wrong with it, I guess, but it just didn't fly like an airplane, it flew like a brick." Over the next few days, the squadron took more familiarization flights; then Mike flew Helldiver number 00080 right out of the factory.

Flying cross-country was harder than anyone had thought. They had to find their way, follow the rules of the airways, and follow a set flight plan. The rules and reports seemed a little bothersome to the pilots of Bombing Six, who had become accustomed to flying out in the Pacific, where "the airways were free, just roam where you want, when you wanted to."

A PRISONER NEVER KNEW WHAT THE DAY MIGHT BRING. FOLLOWING UP ON HIS earlier steps, the camp commandant decided to pay all the American officers for their work. In early March, Captain Austin Shofner signed the forms presented to him, some of which indicated he had received clothing and rations that he had not, and accepted twenty pesos. The camp officials intimated that an account had been created at a bank in Japan where more money had been deposited for him and the other officers. The guards opened a small PX and sold soda water, peanuts, fried bananas, and leaf tobacco. "Supply," Shifty noted unhappily, "was about one-tenth of the demand."

What supplies could be added to their stock were purchased and smuggled out in a work cart to a hiding place. The team also used the money to purchase key equipment on the black market run by Filipinos: nails, a hammer, a screwdriver, a small roll of wire, a compass, a bolo knife, a road map of Mindanao, and field glasses. In the workshop of the penal colony, one man made a cooking pot. Topping the list, the team's machinist crafted a sextant that exceeded McCoy's expectations.

Information about Mindanao was gathered. The detail of men who went to the ocean to make salt had some information, as did the Americans who had been captured on Mindanao. The team's Filipino guides had suggestions and the map that had been purchased provided a general frame of reference. Having picked a rendezvous point in the jungle, the team would set off for Longa-og, a barrio about fifteen miles away. The hamlet was rumored to have some guerrillas. From Longa-og, they would cross the mountains to Cateel, a barrio on the east coast, "where we were told there were some bancas [boats]."

On March 14, the team rehearsed the escape without their supplies and equipment in order to work out the timing of the rendezvous. If caught practicing, they hoped the guards would assume they were trying to steal food and beat them and put them in solitary confinement, but not kill anyone. They set D-day for Sunday, March 28, and waited for the week to pass. A few days later, Hawkins, Dobervich, and Shifty were part of a crew weeding the onion patch. The American officer in charge of the work caught Dobervich stealing onions. He began to lay into Dobervich. An argument began. Hawkins jumped in, and before Shofner knew it Hawkins had punched a ranking officer. The angry man took his report to the American camp commander, who threw Hawk and Dobervich off their work details. Another member of the team, Sam Grashio, talked his way into replacing Hawkins on Shifty's plowing detail; the two continued to cart their gear out to the hiding area, one small piece at a time. McCoy, who could not get overly angry with Hawkins and Dobervich because his own men were stealing chickens by the day, had to go make peace with the U.S. camp commander, who strove to keep the peace as a way of minimizing the death toll.

On Saturday, the twenty-seventh, the rain came down in sheets. Shifty told his team of drovers to rest in the shack since no work could be done. Lieutenant Hosume, the captain of the guard and a man who loved to smack his prisoners around, made an inspection. The prisoners were supposed to be working. He lined the team up and slapped them. He then opened their bags, which were to contain only each man's noon ration of rice. Shofner knew one man had some equipment and he himself had "a bottle containing the entire quinine supply for our escape" in his musette bag.[7] Hosume looked in the bag. He saw the bottle of pills. However, he was looking for forbidden foods, such as fruits or vegetables. With a one-track mind, the guard they called "the Crown Prince of Swat" punched Shofner again and continued on. Shifty said he had just "established a new world's record for holding the breath." Lieutenant Hosume did find a work party carrying stolen food. He ordered all hands to work in the rice fields the next day, Sunday, as punishment.

The punishment forced a delay in their departure. It would not have mattered had it not been for the stashes of equipment hidden near the edges of the fields. The team worked a full week expecting any moment to be discovered. "We were plenty scared."[8]

THE KNOWLEDGE THAT HE VOLUNTEERED HAD SATISFIED CADET SLEDGE FOR a time, and he made steady progress in school. In late March, though, he heard from a friend who had studied chemistry in the V-12 program and had earned an officer's commission. The friend was now an officer in a technical branch, working in a laboratory. The prospect of being a chemist for the Marine Corps made Sledge sick. "With my love and interest in firearms etc.," he wrote his mother, "I'll be doggone if I'm going to be stuck away in some lab and never see any action." He declared he would sooner flunk out and go in as a buck private.

Sledge was too close to his parents, especially his mother, to make his weekly letter to her solely an ultimatum. The Sledge family was a tight-knit family. He took a moment to look forward to seeing them during the Easter break, when they could enjoy the azaleas blooming and hear the wood thrushes sing. He mentioned a letter from his older brother Edward reporting the news of a promotion. Perhaps acknowledging the news of Edward's success set him off. Eugene had "looked forward too long to being in a real outfit," to go very far with pleasant conversation. He wanted his father to get his course of study in V-12 changed to something other than chemistry. "I know father will think me a fool, but I don't care." He hated science and declared that he was not any good at it. "For once in my life, I hope you and Pop realize I made my decision by thinking and that you will . . . try and help me instead of forcing me into something I dislike."

It had all begun a month earlier, when Deacon had insisted Sid go on a blind date. "Why?" he asked. Deacon said he had met this girl and gone around to her house to speak to her mother about a date. The mother had agreed to it provided her daughter Dorothy was accompanied by her younger sister, Shirley. The two sisters went together. "You have got to come with me," Deacon had pleaded. "She's pretty . . . I've seen her." Sid at last agreed to go. The two friends went downtown and met Dorothy and her younger sister, Shirley, who stepped forward with a smile. She reminded Sid of the actress Elizabeth Taylor.

They set off for dinner at a nice restaurant and then to see a movie. Everywhere they went, Sid could feel the jealous eyes of other marines staring at him. One old Aussie shouted, "Give 'er a go, Yank, she's o'r aight'een!" The foursome capped the evening with a visit to the amusement park at St. Kilda. The two couples took the train out to a small house in Glenferrie, where Dorothy and Shirley lived with their mother, "Tuppie," and grandmother, "Nana." Tuppie found a moment to read Sidney Phillips and John Tatum "the Articles of War," regarding her daughters' chastity. Shirley Osborne was sixteen.

None of her rules dimmed their enthusiasm for the girls or for the Osborne family. While both Sid and Deacon went out with other friends and had other adventures, a few nights a week they took the train out to the little house in Glenferrie. Even with both girls working, times were tight in the Osborne home. Shirley's father had served in World War I. The mustard gas he had inhaled in the trenches had eventually killed him. The Osborne family, it turned out, knew all too well the horrors of war, but they did not darken the conversations with it. Deacon and Sid liked to bring over groceries and make a big dinner. One night they took the family to see a movie, *Gone With the Wind*. Tuppie and Nana seemed confused, so Sid tried his best to explain the plot to them. "I could tell I wasn't getting anywhere. They didn't understand what I was talking about."

Rather than blow all of his money having fun, Sid sent most of his back pay home once he received it. When a carton of cigarettes bought in the PX for fifty cents would buy a round of drinks for everyone in a pub, he didn't need much cash. Sid asked his father not to put his money in war bonds, but simply to start a savings account. Sid also asked his platoon commander, Lieutenant Benson, what had happened to the forms each man had filled out, listing the personal items he had lost when the old tub *George F. Elliott* sank. Benson replied that the government had "checked and found that the Rolex watch company had never made that many watches in all of their manufacturing history." The swindlers had been swindled, but life with the Australians was too grand to worry.

As Sid's How Company assembled for reveille one morning on the playing field, a marine came into view. He was not only out of uniform and late for roll call; the marine had a great pile of bedding riding on his shoulders. A few snorts of laughter could be heard in the ranks. As he ran past the company headed for their bunks in the stadium's stands, the men recognized Bob Leckie. Bob, also known as "Lucky," had slept in the park outside the stadium. The laughter grew into "roars of ridicule" as Sid and his buddies surmised that Lucky had not been sleeping in the park alone.[9] Among the First Marines, "walks in the park" had become commonplace. Catcalls from the entire battalion about his flagrant violation serenaded him as Lucky ran to his bunk to get his uniform.

During another of the usual morning drills, this one on March 29, Sid started feeling queer. He went to see the medic, who took one look at him and put him on a truck with some others. The doctors at the hospital diagnosed him with jaundice. They prescribed lots of bed rest and fruit juice. A few days later, Deacon took Shirley to the hospital to visit, but they were turned away. Being refused the chance to visit Sidney did not bother Deacon too much. He had not been able to stop thinking about Shirley for some time. She called him "Wes," a version of his middle name, Wesley.

ON MARCH 30, JUST A FEW DAYS BEFORE D-DAY NUMBER TWO, A YOUNG ARMY medic got a little too careless near the fence. He threw a canteen over the fence to a friend on the other side. One of the guards in the tower fired three shots; the first one killed the medic. The POWs gathered cautiously to find out what had happened. The victim had not been that close to the fence, but he had been close to the guard tower. The Japanese camp officials stated that the medic had been trying to escape. The POWs, whose lives were bordered by men in guard towers, wanted to know why the guards thought a man would try to escape in broad daylight with no food or equipment. The prisoners could only push their outrage so far, though.

On the night of Saturday, April 3, the team met. Casually, slowly, they endeavored to review key details without arousing suspicion. Hawkins and Dobervich were back on the plow squad, so it and the coffee-pickers detail were made up entirely of escapees. They knew the rendezvous point and reviewed the signal to be given to the Filipinos, Ben and Victor, who would be watching them from the church. One last great worry loomed: that their escape would provoke the Japanese into harming other prisoners. After more than a year of pain and suffering, the thought of inflicting harm on their friends came hard. They had done their best to separate their action from the others. Only team members served on the two work details. No one else knew anything about their plans. Most of all, though, was the goal. The team would escape not just for their survival, but to tell the world of the atrocity being committed by the Empire of Japan.

The pledge the team made to one another that night was bigger than any individual. Each member "made a vow if any one of us became ill . . . that would imperil the progress of the group as a whole, that they were to be abandoned. In other words, we had rules to win as a group and if someone had a problem, that was fate." They did not pledge "All for one and one for all," for good reason. Dobervich and others had survived the March of Death on Bataan. The memory of the three men who had been beaten beyond recognition just outside the gate of Cabanatuan haunted all of them. The strong would succeed. Shifty secreted a rusty razor blade on his person. He would slice open the veins in his wrists rather than be captured.

Just before eight a.m. the next morning, the two working parties approached the gate. Shifty gave Ben and Victor the sign. The four-man bull-plowing detail and the six-man coffee-pickers detail checked out at the guard station. McCoy ordered "eyes left" for his formation and gave the guard a snappy salute. They proceeded on their assigned routes until they were out of sight. By eight thirty, the two groups had met at the rendezvous point, a large anthill near the jungle. Excitedly, they "uncovered the gasoline cans and removed our gear, rolled our packs and made ready to leave." Now, where were Ben and Victor? Minutes passed. The guards used roving patrols and lookouts in the sentry tower. On a Sunday morning, they were sure to be slow, but it was only a matter of time.

Half an hour passed. "If they sold us out, they could probably get $10,000 pesos each and become heroes in the Philippines under jap rule." Someone had had to say it, although the idea of a sellout did not adequately explain the delay. The discussion turned to leaving at once, without Ben and Victor. Shifty said, "No. We don't know where we are and where we are going. We have got to have somebody." Fear kicked into overdrive and every man felt the urge to do something. The team started thinking about a strategy to patrol the area around them so they did not get surprised. Another half hour elapsed and Shifty admitted, "The suspense of waiting, unarmed, within 300 yards of the jap barracks was much worse than any heavy artillery barrage."

Ben and Victor hurried over. They had been made to stand at attention while the guards had searched their barracks. The team swung their packs and the feeling of freedom came with a powerful rush. "We literally flew through the jungle for the first hour," Shofner noticed, but it did not last. The guides missed the trail to Longa-og and backtracked to find it. A heavy rain came down, making it harder to find the trail and harder for the enemy to find them. After another hour wasted, they decided to "make our way by compass, northeast. This course would either bring us into the Longa-og trail or to the Japanese railroad which ran almost to Longa-og." Ben and Victor led the way, hacking a path with their bolos. The team carried the Filipinos' gear.

Wading through the jungle, the swamp, several creeks, and a few deep rivers, the team continued until six p.m. Exhaustion could not be allowed to overcome them, though. They had to build sleeping platforms to keep themselves off the ground and out of reach of the deadly double-headed leeches swimming in the water swirling around their ankles. The Filipinos showed them how to cut some lengths of poles and vines and broad leaves and weave them into crude rattan beds. They ate a ration of food and tried to sleep. The driving rain woke them. The singing hordes of mosquitoes woke them. A few of the bunks broke and sent their occupants into the dark water.

Each man breakfasted on six ounces of corned beef before swinging his pack over his shoulder and setting off. Within a half mile, they had sunk hip-deep into the marsh. The mud had a surprising suction. The wild thickets through which they pushed offered no dry spot where one could sit and rest. Within a few hours, the exertion had drained McCoy and his friend Mellnik. Shofner shouldered both of their packs along with his; Shifty was, McCoy admitted, "a tower of strength."[10] By three p.m., McCoy and Mellnik said they could not move another step. The Filipinos spied a large fallen tree, so they made camp on top of it. Again they fashioned beds and dared to light a fire in the wilderness to cook rice and make tea. Shofner watched the hot food and drink revive his team. A debate began about whether to turn back and look for the trail to Longa-og or to continue in the northeast direction. Mellnik wanted to go back, not to find the trail but to turn himself in to the guards. He saw it "as the only chance to survive."[11] Shifty set him straight in no uncertain terms. With that settled, the group still needed to decide its direction. The enemy solved the problem. About 1730, Shofner and the others "heard rifle, machine gun and mortar fire, and also saw some large fires which we concluded were nipa huts burning. We knew this firing came from the japs searching party and presumed they were on the trail we had missed. We took a compass bearing on the fire, determined to go in this new direction in the morning. From the sound we estimated the japs were about 2 miles away."

The mosquito swarms grew fierce at dusk. The nets afforded enough protection to allow the tired men some rest. Well after dark an "eerie sound" awakened them, "the beating of the signal drums by the wild people." Bong-de-de-bong. Bong-de-de-bong. They had heard of the jungle telegraph used by natives, but it sounded more ominous when one was encased inside a swamp. They had heard something moving in the darkness occasionally. Someone asked the guides, "What are they saying?" Shofner interjected, "They're saying bong-de-de-bong, heads-are-available! Heads-are-available!" That brought a chuckle, which broke some of the tension. During the night, a few more beds gave way. "We were not very good woodsmen," Shifty noted.

The next morning the team set off in better spirits with the prospect of exiting the swamp. The water receded somewhat by noon and they waded ashore at about two p.m. In an hour, they found the railway line that was the trail to Longa-og. The infantry training of the marines took control. A scouting party was sent up the trail to the village; an OP was maintained at the spot they had met the track; the rest of the party pulled back five hundred yards and waited. The scouts returned at dark after a hike of three kilometers. They had found some deserted shacks and evidence of a large unit of enemy troops having visited very recently. Were the Japanese farther up the track, the escapees wondered, or had they returned to Davao? As that was discussed, the team inventoried their food supply. Although each man had consumed only his daily allotment—one twelve-ounce can of sardines or corned beef—they had not planned on getting lost. Food was short.

In some ways, the decision of what to do next was made for them. They could not stay there because they had only a few rations left. They could not wade back into the jungle in any direction. Taking the road to the right led them to Davao. Tired and scared men, though, come to agreements slowly. The marines suggested moving out in a tactical formation: the two groups of five men would leapfrog each other. One would be safe in the bush while the other hiked down the track. With a plan for the morning, they began preparing a place to sleep above the silent predators on the forest floor.

The next morning they skipped breakfast and set off in patrol formation, one group leapfrogging the other, up the railroad track. Four kilometers up the track they came to the scene of a firefight. Empty cartridge cases, dried blood, cigarette butts, and hardtack littered the railroad tracks. About five hundred yards farther, they came to a hamlet. Chickens, dogs, and other domesticated animals ran amok, but the inhabitants had fled. Some of the huts, with a roof made of nipa and walls of bamboo, had been set afire in the last day or two. After posting guards, the team went into one of the huts to cook some food in the sandbox. One of the lookouts returned within moments, reporting that he had heard a metallic click. He had whirled around to catch sight of two armed Filipinos in the bushes near the railroad. The Filipinos, upon being seen, had fled in the direction of Longa-og.

Those men may have been guerrillas, but they might also have been guides for the enemy. The team agreed they must move quickly for Longa-og. They had to make contact with the guerrilla forces. The railroad was the only path. Packing up the uncooked food, they set off. They hiked ten kilometers, reaching the village about three p.m. The villagers conducted them to a specific spot and stepped away. They heard a voice shouting in a foreign language and they all dropped to the ground. More yelling caused some of the team to yell back, until one voice rang out clearly: "You're surrounded! Surrender!"

Aside from a few bolo knives, they had no weapons. They held up their arms in surrender. A whistle sounded and fifty armed men stepped out of the bushes. The Filipino guerrillas searched them for weapons. "We told them we were Americans." The hostility did not abate. Ben and Victor, however, slipped into their native tongue and the situation changed quickly. The guerrillas began to believe that Shifty and the others were not spies of some kind. When told how the team had come to the village, however, the guerrilla leader expressed surprise that they had survived the swamp. No locals ever went through it. It teemed with crocodiles.

The Americans told the leader about seeing two armed Filipinos near the railroad. Those men worked for him, the guerrilla replied; they had fired at men they assumed were IJA. "However, the ammunition was faulty and the rifle did not fire." No apology followed. The guerrilla leader at last accepted their identity and introduced himself as Casiano de Juan, captain of the barrio and leader of the local guerrillas. In their brief conversation with him, the escapees nicknamed Casiano "Big Boy." Soon the guerrillas and the escapees all walked back into the village of Longa-og as compatriots.

The villagers welcomed them as friends. The Filipinos' generosity overwhelmed the escapees. Great quantities of fruit, meat, eggs, and more were proffered and gratefully accepted. Big Boy brought them to the barrio's meetinghouse. Other villagers removed the fighting gamecocks that lived there. In the evening, the Filipinos held a feast for the Americans. The escapees got to know Big Boy, who was a sergeant in the Mindanao guerrillas and had escaped from the enemy several times. The emperor had a reward on his head. The Americans had witnessed his toughness; now they saw in him the personification of the Filipino personality: easygoing, warm, kind. For the feast the villagers served the local delicacy, balut. To make balut, the villagers left an egg under a chicken for twenty days, then boiled it. Half formed, the embryo's feathers and beak could be recognized in the goo. The locals bit down on the beaks, which "popped like popcorn," and ate quickly. The Americans knew enough not to slight the honor being paid them. Shifty bit down on one, grinned, and said, "Good."

The carabao steaks went down easier. Resembling a water buffalo, the carabao provided plenty of savory meat. Over the next few days, the men ate every few hours, rested, and washed themselves. In his diary, Shifty described the dishes served at every fabulous meal. All the villagers hated the Japanese and loved Americans. Shifty met a boy who had had the first two fingers on his right hand cut off by the Japanese to prevent him from firing a rifle. At Big Boy's hut they enjoyed drinking tuba, the first alcohol they had tasted in a long time. He told them he would bring them to his superiors when he had made arrangements. He also told them of a radio on Mindanao that communicated with Australia. That got their attention. The group began to discuss changing their plans in light of this dramatic news. They might just make it home after all. As much as the news excited Shifty, he took a few days to relax. Lying in the hut and listening to the rain drum on the roof gave him a deep sense of peace. He slept soundly.

Supplied by the good people of Longa-og, the Americans began the journey to the home of Dr. David Kapangagan, an evacuee from Davao City who could connect them to the guerrilla movement. At every stop along the way, the villagers welcomed them, feted them with music and feasts, let them sleep in their beds. The relaxed and fun life continued at Dr. Kapangagan's house, where they waited for a few days. One night ten or twelve very pretty girls came to invite them to a dance. The Americans walked in the torch parade to the dance, watched the locals perform, and even returned the favor by singing a song. Shifty found himself "called on to do the Tennessee Stomp."

On April 17, Captain Claro Laureta of the Philippine Constabulary arrived. He

Martin K. A. Morgan

affirmed the existence of a large guerrilla force on the northern coast of Mindanao—his constabulary was a part of it—but he refused to confirm the report about the radio communication with Australia. The team listened intently, probing for more answers about the guerrillas, their whereabouts, leadership, goals, and the journey. The trek to the northern coast would take them through a remote area controlled by tribes of Atas and Honobos. "After a meeting all the party decided to change plans and go to the guerrilla headquarters on Northern Mindanao." Captain Laureta organized food and guides for their long journey. On April 21, they set off on the long trek north.

AFFECTION FOR THE SB2C DID NOT GROW ON THE PILOTS OF BOMBING SIX. The manufacturer had suggested the nickname "Helldiver." Its pilots, however, preferred to call it the Beast. It required a lot of attention in level flight and real concentration when landing because of its shaky hold on the air. As part of his April fitness reports, Ray Davis (now a lieutenant commander) asked Lieutenant Micheel to state his preferred duty. Mike said he would prefer to become a fighter pilot on a carrier in the Pacific. He wanted out of El Centro, a backwater training base, and in to the navy's new fighter plane, the Hellcat, which had earned rave reviews. Neither Davis nor apparently the U.S. Navy evinced any interest in letting a skilled dive-bomber pilot get away. In mid-April Bombing Six cut its training schedule short and flew east.

They stopped in Columbus, Ohio, and let the technicians of the Curtiss-Wright check their planes. Mike arrived three days late because of engine trouble. Once the factory engineers gave his plane, number 00080, the all clear, he set out to catch up with his squadron, but ran out of gas and lost two days. He landed at NAS Norfolk, part of the navy's vast complex there, on April 22, well behind the rest of his squadron. The new pilots in Bombing Six had already begun to enjoy an advantage he had not had a year before: practicing carrier landings on a flattop out in the Chesapeake Bay in advance of landing upon their new fleet carrier.

After its new pilots qualified as carrier pilots on a small "jeep" carrier in Chesapeake Bay, Bombing Six landed their SB2Cs aboard the new fleet carrier, USS *Yorktown*, on May 5.[12] *Yorktown* had been commissioned two weeks earlier. Her name recalled the carrier lost at Midway and a proud lineage of U.S. Navy ships dating back one hundred years. The pilots found her passageways crowded with workers and tradesmen of all kinds, completing the installation of the furnishings, fittings and equipment.

Of course she was bigger, the new *Yorktown*. Although not as large as *Saratoga*, *Yorktown*'s flight deck beat *Enterprise*'s by about eighteen feet in length. The longer airstrip pleased Mike, who had always "puckered" at takeoffs more than most. Bombing Six had joined Air Group Five, including thirty-six Hellcats, a scouting squadron that also flew the SB2C and brought the total number of Beasts on board to thirty-six, and eighteen Avengers, the navy's torpedo plane. Jimmy Flatley, one of the most respected fighter pilots of the war, commanded the carrier's air group. His squadrons began practicing their landings on their new carrier as she steamed up and down Chesapeake Bay, preparing for her shakedown cruise.

WHEN SID WAS RELEASED FROM THE HOSPITAL, HE RETURNED TO FIND HIS battalion had left for field exercises. The 2/1 returned a few days later and, when the men of #4 gun squad caught sight of him, they expressed their disappointment that he hadn't died. Sid smiled. Deacon and W.O. shared stories of long marches, extended order drills, and gunnery practice, so Sid was glad he had missed it. Conditioning hikes, though, became a common morning duty, with Lieutenant Benson leading his mortar platoon around and around the Fitzroy Gardens, a beautiful park near the cricket grounds.

The mortar platoon usually had the afternoon off, with long liberties on weekends. Deacon and Sid often went to tea with the Osborne family. One afternoon, though, Sid met up with one of the new guys in the squad, Tex. They took the tram to Young & Jackson, a large pub across the street from the main railway station at the center of town. The pub boasted a painting of a nude young woman named Chloe. While taking a good look at Chloe, Sid drank a pint of beer. Tex downed three scotch and waters. The two walked down the street to another pub. Sid sipped a beer and Tex poured in three drinks. They walked out on the street. Six American sailors were crossing the street toward them."Tex spread his arms and told them to stop right where they were and get back on the other side of the street because this side of the street belonged to us." Tex threatened to swab the deck with them. Horrified, Sid tried to look mean. The sailors decided to skip this fight."Are you trying to get us killed?" Sid asked.

"I can tell which sailors would and would not fight," said Tex. He had a head full of steam as he walked up the street. Sid "let Tex go ahead without me shortly. Why fight unnecessary skirmishes in a long war?"

"WE WERE," SHIFTY GUESSED, "THE FIRST WHITE PEOPLE TO USE THIS TRAIL." THE hike over the mountains on a trail he could not always see followed a few days paddling in a dugout canoe. While the Americans labored, quickly coming to the last of their strength, the Filipinos carried all of the supplies up the slopes with ease. Their encounters with "bushy-headed" people armed with spears, shields, bows and poison-tipped arrows went well. On the far side of the mountains, they bade farewell to most of their guides, climbed into boats, and began floating down the Agusan River toward the northern coast.

The cities of the northern coast of Mindanao, like Butuan and Buenavista, had large guerrilla presences, but also IJA garrisons. The carefree life of the backcountry gave way to vigilance. On May 5, the team arrived in Medina and was guided to Lieutenant Colonel Ernest McClish, an officer in the U.S. Army before the war and now commander of 110th Division, Tenth Military District of the Mindanao guerrilla force. Colonel McClish took them to the home of Governor Panaez, the "Coconut King of the Philippines," for dinner. They sat down at a table with silverware, tablecloths, napkins, and a meal as good as anything in the United States. An eleven-piece orchestra serenaded them. After dinner, McClish gave Shifty a cigar.

The next day, McClish took them all on a long horseback ride to the town of

Gingoog. The radio there was out, so they rode on to a guerrilla outpost in Anakan. From there they sent two messages. One went to the office of the Commander in Chief of U.S. Forces in Australia, General Douglas MacArthur; the other went to the Marine Corps' Australian HQ. Making contact with their headquarters was a glorious moment of achievement. No immediate reply was received. In the evening, after enjoying a fine meal in a house with electric lights, Shifty took a moment to remember. That day, May 6, marked the one-year anniversary of the surrender on Corregidor. He and the others gave thanks. The next day the local Chinese community donated clothing for the Americans, and just in time, too, since a number of parties and fiestas awaited. Shifty and the team attended one in the Chinese area before attending a ball celebrating the coronation of a queen. Shifty got a laugh out of wearing a clean pair of coveralls to a formal ball with women in gowns and men in white evening coats.

On May 10, Lieutenant Commander McCoy and Major Mellnik left the team and proceeded to the headquarters of the Tenth Military District in Misamis, under the command of Colonel Wendell W. Fertig. All of the guerrillas on the island reported to Colonel Fertig, including McClish's division. McCoy and Mellnik hoped to send more messages to Australia and to inquire about transportation off Mindanao. After they departed, Ed Dyess went after them. Colonel McClish induced the remainder of the escapees to help him run his operation. He promoted each member of the team and assigned them jobs. Shifty became Major Austin Shofner of the 110th Division in the Army of the United States. He set about organizing the guerrillas of Mindanao to fight the occupiers.

MANILA JOHN HAD BEEN ENJOYING HIMSELF IN AUSTRALIA. ALTHOUGH HE DIDN'T say much about it, he did usually have to spend part of each payday paying off debts incurred within the last pay period.[13] His buddy J.P. had caused a stir back in March when he allowed his enlistment to expire.[14] Morgan had cashed himself out completely, all $452 worth, which some in the 1/7 must have assumed would be spent on a big drunk. J.P. had a reputation for getting into trouble and for sending his hefty poker winnings home to his wife, Katy. J.P.'s close friends knew, though, that Morgan's parents were in desperate circumstances. A mining accident had completely disabled his father; his mother had to provide full-time care of her husband. J.P. may have mustered out of the corps because he was considering going home to help. His steady pay as a sergeant, however, had won out and he reenlisted the next day.

Manila's own relationship with the corps changed soon thereafter, when he received a temporary citation for the Congressional Medal of Honor on May 7, signed by Admiral Chester Nimitz, Commander in Chief of the U.S. Pacific Fleet. He did not know much about it—his CO would have told him it was America's highest award for valor—nor did he appreciate how it would change his life. Two weeks later, on the parade ground of the Seventh Marines' camp, the regiment held an awards ceremony attended by General Vandegrift, the former CO of the 1st Marine Division, as well as the new CO, General Rupertus. The month of May heralded the onset of winter in the Southern Hemisphere and it grew quite chilly. Still without their Class A Marine Corps uniforms, the men wore the rough wool Eisenhower jackets with their 1st Marine Division patch sewn on the shoulder.

Sergeant John Basilone's years of service had made the forms and conventions of parades, reviews, and inspections familiar. This time, however, he stood not with his platoon but with a small group who were to receive important decorations. Manila knew most of the guys. Mitchell Paige, who had been a sergeant in charge of a machine-gun squad on the Canal, had been in the corps longer than John and they knew each other well. Paige was also about to receive the Medal of Honor for his actions up near the Matanikau River. Colonel Puller strode up and everyone snapped to attention and saluted. Chesty looked at Mitch and said, "Sergeant Paige, you're senior here, oh yes, now you're a looie." Paige had been promoted to second lieutenant before leaving on the Canal and his officer bars were on his collar. With a smile, Chesty said, "You'll always be a sergeant to me. You know the backbone of the Corps is the noncommissioned officer." Turning to John, he said, "Sergeant Basilone, you'll march next to Paige;" then he lined up the others.[15]

When the men of the Seventh Regiment were assembled, Lieutenant Colonel Puller led John, Mitchell Paige, and a handful of others out across the field, followed by the Stars and Stripes and the guidon of the Marine Corps. Chesty, striding along with his oddly shaped chest out, had received a Gold Star in lieu of his third Navy Cross. He was proud that so many of his men in the 1/7 were now being recognized. Billie Joe Crumpton was decorated with the Navy Cross. Cecil Evans had a Silver Star pinned on his breast.[16] J. P. Morgan and others also received Silver Stars, although not necessarily for the same battle as Basilone.

At the ceremony, Lieutenant Mitchell Paige received the Medal of Honor first.[17] Vandegrift read the citation for Platoon Sergeant John Basilone "for extraordinary heroism . . . above and beyond the call of duty," then hung the medal around his neck. Vandegrift told John it was a "great pleasure to deliver the medal" to him in the name of the president of the United States of America.[18]

Official Marine Corps reporters and photographers roamed at will, capturing the moment.[19] They lined up the four winners of the Medal of Honor from

Guadalcanal—Paige and Basilone standing next to General Archer Vandegrift and Colonel Mike Edson—for a photo entitled "Medal of Honor Men."* Edson didn't have his medal with him, so he borrowed a ribbon from Paige. The photographers took a picture of the men shaking hands. They staged a photo of the medal being hung around Manila's neck, this time placing the camera at ground level, looking up between the outstretched arms. They took a portrait of Basilone, looking serious, with the blue and white ribbon around his neck.

Back with his platoon, though, Manila loosened up. While the cameramen snapped photos, the reporters asked questions and got their facts right. They read the citations, too. Everybody had to give their hometown addresses. The reporter who wrote a piece about Private Cecil Evans's Silver Star got good quotes from Basilone, who was only too happy to attest to his friend's courage under fire. "What a guy Evans is. He's only nineteen, has curly hair, and runs around barefoot all the time. We call him Peck's Bad Boy."[20]

To another reporter, John called Dog Company "the best damn company in the world."[21] The reporter quickly realized the "facts bear him out," for the company "lays claim to being the most decorated company." Along with John's medal, Dog Company had three Navy Crosses, four Silver Stars, and eleven Letters of Commendation. All the Navy Crosses went to privates first class like Crumpton. Sergeant J. P. Morgan got a Letter of Commendation from Admiral William Halsey. Captain Rodgers, the CO of Dog Company, received a Silver Star. The 1/7 had a commendation from General Vandegrift: their division had earned a Presidential Unit Citation.

At the reporter's behest, all the men of John's platoon gathered around a .30-caliber Browning water-cooled machine gun. John displayed his medal, Billie Joe Crumpton showed his Navy Cross, and Cecil Evans displayed his Silver Star.[22] John's medal sat in an oblong box. From a powder blue ribbon with white stars hung a large star-shaped medallion. Inset into the medallion was a strange image: a woman with a shield shoving a guy holding some snakes. All the other guys gawked on cue and the camera flashed.

Before the ceremony ended on May 17, Colonel Chesty Puller saluted Basilone. Of all the hoopla on this day, looking the old warrior in the eye and snapping his fingertips to the edge of his brow meant the most to Manila.[23]

*　　*　　*

---

*During World War II both official and unofficial accounts referred to the "winners of the Medal of Honor." Since the war the men who wear it have mounted a concerted effort to change it to the "recipients of the Medal of Honor." The Congressional Medal of Honor, they believe, is not a prize won in a contest.

THE SHAKEDOWN CRUISE OF MICHEEL'S NEW CARRIER, YORKTOWN, GOT OFF TO A hilarious start. The tugs pushed the great ship away from the dock on the morning of May 21 with all of the crew assembled on the flight deck. The bugler began to sound the signals relating to the ritual when an officer grabbed the microphone suddenly and yelled, "You dopey no good sonofabitch! What in the hell did you do that for?"[24] He continued to berate the bugler at some length as everyone on the flight deck began to laugh. The officer doing the yelling was Captain J. J. Clark, the commander of Yorktown. This display proved the word already going around about "Jocko" Clark: he demanded perfection and woe to any sailor who failed to provide it.

Yorktown steamed south for Trinidad later that day, escorted by two destroyers and a submarine because the German U-boats had not been eliminated from the waters off the eastern seaboard. Trouble started a few days later, when Captain Clark came down to the flight deck hopping mad. Unlike most senior navy officers, Jocko Clark had logged a fair amount of time on a carrier flight deck during his early career. He believed his flight deck had not been "spotted" correctly; in other words, his planes had not been positioned efficiently, and he began shouting instructions to the plane pushers on how he wanted his planes spotted.[25] For the next few days, the flight deck officers had their hands full dealing with the captain's demands. Yorktown had two small tractors for use in pushing planes—a novel idea—and these were used to check Clark's flight deck spot against their own.

Since all of the planes were spotted on the stern and took off toward the bow, the deck spot determined the order in which the different types of planes (fighter, bomber, or torpedo) took off. Two other factors mattered, though. Each foot of space saved when creating "the spot," and each minute of time saved while "respotting the deck," made Yorktown a more efficient and more deadly weapon in battle. A few days later, Clark came roaring down from his perch on the island to tell the boys on the flight deck how to do it again. His rounded shoulders and pronounced paunch belied the energy with which he moved. When the captain had it the way he wanted it, he turned to one of his flight deck officers, Lieutenant Henry "Hank" Warren, and said, "Mr. Warren, that's the way to spot a flight deck."

"Joe," Hank Warren asked his assistant, "how much time did that take?"

"About two minutes longer than you, Hank," said Joe.

"How much space did we save?" Hank asked.

The captain's spot, Joe replied, was "eight feet further toward the bow than you were," whereupon Lieutenant Hank Warren faced Jocko Clark. "Captain, I promise never to come up there and try to run that bridge if you'll leave me alone and let me spot the flight deck."[26] After a tense moment, the captain's thick, wide lips broke into a smile. "I promise." The story of Hank getting Jocko to back down was just the kind of juicy story that made it all the way around the ship, even to Mike, who hadn't flown for a few days and wouldn't step into the cockpit for a few more.

Flight operations began in earnest after the ship entered the Gulf of Paria, a large body of water between the island of Trinidad and the coast of Venezuela. The two entrances to the gulf had been blocked with submarine nets, allowing U.S. carriers—and *Yorktown* was one of several new Essex-class carriers preparing for its first combat tour—to focus on testing all of their systems and personnel to the utmost. Mike's flight on May 28, his first in three weeks, was supposed to mark the start of his squadron's final preparation for a combat tour. Instead, it was the beginning of the end of Bombing Six.

The SB2Cs, in Mike's words, "turned out to be a bust. We couldn't get them off the deck. We'd get up into the launch position, the wings would go down, but they wouldn't lock. So we'd have to taxi the plane off . . . to the side of the ship." The next one up might be able to lock its wings, but the plane after that and the one after that couldn't, so the whole launch sequence disintegrated into a mess, as the plane pushers and elevators worked to get the busted ones out of the way. "Most of them never got their wings locked." The ability to fold its wings had been one of the Helldiver's advantages over the Dauntless because it allowed for a tighter deck spot. The sight of four or five men climbing on each wing to weigh it down enough for it to lock, however, failed to inspire confidence.[27]

After a few days of fighting the technology, Captain Clark ordered the Helldivers off his ship. Ray Davis gave Mike the job of going ashore with the faulty planes and seeing what could be done. At an airstrip on Trinidad, Mike and his team spent a week tinkering with the wing-locking mechanism until it worked smoothly. One of the tests they devised involved parking three planes near the SB2Cs and using the propellers to simulate a strong wind. It worked. Even as they were buffeted, the wings snapped down. So they flew back out to the ship, churning through the gulf. The "first time we get in launch position, the wings won't lock down."

Mike was angry at the SB2Cs. He had come to believe the acronym SB2C stood for the plane's rank: Son of a Bitch Second Class. He said nothing as the captain chewed him out, unhappily noting that Clark assumed he had spent the week at a bar instead of working. Clark could not focus on Lieutenant Micheel for long, however. The Helldivers of the bombing and the scouting squadrons revealed other significant flaws. On June 12, a number of them pulled their tail hooks out when they caught the arresting wire upon landing, sending them crashing into the wire barrier—a barrier of last resort that damaged planes and threatened personnel.

Two others developed mechanical trouble and crashed near the ship. Captain Clark expressed his anger in his characteristically blunt style, concluding with, "Kick those things off the ship. I don't want to see any of them on my ship again!" On June 12 he summarily canceled flight operations. His carrier steamed for Trinidad. That night all of the offending SB2Cs were deposited by crane at the airfields. *Yorktown* took off at high speed for Norfolk.

Two weeks after receiving the medal, on June 12, Manila forced himself to write his parents. He described his location as "somewhere where I can enjoy life" so that they would not worry. "I am in the best of health and very happy—for the other day I received the Congressional Medal of Honor. Tell Pop his son is still tough. Tell Don thanks for the prayer they say in school for us."[28] He asked for news about the family and signed off. In the envelope he included a photograph of the medal ceremony. The photo John chose to send showed him wearing his medal and standing next to Billie Joe Crumpton, wearing his Navy Cross.[29]

He received a reply from his parents in late June. They told him that since the news of his medal had broken on June 24, they had been besieged by friends, well-wishers, and reporters and cameramen.[30] Manila's parents, Sal and Dora, included lots of letters. So many of the letters had requested photos of him that Dora had arranged to have a postcard made of him.[31] A lot of the letters came from women whose sons had served on Guadalcanal; they hoped he might have some information about their marines. Sal and Dora sent him copies of the *Raritan Valley News*, which mentioned that Manila John's hometown planned to throw him a big homecoming celebration and also award him a $5,000 bond because, as one headline had it, he had "Held Off Entire Jap Regiment for 3 Days."[32] A huge poster-sized picture of Sergeant John Basilone had been hung on Fifth Avenue in Manhattan. Tony Field, an editor with *Sensation* magazine, had spoken to them about purchasing the life rights to the story of Manila John, to make a movie, pending the approval of John and the USMC.[33]

The news of what was going on back home made him unhappy, even as he and his friend Richard Greer spent the July Fourth holiday with two female friends playing in the snow at a resort called the Australian Alps.[34] When he returned, he wrote his parents again. To all the requests that had been enclosed in the mail to him, he could only apologize with a white lie and say that he had been "kept very busy" since receiving the medal. As for an explanation of why he had been awarded it, he wrote, "I did what any other Marine would have done in my position."[35] He continued.

"I sure would love to come home, but there is still a big job to do over here . . . I'm sending my medal home, so take good care of it." He concluded, "Tell Pop to save some wine for my return." Manila John did not, however, tell his parents the whole truth. Only a few days earlier, he had been found qualified for promotion to gunnery sergeant.[36] With his friend Sergeant Mitch Paige having made the leap to officer, Sergeant Basilone must have felt sure enough of his chances to become very excited. A promotion to the exalted position of "gunny" represented a level of success beyond what he had ever dared to hope. Already, though, another force was at work. His desire to send his new medal home to his parents went unrealized.

When *Yorktown* returned to Norfolk, Bombing Six traded in their SB2Cs for the trusty Dauntless. Other big changes for the carrier's squadrons came from the navy itself. The navy had decided to increase the number of fighters aboard a carrier. America could not continue to lose as many carriers as it had in 1942; more fighters meant more protection from enemy planes. To make room for more Hellcats on *Yorktown*, the scouting squadron was eliminated. The reorganization also recognized that the distinction between bombing and scouting squadrons had existed only in theory, not in practice. While *Yorktown*'s new bombing squadron would be larger than it had been before, it would not be double the size. Some pilots would have to be transferred to other squadrons before the new carrier embarked for the Pacific.

Lieutenant Commander Ray Davis, who had seniority over the officer in command of the scouting squadron, could have chosen to stay with the new Bombing Six. He elected to go ashore and form a new squadron. Mike also went ashore, although in his case the other squadron's flight officer outranked him and elected to stay aboard. Bill Pittman and a few of the other old veterans of Bombing Six opted to go with Ray. They figured their skipper would get them into his new squadron. Once ashore in Norfolk, though, Ray found himself assigned to a desk. Ray and Mike and Bill shared a good laugh about the unexpected turn. Bombing Six had been "tossed to the winds." Mike found himself headed to Bombing Squadron Fourteen, stationed at NAS Wildwood.

In late June 1943, Lieutenant Micheel took a train up the coast a few hundred miles to the village of Rio Grande, not far from the slightly larger town of Wildwood, on the southern tip of New Jersey. He caught a bus past a smelly fish-rendering plant to the base. Located on a long marshy isthmus lined by beaches, NAS Wildwood looked the part of a naval base. Off the runways ran the taxi strips that led to rows of planes parked along the flight line. The giant hangar with its rounded roof had little offices running down either side. In a routine now familiar, he dropped his bags at the BOQ and headed over to report to his squadron commander, Lieutenant Commander Grafton Campbell.

Bombing Fourteen had just begun to exist in fact as well as on paper. Commander Campbell had arrived a few weeks earlier. Pilots had shown up sporadically since then. Mike noticed that his skipper had not yet served in combat. The navy had, however, provided the new squadron with one other seasoned veteran, Lieutenant Harold Buell. Mike knew "Hal" Buell. Hal had been a class or two behind him during pilot training. They had flown together on the second day of the invasion of Guadalcanal, when Mike had gone with Hal's scouting squadron.[37] Hal had spent a few weeks as a member of the Cactus Air Force. Having departed *Enterprise* just as she was struck by bombs on August 24, Buell's group had been forced to land on Guadalcanal. After the Battle of the Eastern Solomons, the group never flew back aboard the carrier. Fighting the Tokyo Express during those crucial days at the end of August and into September, Buell had shipped out before Mike arrived on Cactus in October.

Hardly a day had passed before the navy's new organization caught up with Bombing Fourteen. It merged with Bombing Fifteen to make Bombing Squadron Two. Since neither squadron had had time to develop an identity, the reorganization went smoothly. Campbell promoted his ops officer to executive officer, gave the ops job to Hal Buell, and made Mike his engineering officer. Mike had requested the job because he had already been ops officer and wanted the experience as an engineering officer. His experience wrestling with the SB2C certainly helped. Both Mike and Hal Buell were given a division to lead and the latest version of the Dauntless to fly.

Gregarious and ambitious, Hal Buell began picking the members of his division carefully.[38] He chose those who met his standards for ability and aggressiveness. Although he had bombed the Tokyo Express, Hal badly wanted to sink a flattop and earn the Navy Cross that came with it. He also considered the selection of his wingmen as a matter of survival. Mike noticed that Hal's division became something of a clique unto themselves. When new pilots transferred in, Hal would not take them. He taught his pilots that good dive-bombers didn't drop bombs. Good dive-bombers took their bombs all the way down to fifteen hundred feet and "fired" their bombs into the imperial ships.[39] Commander Campbell, nicknamed "Soupy," liked what he saw of Hal Buell. Buell, however, disliked serving under a skipper who had only just completed flight training and had not been in combat.[40]

Having earned the Navy Cross at Midway, Mike certainly had the admiration of the ensigns in his squadron. The squadron commander, who had Mike's file, would have seen Ray Davis's recommendation that Mike be given command of his own squadron. Had Lieutenant Micheel pulled some rank, few would have looked askance at it. Mike admired Hal's dedication to the mission and the esprit de corps he instilled, but that was not his way. Mike worked with whoever was assigned to him.

All the men in Micheel's division had just come from flight school. The ensigns were as full of themselves as any young group of naval aviators could be expected to be. They wanted to live life to the fullest, whether in the air or in the arms of the young ladies of Wildwood, New Jersey.[41] The pilots attended ground school. The ensigns accepted the necessity of polishing their communication procedures, enjoyed the physical training "to keep us in shape for our nocturnal recreation," but bitched heartily about the boring training films on such riveting topics as "IBP in the OS2U," and "Recognition."

Their division leader decided that his philosophy of training was "you start at the bottom and work up." When the training program began in earnest on June 30, the green pilots found themselves practicing their formation flying before moving on to wingovers, stalls, and other maneuvers that demonstrated a pilot's ability to control his aircraft. They soaked it all up because they loved to fly. His students wanted to get past subjects like navigation to practice tactical maneuvers like dive-bombing, gunnery, and carrier landings.

The ensigns of Bombing Two took every opportunity to zoom over the white sandy beaches bordering Wildwood. It made the women on the beach nervous. As one pilot put it, "There's nothing like scattering half-nude pulchritude." The young pilots took a perverse pride in frequently generating angry phone calls from the town's mayor to Skipper Campbell. If they had one concern, the ensigns feared the war would end before they entered the fray.

When it came to talk of combat, Mike emphasized two skills above all others. He taught them how to conserve gas in a variety of ways—by leaning out the fuel mixture of the engine, by regulating their speed, and so forth. Husbanding their fuel was not something one did in difficult situations. According to Lieutenant Micheel, it was a way of life. During their training flights out over the Atlantic, he also pushed them to read the waves on the water. A good pilot could look at the waves on the water and understand the strength and direction of the prevailing wind. Properly estimating the effect of the wind on his flight path made it possible for a pilot to find his way back to the carrier's deck. Imbuing the young aviators with the bitter lessons of experience was exactly what the navy expected Lieutenants Micheel and Buell to do. While Buell might speak freely of his experiences in combat, Mike wanted his students to concentrate on wave reading and fuel conservation.

Having two such experienced airmen in his squadron could make it difficult for the commander of Bombing Two. As Campbell prepared to take the entire squadron up and practice operating as a unit, he instructed his division leaders that the squadron would fly in a stepped-up formation. This meant that every plane behind Campbell's plane would fly a few feet above and to one side. The normally quiet Lieutenant Micheel voiced concern over the order. His question would have surprised the skipper, since he had recently been trained to fly in a stepped-up formation. Mike said, "Well, I just came from the fleet, and we flew step down. They don't fly stepped up anymore . . . they fly step down." Scouting Six had flown stepped down in the Battle of Midway.[42]

Flying stepped up or stepped down had to do with how the squadron protected itself from attacks by Zeros. Squadrons flew in a V of Vs in order that the guns of all the airplanes were in the best position from which to defend the other aircraft. The relative positions of the planes also had everything to do with how they maintained their tight formation. Since the start of the war, combat pilots had learned that if they flew stepped up, their leaders were below them. When things got tricky, Mike explained, "you never knew where you were when you were over the top of the guy." If you flew below the plane in front of you, however, "you always had him in sight. So that was the way we went."

Mike failed to anticipate that his comments called into question his skipper's ability. Campbell's temper flared. He had graduated from Annapolis. The blood in his veins ran Navy Blue. Micheel was a Johnny-come-lately, a ninety-day wonder. Campbell pulled an instruction manual off his shelf and proffered it. "Show me where you're flying step down." Mike sputtered, knowing without looking what the book said, "Well, they never change those [books] during the war; there wasn't anybody to work on them. There wasn't any grand place where you sent in tactics" to be adopted officially; "they just evolved and if they worked you picked them up. But there wasn't anybody reprinting the tactic books." The disparaging remarks about tactic books might have reminded Campbell of the nickname pilots like Mike had for graduates of Annapolis: "trade school boys." Lieutenant Micheel concluded with a restatement of his experience. Campbell was adamant. Bombing Two flew stepped up.

On July 1, Private First Class Eugene Sledge left Mobile on a train to Atlanta, Georgia, and reported to the commanding officer, Marine Detachment, Navy Training Unit, at the Georgia School of Technology.[43] Eugene's long wait had at last ended and his enthusiasm knew no bounds. The graceful arches of the brick and stone buildings on the campus of Georgia Tech made an impression. Students filled the walks and hallways even in high summer, as Tech had adopted a three-semester schedule to speed students through their courses and thus ease the nation's manpower shortage.[44]

Lieutenant Holmes, the commanding officer of the marine detachment, informed Sledge that he was a private, not a private first class, and assigned him to Harrison Dorm. A modern brick building on the southeastern edge of campus and near the Navy Armory, Harrison appealed to him because it housed only marines.[45] Eugene liked being issued "navy bedding," with which to make up his bunk, and being measured for his uniform. The first rumors he heard about his course work, however, made him wonder if he would have to ask his father to call his friend at the Marine Corps and "cuss him out." Eugene had not come to Tech to study engineering.

The next day, Eugene came close to being kicked out of the V-12 program. The doctor examining him determined that he was underweight. Private Sledge insisted he had just been ill and he would soon regain the weight. The doc passed him. Pleased with his adroit handling of the problem, Eugene began eating more. He wanted to measure up. "Don't let anyone tell you that the Marine Corps has lowered its requirements," he wrote his mother. "If you look at the doc like you aren't feeling well, out you go." The prospect of putting on the uniform of "the best outfit in the world" inspired him to have stationery printed with a Marine Corps logo above his name and to write his friend Sid Phillips.

The demands of service, however, lagged somewhat. The officers in charge of the Navy ROTC Armory plainly had their hands full with Sledge's class, the first class of students for the V-12 program. They had to order the lives of almost a thousand students from the navy, as well as about three hundred marines, and fit them in with the traditional ROTC, or Reserve Officers Training Program. Putting all of these together in the midst of a crowded campus took time.

After a week, the semester began. Reveille awakened the students at 0545. They fell out for calisthenics, led by a navy chief petty officer; then their routine became like that of college students attending Georgia Tech. The steam whistle signaled the class periods every hour from seven fifty-five a.m. to four fifty-five p.m. The V-12 program assigned its students courses in physics and other sciences. Sledge complained about having to take physics and biology, though he liked the economics class on his schedule. After class, they held drill on their parade ground, Rose Bowl Field, on the opposite corner of campus from his dorm. Curfew on military time began at 1930 during the week and the lights went out in Harrison Dorm at 2330.

Attending college in civilian clothes irritated Sledge. He had worn a uniform at Marion Military Institute. Eugene fretted about the arrival of his Marine Corps uniform in part because he and his friends were occasionally asked why they had not signed up to fight. Such questions set him off like a firecracker. Anyone who asked found out in no uncertain terms that Eugene regarded men who wanted to stay out of the war as "yellow." A uniform would solve the problem. As he put it in a letter to his mother, "I'm tired of acting like a marine and dressing like a civilian."

Eugene was surprised and even a bit disappointed at the amount of liberty he enjoyed. Putting it to good use, he put on his sport coat and went walking in downtown Atlanta. Although he found it cold, he liked the city. Its sedate pace and social order had not been disturbed by hordes of workers, like Mobile, where they filled the streets, shops, and restaurants. He found a place that offered Hershey bars for sale—not many shops did—and visited it most every day.

Gene's classmates soon came up with a plan to escape the regimentation of the V-12 program. On the weekends, they pooled their money to rent a hotel room, where they threw a big party and got gloriously drunk and perhaps romantically entangled. Eugene skipped these affairs. He read a great deal, munching on homemade chocolate or one of the other treats his mother sent him every few days. He also wrote his parents every few days. As usual for a man of eighteen years, Sledge had an easier time writing his mother his true feelings than speaking to his father directly, so he addressed them to her. She responded in kind. Since she had also purchased him a subscription to the Mobile newspaper, which he read avidly, they carried on a conversation about their respective lives and that of their country. Most of Eugene's letters also contained requests of some kind, usually for treats and frequently for items he could not find or not afford: a set of clean hand towels, or to have his film rolls developed.

He loved everything about being a marine and wanted more of it. He enjoyed drilling after class, requesting additional assignments, and pushing himself to excel. Although not "one of the boys," Eugene was adept at listening to the others, particularly those in authority, and picking up some of the habits and customs of "salty" marines. The lore of the corps fascinated him. He sought out stories about his corps' glorious defense of Wake Island. He watched the documentary about the Battle of Midway shot by the famed Hollywood director John Ford. Ford's cameramen had been located on Midway when the attack had come.

Ford's cameras caught marines in pillboxes firing .50-caliber machine guns at enemy planes zooming overhead. The explosions of the bombs and the destruction they wrought appeared in full color, as the narrator told of the enemy bombs that had destroyed the hospital and chapel deliberately. Other cameras had been aboard the carriers. The navy pilots, dressed in khaki uniforms with yellow life jackets and cloth helmets, smiled at the audience. The narrator pointed out the "seven meatballs," or imperial battle flags, adorning Jimmy Thach's plane. The film introduced the audience to the throaty buzz of a Dauntless launching off the end of a flight deck, its red dive flaps slightly extended, and the high whine of an enemy plane falling out of the sky. Building to a grand conclusion, the camera panned through the black smoke on Midway, first finding parts of enemy planes littering the airfield. The soundtrack gave way to "My Country, 'Tis of Thee," the choir singing "let Freedom ring," until Old Glory appeared high above the smoke. The choir let the last word ring: "Amen."

Pride in the corps ran rampant through the marines of Harrison Dorm. When the instruction failed to satisfy, though, Eugene went looking for Civil War sites. He took a friend to a battlefield at Stone Mountain. Another weekend, Eugene visited the Atlanta Cyclorama, a mixture of art and music designed to transport visitors back to July 22, 1864, an eventful day in the Battle of Atlanta. He loved it.

A picture from his older brother, though, was all that it took to ruin his V-12 program. Edward sent him a photo of himself with the tank he commanded. It reminded Eugene that Edward was in the war and he was not. It reminded Eugene of the promise his parents had extracted from him. Dr. and Mrs. Sledge were plainly worried by the thinly veiled denunciations of the V-12 program they began to find in their youngest son's letters. When pressed by his parents, he admitted he "had a wonderful opportunity," but he insisted, "I am a Marine now, it's still pretty irksome to be sitting in school. All of us feel the same. So don't get all upset. Every Marine here will be glad when he gets to P.I. [Parris Island], but until then, we are doing what's been assigned us."

BASILONE COULD NOT KEEP THE NEWS OF THE EXCITEMENT BREWING IN RARITAN, New Jersey, to himself. He would have known something was amiss when photographers staged some more photos. One required him to put on his dirty dungarees and his helmet. While he stood pointing off camera toward nothing, the new CO of the 1st Division, General Rupertus, and his aide, both clad in new uniforms, coolly observed. Eventually Manila would have been told that the big splash his story had made back home had attracted the attention of the U.S. Treasury Department. The Treasury raised money to fund the war effort by selling war bonds. In order to get people to purchase bonds, the department had begun to hold war bond rallies with famous people. The Hollywood stars attracted large audiences, but they needed some service personnel as well. Platoon Sergeant John Basilone would join them for a series of rallies known as a War Bond Loan Drive.

The orders came through on July 22, 1943, ordering him to Brisbane for shipment stateside.[46] With time for one last bash, Manila could not wait for the liberty bus. He started drinking at the slop chute on base. With a load of beer, John started clowning around, putting his cap on sideways and pretending he was Napoleon.[47] His friend Richard gave him a hand getting his tie on straight so that he could make it past the guards at the gate and into town. His friends in Charlie and Dog companies wanted to do something for him, so they applied for a furlough for him. They also chipped in to buy him a watch. The donations totaled the princely sum of $200—much of that would have come from the poker winnings of his buddy J. P. Morgan. Time ran out before they could get the watch, so J.P. gave him the money and told him to buy himself one stateside. Manila departed from Brisbane, Queensland, on July 25. To his great luck, his buddy Private First Class Stephen Helstowski, who had served in his platoon before being evacuated from Guadalcanal, joined him on the journey.[48]

SHIFTY'S LIFE AS A GUERRILLA COULD NOT HAVE STARTED BETTER. COLONEL McClish promoted him to deputy chief of staff and made him the operations officer for the 110th Division. Major Shofner traveled throughout the division area, encompassing four provinces in northern Mindanao. By boats known as bancas, in canoes, on horseback, in a car whose engine burned alcohol, he met the leaders of the four understrength regiments. A party, fiesta, or dance required his attendance most every day. The Filipino people and an array of wealthy plantation owners supplied the cadre of U.S. military men with shelter, information, and a fabulous abundance of food. Shifty described the dishes of each meal in glowing detail in his diary.

"In all provinces except Davao," Shofner noted during his inspections, "the Japanese are compelled to stay in a small fortified area surrounded by our forces." While the enemy forces numbered above ten thousand in Davao, Shifty's area of operations held less than one thousand. Unlike Shofner's men, though, the IJA were well trained, disciplined, and well armed. The five thousand farmers and villagers who made up the four regiments of the 110th Division had hidden two thousand small-caliber weapons, most in poor condition. While the guerrillas harassed the enemy garrisons in the major cities, they focused on maintaining peace and order in the areas under their control.

Becoming a successful guerrilla leader, he realized, was not going to be easy.

"There are a thousand obstacles to every task." He saw great potential. His division controlled four landing fields, two large docks, and great swaths of coastline. The division's seven launches and many sailing bancas plied the waters throughout the Mindanao Sea and the Agusan River, the largest river on the island. Most of the road network had been opened to its one diesel truck and four alcohol trucks. One of the region's lakes, Shifty thought, would make a perfect seaplane base.

Shifty's friends Hawkins and Dobervich, and the other members of the escape team, had also been promoted. Their assignments placed them in distant villages, but they saw one another often. McCoy, Mellnik, and Ed Dyess remained at the headquarters of the Tenth Military District, which commanded Shifty's 110th Division and four other divisions. The district took responsibility for all of Mindanao and a few small islands around it. It fielded about twenty thousand men. With only ten thousand rifles and other small arms, each of its soldiers shared his weapon with the others. The Tenth Military District trained its soldiers for war but more frequently used them as a police force. It printed currency that was accepted throughout the island—it had a favorable exchange rate against the money printed by the occupiers. The officers at the headquarters, and those like Shifty at the division level, presided over marriages or imprisoned criminals instead of leading strikes against enemy troops.

Throughout the summer of 1943, Major Shofner and his cohorts played a game of cat and mouse with the enemy on Mindanao. The emperor's soldiers might cause the Americans to move their headquarters, but the enemy never got close. The locals made sure "their army" had plenty of advance warning. The guerrilla officers built their organization as best they could. They spied on the enemy and provided intelligence reports to Tenth Military Headquarters so that it could be radioed back to Australia.

On August 2, Colonel McClish returned from a visit to the headquarters. He brought with him new shoes, socks, underwear, razor blades, cigarettes, and a small amount of ammunition for their rifles and pistols. He told Shifty and the others that the supplies had been dropped off by a U.S. submarine. The thought of it was thrilling. Next McClish revealed that the submarine had picked up McCoy, Mellnik, and Dyess and taken them to Australia. Before departing for freedom, McCoy and Mellnik had given McClish some general statement about helping Shifty and the others; Captain Ed Dyess had written a letter promising to get them out as well. For Shifty Shofner, it was a moment when he found out who his friends were.

LIEUTENANT HOLMES AND HIS NCOS HANDED OUT USMC UNIFORMS TO THE V-12 students on July 20 and Eugene Sledge was thrilled. His new seabag contained full sets of khaki, dungaree, and dress green uniforms. He liked the look of the khaki and figured it would look even better when he got some starch ironed into it. He asked his lieutenant about the dress blue uniform and was told that while blues would not be issued, a marine could purchase a set. Eugene immediately started looking for a set, setting aside money from his pay for it. Later, he put on his "greens," or formal uniform, and took some pictures for his family.

Every day he liked being in the marines more than the day before, marching through close order drills, attending the morning and evening flag ceremonies. At night he studied his *Marine's Handbook* and longed for the day when he'd get his hands on a rifle. He had no interest in smoking, drinking, or carousing. Every Sunday found him attending the North Avenue Presbyterian Church. The cakes his mother sent him allowed him to gain the weight he needed. With his thanks he sent her a USMC service pin for her lapel. He wore the corps' eagle, globe, and anchor with pride.

His uniform eliminated the embarrassment he had felt about being in civilian clothes. While walking in downtown Atlanta, though, he happened to meet a marine. By the way the man dressed, Sledge could tell this marine was a real "salt," or someone who had had lots of overseas duty. When the salt asked Sledge about his own duty, Sledge grew embarrassed as he explained the V-12 program. He figured "the only reason he doesn't laugh is because I am a Marine, and he knows I don't like my duty, any more than he likes hearing about it." When Sledge got back to the dorm, he read a letter from his mother, who was sick at the thought of his brother Edward being sent overseas and into combat. Her concern for Edward's fate irked him. She also expressed concern about her youngest son's attitude toward school.

Eugene understood his battle was with his parents. He loved them, respected them, and enjoyed their company. He appreciated all that they did for him. He treasured the picture he had of his parents and himself on the porch. Eugene had promised them he would complete the V-12 program, and keeping it was important to him. He earned a 100 percent on his first biology quiz.

The promise, however, frustrated him. His enormous drive, intellect, and commitment to his beliefs warred with his filial duty. Gene's mind was fixed on a specific goal: serving in a line company in combat. By August, his anxiety was running at a fever pitch and he began lashing out at easy targets. When a friend from Mobile joined the Seabees, Eugene opined, "The Marines consider them as a bunch of laborers and I've been told they are a pretty crummy lot."* He criticized the press coverage of ma-

---

*A Seabee was a member of a navy construction battalion and took his name from the unit's initials, CB.

rines' contributions to the war effort. "It is a known fact that MacArthur left the 4th Marines as a rearguard in the Philippines. All but 70 were killed," he asserted, and the survivors had become prisoners. He assailed both the United States Congress and the Roosevelt administration for forcing his beloved USMC to accept draftees. "The politicians, and Army, and Navy are still striving, as they have for 169 years, to pull us under & lower our standards."

SID PHILLIPS HAD DRAWN GUARD DUTY IN LATE AUGUST. HE AND SOME OTHERS from the mortar platoon found themselves guarding the Fourth General Hospital in Melbourne. They lived indoors on real beds with clean sheets. Middle-aged Australian ladies cooked them wonderful meals and set the dishes out on platters of china. Pitchers of whole milk dotted the long table. The ladies took such good care of them, "we called them all mother and they loved it."

The mortar platoon rotated among a number of duties, including guarding criminally dangerous military prisoners who were in shackles on the hospital's fourth floor. The main entrance to the hospital was the busiest place for a marine on guard, since every doctor and every nurse wore an officer's insignia and therefore compelled the guard to snap from "parade rest" to "present arms." Sid found he could do his shift of four hours of robotic movements without difficulty. Guarding the hospital was good duty.

One morning while guarding the front door, Sid watched six khaki-colored staff cars pull up at the curb.[49] Army generals and navy admirals began climbing out. Something big was happening. First Lady Eleanor Roosevelt stepped onto the curb wearing the uniform of an army WAC.* Sid snapped to attention, presenting arms, and "popping the leather as loud as I could." His drill instructor from Parris Island would have been proud. Roosevelt approached. Sid thought of the comedy routine on the Canal, "My wife Eleanor hates war," as she stopped in front of him. Her eyes came even with his. "Young man, are you a marine?"

"Yes, ma'am."

"Were you on Guadalcanal?"

"Yes, ma'am."

"Are you being well fed?"

"Yes, ma'am."

"Are you being well cared for?"

---

*WAC stands for Women's Auxiliary Corps, which was connected to the army.

"Yes, ma'am."

"What state are you from?"

"Alabama," came the reply, ringing with pride. The First Lady smiled and said, "I should have known." An officer held the door open and the official party swept inside. Private First Class Phillips "remained stone faced and at present arms until all the brass had passed by. I came back to order arms and parade rest. Then I noticed I was actually slightly quivering."

THE TRAINING SCHEDULE FOR BOMBING TWO OUT ON THE JERSEY COAST WAS rigorous but not intense in the late summer of 1943. Micheel's division of Dauntlesses might fly two or three times on any given day, but there were plenty of days when they did not fly at all. Even including the hours spent in ground school, the schedule left some time for fun.

A lot of the young men came to enjoy living life at high velocity. Hal Buell, by virtue of his seniority and his natural inclinations, became a leader of the wild bunch. He and some of the men in his squadron rented a house off base they dubbed the Snake Ranch. When not scheduled for duty, Hal's division held parties at the ranch, inviting every eligible young woman they could find. Having a bit of fun with naval lingo, one of the snake ranchers described their parties as "a kind of ground school" where "the student mingled shoulder to shoulder with the instructor."[50] Not every ensign got invited to "sit in on the seminars and even to work in the lab," so some pilots made sure that "every night . . . the wolves of Bombing Two sent their howls echoing through the streets and by-ways of Wildwood."[51] The pun, intended, played on the squadron's logo, a wolf named Vertigo.

The owner of the nice hotel in Wildwood often threw parties or dances for the young officers of the NAS Wildwood. The daughter of the owner of the hotel, Mary Jane, began to date one of the pilots of Bombing Two. Mary Jane asked her boyfriend to bring along some of his friends to meet some of hers, and before long a number of Bombing Two pilots hung out at the hotel bar. Mike went a few times. That's where he met a pretty girl named Jean Miller.

Jean worked for the Quartermaster Corps as an accountant in the Navy Yard in South Philadelphia. She came to Wildwood on the weekends. She had trouble getting Mike out on the dance floor from the very beginning, but they began to see one another on the weekends. Her train would get in late on Friday, so they usually met at eight p.m. They usually went to see their friends at the hotel bar; then Mike would take her home on the trolley. "We'd sit on the front porch in the swing," until

Mike looked at his watch and noticed that he had to run to catch the last trolley. By the end of August the two spent their Saturdays and Sundays together. Jean's grandmother's house was about a block and a half from the beach. Jean's mother and her uncle and aunt were also often there, along with her grandmother. Mike enjoyed being with them. Wildwood had a boardwalk like Atlantic City's famous boardwalk, offering all sorts of entertainment and food stands, because the area was a premier vacation destination. It was easy to have fun.

Jean asked her boyfriend to take her up in an airplane. All her girlfriends had been up. Mike was not enthusiastic about the idea. It was against regulations. He tried to argue that he was not qualified to fly the type of aircraft her friends had ridden in. This got him nowhere. "She pestered me." He told her he did not want to do it. Eventually, though, he relented. One Sunday afternoon he took her out to the flight line and said, "There's your airplane." It was an SNJ. She had expected a plane with a door in the fuselage, as her friends had described. Mike said he had not been checked out in the plane she described, the twin-engine SMB. "The crewman gave her a parachute to put on her and she said, 'What do I do?'"

"Climb on the wing." She looked up at the wing and then shot him a peeved look. She could not get up there herself. The crewman gave her a boost up and onto the wing. "What do I do now?"

"The seat's back there," he said. The wing, however, did not extend quite as far back as the rear cockpit. She could not step into it. To get into the rear seat of the SNJ required the use of footholds and handholds. The parachute hanging off her made it tricky. The crewman gave her a hand and Jean made it into the backseat. When Mike at last came over to explain to her how to buckle herself in and what to do in case of— She cut him off. "Forget it. If you go down, I'll go down . . . don't bother telling me what to do." After they took off Jean found she could not close her canopy, which made it rather windy. All of her friends had ridden in a nice plane with a door. It was the last time Jean asked Mike for a plane ride.

THE ARRIVAL OF ONE HUNDRED VETERANS OF THE BATTLE OF GUADALCANAL INTO Los Angeles on August 25 caught the attention of a reporter for the *Seahorse*, a publication of the navy's Small Craft Training Center. Interviewing the marines brought the reporter to Manila John. "To *Seahorse* interviewers, Sergeant Basilone was courteous, although a trifle flustered at all the attention. He is the sort one finds in thousands of high schools across the country—husky, friendly, good company."[52] The reporter asked to see his citation for the Medal of Honor, which Manila produced.

During the interview, John realized he had not read the citation, so he did so for the first time.[53] When asked about "the Jap as a fighting man," he replied, "they're stocky, wiry fighters and they fight for keeps."

Once he got through the *Seahorse* interview and the Marine Corps processing system, John immediately sent his mother a telegram. It was one sentence: "Please wire 50 dollars immediately."[54] The money helped him visit Hollywood the next night. As he walked into the Jade, he saw a girl with flowers in her hair walking out and talked her into staying a while longer. Dorothy worked in Long Beach and they had a fun night.[55] The next morning, he left for a marine base outside of San Diego called Camp Elliott.[56] The officer he met when he reached Camp Elliott may have mentioned that most every day for the past week the Marine Corps Headquarters in Washington, D.C., had telegrammed, asking for information about his arrival.[57]

In a lucky coincidence, he found his younger brother George stationed at Elliott as well. George served with the 4th Marine Division. The two brothers spent two days palling around together.[58] George knew a lot more about what awaited John and could give his older brother, "Bass," the scoop. Reporters had interviewed all the members of his family, his friends, and his former employers and written articles about him. The leaders of Raritan had gotten together to hold Basilone Day. The county judge, head of the organizing committee, promised a $5,000 bond for John and "a roaring welcome—loud enough to echo in Tokyo."[59] According to George, "the town is too small to hold the welcome for you, so they are planning to have it in Duke's Park."[60] Duke's Park meant the grounds of the vast estate of the heiress Doris Duke. All of Raritan, Somerville, and the surrounding area wanted to celebrate their hometown hero, whose Medal of Honor "rated a salute from all officers, including General MacArthur."[61]

On the thirtieth Basilone received his orders. He was to be transferred "immediately by air" to the Marine Barracks, Navy Yard, for "temporary duty" with the USMC's Public Relations Division.[62] The Marine Corps prohibited him "from making any statements to the Press or Radio" and directed him "to maintain proper decorum." He was given a generous per diem of $6 a day. He placed a phone call to Dorothy over in Long Beach but missed her.[63] He had a plane to catch. It left that afternoon and he landed in Washington, D.C., the next morning at ten thirty a.m. A car raced him to the Navy Yard by eleven a.m. on August 31.

IN EARLY SEPTEMBER, THE WOLVES OF BOMBING TWO FLEW THEMSELVES UP THE East Coast to their next duty station, NAS Quonset Point, in Rhode Island. Located on a peninsula in Narragansett Bay near the small town of North Kingstown, Quonset Point would host Bombing Two as well as the squadrons of fighters and torpedo planes that comprised Air Group Two. Having honed their skills at the individual and squadron levels, the pilots now practiced working with the whole team even as they began to practice for their first carrier landings. The necessity of creating an air group that functioned as a team had been one of the lessons learned by the *Enterprise* staff on August 24, 1942, in the carrier battle near Guadalcanal. The first occasion for Bombing Two to fly with the other squadrons proved fun for Mike. As directed, the squadron flew in a stepped-up formation. The other squadrons did not. The air group commander, a veteran of carrier battles, came to see them after they landed. "What are you guys doing?!" he asked. Bombing Two flew stepped down from then on. Lieutenant Commander Campbell had to eat a little crow, but he did not hold it against Mike.

AFTER A MONTH OF BEING THE DEPUTY CHIEF OF STAFF OF A GUERRILLA FORCE, Shifty Shofner wanted to do more. He wanted weapons and equipment sent from Australia so that he could lead the guerrillas in attacks against the Japanese. These attacks would not defeat the enemy troops, he knew. Shofner believed the Tenth Army Group on Mindanao, however, could force the Japanese to station two divisions there to protect its hold. The Japanese would have fewer troops available elsewhere; the Filipinos would be inspired and remain allies of America. The man standing in Shifty's way was not Colonel Wendell Fertig but General Douglas MacArthur. MacArthur believed that a large guerrilla raid would only provoke the Japanese into harming thousands of Filipinos, most of whom were farmers armed with machetes. MacArthur wanted them to be spies. He also wanted Fertig's men to give the Filipinos hope of eventual freedom, so MacArthur sent them lots of matchbooks emblazoned with his likeness and the words "I Shall Return." Austin Shofner believed that MacArthur refused to use the guerrillas because he, the general, found these men to be reminders of his cowardice. MacArthur had fled.

Not all of his fellow escapees saw it the way Shifty did, though. Several of them agreed with army fighter pilot Lieutenant Sam Grashio, who saw no reason to question these orders. When Grashio heard the "bitter remarks about 'Dugout Doug,'" he admitted that the general's departure had been a letdown for the troops and the lack of preparations for war had disgusted him. The situation was more complicated than that, however, and he made some obvious points. President Roosevelt had ordered MacArthur to leave Corregidor, and "it seemed to me mere common sense to save him for the rest of the war rather than let him fall into the hands of the enemy."[64] As a pilot, Sam Grashio had been at Clark Field on the day of the attack and had endured the siege of Bataan. "It always seemed to me," Sam concluded, "that the American government and people, rather than MacArthur and his associates, were mainly responsible for the inadequacy of Philippine defenses." The general had kept promising his men on Bataan that reinforcements were on the way because that had been the only way to keep them fighting. Shofner had a hard time arguing with Sam, whose body weight had dropped to eighty-five pounds during the March of Death and imprisonment. He trusted Sam. For his part, Sam admired Shifty's physical strength and his friend's unshakable optimism. These had been essential to their success. Sam and Austin had to avoid the subject of MacArthur while figuring out what they could achieve as guerrillas.

It took a while for Shifty and the other escapees to figure out that the leader of the guerrillas, Colonel Fertig, communicated with Australia on a daily basis. The colonel had kept it from them because he needed experienced and trained men to run his outfit. Fertig's Tenth Military District was on the front line of the war. He had no intention of letting the HQ in Australia know about the presence of trained infantry officers because he feared they would be recalled.[65]

Washington was filled with the top brass and Manila John Basilone was introduced to lots of admirals and generals. Although attached administratively to the Marine Barracks, Navy Yard, John reported daily to the director of the Division of Public Relations in the Navy Building. The director and his staff had not cut his orders yet, so some of the work was still in progress. They knew they would send John to New York as soon as possible to begin his work as a bond salesman. They were working on getting him involved in the Third War Loan Drive, which had begun months ago.

The U.S. Treasury Department had organized the Third War Loan Drive in association with the Hollywood Victory Committee, an organization representing the motion picture industry.[66] The loan drive was not one thing. It had half a dozen components. An "Airmada" of well-known actors, entertainers, and select military personnel had been organized into a number of "flights," which were staging bond rallies in medium-sized cities. Sabu the Elephant Boy had completed a twenty-six-stop tour.[67] The flights raised millions of dollars. The Hollywood Cavalcade, meantime, was traveling to the biggest cities. The cavalcade included Lucille Ball, Fred Astaire, Betty Hutton, James Cagney, Judy Garland, and many more. The cavalcade raised tens of millions of dollars. The actress Lana Turner raised $5.25 million in bonds by selling 105 kisses for $50,000 each. The slogan for all of the components of the Third War Loan Drive was "Back the Attack."[68]

Before Basilone joined the drive, reporters wanted to interview Manila John. His story had been printed in newspapers across the country since June. The details of his "3-day machine gun rampage" amazed everyone who read it.[69] The twelve-hour battle had become seventy-two hours because of a quote by Private Nash W. Phillips, who had served in Basilone's platoon on the Canal. A reporter had found Phillips recovering from his wounds in a navy hospital in San Diego.[70] The details Phillips had added had become part of the official story. "They stormed his position time and again," Phillips had told them, until thirty-eight bodies surrounded Manila John's foxhole. "Finally he had to move out of there— thirty-eight Jap bodies made it kind of hard to fire over the pile!"[71] The USMC publicity department had adopted Phillips's quote verbatim, rather than use the facts contained in John's Medal of Honor citation. Months before John's return, it had put on the newswire a portrait of John with the caption: "Sgt. John Basilone was awarded the Congressional Medal of Honor for extraordinary heroism in the South Pacific. . . . He stuck by his machine gun for 72 hours without food or sleep and is credited with virtual annihilation of a jap regiment."[72] Most newspapers included the claim that John was the only enlisted marine to be so honored.

The basic story was good but had gotten cold in the past few months. The reporters had interviewed his family and friends and a grade-school teacher and now it was time to hear from the man himself. The first interview took place in D.C. John said he could not tell the reporters much about "the one night blitz." Speaking with reporters made him uncomfortable. He began to perspire. They asked him what he thought of the enemy. He explained that they ran at the machine guns and concluded, "I don't believe they have the brains needed for victory."[73] Trying to explain, he continued. "They looked like a bunch of gorillas rushing us. They ought to have known better than to rush a machine gun that way."[74] As the last questions were asked, he stood up and said, "This is worse than fighting Japs."[75]

It had hardly been a smashing success. No photos were taken. John was wearing the same uniform he had flown to D.C. in because his two seabags had not arrived. Worse, he had diminished the capability of the enemy. The publicists of the navy, marines, and Treasury Department did not want any of its spokespeople to refer to the Japanese as stupid because it diminished the case for buying bonds. The U.S. government needed the money generated by bonds. The navy assigned Lieutenant W. Burns Lee to coordinate John's appearances and to escort him. Burns asked Manila if he had the USMC's dress blue uniform to wear. Although John had once owned a "set of blues," he had changed.[76] "What d'ya think I am, Lieutenant," John replied, "a Navy Yard Marine?"[77] Put another way, Manila thought that the officers in Washington who pushed papers wore dress blues. Marines whose hands were stained with machine-gun oil wore Class As, the greens, when not in dungarees. He refused to wear the blues. Lieutenant Lee did not force him to wear them. The practice of calling the enemy "stupid" and "gorillas," however, stopped henceforth. As for the "3-day blitz" overstatement, the press release that accompanied John kept it as it was, although it quietly corrected the assertion that John had been the first enlisted marine to be awarded the nation's highest award for valor.[78] John was recognized as the only living enlisted man to wear it. The reporters failed to notice, though, that John had not worn the actual medal around his neck. He wore its ribbon bar on his chest.

John and his PR "handler" took the train up to New York and arrived on the afternoon of Friday, September 3, 1943. Unlike Washington, the lights of New York had been dimmed because the lights shone on ships in the harbor and made them targets for German warships.[79] He met his parents. They brought with them Alfred Gaburo, Cochairman of the John Basilone Day Committee.[80] John had once driven one of Gaburo's laundry trucks. They all had a lot of catching up to do. Gaburo would have described the plans for the upcoming parade. John's parents had to have gushed about the attention the medal had brought to them and their family. In July, the prestigious Columbian Union had invited Salvatore and Theodora to a gala at the Robert Treat Hotel in Newark and presented a plaque to them.[81]

The recognition of his parents by a group of New Jersey's most respected and influential citizens would have pleased John, although he may not have been suitably impressed. Such a reaction would have provoked his father to get his attention by calling John the name on his birth certificate, Giovanni.[82]

Giovanni Basilone had grown up in a country that looked down on Italians. White America disliked their religion, their looks, and their social and cultural mores. Although his son had always been called John in public, Salvatore Basilone had been active in organizations like the Sons of Italy, which had celebrated the culture of his homeland. Salvatore, as a man who concerned himself with the relations between the two countries, had known for decades that the goal of America's immigration policy had been to keep immigration from Italy low, while encouraging immigration of those who were more Anglo-Saxon, more Protestant, and more white. His father's bitterness at such injustice was, however, old news for John.

The news Salvatore would have imparted that evening concerned the actions of the government against Italian immigrants since the war against Italy had begun.[83] Thousands of Italians had been arrested. Ten thousand Italians had been forced to leave their homes on the West Coast. Fifty thousand were subject to curfews and ordered to carry ID cards. Most of these people lived on the West Coast and had been classified as Enemy Aliens, a group which included all native Italians who had not completed U.S. citizenship.

The government, however, had not issued any information about its enforcement of Executive Order 9066.[84] The order signed by the president authorized the government to act against the immigrants so named and—horror of horrors—Italian immigrants were equated with Japanese immigrants. The order also created Enemy Alien Custodians. These custodians had restricted fishermen of Italian ancestry in the waters of New Jersey, New York—up and down the eastern seaboard. Italian railroad workers could not work in certain zones. Working with the FBI, the Enemy Alien Custodians arrested men for violating curfews or having a camera in their apartment. There were stories of FBI men coming to homes in New York in the middle of the night and taking men away. If a famous opera singer like Ezio Pinza could be arrested and held on Ellis Island, no son of Italy could rest easy in America.

The official sanctions had encouraged the growth of unofficial discrimination. Some businesses fired people who spoke in Italian to Italian customers. Others simply refused to hire them.[85] All of these realities existed outside of the mainstream media and had therefore become dirty secrets, passed from one immigrant to another. The Italians, the largest foreign-born group in the United States, knew not how to respond. While proud of his heritage, Salvatore Basilone was an equally proud American. He wanted the United States to defeat Italy's dictator, Benito Mussolini, as well as Germany and Japan. Criticizing the government's efforts against those Italians it deemed dangerous would be viewed as unpatriotic. Acknowledging the discrimination was humiliating.

The weight of the world was settling on John's strong shoulders. Sal and Dora and Alfred would have made sure he understood that the story of Manila John Basilone had begun to right these wrongs. In June, when the story had first broken, the navy commander who had briefed the press had said, "I don't fall for all this talk about the Italians being just natural cowards." The United Press International, whose stories ran in newspapers across the country, had pointedly directed its first story at the dictator of Italy, entitling it "Listen, Benito: We're Proud of Buffalo-born Basilone."[86] A few days later the reporters had found their way to the hero's hometown. Asked about his son, Sal spoke to the country on behalf of all Italians.

"Sure, I'm proud. I love my family and I always worry about Johnny, but I love this country almost as much as I love my son and I want this war finished. If Johnny can help hurry it up, then I'm satisfied."[87] Since then, Sal had distanced himself from the groups that celebrated his Italian heritage. Dora had lied to reporters and told them she had been born in Raritan, New Jersey.[88] They stressed that three of their sons were serving in the military, Alphonse, John, and George, without mentioning that the latter two's given names appeared on their birth certificates in Italian: Giovanni and Giorgio.[89]

The next morning, Saturday, September 4, John met with a group of reporters in the navy's pressroom at 90 Church Street in Manhattan.[90] He was smartly turned out in his green Class A uniform, ironed to perfection. He began by admitting that he was "nervous." The admission, and the way he flinched when the camera's flash-bulbs fired, started to win over his audience. In a quiet voice, John outlined what had happened that night. The "bag of 38 Japs" that the writers kept mentioning had not all been killed by him, but also by Billie Joe Crumpton and Cecil Evans. As far as the enemy, "every time the Japs came charging at us they would yell. This would tip us off." Trying to lighten the mood, John continued. "We would yell right back at them, but what we said is 'off the record.' We would also let them have it." The reporters liked that he described the battle "without heroics," but then asked lots of questions in their search for something heroic. He repeated his joke: "This is worse than fighting the Japs."

After the interview, Manila John was taken over to meet the mayor of New York, Fiorello La Guardia, in City Hall.[91] John went around behind the large, ornate desk of one of America's leading politicians. The two men stood side by side, flanked by flags, looking at the reporters, photographers, and a large movie camera assembled on the other side. Mayor La Guardia, a stubby man more than a foot shorter than Basilone, was comfortable working with the media. Ignoring John, he drummed his fingers on the table, chewed his lip, and waited for the signal. When the cameras were ready La Guardia turned to John, looked up into his eyes briefly, then stared at his medal as he said, "Sergeant John Basilone, I am very happy to welcome you, the first enlisted marine to receive the Congressional Medal of Honor, and we're very proud to have you in New York City." As an Italian, the mayor pronounced the *e* on the end of Basilone. La Guardia reached out his hand and gave John's a vigorous shake.

"Tell me, Sergeant, are those japs tough?"

"Yes, they were tough," came the reply, "but the marines were tougher." John delivered his line while looking at the ceiling.

"The marines are always tougher."

"Yes, sir."

"I see you got the Congressional Medal of Honor here," he said as he reached up to touch the ribbon on his chest—the large medal was not hanging around his neck.

"Yes," John said, looking off aimlessly. La Guardia had already turned away, his smile replaced by the harried look of a busy mayor. He looked expectantly to the press, gauging their reaction. Inches away, John waited. The mayor, informed that he had stumbled on his line, turned back to him. The smile flashed. "Tell me, Sergeant, are those japs really tough?"

"Yes, sir, the japs were tough, but the marines were tougher."

"Marines are always tougher!"

"Yes, sir."

"Is this the ribbon of your Congressional Medal of Honor?" Reaching up, the mayor fingered the ribbon.

"Yes." Once again, the mayor dropped his hand like it was hot and looked to the reporters. He had a heated discussion with his advisors and the press corps. He decided to give a short speech. The camera came in tight on his face. John's service had been above and beyond the call of duty, he began, earnestly building toward a conclusion about Americans buying bonds "above and beyond the"—before deciding, "Aw, cut!" He started again, this time smoothly and emphatically exhorting his listeners to "buy bonds above and beyond what we can really afford. We must deprive ourselves of something. We must make some sacrifice. . . ." That seemed to go well, so he set up to make another run at John. La Guardia waited. John waited. The camera pulled back.

"Sergeant, can you tell us something about how you came to get this? You must've mowed 'em down!"

"Yes, sir," John replied to the ceiling. "I was in a good outfit. With good men. I just happened to be there. And any man would have done the same in my place."

"Spoken just like a marine, eh. Sergeant, where does your old man come from?"

"My father comes from Naples."

"And my father comes from Foggia. We're Americans!" They shook hands, and their smiles grew genuine for a moment. The mayor's handlers yelled something. La Guardia flung John's hand down and stepped away. The camera closed in on Manila John's face. Off-screen, La Guardia asked him again to "tell us something about how you came to get this medal." John repeated his line verbatim. They repeated their exchange about where their fathers came from, the camera recording John's earnest delivery, and then it was over. They had spoken at each other, or in the direction of one another, but not with one another. The mayor had played his role and in doing so had shown Manila John how to play his part. The right message had been prepared for the people of New York.

The newspapers the next day played their role. One New York paper featured a large picture of John in its Sunday edition, over the title "A Killer . . . of 38 Japs."[92] The stories had fun with John's discomfort at being interviewed—flashbulbs made him jump more than Japanese—and assured readers that he was properly modest about his accomplishments. Manila John had praised his friends at every turn so that his audience understood "they're a great bunch." After explaining how he had come to have the nickname "Manila," the reporters described his efforts to explain that he was part of a team as modesty. What they could not get from him, they got from Nash Phillips. The Sunday *New York Times* explained how he had killed "38 japs single handed" over two nights.[93] In so doing, Manila John Basilone had "contributed to the virtual annihilation of a Japanese regiment."[94] Use of the word "contributed" covered the contributions of Able Company, which took the brunt of the attack; of the other marines in Charlie, Baker, and Dog companies, some of whom had done everything Manila had; of the soldiers of the 164th Infantry Regiment, who had arrived at a crucial time; of the Eleventh Marines, whose artillery shells rained down on the other side of the wire; and of Cecil and Billie Joe, who had held the ground—surrounded, wounded, brave—long enough for Manila John to reach them.

SEPTEMBER HAD BEGUN MUCH AS AUGUST HAD ENDED. SID'S REGIMENT HAD departed the cricket grounds for training purposes. It was bivouacked about twenty miles outside of Melbourne in fields around the village of Dandenong. It was not too far from the camp of the Seventh Marines. The training had begun in earnest: field problems and conditioning hikes punctuated with inspections and other forms of discipline. Sid had limited opportunities to sample the delights of Melbourne. Living in tents also meant more exposure to the cold, rain, and high winds of winter. One afternoon the sergeant collared Sid and put him on a working party. A truck full of marines drove into the town of Dandenong to unload coal from a train and load it on the truck for use in the stoves of the First Marines. Across the street from the rail yard stood a pub. The sergeant, after swearing all his men to silence, collected two shillings from each man. He took Sid and they went across the street.

At the bar sat a pretty blond woman with a pint of beer in front of her. She was completely topless because she was breast-feeding her baby. Sid thought her well endowed. She gave the two a friendly greeting. The sergeant ordered a quart-sized bottle of Melbourne Bitter for each man in his party. While the barkeep filled the order, the woman gestured toward the infant and told them "the little Yankee bastard's father" was an American sailor on the cruiser *Quincy*. The fact that the Japanese had sunk *Quincy* a year ago off Guadalcanal popped into Sid's head, but he did not say anything. Those naked breasts had him distracted. The young mother started in on American sailors, declaring that they were "no good." Much to her surprise, the two Americans in front of her agreed heartily. Sid's sergeant added that "most American sailors were recruited from prisons in America and had to have marines aboard ships to guard them and make them obey orders."

The sergeant left the bar with the woman's name and address and a promise to come back and see her later. Sid left carrying a burlap sack of beer bottles. The detail finished unloading and loading coal and returned to camp in high spirits, drinking beer and singing "Bless 'em All" and "When This War Is Over We'll All Enlist Again." Deacon caught Sid tipsy, though. A long sermon about "depravity" followed.

ON MONDAY, SEPTEMBER 6, AT THE USMC DIVISION OF PUBLIC RELATIONS, Basilone received his official orders, detailing the bond tour. Manila John would join Flight Number Five of the Airmada, departing New York on September 8. The first events, in Newark on the ninth, would be followed by others in different cities every day for ten days. Flight Five's final event would be held in Basilone's hometown on Sunday, September 19, 1943.[95] The stars of Flight Five began arriving: the actress Virginia Grey, the actors John Garfield and Gene Lockhart, as well as some other service personnel. They put on a show at the Capitol Theatre in Manhattan.[96] They also took part in a nationwide broadcast called "Report to the Nation," which included an address by President Roosevelt.[97] Everyone remembered to repeat the slogan of the Third War Loan Drive: "Back the Attack." One of the remarks that caught the public's attention was an admission from Manila John Basilone that "pieces of my Congressional Medal of Honor belong to the boys who were left behind."[98]

In advance of their arrival in Newark, advertisements announced the "War Veterans Airmada." Ads listed the schedule of events and the names of the "war heroes" and the entertainers who were coming "Out of the Skies to You!"[99] Most of these ads ran in the newspaper, but a navy blimp floated over Newark and dropped "paper bombs." John and the others landed in Newark at ten thirty a.m. The first photo showed the cast of the Airmada in front of their airplane because flying was very glamorous and because the plane was part of the campaign.

The trip from the airport to downtown was like a parade. There was a band to lead them, fire trucks and military units to accompany them, and they sat in open cars. They did not see much in the way of crowds until they approached the site of the rally.[100] Up on the platform, Virginia Grey and John Garfield received a lot of attention. Grey's hairstyle and dress were noted, as well as Garfield's assertion that he "wasn't tough." The two stars began the ceremony by releasing three carrier pigeons, one for each of the Axis Powers; Italy, the lesser threat of the three, had surrendered a few days earlier.* The pigeons carried the message "For Victory—One Down, Two to Go."[101] Joined by the actor Gene Lockhart, they interviewed "the real stars of the show," the "five heroes." After everyone spoke, the troop went back to the hotel and freshened up before appearing at a VIP reception at the Victory Theater and a special showing of the new film *Mr. Lucky*. The surrender of Italy had created a lot of optimism and enthusiasm for the drive. The Treasury representative predicted they would raise more than $1.2 million in Newark, New Jersey.

The next morning, the Airmada took off for Jersey City, followed by New Haven, Providence, Manchester, Worcester, Albany, Syracuse, Rochester, and Scranton on September 18.[102] Visits to City Hall and special dinners with "leading citizens" were added to their days. The events had similar names: "The Million Dollar Luncheon" and "The Million Dollar Bond Hero Premiere." John Garfield frequently introduced Basilone, giving him a big smile and handshake each time, as though they had never met. Garfield told audiences, "Don't let anybody tell you the Italians can't fight. When they have something to fight for they can fight plenty. There are thousands of them in our army and we know."[103] The actor may have been responding to the directives of the Treasury Department. Treasury had decided to hold up its bond tours as symbols of America's melting pot by emphasizing diversity as the strength of America.

The ideal of national unity had a powerful hold on the immigrant communities. In the Airmada audiences were people who had come from all over the world to chase the good life in the United States of America. They had found a country more to their liking than the ones they had left, but they bridled at the barriers they had found to their advancement: their religions and ethnicities. The U.S. Treasury Department made sure the members of all ethnic groups equated buying bonds

---

*The dominant country of the Axis alliance, Adolf Hitler's Germany, decided to prevent the Allied powers from seizing Italy, so the war there would continue.

with proving their loyalty.[104] According to the Treasury, the path to fame and fortune lay open to all loyal Americans. War bonds cost $18.75, but anyone could purchase stamps for a few pennies and work toward owning a bond. It would mature to $25 in ten years. Bonds represented the defense of the American way of life. The newspaper coverage of the Third War Loan Drive noted that the heroes represented all the service branches and "a number of races," although Manila John's skin was the only one darker than milky white.[105]

The newspapers usually held more ink describing the Hollywood stars than the heroes. The stars changed over time—Eddie Bracken and Martha Scott headlined the shows in Albany—and special guests appeared, like the bandleader and songwriter Glenn Miller in New Haven.[106] When it came to the war heroes, the news accounts usually included a photo of Manila John. The caption "Jap Killer Waves Greeting" might run above it and below it a few lines that had phrases like "mowing down nips" and "slaughtering 2,000 Japs."[107] The other veterans received less attention. Seaman First Class Elmer Cornwall, U.S. Navy, "told how he lost 50 pounds while adrift in a lifeboat 36 days with rations for only 15 days."[108] The others had similar tales: they had beaten long odds to survive being shot down or shot up. Manila John, though, was the only one to have beaten the enemy face-to-face.

Basilone liked to tease the navy vets, saying the "swabbies could really tell the sea stories . . . some of those gruesome yarns make me want to buy bonds."[109] If the guys had drinks at the bar at the end of the day, John usually left before it got crazy. Since the Airmada stayed at the nicest hotel in town, a crowd of folks usually showed up in hopes of meeting the Hollywood actors.[110] Not all of the visitors were stargazers, though. Men who had served with John left messages in his box at the front desk.[111] Mothers and girlfriends of men serving overseas showed up to ask about their sons or boyfriends.[112] The mother of Thomas "Chick" McAllister got through the crowds to see him—her son had served with him. About Chick, whose nickname came from his boyish features, John told his mother, "Well, he is not your baby no more."[113] The only type of visitor who ticked John off was "the guy who buttonholed him at the bar and asked, 'What's that blue ribbon with the white stars you're wearing, soldier?'"

"Why, that's for good conduct," John would reply, trying to let the "soldier" crack pass and be friendly, although a wearisome routine seemed to happen in each city. If the guy was middle-aged, he'd start "blowing smoke up your trousers about the First World War. If he's fairly young he starts crying on your shoulder about how he has tried and tried to get in the armed forces but he always gets turned down because of housemaid's knee or adenoids or something."[114]

The Airmada flew back to New York City on Saturday night. The anonymity of the big city offered John the chance to have a quiet dinner. He was not so famous as to be instantly recognized. An elderly woman took pity on the lonely marine she found in the hotel restaurant one evening and treated him to dinner. John never once mentioned the bond tour, the medal, or Guadalcanal. She thought him a nice young man and good company.[115]

On Sunday morning, a car arrived at eight a.m. to take Manila to the place where everyone knew his name, his face, and his story.[116] The actresses and actor who accompanied him were not quite as well known: Virginia O'Brien, Louise Allbritton, and Robert Paige.[117] They came down from New York on Route 29 at seventy miles an hour with a police escort to drive motorists off the road ahead of them. At the traffic light on Somerset Street and Route 31, which signaled the entrance to Raritan, Mayor Peter Mencaroni and Chairman William Slattery of the Township Committee greeted him.

Driving into Raritan, they could see their first stop, St. Ann's Church, from a distance by the crowd out front. John's schedule for the day had been published, so those who could not join him for High Mass waited outside. Manila John met his family at the church they had attended all his life. John had invited his friend Steve Helstowski, who had served with him on Guadalcanal, to join him. Basilone asked the reverend to say mass for "his buddies on Guadalcanal."[118] In his sermon, Reverend Graham declared John's "life will be a guide to American youth. God spared him for some big work."[119] Afterward, the reporters wanted to know what it was all about. John said he had prayed for all servicemen and for one marine in particular, a guy "who used to romp around in the same foxhole with me, but didn't come back."[120] He did not give a name. John had Steve stay close with him as they left for a meeting with "dignitaries," the members of the John Basilone Day Committee, before heading off for lunch.

John's table at lunch included Steve, his parents, and the two reverends from the church. He had some good news for his mother. After he completed the "Navy Incentive Tour," which began the next day, he would have a month's furlough.[121] After the meal they drove to nearby Somerville, where the parade started at one p.m.

In the convertible, Steve sat in the passenger seat up front. John's parents sat in the backseat, and Manila John Basilone sat on the back of the car, where everyone could see him. A detail of female marines flanked the car, which found its place in the long line. Twelve marching bands were interspersed amid a great variety of civic and military organizations. Numerous contingents of Italian-American societies marched. A navy blimp flew over the proceedings as Manila John's car drove two miles through thirty thousand people. He waved the whole time, smiling and occasionally blowing a kiss.[122] Both Somerville and Raritan had been bedecked for the occasion. One storefront featured a "Jap graveyard with 38 tombstones and a machine gun, all against a Basilone picture."[123] Another shop had hung two large portraits side by side: General Douglas MacArthur and Manila John Basilone.[124]

A large crowd had already assembled when John's car pulled into the grounds of Doris Duke Park, just across the river from downtown Raritan. He and his parents and Steve Helstowski made their way to the reviewing stand. Among the honored guests seated there was sixty-six-year-old John M. Rilley of Mountainville, who had won the Congressional Medal of Honor in the Spanish-American War.[125] America's victory against Spain had enabled the extension of her sovereignty over the Philippine Islands and thus over John's beloved city, Manila. Harry Hershfield, a famous humorist and host of a national radio program, served as master of ceremonies. Once he stepped to the microphone, he kept the program rolling along. All the speakers praised the heroism of Manila John Basilone and held him up as an example for all Americans. In between the speechifying, entertainers came on to enliven the proceedings: the comedian Danny Thomas performed during one break; Maurice Rocco, described as a "Negro boogie-woogie pianist who shuns the piano stool," entertained during another.[126]

On her way to the podium, the actress Louise Allbritton stopped to give Basilone, who was seated, a peck on the cheek. She turned to the podium but the crowd's reaction, as well as the enthusiasm of the assembled reporters and photographers, caused her to turn back, grab John's arm with both hands, and tug. He stood up slowly. She signaled the crowd to "watch this," and made to kiss him on the lips. John did not want to kiss her. Her kiss meant as much as Mayor La Guardia's handshake. He brushed her off and turned away slightly, smiling bashfully. She kissed him on the side of the mouth and the crowd laughed heartily. "Ah," sighed Miss Allbritton, when the operation was completed. "I've always wanted to kiss a hero." The sergeant was speechless.[127] Reporters thought the actress "stole the spotlight" and concluded that John, who up to that time had "had the situation well in hand," going through the parade and ceremony "with the same courage with which he had faced the japs," had been "awed by the kiss." Another noted "a good many gals present were envious."

At last the organizer of the event, Judge George Allgair, stepped to the rostrum. He turned to his right to address John, who joined him. The audience began to stand and cheer. Cameramen in the front row stood and their flashbulbs began going off. Allgair could hardly be seen or heard. When the judge presented the five bonds of $1,000 "on behalf of the good people of Raritan," John began to pale. The easy smile faded as the judge said the bonds represented "a pledge of their eternal love and devotion to you."[128] A practiced hand at live events, though, Manila paused so the cameramen could get a photo of him accepting the bonds.

When the man of the hour came to the microphone the crowd cheered. He gave them a big, handsome smile and the applause grew and grew into thunder. One of their own, a tailor's son, had become a rich man, a famous man with famous friends. Little did they know that this was one of only a few occasions when he hung the medal around his neck, so they could see the actual medal, rather than just wearing its ribbon on his breast. "Jersey's #1 Hero" let the smile fade slowly and looked out into the middle distance. After thanking the judge and "the good home folks of Raritan," he said, "Really, it's all a dream to me. I really don't know what to say." He forgot the notes he had in his pocket.[129] So he slipped back into more comfortable territory, letting them know that "my buddies" on the front lines appreciated people "backing the attack and buying war bonds." He had intended to say, "The Congressional Medal of Honor is a part of every Marine that so heroically fought on Guadalcanal." Overwhelmed, he introduced his friend Steve, "a boy who played in the same foxhole, fought next to me, and who is on sick leave from a hospital." Steve came up and stood next to him. John concluded, "And thank you all from the bottom of my heart."

His mother, Dora, came to the microphone. John stood behind her, his hands on her shoulders, whispering suggestions for what to say. She struggled to find her voice, but finally they both gave up, and John came around beside her and said into the microphone: "Just like a Basilone—bashful." The crowd loved it. His father stepped forward. Salvatore kept his remarks fairly short, delivered in a dignified manner and entirely in his native Italian. While he knew many in the audience spoke Italian, he intended to make a point to those who did not.

The big event concluded with an original song, performed by Ms. Catherine Mastice, entitled "Manila John."[130] John looked a little dubious as she began to sing. The refrain, "Ma-nil-a John, Ma-nil-a John, son of Lib-er-ty / Glo-ry has been bravely won and made your broth-ers free," washed over the crowd.[131] The Basilone family went back to their house, a duplex in the center of town and not far from the park. The family held an open house "for the many friends of their hero son."[132] A crowd covered their lawn and spilled into the street. Cameramen filmed Manila John standing outside, alternately nervously eyeing the camera and shaking hands with well-wishers. Someone asked him to kiss his mother. Happy to oblige, John kissed her and gave his father a kiss, then kissed them both again.

The next morning, the newspapers listed the total bond sales of Basilone Day at $1.3 million. Manila went back to work. A photographer from *Life* magazine took photos of him shaving, making sure to get a shot showing each of his tattoos. A reporter from *Parade* magazine joined the representatives from *Life*, each digging deep to develop big stories on him. They had arrived before Basilone Day and would remain in Raritan for the rest of the week. After breakfast, Manila John began his work with the Navy Incentive Tour. While the tour itself would not begin full-time for a week, he visited some of the factories in cities around Raritan.

Meeting the workers on the shop floor or in the cafeteria, he was to assure them that the clothing, equipment, or armaments they manufactured for the War Department meant success on the battlefield. He also was told to thank them for working overtime. The Johns-Manville Company, which had purchased $500,000 in bonds for Basilone Day, manufactured the asbestos gloves machine gunners wore when handling hot machine guns. The asbestos company produced an advertisement featuring Manila holding the asbestos gloves. "But for these asbestos gloves," the caption read, "I would be here today with my hands and arms still blistered."[133] At lunch, "Manila John" was introduced to the company's head chef, "Filipino Phil" Abarientos, an immigrant himself.

Manila found the new job just as embarrassing as the old one. Being held up as the epitome of America's youth made him uncomfortable. Being the representative of the combat soldier meant not being a combat soldier.[134] When he came home, the reporters were waiting to ask him some more questions. The photographer from *Life* took a photo of him eating his mother's spaghetti.

SEPTEMBER HAD STARTED OUT ON A GOOD NOTE FOR EUGENE. THE MARINE detachment at Georgia Tech had received a new commanding officer, Captain Donald Payzant. At the ceremonial review Private Sledge read the symbols on Captain Payzant's uniform. The campaign ribbons and service awards were pinned on his left breast, the rank on his collar. The patch of the 1st Marine Division, sewn on the right shoulder, proclaimed a word known throughout the Western world: Guadalcanal. Payzant gave Eugene exactly what he wanted—more discipline and higher expectations. The veteran treated his charges "like men and not a bunch of boys"; if one of them failed to measure up, Payzant dressed him down fast.

One afternoon in late September, Sledge mentioned to Captain Payzant that his good friend Sid Phillips was a marine. Sid's frequent letters omitted any information about where he was, of course, but Sid had recently sent his sister Katherine a metal plate covered in Japanese lettering. Sid said he had pried it off a downed Zero. Captain Payzant replied that he knew Private Sidney Phillips rather well. Sid served in H/2/1, the company Payzant had commanded on Guadalcanal.[135] The shock of the "Gee, ain't it a small world" reaction preceded a ferocious curiosity to know more about Sid's life. Payzant likely shared a memory or two of the #4 gun squad. With the stories came a realization: Sid had been a part of the great victory, the first time the Imperial Japanese Army had been licked, a victory won by the United States Marine Corps. Eugene, who had just bought a leather desk set for Sid's Christmas present, decided to write him later.

That afternoon Payzant posted the names of the men who had been flunked out and were leaving for boot camp at Parris Island. The list did not include Private Eugene Sledge. Gene stared at the list, conflicting emotions churning inside of him. He wrote his mother that evening that he still might flunk out because of his struggles with physics. "I hate to leave here by failure," he continued, "but I'll be glad to do so." He wanted to be like Sidney Phillips and "get into the brawl." Then he opened up to her with his soul. "When I'm through P.I. [Parris Island], I'll really have self-confidence. I'll have reason for it. I'll be a man then, but this fooling around isn't good for anyone."

His mother, who did not wish to see her son become cannon fodder, astutely sidestepped the raging desire inside her son to become a man. She maintained the issue at hand had to do with keeping one's promise to one's parents. Dr. and Mrs. Sledge had fulfilled their part of the bargain. A week later his letter to her began, "I got your letter of the other day and appreciated it. I am thoroughly ashamed for saying what I did and I apologize. No one could ask for better parents than I have." Although he repeated his desire to leave the program, he moved on quickly to other news. Sid's sister Katherine had visited him. They had had a grand time swapping news about Sid and his friends. Katherine declared that Eugene heard from her brother "more than anyone else." With a semester break coming up at the end of October, Eugene spent part of this letter and the next making arrangements for his mother to visit him in Atlanta. After he showed her Georgia Tech, the two planned to travel back to Mobile. "I dream of it," he wrote his mother, "by the hour."

MANILA JOHN'S LIFE MADE GOOD COPY. LIKE MILLIONS OF HIS FELLOW COUNTRYmen, he had been born into a large family of limited means, the son of an immigrant. His struggles to find himself were readily apparent and, in light of his great success, his false starts took on a warm glow. The story of a boy who had dropped out of school after the eighth grade, of the young man who had quit a number of jobs, had a happy ending. During the lead-up to Basilone Day, lots of reporters had dug into every facet of his life—the rambunctious kid chased by a bull in a field; the likable, smiling young man who drove a laundry truck. They interviewed his youngest brother, his former employers, his schoolteachers. His mother, Dora, remembered Johnny's first spanking: "he had been stealing apples and I smacked him good," she said.[136] Neighbors noted instances when Johnny had exhibited bravery even as a boy. The copy flowed into newsprint in the cities of eastern New Jersey and elsewhere.

In the week after the Basilone Day parade, the reporters from *Life* magazine and other news outlets wanted more from the man himself. While asking him about his days as a golf caddie, they uncovered an interesting connection. John told them that he had carried bags for wealthy and influential Japanese businessmen. Manila recalled, "The Japs always carried and used cameras while on the course, which has a wonderful view of the surrounding factories, railroads and canals. They never failed to smile politely and make room for other, faster players coming through."[137] Their behavior had seemed odd to him at the time; now it seemed treasonous.

Even back in the mid-1930s he had "smelled a fight coming" and joined the army. After his hitch was up, he decided "the army's not tough enough for me." The reporters and photographers studied the tattoos he'd acquired while in the army in great detail. "As mementos of his first enlistment he had two fine, large, lush tattoos, one on each arm," one reporter later wrote. "The right upper arm shows, in delicate modulations of blue and red inks, the head and shoulders of a full-blown Wild West girl. The left arm, in equally bold markings, bears a sword plunged into a human heart, the whole entwined with stars and flowers and a ribbon on which is written, 'Death Before Dishonor.'"[138]

The interviews allowed John to dispel one of the false stories that his own family had begun. Back in June, the Basilones had told reporters that Manila John "held several Army boxing championships."[139] When asked for details, John said he had tried boxing as a middleweight in the Golden Gloves program, but he had not been "particularly successful."[140] The matter dropped. When a reporter asked him later what he intended to do with his $5,000 war bond, he replied, "When the right girl comes along I'm going to buy a ten room house, and I'm going to have a bambino for each room."[141]

Of course, the reporters eventually got around to discussing the night of October 24. John had not learned to elaborate much on it. Sometimes he would admit that he had been scared he wouldn't make it, like when he ran the hundred-yard dash for more belts of ammunition. At other moments, he'd insist, "I wasn't scared—didn't have time to be. Besides, I had my men to worry about. If you don't keep a cool head, you won't have any head to worry about."[142] He made clear that "the next day, the japs fell back," without directly stating that his battle had not lasted three days as previously reported.

When pushed by the writer James Golden over the course of a four-day interview "to talk about himself and his heroics," John said: "Look, Golden, forget about my part. There was not a man on the canal that night who doesn't own a piece of that medal awarded me."[143] The blunt assertion did not stop the writer from pushing harder to get the story. After all, Golden figured, John must have done something extraordinary to win the Medal of Honor. Golden eventually concluded that John was "simply . . . too modest." Manila John had not even known what exactly he had done to merit the Medal of Honor until he read the medal citation signed by Roosevelt months later. Golden talked John into pulling out his old set of blues and wearing them with his medal hung around his neck for a photo. When Golden's article appeared, it repeated the same story as the others, describing Manila John as "a man-sized marine."[144]

The big interviews with *Life* and *Parade* and the meetings with the local industries completed, John prepared to travel around to other factories on the Navy Incentive Tour. Before setting off, John sent a note to J.P., Greer, and his friends in Dog Company.[145] He wrote them about the morning in D.C. when a corporal had walked into his room and inquired, "Sergeant Basilone, would you like to get up this morning?"[146] John knew his buddies would howl over that one. Manila also convinced his sister Mary to write a letter to Greer's family to let them know some news about their son Richard.[147] He had not forgotten the promise he had made to Greer back in Australia. On September 27, he traveled back to the navy's office in Manhattan and reported in to the Inspector of Naval Material.

ON SEPTEMBER 27, LIEUTENANT BENSON ORDERED HIS PLATOON OF 81MM mortarmen to pack their gear. They were boarding ship that night. No one in the #4 gun squad was surprised; they had been preparing for weeks. The news that the 1st Marine Division also had been transferred to General MacArthur's command for its next operation, however, came like a thunderclap. Barks of derision followed Benson's announcement. Army fatigue hats were issued. Sid threw the hat away and boarded the truck. The 2/1 arrived at Queen's Pier in downtown Melbourne at five thirty p.m. Their gear did not arrive until eleven p.m. Sid and Deacon went on a working party, of course, until the wee hours. The next day brought more of the same as they loaded their ship, one of the navy's new troop transports called a Liberty Ship. The good news came at the end of the day, when all hands got liberty.

The veterans of Guadalcanal had a very clear expectation of what awaited them and therefore made the most of it. Deacon noted in his diary, "everybody drunk tonight." Deacon went to see all of his girlfriends before going over to Glenferrie to visit Shirley and her family. Sid didn't go. He had said his good-byes weeks earlier.

At inspection the next morning, Lieutenant Benson and the top sergeant were both caught drunk. A lot of yelling ensued. A number of summary courts-martial were issued. By evening they had sorted it out and boarded the ship. A large crowd had gathered, a "waving, crying, flag-waving mob" on the dock. The local police and the Australian army's military police (MPs) were called out to keep them back. On deck, the marines blew air into their remaining prophylactics and let them drift to shore. Sid thought inflated condoms might just be going too far. The ship cast off and stood out from Melbourne's great harbor that same evening. For the next week, it steamed along the Great Barrier Reef, host to a battalion of marines cursing Liberty Ships, C rations, and "Dugout Doug." The men of the 2/1 figured they were headed for Rabaul or Bougainville. Rabaul was six hundred miles from Guadalcanal; Bougainville was even less. By implication, not very much progress had been made in the ten months since the #4 gun squad had last steamed through the Pacific. Looking forward to another six months stuck in a jungle, a crowd of marines took over Deacon's bunk and played for stakes as high as £100.

THE NAVY INCENTIVE TOUR HAD TURNED OUT TO BE QUIET AND BORING, WITH the occasional interview. The reporters may have worn Manila down because his resolution faded. In New York on October 15, the reporter Julia McCarthy tried to peel away some of the myths. She asked, "Didn't you personally kill thirty-eight Japanese, or have we been told wrong?" Before he could answer, she followed it with another: Had Manila really moved his machine gun because he had piled up so many dead? John nodded; all that was true. What about the rumor, McCarthy continued, that he had been offered a commission? John "at first admitted, then denied a report he turned down a chance to become a second lieutenant."[148] His denial may have come from a desire to protect himself from being criticized for declining the opportunity for advancement. "The title I like best is 'Sarge,'" he explained, "and I like to be in the ranks."[149]

The incentive tour proved to have lots of holes in it, so John frequently returned to D.C. He began dating one of the female marines working in the Navy Building. When the final tour event ended on October 19, he was given a month's furlough, so he moved back to the three-bedroom duplex in Raritan where his parents had raised ten children.[150] Most of his older brothers and sisters had long since moved out, though. Manila and his younger brother Don, who was just a boy, shared a room. Two sisters lived in the other.[151]

All of the news stories had been published by mid-October. His mother had a large scrapbook, although it's unlikely John ever read it. The long interviews had not changed the coverage very much. The Basilone household received a lot of fan mail in October. The early articles in the summer had gotten a few people to write John and his family. The photographic essay in *Life* and the national radio broadcasts, however, generated lots of mail. Mothers wrote to congratulate his parents. The parents of men in his outfit wrote to congratulate him. They sent clippings; they wanted to know if Basilone had seen their boys in the South Pacific. Kids wrote for autographs. Old girlfriends wanted to catch up. Women he had met on the bond tour wanted to know how it all went. A dozen women sent pictures to John and introduced themselves to him. More than a few struggled with how to start a letter to a hero they did not know. Each acknowledged that he was being besieged by letters, but as one wrote, "I'm keeping my fingers crossed a little and hope you'll answer this letter, crummy and dull as it is."[152]

John enjoyed reading the letters, which his mother saved for him. Some friends from his hitch in the army wrote to congratulate him. They were proud to have soldiered with him. Of course, being old buddies, they had to tease him, too. "The only part that bothers me is that you had to be in the marines," said one.[153] Everyone—old friends, friends of friends, former neighbors, former teachers, strange women, fans—all of them begged him to write them back, to call them, to let them know he had heard from them. They acknowledged how busy he was, but pleaded for a visit. They also called his house, called his brothers, and left word with his cousins.

Among the mail came a slick brochure from the War Activities Committee of the Motion Picture Industry, wrapping up the success of its Third War Loan Campaign. Flight Five of the Airmada, featuring Manila John, John Garfield, Virginia Grey, and others, had sold just over $36 million in war bonds. A few others had a higher total. Flight Three had topped them all with $94 million in bond sales.[154]

In late October, John went up to visit his friend Stephen Helstowski in Pittsfield, Massachusetts.[155] The real reason, as Steve knew, was for John to meet Steve's sister Helen. He had been infatuated with her since he received her letters on Guadalcanal. Since his return to the States, Basilone had spoken of her several times to the press with such enthusiasm, it was reported that he would marry Helen Helstowski.[156] He spent a few days there, double-dating with Steve and his girlfriend. They got along very well and the relationship grew serious.[157] He could not stay long, though. In early November he boarded a train for Raritan.[158] There was more work to be done.

EUGENE SLEDGE'S HOLIDAY BREAK FROM THE V-12 PROGRAM DID NOT GO AS HE expected. He returned to Georgia Tech three days early. Whatever the reason he gave his family, the tension inside of him resulted from the secret he was keeping from them. He had flunked both physics and biology and earned Cs in English and economics. So far as Captain Payzant could tell, Private Sledge was "below average" in intelligence and "not inclined to study," nor did he possess the "necessary officer qualities." The dean of the college agreed with Payzant's recommendation that Sledge be reassigned. On October 31, 1943, Private Sledge and forty-four of his colleagues were put under the command of Corporal James Holt, who escorted them to the Marine Corps base in San Diego "for recruit training and general service."

The recruits shipped out the very next day. Their train to San Diego stopped in Mobile for a few hours before steaming across the Southwest. Eugene did not attempt to phone his parents. He feared their reaction. He waited to write to them until the end of his first complete day of boot camp at the USMC Recruit Depot, which was also his twentieth birthday. The letter explained that he had not flunked out. Upon reviewing his file, Captain Payzant had decided that Sledge was not prepared for the engineering course required in the second semester, since he had had no previous courses it in. "At the last minute," Sledge had been "reassigned." Although Gene had asked to remain in the program, the captain had sent him to boot camp. "So you see," Eugene concluded his first letter to his parents, "I don't feel bad about coming here." He described his delightful train trip across the country. The mountains of Arizona had been especially beautiful, leading him to suggest a family trip to visit them after the war.

THE BATTALIONS OF THE 1ST MARINE DIVISION WERE DISPERSED AFTER THEIR troop transports had steamed back within range of "subs and jap heavy bombers" in mid-October. Some units found themselves on the eastern tip of New Guinea. Sid's 2/1 built their bivouac on Goodenough Island, one of a small group of islands near the tip of New Guinea and firmly under the command of MacArthur. One look at Goodenough Island and most concluded the 1st Division was "back in the boonies again!"[159] Sidney saw a "beautiful island with mountains which seemed to touch the sky." They set up their bivouac near the base of a mountain, pausing every few min-

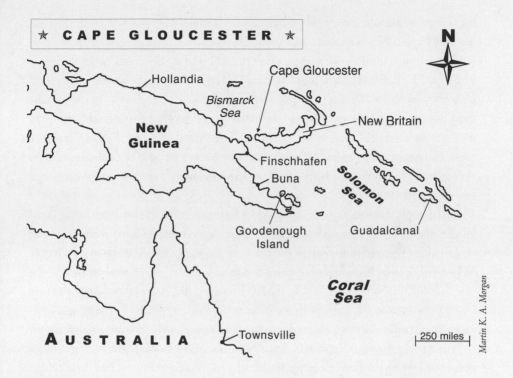

utes because of the enervating heat. A clear, cold mountain stream beckoned them in the afternoon. Being near an airstrip and a river made it all seem familiar, although this time there were no enemy forces on the island—just "gooks," the marines' popular slang word for any nonwhites.

While they awaited MacArthur's orders, the marines of the 2/1 hiked through a jungle dotted with small villages to stay in shape. One afternoon during a ten-minute halt, Sid spied some sugarcane nearby. He walked over and cut some stalks, handing them out to all the Southern boys. A few moments of joyful chewing caught people's attention, so they "taught the Yankees to peel the cane and cut it into chewable-sized pieces and soon had the whole platoon, including officers, chewing sugarcane. The Yankees thought we were brilliant."

The exercises on Goodenough also included an introduction to the LST, or Landing Ship Tank. Essentially a giant Higgins boat, the LST had a very shallow draft, allowing it to beach itself onshore. The tall bow doors swung open, and a ramp came down allowing trucks, jeeps, hundreds of men, and equipment to pour forth. The division's new Sherman tanks, far larger than the old Stuart tanks and mounting 75mm main cannons, made quite an impression. The practice landings took place at Papua, New Guinea, on October 24. These landings proceeded in the prescribed manner until the afternoon when the 2/1 and its Sherman tanks arrived at a village. The natives looked to Sid as "nine-tenths white and the women all dressed only in grass skirts. They all came to smilingly gawk at us and we were delightedly gawking at them when our officers proceeded to get us off of that island faster than we had come ashore." No fraternization would be permitted. As the LST steamed away, Sid heard someone say, "There must have been a lot of active missionaries on that island." When the 2/1 landed back on Goodenough, "as usual H Company had to unload the ship."

Although close enough to the front to have air raids, How Company enjoyed all the discipline of a bivouac area. When they cooled off too long in the river and returned to camp ten minutes late, the gunnery sergeant ordered them to miss lunch. When the colonel inspected their tents and found a mess cup in their trash pile, the platoon was put on report. These lapses, however, did not prevent Deacon from being promoted to sergeant. With the promotion came a transfer to the 60mm mortars. The 81mm mortars practiced on the same range as the 60mm, though, so for the time being the two friends still saw a lot of one another. Out on the range, the #4 gun squad set up the fastest, changed azimuths most accurately, and laid their bombs on the target in the fewest number of rounds. Before departing Goodenough, they witnessed a demonstration of the new bazookas and Bangalore torpedoes. Watching in fascination, Sid forgot for a moment about the endless rifle inspections, the piles of red ants, and the deluges of rain that threatened to drown him while hiking.

A FAIR NUMBER OF LIEUTENANT MICHEEL'S GREEN PILOTS MISJUDGED THEIR approaches and flopped or skidded into Narragansett Bay.[160] A carrier landing bounce drill, conducted on a runway painted with a ship's outline, demanded a high level of precision and timing. A Landing Signal Officer stood on his corner of the outline with his large paddles, waving in the Dauntlesses of Bombing Two. They landed tail first, trying to hit the spot where the arresting wires would lie on a real flight deck, then powered up immediately to climb back into the sky, get into the groove, and repeat it. On other days they made dummy bombing runs against any Atlantic convoys in the neighborhood, or rehearsed coordinated attacks with army units marching on Cape Cod. The nights of the Snake Ranch had ended. With a big city nearby, and with Boston and New York within range of any officer clutching a two-day pass, finding good places to get drunk and chat up women came easily.

Not one to live the wild life, Mike looked upon all these shenanigans with a veteran's aplomb. "I'm not getting shot at. So that's good." That fall he passed the one-thousand-hour mark in flight time and his skipper recommended his promotion, describing his "quiet, even and pleasant disposition and strong character." Mike's experience had been "very helpful to the other pilots of the squadron." Vernon Micheel, now a full lieutenant in the United States Navy, had become a senior naval aviator.

Jean had stayed in touch with him. She arranged to come up to see him with a friend of hers, but it fell through at the last minute. Later in October, though, Bombing Two received orders to prepare to ship out to the West Coast. The wolves began to receive longer passes. One night on the phone Jean said, "Why don't you come down and visit me one weekend?" Mike agreed. A few days later he got on the train and was walking down the aisle when he saw Richey, one of his squadron mates. Mike sat down and started making conversation. "Where are you going?" Richey said he was going to Philadelphia. Mike asked, "Where are you going in Philadelphia?" Richey said Germantown. Mike said, "Well, so am I. Who are you going to see?"

"Jean Miller."

"Who?!"

"Jean Miller," Richey repeated. Catching himself, Mike let a moment pass before he asked casually, "What's Jean look like?"

"Oh, she's about so tall with long hair down to her shoulder, henna colored hair. She's an athletic build." That sounded like a spot-on match.

"Oh, OK, well, see you later, Richey." Mike found a reason to find another seat. Getting off the train, "the first thing I did I went to the telephone and I called up and Jean answered the phone. I said, 'I'm at North Philly station, were you expecting me this weekend?!'

"'Yeah. Why are you talking like that?'

"'Well, I just came down on a train with Richey and he says he's going to see a Jean Miller.'

"'Oh,' she says, 'I know her, she . . . lives over in the next neighborhood.'" Jean went on to explain, the relief evident in her voice, that people often mixed up her and the other Jean. It took a little assurance to convince Mike. He had been ready to get back on the train. Everything turned out all right, though. When the weekend ended, they said good-bye with the understanding that he was headed off to the war. In one way this fact had always been there, since Lieutenant Micheel refused to think beyond the war. He was not one to speculate about the future he did not control. Jean had already guessed that she should not expect too many letters from her quiet Mike while he was away.[161]

On October 24, 1943, the orders came through for the pilots of Bombing Two to fly their aircraft to Alameda, California. Before they left, they took a squadron photo in front of their mascot, Vertigo, the Sea Wolf. Mike called Jean to say good-bye. On the thirty-first, he and his new, regular rear seat gunner, Aviation Machinist's Mate First Class Charles Hart, flew across America, toward the Pacific.

PRIVATE EUGENE SLEDGE MADE NO ATTEMPT TO HIDE HIS DELIGHT AT BEING IN boot camp in his letters home. Everything looked perfect. The Spanish influence on the Recruit Depot's architecture, with terra-cotta roof tiles and courtyards framed by arched walkways, held all the allure of the new and the exotic. The important buildings had been painted in camouflage. Recruit Platoon 984, to which Sledge and sixty-three others were joined summarily, assembled in front of their drill instructor (DI) that first evening. "You're okay in my book," the DI began, "because you are a complete volunteer platoon." The DI stopped his talk for a moment, interrupted by a boot from another platoon standing at attention and uttering "Yes, sir" constantly. After draping a steel bucket over the boot's head, the DI declared his surprise at the "fine physical shape" his new platoon was in. He promised them Platoon 984 "would be treated better than the draftees," because they had had "guts enough to get into the Corps without being drafted." The face of every man in 984 shone with the praise even as it likely betrayed a trace of concern about the man with the bucket over his head yelling "Yes, sir!" over and over again.

Being demoted again, this time from private to "boot," did not bother Eugene a bit. He prepared himself to "catch plenty of sand." In his formal induction interview, Eugene neglected to mention his membership in his high school band and his tennis lessons at Marion, instead choosing to assert that his sports had been boxing and football. Sledge had not come all this way to play in the band. He set his sights on getting into Sea School after boot camp. Sea School prepared marines to serve on the navy's battlewagons and carriers.

His platoon moved into some tents near the edge of the base, next to a large factory that produced B-24 bombers. Every few minutes, one of the big four-engine planes rolled off the assembly line and roared overhead. The tents leaked, so Platoon 984 left ponchos on their beds to keep them dry. The damp bed and hard training soon gave Gene the first of a number of colds and fevers. In spite of his fastidiousness about his dress and hygiene, he loved it. He gave himself over to the Marine Corps, hustling for all he was worth. The lessons learned at Marion Military Institute and from Captain Payzant helped him negotiate the treacherous terrain of a boot, where any missteps brought instant punishment. He felt sorry for those men who had had no such preparation.

While those in the 984 with no prior training had a harder time adjusting to the discipline, Eugene's problem was with his parents. Due to the lag in letters created by his sudden departure, he had not heard their reaction. Amid all of his breezy letters about boot camp, he made sure to build his case. About a thousand men from V-12 had been "gyped like I was." Every one of them agreed the officer training program had problems. Eugene Sledge, however, was not a good liar. In one of his first letters, even as he explained again how he had been let go because he lacked training in engineering, he included the lines "For yours and father's sake I will always be sorry I was a failure. But I have one consolation, that is if I had passed everything I'd still be here anyway. So you see, I'm really not a failure." While the depth of his relationship with them may have caused him to inadvertently admit he had flunked out, it did not prevent him from offering what amounted to a bribe: "if I have to sell eggs and chickens do it, I'm going to get a degree in history or business after the war."

The fateful reply arrived at Eugene's mail call on November 16. Dr. and Mrs. Sledge had acknowledged his transfer. He replied at once, opening his letter with "I got your two letters today and boy it was like a blood transfusion to hear from home. You can't realize how relieved I am to know you realize that it wasn't my fault because I am here." He shared their disappointment. He knew that his sudden departure had given them a scare. He appreciated their surprise that he had not phoned home while in the Mobile train station. Being denied permission to use the phone had made him sick. Now that they understood, though, he had a clear conscience. He dropped it, smartly, and wrote letters describing his life as a boot and the rigors of extended order drill. After listing the types of candy he would like to receive and letting them know he did not need his dress blue uniform sent, he agreed with his mother's choice for the new watch she wanted to purchase for him. With his gold watch locked away for the time being, "an American shock and waterproof is just the type. Don't pay too much for it."

As usual, he asked for the news from home and wondered about the health of his horse, Cricket, and his dog, Deacon. He knew his father had been out in the countryside, hunting ducks and squirrels, and Gene sorely missed being with him. The highlight of the week was the appearance of the comedian and movie star Bob Hope, who had given a show at the base theater. Although the boots had not been allowed to attend the show, Hope had walked out on the outdoor stage afterward.

Bob brought with him the comedian Jerry Colonna and a few beautiful actresses and singers. They performed an abbreviated version of their show. Looking out at all the young men, Hope observed their hair had been cut so short, "they must have cut it from the inside."

ALTHOUGH HE WAS OFFICIALLY ON FURLOUGH UNTIL THE END OF NOVEMBER, Manila John's public relations duties continued on a sporadic basis. On November 9, he and his brothers Carlo and Angelo went into Manhattan to record a radio show.[162] The three brothers read from their scripts. The central story involved Manila John talking about the night he "killed all those japs." He said little beyond "we kept our guns going until we had them licked," and had his brother Carlo say, "You and your crew killed thirty-eight japs right in front of your emplacement." The oblique reference to Cecil and Billie Joe represented a small victory, as did having the announcer pronounce the name Basilone correctly, with the final *e* enunciated. The radio program used the viewers' interest in his story as the backdrop for John praising all of the war workers who "gave us the stuff to fight with."

The conclusion began with Carlo, who said, "I'll never forget that Sunday you left home for overseas. Remember? All of us kids at mom's house and after putting away all that grub, you got up to go . . ." Angelo jumped in at this point, with "And all you said was 'Goodbye folks—be seeing you in the funnies.'" The three laughed as scripted, "ha, ha, ha," as they papered over the tense night three years ago when John had informed their parents he had quit his job and joined the marines. Sal and Dora had not been happy. Angelo continued. "That's just what happened, so help me. One day my kids were reading the comics, and there you were: Sergeant John Basilone, a hero." John said, "Yeah, sure, sure," and their laughter came more easily as the program ended.

The next day, the birthday of the United States Marine Corps, would have also brought a laugh from Manila, if only to himself. As part of a radio tribute to his corps, John urged young women to join the marines.[163] Since he was receiving a stream of letters from a certain Corporal Carolyn Orchovic of the USMC's Women's Reserve, who was wondering when he would return to D.C. so they could continue dating, he obviously had nothing against women in uniform.[164] He went to headquarters in D.C. whenever ordered; otherwise he lived in Raritan.

Life in the home he had grown up in grew uncomfortable slowly. He liked people, and everywhere he went in Raritan, everybody knew Manila John. His friends and family knew he had a long furlough, assumed the Marine Corps would give him a cushy job eventually, and believed he was set for life. When asked about the public events, he would say, "I feel like a bull thrower."[165] Everyone had a laugh at that. John did not elaborate. The truth was his future did not look clear to him. The brass liked having him available for public relations duties and had extended his furlough to make that easier. When officers did speak with him about future options, these included being an instructor at the marine base in New York City or going back to D.C. and serving in the guard company of the Navy Yard. Both of these options represented more public appearances, more time in dress uniforms, more time spent behind a desk or in a room with officers and less time outside with the infantry. He began going for long walks late at night. The physical activity settled him down, allowed him to think. He also kept a bottle of scotch on his nightstand.[166] His close friends and his family had seen these signs before—years earlier his long walks had preceded him quitting a job. John's growing discomfort, however, mystified friends and family. Manila John had it all. Their views perhaps persuaded him not to seek anyone's advice. He told his younger sister Mary, "I had to make up my own mind."[167]

In mid-November the mailman brought John a note from Dog Company. They had passed around his letter to them. "You didn't forget the boys," they affirmed, and used the phrase they heard in Melbourne, "Good on you, Yank." After teasing "the medal kid" about having "too many women," his friends tried to pass along a little news of their own: "all the liberty is finished & you can guess what that means."[168] It was not much of a guess. Dog Company had gone back to the war.

IN SHOFNER'S DIARY OF HIS LIFE AS A GUERRILLA ON MINDANAO, MORE ENTRIES concerned fiestas than firefights. He and the officers above him wanted to move beyond scouting and spying. The Filipino people expected their guerrillas to attack the enemy. MacArthur's headquarters in Australia, however, made it clear that the guerrilla units were not to attack Japanese targets. The submarines sent to Mindanao held some small arms and some ammunition, but nothing larger and not in great numbers. Although Shofner and his immediate officers tended to blame Australia, their problems went beyond equipment to organizing and training. The leaders of the various bands of guerrillas often squabbled with one another about methods, goals, and the chain of command. Simply maintaining a regular schedule of radio reports to Australia often proved difficult. In recognition of this, Shofner spent part of his time engaged in propaganda aimed at maintaining the loyalty of the Filipinos. He thrived in the make-it-up-as-you-go-along world of a guerrilla.

His job involved politics, economics, and religion. It also had its advantages. "Everything fouled so bad," Shofner wrote one Friday, he had "decided to take a day off and start fresh Monday."

His life as a guerrilla leader came to an end when the USMC HQ in Australia ordered Colonel Wendell Fertig to return him, Mike Dobervich, and Jack Hawkins. The other four remaining escapees would also return, separately. Shifty's job as deputy chief of operations ended on November 1. He began awaiting his submarine home in the village of Rizal, where he had spent much of his time. Thirteen days passed before he heard definite news. Another two passed before "D-day," when everything went wrong.

The truck that ran on alcohol ran out of alcohol. The bike had a flat. Shifty walked most of the way to the rendezvous site until he found a bicycle to "commandeer." At the harbor he found Jack Hawkins, Mike Dobervich, and a few Filipino guerrillas awaiting transport. Colonel Fertig also arrived, late. His horse had run away. Scouts had been placed on the roads for miles around them. They felt safe from the Japanese. The anticipation must have been nearly overwhelming. Dobervich sent up the all clear signal for the sub too early and incurred the wrath of his friends until USS Narwhal surfaced at five twenty-five p.m. Shofner lost a bet to Fertig on the time and handed over one Philippine peso.

Unloading the sub took over four hours at top speed. A large number of guerrillas handled the boxes of medicine, ammunition, and the "I Shall Return" matchbooks Shifty despised. The escapees said good-bye to Colonel Fertig and good-bye to many Filipino friends who had risked their lives to protect them. As the Narwhal cast off from the dock, the band played "God Bless America." The next morning Shofner wrote in his diary that the submarine "went through Surigao straights into Pacific . . . all well."

Although he would have to learn to like the sub's soft bed, the familiar food and the hot coffee were most welcome. The ship's captain, Lieutenant Commander Parsons, hailed from Shelbyville, Shofner's hometown, and his mother's maiden name was Shofner. They had some catching up to do. The sub made its best speed while on the surface. Twice they spotted planes. The second time a pair of enemy planes approached within four miles, coming in low and fast right at them. The skipper bellowed orders and Narwhal's bow pointed down. She ended the dive to 150 feet with a sharp turn. No bombs were heard. The captain told them he was taking them to Port Darwin and, barring any more disturbances, they would arrive on November 22; from there, a plane would take them to MacArthur's headquarters in Brisbane. Shofner borrowed a book about the marines on Guadalcanal to keep himself entertained.* When *Narwhal* crossed the equator, Shofner and his friends were delighted to learn they had become "shellbacks."

SLEDGE'S HAPPINESS DISAPPEARED IN AN INSTANT. JUST BEFORE THANKSGIVING, he received a letter from his parents. They had received a letter from the V-12 program at Georgia Tech advising them that their son had flunked out and been transferred. His parents accused him of lying to them. He felt terrible, but there was no going back. He launched a campaign to convince them he had neither lied nor flunked out. The explanations grew lengthy. The letter they had received from the V-12 program was explained away by relating the story of one of his friends in boot camp. This "boy," Eugene claimed, had passed his courses in Atlanta, but had requested a transfer. This boy's parents had received a letter stating their son had flunked out. While the unnamed boy was obviously "crazy," and Sledge himself had "wanted to become an officer," this story proved that "no matter why anyone left, his parents received the same letter."

Although they continued to correspond about other matters, and the packages of goodies continued to arrive, Dr. and Mrs. Sledge remained unconvinced. Their youngest son pushed harder. "I might not be a credit to the Sledge name," he said, "but I've never lied to you or pop. And I didn't lie about my leaving Tech. If I had failed, I promise you I would admit it. . . ." Gene increased the pressure. "I guess you know, I've got a lot of danger to face before I come home again. I'll face it like a Sledge should, and I won't fail to hold up the name. But please believe me, for I've told you the absolute truth."

The ordeal of boot camp, meantime, had begun to change. Platoon 984 took its turn at the rifle range in late November. Their day still began with the DI waking them up at five a.m. Every last man in Sledge's hut, all nineteen of them, immediately lit a cigarette and began coughing. Sledge thought they were crazy. Smoking's ill effects were readily apparent. After chow, the DI turned them over to the instructors on the rifle range. These marines were concerned with teaching the boots to shoot straight. Eugene, whose passion for firearms went back to his earliest days, ate it up. When asked about the largest caliber he had fired to date, Sledge proudly described his .54-caliber muzzle loader. Absorbing every detail of the instruction, he set his

---

Into the Valley by John Hersey was published in February 1943. It detailed the Third Battle of the Matanikau, in which Chesty Puller's Seventh Marines (led by the marines of Basilone's Charlie Company) won their first clear victory. Richard Tregaskis's *Guadalcanal Diary* was also published in 1943.

sights on earning the highest rank, Expert, when his platoon fired for record. Scoring that high would help him earn the right to go to Sea School, his first choice of duty assignments.

The training with the M1 rifle brought back a flood of happy memories of hunting with his father. He wanted to tell his father about his training so he would "understand why Marines are the best riflemen in the world." In the evening, as he listened to the others in his hut talk about their parents, he realized how lucky he and his brother Edward had been. Eugene wrote to tell them about an argument his hut mates and he had had about where they would like to go on their first liberty. "You can bet I said I'd go home & stay there as much as possible. We have the most beautiful home & finest & happiest family I ever knew of. We really have a lot to be thankful for and I really am." He spoke of going to college upon his return. However, Eugene never let go of his demand that his parents accept his explanation about his departure from the V-12 program. Dropping the subject was not good enough.

An escort ship led their submarine through the minefield and into Port Darwin. A lieutenant colonel in the USMC met Shofner, Hawkins, and Dobervich onshore and brought them to an unmarked house. As he doled out Red Cross packages, the colonel told them they were flying to a hospital in Brisbane the following day. He also ordered them not to divulge any information about themselves to anyone. From what Shofner could see, the armed forces in Darwin enjoyed such a level of comfort "I do not believe these people are doing any fighting." The hospital in Brisbane turned out to be very impressive. On November 24, Shifty slept late, took his first hot shower and shave in two years, and had ice cream for lunch. The doctors began to run tests. His duties included getting new uniforms and a haircut; having his teeth cleaned; and writing a report about the Japanese prisoner-of-war camps. He also played poker against all comers in his ward. He lost $17 on a run of terrible cards.

At the end of the month, the hospital discharged him, Hawkins, and Dobervich. They received orders to return to the United States and were given a class-three priority for seats on naval air transport planes. A few days later Shofner delivered a series of reports to Brigadier General C. A. Willoughby, the intelligence officer, or G-2, of the General Headquarters for the South West Pacific Areas. Based on the entries of his daily diary, he had written a record of events in the POW camps from May 6, 1942, to April 4, 1943; an account of their escape; and a document entitled "Service with Guerrilla Forces in the 10th Military District, Philippine Islands: May 11 to November 15, 1943."[169]

As the senior officer of his contingent of the escapees, Captain Shofner would have considered it his duty to prepare a report. All of the ten men shared the intense desire to let the world know the atrocity being committed, and a military report written in a timely fashion formed a foundation for publicity. Publicity in Shofner's mind would produce legal redress and spur military action against Japan. As the only one to have kept a diary, Shofner could write with a level of specificity others could not match. The final part to his report, "Recommendations for the Philippine Islands," demonstrated his strength of purpose and high level of energy.

Shofner's three-page memorandum detailed the means by which the United States could strengthen the guerrilla forces and use them to prepare the way for the U.S. invasion. This included sending a large cadre of officers to take command of the guerrilla forces at all levels. He recommended that a general be put in command. His note that the rank of general might be "temporary if necessary," combined with his insistence on the necessity of "experience," suggested that he had someone in mind for the job. His own experience had taught him "the Filipino soldiers are good fighters under American officers." However, "the average Filipino must be treated as a child." Americans also needed to understand "extreme patience as the ways of the East are mysterious." The equipment needed for this mission was spelled out in a long, prioritized list. "Bullets are the best propaganda," he insisted. Much of the list was devoted to sabotage equipment, ammunition and guns, although he itemized the medicines, clothing, and various types of communications equipment, including mimeograph machines. A final page covered the long list of incidentals like raincoats, buttons, and flashlights.

While his memo focused on protecting the Filipinos' faith in America and creating a force capable of isolating the enemy, Shofner included the plight of the POWs in his plan of action as well. Vitamin tablets should be sent to the camps "immediately," because some of it would make it to the prisoners and their needs were "urgent." It had to be done before Japan moved all of the POWs to camps on the island of Formosa, well inside the empire. This threat had been heard many times in Cabanatuan. One outcome of his plans for the guerrillas on Mindanao, a reader would have inferred, would be to move beyond the relief of the POWs to their rescue.

Before departing, the three marines were driven to the office of the commander of the South West Pacific Areas, General Douglas MacArthur. The general had already heard of the plight of the POWs from Commander McCoy and his friends. The marines affirmed the truth of McCoy's story. Shofner disclosed that he had kept a list of all the POWs he felt had betrayed their oaths to their country. MacArthur gave a vague reply about ensuring returning POWs received proper acknowledgment for their service. The discussion, however, turned away from the war. MacArthur's wife, Jean Faircloth MacArthur, was a distant relative of the Shofner clan. Next came the unexpected. The general decorated him, Hawkins, and Dobervich with the Distinguished Service Cross. As he pinned the U.S. Army's highest award for bravery on Shofner, the general said, "Never during my long and illustrious career have I presented a more deserved" award. The citation, dated that day, December 6, had been awarded not to the captain who had been captured on Corregidor, nor to the lieutenant colonel of the guerrillas, but to Major Austin Shofner of the USMC. He had received an official promotion. Major Austin Shofner's citation, "for extraordinary heroism in actions in the Philippine Islands," described his escape from the camp, his volunteer service as a guerrilla, and praised his delivery "of information of great military value on the defense of Corregidor and the treatment of our prisoners of war in Japanese hands."

After Shofner, Hawkins, and Dobervich left the general's presence, the new major vented his disgust. MacArthur had dared speak of his "illustrious career" to men who had endured the results of his failure.[170] Being Shifty, he later poked fun at the general's carefully cultivated aura of power, quipping that during the meeting he had felt like MacArthur was "God and I was the right hand angel. It took me 48 hours before I could have a dirty thought." The PBY bearing the three heroes departed Brisbane on December 9, making stops at Noumea, Efate, and elsewhere along the chain before landing in Hawaii on December 14.

MANILA JOHN REPORTED TO THE NAVY'S WAR BOND OFFICE IN MANHATTAN on December 6 to prepare for the Pearl Harbor Day bond drive. On the anniversary of the attack, he traveled upstate to a bond rally in the town of New Windsor. With each bond sold, he autographed a special preprinted flyer, dedicated to the person who bought it. The front side of the flyer explained why it was important to buy bonds and thanked the donor. The reverse quoted from the citation for John's medal. It also described how he "had a machine gun on the go for three days and three nights without sleep, rest or food"; and how he had "killed 38 japs near his hole with a pistol."[171] At least the flyer to which he signed his name correctly identified him as "the only living enlisted Marine wearing the coveted Congressional Medal of Honor." After a cold day riding in a jeep and thanking bond buyers, he returned to the city to attend another big gala thrown by the National Association of Manufacturers (NAM) at the Waldorf-Astoria, one of the great hotels of New York.

As befitted one of the nation's most powerful industry associations, the NAM held a very fancy affair for the four thousand members attending its "second War Congress." The remarks by its speakers were recorded for an international radio broadcast. The chairman of General Motors informed his audience that GM was ready to invest $500 million into "postwar America."[172] Lieutenant General A. A. Vandegrift, identified as the Commandant of the Marine Corps although his tenure would not begin until the new year, said that victory over Japan would "demand the best kind of teamwork."[173] John sat on the dais next to another sergeant, William Downs, who had lost a leg in the air war over Stuttgart, Germany. Both men gave short speeches as a part of thanking their hosts.[174]

In order to make Manila John available to attend the NAM event, the USMC had extended his leave again, to December 26. So he returned home to Raritan for another twenty days of furlough. One of the letters that arrived during that period came from his friend Richard Greer.[175] Greer started by giving him the Dog Company news—who was now sergeant of which platoon, who had gotten busted in rank, who "broke his hand on somebody's jaw." Their pet, Jockstrap, was still with Dog Company. J. P. Morgan sent his regards but would not write. The boys were near the ocean and were once again bathing in a river. They saw lots of "fuzzy wuzzies," or natives, mostly males but sometimes females. "The young are black, bushy headed with those pointed breast and the old gals are baggy and their breast hang down to their waist."

Even out in the boonies, Greer said they had read a news report stating John would soon marry Helen Helstowski, Steve's sister. Along with demanding to know "the dope," Greer teased him. Like all good jokes, there was some truth and some lies mixed together. "We thaught you had a wife and kids in Minila to take care of let alone one in the states. Ever hear from Nora? Or the gook gal you ran up a coconut tree about eighteen months ago? I believe Morgan dragged you out of the church in Georgia once time. Boy you've had some close calls but this time its news and you're _____." Greer closed the letter by saying that they all wanted to hear from him. Having written letters for John, Greer knew his friend all too well, so he ordered Manila to "get somebody to do it if you won't."

THE MONTHS SPENT AT NAVAL AIR STATION SANTA ROSA, JUST NORTH OF SAN Francisco, had been very much like the months of training at NAS Quonset Point, Rhode Island. The naval aviators of Bombing Two gained confidence faster than competency. They referred to their Dauntlesses in disparaging terms. They expressed their concern that they were missing the war. The arrival of another award for Lieutenant Vernon Micheel could have only convinced them they were right. Mike received notice from the navy that he was entitled to wear the Presidential Unit Citation for his service aboard *Enterprise*, which had "participated in nearly every major carrier engagement in the first year of the war."

It escaped no one's attention that none of the U.S. carriers had merited that kind of award for their actions in 1943. There had not been any major carrier engagements and the end of the year was fast approaching. A look at the map showed the United States in control of the Gilberts and the Solomon Islands. A vast ocean dotted with hundreds of islands separated them from Tokyo. One afternoon the wolves found out they were going to do their share to get there. In mid-December they packed their Dauntlesses hurriedly and flew down to Alameda. Instead of an immediate departure, they found themselves in a barracks near the wharf. Being so close to San Francisco, and not being ones to sit idle, most of the wolves raised such a drunken ruckus that the whole squadron was put on report. The warning made little impression on the ringleaders. They knew Uncle Sam had a job waiting for them. A few days before Christmas a crane began to load their airplanes on a small aircraft carrier, known as a "jeep" carrier. The pilots of Bombing Two walked aboard. "Marines stood on the dock with sub-machine guns," the ensigns noted sarcastically, "as if to prevent dangerous criminals from a last minute escape."[176] After sailing under the Golden Gate Bridge, Bombing Two would spend Christmas 1943 cramped in a small space on the way to Pearl Harbor.

SHOFNER AND HIS FRIENDS MADE GOOD TIME FLYING ACROSS THE PACIFIC ON A class-three priority. They landed at Pearl Harbor on December 14. On their way to Washington, they changed planes in Chattanooga, Tennessee. Shofner walked into the airport. "Behind the Pennsylvania Central Airline counter Shofner saw . . . Kathleen King, his sweetheart."[177] They had begun dating while attending the University of Tennessee. He got in line. Jack Hawkins watched as he walked up to her. She caught sight of him and fainted. The man she knew had lost some of his strength, with lines etched into deeply tanned skin. He had lost some teeth. The last word from him had come a year ago, a postcard letting his family know he was a prisoner. Here he was out of the blue and he had a plane to catch. He had been ordered not to reveal his ordeal. Shofner was allowed to share good news: after he and the others reported in to the chief of naval operations, they would receive furloughs. He would see her soon.

A car met their plane when it landed in D.C. and took them to the Willard Hotel. In the main dining room of the hotel, Major Shofner felt out of place "with a complexion more brown than that normally allowed a guest of the Willard." At least some of the guests, however, must have recognized him—if not by the DSC, the Silver Star, the Purple Heart, and rows of campaign ribbons, then by his uniform and rank—as a veteran returned from the Pacific. The three marines were allowed a few days of rest. After completing some paperwork, Shofner got paid and decided to treat himself to a new pair of shoes. He had to admit to the shoe salesman that he had never heard of ration cards. He could not purchase shoes without them. It was one of those little things that made him think his transition would not be entirely easy.

The big meeting came on December 22, when the three friends went to see General Archer Vandegrift, the incoming commandant of the Marine Corps. The officers of his staff welcomed them, as did the general, until at length each escapee had a moment alone with Vandegrift. Along with the words of praise, the general offered the idea of Major Shofner working with a Hollywood studio on a film about the great story. It certainly had all the elements for a great movie. Austin came clean. One morning in Cabanatuan Prisoner of War Camp Number One, Shifty replied, he had decided to consider the war against the Japanese as a football game. His desire "to get back into the game, and to win . . . had kept him going." He "did not want to be cheated out of his opportunity to bring the battle to the Japanese." The general granted his request. As the meeting concluded, Vandegrift and his staff informed all three men that they would receive a two-month furlough. Even as he spoke, Vandegrift said, their families were being notified of their return. When their furloughs ended in late February, Major Shofner and Captain Dobervich would report to the Senior School of the Command Staff College of the Marine Corps in Quantico, Virginia. Captain Jack Hawkins would go out to Hollywood, California, and develop a movie about their experiences with the legendary film producer Darryl F. Zanuck.[178]

For the time being, however, they would have to continue to keep the secret of Cabanatuan, of the March of Death on Bataan, of their escape. The burning desire to tell their countrymen had helped sustain them. Now that they were home, they were ordered not to speak of it. Shofner was not told why, exactly, he had to keep his mouth shut. Everyone of prominence in Washington knew about it. He guessed that it had to do with President Roosevelt's decision to beat Germany first. Roosevelt wanted Americans to continue to focus on Germany, rather than on Japan. Whatever the reason, Austin Shofner's year did not end on a high note, but with frustration.

On December 23 he said good-bye to his two comrades, with whom he had endured so much, and boarded a flight for Nashville. His parents met him and drove him to Shelbyville. The thin line of blacktop made for a four-hour drive, so he had plenty of time to tell them "what he dared." Sharing the story of his war was a moment steeped in generations of family tradition. The land upon which their home stood had been granted to a Shofner for his service in the Revolutionary War. Austin's grandfather had served in the cavalry led by Nathan Bedford Forrest during the Civil War. As the car neared their home, it passed an oil truck driven by one of Austin's teammates from his high school football team. They exchanged a wave. The car pulled into the drive. Austin was home. His mother began preparing dinner. In the driveway came the oil truck, followed by the cars of more friends. The homecoming lasted late into the evening and continued the next day as aunts, uncles, cousins, and more came for a visit.

The party proved too much too soon. All that he had suffered at the hands of his captors could not be washed away by a few weeks of hot showers, nor bound up by a clean dress uniform, nor healed by his parents' warm embrace. Months as a guerrilla had helped him, but sometime that day, Christmas Eve of 1943, Austin's family watched as he "collapsed into a state of near total mental and physical exhaustion."

EVENTUALLY EUGENE SLEDGE'S PARENTS STATED THAT THEY BELIEVED HIM: HE had been kicked out of the V-12 program against his will. Now all he had to worry about was the weather, since the daily rains were hindering his platoon's rifle instruction and the final test was approaching. Then a camp doctor determined that one of the members of Platoon 984 had spinal meningitis and quarantined the lot of them for three days. Eugene passed the time reading the Mobile newspaper and writing his friends and family. "From what the papers say," he joked, "I am safer out here than in Mobile with all the ship workers. When all of us come home I really hope all those people have left town for good." The newspapers had also carried stories about the marine invasion of Tarawa in the Gilbert Islands. The marines had suffered more casualties in three days there than in six months on Guadalcanal, a disturbing fact that no one at the Recruit Depot could explain to him, except to say "something went radically wrong."

When the quarantine ended, Platoon 984 shot for record, meaning their scores would be entered into their personnel files and affect their respective futures. Eugene shot 300 out of a possible 340, just shy of Expert. Although disappointed to rank only Sharpshooter, he had been around long enough to know that in this category, the one prized by the Marine Corps above all others, his score placed him above the average. The platoon left the rifle range and returned to its huts for the final week of training. The NCOs gave a lecture on the Japanese use of sabers. Sledge "thought that's absolutely got to be the most ridiculous thing. That was in the Civil War when people were running around waving a saber at people." The boots eased through the last few days. Sledge was allowed to take communion for the first time since his arrival and spent every last dollar he had ordering Christmas presents for his family.

A number of Christmas presents for him, carefully selected and beautifully wrapped, began to arrive as Christmas approached. Boot camp officially ended for Platoon 984 on December 24. Along with being recognized as a Sharpshooter, Eugene had scored a perfect 5 in "obedience" and "sobriety," and 4s in the other categories, like "military efficiency" and "intelligence." Although he already had worn the eagle, globe, and anchor emblem, Sledge attached it to his collar not as a student but as a United States Marine. He had been promoted to Private First Class. He would depart for Camp Elliott, a training base nearby, on Christmas Day.

In mid-December, Sid Phillips's company had the chance to review their next assignment while studying a physical, three-dimensional map of the island of New Britain. The big enemy base of Rabaul sat on one end of the long thin scythe of an island. Reports of the slow devastation of Rabaul by U.S. planes had been reaching them for two months. The 1st Marine Division would storm ashore on the other end of New Britain, on Cape Gloucester, near New Guinea. The advance had already begun. In the course of the past two weeks, his division had leapfrogged up the northern coast of New Guinea. Each stop had involved unloading the ship, making camp, breaking camp, and reloading. As they neared the point of New Guinea that almost touched Cape Gloucester, the air raid alerts were no longer false alarms. Enemy bombers appeared overhead on occasion.

As December came to a close, Sid's 2nd Battalion, First Marines, learned that not all of the division would go ashore at Cape Gloucester. Their battalion, reinforced with some supporting units to form a landing team (LT-21), would seize a beachhead near the village of Tauali, eight miles from the main invasion site. The 2/1 would block one of the island's main trails and thereby prevent the enemy from either resupplying its forces at the main beachhead or withdrawing from that position.[179] One last leapfrog brought them and the rest of the First Marines to Finschhafen; the next one would take them into combat. Not so long ago, Finschhafen had been in the enemy's hands. The site of the battle interested Sid and Deacon because it was still littered with weapons, ordnance, and equipment. Through the port came battered ships and wounded men on their way to rear areas.

On December 23, the NCOs ordered the #4 gun squad to turn in all of their khaki uniforms, all excess clothes, and all personal effects they wished to save. Amid the equipment they were authorized to take with them were their new jungle hammocks. Sid liked his hammock. A waterproof tarp and a mosquito net covered the hammock's sleeping area. At last the U.S. military had figured out how to provide its troops with a convenient means of escaping the wet and muddy ground. Before Christmas service that evening, they learned that Cape Gloucester had been bombed by one hundred Liberators, the four-engine bombers of the army air corps.

Christmas Eve found the 2/1 in a flurry of action as they made final preparations. Each man received ammunition, salt pills, Halazone tablets (for water purification), Atabrine, and some of the army's good K rations. Christmas packages from the Red Cross were also distributed. "Headquarters Company," Deacon observed of the distribution, "got the best as usual." In the evening, Lieutenant Colonel James Masters, Sr., gave his battalion landing team a talk. Masters had just come over from the States, so he was green. The word was he had lost a brother at Wake Island. Masters ordered his men to "kill the bastards whenever we could." He reminded Sidney Phillips of his father. "I liked the man immediately; he hated the Japanese just like the rest of us." One of Sid's friends took to calling their battalion "Masters's Bastards."

The air raid alert went off a few times that night. It sounded again at four a.m., a half hour before reveille sounded on Christmas Day. After chow, they set about policing up their camp. The NCOs inspected their packs. How Company walked up the gangways of LCI 30 at two twenty p.m. Unlike the LCT with which they had trained, the LCI looked like a regular ship, although on either side of its bow a set of stairs could be lowered to water level. Sid's ship steamed out of port at three p.m. bound for New Britain, accompanied by the four other LCIs, twelve LCTs, and fourteen LCMs carrying the marines and equipment of LT-21. Two destroyers escorted the convoy, which used the cover of darkness to cross the Dampier Straits.

THE PRESSURE HAD BEEN BUILDING INSIDE OF JOHN BASILONE FOR SOME TIME. As the date approached for his return to duty, December 26, the discussion became pointed. His family and friends could see his discomfort with the situation as it existed. They had heard he had turned down an offer to be promoted to second lieutenant. None of them understood his unease. His future looked so bright. The $5,000 war bond meant that he could afford to set himself up properly with a fine home and a car. As for the war, he had done his part. It was "somebody else's turn."[180] John should accept a cushy job, enjoy his hard-won success, and be near his family.

All of it made perfect sense to everyone except John. He was thinking of settling down with the right girl and even of starting a family eventually. However, he had had a glimpse of the life that awaited him at Marine Corps Headquarters. It involved sitting behind a desk and filing reports. John had dropped out of the eighth grade for a reason. Although the Marine Corps knew his weakness in administrative work, it seemed willing to ignore it.[181] Providing ceremonial security details for high-ranking officers and special events meant observing protocols and strict military decorum. Neatness and military bearing had never been John's strong suits; in D.C. they were inescapable. Outside the buildings, officers saluted when they recognized him, as a mark of respect for the thin blue ribbon bar with white stars that hung above all the other medals on his Class A uniform. In Raritan, Manila John was a famous hero and a credit to the Italian community. The John Basilone Day Committee wanted to raise money to build the John Basilone Public Library. John, however, regarded himself as a "professional marine." He wanted to get back to the life that made sense to him.

He could not put all that into words. Just before Christmas, he told his mother he was going to ask to be reassigned. "I don't want to go to Washington, but I have to go for two days to tell them."[182] He did not want a desk job. His older brothers, Carlo and Angelo, tried to talk him out of it. "Johnny, don't go back. You did enough. Why go back?" Angelo asked.[183] John had been offered a job as a machine-gun in- structor as well. He was good at that and it was safe. John obviously viewed the job of instructor as meaning more of the same: being on call whenever the Treasury Department or the Marine Corps needed a hero. He told his family he was "fed up with being an exhibition piece."[184] For all of those who were so passionate about the Medal of Honor and what it meant, he offered to give it to the parade committee for display at the local library if they thought it would help.[185] The idea would have seemed almost sacrilegious to his family.

The decision to return to a line company had come hard—not because he did not know what he wanted, but because of the expectations of others. Sergeant John Basilone left Raritan the day after Christmas, a Sunday. As soon as he could that next week, he went to Lieutenant General Vandegrift. Vandegrift, also a holder of the Medal of Honor for his service on Guadalcanal, always tried to make time for the men who had stood with him on the Canal. He was pleased to hear John say, "There is still a big job to be done over there and I want to be in at the finish."[186] General Vandegrift promised him he "would be among the first Marines to land in Tokyo."[187]

ACT IV

"HAZE GRAY AND UNDERWAY"

December 1943–June 1945

MOST OF 1943 HAD PASSED IN A SLOW, GRINDING WARFARE CONDUCTED BY America and her allies along the periphery of the Japanese empire. Less noticeably, the enemy had struggled to make up its losses in weapons and men. As the Imperial Navy shrank, the U.S. Navy experienced an unprecedented expansion. The war entered a new phase in late 1943 because Americans in factories, laboratories, and training camps had spent the last two years producing a vast arsenal of military weapons and equipment, as well as men and women trained to use them. The arrival of this awesome power fueled two separate drives aimed at Tokyo: one led by General Douglas MacArthur through the South Pacific; the other by Admiral Chester Nimitz through the central Pacific. The onslaught reduced the Empire of Japan to one set of military tactics.

THE PASSWORD FOR DECEMBER 26, D-DAY ON CAPE GLOUCESTER, WAS "GUADAL-canal." Just after five a.m. the mortar platoon watched a long stream of bombers off to their left and assumed they were bombing the main invasion beaches. The two destroyers nearby began firing their five-inch guns at the beach at seven thirty. Sid heard a friend beg Uncle Sam "not to be too thrifty" and fire more rounds, damn the expense. The shelling, however, halted after fifteen minutes and a squadron of fifteen medium bombers bombed and strafed the beach.[1] The bombers' fighter escort shot down eight enemy airplanes. The 2/1 landed at 8:05 a.m. against no opposition. Sid walked down the portside stairs and through knee-deep water to shore. The word was "the japs fled leaving everything." Abandoned packs, rifles, ammunition, and supplies indicated the enemy had occupied the area just prior to the morning's assault. The enemy's departure made more and more sense as the marines discovered the level of destruction wrought by the bombardment. All hands turned to the work of setting up the perimeter, unloading the ships, and getting their camp organized. Inexplicably, no chow had been unloaded for lunch.

The object of their invasion, the coastal trail, turned out to be "nothing more than a single footpath," so far as Sid could tell. The trail ran along a ridge about twelve hundred yards inland, paralleling the ocean. The 2/1 made the ridge and its section of trail the apex of its semicircular perimeter, with the line running back toward the beach on both sides. The perimeter enclosed an area of about three city blocks, all of it on an angle from the shore to the ridge. Beyond the ridge, the ground rose precipitously upward to the top of nearby Mount Talawe, at sixty-six hundred

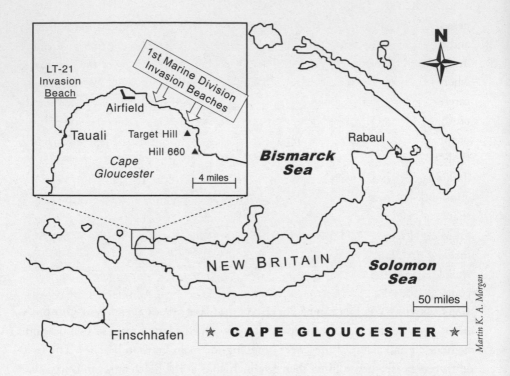

LT-21
Invasion
Beach

1st Marine Division
Invasion Beaches

Airfield

Tauali

Target Hill ▲

Hill 660 ▲

Cape
Gloucester

4 miles

Rabaul

**Bismarck
Sea**

N

NEW BRITAIN

**Solomon
Sea**

50 miles

Finschhafen

★ **CAPE GLOUCESTER** ★

Martin K. A. Morgan

feet. In the center of his perimeter, Colonel Masters put his 81mm mortar crews and a battery of 75mm guns. The day after the invasion, the #4 gun squad continued building their firing positions in the rain. It rained two and one-half inches that day, the water finding its way through the dense underbrush to the sharp ravines leading to the sea. The rain and the work continued the next two days. The working parties beat back and tramped down the mass of vegetation, which grew thicker and denser than the jungle of Guadalcanal. They strung barbed wire. They enjoyed eating the K rations, a step up from the C rations, although K rations convinced them the army got the best chow. They were glad when the cooks got their galleys operational on the twenty-eighth. Shots rang out along the perimeter several times that morning, and three patrols had reported skirmishes by noon. Marines manning the lines in Company E's sector saw enemy soldiers moving toward them. It was only a matter of time. Sid and all the others not manning foxholes on the line swung in their hammocks that evening, grateful for a dry place to sleep.

In the steady rain of the next day, another patrol contacted a large enemy force near the village of Tauali. A gale gathered around them in the afternoon and darkness came quickly. Just after midnight, during "a wild howling monsoon lightning and rain storm," the shit hit the fan on the right flank. The observation post called in the coordinates; the spotter asked for a barrage along that side of the perimeter, where G and H companies' lines met.[2] A fire mission so close to marines demanded careful leveling of the bubbles in the gun sights, the correct number of increments on the bottom of each shell, and precise calculations based on the range card. Each of the gun squads had been issued a one-cell flashlight for just such a contingency. Only Sid's worked, though. He moved from gun to gun as the others groped in the darkness. To get the rounds up and out of the jungle canopy, Sid had to keep the guns above a seventy-five-degree elevation. The big 75mm howitzers nearby lacked that trajectory and were therefore useless. The 81mms provided the fire support. An experienced gunner, Sid likened the job of firing a mortar in a jungle to standing inside a barn and "throwing rocks at the enemy . . . through holes in the roof." He walked the bursts to within fifteen yards of the front line. Some moments his squad could hear marines on the perimeter "pouring lead"; at other moments the concussions mixed with the thunder and became confusing. The soft cough of the 60mm mortars, being directed by his friend Deacon out there in the darkness, could not be heard at all.

Over the telephone came news of hand-to-hand fighting and a running total of banzai charges. Some of the men in Sid's OP were hit. The battle slackened after the fifth charge and stopped at about seven thirty a.m. The #4 gun squad dug out the base plate of their mortar. The concussions had forced it deep into the mud. Colonel Masters came to congratulate his 81mm mortar platoon on a fine performance. Masters asked his mortarmen to introduce themselves. He asked Private First Class Phillips to show him the one flashlight that had worked. It was a proud moment in an otherwise depressing situation. Instead of hot chow for breakfast—the cooks and the mess men had spent the night carrying ammo—they received more of the wax-paper cartons marked "U.S. Army Field Ration K" above a list of its contents. Slipping and struggling through the mud came the stretcher bearers, bringing back the dead and wounded. How Company had been hit hardest—of the six killed in action, four came from H Company; sixteen of the nineteen wounded had been How Company men. The surgical tent happened to be near the 81mm mortar platoon, so Sid got a good look at his friends' suffering. He felt helpless. They were in agony. He hated the feeling of not knowing what to do. In that moment a desire to learn to heal came to him.

The 81mm gun squads spent the morning cleaning up the mess around their mortars—most of it the packaging that encased their shells. Yellow range cards, one per canister, were strewn about. A few of them had been kissed by girls in the ammunition factory, imprinting the shape of their lips in red. Under the red lips the girls wrote messages like "Love you, Betty." Scrambling after these cards made the work go faster. "These cards were prized and passed around in the rain for everyone to kiss the red lip imprint and make obscene remarks about Betty." How Company prepared for another attack. The enemy body count arrived later. Someone said it was 185 and that "more japs were killed inside our line than outside."[3] Five wounded Japanese had become POWs.

The enemy that the marines could not kill or capture was the rain. It drilled them relentlessly. The area inside LT-21's perimeter had become a morass of mud. Sid and W.O. and the rest of #4 gun squad threw away their underclothes and socks, wearing only their "dungarees and boondockers and helmets just like we had done on Guadalcanal." The rain fed a dense thicket of jungle, which they had taken to calling the green inferno. The infinite shape and variety of green vegetation could drive a man to distraction. Sid saw it a bit differently. The heavy rains faded the color of his dungarees. Storm clouds darkened the jungle around him until he saw only shades of black and white.

PRIVATE FIRST CLASS EUGENE SLEDGE HAD HOPED TO STAY AT THE RECRUIT Depot in San Diego and receive training at its Sea School, where a marine learned how to serve in a detachment aboard a navy ship. A marine's duties on board a battleship or a carrier included a fair amount of ceremony, like serving in an Honor Guard, along with providing security and handling some of the ship's AA guns. Sledge thought the most elite marines went to Sea School and was disappointed not to have made it. He arrived at Camp Elliott, outside San Diego, on Christmas Day and learned that it trained tankers as well as infantry. Relieved to be assigned a bunk in a big barracks "with hot showers, good lights, and steam heat," he recovered from a fever and set his sights on getting into the tank or the artillery corps. The Marine Corps quickly decided that Private First Class Sledge would make a fine mortarman, and assigned him to Company E of its infantry battalion.

New Year's Day marked his first liberty since boot camp. He considered traveling into Los Angeles. Every man he spoke to, though, planned to go there "after women and whisky." He chose to visit the base library and write his parents to tell them he "was lucky to get in the best branch of the Corps. That is 60mm mortars. It is about the safest thing next to a desk job." That last observation was surely intended to assuage the concerns of his mother, to whom he also promised to be safe and to try to make corporal. He asked her to please send him his dress blue uniform, including for her benefit a detailed list of the items and packing instructions.

After ten days of training to be light artillery support for the infantry, E Company got up at five thirty a.m. and prepared to join the battalion for its first amphibious training exercise. Carrying the full complement of personal gear—pack, helmet, canteen, and M1—they boarded trucks for the twenty-mile ride to the shore of San Diego Bay. To give their training more authenticity, the wharves had been draped with cargo nets. The marines put on their life belts and climbed down the nets into Higgins boats.

Eugene's boat circled out in the bay for half an hour. He recognized several species of birds. At last the flotilla of small amphibious craft motored west through the dozens of large ships at anchor. Gene counted four enormous aircraft carriers as his boat went around North Island and out into the Pacific Ocean. The flotilla continued west for about a mile, where the powerful ocean swells took hold of the same landing craft, before turning back toward the coast. Another delay, inexplicable as always, began. Sledge noted a number of marines looking decidedly green around the gills.

The command boat flashed the signal, and the waves of boats roared toward North Island. Sledge's lieutenant ordered his three squads of eleven men to get below the gunwales. At the breakers, they hit a sandbar. The coxswain waited for the next wave to lift his boat; then he gunned the engine and got them close to the beach. Racing down the ramp, Eugene almost tripped on the man in front of him, who had sprawled into the knee-deep surf. He caught himself, however, and raced onto shore.

The marines of Easy Company threw themselves on the ground and awaited orders. After a few minutes, an officer came up and congratulated them. He pointed down the road and said, "Go get your chow." Leaving their rifles stacked, they walked over and formed a line for sandwiches and coffee. Hours passed. Sledge dried his dungarees as best he could, then went to examine a Japanese landing craft. It had several bullet holes in it. Compared to the Higgins boat, the enemy's landing craft appeared clumsy. An LCM (a larger version of the Higgins boat made for carrying a tank) arrived and E Company climbed aboard for the ride home. In describing it to his parents, he wrote, "We really learned a lot & feel pretty 'salty' now. Next time we will probably take our mortars with us."

The training satisfied Private First Class Sledge. He liked the 60mm mortar, although when another chance came up to become a tanker, he ran to sign up. His blues arrived, carefully tailored, just in time to wear them to a concert by the philharmonic orchestra.

The arrival of a battalion of paratroopers caught his interest. The paratroops had fought on Bougainville and were only too happy to tell the new marines all about jungle fighting. They were tough, hardened veterans who spoke of banzai charges in disparaging terms. Sledge found their opinion of MacArthur's soldiers not much higher. In the course of a story, one trooper remarked that "army discipline was pretty much a joke." The paratroopers also happily parted with their specialized knives and jump boots in exchange for pairs of nice leather shoes and other civilian accoutrement—the veterans had a month's furlough coming to them. Eugene traded for the jump boots. As he came to know Camp Elliott he also sought out other men from Mobile. One of them told him tales of flying in a Dauntless as the tail gunner in the Solomon Islands. Each bit of news about his new profession he carefully gathered, weighed, and remembered. Excelling in the Marine Corps meant learning from the "old salts," and Gene strove to excel.

BOMBING TWO'S SHIP HAD DOCKED AT PEARL HARBOR, THE NEXUS OF THE CAR-rier war. Cranes unloaded their planes and mechanics prepared them for flight. As soon as was possible, they flew east to NAS Hilo, a naval air station recently carved out of the dense tropical rain forest and the hard black volcanic rock lining the coast of Hawaii. A brass band tried mightily to play "Aloha" as a welcome, on behalf of the citizens of the small town of the same name. From the windows of their quarters, they could see the ocean in one direction and two great volcanic mountains (Mauna Loa and Mauna Kea) in the other. Micheel liked the small town, although it was quiet. Many of Hilo's citizens were of Japanese descent and not all of them spoke English. The pilots in his squadron would have preferred to be closer to the bright lights of Honolulu than on "the big island" of Hawaii. Their New Year's Eve party had not been worthy of note. Still, they admitted they had moved to paradise.

Their training regimen resumed in January. No one knew how long it would last. When their air group's fighter squadron arrived at Hilo, they saw that as a good sign. Given the navy's emphasis on the air group as a team, instead of a collection of squadrons, the assembly of Air Group Two meant that someday soon an empty aircraft carrier would show up. The skipper, aided by veterans like Mike and Buell, strove to make this training pay off. The bombing skills of their squadron had not become so sharp that they could avoid the occasional miss. During one exercise on the far side of the island, they practiced supporting ground troops near the marine base called Camp Tarawa. One of their practice bombs, which emitted only smoke, "was noticed fumigating the friendly marine camp."[4] Navigation exercises required a long flight to be effective because the two volcanoes near Hilo stood nearly fourteen thousand feet and were visible for fifty miles.

Along with stressing the mathematics of navigation, Lieutenant Micheel emphasized fuel conservation to the pilots in his wing. Their survival would depend upon their ability to do more than simply select the "auto-lean" setting on their fuel mixture. A good pilot experimented with his machine, sliding the control to a dash near "idle cut-off."[5] Leaning out the fuel mixture saved gasoline, but it also increased the cylinder head temperature. The RPMs would drop off as well. The pilot had to compensate for these, had to make wise choices about speed and altitude, had to dial in the proper trim. Knowing how far to push it and when, and why—these questions required the judgment that experience alone could produce. Bombing Two had had ample time to gain that experience, unlike Scouting Six's Ensign John Lough and so many others who had flown at Midway.

Lieutenant Micheel never mentioned Lough in his instruction. It was not his style. Perhaps he knew better. The pilots of Bombing Two had the prerequisite for success, confidence, in abundance. The wolves loved to fly and they loved being pilots. Their big joke was about life in their boring little town. "Culture raised its shiny dome in Hilo; it had to." On their off days they acted like tourists, visiting sites of Hawaiian culture or taking scenic drives in rented cars. They scouted many locations like the trained navigators they were. It took a few weeks, but the wolves finally threw themselves a "Squadron Party" at the Hilo Country Club. "The orchestra was small but," one wolf reported, "the drinks were heavy."[6] Many desirable young ladies attended, new friendships were made, and "culture passed away just as quickly as it had unexpectedly arrived."[7]

PATROLS FROM MASTERS'S BASTARDS CONTINUED TO ENCOUNTER SMALL ENEMY forces out in the jungle of Cape Gloucester. They found enemy troops sitting on logs and eating coconuts, found them sleeping with no one standing sentry. One patrol killed a column of IJA soldiers who had been marching on the trail without a man on point. Another found equipment stashes that included USMC items taken from the Philippines. Although Washing Machine Charlie often threatened harm at night, rarely did the air raid alert end with bombs being dropped. The marines on Cape Gloucester began to win handily in early January. The rough seas made resupply by ship difficult, though. On the morning of January 3, Colonel Masters had B-17s air-drop crates of mortar ammunition and some other critical supplies inside the perimeter.

One Japanese officer had come to their lines carrying a "flag of truce" and surrendered.[8] Every veteran of the Canal, though, knew this was an isolated occurrence and remained on the alert for the next onslaught. Enemy artillery ranged in on LT-21's perimeter on a few occasions. Much of it landed in the surf behind them. The OP called the 81mm mortar platoon to provide "counter-battery fire," to destroy the enemy artillery. They set the azimuth and range and fired a few white phosphorus rounds. The OP called in a correction and the whole battery of 81mms cut loose with a concentration of forty rounds from each of the #4 guns. The enemy battery fell silent only for a short time. At least when it resumed, the aim was still lousy. A rumor went around that the Japanese officer who had surrendered had offered to bring in five hundred more men and Colonel Masters had turned him down.

On the fifth, a Wednesday, word came to stand by: enemy troops had snuck inside the perimeter. "No shooting tonight," ordered Colonel Masters. "Get a knife or a bayonet and slit the yellow bastard's throat, draw blood." Nothing more came of the alarm, though, except a lot of lost sleep.

The occasional skirmishes with small bands of the enemy did not warrant the continued presence of Masters's Bastards astride the trail near Tauali. A combat force went north along the trail to the village of Sag Sag, said to be an enemy stronghold. The captain leading it decided the natives there were cooperating with the Japanese and he ordered the village burned. Pushing north, his patrol met another coming south, sent from its regiment. The trail between them was clear. LT-21 had completed its mission and would rejoin the 1st Division. Amphibious craft of various types began arriving offshore. The high seas delayed their beaching; eventually they came in and working parties began to load the gear. Although enemy planes from Rabaul still caused air raids occasionally, the word was that the U.S. fleet had "pulled into Rabaul Harbor in plain daylight and shelled them. That place must be deserted by now."

While their equipment went by ship, the men of LT-21 were ordered to march to the division's perimeter, where they would lose their support units and become the 2/1 again. Hiking along the thin trail leading north through the inferno proved a two-day ordeal. "Slipping and cursing" his way along "in single file carrying a full pack and a 46 pound mortar bipod," Sid came face-to-face with Colonel Masters. The colonel recognized Private First Class Sidney Phillips from the flashlight incident. "Phillips, are you tired?"

"No, sir."

"You look tired to me." Masters called a ten-minute break and stunned Sid. "He calls a ten-minute break because one of his privates looks tired?" Sid had no sooner dropped his gear and sat down than someone called out, "Come look." He walked

Higgins boats deliver marines for an amphibious assault.

(*left to right*) PFC Robert Leckie (James Badge Dale), PFC C. B. "Runner" Conley (Keith Nobbs), and PFC Lou "Chuckler" Juergens (Joshua Helman) storm the beach at Guadalcanal.

Sgt. John Basilone (Jon Seda) *(left)* and Cpl. J. P. Morgan (Josh Bitton) survey the scene.

Marines traverse Guadalcanal.

2nd LT G. B. Corrigan (Henry Nixon) *(center)* leads the charge on Guadalcanal.

Marines check for survivors following a battle on Guadalcanal.

(left to right) PFC Robert Leckie (James Badge Dale), PFC Bill "Hoosier" Smith, PFC Lou "Chuckler" Juergens (Joshua Helman), and PFC Sidney Phillips (Ashton Holmes) check out an abandoned Japanese emplacement on Guadalcanal.

PFC Robert Leckie (James Badge Dale) stares over his machine gun.

Marines storm the beach.

(left to right) PFC C. B. "Runner" Conley (Keith Nobbs), PFC Robert Leckie (James Badge Dale), and PFC Bill "Hoosier" Smith receive a warm welcome upon arriving in Melbourne, Australia.

PFC Lou "Chuckle" Juergens (Joshua Helman) receives a taste of home from an ice-cream vendor in Melbourne, Australia.

PFC Sidney Phillips (Ashton Holmes) and Gwen (Isabel Lucas) enjoy a day of relaxation in Melbourne, Australia.

Sgt. John Basilone (Jon Seda) attends a War Bond luncheon.

Sgt. John Basilone (Jon Seda) marries Lena Riggi (Annie Parisse) in San Diego.

Sgt. John Basilone (Jon Seda) and starlet Virginia Grey (Anna Torv) embark on a War Bond tour.

(left to right) Hope (Penny McNamee) and Gwen (Isabel Lucas) bid farewell to the Marines as they depart Melbourne, Australia.

(*left to right*) Cpl. Robert Burgin (Martin McCann) and PFC M. B. "Snafu" Shelton (Rami Malek) on Peleliu.

Marines heading into the hills of Peleliu pass others who have already experienced the horrors there.

PFC Eugene Sledge (Joseph Mazzello) contemplates the horrific reality of war.

PFC Eugene Sledge (Joseph Mazzello) *(left)* and PFC M. B. "Snafu" Shelton (Rami Malek) *(center)* traverse the rocky terrain of Okinawa.

PFC Eugene Sledge (Joseph Mazzello) reads a letter from home in the mud of Okinawa.

Sgt. John Basilone (Jon Seda) explodes out of a hole on Iwo Jima.

Sgt. John Basilone (Jon Seda) falls after being shot as he storms the beach on Iwo Jima.

Sgt. John Basilone (Jon Seda) lies dying on the black sand beaches of Iwo Jima.

Robert Leckie (James Badge Dale), home from the war, courts his future wife, Vera Keller (Caroline Dhavernas).

PFC Sidney Phillips (Ashton Holmes) enjoys a party back home in Mobile, Alabama.

PFC Eugene Sledge (Joseph Mazzello) hugs his mother when he returns home to Mobile, Alabama.

less than twenty yards to a camouflaged seaplane hangar. Approaching it "gave me the creeps and I slipped a round in the chamber of my carbine." Others followed suit. Inside, they found a dock, drums of gasoline, a propeller, and other equipment. Even without the floatplane at the dock, "we knew we had found one of Washing Machine Charlie's home ports." It proved one of the few moments of relief from the hard slog north.

THE TRANSFER CAME THROUGH ON JANUARY 13. JOHN DEPARTED D.C. WITH JUST $7 left in his account as he took a train west to join his new outfit, the Twenty-seventh Infantry Regiment of the 5th Marine Division. He stepped off in Ocean-side, a small town just north of San Diego. Accustomed to making his way around, he caught a ride to Camp Pendleton. No central reception area crowded the main gate. It was a few miles before he saw any buildings at all. The road wound through the arid countryside, passing tent cities, regimental and battalion headquarters, and row after row of war machinery. The units of the division were housed in a number of camps spread out over the two hundred square miles.[9]

He found the headquarters of the Twenty-seventh Regiment housed in a wooden-frame two-story building about ten miles from the front gate.[10] The regimental staff was consumed with organizing itself and its new division, the 5th. Few of the officers and men had arrived. Those who had arrived had their hands full building a division from the top down.[11] The 5th Marine Division was just days away from becoming officially activated. The 4th Marine Division had departed a few days ago for its first overseas deployment. Sergeant Basilone reported in to the assistant to the adjutant.

With a division being built from scratch as quickly as possible, a sergeant with experience could have found any number of billets for himself. John made sure to ask to be assigned to a machine-gun platoon.[12] The assistant went to check with the adjutant, who came out of his office to say hello. He readily assented to John's request, and pretty soon John was headed down the road to the 1st Battalion. The battalion staff officers weren't quite sure what to make of John. The CO, Lieutenant Colonel Justin Duryea, saw a marine walking around with "only half a uniform on" and asked his sergeant, "Who is he?" When told his name and the medal he held, Duryea cracked that they should all go over and bow to their hero.[13] John again made it clear that he had not come all this way to do paperwork, and he was assigned to Baker Company's machine-gun platoon for the time being.[14] Some-time soon after his arrival, John caught sight of "the long line of machine guns parked in the aisle" and was thrilled to be home. "I felt like kissing the heavies on their water jackets."[15]

Baker Company's skipper, Captain Wilfred S. Le Francois, had a lot of paperwork and few men. He had earned his bars, though, serving with the 2nd Raider Battalion on the Makin Island Raid back in 1942.[16] Directing John to Baker Company's quarters, he would have added that the Twenty-seventh Regiment was lucky to be quartered in wooden barracks. The Twenty-eighth Marines, also in the 5th Division, had been assigned tents in an area called Las Pulgas, which was Spanish for "the Fleas."[17]

The long wooden barracks, a few hundred yards from another just like it, had been painted a dull cream color. In the center of the long side were two large double doors. Inside, a stairwell divided the two-storied building into four large sections. Each platoon had one quarter. After opening the door to one of these, John went through a short hallway. The left-hand side had small rooms for the platoon's NCOs; they got some privacy. The heads and showers took up the right side. Farther along, the hallway entered a large open room with metal double-decker bunks running down each side. Each bunk had two wooden footlockers, one in front and one in the back aisle by the wall. A row of lightbulbs ran down the center aisle. Most of the light came through the windows. The room held enough bunks for an entire platoon, but John found just two men there, sleeping. One marine jumped to attention, obviously freshly minted. The other moved more slowly, evidently hungover.

"I'm John Basilone." The announcement had no effect on the drunk, but the young one looked like he might faint. "I'm going to be in B Company and I'm going to be in machine guns. I'm going to be the machine-gun instructor." His manner was calm and easy, even friendly. He asked for their names and ranks.[18] With obvious glee the young private said, "I'm in B Company, too."[19] It was clear that neither of his charges had received any orders or knew what was going on.

"How long have you been here?"

"Three days."

"Don't worry. Other Marines will be arriving in a few days. We're forming the 5th Marine Division, best one in the Corps."[20] John went off to find a rack in the sergeants' area. The next morning, he marched his two-man company down to the mess hall, had chow, and marched them back. At the door of the barracks, he said, "I want this whole place squared away when I get back." His two marines went to work, mopping the wooden deck with pine oil and washing cobwebs from the windows. There was plenty for them to do. As for himself, John set about getting his skipper to approve a loan from the USMC. He was broke.

John wrote his parents. He was waiting to be assigned to an outfit, but "I know I will be in a machine gun co. again which I want to be." His brother George, with the 4th Division, had shipped out two days before he arrived. He liked being out in the country. "The days here is hot, but the nights are cold."[21] The nights grew quiet, so "one thing you can get plenty of sleep." He included a request as a postscript. "Mom you know some of those letters I got home will you look through them and see if you can find some that girls had writen me from Calif and send them to me. Love and kisses to all. Love always, Johnny."[22]

THE SECOND DAY OF HIKING THE TRAIL AROUND CAPE GLOUCESTER TOOK LESS time because the 2/1 only had three miles to hike. The commanding general of the 1st Marine Division, General Rupertus, passed the column, accompanied by General Kreuger, a top army general. The brass elicited about as much comment from the marines slogging through the mud as the 2/1 itself received when it arrived at the division's perimeter. Sid's How Company set up camp in a muddy open area pockmarked with shell craters. The jagged stumps of the forest that had once stood there littered the land. Their personal gear, including their hammocks, had been brought around by ship. As men began to remove theirs from the pile, it turned out that about a quarter of them were missing. The main news from the marines around them concerned the Seventh Marines. Several of them had been found beheaded earlier that day.

The next morning the 2/1 received supplies from the PX: cigarettes, candy, and toilet articles, along with the news they were headed for the fighting up at Hill 660. They heard the company they would soon relieve, K Company, "has only 61 men left, no officers, but they killed over 200 Japs." As they thought about what awaited them, Hill 660 received a violent storm of artillery shells. The walk up to the hill the next day found them floundering through knee-deep mud. It got worse. How Company waded into the aftermath of the violent battle for a portion of Hill 660. "We are at the don't care position now, the very air is putrid from rotting human flesh. It is theirs and ours, several foxholes are filled with dead, equipment lying everywhere." They found places amid the silent misery to set up their guns and their bivouac.

The silence did not last. As usual, the Japanese waited until the middle of the night to attack. The U.S. artillery exploded so much ordnance on the crest in three and one-half hours that men in How Company wondered if "the elevation of 660 was knocked down 100 feet." Sid's mortar platoon waited it out, swatting mosquitoes. The rain and the shelling continued steadily for the next two days. The enemy counterattacks seemed like proof of his desperation. The IJA units had been cut off. The constant thunder of the Marine Corps' big guns assured the men on Hill 660 that nothing was going to be alive on the other side.

Without an active role in the battle, though, the men got bored. Sid and W.O. sloshed their way five hundred yards down a trail and found the remains of "a Jap hospital tent about 10 by 20, abandoned, dead Jap soldiers in uniform on canvas stretchers in line on the deck . . . all reduced to skeletons, no odor except for the strange odor like Colgate tooth powder." A folding table held medical equipment of all types and Sid examined glass syringes, ampoules, and a "beautiful binocular microscope." He looked back at the ground. "All of the dead Japs still had on wrapped leggings and uniforms." The hunt for souvenirs gathered speed in the following days. Some marines began digging up graves after they found out the cadavers held some of the best trophies. It took longer—the stench made them stop and puke before they could dig some more, then puke again, then dig deeper.

A major in battalion HQ put a stop to the forays to the enemy's former bivouacs, storage sites, and hospital. No one could leave the area without the major's permission. The boredom increased. Scuttlebutt from a well-placed source said they would return to Melbourne, but did not say when. The mess served real pot roast for dinner the night before the sun came out—not just a glint, but strong and clear—for the first time in a month. On January 21, the men rushed to set their clothing and blankets out to dry in the hot sun. The beautiful and welcome day ended with an air raid at eight p.m. The AA guns of the Eleventh Marines sent up constellations of red bursts in the dark sky and Washing Machine Charlie departed.

Around midnight, Sid took his turn at the guard with his friend Les. They sat in the darkness next to the phone for their platoon "and fed the mosquitoes." The telephone rang. Battalion HQ informed them that "we have night fighters in the air, and if there was a condition red (air raid alert) they would call and let us know." After a time, Les and Sid heard the "drone of aircraft overhead" and they both observed "that it really did sound like Washing Machine Charlie." They waited for the phone to ring. Charlie flew right at them and dropped three bombs "almost in our pocket." The thunder of the AA guns followed quickly. Unfazed, Charlie and his friends motored over the area and scattered more shells around the marines' area. The men of How Company cursed as they ran from their hammocks to their holes.

At the mortar platoon's roll call the next morning, Lieutenant Benson informed Sid and Les that they "were on permanent mess duty for ever and ever." Attempts to explain gained them nothing. Benny refused to hear them. Everyone knew Benny was going to punish them because of the damage to his precious hammock caused by him ripping it open when the bombs went off. They also knew that the severity of the punishment came from the desire of Benson and his boss, Lieutenant Gaze Sotak, to pay Sid back for an incident that had occurred months ago. Back in Australia, Lieutenant Sotak had wanted to use Sid as a witness in a court-martial of Sid's friend Whitfield. In a small town outside Melbourne, Sotak had given Whitfield a "mean and stupid order" and Whitfield had told Sotak where he could shove it. The lieutenant took one look at Whitfield's massive frame and decided to get him for insubordination. When pressed to bear witness, Private First Class Sidney Phillips had said his "hearing was bad but if Whitfield would repeat it I would listen closely this time."

Officers almost always win. Lieutenant Gaze Sotak had the last laugh as Sid and Les grabbed their gear and set off for the bivouac of the battalion mess men about two hundred yards away. The mess men gave them the lowliest job, that of "pot walloping." They stood in the creek near the kitchen and scrubbed the large pots with rags and sand and small stones. "It really wasn't hard work," Sid observed. "Japs were no longer a problem." In the chow line they might hear the latest dope: how the Fifth Marines had met resistance up the coast; that the Seventh Marines "has a promise to be home by Father's Day"; or that the "japs landed a reinforced regiment last night" and were massing along the 2/1's line. None of that seemed to matter too much to a pot walloper.

At the end of January, the 2/1 moved up to the top of Hill 660, where the Fifth Marines and the Seventh Marines had fought great battles. While the rest of How Company surveyed the devastation, Sid and Les found themselves setting up camp near another creek. The two Cinderellas realized too late that all the best trees for swinging their hammocks had been taken. They had to tie their hammocks to trees farther up the ridge. The next night a storm blew in and grew in intensity until the rain poured like a waterfall. The flowing water washed the earth from the roots of the trees and the wind pushed them over.

Sid lay nude in his hammock, wrapped in his wool blanket, hoping for the best. In the morning, he unzipped and put on his sopping clothes. He and Les Clark looked down to the battalion mess and "dissolved into fits of laughter." The cooks' "hammocks were shreds, their clothes were gone, and their weapons were gone. The mess tent, stoves, pits and cases of food were gone, but Clark and I were high and safe and crying in delight." The creek, swollen into a powerful river by the torrent, had swept it all away. When the water had risen to the level of the cooks' hammocks, they had had to abandon their warm, dry beds and climb naked into the trees, waiting for morning and help. Sid and Les would help but, being marines, first they would enjoy a good laugh at the expense of the naked men in the trees. A lighter, normal rain began later that morning.

WHILE RECOVERING AT HOME MAJOR SHOFNER RECEIVED A TELEGRAM ON JANUary 27 from the Marine Corps. "Public release of your experience will be made shortly by Washington." The country would soon know of the atrocity that had killed so many men. It would have been great news had it not been for the accompanying orders. "You are not repeat not to grant press interviews without contacting your nearest Navy or Marine Corps public relations officer and care must be taken not to describe any experiences after your escape or any means whereby you escaped. . . ." Another telegram followed two days later "to include newsreels." Were these orders logical? A public release of the story should have rendered further secrecy unnecessary. Something was up.

The telegrams would have stimulated another discussion in the Shofner household about the war in general and of U.S. POWs in particular. As the family of a POW, they had paid keen attention to the developments. Aside from Austin's letters, they had received two letters from the Marine Corps. One had advised them of his Silver Star; the other that he had been listed as Missing in Action. Aside from that, much of what they had learned about Japan's conquest of the Philippines had come from General MacArthur. His communiqués of 1942 had described the heroic defense and burnished his national reputation as one of the country's outstanding generals. After the defeat, little in the way of hard news had arrived.

Most commentators had agreed with Governor Thomas Dewey of New York, who explained that the defeat had not been the commander's fault. General MacArthur, Dewey stated, had "performed [a] miracle with inadequate supplies, inadequate air force, and inadequate ground forces."[23] The editorialists could not explain what had happened in the Philippines since the surrender. In June 1943 the film studio MGM released a film entitled Bataan starring one of its leading men, Robert Taylor. This major studio release followed the shorter film Letter from Bataan, released in September 1942.[24] These films had helped establish the public's perception of the loss of the Philippines, Wake Island, and Guam. The U.S. military, particularly its army, had fought a gallant yet doomed fight. This understanding, produced by the filmmakers in Hollywood under the direction of the government, was intended to focus the public's energies on the war effort.

Hollywood had not, however, been able to resolve two nagging questions: Why had there been a surrender? Were Americans less brave than the Japanese? These doubts had smoldered within the national consciousness, causing thousands of families like the Shofners no end of heartache.

The concerns of the families of the POWs had received the full attention of their members of Congress.[25] In the fall of 1943, just a month before Shofner and his friends escaped to Australia, a bill had been introduced into Congress "to provide for the promotion of certain prisoners of war."[26] Since many of the soldiers in the POW camps served in the New Mexico National Guard, the senator from New Mexico had introduced the legislation to make sure any man "who is now a prisoner of war, shall be advanced one grade" in rank for every year of his captivity. The Honorable Dennis Chavez wanted justice for the men of his state and others who "through no fault of their own are now prisoners of war." Since everyone understood that "they didn't have the wherewithal with which to fight," then the POWs should be entitled to the same schedule of promotions that the "swivel chair officers" in Washington, D.C., were receiving.

Senator Chavez's bill, watched with interest by all members of Congress, had been opposed by the War Department. In November 1943, Secretary of War Henry L. Stimson had sent a letter to the Chairman of the Senate Committee on Military Affairs explaining that it could not provide for blanket promotions for men because it could not "distinguish between those men who, by virtue of having fought to the last, might be deserving of a reward in the form of a promotion and those who surrendered in circumstances under which they might reasonably have been expected to resist."[27] Secretary Stimson was not prepared to absolve the POWs of responsibility for defeat.

His letter had ignited controversy within the country, especially in the families of the POWs and in states like New Mexico, which had hundreds of men listed as missing in action. Armed with letters from lots of angry families, Chavez had led a growing number of congressmen willing to take on Stimson.

The question about the surrender had naturally devolved into a debate over whether or not MacArthur's army had been supplied by their government with the tools to win. Chavez's group had the upper hand. No ships had been sent to aid MacArthur. Moreover, the troops had not surrendered; General Wainwright had ordered it. Stimson's War Department could not argue that its army in the Philippines had been well equipped because in hindsight it was not true. Moreover, such an argument implied American boys were cowards. Nor could Stimson blame General MacArthur. The Roosevelt administration, after extracting the general from Corregidor, had entrusted the defense of Australia and the leadership of the U.S. Army to him.

Helping his family to appreciate MacArthur's role in the Philippines was something Austin Shofner would have undertaken with great passion. He looked forward to the moment when the nation learned the truth about Douglas MacArthur. For the Shofner family, that moment came when they received the February 7, 1944, issue of *Life* magazine. It carried a long story on page 25 under the headline "Prisoners of Japan: Ten Americans Who Escaped Recently from the Philippines Report on the Atrocities Committed by the Japanese in Their Prisoner of War Camps." Although it included photos of each of the ten escapees, only two of them contributed to the article. Commander Melvyn McCoy and Lieutenant Colonel Stephen Mellnik had "finally broken" the silence about the fate of America's army in the Philippines. Their story, dictated from their hospital beds, had been sent to the secretary of the navy, who had forwarded it on to President Roosevelt. The publisher of *Life* magazine loved the scoop. "In the third year of war, censorship finally lifted the curtain on what happened at Corregidor and Bataan after the American surrender."

Life magazine had not, however, lifted the veil concealing the story of the POWs. Its story followed a week's worth of stories appearing in the *Chicago Tribune* and the one hundred newspapers affiliated with it. The *Tribune's* series would continue for the rest of February, detailing the story of Lieutenant Colonel William E. "Ed" Dyess, the army air corps pilot who had returned with McCoy and Mellnik. The way Colonel Dyess began his story indicated that he had a different message from that offered by McCoy and Mellnik in *Life*.

Dyess began his account two days before the Japanese attack on the Philippines in order to impress upon the reader that the U.S. forces in the Far East had been expecting a Japanese attack. At great length he detailed the quick destruction of American military might on Luzon, followed by its slow disintegration on the peninsula of Bataan. At every turn, he made it plain that valor could not mitigate the huge deficits in numbers, arms, and matériel that the Americans and Filipinos had faced. The big joke in the air corps had been a note written to President Roosevelt: "Dear Mr. President: Please send us another P-40. The one we have is all shot up."[28] Dyess described catching and eating lizards after their rations ran out. As Ed Dyess made clear that the Americans had been abandoned by their country, the *Chicago Tribune* published tables showing the hundreds of millions of dollars in tanks, aircraft, and artillery the United States had sent to Great Britain, the Soviet Union and other allies at the same moment. The facts set the Roosevelt administration's "Europe First" policy in stark relief. America's real enemy was the Empire of Japan.

When Dyess's series came to the surrender, it overlapped with McCoy's and Mellnik's story. The *Life* magazine article had omitted the start of the war entirely, thereby evading any questions as to how the defeat had come to pass, and focused on Japan's treatment of POWs. It grabbed readers' attention with specific atrocities from the March of Death from Bataan. The second page featured an artist's rendering of one horror. The caption under the picture explained: "Americans were forced to bury other Americans alive. At the point of jap bayonets this man is forced to hit a countryman with a shovel and bury him." A long description of the conditions in the POW camp followed. The Japanese had killed five thousand helpless Americans. Mellnik and McCoy believed that "not more than 10% of the American military prisoners in the Philippines will survive another year of the conditions which existed at the time of our escape."

Amid promises that none of these descriptions had been exaggerated, the authors explained at length that all of this had occurred as the deliberate policy of the Imperial Japanese government. McCoy and Mellnik wanted to establish these facts for the record to prevent the Japanese from claiming that these atrocities had never happened, or that its political leadership had not been aware of conditions in these camps. In this way the article might create pressure on the Japanese government to take better care of the men. Most of all, though, the escapees wanted to increase the American people's feeling of urgency and necessity to make a supreme effort in the war.

The story of the monstrous cruelty committed at Cabanatuan and elsewhere caused the national sensation of which all POWs, not just the ten who had escaped, had dreamed. The editorial page of the *Chicago Tribune* declared that in the Pacific, the United States faced "the task of dealing not merely with Hitler and his gangsters, but with a race of Hitlers who have made gangsterism their state religion."[29] Congressmen used words like "revenge" and issued pledges to "ruin Japan" by bombing Tokyo. The public bought more bonds to quicken the pace with which America destroyed the hated enemy.[30] The gift that McCoy, Dyess, Shofner, and the others had so desperately wanted to give the men left behind in Cabanatuan had been delivered.

The stories from the escapees also fed the ongoing debate in Congress about the promotion of the POWs. Senator Chavez and his allies believed they had all the proof needed to justify the promotions. The families became more strident because they considered the promotion issue to be recognition of their sons' and brothers' sacrifices. Interviewed by congressmen who visited him in New Guinea, MacArthur told them his men "didn't surrender . . . they fought until they were too weak to stand and fight any longer."[31] His comments seemed to support the idea of promoting the POWs.

Austin Shofner saw the promotion debate as a sideshow. As escapees, he and the others had proven their courage and had been promptly promoted upon return. The manner in which Melvyn McCoy and Stephen Mellnik had become famous as the leaders of the escape rankled him, though he said nothing. Shofner wanted the public's fury at the debacle on Bataan to be directed toward a frank appraisal of the leadership of General Douglas MacArthur. From what he had seen, the Japanese invasion need not have led to the March of Death. MacArthur and his staff had allowed their air force to be destroyed on the ground a full nine hours after learning of the enemy's offensive. The defense strategy he had crafted had descended into a rout. Hundreds of tons of foodstuffs had never made it to Bataan. Tens of thousands of men had paid a huge price for the mistakes made by MacArthur. This accounting, however, did not occur.

In the national discussion that followed its appearance, pity for the POWs' suffering gave way to acceptance that the American troops had not been equipped to fight Japan. Left unsaid, but certainly part of the public's calculations, was the growing realization that war demanded sacrifice, even callous sacrifice. In the estimation of many knowledgeable observers, the men who had fought on Bataan and Corregidor had slowed the enemy's advance and given the United States time to prepare for war; they had lifted morale in the United States and had inspired her troops like nothing "since the Alamo."[32] This logic placed them in one of America's favorite stories: the gallant stand of the lost cause. It removed from the POWs the stigma of shame. The tide turned against Secretary Stimson. The families of the POWs, who had for so long been outraged and heartsick, would be mollified.

A potent blend of mythology, patriotism, practical necessity, and skillful public relations overwhelmed all those who, like Shifty Shofner, had experienced a different truth. The public understood that the sacrifice had been an unfortunate necessity and, once the blot of cowardice had been removed, moved on. Public opinion on the fate of the Philippines contrasted sharply with the disdain with which Americans regarded Admiral Kimmel and General Short, the two commanders of U.S. forces in Hawaii on December 7, 1941. These leaders had been summarily relieved of duty in the wake of the attack upon Pearl Harbor, their careers ruined. Douglas MacArthur had been awarded the Medal of Honor "for the heroic conduct of defensive and offensive operations on the Bataan Peninsula."

ON FEBRUARY 10, EUGENE SLEDGE COMPLETED HIS TRAINING WITH A TEST OF HIS skill on the 60mm mortar. He scored a 94, two points shy of being certified as Expert. It angered him to have come so close because it reminded him of his rifle test, but also because an Expert rating would help him make corporal quicker. Gene was pushing hard, as usual. He had only just witnessed a live-fire exercise and would not fire a live round himself for another week. Although his request for a transfer to the tank corps had not been granted, he was enjoying the life of a marine.

His platoon had been issued carbines (lightweight semiautomatic rifles), a sure sign they would ship out soon. Most of his platoon "armed themselves to the teeth" with pistols and knives. Censorship forbade him from being too obvious about his imminent departure, but the signs were in his letters. He got some pictures taken in his blues and sent them home along with a box of nonessential items he could not take with him. He thanked his parents for hiring someone to have his room "done over" in preparation for his return and reminded his father about his request for a .45 automatic pistol. Eugene could hardly wait to ship out. He closed a letter to his mother with "Love you & pop more than tongue can tell & heart can wish." In mid-February Private First Class Sledge was placed into the Forty-sixth Replacement Battalion. A week later, his replacement battalion shipped out on USS *President Polk*.

Out at sea Eugene read a lot, mostly the New Testament to renew his faith, and a few outdoor sporting magazines, which reminded him of all the great hunting trips he had had with his father. Standing in the hot sun watching the trackless Pacific, he felt the pride he had wanted to feel of doing his part for his country. The passing days gave him a marine's deep tan, sea legs, and something else Gene had wanted so badly he could only now admit it. He was catching up to his older brother Edward, who had shipped out for England in November.

THE RUMOR ARRIVED IN HILO DAYS BEFORE THE AIRPLANES DID. IN EARLY February Bombing Two traded in their Dauntlesses for SB2C Helldivers. Trading in the old Dauntlesses for the navy's modern dive-bomber meant an imminent deployment to a carrier. Everybody liked the idea, especially the young wolves. The Helldiver carried more bombs, flew faster, and had four 20mm cannons. Rumors about the Beast did not intimidate them. It "had wings, an engine . . . and various other things."[33] The Helldivers they received had not come directly from the factory. Walking up to them on the flight line, Mike's preflight check confirmed his first impression: "they sent us some old junkers." The condition of the airplanes concerned Mike both as a pilot and as the squadron's engineering officer.

The skipper of Bombing Two looked to Mike as the key officer to lead the transition because he was the only one who had flown the SB2C. The squadron was informed it had a month to get carrier qualified with the SB2C. Lieutenant Micheel told them about the high stall speed, which meant they had to carry more speed into their landing approach. He led the flights off their airfield, nestled between the ocean and two tall volcanoes, to show them how impossible it was to dial in the right trim on the Beast. The Dauntless could be trimmed to fly straight and stable; the SB2C could not. A pilot had to keep an eye on the SB2C. Before long, Mike became as busy being the engineering officer as the flight instructor. The aircraft suffered from the same malady that had gotten them and Mike kicked off the *Yorktown* a year ago: the wing lock.

The manufacturers of the Helldiver, Curtiss-Wright, had solved the problem of the locking wing by installing a wing lock lever inside the cockpit. When the wings were let down in flight position, the locking pins inside the wings were inserted. To lock the locking pins in position, the pilot pushed in the wing lock lever down by his feet. The lever, though, had a problem caused by the plane's vibration. Mike and his comrades noticed "you'd be flying along and pretty soon you'd see that thing moving out so you'd sit up here and boot it back in." Lieutenant Micheel found himself in the hangar with the mechanics. One of the crew's chief warrant officers wondered, "Why don't you put a bungee on it?" Mike tried it. It held the wing lock lever in place and also allowed it to be unlocked quickly. All of the cockpits were outfitted so that the bungee cord could be connected to the lever on one end and a secure bit of metal on the other.

New SB2Cs, fitted with improved wing lock levers, arrived to replace the old ones they had trained in. The Beast, however, had not earned the pilots' trust the way the Dauntless had. The squadron's skipper, Campbell, reported to his superiors that "most pilots felt that it was a decided change for the worse. The reputation of the SB2C was bad and on the whole the pilots did not trust the plane and felt that they would be unable to dive accurately therein."[34] It was too late. The air group's other squadron, the torpedo planes, arrived. Air Group Two's CO explained that they had been assigned duty aboard USS *Hornet* because the air group currently embarked on *Hornet* "isn't doing very well and we're going to go replace them."

THE MARINES WHO WOULD MAKE UP BAKER COMPANY TRICKLED INTO CAMP Pendleton from a variety of sources. The men who had been paramarines arrived with their trousers tucked into their jump boots. Others, usually NCOs, had been yanked from behind their desks in D.C.; these men frequently carried some extra pounds around their waists, but at least they did not have a chip on their shoulders like the men who had been picked to be paratroopers. Those marines considered themselves elite, even if they had not seen action. A few veterans of the war, like John Basilone, found themselves salted into Baker Company, 1st Battalion, Twenty-seventh Marines. One of the new men, Corporal Tremulis, had manned a 20mm antiaircraft gun along the flight deck of USS *Yorktown*. He had had to swim in the open ocean when the captain had ordered the ship abandoned during the Battle of Midway.[35]

The majority of the men flooding into the 1/27 in late January, though, came from boot camp. They found their new battalion slightly chaotic. Some routine was imposed through the physical training held each morning out in front of their barracks. One afternoon, Captain Le Francois went on liberty in San Diego and failed to return. Officially listed as absent without leave, Le Francois had "gone over the hill," in marine parlance. Experienced men going AWOL was not an isolated occurrence, although most returned eventually—happy to be busted in rank for a few extra days of liberty.[36] Baker Company received a second skipper and never heard of Le Francois again.

The 5th Division HQ set out a formal training schedule on February 8, even before all the men had arrived.[37] The schedule began with the physical conditioning of the individual, training the individual with his weapon (snapping in), and training the individual for his job within the squad. The squad hiked to each of the firing ranges scattered about the vast grounds of Camp Pendleton. While most divisions trained five days a week, the 5th Division HQ decided to speed up the training cycle by working ten days on and three days off.[38] The marines in John's machine-gun platoon concentrated on the .30-caliber air-cooled Browning Machine Gun.

One afternoon on the machine-gun range Sergeant Basilone watched Private Charles Tatum, the seventeen-year-old he had met on his first day with Baker Company, whipping the gun back and forth like it was a hose. The sergeant tapped the private on the shoulder and said, "Tatum, you're probably the worst machine gunner in the Marine Corps. You got to be gentle with it. Don't spray it."[39] He repeated the earlier admonishments against burning out the barrel. "Fire it in bursts. Don't spray it. Treat it gently." The machine gun was not an all-powerful weapon. Tatum listened in rapt attention.

Every marine knew the name Manila John Basilone and knew his story. It conjured up images of "brute strength and determination."[40] The men of Baker Company, though, came to know a sergeant who did not take himself too seriously, much less consider himself special. He fit in. The words "Medal of Honor" never came out of his mouth so no one got to know "Manila John."[41] The men in his platoon addressed him as Sergeant. Other sergeants called him John since none of them went back far enough with him to call him "Manila." He did not encourage anyone to call him that.[42] Perhaps he felt the name belonged to the legend.

The happiness and good cheer that the men noticed marked the return of John's natural disposition.[43] In mid-February, the 1st Battalion returned to its barracks after completing one of their first bivouacs. After giving them some time to get squared away, Colonel Butler then called his battalion into formation for an inspection. The men reported with their khakis pressed, field scarves tied as prescribed, their fingernails clean, their shoelaces of uniform length. They carried no packs, only their cartridge belts and personal weapons. The companies passed in review of the battalion CO, Colonel Butler. Baker Company's lieutenant called out, "Eyes right!" and saluted as they passed the colonel.[44] Colonel Butler inspected each man and his weapon. The company commander followed along. Inspecting hundreds of marines took time. The colonel liked what he saw. He praised the men for a great job and promised them steak and eggs as a reward.[45] He then asked Sergeant John Basilone to step forward. He did. The colonel handed him some papers and said, "It's now Gunnery Sergeant John Basilone."[46]

This promotion was the moment he had been working toward. Before the war began, men had dedicated most of their lives to reaching the exalted position of a gunnery sergeant. Henceforth, he would be called Gunny. In the world of men who trained hard and fought wars, the gunny had authority, a certain amount of autonomy, and a lot of respect. Officers like Colonel Chesty Puller often stated that the senior NCOs were the "backbone of the Corps." The promotion came with the princely sum of $158.90 per month in pay, including an extra $2 "for Medal of Honor."[47] Since Baker Company had recently been assigned a gunnery sergeant, John was transferred to Charlie Company. Basilone moved his seabag into the barracks of C/1/27 about a hundred yards away. He was right where he wanted to be.

THE TROOPSHIP STEAMED TO THE DOCK OF A BUSY PORT. EUGENE SLEDGE AND THE other marines of the replacement draft disembarked. Rows of tents of the replacement depot at Noumea, New Caledonia, awaited them. Situated near the Old Mission Church, the camp had a mess hall serving the best food Sledge had ever had in the corps, including fruit juice. There were a lot of rules and the usual delay in finding out what happened next. Men came and went at the replacement depot, so there was little camaraderie. Aside from some physical training, there was little to do. Days turned into weeks before he was even processed completely into the system.[48]

Until his mail caught up with him, Sledge contented himself with reading what he had brought with him. He enjoyed looking at the selection of photos of his family, his horse and dogs, his prized gun collection, his house. He could picture in his mind the pretty azaleas and japonicas blooming on the grounds of Georgia Cottage. He walked into the town of Noumea often. He found the architecture identical to New Orleans' French Quarter and stepped around every corner expecting to see the Cabildo, one of New Orleans' landmarks. In the evening, he might visit the Red Cross to get some free V-mail paper, although he did not care for "dehydrated letters" and found writing difficult since "everything was a secret." He looked forward to being assigned into an outfit and began to hope that it might be the same as Sidney Phillips's unit. After a few weeks he received his first mail call and a letter from Sidney. Although he expected to be rotated home, Sid joked that he would stay if Eugene was put into his outfit.

Major Shofner's furlough ended on February 27. He reported to the Pentagon for a few days before reporting to the commandant of Marine Corps Schools. The corps had a lot to teach him about the evolutions in theory, practice, and weaponry of war. During the following months, requests for public appearances from the office of the USMC's Director of Public Relations interrupted his instruction. Shofner, and the other escapees, stood up at these events to embody the bravery of the men of the Philippines. Whenever one of the escapees appeared in public, the families of the missing in action surrounded them, pleading for any information— Do you recall this name? Do you recognize the face in this photo?[49] Those faces of loved ones in photos must have brought the horror back to the fore of his consciousness. It must have been difficult to return to class. Few of the other students received a letter directly from General Vandegrift, who wrote him to express "my deep appreciation of your devotion to duty and your heroic conduct." Vandegrift enclosed Shofner's second Silver Star, this one with the army device.

The recognition and the preparation to return to combat delighted Shofner. Demonstrating a keen understanding of the way large bureaucracies worked, though, his reply to the commandant of the Marine Corps included "data about my services not shown on any muster roll." The muster roll, a sacrosanct document produced monthly by each unit in the corps, was the basis for calculating a marine's monthly pay, his experience in the different types of command (for example, service as a division operations officer, or G-3), promotions, length of service, and the like. Shifty intended to receive the credit for all of his service, including his time as "deputy chief of staff," and as a "G-3."

Shifty also sought to receive reimbursement for the personal items he had been ordered to abandon on that awful Christmas Day back 1941, at a warehouse in Olongapo. In twelve pages, he detailed his collection of carved ivory, his array of evening suits, and all the other contents of his trunks. Calculating in some loss due to "depreciation," his list of personal property "lost, damaged or destroyed by operations of war" totaled $2,621.90.

IN RESPONSE TO THE CONTINUING INTEREST IN GUNNERY SERGEANT JOHN Basilone, he sat down with one of the corps' public relations specialists to produce a statement that could be sent to those who requested interviews.[50] Acknowledging that he had received both fame and fortune, he struggled to find a way to express how he felt about giving war bond speeches. He couldn't call it what he wanted to call it. The ghostwriter probably suggested the word "hippodrome." An unusual word for someone who had not attended high school, it referred to a game in which the results are fixed in advance. Set in opposition to his obvious joy at being back with the combat troops, the word's disparaging meaning came through clearly.

John felt compelled to deny that he "liked to slog around the South Pacific and let little monkey-faced characters shoot at me any more than the next Marine ... but, if it's all the same with everybody, I'd much rather spend the rest of the war overseas. I think all real Marines, who are not physically disqualified, feel about the same way." His exasperation at the endless questions he had received from his friends, family, reporters, and even other marines had forced him to explain in detail why he had requested a return to the Fleet Marine Force. "It has been my ambition ever since Pearl Harbor to be with the outfit that recaptured Manila. I kept thinking of how awful it would be if some Marines made a landing on Dewey Boulevard on the Manila waterfront and Manila John Basilone wasn't among them." Once the war ended he would take his $5,000 bond money and buy a restaurant or a farm, and renew the relationship with his "girl back East."

The girl was not named in the article, but John was referring to Helen Helstowski of Pittsfield, Pennsylvania.[51] He heard from her "every other day"; he wrote his parents, teasing his mother with the line "maybe there will be a wedding soon?" John included a newspaper clipping in the letter about his brother George, who had survived the 4th Division's invasion of the Marshall Islands in late January. As far as himself, "well, we ain't doing much down here still waiting for more men to train." Regardless of the number of men in Charlie Company, Gunny Basilone had them outside training. One afternoon he spied an old friend from Dog Company, Clinton

Watters. He went over and said hello. As they got caught up—Clint had contracted jaundice in Samoa and missed the Canal—John asked him why he was in a rifle platoon. When Clint said something about going where he was sent, John said he'd fix that. The next day, Sergeant Watters reported for duty with the C/1/27.[52]

Clint had not been particularly close to John when they had been in Dog Company. He had been a private during their training in New River and he had missed the big show. He was, however, someone John knew from before he had become a celebrity. After work they often went out for a beer and some fun. John wore his khaki uniform, which had no insignia other than his sergeant stripes. Wherever they went, John would get approached by civilians, marines, and other service personnel. He understood their desire to meet a hero and made sure to shake a hand or say hello.[53] Both Clint and John had a few sea stories to share with one another. Watters had been put into the Raiders and had seen action in Bougainville and other islands in the Solomons. John told a few fun stories. As for the medal, he told Clint about the moment Chesty Puller saluted him.[54]

Clint didn't join John on the night of February 23, when he went down the road to the Carlsbad Hotel in the nearby village of Carlsbad. It was a beautiful hotel, fairly new, in the Spanish missionary style. A lot more stylish and expensive than the places John frequented, the small bar off the main lobby usually hosted wealthy visitors who had driven down the coast highway from L.A. He and some friends were standing at the bar when Myra King, a member of the Women's Reserve of the USMC, said hello. Myra introduced her group of friends to his.[55] One of the women seated at the table caught his eye. Her friends called her by her last name, Riggi. Also a member of the marines' auxiliary branch, Lena Riggi wore little makeup and dressed in comfortable clothes. He found her dark brown eyes, set off by waves of jet black hair, beautiful. While the appearance of Manila John Basilone left some of her friends "breathless," Riggi's face betrayed her reaction: "So what?"[56]

The women invited John and his friends to join them and they did. Although Lena did not say much, what she did say had a forthrightness to it. The manner of her speech, John likely noticed, suggested a background similar to his own. He eventually asked Lena if he could take her home. "No," she replied, "you didn't bring me here. I'm not going home with ya."[57] He asked about seeing her again. Lena told him that she was going on liberty for five days. He asked if he could call her when she came back. She agreed, thinking "he could have any girl he wanted to" so he'd never call. John wrote down the phone number of the officers' mess where Lena worked on a matchbook cover.[58]

*   *   *

WHEN THE ORDERS ARRIVED TO REPORT TO USS *HORNET* FOR "CARRIER OPERA-
tions," all the wolves of Bombing Two smiled. "The orphans," Micheel's friend Lieutenant Hal Buell later said, "had found a home."[59] Privately, Lieutenant Vernon
"Mike" Micheel wished his ensigns had had more training time in the Beast. In early
March they flew over to Ford Island, in Pearl Harbor, to meet their ship. They also
met the members of the air group they were replacing, Air Group Fifteen. Bombing Two knew the pilots in Bombing Fifteen because both squadrons had trained
at NAS Wildwood. At the officers' club, the new *Hornet* pilots got the word from
the old *Hornet* pilots. Fifteen had joined the carrier soon after its commissioning in
November 1943, and had gone through months of training under Captain Miles
Browning only to be summarily replaced upon arrival in Pearl Harbor, before the
first combat cruise. In the course of a few "Happy Hours," they told the men of
Bombing Two what an awful, belligerent, and vindictive dictator the ship's captain
was. Captain Browning had made *Hornet* a very unhappy ship.

During the Battle of Midway two years earlier, Browning had served aboard *Enterprise*. His critical role in the great victory at Midway had earned him a DSC, and a
service-wide reputation, and put him in line to command a carrier. The new Essex-
class carrier *Hornet* was his first.[60] The wolves' qualifications aboard Browning's carrier began on March 9 and went smoother than Micheel had dared hope. The pilots
made their three successful landings. The longer they spent aboard, though, the
clearer they came to see the crew's discontent. The attitude came from the top. The
captain's capriciousness had everyone unsettled and mistrustful.

The prospect of working for such a captain pleased no one in Air Group Two
or its bombing squadron. Mike's immediate future took another startling turn when
he discovered that the admiral who arrived to hang his flag from the flattop's staff
was none other than Rear Admiral J. J. "Jocko" Clark. A year previously Clark had
vociferously expressed his unhappiness with Lieutenant Micheel's performance on
Yorktown. Mike figured Clark might not recall him, since the problems with the
Beast had caused the admiral to yell at a lot of people that summer, but he decided
to stay out of Jocko's way just in case. Luckily, his job did not demand contact with
Captain Browning or Admiral Clark. Micheel's responsibilities were the training of
the men in his division and the maintenance of the airplanes in his squadron. He
focused on the mission and so did his pilots, who weren't going to let the top brass
ruin their tour. Micheel found their enthusiasm infectious, and a week of training
exercises went quickly. He embarked on his second combat tour with more than one

thousand hours of flight time and sixty-five carrier landings under his belt. He felt like a hotshot navy pilot. "I had this thing all figured out."

The front line of the navy's carrier war lay pretty far across the Pacific Ocean in March of 1944. *Hornet* sortied from Pearl Harbor at eight forty a.m. on the fifteenth and joined up with her destroyer escorts and three other aircraft carriers. They steamed southeast for five days, conducting gunnery practice and other drills. Another flattop with its task group sailed about thirty miles south of them.[61] They entered Majuro Atoll in the Marshall Islands on the morning of March 20. A thin strip of coral ran in almost a complete circle, encompassing more than twenty miles of lagoon. The opening on Majuro's northern side allowed the supporting vessels of the U.S. Navy's great carrier fleet access to a perfect anchorage in the middle of the Pacific Ocean. The pilots of Bombing Two, as their flattop steamed into the lagoon, saw what looked like "the entire Pacific Fleet."[62] *Hornet* joined a task group made up of one other fleet carrier like theirs, two smaller carriers, and their escorts. Task Group 58.2 got under way soon after, steaming to the Palau Islands for the first combat mission. Two more task groups joined them at three p.m. along with the commander of the Fifth Fleet, Admiral Spruance.

With more pilots than planes in his squadron, Mike had not flown much since they departed Pearl Harbor. The new men needed all the experience they could get. When they departed Majuro, though, the air group commander scheduled a "group grope" to see how well his squadrons worked together in a coordinated attack. Micheel took off in his Helldiver and gained altitude, joining up his division. As he gained altitude, the great fleet came into view. "I never saw such a number of ships in my life." Comparing the sight before him with his memory of his first combat tour, "the difference was just phenomenal, how big our fleets were and how many ships we had. It seemed like they were all over. They were out 40 miles ahead." Thinking of all those trained pilots on all those carriers surrounded by all those support ships gave him a surge of confidence. "How could we lose?" The sight may have awed the wolves behind him as well, since the group grope went poorly.[63] The problems went beyond a lack of concentration. Several of their Helldivers proved defective. Captain Browning had them pushed over the side.[64]

The training of Air Group Two, however, ended with that flight. The task force had been handed Operation Desecrate One, to destroy the enemy's offensive capabilities in the Palau Islands. The Palaus needed to be neutralized to facilitate General MacArthur's advance along the northern coast of New Guinea. The task force did not sail straight west from Majuro, though. Instead, it dipped south to stay clear of the big enemy base at Truk, and crossed the equator on March 25. Even with combat imminent, the ship's company took the opportunity afforded by crossing the equator to initiate those men who were making their first crossing. Veterans of Guadalcanal, Lieutenants Buell and Micheel had crossed the equator in 1942. Unfortunately, they lacked properly validated identification as a shellback from King Neptune, so they received their share of hazing along with the rest of the wolves. They endured an abbreviated ceremony, however. On *Hornet*, the pollywogs outnumbered the shellbacks by a considerable number, so the ritual humiliation could only be pushed so far.

Another task group joined them on the twenty-sixth, pushing the number of flattops to eleven. *Hornet* pulled alongside *Kankakee* to receive fuel oil and aviation gasoline. Topping off the fuel tanks, like the increased frequency of Combat Air Patrol (CAP) and the antisubmarine (ASW) searches, signified the final steps in long months of preparation. On the twenty-eighth one of the scouts spotted a Japanese two-engine bomber, called a Betty.[65] The U.S. pilot, in a torpedo plane, took off after the enemy scout. The Betty dropped her load of bombs and fled. Her escape meant the enemy knew the big fleet was bearing down on them. Another Betty spotted them the next day. Close to enemy airfields, *Hornet* went to general quarters for the remainder of the day; the task force prepared for an enemy counterstrike. It arrived at eight forty-six p.m. No fighters went up to challenge them because the task force commander did not want to risk flight operations at night. The carriers commenced emergency maneuvers while the battlewagons belched showers of flak. None of the stalkers got close. Word came down from the bridge that the attack on the Palau Islands was being moved up to March 30, the next day.

IN EARLY MARCH, SOON AFTER LENA RIGGI RETURNED FROM HER LEAVE, JOHN called her at work. They talked for a bit before he asked her what time she got off work. She agreed to meet him that evening at the USO in Oceanside.[66] At the club, John attracted a crowd. Lena decided that he had chosen her, so she did not need to get jealous at all the women crowding around him. A time to talk did come and they found a fair amount of common ground other than the Marine Corps. Her parents had both immigrated to the United States from Italy. Her mother had given birth to five boys and one girl. She had grown up on a farm outside of Portland, Oregon, and had learned to do everything her older brothers had done.[67] She had eventually escaped the farm, moved to Portland and found work.[68] Working as a clerk at Montgomery Ward, a department store, had bored her. "One morning I woke up," she said, "and I said to my girlfriend who was in the front apartment, 'You know what? I'm going to join the service.'" She set off that morning and had happened upon a

Marine Corps Recruitment Center, enlisting on July 5, 1943.[69] Her story would have reminded John of his own search for direction on July 6, 1940, which had led him to the USMC.

Like him, Lena had trained in New River, North Carolina, before being transferred to Pendleton. She had arrived in late January to discover that women had only just begun to be posted there.[70] As a field cook, she would become a sergeant officially once the auxiliary formalized its rank system.[71] Her directness gave way to a sense of fun as she got to know him. He liked to laugh, was unpretentious, and was obviously close to his family. They shared an interest in playing sports and even ranked them similarly—their two favorites were softball and golf.[72] John did not need to say much about his medal or the Canal, so when it came up he said, "My men earned it. I am just wearing it for them."[73] At the end of their first date she would not kiss him good night. She had, however, taken to calling him Johnny.[74] He stopped over to see her at the officers' mess after work a day or two later.[75] Her friends liked him immediately. He obviously did not share the opinion of other guys at Pendleton, who referred to female marines as BAMs: Broad Assed Marines.

ON MARCH 30, BOMBING TWO ASSEMBLED IN THEIR READY ROOM TO THE sound of the general quarters Klaxon. Campbell briefed them on the strike again. Bombing Two would not fly as a squadron. Two divisions of six planes each would comprise the first sortie. The next two divisions would fly the second strike. The map of the Palau Island chain had a lot of strange names, like Babelthuap. Campbell, leading one division, and Buell, leading the other, would join up with some of their air group's fighter and torpedo planes to hit the enemy's ships in the harbor of the island of Koror. The enemy knew they were coming. As Campbell went over the details of the raid as displayed on the blackboard and the Teletype—headings, distances, code words, and the like—the assigned pilots scribbled furiously, letting out the occasional "Dammit! Down in front."[76] The loudspeaker blared, "Pilots, man your planes." With parachutes hanging off their backsides, the pilots of divisions one and two walked to the flight deck for the squadron's first mission. Micheel and the remaining pilots would have found a spot on Vulture's Row to watch the launch before going back to the ready room to wait.

With the tension of combat added to the men's natural exuberance, one of the wolves described the life in the ready room as "a cross between the Roman Coliseum in its heyday and Barnum's freak show."[77] The truth was much less exciting, however, as they smoked cigarettes, played acey-deucey (backgammon), and prepared for the next mission. Eager pilots engaged in a fair amount of shoptalk, where the qualities of each type of aircraft—like its wing loading and wing aspect—were compared. A few hammocks swung from the ceiling. Down in the ship's store, cigarettes sold for seven cents a pack. Across the passageway outside, a young black man operated a small pantry. Seaman Roland E. Williams prepared light meals for flight crews when the wardroom was closed, and looked forward to the day when the war ended and he could go to hairdresser school. Other seamen cleaned the pilots' staterooms and did their laundry. On the flight deck above their ready room, teams of men spotted aircraft and handled the takeoffs and landings of the CAP and ASW missions. *Hornet* did not turn into the wind to launch these single-plane missions; it threw them into the air with its catapult.

The first strike returned almost three hours later and their news was mostly good. In the island's harbor the Helldivers had found eight enemy ships, most of which were five-thousand- to eight-thousand-ton transports, with one destroyer and one sampan. Bombing Two had scored two hits on two ships, one hit apiece on two others, but missed the destroyer. The sampan had been thoroughly strafed— and that was saying something with the SB2C's 20mm cannon; the pilots found "their destructive power . . . tremendous."[78] Though enemy fighters were known to be operating off the nearby island of Peleliu, the only enemy plane spotted had been one "Tojo." It had fled. The enemy's antiaircraft fire, though, had been intense. One of their planes had not returned. The pilot and gunner, last seen as their plane entered its dive, were listed as missing in action.

Later that day Mike's turn came to take the Helldiver into combat. He led the second division and the squadron's XO led the first.[79] The target was the airfield on the tiny island of Peleliu, 112 miles away. On the map, the airfield's runways looked like a giant number 4 etched into the base of an irregular-shaped island. The Beasts were being loaded with a thousand-pound bomb in the bomb bay and a hundred-pound bomb under each wing. The smaller bombs had an instantaneous fuse setting, to increase the splatter. The larger one had a .1-second delay to give it more destructive power against walls. Visibility was unrestricted. Eight fighters and seven torpedo planes would accompany them. The enemy had demonstrated an effective antiaircraft defense. Pilots in the ready rooms, as they began to copy down important information onto their Ouija Boards, must have begun to pay particular attention to the location of the rescue submarine. The navy had started placing a sub in the vicinity of the strike zone to rescue downed flight crews.

Mike found the mission less than challenging. "Now here I am, been through two squadrons that I trained, and they give us a little target like Palau." After years of training to hit moving ships, the prospect of hitting an airfield and its hangars made him laugh. "My God," he exclaimed, "miss an airfield?" The call came to man their planes.

Up the stairs and out on the flight deck, the pilots walked to the stern. The wind carried the astringent odors of aviation fuel and exhaust. The Helldivers had been jammed on the stern, their wings in the up position to make room for more. The Hellcats and Avengers took off before him, as did the XO's division. Moving up to the launch position, he pushed a button and the wings came down. The plane captain and another deckhand made sure they were locked. Mike taxied forward; the nose of the Beast obstructed his forward view.

He grew nervous as he got to the spot. Sure, the SB2C Helldiver had a lot more horsepower than his old Dauntless, but the air group commander and Captain Browning "took it away from you by giving you a shorter deck." They wanted more planes spotted on the deck ready for takeoff. More planes on the rear of the flight deck in turn pushed the spot from which Mike would begin his takeoff farther forward. He did not like the idea that they had figured exactly "how many feet to take you off so you didn't sink. . . ." The run-up of the engine sounded fine. At full power the plane shook with pent-up energy. The flight director pointed to the bow and ducked. Mike released the brakes, and the Beast rolled forward. Gaining speed, the tail came up level behind him, allowing him to see straight ahead. The edge looked too close. When he cleared the bow of the ship, the aircraft dropped. He realized he was right; "it was maybe 20 feet off of the deck before you got flying speed." As quickly as possible, Mike made a gentle turn to starboard to make the wind better for the pilot behind him. He also had to unbuckle himself so he could reach way down by his feet to pull the handle to retract the landing gear.

Circling, he noticed two other carriers also in the midst of a launch a few miles away. He noted some heavy cumulus clouds. The Hellcats and Avengers circled with him. Only nine of the twelve Helldivers scheduled joined up—more technical problems—and off they went. The flight to the target took less than an hour. The leader had to find the right tiny island amid a great scattering of tiny green islands and atolls. It took a little concentration. They came in an endless variety of shapes, surrounded by the pale blue of shallow water and white coral reefs. The main harbor on the main island was easy to spot: burning Japanese ships filled the water and U.S. planes filled the sky.

The XO led his strike in from the northeast. As he approached the target, he took the planes into a shallow dive to gain speed. The wolves adjusted the settings on their engines and props, then trimmed their planes for the dive. They were at about ninety-five hundred feet when they aligned themselves along Peleliu's northeast-to-southwest runway. The great white 4 stood out clearly amid the green canopy. Micheel peeled off and pointed his plane at the airfield below. As his airspeed indicator slid toward three hundred knots, a fighter plane went roaring by him, strafing the ground to help slow the enemy's AA guns. His speed increased with every second. "I'm going down in, on my diving run, and I'm maybe about 4,000 feet. Pow! I feel something hit the airplane. I look out and . . . my starboard wing's on fire." Mike thought he might as well finish the dive at this point; "maybe it [the fire] will go out." At about two thousand feet he released his thousand-pound center bomb and pulled back on the stick with both hands. Gravity gave his body a tight squeeze.

"When I pull out and head out to sea, I can see the fire has gone out, and my aileron wire is unraveling. . . ." He might lose control at any moment. He got on the intercom. "Prepare to ditch at sea! We're going to land next to the survival submarine."

"Oh, sir," John Hart, the gunner, protested, "I hope we can get back to the ship. I've been shot and I'm bleeding and I can't reach the life raft and I can't swim. So I hope we can go back to the ship." Mike looked over and saw "a great big hole in the wing." He could see the aileron wire flipping around. If it snapped, he might not be able to slide his plane smoothly to a stop near the rescue sub. On the other hand, his gunner was wounded. If the landing went wrong—which was likely during a water landing—John might not make it out before the plane sank.

"Well, we'll try to get back," he said into the intercom. "I don't know if that aileron is going to hold or not. If it goes and I can catch it with my rudder I'll be all right." He turned toward the carrier. The flight back lasted most of an hour, until the welcome sight of the task group hove into view. Mike called down to his carrier to let them know he had a wounded gunner. He listed the damage to his aircraft, so they would know how serious it was. His request for immediate clearance to land, however, was denied. "Wait." Then a pause, and then the controller said, "Go to five thousand feet . . . and dog." From Mike's damage report, Hornet's air controller knew it was likely he would crash on the deck. So Mike would circle the ship until all the others landed and a large crash barrier was raised.

As he circled, Mike had time to think. He had plenty of gas. As long as his aileron held he was fine. As serious as the hole in his wing was the loss of hydraulic fluid, which the fire had consumed. Without his hydraulics, Mike's plane would lack landing flaps, which give the wings more lift at slow speeds. Hydraulics also powered his landing gear, so he would have to crank his wheels down by hand. Once the wheels went down, he had to land on the carrier. He could not land in the water because the wheels and struts would catch the water and slam the nose of the plane into the water. In the ensuing collision, the plane would often flip over on its back before sinking. A new concern shook him: What if only one wheel locked into place? Mike got on the radio. "You didn't forget I'm here?"

"No, sir," the controller replied, "you're going to be the last plane to land. We're going to put up the barricade for you." In order to land, Mike had to know the speed at which the plane would stall. A stall meant total loss of control over the aircraft. He began to experiment, slowing down to just the moment of stall, then catching it and speeding up again, and so on. He wanted to get a precise figure, knowing that he would have to add in some speed to compensate for the extra drag created when he lowered the wheels. "I figure out, well, I got to go about twenty knots faster when I come in than I do normally." After a time the call came and Mike brought the Beast into the landing pattern. He lowered his wheels as he flew the downwind leg.

Making a classic carrier approach, Mike flew alongside the carrier, with it headed in the opposite direction off to his left, or port. He lowered his tail hook. "I know I'm fast. When I get right up there to the ship, I . . . turn my wing up so that those guys on the bridge that are watching can see the hole in my wing!" Even before Mike could begin to make the final turn to come up behind the ship, the LSO waved him off. "So then he gets on the radio and he tells me, 'You're way too fast. You got to slow it down.'" Mike circled the ship at low altitude, setting up for another pass, trying to find the right spot between stall speed and excessive speed. Once again, though, the LSO waved him out of the groove. He told Mike over the radio to take a longer approach. Instead of making a ninety-degree turn off the stern of the ship, Mike would fly straight and level toward it, just like an airplane landing at an airfield. A land-based plane, though, landed on its front wheels; a carrier plane landed by catching its rear hook. Placing a plane in the attitude to catch an arresting wire meant that the nose blocked the pilot's vision forward and the wings blocked his vision below. This was why carrier pilots normally made a sharp turn to land—the turn dropped the port wing and allowed them to see the deck and the LSO until almost the last second. No turn meant no forward vision.

The LSO, an experienced aviator who had undergone advanced training, knew exactly what he was asking of the pilot. Thankfully this pilot had a thousand hours of air time and had spent a month of high stress on Guadalcanal. Mike made the long, straight approach from the stern. "My Landing Signal Officer just let me have my speed, but he just cut me sooner, so I would glide further before I hit. Normally when you come aboard, you're almost over the end of the carrier deck and he gives you a cut . . . you're right there: bang, bang! But this time he gave me a cut way out, and I could see the stern of the ship!" At the LSO's cut signal, Mike yanked the throttle back to zero. The engine's roar faded. "Oh, I had to trust him. I can't do anything else. I just got to do what he tells me. He knows what he's doing, that's what he's there for." The Beast glided for a long, quiet moment. The carrier's island rose quickly in the right-hand window. The cut had been timed perfectly and it "plops me right in on the deck." The tail hook caught the wire.

Mike looked up to see the crash fences in front of him flop down. He throttled forward, then climbed out and let the plane handlers take over. A medical team rushed forward and took his gunner, John, below to sick bay. Micheel went to the ready room to be debriefed. After such a feat, a pilot would receive a warm welcome from his squadron. While the ensigns might have been impressed with Lieutenant Micheel's landing, his skipper was impressed that Mike had completed his dive on the target with a burning wing. The other pilots had confirmed that Mike's thousand-pound bomb had "hit almost dead center of the intersection of the two main runways on Peleliu."[80] This was the example a division leader set for the men on his wing. The enemy would have a hard time coming after *Hornet* because Mike's first instinct had been to press home the attack. To Campbell, Lieutenant Micheel's "skilled airmanship and courageous devotion to duty in the face of heavy and accurate antiaircraft fire were in keeping with the highest traditions of the United States Naval Service."[81]

While giving his report Micheel learned that his had not been the only plane to get hit with a burst of AA fire. One other had sustained less damage than his. A third Helldiver had burst into flames over Peleliu. The pilot, John Houston, had rolled it over so he and his gunner could get out quickly. Two parachutes were seen to open. Houston and his gunner landed in the water a hundred yards off the enemy's shore, too close to be rescued.[82]

"After I had had my debrief, I went down to the hangar deck and looked at my airplane." The mechanics had kept the wings down in order to study the damage. "So I got up there and put my head through the hole in the wing, I could turn all the way around, my shoulders could turn all the way around inside that hole." No wonder he had come in a little fast. Up close, he could also see that the SB2C had three cables to control the aileron and only one had been nicked. Even the damaged wire had not unraveled that much; it had only looked that way as it whipped in the wind. Back in the rear seat compartment, the shell that had maimed John had blown off the left handle of his .30-cal machine gun. At that, "I went down to see my gunner and guys were coming out of the sick bay and they said, 'Oh, he's okay, there's nothing wrong with him, he's okay.'"

"What do you mean 'nothing wrong with him'?"

"Well, he just lost his index finger."

"You mean," Mike asked, "he couldn't pull out that life raft because he lost his finger?"

"Well, he was scared. He was in shock. He didn't know what had happened. He was bleeding . . ." Thinking it over, Mike did not blame John for not wanting to attempt a water landing. He had not liked the idea either, but the aileron wire had "scared the daylights" out of him. As the tension eased, he began to laugh at himself. "I thought I was a hotshot. I had this thing all figured out. Then the first thing you know I got a bullet through my wing that set me on fire." He resolved not to be so smug, to understand it could happen to him, regardless of his skill. The first strike of his second combat tour "changed my mind all over again, and then I was always careful, an apprehensive pilot." A little before nine p.m. enemy planes approached the task force. None of them got close to *Hornet*, but the ship stayed at general quarters until eleven p.m., and that cut into everyone's sleep.

When Mike reported to the ready room the next day, he learned that John Hart had resigned from flying. Rear seat gunners volunteered for the job, so they had the right to return to being an ordinary aviation mechanic again. Hart had flown with Mike since August, but one combat mission had been enough. Another airman volunteered and flew with him on a strike at a spot called Corro. The carrier had another busy day, much of it successful. One of the torpedo planes, however, went off the end of the flight deck and crashed into the water.

On the third day of combat, April 1, the air group shifted its attention away from the Palau Islands to Woleai Atoll. Micheel did not participate. During the nine a.m. launch one Beast failed so badly on takeoff that the pilot "essentially taxied off the bow."[83] The plane and her crew disappeared before the guard destroyer could get to them. Both men had wives and children. A second mission against Woleai cost another Helldiver from AA fire. Before lunchtime, the carriers and their air groups had completed their assignment and set sail for Majuro.

In the ready room, Skipper Campbell began chewing out Hal Buell, who led the second division in Campbell's strike. Campbell told Hal he was not to dive in advance of Campbell's division, but to follow his lead. If the skipper expected Hal to accept this, he had read him wrong. Hal looked him in the eye and told him the leader was not supposed to slow down their attack by circling the target—that just gave the enemy gunners more time to sight in their AA guns. Proper technique dictated a high-speed approach—descending from the cruising altitude to the diving altitude—followed immediately by the dive. "You want to get over the top of the target and out!" Campbell could not accept this challenge to his authority. The two ended up going to the air group commander. Campbell had rank on his side. Hal was a seasoned veteran who knew the doctrine. As a division leader himself, Mike could have been drawn into the confrontation, but refused. He got along well with "Soupy" Campbell. He agreed with Buell. Micheel had been around enough to know the flap would work itself out as such things usually did: Hal would be told to follow orders and Campbell would stop circling the target.

After three days, America's first strike into the Palau Islands ended in complete success. The enemy in the Palau Islands could not threaten MacArthur's advance up the New Guinea coast; 130,000 tons of enemy shipping had been sunk; and dozens of planes had been shot down and more strafed on the ground. The task force had lost about two dozen planes, although the subs had picked up a number of downed crews. It bothered Mike that operational losses had outnumbered the airplanes lost to enemy fighters or AA fire. Steaming back to Majuro, scuttlebutt had it that they would hit New Guinea next.[84] First they had a chance to get off the ship and onto the Majuro Atoll while the ships received supplies and gasoline. The men played baseball on the beach or went swimming, but there wasn't much to Majuro. One of the wolves surely defined the word "atoll" for his friends—no women atoll, no whiskey atoll, nothin' atoll.

As BAD AS THE RAIN ON CAPE GLOUCESTER HAD BEEN, IN MARCH THE MORTAR-men of the 2/1 had to admit "the rainy season seems to have only begun now." It rained hard. It rained daily. The rain created the seas of mud that slowed the pace of infantry warfare. The air raid siren sounded occasionally, although seldom did planes arrive. The only troops of the IJA the marines saw were those strung up in the native villages—each village had captured five or six alive. The natives "beat the mortal shit out of every jap they catch," exacting retribution for the injuries the invaders had once inflicted on them. To keep busy, the 2/1 had classes on weapons, had inspections, and worked on their camp.

Sid, as a member of the kitchen team, had seen his popularity sink. The men hated eating the same food every day. Twice in the past two months, steak and eggs had been served to break the monotony of warmed-up K and C rations. In early April, the cooks tried serving fish as an entrée. Deacon took one look at it and told the cooks, "They can jam that salmon up their ass as far as I am concerned." When John Wesley "Deacon" Tatum used foul language, the situation had obviously gotten bad. The regimental HQ tried to improve the situation. It issued cigarettes, toothpaste, and other treats. It offered the men a chance to draw out some of their money. No one wanted any. It began showing movies at night, the one bright spot in the jungle.

The night of April 5 they offered a double feature. The rain abated, and that allowed the men to watch them before bed. At about four a.m. a huge crash woke up Sid. Someone yelled, "Tree on a man." Sid climbed out of his hammock to see a huge tree, with a trunk perhaps ten feet in diameter and fifty feet tall, lying on a tent twenty feet from him. The galley men grabbed their Coleman lanterns and the whole of H Company came to help. The tree had crushed the legs of one man in the tent. Deacon and W.O. were with Sid when the company moved the trunk, freeing the injured man and extracting a body out from underneath. The dead body had been Don Rouse, one of the original members of the #4 gun squad.

Later that morning Lieutenant Benson gave Sid the job of going through Rouse's personal effects as a team of Seabees showed up and began to inspect the forest in and around camp. Two of them carried a giant chain saw like a stretcher team. They cut the tree that had killed Rouse into pieces. In Don's possessions Sid found a piece of propaganda that had been dropped on them by the Japanese back in New Guinea. Don had a copy because he had been moved over to the company's intelligence section. Given the propaganda's pornographic content—the Japanese had mistaken the marines for Aussies and had intended to sow discord among the Allies with it—Sid took it to Benson. Benny told him to keep it; he already had one.

Apparently the rain had weakened the hold of the trees in the earth. All of the top-heavy ones had to come down. A Seabee from Oregon dropped trees with precision, not even asking for the tents to be moved. The company held the funeral at two p.m. for Private First Class Don Rouse of Biloxi, Mississippi. They buried his body in the cemetery. The headstones they erected would not last long in the jungle on Cape Gloucester. Nothing man-made lasted within the green inferno. Next to the tents the Seabees cut the felled trees into logs and the marines rolled them out of their way.

A few nights later How Company learned lists were being drawn up for rotation home. A furlough system had also been established for those who qualified, although applying for a furlough meant delaying one's rotation stateside. Neither would happen until they departed Cape Gloucester, New Britain. The first reliable news about their departure reached the men on Easter Sunday, April 9. A senior NCO called a special meeting to announce the army's 40th Division would relieve them in seven to ten days. The 1st Division would either go to Noumea, Guadalcanal, or some island in the Russells.

EASTER SUNDAY FOUND PRIVATE FIRST CLASS EUGENE SLEDGE STILL STUCK IN the replacement battalion camp in Noumea, New Caledonia. The Red Cross held services. Attending church brought him joy and fond memories of attending the

Government Street Presbyterian Church in Mobile with his family. As he told his father in a letter written on that day, "You and mummie have given Edward and I a pure Christian outlook on life that we will never lose no matter where we are."

The replacement battalion made long marches into the mountains outside of town. They hiked eighteen miles fast enough that Sledge felt "sure Stonewall's Foot Cavalry would have thought us pretty good."* His sharp eyes did not miss the cockatoos and parakeets in the trees. The birds' brilliant plumage as well as their scolding replies to any disturbances on the ground below delighted him. Later, when the marines practiced their amphibious maneuvers, he noticed the tiny shells and took interest in the sea life.

Now that he was overseas, Eugene permitted himself to talk the talk of a marine. To a friend in Mobile who had "just joined the best outfit in the world," he counseled, you "will find the furloughs few and the work pretty hard. But when it's all over he can say he was a Marine. I'm proud to say that right now." To his aunt, who had had the temerity to suggest that Gene "looked like an R.A.F. fighter pilot" in a recent photo, he declared, "If a man told me that I'd grab him by the stacking swivel & blacken his sights. In other words—push his face in. Not that I have anything against the R.A.F. But I'm in an outfit with 169 years of fighting spirit & tradition behind it and I don't care to be told I resemble a 'fly-fly glamour' boy." His pride in the Marine Corps only seemed unbounded, however. He drew the line at tattoos. A lot of the men in camp had had the eagle, globe, and anchor etched into their arms or chests, but he knew his parents would be "horrified."

Private First Class Sledge also quickly adopted the fighting man's disgust at receiving bad news from home. "When I'm down here doing the best I can," he advised his mother, he didn't want to hear about "strikes, racial trouble, or political bickering." He liked the clippings from the newspaper she sent that were about hunting or history, but he asked her to stop sending him news about the war—the recreation room was full of it and he was sick of it. So far as politics went, "When we win the war I hope the politicians have left enough of America for us fellows to live peacefully in."

HORNET SAILED OUT OF MAJURO ON APRIL 11 ON THE WAY TO HELP GENERAL MacArthur's army move farther up the northern coast of New Guinea. Due to a

---

*Thomas Jonathan "Stonewall" Jackson became one of the most revered Confederate generals of the American Civil War, renowned for his brilliant military tactics.

shake-up in command, Micheel's flattop had become the flagship of Task Group 58.1, which included USS *Bataan* and two other light carriers, under the command of Jocko Clark. The task group sailed with the other task groups of Task Force 58, a force totaling twelve carriers and dozens of escorts. In offensive capability, it had no equal.

Sailing with an armada of cruisers, destroyers, and other carriers made launching sorties more difficult. The carrier had to turn into the wind, whatever its direction, and speed up. The speed of the carriers made life difficult for the slower vessels. On the trip to New Guinea, Admiral Clark informed his task group that his "flipper turn" was now standard operating procedure. As a carrier commander, Clark had invented "the flipper turn," in which his carrier exited the group formation at twenty-five knots while the other ships held steady at eighteen knots.[85] It saved fuel. Now that he commanded 58.1, Jocko Clark decreed the entire task group make the flipper turn, whose prosaic name was changed to "Modified Baker" to fit better with naval lingo. Jocko, a former pilot, ordered the change because he put the needs of his carriers first. His plan angered the captains of the battleships, cruisers, and destroyers, who had "to give way" to the carriers.[86] Modified Baker represented another marker in the destruction of centuries of navy tradition and doctrine. The line of great battlewagons had once ruled the seas. Breaking that line meant the battleships were no longer preparing to fight the decisive fleet engagement; their guns existed to protect the carriers from enemy aircraft. Admiral Mitscher, in command of all of the task groups, also wore the Golden Wings of a naval aviator. Mitscher observed Jocko's 58.1 execute the flipper turn, decided it worked better than any other, and ordered it adopted by all the task groups of the Fifth Fleet.

In the Bombing Two ready room, Campbell showed his men a map of New Guinea and of MacArthur's target, Hollandia. As usual, they would help the soldiers by destroying several airfields nearby. Reports by army reconnaissance estimated Japanese strength at 350 aircraft. While other squadrons hit Hollandia itself, the wolves were assigned to strike bases about 120 miles farther west along the coast. Part of the preflight briefing concerned the location of a place to land or to bail out over in the case of trouble. Hitting targets on the coast of New Guinea gave them a lot more options than the Palau Islands had, but Mike warned his guys with a grin, "Don't land in the jungle because there's aborigines in the jungle . . . man eaters!" As they approached New Guinea, they again found themselves within the range of enemy planes. The Combat Air Patrol (CAP) began to have bogeys to chase down. The bogeys came in singles, though, not in squadrons.

An unexpected ruckus broke out early in the morning of April 19, the day before the next combat mission. As the ship turned into the wind to launch some routine ASW scouts, general quarters sounded.[87] Mike and the other pilots had to remain in the ready room. It turned out that the carrier had turned into the path of another ship of the task group. More of the story came in later, when Hal Buell returned from his routine ASW search. He had seen two ships almost collide with *Hornet*. He had been sitting in his plane, the engine idling, when he had looked over the starboard (right) side of the ship to see the prow of another charging at him through the darkness. It had slid past with perhaps twenty feet to spare. Just as he had gushed relief, another one appeared; its prow "appeared as tall as our flight deck" and "on a direct collision course." Hal had cut the engine, released his harness and jumped from his plane. He watched as the tanker threw itself into reverse, sliding past "our stern with only inches to spare; I could have jumped from our fantail onto her bridge deck. . . ." From the bridge word came that Captain Browning had been at the helm when this happened and had gotten an earful from Admiral Clark, "who had run to the bridge in his bathrobe."[88] It ended with Jocko warning Browning, "Don't you ever do that again."[89] The ship's captain walked away, shaking his head.

Beginning on April 20, the airplanes of Task Force 58.1 spent four days hitting targets at Sawar, Sarmi, and Wakde Island. The weather was terrible, with a ceiling so low that the Helldivers began their dives from four thousand feet.[90] The low altitude helped the enemy gunners on the ground. In a few days, the wolves lost eight planes.[91] Mistakes and malfunctions accounted for more losses than enemy AA fire. Two planes collided. Another had engine trouble soon after takeoff and crashed while attempting to get back aboard. The pilot survived; his gunner did not. Another plane failed on takeoff and fell into the ocean. His gunner got out, but the pilot's body had to be pulled from it. Blunt-force trauma to the head had killed him. Every pilot knew why: the handle to pull up the wheels was beyond most pilots' reach. Pilots had begun taking off with their shoulder straps unbuckled, so they could get their wheels up quickly. Getting the gear up quickly helped the Helldiver reach flying speed faster and thus reduced the chances of hitting the water. Without his straps on, Lieutenant Bosworth had sustained a severe blow to the head when his Beast fell off the end of the bow and hit the water 52.3 feet below.

The accident prompted the skipper to make sure the navy understood the problem. Campbell also asked for immediate assistance in extending the handle. The pilots had to be able to bring up the wheels while remaining strapped in. When another SB2C failed on takeoff and hit the water, the pilot had his shoulder strap on. When he was fished out of the water, he described being "trapped in the cockpit and dragged thirty to forty feet below the surface before he could fight clear."[92] The crash brought Hal Buell and Mike Micheel together for a talk. Something had to be done. Their air group had suffered ten crashes. After reviewing the circumstances of each, the two veterans decided the pilot had been at fault in one or two; "insufficient wind" over the flight deck had caused the others. While the ship's other planes, the Hellcats and the Avengers, seemingly jumped off the deck in a light breeze, a fully loaded SB2C demanded lots of wind and lots of flight deck. Buell did not think their squadron CO, Campbell, appreciated the danger and recommended going over his head to the air group commander. Mike agreed. Roy Johnson, the CAG, listened carefully to his veterans and decided they were correct. He found a way to convince Captain Miles Browning to either get twenty-five to thirty knots of wind or allow the Helldivers to fly with a fifteen-hundred-pound payload of bombs instead of two thousand pounds. Skipper Campbell of Bombing Two found out about the meeting, of course, and he blamed Buell.

Their task group spent a few more days in the area, providing air cover and escort services in support of MacArthur's attack. From the radio news programs, it soon became evident that "MacArthur's public relations department was extolling the accomplishments of the Army's invasion of Hollandia but there wasn't one word about the Navy's support."[93] The wolves could only shake their heads in disgust at the unabashed machinations of "Dugout Doug." Some of the frustration they felt, however, resulted from the feeling that their strikes had not been effective. The exact locations of the enemy installations had not been known in advance. Their targets on the ground had been "heavily covered by coconut trees," and well dispersed. "Dives were therefore made," Campbell complained, "on areas of the island rather than a specific target. In most cases it was a matter of luck whether a valuable target was hit and destroyed."[94]

JOHN BASILONE WROTE HIS FAMILY AGAIN IN APRIL—OBVIOUSLY HIS MOTHER had given him a stern lecture about writing more often—to tell them he had spent the first part of the month out in the fields of Camp Pendleton.[95] Living out of his backpack for two weeks had been easy. "I'm feeling fine only I got a lot of sun burn. I'm as Black as the ace of Spades." As usual he spent most of his short letter inquiring about his family—his grandmother, who was ill; his father, who had been hired by a prestigious clothing store; his brothers and sisters. His brother Al had joined the marines. Johnny asked his mother to "tell him all the luck in the world for me." He signed his letters, "Love and Kisses, your loving son Johnny." He asked his mother to send a copy of *Parade* magazine: "I want to show it to the boys."[96]

"The boys" were some of the sergeants in his company: Clinton Watters, Jack

Wheeler, Rinaldo Martini, and Edward Johnston. These were his buddies in Charlie Company, which was just back from field maneuvers in the boondocks. The NCOs had to get their green marines accustomed to firing live ammunition, conducting patrols, and infiltrating enemy positions at night, crawling under fire.[97] Out in the field the marines of Charlie Company found their attention focused on their gunnery sergeant. Basilone was special. All of his fame and fortune made a few things self-evident to the men just out of boot camp. He loved being a marine. He believed the war was a worthy endeavor. He would always do his best. These truths stayed with them even as the glitter of fame gave way to the familiarity born of camping in the field. Not that a private first class ever got too familiar with a senior NCO, only that the gunny's easy way with everyone broke down the stereotype of Manila John.[98] Most of all, he made it clear that he would have to depend on them, too, when the shooting started. Mutual trust created a team, not adulation.

Johnny relied on his sergeants—Clint, Ed, Jack, and Rinaldo—to help him with the company's administration and with the guidebooks used to explain theory to the men. He taught his men how to operate and maintain the Browning .30-cal light machine gun by demonstrating it to them. The new air-cooled Brownings weighed a lot less than the old water-cooled models, and that helped a lot as they moved in support of the advancing fire teams. His enthusiasm for machine guns and for the physical demands of field problems impressed his men. They became imbued with his understanding of what being a marine meant. Charlie Company knew their gunny was going to be out in front.

Back in camp, they could see him at the slop chute on base or at a beer hall in Oceanside, drinking a beer "with all the gusto of a millionaire guzzling champagne."[99] If Lena had to work, he'd be there with Clint, Ed, Jack, and Rinaldo. Ed had played some semipro baseball and was the best athlete. Jack was the quiet one. Rinaldo had ridden the rails as a hobo so long he claimed to have no hometown.[100] When Johnny came back to camp with his garrison cap on sideways, doing his impression of Napoleon, his friends knew he was just goofing off. It looked different to marines in the other companies of 1st Battalion, however. Now the air carried a whiff of "Oh, he gets away with it because he's a Medal of Honor winner."[101]

RATHER THAN RETURN TO THE FLEET ANCHORAGE AT MAJURO WHEN THEIR New Guinea mission ended, the ships of Task Force 58 blasted through a fearsome storm, bound for the island of Truk in the Caroline Island chain. Everyone in the navy knew of Truk's fearsome reputation as the enemy's great forward fleet anchorage. The air force's B-24s had been working it over for some time, and the carrier fleet had hit it previously. The Imperial Navy had sent more planes there, though, and the wolves still feared it.[102] As *Hornet* steamed north, Bombing Two began reviewing maps, becoming familiar with the several atolls that made up the location known as Truk. Their new maps noted every building, their function, and type of construction. In the briefings, the skipper made clear that a massive fighter sweep would be launched first, in order to clear out the enemy fighters, so the dive-bombers could do their job. The ship would launch them about a hundred miles from their targets.

Before dawn on April 29, *Hornet* came to course one hundred degrees True, her speed twenty-five knots. The fighters took off from all the carriers in the group.[103] During the course of that morning, they shot down fifty-nine enemy fighters, and destroyed another thirty-four on the ground. When Campbell led the first of Bombing Two's missions, a few Zeros made passes at them, but the wolves' problems came not from enemy planes during the following days. In eleven strikes against Truk and other enemy bases in the Caroline Island chain, the enemy AA guns took a lot of bites out of their planes. Mike led four strikes, punishing any signs of life with five-hundred-pound bombs. On one sortie, an enemy gunner blew another hole in his wing, but the shell failed to explode. It left a three-inch hole in the leading edge of his left wing. He hardly noticed. Other squadrons, however, lost a lot of guys to the heavy AA fire. News of the losses on the other carriers came slowly to the squadron ready room, usually arriving in dribs and drabs. Pilots needed to know. More than half of the forty-six airmen shot down were rescued. The rescue submarine USS *Tang* picked up twenty-two by itself. Floatplanes launched from the cruisers picked up others, an idea Admiral Clark in his flag bridge atop *Hornet*'s island had put into action.

The neutralization of the enemy's ocean fortress went well, but the Beast did not hold up under the strain. Several planes collapsed upon landing, one of them catching fire and later pushed overboard. The Helldiver's bomb release mechanism had begun sticking.[104] On the last day of their mission, the problem became severe. In one instance, a pilot landed on *Hornet* with a hundred-pound bomb still attached under his wing. He had tried all manner of maneuvers to shake it loose on the return flight, with no success. As soon as he slammed into the carrier's deck, though, it disengaged and rolled down the deck and exploded. Two men died. The damage to the deck was repaired temporarily within twenty minutes, allowing flight operations to continue. Later that day another pilot landed with a five-hundred-pound bomb in his center rack. This bomb also detached upon impact, fell through the airplane's closed bomb bay doors, rolled underneath the spinning propeller and up the deck.[105] All hands jumped off the deck and down onto the catwalk that surrounded it. When nothing happened, one of the wolves peeked over the edge. The flight deck "looked like a ghost town."[106] Finally, the deck crew got a cart and disposed of it.

Reviewing the reports and photographs taken on the last sortie, the senior staff decided their mission had been accomplished. On the evening of May 1, Task Force 58 broke off contact and steamed back to the Marshall Islands. The wolves could stand down.

A FEW DAYS BEFORE SID PHILLIPS AND THE REST OF THE 2/1 DEPARTED CAPE Gloucester, they knew they were headed for the Russell Islands near Guadalcanal. The Canal had grown into a large U.S. base. Hope of returning to Melbourne had been dashed. The news helped provoke a fair amount of angry mutters—what Sid called "gum beating" because it served no purpose—as the working parties loaded the ships. The 2/1 boarded *President Adams* on April 24 and sailed the next day. The stifling heat made it hard to breathe down in the holds where the bunks were. The ship's galley served big pork chops that night and cold ice cream the next, making it easier to enjoy the trip. Two sub chasers and two destroyers guarded the ten transports hauling the 1st Division off the green inferno and depositing them on what scuttlebutt called Buvuvu Island, which turned out to be incorrect. The 1st Division extracted itself from MacArthur's control and rejoined the U.S. Navy on April 28, 1944, when it landed on Pavuvu in the Russell Islands.

The disembarkation began at nine a.m. They found themselves on a small island covered mostly by a coconut plantation. The only camp in sight belonged to the 15th Field Depot Battalion. The marines had to build their own. The idea of being required to build one's own rest camp angered everyone. Working parties fell out to erect tents in long rows. They discovered they first had to clean up piles of rotting coconuts. The long first day ended on a bright spot. The new ten-in-one rations were issued. Created to sustain ten men for one meal or vice versa, they had been tasted by the marines and judged to be an improvement in field chow. The hard work continued for days, though, as the men began hauling crushed coral. Colonel Lewis "Chesty" Puller, who had taken command of the First Regiment back on Cape Gloucester, decreed that they could not use the jeeps to haul coral. Staggering along with helmets full of coral, Sid and W.O. "felt like Chinese coolies." They spread the coral along the footpaths and at the bottom of their tents in an effort to reduce the amount of time spent walking in the mud. The engineers strung lights in the tents, beginning with those of the officers and NCOs first.

When the 15th Field Depot unit moved over to Banika on May 4, the marines rushed to grab any of the boxes, tables, or construction materials they left behind. The veterans knew that every little bit of comfort helped. Most nights, one or more of the regiments and often the division HQ showed a film. The projectors tended to break down, though. The entertainment on the evening of May 9 received everyone's full attention. A drawing was held to determine who in the 2/1 would get rotated stateside. In the mortar platoon about thirty pieces of paper were put into a helmet. Half of them had a number on them. The colonel announced that if a man drew a piece with a number, he went home; if he drew two pieces of paper, he forfeited his chance. Every marine "felt very carefully before they withdrew a piece." Both Sid and W.O. won, as did Lieutenant Benson. Their friend Deacon, now a sergeant, did not, nor did any other member of the #4 gun. Deacon noticed the colonel gave tickets home to a number of marines considered "mentally and physically unfit," as well as those with "domestic trouble."

Colonel Puller's tent happened to stand near the regimental mess hall and just a few feet from the series of washing tubs that Private First Class Sidney Phillips kept full of hot water for the men to wash and rinse their mess kits. In the afternoon before chow, Puller would come out of his tent and see Sid at work, lighting the fires under the "GI cans." He asked Sid how he had come to be on mess duty and laughed heartily when he heard the story. The colonel's stature, at "maybe five six," surprised Sid, since Chesty Puller was a legend of the corps. "The thing that impressed me most about him was how genuinely friendly he was." With a stubby pipe clamped in his mouth, he'd say hello to anyone. He asked Sid about his family, his hometown, and his plans. "When I told him I wanted to go to medical school, I remember he said that wouldn't be easy, but there was no reason why I couldn't make it if that was what I really wanted." Sid felt very lucky to have the chance to speak with such "a great American," as he stoked the fires so the water boiled to the point that "it was hazardous to approach the GI cans at chow time. I couldn't be reprimanded for doing too good a job."

Colonel Puller held his first inspection of his regiment's camp on May 20. He expected his marines to have themselves squared away and he took his time making sure they were. His men learned what to expect.[107] On May 21, the battalions began receiving their share of the fourteen hundred replacements that had arrived. Puller put the First on a training schedule. Reveille blew at five thirty a.m., followed by physical drill, and then chow. The work for the working parties looked endless to everyone but Sid and W.O. On May 23, they turned in their gear. All the guys who were going home had been assigned to a "casual company."

*   *   *

EARLY MAY HAD PASSED IN ALMOST A PACIFIC IDYLL FOR BOMBING SQUADRON Two. Eniwetok Atoll in the Marshalls had become an important base, which meant lots of Seabees had come to build the base, which meant there was an officers' club serving cold beer. The wolves liked to have parties. A few of the more intrepid pilots went to see the bunkers where the Japanese had fought the 4th Marine Division.

One night in mid-May a few thousand members of the ship's crew crowded into the hangar deck to watch a movie. A deck full of folding chairs in the darkened expanse made a great theater. When the opening cartoon ended, "a loud hissing noise" erupted from the back of the room. "A cry of 'It's a bomb' started a human tidal wave action rolling from the rear toward the front."[108] The wave of panic crashed through the wooden chairs until the lights came on. The sight of bodies sprawled all over his hangar incensed Admiral Clark. Mindless fear had no place aboard a warship. Some thirty men had to be sent to sick bay. One seaman was fished out of the bay. When at last things got squared away, the film began again.

Two days later, the body of a *Hornet* seaman was found floating in the harbor. The story quickly came out that another seaman, one who had been pulled from the water during the melee at the movie, had reported seeing someone else in the water. No muster had been held and no search had been launched at that time. The chairs had been reset and the movie shown. While a court of inquiry was convened to investigate the death, *Hornet* set sail for Majuro to rendezvous with the rest of the fleet. Scuttlebutt about the movie riot and the next mission flowed through the Bombing Two ready room. The court of inquiry came back with a bland statement about an accident. Admiral Clark directed it to convene again and this time to "assign blame."[109] At Majuro the carrier began to take on fuel and supplies for another sortie. On May 30 the commander of the carrier fleet, Admiral Mitscher, relieved Captain Miles Browning of command. Captain W. D. Sample reported aboard Admiral Clark's flagship at ten thirty-eight a.m.

Stories about the irascible Miles Browning all had to be told. A few instances of poor seamanship and many examples of petty cruelty while aboard *Hornet* contrasted sharply with the prevailing opinion within the navy: Browning's brilliant mind had created the victory at Midway—a victory so massive, it had changed the course of the Pacific War. The word was Mitscher had sent Browning to command the naval air station at Leavenworth, Kansas. In other words, his career had just ended. On the topic of how such a hero could be dismissed so quickly and completely, everyone had an opinion. Stories of Browning's excessive drinking and even a case of adultery also wafted through.[110] Lieutenant Micheel stayed out of it. He did not, however, regret the loss of a captain who had shortened his pilots' flight deck and who often failed to provide them twenty-five knots of headwind during the launch. Mike measured his life expectancy in those few extra feet of deck and knots of wind.

The new captain, Sample, made a good first impression on his air group. Two days after he arrived, representatives of the Marine Corps came on board to brief the carrier's air group officers on Operation Forager, the invasion of the Mariana Islands. To stop this amphibious assault, Japan would send her carrier fleet. Aircraft carriers had not clashed since October 1942, when they had traded punches in the waters around Guadalcanal.

OUT IN THE FIELDS OF CAMP PENDLETON, THE TRAINING OF BASILONE'S MARINES shifted again. The individual's proficiency with his weapons and the squad's integration gave way in early June. The training cycle focused more on the battalion-level field problems.[111] These included the use of heavy mortars, 37mms, and half-tracks carrying 75mm howitzers. The next step, to a regimental-size exercise, came soon after. Units from artillery, engineers, motor transports, MPs, and others had been attached to the Twenty-seventh. The reinforced regiment became designated a regimental combat team (RCT). Topside intended each of the three RCTs of the 5th Division to have everything it needed to sustain itself in combat.

After a day's work in the field, Gunny Basilone went out with his girlfriend, Lena, whenever she could get away. Sometimes he and his friends stopped by her mess hall to say hello and beg for some good chow. He made sure his weekend liberties coincided with hers, and they'd go into Los Angeles and stay at the Biltmore Hotel. To Lena it felt like "we were never alone," because everyone tagged along.[112] Other women often pestered her with "How in the world did you get him?"

"I don't know, you kids chased after him. That's why you didn't succeed. Play hard to get," Lena said with a laugh. Her sense of fun fit in well with Johnny and his friends. Dancing, drinking, seeing shows, and carrying on, it all got packed into a forty-eight-hour pass. After one of those fun weekends in early June, Johnny came to Lena's room. As she finished packing her bag, she mentioned that she was going on leave to Oregon to visit relatives. "Let's get married and go to Oregon together," he suggested.[113]

"Okay," Lena replied. Noting his offhand manner, she paid it little attention. They caught a train from L.A. to Oceanside. At the bus depot, waiting for their ride to camp, Johnny asked Lena if she was going to tell everyone the news. "I thought you were kidding," she said.

"No, I meant it," he said.[114] So had she.

*　　*　　*

FROM THE RELATIVE SAFETY OF HIS KITCHEN MESS DUTY, SID WATCHED THE FIRST
Marines begin a training regime. Reveille sounded at five thirty a.m. in the dingy
tent camp on Pavuvu and the men went through physical drill before chow. How
Company's Lieutenant McGrath decided to exceed Colonel Puller's expectations
and hold an inspection of some type (clothing, tents, or equipment) most every day.
Deacon and the guys who were staying for another battle uttered dark threats about
McGrath as they slaved over details like putting the new cloth camouflage covers on
their helmets. They used their ponchos to haul away the piles of stinking coconuts
and dug more trenches to drain the rainwater away from their tents. Free time came
late in the afternoon.

Somehow, Sid knew he would never escape this "monstrous mud hole." After
two years in the boonies, though, he and the other "old timers had become experts
at making and hiding jungle juice." Accumulating or stealing enough canned fruit to
make the liquor proved tricky but not insurmountable. With Deacon distracted by
his duties as a sergeant in the 60mm mortar section, Sid's #4 gun squad had a party
"whenever a new batch was ready." Boredom also drove him to the hut of his friend
Bob Leckie. The marine gunner known as Lucky had a collection of books he called
the Pacific Library of Congress. Lucky would loan Sidney books, but he was a stick-
ler on their being returned. Late in May a ship came in bringing more replacements.
It departed on June 1 with W. O. Brown aboard. He and the others in the first half
of the rotation had shipped out for stateside duty. The sight of it did not convince
Sid he was "ever really going to leave Pavuvu." His ticket home still felt like a dream
from which he would be rudely awakened.

EUGENE SLEDGE HAD CHAFED UNDER THE LONG DELAY, WANTING TO GET INTO
a good outfit and "see some of the Pacific." Other marines from the replacement depot
in Noumea had gotten assignments, some to the 1st Division, and he was jealous,
although he had read in the newspapers about U.S. forces being sent to China, and
that appealed to him, too. Occasionally a USO show passed through to relieve the
tedium and he saw the likes of "Eddie the Banjo King" before at last getting the word.
He embarked on USS *General R. I. Howze*, which sailed north from Noumea and arrived at the small dock of Pavuvu on Thursday, June 1. Eugene Sledge was assigned
to the mortar section of King Company, 3rd Battalion, Fifth Marines (K/3/5) of
the storied 1st Marine Division. Gene knew the Marine Corps had, up until 1940,

always operated as regiments, not divisions. He knew the Fifth Marines were one of the oldest and most decorated regiments in the corps. Joining such an elite force thrilled Private First Class Sledge.

As he walked through the rows and columns of eight-man tents looking for King Company's street, he saw tired men in ragged dungarees. The tents and other equipment looked careworn. The camp at Pavuvu made what he had left in Noumea look good.

He found his way to King Company's platoon mortar leader, a Lieutenant Ellington, who hailed from Birmingham and had attended Marion Military before OCS. "Son," his lieutenant said, "you will find that most of your time overseas will be just like it is here." Eugene assumed the lieutenant meant that most of his life would be boring, but that was only partially correct. It also could be translated as "get used to living in the boonies, kid." The lieutenant turned him over to Johnnie Marmet, the sergeant of the mortar platoon. Sergeant Marmet assigned him to one of his 60mm mortar squads. Corporal R. V. Burgin ran #2 gun. Everybody called the corporal Burgin or Burgie, because lots of guys were known by their last names and also because R.V. stood for Romus Valton. Tall and thin like a bullwhip, R. V. Burgin delivered his short, chopped sentences in a spare Texas accent. The lack of inflection conveyed a no-nonsense attitude. Sledge would have begun by calling him Corporal Burgin.

Burgin and the others in King Company had a yellow hue to their skin and purple blotches where the corpsman had rubbed medicine on their infected flesh. Burgin's toes had begun to rot on Gloucester and he had lost two toenails.[115] The first impression startled Gene, although some good news came in the form of Private First Class Merriell "Snafu" Shelton. Snafu, #2 gun's gunner, hailed from Hammond, Louisiana. Southerners (not Yankees) led his squad, Gene noted happily. A walk through the chow line revealed to Eugene that the food quality had also diminished on the short trip from Noumea. Most of the contents had been dehydrated—powdered eggs, powdered potatoes. Men in the line considered Spam, the "pre-cooked meat product," a welcome relief from heated C rations. At some point Sledge made the mistake of complaining. The smoldering anger just under the surface of R. V. Burgin's demeanor cut loose in a hail of cusswords. He had spent four months on Cape Gloucester and it made Pavuvu look good. Gene and the other fresh-faced boys accustomed to clean white sheets, he advised, had better keep their mouths shut.

The Southerners of #2 gun soon found out about the new guy's background and education. They started razzing him about being "a college boy." Burgin had grown up on a farm without running water and electricity. Snafu had dropped out in the seventh grade and gone to work.[116] Unlike them, Eugene had led a sheltered and privileged life. "The only damn job you ever had at home," Burgin surmised matter-of-factly, "was feeding the dog." Sledge took it on the chin as he was supposed to do. He and the other new men also took over the grunt work of hauling away coconuts and carrying in crushed coral.

Two days passed before Eugene had a chance to go find Sid. Finding his best friend amid the entire 1st Marine Division and its attached units took some doing, but he ran into someone who knew Sid.

THE DAY AFTER W.O. LEFT, SID WAS SITTING ON HIS COT "WHEN I NOTICED SOMEONE coming down the company street looking in each tent. I recognized 'Ugin' about three tents away and ran into the company street and screamed 'Ugin' as loud as I could. He ran, and I ran, and we hugged each other and pounded on each other and rolled around wrestling on the ground shouting and screaming. A large crowd gathered thinking we were fighting, and I introduced him around and then we got back to pounding on each other."

AFTER THE BIG WELCOME, EUGENE DISCOVERED THAT SID WAS "JUST LIKE HE always was." However miraculous their meeting on Pavuvu might be, their connection meant even more. After a long day of drill and drudgery, Eugene would go find Sid stoking the fires under his cauldrons well past the point of necessity. They talked about guns, they talked about their dismay at Mobile becoming such a "wild place," and they talked about the war. The veteran told his buddy about Cape Gloucester, where the enemy was on the run. Sid confirmed Ugin's understanding of the life of a United States Marine. Nine-tenths of his time would be spent just as it was at this moment. "The newspapers lead people to believe that a man is under fire all the time," Gene learned, "when he is probably sitting on his bunk reading a funny paper . . . I am just as safe now as if I were home."

Sledge wrote his parents what he learned from Sid. He wanted them to know they bore the hardship in war, because marines "only worried when they were in actual danger, while the parents of marines worried all the time." He described his life as "living in a good tent, eating good food, taking a shower every day, and working." Gene left out the ongoing efforts to kill the legions of rats. The camp on Pavuvu provided him with plenty of hard candy, so in a letter written by the light of a "beer bottle smudge pot," he asked his mother to send him chocolate, Fig Newtons, and more magazines. He also made sure to tell his parents about one of his conversations with Sid in which they had talked about some of their other friends. When he had mentioned that their friend Billy had remained in the V-12 program, Eugene said Sid had concluded, "That boy is yellow." The judgment had shocked him, since no one who knew Sid expected him to say something that harsh about a friend. Eugene, of course, had a reason for telling his parents of it.

Ugin confided in his old friend that he had deliberately flunked out of the V-12 program.[117] The thought of ending the war as a second lieutenant who had never even seen a rifle range had been more than he could bear. Sid respected him for volunteering and knew he'd be fine, but in his heart Sid also knew Eugene was too sensitive of heart and too serious of mind for the "slings and arrows of outrageous fortune" that went with being a Raggedy-Assed Marine. Eugene was so excited to be with someone who would talk about something other than whiskey and women. Sid did show Ugin a picture of his girlfriend he had in Australia, Shirley Finley. He never expected to see her again. The colonel had told him he was going home. Sledge said "she was very pretty."

Once Sid finished his mess duty, the pair usually went to see one of the movies playing, finding seats on the rows of coconut logs. During the love scenes, jokers in the audience "tried to out perform the script" with a few well-placed obscenities. Sid found the improvisations hilarious. On the night of June 6 the movie was entitled *This Land Is Mine*. It concerned a schoolteacher in France who is forced by the Nazi regime to take action against it. The picture stopped. This time, the machine had not broken. An officer announced the news of the second front, the Allied invasion of occupied France. "The earth literally rocked with yells."[118]

News of the Allied invasion in Normandy caused Eugene to think of his brother Edward, who had been stationed in England, from whence the invasion had been launched. He looked up to his older brother, who had earned a degree at the Citadel, a prestigious military school, and become an officer. His mother had sent him a portrait of Edward, who looked dashing and impressive in his uniform. Gene kept it by his bed. Next to Edward, he thought, "I've never done anything to amount to a hill of beans." One small step he could make, he took. He sent his father a money order as a gift. He asked his "Pop" to spend the money on anything he wanted, so long as it was not a bond for his youngest son, Eugene. The gift, intended to demonstrate "my appreciation for the millions of things you & mother did for me," imitated the gift Edward had given their father back in April.

*　　*　　*

THREE NEW FLEET CARRIERS JOINED ADMIRAL SPRUANCE'S FIFTH FLEET IN THE great lagoon of Majuro, allowing him to create Task Group 58.4. The admiral and his carrier commander, Admiral Mitscher, shuffled the assignments a bit. USS *Yorktown*, Micheel's old ship, joined *Hornet*'s Task Group 58.1, which also included the two light carriers *Belleau Wood* and *Bataan*. The other two task groups (58.2 and 58.3) each had four carriers. A grand total of fifteen aircraft carriers, emblazoned with a camouflage of aggressive geometric shapes, swung at anchor together.

At twelve thirty-two p.m. on June 6, 1944, the United States Navy's fleet of fast carriers and a vast array of escort ships stood out from Majuro, setting sail for the Empire of Japan.[119] For the tip of his spear, Mitscher selected his most aggressive admiral in command of his most competent task group. He chose Admiral J. J. "Jocko" Clark, who credited his Cherokee blood for his fighting spirit. A reporter traveling with the fleet described Clark as "a mercurial, glandular man" who "has a long, floppy lower lip which protrudes far out when he is angry."[120]

With Clark's *Hornet* in the van, the fleet's trip to the chain of islands known as the Marianas took five days. The rhythm of battle began on the eleventh with the carriers refueling their escort fleet at five a.m. *Hornet* launched her CAP and ASW at about eight thirty a.m. The fighters found three enemy planes during the course of the afternoon and shot them down. Everyone assumed the enemy on the islands knew they were coming. In the afternoon, fifteen fighters took off and joined up with two hundred Hellcats from the other carriers to sweep the four islands of the Marianas with airfields (Guam, Saipan, Tinian, and Rota) clean of enemy fighters. Fourteen of the fifteen *Hornet* Hellcats returned at six forty-four p.m.; heavy AA fire had forced one to land on the water near the island of Guam. For this type of emergency, Mike's skipper, Campbell, had accompanied the strike with some life rafts in his bomb bay. The pilot went in close to shore, though, with too many AA guns nearby to attempt a boat drop. The rescue submarine promptly came in submerged and got him. Admiral Clark ordered his task group to pull back to the south for the night.

The fleet pulled away from the Marianas because the Japanese would find a way to attack at night, even though they had lost about 150 airplanes that day. A bogey appeared just before two a.m. The Hellcats equipped for night fighting had a difficult task. They had learned to launch and land at night, but finding the enemy— even with radar—proved difficult. The bogey disappeared.

Bombing Two's day started at two a.m. with breakfast. The wolves assembled in the ready room by three a.m. and the first strike flew off the deck beginning at five a.m.[121] For the next three days, Mike's squadron struck the airfields, beach defenses, and villages of Guam and nearby Rota as many as five times in a day. So many missions placed a real burden on the squadron's mechanics because the SB2C took more man-hours to prepare for flight than other types of planes.[122] After each mission, fewer and fewer of the planes would be available for the next one. Too many radial engines could not be throttled up to full power.

The scarcity of aircraft produced competition. Most pilots clamored for every chance to fly. As flight officer, Lieutenant Hal Buell had some say in who flew and who did not, as did the skipper. The wolves knew a pilot needed to fly a certain number of combat missions to earn an Air Medal, and that a certain number of Air Medals entitled one to a Distinguished Flying Cross, the coveted DFC, one step below the Navy Cross. In June of 1944, a pilot's confidence came a bit cheaper than in 1942. The gigantic Fifth Fleet, with its overwhelming superiority, surrounded by dozens of destroyers and submarines dedicated to rescuing downed airmen, could certainly overheat a man's dedication and turn it into a desire more personal and more foolish. Lieutenant Hal Buell made no bones about it. He "coveted a major decoration in the worst way."[123]

Mike did not ascribe his fellow pilots' enthusiasm to being "award hungry" necessarily, nor did he criticize those who were. The wolves were exactly what the naval aviation program had been designed to produce: highly motivated, aggressive, and thoroughly trained dive-bomber pilots. Buell had proven himself in several carrier battles and on Guadalcanal. The new men knew the dangers. Enemy AA fire on Guam and Rota claimed one plane from Bombing Two and scored hits on a few others. The squadron also lost six SB2Cs to "operational losses." Two of those losses occurred during takeoff. Both of the rear seat gunners were recovered, but only one pilot had survived. None of these losses surprised the men of Bombing Two. Clamoring to fly the Beast, therefore, took courage.

The squadron's flight officer did not, however, receive requests from Lieutenant Micheel. While others took issue with Buell's flight schedule, Mike "just went along with them. When it was my turn I went. I didn't scream for any." A cynic might have thought Lieutenant Micheel lacked an aggressive spirit, or perhaps that he was a little too comfortable with the knowledge that the Navy Cross he wore could never be awarded on the basis of the number of missions. A cynic would have been wrong. Mike led his division on four of the eighteen missions flown, taking them in fast. He pushed the Beast all the way down in his dives, through heavy flak, occasionally through heavy clouds. Of the half dozen important hits scored by Bombing Two during its raids, Mike got two confirmed: one on Guam's big ammunition dump and another on a shore battery of #4 guns guarded by intense AA batteries at the northeast corner of Oca Point.[124] As a result the enemy had fewer big guns and less ammunition with which to stop the marines' amphibious assault, scheduled to begin June 15.

The pilots had been briefed that their strikes against the Marianas, and the imminent invasion of Saipan, would bring the Imperial Japanese carrier fleet against them. The possibility of at last confronting the flattops had hung over every mission. For the first two days, the searches came up empty, but late on the twelfth one of the U.S. planes spotted an IJN convoy headed toward Guam. Hal Buell led a search team "to relocate the enemy" in advance of a full strike being assembled. He and his men flew to the extreme edge of the SB2C's range and just did spot the surface fleet before their fuel supply forced their return. Four of the scout planes had to land on the first carrier they came to, *Bataan*. The fourth landed wrong, plunged through the barriers, and destroyed all four Helldivers. The next day, *Hornet* launched a "special strike" of six fighters and two dive-bombers. The strike found the enemy convoy, comprised of four destroyers and two troop transports, and left two of the ships "burning fiercely."[125] Mike, meantime, took a division down to the town square in Agana, the largest town on Guam, to drop leaflets. The Japanese knew the Americans were coming. The Americans wanted the native Chamorro to have a chance to prepare themselves.

While the fleet continued to prepare Saipan and Guam for invasion, Clark's Task Group 58.1 began the morning of June 14 with a course change to 000 degrees. A ship came alongside to deliver fuel and aviation gasoline. Another escort came alongside to get some wolves. It brought them to a nearby escort carrier, and later that day they flew home with seven new Helldivers, some new Hellcats, and some replacement pilots. Word of the next mission, hitting the Bonin Islands to the north, also arrived. The enemy could use the airfields in the Bonins to shuttle planes from Tokyo to the Marianas. The task of denying the Japanese their reinforcements created a terse exchange between Admiral Clark on *Hornet* and Admiral Harrill, in command of Task Group 58.4. Harrill had been ordered to sail his group with Clark's to the Bonin strike. Harrill did not want to go, citing bad weather and lack of fuel.[126] At about twelve thirty p.m., Clark got in the backseat of an SB2C and was catapulted off the runway so he could speak to the reluctant admiral in person. He returned a few hours later. The gist of the two admirals' conversation became common knowledge. Every sailor could fill in the blanks on what Jocko said and the manner in which he said it. Preparation on *Hornet* continued. A little after four p.m., the carrier "jettisoned dud airplanes."[127] In the ready rooms, the pilots studied their charts and reviewed their upcoming mission. While the rest of the fleet continued to pound targets on Saipan and Guam, they would cut off one of Japan's supply routes.

The Bonin Islands held a communications center, a port, and an airfield. At six forty p.m. *Hornet* steamed north, leading Task Group 58.1 toward Chichi Jima and Iwo Jima, five hundred miles from mainland Japan. Task Group 58.4 followed. Jocko had persuaded Harrill to do his duty.

ONE DAY IN MID-JUNE, JOHNNY FOUND A MOMENT DURING THE LONG DAYS OF training at Camp Pendleton to write the longest letter of his war. "Dearest Mother," he began, "I have a long story to tell you hear it goes. First when I came down here I met a girl and have been going with her ever since, She is a very nice kid and she is Italian too. She has the prettiest eyes and hair that you have ever seen. Well mom we are going to be married on Weds 12th of July. I was trying to get enough of a leave to come home but cait get it. So we are going to her place for a few days which is in Orgon. We are being married in a Catholic Church in Oceanside Calif that is about 10 mi from camp. She also is a Marine so you see I'm keeping it in the family. I wish you could be here for the wedding. I just got back from seeing the priest and he was very nice, he asked about you and Pop. She is going to wear a Vail for the wedding. Mom don't think that I'm rushing things to fast, but you see it is the only time that I can get a 7 day leave. Mom I know you will like her when you meet her. One thing mom she really can cook for that's what she does down here. The boys down here have been kidding me as soon as they found out about us getting married. Mom don't forget to wire me, did you get the telegram I sent you about my Baptism paper. I'll send you a picture of the wedding as soon as it gets finish. Mother to know that you and pop aprove of this is going to make me very happy. So I'll be wanting to hear from you in a wire soon. Her name is Sgt. L. Riggi which will soon be Basilone. I wrote to Helen and told her about it too so I hope she isn't hurt. Mom you know that I'm a family man just like you and pop. I want to have children so when the war is over I can relax. Regards to all. Tell the rest of the kids about me will you. Love and Kisses your loving son always Johnny." [128]

AUSTIN "SHIFTY" SHOFNER GRADUATED FROM THE USMC COMMAND AND STAFF School on June 14. During the previous months of training, he also had attended the public functions requested by his superiors. The corps meantime completed its calculation as to his back pay. It had sent him $4,531 in back pay, along with several pages of accounting. Shifty no doubt examined the dates and pay grades carefully. Through it all, he had received very high marks in his Officer Fitness Reports, particularly in the category of "loyalty." The corps had seen fit to promote him to lieutenant colonel. Yet on the final fitness report, his marks in the areas of "attention to duty, cooperation, intelligence and judgment and common sense" had dropped into the average range. Worst of all, his commander had indicated that he did not "particularly desire to have him," nor would he be "glad to have him"; he would be "willing to have him" serve in his unit in combat. It was not a glowing report.

The report did not slow him down, though. On June 15, Lieutenant Colonel Shofner began his journey back to the Pacific. Halftime had ended.

INTERCEPTS OF JAPANESE COMMUNICATIONS DETAILED THE ENEMY'S INTENTIONS and these were passed on to Clark's task group. The enemy had sent a great number of airplanes to the airfield on Iwo Jima to form the basis of a strike on the Fifth Fleet off Saipan. Eliminating Japan's offensive military capability meant destroying those planes as well as the radar and communications installations at Chichi Jima. Word reached *Hornet* on June 14 that the enemy fleet carriers had been sighted. They were steaming toward the Marianas to stop the invasion. The pilots of Bombing Two worried they would miss a big carrier battle shaping up to the south. Admiral Clark apparently agreed, because Task Group 58.1 sped up. It was announced that the fighter sweep would launch a day earlier than scheduled. The weather turned bad on June 15, but the attack proceeded. The deck's catapult threw off the CAP and ASW patrols first. At one thirty p.m., about 135 miles from Iwo Jima, a fighter sweep took off to catch the enemy by surprise. A strike of twenty-two Helldivers, twelve torpedo planes, and seven fighters followed quickly. The heavy seas had the deck pitching and rolling, so each takeoff had to be timed so that the plane arrived at the bow at the same moment that the bow pointed upward. A wind of fourteen to eighteen knots helped.

Mike waited it out with the others in the ready room. The scouts returned, excited to have flown north of Chichi Jima and therefore very close to Japan itself— unlike their earlier strikes at the other enemy redoubts, like Truk, *Hornet* pilots were blazing the trail to Tokyo. The Hellcats' sweep had gone so well, it had created a rare phenomenon, the Ace-in-a-Day. Lieutenant Lloyd Barnard had five confirmed kills in the one action.[129] The dive-bombers returned with tales of a difficult afternoon. The squall lines had intimidated Campbell, who had led his wing on a bizarre flight around and up and down as he flew around the worst parts of the storm. The flight to Chichi Jima had taken two hours. Once there, the AA guns had given them a hot reception. Diving through the cloud cover had thrown off their aim—they claimed a few hits on the seaplane base and on Omura Town, but the eight to ten ships moored in Futami Ko Harbor had been missed. One Helldiver, Dan Galvin's, had been shot down. The sortie returned to find a flight deck that looked like it was pitching thirty degrees in the waves.[130] The skipper reported that "the fatigue occasioned by the flying at the extreme range of the plane through bad weather and over rough seas cannot be overstated."[131]

The next morning the gale still blew as the flattops steamed toward the targets. At about noon, Task Group 58.1 turned east and found some clear sky. Mike got his chance. He would lead Bombing Two's strike on Iwo Jima. While squadrons from the other flattops attacked the villages of Motoyama and Minami, and the other airfields under construction, he sortied for the main airfield, Motoyama Number One. In the squadron's ready room, word came that U.S. submarines had spotted the enemy's carrier fleet steaming through the Philippine Islands on their way to Saipan. The key carrier battle might happen without them. They also heard that the airplanes from the other carrier task group, Admiral Harrill's 58.4, would not participate in this mission because of foul weather.

Hornet and her three accomplices put up seventy-six aircraft: Helldivers, Hellcats, and Avengers. Lieutenant Micheel led his strike in from the north, and as they got close, he gathered speed by descending from sixteen thousand to ten thousand feet. Visibility improved and he could see the small island with the volcano at its tip. Mike's mistrust of the Beast led him to wonder, as he peeled over in his dive and felt gravity pull him, what would happen if his dive brakes failed to open. The AA flak did not get bad until his plane passed through eight thousand feet.[132] The strike leader took his team all the way down to two thousand feet before releasing their bombs. His thousand-pounder scored "a direct hit on a large enemy hangar" just off the southern end of the runway at Motoyama Number One.[133] The wingmen scored confirmed hits on other parts of the airfield. The wolves noticed a lot of aircraft on the ground that had survived the air battle. Mike led his guys on some strafing runs. The 20mm cannon burned through targets like a buzz saw, but aiming it meant pointing the plane at the ground. Flying at two hundred knots below a thousand feet, Mike strafed by making quick little dips and triggering quicker little burps. Back in the ready room, the skipper praised their work. Word was the other task group, 58.4, had started south without them.

June 17 dawned with better flying weather. The early sortie comprised twenty planes flying a huge search sector of 150 degrees to 240 degrees, or "the area generally west of the Marianas," with the mission "to detect the approach of the suspected enemy fleet."[134] Attacks on "the Jimas" had ended and everyone knew why. The Fifth Fleet, still stationed off the Marianas to protect the marine landing on Saipan, needed Task Group 58.1 to return for the battle with the approaching enemy fleet.

Admiral Clark had *Hornet* fuel up all of his escorts in preparation for battle before ordering full speed ahead. U.S. submarines had reported nine Imperial Japanese carriers, six battleships, thirteen cruisers, and twenty-seven destroyers churning toward Saipan, in the Marianas. Airfields in the Philippines held hundreds of more enemy aircraft. A carrier battle as big as all the others put together looked to be on the horizon. Later that day some pilots would have caught a whiff of "hot dope," or inside information. Admiral Clark had discussed the idea of steaming more west than south in order to place his task group and Harrill's 58.4 in a position behind the Imperial Navy.[135] *Yorktown's* captain endorsed the idea; Admiral Harrill rejected it and had continued to steam south toward the other carriers, well ahead of *Hornet*, *Yorktown*, and their comrades.

Apparently Clark decided not to take on the enemy's fleet of nine aircraft carriers on his own, because at ten thirty-two the next morning, Task Group 58.1 rejoined 58.2, 58.3, 58.4, and 58.7 on a line running just west of Saipan. The U.S. flattops carried a total of 950 planes, in the midst of six hundred ships and submarines. An armada such as the world had never seen, the Fifth Fleet eagerly awaited a showdown. The scouts flew search sectors of 350 miles to prevent surprises and to provide the United States the opportunity to launch the first sortie. The scouts returned empty-handed and the radar screens picked up only the occasional bogey. A submarine reported sinking an enemy flattop, so they were out there, somewhere. Admiral Jocko Clark and many of his naval aviators concluded the moment had come to steam west and find them. The Fifth Fleet, though, turned east at dusk, into the wind to catch their last scouts, away from the enemy, and much to the consternation of eager naval aviators.

The adrenaline of expectation started pumping early the next day. A few bogeys rose from airfields on Guam, less than a hundred miles away from the U.S. carriers. Their presence came as a surprise. Obviously they had come from the Philippines the previous day and they were heard to report the U.S. fleet's position. An early flight of navy fighters found lots of enemy planes on Guam and another eight Hellcats were dispatched at nine fifty-three a.m. A report of a "large group of bogeys at 250°, 110 miles" was received at ten fifteen a.m. These had been launched from the enemy carriers. Hal Buell, set to lead a strike of fourteen dive-bombers accompanied by twelve Hellcats and seven Avengers, got the order to "clear flight deck of aircraft and neutralize Guam airfields." With enemy inbound, the admiral wanted the deck ready for fighter operations. The deck crews had been so busy with Hellcats they had not completed arming Buell's planes. Most of them left without a bomb in their bay.

Out on the horizon, the screening ships fired black clouds of AA flak into the air at intervals throughout the day. The fighter strikes came and went hour after hour, with the first rumors of victory beginning to resound in passageways below-decks. *Hornet's* radar picked up the third wave of bogeys just before one p.m., when Buell's planes began returning. A cruiser off the carrier's port quarter cut loose with a barrage of flak. In the debriefing, Buell admitted that most of his planes had simply circled overhead. They had planted four bombs on the airfield of Agana, Guam's largest city.

The waves of enemy fighters had been handled easily by the Hellcats. Hundreds of Zeros, or "Zekes," "Vals," and "Kates" of the Imperial Japanese Navy had gone down in flames. Denying the few enemy survivors access to the airfields on Guam would drive another stake into the heart of the Japanese carrier fleet. Micheel walked out on the flight deck just after two p.m. to lead fourteen Helldivers against Guam.[136] His Ouija Board held the details for the destruction of Orote airfield and his plane had been loaded with one thousand pounds of TNT. Being first to launch meant getting the shortest deck. The twenty-foot drop off the bow forced Mike to pucker until the ungainly Beast gained flying speed.

Twelve Hellcats and seven Avengers accompanied Mike's sortie. They flew through heavy clouds. The target lay a shade less than a hundred miles distant. The ships would steam east behind them, making Point Option, where they would meet back with their flattop, closer. He took them in from the south. The Japanese fired a thunderous chorus of AA guns. He flipped over into his dive and went down, watching the target become clear. On the end of the airfield a large phony airplane had been erected. He aimed for a large battery of AA guns and toggled the release higher than usual, at five thousand feet. Mike pulled out and swung around to watch. As strike leader he had to report. Six explosions ruined the runway and five others detonated near the batteries of big guns.

They returned about two hours later to find their carrier furiously moving aircraft. Mike and half of his striking force landed. They and their planes were hustled below. Another wave of bogeys had just appeared on *Hornet's* radar screen. The cruiser off their carrier's port quarter began firing AA guns. A wave of fighters landed. The ship's deck catapult threw a sortie of Hellcats off; then Buell led fourteen wolves aloft. In the ready room, more reports of a massive victory filtered in. The fighters were shooting down enemy planes by the hundreds, if the initial reports were to be believed. The remainder of Micheel's strike landed with bad news. One of his group was MIA. Another pilot reported that he had lost his rear seat gunner. AA fire had hit his plane and set it afire. He had ordered the gunner to jump out, which the airman, Arne Ulin, promptly did. It looked like Arne's parachute had come down at least two miles from the island and not far from the rescue sub. The pilot had decided he could fly his plane back and had done so.

The big day ended with the Hellcats of Clark's Task Group 58.1 accounting for one-fourth of the 402 "confirmed" kills for the entire task force.* More fighter pilots became Aces-in-a-Day. The United States lost thirty-one aircraft, although some of the pilots had been rescued, and a few dozen sailors on those few ships the enemy had managed to reach. The Helldiver pilots must have felt some disappointment not to have had more of a role. They received good news: the task forces, led by 58.1, were going to churn westward all night long and hunt down the enemy flattops in the Philippine Sea. The fighters had had their turn; now the dive-bombers wanted to finish the job. At long last, the wolves would get a chance to fulfill the mission for which their dive-bombers had been created. They were heartily sick of bombing airfields.

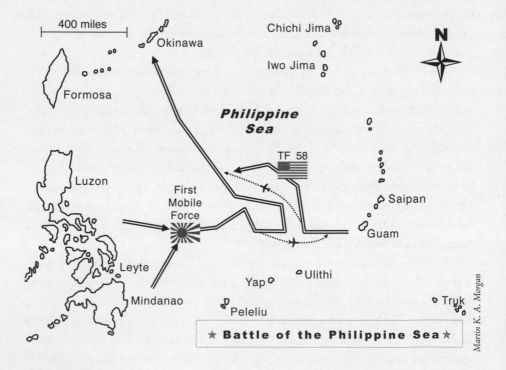

★ **Battle of the Philippine Sea** ★

Martin K. A. Morgan

---

*The victory became known later as the Great Marianas Turkey Shoot, phase one in the Battle of the Philippine Sea. As in all air combat, the number of kills was overstated. In this battle, though, the size of the victory was not.

The phone rang in each of the pilots' staterooms at four thirty a.m. When a pilot answered it, he would hear: "This is the Duty Officer. GQ in twenty minutes."[137] He got dressed and climbed the ladder to Ready Room Four before the alarm sounded general quarters and all hands reported to their battle stations. Twenty minutes later, the catapults threw off eight fighters and four Helldivers—their bomb bays empty to increase their range—for a 325-mile search pattern covering sector 285 degrees to 325 degrees. Hours later Search One returned. No carriers had been sighted. Search Two took off after lunch. The presentation of medals to some of the Hellcat pilots, who had scored the great victory the day before, enlivened the long day's wait. At three forty-nine p.m. *Hornet* "received report of enemy fleet at Lat. 15° 00' N, Long. 135° 25' E, course 270°, speed 20 knots."[138] Moments later, Jocko ordered his air group to take off. A deckload of planes had been prepared: fifteen Hellcats, eight Avengers, and fourteen SB2C Helldivers. Commander Campbell, who had always led the first strike against new targets, led this one with Buell in charge of the second division. Working through their navigation, the wolves realized this mission required them to fly close to their maximum range and return at dusk or beyond. They talked a lot about how to conserve their fuel. Instead of circling the ship after takeoff, Campbell would fly the heading to the target at a minimum speed to allow his men to catch up. The first plane launched at four nineteen p.m.

Micheel and those scheduled on the second strike would have watched the first. This was too important. The wings came down and were locked in position as the SB2C taxied forward. Up on the PriFly, a board with new navigation information was put up. It announced that the enemy carriers were another degree of latitude, or 60 miles, farther away. The round-trip had just increased an additional 120 miles. The pilots of Bombing Two, along with Fighting Two and Torpedo Two and all the other strike groups of all the other carriers, knew strike number one was in big trouble before it took off.

A familiar feeling crept over Lieutenant Vernon Micheel. "Oh, always the same ol' stuff. They'd launch us further than we could really go safely." The airplanes were bigger and faster and there were more of them, but on this mission "we knew it was going to end in the dark when they got back." The deckhands began loading aircraft on *Hornet's* three elevators and sending them up to the flight deck. Down in the squadron's ready room, the pilots of Mike's sortie "were gouging around every place to get colored ammunition. They were just taking it by the fistfuls." Firing colored ammo with their .38 pistols would help the destroyers find them floating at night in the Pacific. Fire a white bullet and "they might not come near you." A blue one or red one would attract a friendly ship. Fear had made them a little crazy, though.

With respect for their experience, Mike suggested that bulging pockets of colored ammunition "might be detrimental." In other words, if they landed in the water at night, they might not have time to get the life raft deployed. In that case, all a man would have was his Mae West life preserver. "You might well have to throw all that stuff out of your suit to stay buoyant." He said all that and it didn't work; he stuffed his pockets full of ammo, too.

Hornet steamed into the wind. The daylight already had that late-afternoon quality to it. Mike climbed onto the port wing of the Beast; the plane captain stood on the starboard wing. Mike put his left toe in the step on the fuselage and swung his leg into the cockpit, then sat down while the captain helped him arrange his chute behind him, get into his harness, and connect his oxygen and radio cords. The veteran ran through his checklist. His dive-bomber was number one for take-off after his fighter escort. The props on the Hellcats began turning over. "I was sitting there just puckering away," wondering "why every time you're going to go on a tough strike, you're going to be short on gas." Once the launch began it would go quickly. The plane captain would have yelled "Clear!" so Micheel could start his engine and prepare to taxi. It would be full dark before he reached the enemy carriers. "We were out of range . . . so I was afraid." In that moment an "Angel of Mercy" intervened and saved him from the mission he was pretty certain he would not survive. As the first Hellcat revved its engines for the flight director, the admiral scrubbed it. The relief came out of Micheel with an "Oh boy. . . ." The deckhands began clearing the deck for the return of Strike 1A. *Hornet* swung around onto course 270 degrees, the last known course of the enemy, and tried to close with her Helldivers, Hellcats, and Avengers.

Mike decided to wait outside for his friends. He knew if they had found the enemy, there would be very little daylight remaining. Whatever they had encountered with the enemy CAP and AA, Bombing Two would have to get down, get out, and join up before full dark. Joining up after dark would be difficult because the little white running lights started to resemble little white stars. Unfortunately, the moon was not lighting the night sky on this evening. Mike knew what it felt like to be that pilot, flying in the darkness. Life came down to fine-tuning the engine and dialing in the right trim, while ignoring the urges to climb higher or go faster and ignoring the fear produced by not being able to distinguish the sea from the sky. The plane's homing device, the YE/ZB, had a good range and its radar would help once a man got close. Inside the ship, cryptic radio messages began to be received. "I'm hit," and "I'm out of gas, going into water."

Jocko Clark, the admiral who had ordered his squadrons to attack even before he had heard from his CO, knew what was happening. His flagship, USS *Hornet*, turned on her white truck lights at seven fifty-nine p.m. The massive illumination made her a perfect target for enemy submarines, but it had to be done. The pilots deserved it. The Landing Signal Officer (LSO) took his place on the aft port quarter, his lighted paddles ready to guide the boys in. Mike heard the approach of aircraft; the first two arrived very close together. "I sat up there on one of those catwalks and watched those guys trying to come in two at a time . . . those guys were racing for a spot in the landing pattern to get aboard." One plane got the cut from the LSO. Plane two lengthened out his final downwind turn to give plane one a chance to clear the deck. Out of the darkness a third plane dashed in ahead of plane two. Mike did not blame him—plane three might not have even seen plane two in the darkness. More planes approached, their pilots expecting their tanks to run dry any second. He could see discipline giving way to "me or you." The landing pattern became a melee. It hurt too much to watch. "I just got out of there." Down in the ready room, he heard that the "screening vessels began firing star shells and turned on searchlights to aid returning planes in locating the task force."[139] That began at a quarter to nine. The radio messages from men going down somewhere out there were heartbreaking. In the next hour, two crash landings and a shift in wind direction caused costly delays, as the deckhands pushed the wreckage over the side and the captain brought the ship about. One aircraft landed in the water near the starboard bow. At ten fifteen the LSO waved in the last plane, "no others being in the air."[140]

In the dark waters around the ships the rescue of downed pilots and airmen continued as Air Group Two counted noses. One Helldiver had been hit making its dive on the target. Two of fifteen Hellcats and one of four Avengers were missing. The SB2Cs presented the biggest problem: nine of the fourteen Helldivers failed to land on a flattop.[141] A total of nine *Hornet* planes had crashed while landing, killing one airman. As usual, the Beast had the worst record: only one of fourteen would be ready to fly the following day. Reports of Air Group Two planes on other carriers began to arrive.

General quarters sounded at five twenty-two a.m. the next morning. Some of the news heard in the squadron's room was good: the wolves had been credited with eight to ten hits on a carrier of the Shokaku class, an Imperial Japanese Fleet carrier. The escort ships and a few other flattops had, however, escaped. No new contact reports had come in. The admiral expected the IJN to sail north, toward Japan. Micheel led nine dive-bombers, accompanied by a number of fighters and torpedo planes, on a mission "to strike enemy fleet if within range."[142] In his logbook, though, he noted a slightly different priority: "search for buddies and Jap fleet."[143] Headed north, he saw "numerous oil slicks . . . and considerable wreckage." When he had consumed half of his gasoline, he turned around and flew back.

He found *Hornet* to be a happy ship.[144] All of the air group had been accounted for. Five planes flew back aboard, having landed on other carriers the previous night. Only one of these returnees was a dive-bomber. In another amazing turn of events, destroyers had recovered the eight pilots and airmen of Bombing Two who had landed in the water. Lieutenant Hal Buell, however, stepped aboard *Hornet* after crash-landing on the deck of *Lexington*. Ashen and wincing in pain, Hal had been wounded by shrapnel. He had also accidentally killed a Bombing Two gunner. It had happened in the crash. Buell had been about to get his cut when he got a wave-off instead. In that split second, Buell thought about his Beast, with a big hole in its wing and no gas in its tank.[145] He cut the throttle. His tail hook missed, and his plane bounced over two of the wire safety gates and landed on top of his friend Dave Stear's Helldiver. His plane killed Dave's gunner and one of the plane pushers. Some of the men aboard *Lexington* had angrily denounced Buell. They thought he had cut in when he should not have.[146]

Hal Buell came home to a warm welcome on his carrier, though. No one wanted to talk too much about the return landings for a near-suicidal mission. Hal had done what he had set out to do. He had put himself ahead of Campbell's division by plotting his own course and by flying at a lower altitude. As the strike groups had arrived over the top of one of three groups of IJN ships, Lieutenant Buell began his high-speed approach as he asked for and received permission to attack—not from his skipper, but from the air group commander.[147] Buell's division had pushed over from 13,500 feet into very heavy enemy AA fire. Red, green, and orange puffs of AA, "as well as white phosphorus streamer shells," were aimed at them. Set against the darkening sky, the pyrotechnics were unlike anything anyone had seen. While the fighters watched and a photographic plane off of *Bataan* snapped pictures, "a cone of fire focused on Lieutenant Buell's section."[148] The enemy carrier had swung hard to starboard and had completed a ninety-degree turn before he released. Buell managed to run his division over its length and ignite its destruction with several well-placed thousand-pound bombs.[149] Campbell had followed with several more. No formal rendezvous had followed. A few enemy planes briefly attacked as the pilots raced for their ship. The flak had chased them for fifteen miles. One of those bursts had blown a large hole in Buell's wing and lodged some sharp bits of metal in his back.

Others told equally scary stories of landing at night in the Pacific. The discussions about the previous night's mission, the most dramatic of their tour of duty thus far, had only just begun. *Hornet* refueled. The scouts failed to find the remainder of the enemy fleet. Still steaming north the next morning, the sailors standing watch "began spotting numerous life rafts, the ship being in the area where pilots were forced to land in the water the night of 20 June. Screening destroyers were sent out to investigate."[150] A lot of carriers had downed pilots. Once the destroyers had checked all the rafts and the searches failed to find more, the carrier fleet gave up the chase. Every carrier task group retired after the battle, steaming back to the fleet anchorage, except for Jocko's group. *Hornet* and her companions set sail for Iwo Jima. The fighter sweep launched just before six a.m. on June 24.

THE MARINES ON PAVUVU HAD HEARD ALL ABOUT THE CARRIER BATTLE IN THE Philippine Sea, with "better than 300 nip planes down," almost as it happened. Some news came every night with the movies; some hot dope came through more official channels. The 2nd and the 4th divisions had landed on Saipan. Unlike the experience at Guadalcanal and Gloucester, though, those divisions had not walked ashore. Word that the army air corps' B-29s had detonated hundreds of tons of bombs on Tokyo arrived on Pavuvu on June 16 and brightened everyone's day.

Eugene and Sid got together most afternoons. They made plans for after the war. More immediately, Sid promised to carry Eugene's seashell collection home to Eugene's mother and to visit the Sledges upon his return if—Sid smiled—his own parents ever let him out of the house again. On the night of Sid's two-year anniversary of being overseas, June 22, the outdoor theater showed *Gung Ho*. The film depicted a USMC Raider Battalion's raid on Makin Island, which had occurred about the same time as the 1st Division landed on Guadalcanal. The marines threw themselves on barbed-wire fences to allow others to climb over them. They ran headlong at Japanese machine guns—bravely getting mowed down until one marine took off his shirt and ran at the bunker half naked with a grenade. The bloodless violence and corresponding level of bravery generally failed to impress the veterans of the 1st Division.

Sid and Gene had a last afternoon together before Private First Class Sidney Phillips reported aboard a troopship. The ship steamed away from Pavuvu's steel pier on June 24. The division, perhaps understanding that a lot of marines would have liked to have sailed home, served each man two fried eggs and a cup of cocoa. Sledge lounged the next day, Sunday, reading a Sunday edition of the Mobile newspaper, studying the map of the Pacific, and enjoying his photographs of home. Sid had promised to go to their favorite Civil War site and take some photos and send them to him. Gene wrote his parents, asking them to let Sid borrow anything in his room, including his good camera. A visit to Eugene's parents meant Sidney would get grilled by them, but Sledge liked the idea of Sid telling his parents everything that he could not put in a letter because of censorship. "Believe everything he tells you," he wrote his parents, "& don't think he is trying to stop you from worrying about me. He'll tell the truth." The loss of Sid, though, meant that Eugene Sledge's only friends in the world were the men of King Company, 3rd Battalion, Fifth Marines, 1st Marine Division.

ON JUNE 29, JOHNNY SPENT THREE DAYS IN THE SICK BAY OF CAMP PENDLETON. He had fever, chills, vomiting, and headaches. He had had malaria on the Canal, so its appearance elicited little interest from the medical staff treating him. The recurrence may have been brought on by the pressure he now found himself under. He was about to get everything he wanted.

Johnny and Lena Mae had been busy planning their wedding. They had visited with the regimental chaplain to see about getting married. The chaplain had agreed to preside over their marriage in the chapel on Camp Pendleton after Lena underwent two weeks of "instruction."[151] Lena was having none of it.

"Have you ever been married?" she asked the chaplain.

"Of course not."

"In that case, what can you tell me? You've never been married. You can't tell me nothing." The challenge was classic Lena. She knew they didn't have two weeks to wait. They had to get married before they got their leaves. She also wanted to get married in a church with a long aisle, not on the base. So John went around one morning to see the chaplain of the Twenty-eighth Marines, Father Paul Bradley. Bradley, about John's age, understood and agreed.[152] Lena booked the nearby St. Mary's Star of the Sea Church, in Oceanside, for the evening of July 11.

Along with the pressure of getting married came another momentous decision. On July 6 his four-year enlistment in the USMC would expire. It's likely no one knew that his enlistment was up because in the wake of the attack on Pearl Harbor everybody had signed up for the duration of the war plus six months. This fact kept service personnel from having conversations about "when are you getting out?" The end of his enlistment brought back a familiar feeling. His family and friends back in Raritan had not even wanted him to request reassignment from D.C. Every marine at Camp Pendleton had found his return to a line unit remarkable. He did not enjoy being remarkable.

John's great gift, however, was to know himself. Being a gunny made him happy.

He also felt a strong duty to the men of Charlie Company, 1st Battalion, Twenty-seventh Marines. He may have always known he would "ship over," or reenlist, but at some point he had to tell Lena, "I've got to go back overseas. I have men in my platoon that have never been there before." Lena understood that "he couldn't send them over there and let something happen to them."[153] On July 3, Gunnery Sergeant John Basilone quietly shipped over for another two years of service. His contract with the USMC stated that he would "further oblige myself to serve until 6 months after the end of the war or national emergency if so required."[154] Four days later, Johnny and Lena went and got their marriage certificate. He bought her the wedding ring. It cost six dollars.[155] The next day, the AP wire service carried a story picked up by various newspapers around the country and especially those in New Jersey: "Guadalcanal Hero to Wed."[156]

In observance of Independence Day, the 1st Division handed out a beer ration to all hands on July 3. Sledge sold his ration, as usual, and watched as the boys had a big night of merrymaking. Some sang, others played poker, and others took in the movie starring Frank Sinatra. When the famous singer appeared on-screen, men in the audience feigned swoons of rapture. Gene enjoyed their jokes more than Sinatra's acting.

The guys in Sledge's tent woke up hungover on Tuesday, July 4. In the afternoon, ice cream was served in the division movie area. On the small, crude stage, six Red Cross women doled out scoops as fast as they could. A huge crowd had gathered. Eugene could not tell if they were there to see the women or get a scoop. No officer had bothered to impose order, so the great mass heaved itself against the stage. The convulsions gave way to a riot. Watching the MPs struggle in vain to stop the fights breaking out came as no surprise, although it disgusted him. Two men were knocked out cold and a third fell victim to heatstroke before Eugene decided not to attempt to get ice cream.

He returned to his tent, weary from the heat. Someone had rolled up the side flaps of the tent, allowing air to circulate as they lay on their bunks. "In normal times," Gene concluded, "I am sure a white man, if he was sane, wouldn't live in this part of the world." The heat made him want to be in France with Edward. A stream of packages loaded with treats improved life inside Sledge's tent. If it wasn't cookies or cake, Sledge had copies of *Reader's Digest* and *Muzzle Blast* magazine (about antique firearms) to loan. The reading material was eaten up with every bit of relish as the food because it staved off boredom.

While lying on his bunk he heard one of his buddies let out an angry whoop. A big rat was under his bunk. In a fit of rage, the friend found a large stick and attacked. The rat ran out of the tent, followed closely by his attacker, who was yelling, "Kill him! Kill him!" Across the company street they went, the rat searching for cover from the blows. They went through five open tents, throwing everything into confusion. Surprised marines demanded to know what the hell was going on, until at last the angry marine dealt the rat a big blow, the "Coup de Grace," Eugene called it, ending the battle much to the enjoyment of the gawkers.

SHIFTY STEPPED OFF THE BOAT ON JULY 7. THE TRIP TO PAVUVU HAD TAKEN Lieutenant Colonel Shofner three weeks. One look must have made him feel right at home—he was back in the boonies for the start of the second half of his war. Protocol required him to report to the regimental headquarters. Colonel Harold D. "Bucky" Harris commanded the Fifth Marines, to which Shofner had been assigned. Colonel Harris had served on Guadalcanal as an assistant chief of staff and had worked his way up through Cape Gloucester to take command of the regiment. Shofner met Bucky Harris's staff as well as the other battalion commanders. When appropriate he would go to the division's HQ and meet General Rupertus and his staff. Almost all of them were veterans of the Canal. Shifty also looked for his cousin who served with the Eleventh Marines, the division's artillery regiment.

While welcoming Colonel Shofner to Pavuvu, a place everyone acknowledged was "more of a hog farm than a rest camp," Bucky Harris and his staff would have described it as the only choice.[157] Although the huge base at Guadalcanal had Quonset huts with lights and plenty of good chow, it had had drawbacks. Rupertus's boss, General Geiger, had feared that his men would have been put to work as stevedores if he had stationed them on the Canal. Geiger wanted his men to rest after the campaign on Cape Gloucester. He also wanted to make sure they were free to begin training. As for a rest camp in Australia, Shofner heard that keeping the 1st Marine Division out of Australia meant keeping it out of the control of General Douglas MacArthur.

The marines were still bitter about having had to serve under MacArthur and support his New Guinea Campaign. The jungles of Cape Gloucester had been a dead end, they told him, where "more men were hurt from falling trees than by enemy action." The division staff had already begun planning for the next campaign. The target promised to be an escape from the rain forest and the plague of malaria. It would not, however, represent an escape from General MacArthur, for the coming operation would support another MacArthur campaign, this time his invasion of the island of Mindanao. This news thrilled Shofner, even if it meant helping MacArthur. If Shifty could not liberate the Davao Penal Colony on Mindanao himself, at least he would help make its liberation possible.

The 1st Division would neutralize the threats to MacArthur's flank coming from the island of Peleliu, in the Palau Island chain, as well as the islands of Yap and Ulithi Atoll. Aircraft based in these locations could strike Mindanao. "General MacArthur," the marines had been informed, "believed that he could not mount an amphibious campaign against the Philippines unless this potential threat to his lines of communication was eliminated."[158] Not every marine agreed with MacArthur. Other ideas about what the next target should be made for conversation around the officers' mess, with or without references to General MacArthur, especially when the chatter was leavened by a sprinkle of gossip from the highest levels. Admiral Halsey had recommended speeding up the war by skipping past the Philippines and striking Formosa or Japan.

Dinners inside the crude officers' mess also would have been enlivened by descriptions of the beautiful women of Australia and New Zealand. When the discussions turned to life on Pavuvu, Shofner caught a hint from the others: "if you think this is bad, you should have seen it when we arrived." It surprised him. They knew he had been a prisoner of Hirohito. Their knowledge obviously lacked detail if they thought conditions on Pavuvu put him off. He began to feel a little out of step with his fellow officers and the feeling did not fade. After a time he realized the root of it. Even though his war experiences had earned him their respect, he was not going to be immediately "admitted to the fold." The men of the 1st Marine Division had gone through a lot together. Guadalcanal came up in most conversations, either as their beginning or their end. The Canal had forged a bond that he did not share.

The Canal veterans, however, were rotating home in record numbers. In a short span of time, the division received some 260 officers and 4,600 enlisted men to replace those sailing stateside. At all levels, the new men were mixed in with the vets. Bucky Harris assigned Colonel Shofner to command the 3rd Battalion, Fifth Marines (3/5). Shifty walked over to his HQ to meet the officers of the 3/5.

His battalion HQ comprised the men of the Headquarters and Services Company (H&S Co.). Sixteen officers, supported by NCOs and enlisted personnel, supported and directed the work of the battalion's three rifle companies: Item, King, and Love.* Most of his officers, including his executive officer, had joined the battalion

---

*The 3rd Battalion of a regiment in the Marine Corps did not have a Company J, reputedly because in the days of handwritten messages, J could be confused with I.

after the Canal and some after Gloucester.[159] The "lean mixture" of combat veterans in the 3/5 alarmed him. At least King Company, led by Captain Andrew A. Haldane, had an experienced leader. Haldane had fought on the Canal as a lieutenant with a different unit and had a good reputation. When asked about his officers, Haldane would have gone through his list of platoon leaders. The K/3/5 had a few experienced officers. His executive officer, First Lieutenant Thomas J. Stanley, had served with King on Cape Gloucester, as had his mortar section leader, Second Lieutenant Charles C. Ellington.[160] A few of his senior NCOs had proven themselves on the Canal.

Junior officers were not likely to complain to a new CO. If asked, Haldane and the others on the battalion staff would have admitted that the morale of the men had "hit an all time low."[161] Every officer knew it. The past few months had been spent clearing rotting coconuts and dragging buckets of crushed coral to make roads and paths. More work remained. The battle against the rats and crabs was being lost. In the meantime, everybody knew that the service troops on the islands nearby (Banika and Guadalcanal) were eating and drinking much better than the combat marines. Fresh meat appeared on the mess tables once a week on Pavuvu and beer was limited to only a few cans a week.

Shifty could not change the conditions on Pavuvu. Speeches about life as a POW in Cabanatuan, he knew, would not help. They had either heard about his story or had read it in *Life* magazine. When at last he stood in front of his battalion, he made sure his marines understood that he "had a score to settle with the Japanese."

ON THE AFTERNOON OF JULY 10, JOHN BASILONE AND HIS TWO GROOMSMEN—THE sergeants in charge of his machine-gun sections (Clint and Rinaldo)—donned their Class A dress green uniforms with the 5th Division's Spearhead patch on the shoulder.[162] John had chosen Clinton Watters, the old D Company man, as his best man. Lena's maids, also all marines, wore their white dress uniforms, except for Mary Lambert, her maid of honor.[163]

Lena arrived late to the church, visibly frustrated, wearing a wedding gown of eggshell taffeta. John's other machine-gun section leader, Ed Johnston, met her. He was going to give her away.[164] Lena walked up the aisle with Ed, thinking, "I always wanted a long aisle. Now I wish it wasn't so long.[165] As she reached the altar John gave her a big smile. Her tears dried. They said their vows looking straight into one another's eyes. "Until death do us part." John got the nod from the father and kissed his bride.[166]

Afterward they held their reception at the Carlsbad Hotel. Lena explained that her ride to the church, a cabbie with whom she had made a deal, had forgotten her. Her frantic attempts to get in touch with her cabbie seemed funny now in the warm glow of their reception. A lot of their friends left after a turn on the dance floor and a drink or two—the Carlsbad charged a lot for a drink. The wedding party stayed for dinner and the couple spent the night. The next morning, Mr. and Mrs. Basilone left early to catch the train for Salem, Oregon.[167] She wanted to introduce him to her brothers.

LIEUTENANT MICHEEL SPENT THE AFTERNOON OF JULY 10 ON A BOMBING MISSION over the island of Rota in the Marianas, as part of the preparation for the marine invasion of nearby Guam. The preparations had begun on July 1 when, following a short rest at the fleet anchorage, Clark's task group had gone back to the Bonin Islands for several days. Intent upon cutting off Guam from the empire just as they had with Saipan, the wolves had spent a few days destroying the repaired airfield and the new airplanes on Iwo Jima. They attacked the ships and the radar station on Chichi Jima. Enemy AA guns had been a big problem, especially over the latter island. The bombing run on Chichi Jima had cost Lieutenant Micheel his wingman. Along with losing men to AA fire, the wolves had also lost a couple of pilots because they had attempted to perform a "victory roll" and had spun into the sea. Commander Campbell had issued an edict: no more victory rolls. The problems had subsided with their return to Guam and Rota a few days earlier. The enemy AA fire here was not too heavy.

On this afternoon with a few cumulus clouds dotting the sky above Rota, Mike led his division against the island's sugar mill. They scored a few hits and began the short eighty-mile trip back to *Hornet*. Ensign William Doherty called him on the radio to report trouble with his SB2C. He could not control his ailerons.[168] Like a good pilot, Ensign Doherty had investigated the situation. With both ailerons locked in the up position he could maintain a level flight path. The rudder allowed him to turn the aircraft without ailerons, although not very effectively. Doherty slowed his plane down to see how it performed at landing speed. As he slowed down to 100 knots, Doherty radioed Lieutenant Micheel that the SB2C became "very sluggish and definitely not safe" because of the drag above each wing. When he put his wheels down, he had to increase his speed to 120 knots to remain aloft. A carrier landing at 120 knots was out of the question, so Mike directed Doherty to make a landing at the airstrip on nearby Saipan. Enough of Saipan had been secured by this time that its airfield, Isley Field, had been designated as an emergency strip. The length of Isley's airstrip allowed a high-speed landing. Even with that, though, Doherty still did not trust the Beast with the wheels down, so he kept them up and slid it in on its belly.

Ensign Doherty's problem resembled a problem Ensign Reynolds had had recently. After a sharp dive over Guam, Reynolds's plane had "snapped violently over on its back, causing him to black out momentarily." He had recovered and righted his SB2C. "By holding his right rudder and using full right aileron he was able to return to the formation. Here he noticed that at low speeds the left aileron flapped up and down, with control being maintained only on the right aileron. He climbed to 9500 ft. where he and his gunner parachuted safely in front of the task group formation, being recovered by destroyers."

Noting the similarity of Reynolds's and Doherty's problems, Campbell told his engineering officer, Lieutenant Micheel, to "go find out what's wrong with these planes." The manufacturer of the Helldiver, Curtiss-Wright, had a representative on board *Hornet*. He climbed into the back of an Avenger on July 11 and Mike flew them both to Saipan. Ensign Doherty would have greeted them with some enthusiasm. Saipan's airfield may have been secure, but the island was not safe. Only three days previously, more than three thousand Japanese soldiers had launched a suicide charge against the army and marine lines.

The aircraft company man knew exactly what to examine. It took him only a few moments before he said, "I found the answer." Inside the wing, the wire controlling the ailerons ran through a bell crank. Both bell cranks on Doherty's plane had snapped. Mike examined them and saw they were made out of a white metal. Reynolds's plane had obviously snapped only one bell crank in his dive, and when he had tried to pull them flush, the one that had not moved had sent his plane into a roll. Mike said, "Well, what's the solution?"

"Get more bell cranks." It seemed simple enough. Mike's borrowed Avenger had room for all three, so they flew back to *Hornet*. After hearing his engineering officer's report, Campbell checked his documents and found Change Order No. 71, dated June 3, had specified "steel bell cranks and aileron push rods."[169] Put another way, more than a month ago, Curtiss-Wright knew the bell cranks were failing. The company's representative had said nothing. Bombing Two had received many new SB2Cs in late June to replace those lost during the Battle of the Philippine Sea. These aircraft had had defective bell cranks. As the import of all this became understood, the aircraft rep would have found himself in hot water. Steep dives caused the bell cranks to fail. A failure on one side had made it look like the pilot was attempting to perform a victory roll as he pulled out of the dive. "It is possible," the skipper reported to the air group commander, "that many previous losses over the target were the result of this failure rather than of enemy antiaircraft fire as previously supposed." The truth was "hard on a bombing squadron's morale."

Campbell recommended that the SB2C "be restricted from dive bombing or high speed attacks of any sort . . ." until the defective parts were replaced. The ship's storerooms contained no spare bell cranks. Mike watched as "the guy from Curtis Wright went down to the engineering department and started manufacturing them out of steel." He fixed about half of them on July 13, which he hoped would last until new parts arrived. *Hornet* spent the thirteenth refueling. On July 14, Lieutenant Micheel was among those who climbed back into a Helldiver to continue their missions against Guam and Rota. Admiral Clark's flagship had not missed a beat. "Dives," Campbell noted, "were made from a comparatively shallow angle. . . ."

THE MASS DEPARTURES AND THE FLOOD OF REPLACEMENTS CREATED A LOT OF change within the 1st Division. Experienced men were promoted, creating the need for reassignments. On July 16, King Company's mortar platoon held a contest. Lieutenant Ellington, who commanded the platoon, tested each man's proficiency with the 60mm mortar. Private First Class Eugene Sledge won. He now served next to Snafu Shelton on #2 gun. Snafu served as gunner and Corporal Burgin ran the squad, which included a number of ammo carriers.

Sledge might have been a college boy who could compute an azimuth faster than the others, but he was also a volunteer. That made it easier for him to get to know the men in his squad. Snafu Shelton enjoyed smoking and drinking, was a whiz at poker from his years serving drinks in a saloon called the 400 Club, and spoke with an accent few could decipher. Snafu did not know the names of the towns in which his parents had been born.[170] Corporal Burgin had been a traveling salesman for a few years after high school. Burgin had volunteered for the Marine Corps on November 13, 1942, because he had to—it was either that or be drafted.[171] He shared with Sledge a strong faith, for all of his bluster. Both Snafu and R.V. had missed Guadalcanal, joining King Company while in Australia. Merriell Shelton had earned his nickname, Snafu, in Australia for his wild behavior.*

Their time in Australia entitled Snafu and Burgin to use Aussie slang, like "cobber" for buddy, but they idolized men like Sergeants Johnnie Marmet and Hank Boyes, both of whom had fought the battle of Guadalcanal. Marmet's stories about

---

*A popular acronym in all branches of the U.S. armed services in World War II, SNAFU stood for "Situation Normal, All Fouled Up."

the Canal fascinated Burgin. King Company, however, had only a few men like Marmet and fewer still of "the Old Breed," or the men who had been in the corps before the war. Eugene Sledge, in turn, looked up to Snafu and "Burgie" because they had served on Cape Gloucester.

Sledge wanted to hear about Gloucester. King Company, led by Captain Haldane, had repulsed half a dozen banzai charges the night after they landed. "Before the banzai charge"—Burgin told the story easily—"the japs—they had one jap out there that could speak English and our platoon sergeant, Harry Raider, was in charge of the machine guns. And, this jap would say, 'Harry, Harry, why you no shoot? Harry, why you no shoot?' In a very calm voice Raider said, 'Give him a short burst of about 250 rounds.'" The burst had let the enemy know the machine gun's position. Before dawn the charge had come. "One of the japs come in . . . to the foxhole where I was at. I stuck my bayonet in his upper stomach and shot him off . . . and just threw him over my shoulder, and I think I got about three rounds off on him before I lost him . . . I think I stuck that bayonet all the way through him. And, later on in—in the morning in the same banzai charge I killed one jap that was within three feet of me, just right in—almost right in my face . . . I don't remember how many japs that we killed that night, but it—it was a bunch of them, it was a lot of japs that . . . committed suicide that night."

Killing the enemy bothered Burgin about as much as "killing a mad dog." He hated the Japanese for the brutality they inflicted on marines. He did not take prisoners. Along with explaining banzai charges, Burgie may have told Sledge and the other new men about fighting in the jungle: the snipers in the trees, the shooting lanes cut through the jungle, the enemy's trick of yelling for a corpsman during a battle. Corporal Romus Valton Burgin also taught his men not to expect him to repeat an order. When Gene's friend Private First Class Jay de L'Eau started having trouble getting out of his bunk in the morning, Burgin walked in, dumped a pail of water on Jay, flipped his bunk over, and walked out without saying a word.

The men of King Company trained together and played together and lived together. Pavuvu offered no alternatives. Gene began to become a part of his #2 gun squad. He missed Sid, of course, and was delighted to receive a letter from him in mid-July. Sid wrote to tell him he had made it to the West Coast. America, he confided, had never looked so beautiful. Sid also repeated his promise to send Gene anything he needed. The letter caused Eugene to imagine Sid's arrival in Mobile. The image made him smile. Sidney Phillips had done his share and deserved his homecoming. Eugene trusted his friend to set the civilians straight on what the war was really like. After careful consideration Sledge decided that it did not matter that Sid came from a low ranking in Mobile society. "He is the best friend I have."

SID'S TROOPSHIP HAD PULLED INTO SAN DIEGO HARBOR ON A SUNNY MORN-ing in mid-July. On the dock, the marine band struck up "Semper Fidelis" and "Stars and Stripes Forever," as the grizzled vets stepped down the gangway. When the band burst into "Dixie," Sid Phillips got choked up. It had been so long since he had heard a live band. It had been so long since he had been home. Some men knelt to kiss the dock. Trucks took the veterans to the USMC Recruit Depot in San Diego. They dropped their gear, such as it was, in a tent camp.

For chow, they walked over to the great mess hall. Sid noticed that he and the other "lean Atabrine-yellow old timers" attracted a fair amount of attention from the endless numbers of clean-cut young marines in the line for the cafeteria. Sid and a cobber grabbed their trays and walked along until they came to the lettuce. "We asked if there was any limit on the lettuce, and when told there was not, we loaded our trays with nothing but lettuce. The lettuce was cut into one fourth heads, and we went again and again for more. A crowd of curious mess men gathered around us and watched us eat lettuce, and eat lettuce and eat lettuce. We hadn't had any lettuce for over two years; Australians didn't eat lettuce."

FOR COLONEL SHOFNER, THE WORK NEVER ENDED ON PAVUVU. ONCE THE briefings started in earnest, he learned the plans for the next operation were still being worked out between the 1st Division's CO, the CO of the provisional corps to which the 1st was attached, and the navy. Each had their own interpretation of the orders that had come from the office of the Commander in Chief, Pacific Ocean Areas, Admiral Nimitz, in May.

The campaign had been originally conceived to include three main islands in the Palau group (Angaur, Peleliu, and Babelthuap), as well as the Japanese bases on Yap and Ulithi. After much discussion, the mission became focused on those islands that held airfields: Angaur, Peleliu, and an islet just off Peleliu called Ngesebus. The other targets were dropped because their enemy garrisons posed no threat. Ulithi remained, however, because it would be easy to take and provide a magnificent fleet anchorage. The 1st Division would seize some of these objectives as part of the X-Ray Provisional Corps, which included some other units, most notably a regi-mental combat team (RCT) from the army's 81st Infantry Division.

The CO of the 1st Marine Division fought with his navy counterparts on the order in which the objectives should be taken. The navy wanted the island of Angaur taken first. General Rupertus insisted that Peleliu and Ngesebus be first. Rupertus not only disagreed with the navy, he also disliked his own assistant division commander, Brigadier General Oliver Smith. Smith, who had been working on the plans longer than Rupertus, was removed from the process.[172] Rupertus also insisted that his division could take Peleliu by itself. He flatly refused to include the army's 81st RCT. Rupertus planned to assault Peleliu with two regiments from his division, with his remaining regiment as reserve. So far as he was concerned, the doggies could take Angaur afterward. These were big fights to be having in July for an operation set to begin on September 15.

While the outcome of the strategic catfight would affect the tactical invasion plans, the marine battalion commanders like Shofner had been told they would invade Peleliu and there were a lot of parts to it they could work on. Bucky Harris, Shofner's CO, had helped glue a mass of photographs of Peleliu onto sheets of plywood to create a huge portrait of the target. Taken by navy pilots in March and later by army bomber crews, the photographs allowed terrain features to be studied. Photos of the beaches had been taken by USS *Seawolf*, a submarine, affording a ground-level view of the immediate objective. Along with the images, the senior officers consulted a map of Peleliu drawn to the scale of 1 to 20,000. Comparisons of this detailed information to the hand-drawn, grossly inaccurate map of Guadalcanal that Vandegrift had carried ashore on August 7, 1942, were surely drawn by Harris.

Peleliu had a lot of beaches suitable for amphibious assault. The planners had long been drawn to the western edge of the island, where the beach ran essentially twenty-two hundred yards in length. Made of hard coral, the beach rose only slightly from the water's edge to the scrub jungle. Although the enemy had cut the ground with lengths of antitank ditches and erected minefields and log barriers, the LVTs and amphibious tanks could roll over flat ground all the way to the airfield. The island's entire road system found its locus at the village on the north side of the airfield. North of the village of Asias, aerial reconnaissance had revealed high ground. The jungle canopy obscured the hills, but any trained artillerist would emplace his guns up there to command the airfield and the beaches.

The 1st Division had confronted IJA positions on the high ground on Cape Gloucester. It had never crossed a barrier reef, however. The reef that encircled Peleliu undulated off the western shoreline about four hundred to six hundred yards. In his studies at the USMC Command and Staff School, Shofner would certainly have learned that a reef just like this one had been a key factor in the debacle of the invasion of Tarawa. It had inhibited the speed of the assault. Speed and power were the keys to success in any amphibious operation. The Japanese could be expected to use Peleliu's reef to their advantage. A lot of specialized amphibious equipment had been developed since Tarawa, however, and the senior staff spent a lot of time planning for its use.

The specialized equipment of most immediate concern to a battalion commander was the LVT, or amtrac. The tracks of these vehicles would carry his men over the reef and onto shore. A few of them, instead of carrying marines, carried a 37mm antitank gun. These new LVTs would drive inland with the men while the troop carriers went back out to the reef to get more men. It all sounded great to Shofner, except that the 1st Division had nowhere close to the number of amtracs it needed. None of the new LVTs had arrived. He did not have enough marines who knew how to drive an LVT and no one could train on the new ones. In desperation, the staff gave some enlisted men the new LVT's operations manuals to read.

Training the men proved difficult on the tiny island of Pavuvu. Shofner informed his officers that the men of the 3/5 "had to be drilled so that they could do their job when exhausted, afraid, wounded, hungry and thirsty, and in shock from the violence of battle." While his officers no doubt agreed, there were some problems. Battalion-sized exercises were out. The island was so small that attempts to hold large-scale field problems had seen men "slipping between the tents and mess halls of their bivouac area."[173] As a former guerrilla leader, Shofner had become accustomed to making do with whatever was available.

Of necessity, training on Pavuvu focused on the individual, the platoon, and the company. An infiltration course forced men to crawl forward under live fire. Instructors demonstrated techniques for hand-to-hand fighting with knives, bayonets, and anything handy. Time on the rifle range included practice throwing grenades as well as an introduction to other weapons that the rifle platoons had begun to receive in quantity: the bazookas and the portable flamethrower.

Colonel Shofner believed physical conditioning to be the essential ingredient for successful combat troops. The challenges he had endured on Corregidor, in Cabanatuan, and across Mindanao had taught him how "to make men give more than they thought they had." He intended to lead men into battle who had the strength to fight. Once again, though, the size of Pavuvu limited his options. Long hikes with full packs and equipment had long been used to harden marines for the rigors of combat. In order to have the men march with full packs, most officers put their columns on the shore road. Since the road only circled part of the island, they marched in a circle, down one side of the road and up the other clockwise, while other units did the same counterclockwise. The marching units kept bumping into one another.

Shofner began to earn a reputation among the other battalion commanders as a hard driver, an officer particularly demanding of his captains and lieutenants.[174] Harris and the other senior officers, however, were impressed by Shifty's efforts with his men and his grasp of his responsibilities in the upcoming campaign. The NCOs of the 3/5 like Hank Boyes and the battalion's enlisted men like Eugene Sledge thought Shofner was terrific.[175]

AFTER WEEKS OF TURNING GUAM INTO A ROCK PILE, BOMBING TWO SUPPORTED the 3rd Marine Division's landing there on July 21. Lieutenant Micheel took off at five fifty a.m. with nine Helldivers, thirteen Hellcats, and six Avengers on his wing. He led them to Point Nan, on the northern tip of the island, before reporting in to the commander of support aircraft, who had them circle at ten thousand feet until he was ready. The first target was the Red Landing Beaches. The dive-bombers swooped down in shallow dives to drop the five-hundred-pound general-purpose bomb in their belly racks. The second target turned out to be a ridge with defensive positions set into it. At his release point about two thousand feet above it, Mike noticed "the ridges . . . were well covered with bomb hits." He released the bombs in the wing racks. No flak burst around him. The strike group began landing aboard at eight thirty-four a.m. He didn't fly again that day or the next. On July 22, the task group set off for the next mission: the island of Yap. During a busy week of strike missions there, Lieutenant Micheel made his one hundredth carrier landing.

All of the Beast's problems remained: its 20mm cannon jammed 30 percent of the time and Bombing Two had stopped using the bomb racks because of their tendency to release the bomb not on the target but on *Hornet's* flight deck during landing. Worse, the Beast killed another of Micheel's comrades that week. "As the plane started to nose up out of its dive," the skipper reported to the air group commander, "the left wing was seen to drop, and the plane rolled onto its back and plummeted vertically to the ground. As there was no AA fire at the time of this attack, it is presumed that the failure of the aileron bell crank was responsible for the crash." The wolves eased the angle of their dives to forty-five degrees. Their bombs started falling short of their targets.

*   *   *

AT DINNER ONE EVENING SHOFNER HAPPENED TO BE SITTING NEAR CHESTY Puller when a messenger arrived. Lieutenant Colonel Sam Puller, Chesty's younger brother, had been killed during the invasion of Guam. Chesty became reflective, and he invited Shofner to have a drink. He wanted to spend some time with an old China marine like himself. Chesty had been the executive officer of the 2nd Battalion, Fourth Marines, when Shofner arrived in Shanghai in June of 1941. Puller spent the night "nursing a bottle of bourbon and telling Shofner stories about Lou and Sam Puller growing up in Tidewater Virginia."

Puller and Shofner's next assignment had come into focus quickly with the arrival of some new information and the return of General Geiger, the commander of the X-Ray Amphibious Force, now called the Third Amphibious Corps. Geiger learned from documents captured on Saipan that the enemy garrison on Peleliu numbered eleven thousand men, a lot more than previously expected. In late July, frogmen had swum close to the beaches looking for mines and other obstacles. The western beaches had not been heavily fortified. General Geiger forced some changes on General Rupertus of the 1st Division.

The idea of a second landing, to catch the enemy in a pincer movement, was abandoned once and for all. Geiger also revised Rupertus's plan to employ two of his regiments and hold the third in reserve. More marines were needed. All three infantry regiments of the division would land abreast of one another. One battalion would remain in reserve. Geiger did not, however, force Rupertus to include the soldiers. Since the other island target, Angaur, would not be invaded until the marines had a firm hold on Peleliu, Geiger designated the 81st RCT as the marines' reserve. He and Rupertus thought that would suffice. As a recent graduate of the USMC's school, though, Shofner would have known that the optimum ratio of attackers to defenders in an amphibious operation is three to one. The 1st Division's three regiments would not quite muster a one-to-one ratio.

Part of the discrepancy in ground troops would be made up by the Fifth Fleet. The navy's carrier-based aircraft had struck Peleliu hard already and would soon return. Days before the invasion, the fleet's great battlewagons would circle the tiny island. Salvos from dozens of five-inch, twelve-inch, and sixteen-inch guns—the latter far larger and more destructive than land-based artillery—would unleash a firestorm of unheard-of proportions. Nothing would survive. The Japanese empire had no navy with which to impede, much less threaten, the U.S. fleet, although the admirals certainly looked forward to the next sortie by the remaining Japanese carriers so as to complete the job left unfinished near Saipan. Men had taken to calling the carrier battle near Saipan "the Great Marianas Turkey Shoot" because scores of

Japanese pilots had been killed. Peleliu, well south of the Marianas, was not expected to become the setting for the final carrier battle. The Japanese, however, had to stand and fight sometime, somewhere.

The Japanese on Peleliu who survived the Fifth Fleet's shellacking would be overwhelmed by speed. At 4.5 mph, the waterborne speed of an amtrac did not seem like much. The staff estimated the trip from the reef to the beach would take fifteen minutes. Enough LVTs had been promised, though, to create a giant conveyor belt. At H hour, amtracs with the 37mm antitank guns would crawl ashore and drive inland to blow up bunkers. One minute later the first wave of marine riflemen would land, with more waves landing every five minutes. In twenty minutes, five battalions of forty-five hundred men would be on their assigned beaches. Immediate fire support would come from the division's tanks, whose flotation devices enabled them to make the trip from the reef to shore, as well as from the 75mm pack howitzers loaded in some of the amtracs. The regimental weapons companies would begin landing five minutes later, their larger 105mm howitzers brought in by "ducks" (floating trucks officially designated DUKWs) fitted with a mechanical hoist. In the meantime, the empty amtracs would drive back out to the reef, pick up more troops, and return. Eighty-five minutes after H hour, three more infantry battalions would be ashore. Eight thousand combat marines would sweep across Peleliu as the first of the division's seventeen thousand support troops landed to provide the supplies and logistics to sustain the drive.

Colonel Shofner, who had fought the enemy with a few rusty World War I Enfield rifles as a guerrilla on Mindanao, must have been amazed by the sophistication of the technologies and organizations that made such offensive might possible. Even better, he could control some of it himself. Shofner would come ashore with his own team from JASCO (Joint Assault Signal Company). It consisted of a naval gunfire officer, an aviation liaison officer, and a shore party officer, as well as their assistants and communications equipment. "Once ashore," the assault plan stated, "the Battalion Commander had only to turn to an officer at his side and heavy guns firing shells up to 16 inch or planes capable of bombing, strafing, or launching rockets were at his disposal."[176] Now that was fire support.

Harris picked Shofner's 3/5 to land at H hour, next to the 1/5. The 2/5 would land behind them. The Fifth would drive across the great flat plain of Peleliu, some of it jungle and some of it the airfield. By reaching the far shore, the Fifth Marines would cut the defenders in half and be in possession of most of the airfield. On Shofner's right, battalions of the Seventh Marines would assault the rocky little southern tip of the island. Once they secured the tip, the Seventh would turn north, cross through the Fifth's area, and help Chesty Puller's First Marines. The First Regiment, because it would come across Peleliu's northern beaches, faced the challenge of seizing the high ground north of the airfield as well as the enemy's main troop concentration. The invasion barrage by the navy's battlewagons would engage the enemy bunkers on the ridge while the marines stormed ashore. Four hours after landing, the 155mm artillery of the Eleventh Marine Regiment would have come ashore behind the Fifth and stood ready to mass fire on any hard points in front of the First or the Fifth.

Shifty's battalion's landing on Orange Beach Two would be led by Item and King companies, with Love Company following. His company commanders received maps of their specific areas with scales of 1 to 5,000 and 1 to 10,000. The rifle companies trained for their specific missions as best they could on a tiny island with too few LVTs and too few tanks. When the assault LVTs arrived, they mounted a snub-nosed 75mm howitzer, not a 37mm antitank gun as shown in the operator manuals distributed to the men who were learning to drive them.

EUGENE SLEDGE NOTED NO SPECIAL INTENSITY OF THE TRAINING LATE IN THE summer. He did notice an additional sergeant had joined K/3/5. Sergeant "Pop" Haney had a reputation for being more than a little loony, or "Asiatic," as the saying went. Burgin called him a "crazy jap killer," because Pop Haney had earned a Silver Star on Cape Gloucester. The word was Haney had served with King Company in World War I. He kept being rotated or transferred, but whenever the shooting was about to start, Pop came back to King. With only twenty-four veterans of the Canal in his 240-man company, Captain Haldane gave Haney permission to attach again.[177] The old and grizzled vet joined the young marines on their marches, mostly keeping to himself.

Eugene kept his mind off the drudgery and boredom of training by watching for birds. The habits and mannerisms of the blue kingfishers and white cockatoos delighted him. As on New Caledonia, the cockatoos seemed to look down from the coconut trees with resentment. "I think the birds are the only ones who want the groves. I know I don't." The red parakeets left red streaks as they flew through the jungle. A marine caught one and he let Gene put it on his shoulder. The bird "climbed on my arms and head and had a big-time scratching in my hair." In the evening, Gene might relax by watching the bats leave their nests high up in the palms to hunt. Sergeant Pop Haney, meanwhile, frequently decided that he had not performed well during the day and assigned himself extra guard duty or conducted a bayonet drill solo.[178] The sight of Pop disciplining himself struck everyone as weird. Pop's vigorous use of a GI brush—with bristles so stiff they'd remove skin—to scrub his body clean was painful to watch. Sledge, who had memorized many of Rudyard Kipling's poems about fighting men with his friend Sid, must have seen the resemblance Pop Haney bore to Kipling's famous character Gunga Din.

The arrival of Pop Haney and more LVTs brought lots of scuttlebutt about the upcoming mission. As Eugene anticipated his first taste of combat, he received a newspaper clipping announcing that Lieutenant Edward Sledge had been awarded the Silver Star. Gene read the citation aloud to the men in his tent and showed the clipping's photo of Ed accepting the award. Gene knew he should be and was proud of his older brother, but the hill he felt he had to climb had become steeper.

SID PHILLIPS HAD GIVEN UP TRYING TO CALL HOME. LONG LINES OF MARINES stood in front of the few phones at the San Diego Recruit Depot. He sent a letter saying he "was back in the U.S.A. and would be home as soon as we are processed." In early August he departed on a troop train that wound its way through New Orleans. Sid stepped off in Meridian, saying good-bye to "Benny," Lieutenant Carl Benson, who had trained the #4 gun squad and had commanded the 81mm mortar platoon. The months of pot walloping to which Benny had condemned him left no hard feelings with Sid.

A bus took Sidney home to Mobile. He called home from the station. His family arrived soon thereafter. All of his hopes for a joyous reunion came true. "My family treated me like I had returned from the grave, and we stayed up and talked until almost to dawn." Sid found it hard to speak at first. Years of service with the Raggedy-Assed Marines, where most every other word was a cussword, forced him to concentrate on his speech to prevent something dreadful from tumbling out of his mouth. At last everyone went off to bed and he lay in his bed, in the room in which he had grown up, unable to close his eyes. He had a whole month of furlough before his war began again.

BOMBING TWO AND ITS TASK GROUP SPENT EARLY AUGUST BACK IN THE BONIN Islands. Lieutenant Micheel and his division made the third strike on a convoy of four troop transports and their escort destroyers in the port of Chichi Jima. The target brought out the reckless streak in them. The wolves increased their dive angles somewhat to score hits. Clouds of AA flak boiled around them as the Helldivers dropped down into the steep-sided bowl that was Chichi Jima's harbor. They scored two hits and two near misses with their five-hundred-pound bombs. The sorties continued until all of the enemy ships had been sunk. All of the squadrons of Admiral Jocko Clark's Task Group 58.1 roamed at will around the Bonins, seeking out any resistance on Iwo Jima, Haha Jima, Ototo Jima—it turned out that the Japanese word for "island" was "jima."

By early August 1944, Task Group 58.1 owned "the Jimas," just five hundred miles from Tokyo. The men of Air Group Two decided to create the "Jocko-Jima Development Corp." They printed certificates of their initial stock offering, one for each *Hornet* pilot, certifying the holder of one share in a company that offered "Choice Locations of All types in Iwo, Chichi, Haha & Muko Jima."[179] The corporation's president, Jocko Clark, signed the certificates and sent stock share number one to his boss, Admiral Mitscher.

Clark took his carrier group back to Saipan where, on August 9, Admiral Mitscher came aboard the *Hornet*. All hands gathered on the flight deck in their dress uniforms. Mitscher presented numerous awards to the men of TG 58.1, including Navy Crosses for Admiral Jocko Clark, Lieutenant Commander Campbell, and Hal Buell. Buell had earned his for firing a bomb into an Imperial Japanese Fleet carrier in the Philippine Sea.

WHILE MR. AND MRS. BASILONE ENJOYED THEIR HONEYMOON IN OREGON, President Roosevelt had visited Camp Pendleton to watch the Twenty-sixth Marines practice a full-scale amphibious assault on the Pacific coast. Days later, the Twenty-sixth had loaded up and shipped out, to become the floating reserve for the Third Marines' invasion of Guam. The regiment's departure, as the Basilones learned upon their return, had not noticeably increased the number of available apartments to rent in the town of Oceanside. "The superintendents and landlords all said the same thing; we're all full up."[180] Lena thought John should be a bit more assertive. "Tell 'em who you are, you'll get one."

"No," he replied, "I ain't gonna use my name to get no apartment."[181] So they continued to live in separate barracks on base. Lena began the process of changing her last name in her official USMC file. John used his last name to bail a few of his marines out of jail for drinking or fighting.[182] The regiment's impending departure had encouraged the marines of Charlie Company to be a little overly energetic.

On August 11, they got word they were leaving the next day on buses for the port of San Diego. Johnny found his wife on duty, cooking for the officers' mess. "We might be shipping out," said John, "so I wanted to be with you."[183] Lena's friend, who had an apartment in Oceanside, said, "Why don't you take my key and use my room tonight?" Lena accepted. John hung around for her shift to end. The phone rang. It was for John. He had to go back immediately.[184] They knew this was it. He was shipping out and it would be months before he saw her again. "I'll be back," he said.

Just after three a.m., the buses carrying two regiments of the 5th Division began rolling out the gate of Camp Pendleton and down the coast highway. As the morning wore on, the word got out. Wives and kids and friends lined the road beyond the gate, waving and cheering as hard as they could as the buses passed.[185] At the docks in San Diego, long lines of marines carried their rifles, packs, and machine guns up the gangways of the troopships. John's ship, USS *Baxter*, departed on August 12, making its way around North Island and into the open sea. With the ship safely under way, a number of dogs appeared on deck—all mascots smuggled aboard.[186] The next day they learned over the ship's public address system that they were bound for the town of Hilo, on the big island of Hawaii.

Baxter's Higgins boats took the 1/27 into shore at Hilo a week later. No beautiful native women in grass skirts danced for them.[187] They were told to wait. Word came that a polio infection had broken out. The 1st Battalion was quarantined just off the beach in a public park. So they set up their pup tents, dug slit trenches, and waited. The stores across the street, some of which had signs in Japanese, were off-limits. The quarantine order had a hard time sticking, though, when the guys ran out of cigarettes and candy. There was too much time to kill. A rumor ran around that when the marines of the 2nd Division had unloaded here after Tarawa, some of them had seen Japanese faces in the crowd. The Japanese supposedly had cheered when they saw how badly mauled the marines had been. So the marines had fired into the crowd.[188]

WEEKS OF STAFF WORK AND SOME BASIC MATHEMATICS PRODUCED A DETAILED plan of assault on Peleliu. The "Shofner Group" consisted of the 3rd Battalion, Fifth Marines, totaling 38 officers and 885 enlisted men. To the 3/5 had been attached a platoon of engineers, a platoon of artillery, some pioneers (who unloaded ships), and his JASCO team (who communicated with ships and aircraft). His group also included the amtrac crews driving them to shore and the DUKW crews supporting their assault, so the total reached 1,300 men and 60 officers.[189] More than 250 of them, however, drove vehicles. Half of these men expected to serve on the front line in combat.

The combat marines of the 3/5 would come ashore in six waves. Thirteen of the amtracs with the 75mm cannon would land first. Eight LVTs carrying about 192 riflemen landed in wave two. Wave three had twelve amtracs carrying 288 fully equipped marines. Five more of the amtracs with the cannons landed on wave four, followed by twelve amtracs of wave five. The DUKWs carrying the artillery arrived as wave six. This left Shofner with two LVTs to carry ammo; one DUKW to carry the main radio; one LVT to carry part of the division staff; and one amtrac for himself and his battalion HQ. These were scheduled to arrive after the fourth wave. Shofner, under the guidance of his regimental team, also worked out the order of another six waves, by which the reserve company of his battalion (Love Company) and the other essential elements of the Fifth Regiment arrived.

Loading all of these waves had not been worked out because the navy had not sent along detailed information about the number and type of ships. The seventeen troop transport ships for the division arrived August 10, so the staff of Transport Group Three came ashore to work with the marines. The Shofner Group would sail to Peleliu in LSTs, which also carried their LVTs. The flotilla of thirty LSTs for the division arrived on August 11. Assigning his assault teams was easy: King Company would go aboard LST 661, Item on 268, and Love and Headquarters on 271 and 276. The marine officers had come up with a creative way to bring more of their necessary cargo—ammo, spools of barbed wire, drums of drinking water—by loading them first, adding a protective layer, and driving the LVTs in on top. The navy captains rejected the idea of "under-stowing," which just added to the challenge of working out all of these details quickly.[190]

Like all battalion commanders, Shofner had to fight to get what he needed aboard ship, had to find solutions to a hundred other problems, and had to keep his men on a training schedule. In late August his boss, Bucky Harris, began to worry about Shofner's agitated state.[191] The stress seemed to be getting the better of Lieutenant Colonel Shofner, and the stress level only increased. The navy informed the 1st Division that, due to limited space, it could only carry thirty of the marines' forty-six tanks. Although each of his assault squads was entitled to a flamethrower, not enough of the improved M2-2 flamethrowers had arrived. Once the marines at last embarked on their ships, someone discovered that the troopships had loaded improperly. The follow-up waves of the Fifth Marines and the Seventh Marines would—unless they changed—have to cross one another on the trip to shore, making it quite likely they would land on the wrong beaches. It had to be rectified. On nine ships, the marines unloaded off of one and loaded onto another. With all of the problems, though, the marines departed Pavuvu on schedule. Their ships lifted anchors on August 26 for the short trip to Guadalcanal.

*　　*　　*

Task Force 58, the aircraft carriers of the Fifth Fleet, returned to anchorage in the Marshall Islands, specifically the atolls of Eniwetok and Majuro, in early August. All hands enjoyed some time off. A USO show, featuring "five real live girls," performed. Fresh food arrived and was served immediately. When the rest period ended and Bombing Two started to prepare for the next mission, they learned that some big changes had occurred. The navy had decided to give Admirals Mitscher and Clark a rest. Their Task Force, 58, would become known as Task Force 38, as Admiral Bill Halsey took over the helm. Jocko Clark's Task Group 58.1 would become 38.1 under Admiral "Slew" McCain and his leadership team. Clark would remain aboard for a time while McCain and his staff learned the ropes. Another big change, instigated by Clark, arrived simultaneously.

As the new version of the Helldiver, the SB2C-3, arrived at the atoll to replace the older and problematic "dash twos" of Micheel's squadron, fewer of them came aboard Hornet. Clark had had it with the Beast. If the Helldiver could only carry one five-hundred-pound bomb on the centerline rack because of technical malfunctions, the dive-bomber pilots might as well fly Hellcats, the navy's fighter aircraft. It could carry the five hundred pounds, although it lacked a bomb bay. In mid-August Bombing Two received fifteen fewer SB2C-3s and fifteen more F6F Hellcats. The latter would become a new group: the fighter-bombers.

The skipper of Bombing Two gave Lieutenant Micheel command of Hornet's new fighter-bomber wing, which was something of an experiment.[192] Lieutenant Commander Campbell might have handed the plum assignment to his executive officer, but for some time now Campbell had acknowledged that Lieutenant Micheel would make a superior squadron leader. Command of Fighter-Bomber Two represented a big step toward that. The former dairy farmer from Iowa had earned the respect of the Annapolis man after all.

On August 26, 1944, Lieutenant Micheel finally escaped the Beast. Mike selected nineteen pilots from Bombing Two to join him as he began operational training in the F6F Hellcat, the navy's fighter. From the airstrip on Eniwetok, they tested the F6F's capabilities as a dive-bomber. Test "hops" acquainted them with their new aircraft. At idle, the aircraft had a distinctive, unbalanced sound because its Pratt & Whitney R2800 engine had eighteen cylinders and ten exhaust outlets.[193] Mike immediately loved it. The Hellcat throbbed with power, raced across the sky with tremendous speed, and turned with agility and grace. It flew smoothly, allowing its pilots to trust it. "It's like a Cadillac and a Ford," Mike said, trying to compare the F6F with the SB2C, "or maybe I ought to say a Cadillac and a Mack truck!"

The task group had a schedule to keep, as usual, so Micheel's training period was abbreviated. They flew formation, made a few gunnery passes; the next day they tried six to eight practice landings on the atoll's airfield. Training ended on the twenty-eighth when the word came from on high, probably from Jocko, "Now get aboard!" On the twenty-ninth, he and his men took off from the flattop to practice runs on a sled towed behind the ship. Mike made his first carrier landing in the F6F Hellcat, the 103rd carrier landing of his lifetime, that day. It was his fighter-bomber group's one and only practice landing.

Armed with four air groups, *Hornet* and her task group steamed for Peleliu. During the trip, Mike was asked to cut his team from twenty to thirteen pilots as the experiment evolved. The task group steamed nearly directly west, no longer circling south to avoid the enemy bases on Truk or Yap. On September 7, the air group commander decided a fighter sweep was unnecessary. At 0531 with the island bearing 331 degrees, at a distance of eighty miles, *Hornet* set up a huge strike of fighters, then fighter-bombers, then torpedo planes and a deckload of SB2Cs. The eight Hellcats of Lieutenant Micheel's strike carried the same load as SB2Cs carried, only they leapt off the flight deck and charged into the sky. Strike groups from two other carrier squadrons rendezvoused with them. The big formation made visual contact at 7:05 a.m. Aircraft from *Wasp* went first while Air Group Two circled east of the island. From his vantage point, Micheel could see that the enemy AA flak had dropped off considerably since the last time he had sortied for Peleliu.

The strictures about radio silence had long since lapsed. Micheel got a call when the other squadron completed its mission and his wing was on deck. He brought his Hellcats around from the north, increasing speed as he nosed down to nine thousand feet before breaking into a seventy-degree dive. He and the two planes on his wing pointed their bombs at an AA battery on the tip of the small island a stone's throw from Peleliu called Ngesebus. As he fell below three thousand feet at 430 knots indicated airspeed, Mike would have noticed the small bridge that connected the two islands as he released the bomb. He pulled out at two thousand feet and felt the F6F roar back skyward. The new antiblackout suits made it a lot easier to withstand the terrific g-force experienced in a pullout. In front of him the SB2Cs of Bombing Two were hitting the main island of Peleliu. Behind him and his wingmen the other fighter-bombers aimed for revetments and bunkers around the airfield on Ngesebus. Micheel's team rendezvoused with the others two miles east of the target and all returned. In the reports on their missions all of the air group pilots admitted they could not discern the amount of damage they had inflicted on their targets. Peleliu and Ngesebus "appeared to be badly damaged by previous attacks."

The afternoon strikes took off to hit Angaur, the most southern of the Palau chain, which also had an airfield. The pilots of Bombing Two reported that their new SB2Cs, the dash threes, performed better than the SB2C-2s. The task group retired to the east that night, the standard procedure to make a night attack difficult for enemy aircraft. The only bogeys, though, turned out to be friendlies. The next day, September 8, while the squadrons made a few more strikes just for good measure, Admiral Clark's task group continued west, bound for the island of Mindanao, in the Philippines. The destroyers and battlewagons, which had been escorting the flattops for months, took the opportunity to surround Peleliu and shell every target on their maps.

THE 1ST MARINE DIVISION AND THE REGIMENTAL COMBAT TEAM (RCT) OF the 81st Infantry Division—together the Third Amphibious Corps—conducted its practice landings on Guadalcanal on August 27 through 29. Carrier air support, naval gunfire (NGF), and all the amphibious craft delivered the punch that General Rupertus intended on the western end of the famous island. The exercises went well. Afterward, the marines were allowed to visit the big military base and its PX, which offered all sorts of delights.[194] Few of them had ever been to Guadalcanal before, but by 1944 the women of the Red Cross had been stationed there for almost a year.[195] Most marine units passed through the Canal on their way somewhere else. Burgin got to the PX and managed to eat a handful of ice-cream bars.

The fun ended on September 4, when the 3/5 boarded their LSTs and steamed northeast toward Peleliu through several days of rain. The LSTs, called Large Slow Targets for a reason, departed first; the other ships would catch them easily en route. Sledge's LST 661 had a Landing Craft Tank lashed on the weather deck, as well as two large pontoons used for making a floating dock after the assault. The 661 would become the LVT repair ship after discharging its cargo, so a large crane and piles of maintenance equipment left little free space. Below the main deck, on either side of the big hold filled with the amtracs, were two long aisles filled with metal bunks where King Company slept. An LST had the flat bottom of an amphibious craft, giving it the seagoing stability of a cork. Luckily the rain and heavy seas cleared on September 7. The men at the point of the Third Amphibious Corps sailed through twenty-one hundred miles of calm ocean ahead of schedule. Every day on the aft deck, Sergeant Pop Haney conducted his one-man bayonet drill.[196]

LIEUTENANT COLONEL SHOFNER LOOKED FORWARD TO COMBAT. HE WOULD LEAD a massive offensive. Its destructive power exceeded what he had endured on Corregidor. Although his troops were not landing on Mindanao, Shifty could take comfort that this assault marked the opening salvo of the invasion of Mindanao, scheduled for mid-October. The POWs at the Davao Penal Colony would soon be free. Shofner's state of mind did not come across as ferociousness to his regimental CO, Bucky Harris, though. Harris could see his 3/5 commander making every effort to succeed, but a high level of irritability seemed to be affecting his leadership.

THE FINAL DAY OF SID PHILLIPS'S ONE-MONTH LEAVE IN MOBILE HAD COME quickly. He had spent a lot of time with his friends, enjoying every moment, every glass of clean water, every moment in a dry bed with clean sheets. Dr. and Mrs. Sledge had loaned him Gene's car. Dr. Sledge used it for bird hunting, so it smelled like wet dog. Sid had driven it down to the courthouse, "took the drivers test, told the policeman a bunch of war stories, and drove away with a driver's license." The good doctor had kindly left it with a full tank, which meant a lot since gasoline was still rationed.

The last day of his leave found him and his friend George strolling through the Merchant's Bank. George stopped to say hello to one of the tellers. Sid recognized her immediately. Her name was Mary Houston. "I nearly collapsed right on the floor." It had been years since he had seen her in Murphy High School and he had just assumed she had married. "She was even prettier than I remembered." Sid walked out of the bank kicking himself for drinking beer with the boys on the Gulf while he could have been trying to make time with Mary Houston. He boarded a bus the next day, bound for his next duty station: the Naval Air Station at Boca Chica, Florida. All the seats were filled. Private First Class Phillips stood in the bus's center aisle for twenty-four hours.

BY TRUCK AND BY TRAIN, SERGEANT BASILONE'S 1/27 DEPARTED HILO FOR THEIR camp. The old salts knew they were approaching their new base when their vehicles exited the lush rain forest and entered a high desert. Of course Camp Tarawa, named by the 2nd Marine Division, had been built in the desert, a dozen miles from the sea. The wind blew reddish volcanic ash against a few buildings, a few Quonset huts, and a great sea of eight-man tents.[197] Leave it to the Marine Corps to find the ugliest part of Hawaii. "No wonder," said one wag, "the 2nd Division was so happy to invade Saipan. . . ."[198] The Twenty-sixth Regiment had arrived first and taken the best part of the camp. The Twenty-seventh Regiment at least got the second choice and left the hindquarter to the Twenty-eighth.

John wrote his family, who must have been astonished to see that he was keeping his promise to write often. "Dearest Mother and Dad and all," he told them, "I'm back in the South West Pacific." After inquiring after everyone's health, he asked, "Have you heard from my wife, I sure wish she can get time off and come to see you all. For she sure [would] love to go to Raritan and see you all. How do you like our wedding picture." He hoped to get to see his brother George, whose 4th Division was also stationed in the Hawaiian Islands. "Mom you should see me now I got all my hair cut off and am getting black as a negro." The gunny, his buddies Clint, Ed, and Rinaldo, and the machine gunners in his section had also shaved their heads bald, on a lark.[199] John wasn't sure what he could write that would get past the censor. "It is a beautiful place its hot in the days and cold in the nights." He sent them all hugs and kisses and "Don't forget," he signed off, to write him soon and to send one "also to my wife."[200]

TASK FORCE 38 HAD ROAMED AT WILL ALONG THE PHILIPPINE COAST. ITS ATTACKS on Mindanao, which began September 9, had met little resistance, much to everyone's surprise.[201] Air Group Two shot up the small ships they found in Davao Harbor and ignited the planes they found parked on the airfields near the city. Although six days had been scheduled, Mindanao took only two. Up the island chain the fleet steamed, hitting Leyte and waiting for the Japanese to respond. Micheel led his fighter-bombers across Leyte to the island of Negros, on the western side of the Philippines. While his group strafed a sampan, Micheel spotted two enemy fighters and went after them. He made several gunnery passes, but they escaped. The squadrons of Air Group Two saw more planes lining the runways than they encountered in the sky. On September 12, one of the fighter pilots went down near the island of Leyte. He arrived back aboard *Hornet* the same day; having made it to shore in his rubber boat, he had been picked up by guerrillas. The guerrillas had contacted the fleet and had him home by lunchtime.

The returned pilot, Ensign Thomas Tillar, brought with him news from the locals that the Japanese airfields of Leyte had been emptied. His report confirmed the experience of the pilots thus far. The war was not here. Admiral Clark sent Tillar's report on to the new carrier commander, Admiral Bill Halsey.* The wolves kept up the chase. Lieutenant Micheel made a run in an SB2C that same day, diving through

---

*That day, September 11, 1944, Admiral Halsey sent a recommendation to Admiral Nimitz that the invasion of Mindanao be canceled. On September 14, with General MacArthur's approval, a new strategic plan was approved, calling for the army to bypass Mindanao and invade Leyte on October 20.

some "meager" AA fire to destroy four planes he spotted on Saravia Airfield on Ne-gros Island. Upon his return, Mike brought his plane around the end of *Hornet*, took the cut, and caught a wire. The wire pulled the tail hook off, sending the SB2C into the crash barrier. The spinning prop tore itself into pieces as deckhands dove for cover. It was the last time Mike flew the Beast.

The occasional enemy plane came within the ship's radar as *Hornet* steamed south. On September 14, Micheel's fighter-bomber group met in the ready room before five thirty a.m. to get their assignment. "With Davao bearing 284°, 112 miles," Strike 1 would launch at six a.m. A solid wall of clouds blocked the sky at thirteen thousand feet. At five thousand feet they could get good visibility. The leader of the fighter sweep, a few minutes ahead of Micheel's group and Buell's SB2Cs, radioed that he had spotted an enemy destroyer in the gulf outside the harbor of Davao. Micheel, behind Buell, watched him break his eleven Helldivers to port. As he ap-proached Davao, he saw Buell's wing coming north, toward them. While Mike's team circled, Buell scored a direct hit on the destroyer. Others followed. The destroyer threw up a fair amount of AA fire, but to no effect. The Beasts blew the aft portion of the ship off, and then it "settled rapidly by the stern, disappearing under the water, bow last, inside of two to three minutes. . . ."[202] Mike and his comrades worked over the airfield, looking for revetments hiding aircraft or storage tanks. He took them out over the gulf, where Buell's team were circling over the oil slick—all that was left of the IJN destroyer—and they turned toward *Hornet*. Later, the skipper would lead in another strike, just to make sure the enemy knew: the port of Davao was now closed. Mindanao had been cut off from the Empire of Japan.

Somewhere out of sight but close by, six escort carriers steamed, providing security to the Shofner Group. Lieutenant Colonel Shofner's marines would have lots of close air support. Another four of the navy's smaller carriers waited for them off Peleliu. These carriers, operating with five battleships, four cruisers, and fourteen destroyers, had begun plastering Peleliu on September 12. On D-day minus 1, or September 14, the LSTs neared the target. The troop trans-ports, which had left the Canal well after them, caught up. Shofner and the other officers opened a sealed letter from the commanding officer of the 1st Marine Divi-sion. In it, General Rupertus informed his troops that the battle for Peleliu would be "extremely tough but short, not more than four days." While this message was delivered to all of the marines, men at Shofner's level would have heard another bit of good news. The big navy guns providing the preinvasion bombardment (NGF) had begun to run out of targets. It was a welcome change from the last report received before departing Pavuvu: aerial photographic reconnaissance had spotted tank tracks up near the airport. The division's tanks had been shifted north, out of Shofner's immediate zone of operations.

ON AND OFF DURING THE TRIP, EUGENE SLEDGE HAD TRIED TO READ HIS NEW book, *River Out of Eden*, about a boy's adventure traveling up the Mississippi River on a flatboat. On D-day minus 1, though, he wrote some V-mails. He wrote Sid, thanking him for the photos of Spanish Fort and continuing to make plans for their trip after the war to visit Civil War battlefields. Gene also described the scene around him on the weather deck: groups of card players crowded every corner. The sergeants of King Company stepped over and around the bodies, bellowing orders that seemed to always begin with "You people!"[203] Gene's description made it by the censor easily, even though it informed Private First Class Phillips that his friend Ugin would soon be in harm's way.

Eugene also wrote his parents a letter, one much shorter than his usual. He never once betrayed any hint of where he was or what the next day held. Most of it consisted of a continuation of his Christmas wish list, since his parents would purchase his gifts early in an attempt to mail them in time. He reminded his mother of their trip to New Orleans, the memory of it a treasure to him. As dusk gave way to darkness, few men moved below to sleep. The cool breeze on deck provided some relief from the heat. Those who could not sleep could pace. The low baritone hum of the engines had been forgotten about until they switched off. The quiet felt sudden and ominous.[204]

ON SEPTEMBER 14, JOHN BASILONE "PULLED RANK." WHEN HE FOUND OUT THAT there was a fair amount of air traffic between his base on Hawaii and his brother's base on Maui, he requested a ride.[205] John flew over to see George, who was training with the 4th Division. They had last seen one another in August 1943. George had participated in the invasion of Kwajalein, in the Marshall Islands, and in the invasion of Saipan, in the Marianas. Unlike John, though, George did not serve in a rifle company.[206] He handled supplies. John sent both his mother and his wife a photo of him and George. Dora Basilone allowed the newspaper to use her copy of the photo in a small news item entitled "Basilones Meet in the Pacific."

*   *   *

After breakfast, more than a few K/3/5 men climbed a ladder topside. They watched the sun rise behind Peleliu, framing the dark little island, and shining into their eyes. With each passing moment the volume of the bombardment grew. The great thundering cannons of the battleships punctuated the faster, point-blank shooting of the destroyers and the angry buzz of the navy planes on their bombing runs. The staccato blended into a vast storm. Each marine told himself that this violence was a good thing. No enemy could survive such fury. The island disappeared inside a dark pall of smoke and debris, lit by fires churning underneath. Apprehension grew inside them. It was all so big, so far beyond the power of the individual. "Everybody below-deck."[207] Noticing that some of the new men in his squad seemed nervous, Burgin told them, "Just keep your calm and everything will turn out all right. Just do your job."

Down the ladder and into the metal cavern of the LST, the men of King Company found their thirteen amtracs.[208] The engines' exhaust fouled the air. The three nearest the bow door had a cannon mounted on them. The next four LVTs were newer models with rear ramps; these also carried King's 37mm antitank guns. The marines in the six remaining amtracs had to climb up the sides to get in. Sledge's #2 gun squad was assigned LVT 13. It would be in the second wave of amtracs carrying troops. A light opened at the far end of the chamber. The engines gunned, and one by one they drove out toward daylight.

After their craft splashed into the ocean, the heads of the mortarmen were about the height of sea level. Everything loomed above them. Swabbies in T-shirts took in the scene with keen interest, a cup of coffee in one hand.[209] A few waved cheerfully at the helmeted figures below. The other three LSTs of the 3rd Battalion lay at anchor nearby, disgorging assault craft as well. The amtracs churned slowly toward their positions. Inside the assault craft, the noise of bombardment began to separate the men. Only by yelling in a man's ear could Sledge communicate. Snafu offered Sledge a cigarette. Sledge said he did not smoke. To which Snafu replied, "You will."[210] Burgin laughed.

Shofner climbed into his amtrac to ride in with wave three, or the second troop wave. Once in the water, he could not see much, but all seemed to be well. The NGF had begun firing precisely at five thirty a.m. and continued to fire shells over his head. The calm sea stirred with each titanic broadside of the battleships, as the recoil rocked the ship and created a wave. At 0800, the circle of assault LVTs broke, fanned out into a line, and started toward the beach.[211] The small circle of wave two followed and then his own trip began.

THE FIRST QUESTIONS THAT CAME TO SLEDGE'S MIND WERE "WOULD I DO MY duty or be a coward? Could I kill?"[212] The salvos of the big guns and their attendant concussions isolated each man. It was so loud, so intense, Sledge could hardly think. "Would I ever see my family again?" The great forces unleashed the first flush of panic at the thought of being tiny and vulnerable amid the unforgiving steel. Sledge's amtrac came to the coral reef and began to crawl over it.[213] The engine stalled. A few moments passed. Explosions sent geysers of water in the air nearby—the enemy was shooting back. The powerful fear it awakened within him surprised him: "you wonder why someone wouldn't have thought of it sooner . . . for the first time I thought, My God, that metal will absolutely tear through somebody's flesh." He went weak from fear and braced himself against the side of the tractor. Terror, frantic and certain, gripped him so hard, he thought, "I might wet my pants."[214] The engine came to life. Up and over the reef they went. Peeking over the rim, the mortarmen could see amtracs had been hit and were burning. Eugene "saw several amtracs get hit and it was just awful because Marines just got blown into the air and some of the amtracs burst into flame . . . I found solace in just cussing the Japs."[215] Individual marines were bobbing in the water, struggling to get to shore. Fires burned onshore, roiling beneath a tall cliff of black smoke. The sight of it made the eyes of the combat veterans, like Burgin, grow wide. This was a new level of danger. Burgin said to himself, "God, take care of me, I'm yours." A stream of bullets smacked into the front of the craft. Someone yelled, "Keep your heads down or they'll get blown off."

THE TWO WAVES OF AMTRACS AHEAD OF SHOFNER HAD BEGUN TO BUNCH UP. Inside the reef, large "coral boulders" combined with some man-made obstacles narrowed the open tidal area into a few avenues of approach. Most of the amtracs crowded into the free lanes as others bellied up on the coral boulders and became stuck.[216] Nearing shore, they came under fire from a 47mm antiboat gun firing from a tiny islet jutting out from shore to their right.[217] The ships' batteries could not hit it because it was located behind the islet, and the carrier planes above could not see it. Its fire devastated the fleet of amtracs using beaches Orange Two and Orange Three.

THE AMTRAC CRAWLED OUT OF THE WATER AND STOPPED. SLEDGE HEARD, "HIT the beach!"[218] The mortar squad clambered over the side of their LVT. He followed Snafu, but lost his footing and landed on the beach in a heap. Every shell, every white stream of machine-gun bullets seemed to be aimed directly at them. Although the beach was white and smooth, it consisted not of sand but of hard coral. The burdens of his rifle, apron of 60mm mortar shells, and personal equipment became ungainly in the storm and Gene struggled to catch up with the squad. Strands of barbed wire, attached to metal stakes, crisscrossed the area, preventing men from crawling.

Across the strip of white coral he came to a shelf of vegetation, most of which was burning or had been burnt. Sledge nearly stepped on a land mine. He noted the inches separating his foot from the triggering plate. He looked up and saw a marine step on one "and he just atomized, just disappeared." Inside the copse of coconut trees, broken and angular, the men of King Company ran into the tank trap.[219] The depth kept them out of the line of fire. One of King's sergeants, Hank Boyes, noticed "everyone was very content to stay there in what seemed a safe spot."[220] Bullets passed over their heads. Gene said, "Burgin, give me a cigarette."

"Gene, you don't smoke."

"Give me a cigarette." Burgin handed him one. Gene "took it and I looked at him, and he had it between his lips. I looked back a few seconds later and he was chewing it, that's how nervous he was." Burgin saw Sledge's eyes "bugged out" and told him not to pay too much attention to the bullets snapping overhead. "Like hell," Gene said, "those are real bullets."[221]

THE CO OF 3RD BATTALION LANDED AND FOUND A LOT OF MARINES WAITING FOR other marines to move forward. Shofner stood up and yelled, "Come on, there's not a Jap alive on the island!"[222] He ran forward to a shell hole twenty-five yards in from the shore. He had his carbine, map case, and a radioman.[223] He tried to get a handle on the situation. Item Company had moved inland. His other company, King, was confused. His junior officers were struggling to get their men organized. The noise made verbal communication all but impossible. All of their training in small-unit tactics relied on the integrity of the squads and platoons. Time passed. Part of one platoon came in from the left, where Item had landed.[224] After fifteen minutes, they identified the holdup. The antiboat gun off to their right had driven amtracs of the Seventh Marines onto Shofner's section of beach. Worse, the unit of the Seventh that had landed with them was King Company, 3rd Battalion. Two King Companies were struggling to get their men sorted out. The amtrac containing Shofner's communications equipment was hit. Some of the men swam ashore, but without the bulky machinery. Just as Shofner's platoons prepared to move out, the enemy mortars began exploding all around them. A shell killed Shofner's executive officer. Movement in King's area of the beach stopped. The last of Item, to the left, moved out.

The barrage lasted thirty minutes. The drive inland began when it lifted. Shofner pushed forward to an antitank trench and established the 3/5's command post, although, without a powerful radio, his knowledge of and control over events became limited. The radio carried by his assistant might reach his company commanders, the colonel leading the 1/5, or even the regiment, or it might not. He needed runners. He wrote a message and gave it to a runner to give to division CP: "3/5 progressing in tight contact with" the Seventh Marines. "Urgently require communication personnel," and "Request latest in progress" of First Marines.[225] Some updates reached him. Item Company had attained its objective and was tied in with the 1/5, to his left. The 1/5 had halted because the unit on its left, the First Marines, had been halted by fierce resistance. To Shofner's right, King Company had begun to push forward.

THE NEXT PUSH OF KING TOOK IT OUT OF THE DITCH AND THROUGH THE SCRUB. To one of the riflemen, it did not look like anybody "knew where they were going. It was just: jump in a hole, stay there, and look at everybody else. If they moved, you moved."[226] The dense thickets kept visibility low. The cannonading continued around them. The mortarmen carried their rifles at the ready, waiting to meet the enemy, trying to keep together in the tangle of dense brush. They came upon the skirmish line of the riflemen, who had stopped at the edge of the vast clearing that held the airfield.[227] A number of pillboxes barred the way. Sergeant Hank Boyes was yelling for his men to shift their line of advance to the right. King was not tied in with the 3/7 on its right and the gap was dangerous.[228]

SHOFNER "WAS TORN BETWEEN HIS REQUIREMENTS TO MAINTAIN CONTACT WITH his higher headquarters, the Fifth Marines, and his need to keep his rifle companies in a coordinated effort against a possible Japanese counterattack." Love Company landed and he sent it to cover a gap emerging between Item on the left and King on the right. His battalion was at last pushing inland. Shofner may have heard that half of the tanks had been hit before they reached the shore. The 2/5, the last of the regiment's three battalions to land, began arriving just before ten a.m. It began to march into the gap between the 1/5 on the far left and Shofner's 3/5 on the right.

AT THE EDGE OF A GREAT OPEN PLAIN, CORPORAL BURGIN AND HIS #2 MORTAR squad had caught up to some riflemen. Burgin saw an enemy artillery piece near the airstrip. As he watched, the Japanese crew rotated positions every time the gun fired. It seemed odd that each man had to take a turn hefting ammunition; there was no set gunner. Each of the crew exceeded six feet in height, though, so they made good targets. Burgin got his men to start "picking them off one at a time." The attack began to gather steam and the push developed around to his right, where the field gave way to jungle. A marine tank appeared. It mistook King Company for the enemy and began to come at them. The #2 gun squad began to yell their unit name, but it seemed hopeless. The Sherman tank had no infantry around it to hear them.

Staring down the barrel of the Sherman's 75mm shocked everybody. One marine near it ran over to stop it. He was hit by something and fell. Sergeant Hank Boyes got around to the back of the tank, where the phone was. He jumped up on the back of the tank, which put him in an exposed position. The phone must have been broken. Most of King Company watched in amazement as he rode it like a cowboy. The enemy concentrated its fire on the most direct threat: Boyes's tank. Boyes directed the Sherman's fire at the artillery piece and three other pillboxes, the tank's 75mm shells penetrating inside and exploding each in turn.[229] The assault continued to the right, away from the airfield and into the jungle.

With the 2/5 taking over on his left flank, Shofner had pulled Item Company off the left flank, brought it around the back of Love Company, and sent it forward to connect Love to King. He heard about King encountering some bunkers and called in an air strike.[230] King had resumed the advance when Shofner received a radio message from the Seventh Marines on his right flank. The 3/7's CO said his "left flank unit was on a north-south trail about 200 yards ahead of 3/5's right flank element."[231] The two officers agreed that the 3/7 would hold its position until King reached them. Shofner sent an order for Item and King to press forward.

A hundred yards brought King's rifle squads to a large trail running perpendicular to their eastward advance. They halted there for a time. Captain Haldane needed to get connected to the units on either side of him. Item Company came up on his left. Both companies advanced across the trail and eastward again through the brush.[232] King Company's first platoon halted before noon, when they could see water ahead of them. They had nearly crossed the island. The other parts of the company caught up as an hour passed. No one had contact with the battalion CP.[233] The water levels in the two canteens of water each man carried began to get low. The heat and the physical exertion made each man in #2 mortar "wringing wet with sweat."[234] They prepared to defend themselves from a counterattack.

ABOUT THREE P.M., SHOFNER DID NOT KNOW EXACTLY WHERE HIS KING Company was, but he heard where it wasn't. The 3/7's CO radioed Shofner that "the position of 3/7's left-wing unit had been given incorrectly."[235] It had not advanced as far as he had told Shofner earlier. His unit was not in contact with Shofner's King. That meant that the 3/5's assault teams were well out in front of the entire division's front line, exposed on both flanks to enemy attack. When he understood the situation, Shofner ordered Company K to bend its right flank back in an effort to tie in with the 3/7. He had also become worried about Item, in the center of his line. Love Company, on his left, was fine: in touch with its flank, the Fifth Marines, and making steady progress across the airfield.

BURGIN HAD SLEDGE AND SNAFU SET UP THE GUN ON THE FAR SIDE OF THE VAST open plain that held the airstrip. They found a crater for their gun position. "Snafu put the gun down, flipped the buckle on the strap, opened the bipod out, stretched the legs out, tightened them up, snapped the sight on." A simple device, the sight had two bubbles that were leveled for elevation and windage. Snafu "took a quick compass reading on an area that they told us to fire on and we put a stake out there at the edge of this crater."[236] The order came to fire. Snafu looked at the range card that stated the number of increments. Sledge "repeated the range and pulled off the right number of increments to leave on the correct number, pulled the safety wire and held the shell up" with his left hand. The thumb on the left hand held down the shell's firing pin. When he let it go, it slid down the tube, hit the bottom, and discharged with a soft hollow whisper. The order came to cease fire or secure. The mortar team waited. The heat was crushing. The old salts predicted the enemy "would pull a banzai tonight and try to push us off the island. We'll tear 'em up."[237]

Sledge looked north, across the great distance of the airfield. He saw some vehicles moving amid the explosions. "What are all those amtracs doing out there next to the jap lines?"

"Hey, you idiot," Snafu replied, "those are jap tanks." Sledge felt his heart nearly stop at the thought of enemy tanks.[238]

*　　*　　*

As late as five p.m., Shofner was still struggling with a faulty communications network to get his men tied in properly. The communications officer of the Fifth Regiment arrived. The two had begun to sort out a solution when a mortar shell exploded near them. Shofner's "mouth was dry and his breath was short, he had no feeling in his left arm and he looked down and could see the bones of his forearm, the skin and muscle torn away by shrapnel. He looked up and tried to speak but there was no one to speak to. Then, as if in slow motion, he saw Marines from the adjacent units spill over into the shell crater. He heard the cry for corpsman, and he heard some Marine yell that 'the damned japs had got Shifty.' Then things went black."

He awoke on a stretcher, being carried across the beach and onto a Higgins boat. His arm had been bandaged and he was receiving plasma. Shofner "tried to protest, but his head was in a cloud, and he suspected he [had] received a shot of morphine." A marine said, "Don't worry, Mac. You'll be OK." Unconsciousness slipped over Shifty again. When his eyes opened again, he saw he was lying in the cavernous amtrac deck of an LST. His head ached badly. He "felt the sheets under him. He was naked except for his bed linen. His left arm throbbed." The navy's medical teams moved quickly to handle a lot of wounded men. A corpsman noticed he had awakened and called over to his supervisor, "Well, Colonel Shofner, you are a lucky man"; he would make a full recovery. Austin wanted to know what had happened and was told he "was the sole survivor of his command group." Colonel Shofner asked about returning to his unit. The corpsman "became evasive and suggested that he rest for a while."

The enemy tanks never got very far south. The great white airfield and the plain that encompassed it were mostly empty. Although the sound of the big guns filled the air, Sledge and his mortar team were threatened mostly by small-arms fire. With his rifle platoons already committed, King Company's skipper, Captain Haldane, ordered his headquarters personnel to help tie his line in with the Seventh Marines, but to no avail. The skipper ordered his company into a perimeter defense. The hard white coral could not be dug out by hand. Marines picked up what chunks of coral they could to provide some small cover for their bodies. Darkness found King Company still in an exposed position, still not tied in with either the left or the right, but ready to hold their ground.[239] The big fear was a banzai attack. King had strung its barbed wire, the mortars and machine guns had registered sound rounds, and Captain Haldane had a telephone line back to the artillery. As far as Eugene Sledge could tell, though, "we were alone and confused in the middle of a rumbling chaos with snipers everywhere and with no contact with any other units. I thought all of us would be lost."[240]

The small-arms fire slackened as it grew dark. After a couple hours, the word came to pack up, King was pulling back. Battalion wanted it tied in with Item on the left and the unit of the Seventh on the right before the banzai attack began. Stumbling in the dark through the wild thickets and scrub jungle along the edge of the field made for a lot of cursing, but they moved close enough to the right spot to be allowed to dig in.[241]

Although not properly tied in with Item, Love Company, or the Seventh Marines, King Company marines began to string barbed wire along the edge of the airfield to hold off the banzai attack.[242] The sound of howitzers and the naval gunfire and heavy mortars and machine guns continued all night long. Much of it emanated from the north end of the airfield and from the ships offshore, although enemy mortars rained on the beach. The navy ships also fired huge flares, which swung slowly in the sky as they fell, skittering shadows across a broken and burning landscape.[243] The marines of the #2 gun squad piled rocks around themselves and slid into shell holes to get below the line of fire. In the darkness, Sledge took off his boots because his feet were sloshing in his sweat. Snafu yelled, "What the hell you doing, you better get those damn boots back on . . . By God, you don't never know when you're going to have to take off [running]."[244] Lying nearby, Burgin laughed as Snafu cursed the new guy for being "a stupid son of a bitch." Corporal Burgin expected the enemy charge to come, just like on Gloucester. He worried about the dwindling levels of water in his squad's canteens and began chewing on a salt tablet.

In the early hours of September 16, Burgin was proved right: a charge did come. A ferocious concentration of machine-gun fire on his left, the guns of the 2/5, knocked down the dark shapes of running men.[245] The #2 gun shot up a lot of illumination rounds, each lasting about thirty seconds. With a few flares hanging up there, it was light enough to see that no hordes of Japanese were running at King. The cacophony of hard fighting continued on both sides of them.

When dawn broke, those still trying to sleep had to abandon it. The canteens of Burgin's mortar crew were empty. The support teams brought up water in five-gallon cans and fifty-gallon drums and everyone was mad to get it. The first sip brought a nasty shock to the #2 gun. It tasted like diesel. Some of the guys around them drank it anyway. Burgin joked that he could blow on a match and be a flamethrower. Stomach cramps followed and a few puked. As usual, though, a trooper's fate hung in the luck of the draw. Other squads in King Company received two canteens of clean water.[246]

The task facing them was to cross the airfield. It looked like a long way. Burgin guessed it was over three hundred yards. At the signal, the skirmish lines of marines ran out into the open field and across the hard white coral runway. The Japanese unleashed a barrage upon them as expected. Large shells, mortars, and machine-gun bullets cut the air around them as the marines ran east for all they were worth. Much of the enemy's fire came from its positions on the northern end of the airfield, to King's left. Most of their regiment and all of the First Marines, therefore, stood between King and the guns. Love Company ran on their immediate left. Every step felt like their last. As he ran, Gene "was reciting the 23 Psalm and Snafu was right next to me and I couldn't hear what he was saying, but most of it was cussing."[247] Burgin watched the white tracers flash past him until he found cover on the far side. "I don't know how we didn't all get killed—I really don't."[248] No one else did either.

The thick scrub they entered slowed their progress toward the ocean, but resistance was light. They came to a wild thicket of mangrove swamp that marked the shoreline. King tied in with the Seventh Marines on their right. The Seventh had its hands full with securing the southern tip of the island. To their left, farther north along the eastern shore, Love Company tied in with them. Item Company, the other component of the 3/5, marched still farther north. King Company dug in as ordered, out of sight and away from the battle.[249]

With time to catch his breath and reflect, Sledge realized the last thirty-six hours had been "the defining moment in my life."[250] Much of what he thought he knew—from the Civil War books he had read to the "Barrack-Room Ballads" he had memorized—had had nothing to do with the carnage, the chaos, the electric fear threatening to engulf him. Gene had watched a wounded marine die and was aghast at the waste and inhumanity. He had watched two marines pluck souvenirs from two dead Japanese and wondered whether the war would "dehumanize me." He needed to process these experiences. He felt a duty to document his battle for his family, so they would know what the future books about Peleliu left out. Eugene B. Sledge decided to write himself notes in his pocket Bible so that he would not forget the horrors he witnessed.[251] "The attack across Peleliu's airfield," E. B. Sledge later wrote from those notes, "was the worst combat experience I had during the entire war."[252]

He had seen marines fall during his run across the airfield, even though he had tried to look straight ahead as he ran. The number of wounded went uncounted because the invasion day's tally and the fierce battle the First Marines were having up north had overwhelmed the system.* One marine had been killed for sure, though.

---

*The Fifth Regiment landed with 3,227 men and officers. It sustained about 250 casualties during D-day and D + 1, the highest two-day total of the regiment during the campaign.

Private First Class Robert Oswalt, Gene's friend, had been hit in the head by a bullet or a fragment from a shell.

The big guns found King's position before dark. Burgin lay on his stomach, hugging the earth and listening to the quick swishing noises and feeling the concussions. He thought those shells were so big he could see them. Chunks of coral, mud, and mangrove splattered down upon the men of #2 gun. The size of the explosions left them sick with fear. A line of communication wire had been tied to a phone in Burgin's foxhole. It connected him to the other platoons, Haldane's company CP, and from there further back to battalion. Burgin got on the phone, heard someone answer (he wasn't sure who), and reported that his position was taking friendly fire. He heard the man reply, "No, that's not ours—that's jap."

"No, that's ours," Burgin replied, and began cursing. "I know where we just came from, and that artillery is coming where we've already been, so I know it's ours. So get it ceased." The other marine remained unconvinced. Burgin could tell the shells were 155s and yelled, "If you're going to fire . . . go out a little further than that because you're going to kill my whole damn bunch."[253] The barrage increased and worsened. Shells burst about twenty or thirty feet above the ground, sending searing shards of metal down upon them. King had almost no cover. They could only hold on and wait till it ended.

As the shelling, both U.S. and Japanese, slackened, the marines tried to get water. Some found a grayish liquid in the bottom of some of the deeper shell holes— the water table was very high on Peleliu. The men who drank it became sick, even the ones who strained out the big particles by keeping their teeth closed. In the mortar squads, Stepnowski, a big guy from Georgia they called Ski, dropped out. The heat and the dehydration were too much. He was turned over to the medics, who took him back. Lack of water caused one-third of the casualties.[254] Sledge noted that the big men tended to give in to heat exhaustion more often than those of slighter build. The day ended with stringing barbed wire in preparation for a banzai attack.

When the night passed without an attack, King Company had so far gotten off easier than others and some of them knew it—not E. B. Sledge, however. The dead and wounded men he had seen and the punishing concussions of high explosives left him terrified. He hung on gamely, lugging mortar shells and preparing to fire the #2 gun. During the next day, they watched as the ridge to the north took a horrendous pounding from the ships' guns, from navy planes, and from the howitzers of the Eleventh Marines. King marched toward the ridge that morning, behind the rest of the 3/5. Along the east side of the airfield, they saw millions of jagged shards of metal—

shrapnel—covering it.[255] The wreckage of airplanes included more than two dozen medium bombers and dozens of fighters.[256] King arrived at the junction of the cross runway. Item Company dug in there, inexplicably, while Love and King closed with the village that draped around the north end of the airfield. The volume of small-arms fire picked up precipitously. They were not on the front line yet, though. The 2/5 was ahead of them and, beyond them, units of the First Marines.[257]

King soon moved along the eastern edge of a mad jumble of craters, airstrip, and demolished buildings. Most buildings were farther west, on their left. Love Company was over there, tied in with units of the First Marines, in the thick of the fighting by the sounds of it. Item Company remained behind them. By the end of the day, #2 gun had advanced through the small collection of buildings to a point where they could see the northern ridges. King tied in with elements of the 2/5.[258] To their left, west, were the ridges; to the north and to the east, roads led into terra incognita. They watched the other units attempt to move north. "Anytime anybody got up, the Japanese started throwing not just machine-gun or rifle fire, but shell fire."[259] Watching it happen, Gene could not see the enemy positions, only a riot of confusion, fear, and pain. The Japanese fired so many weapons, the coral ridges were so impregnable, he thought, "we had absolutely hit a stone wall." The soft malice of the incoming mortar rounds sounded to him like "some goulish witch telling you that 'Well, I may not get you this time, but I'll get you next time.'" The sound of combat never ceased that night, although the enemy again failed to mount a banzai charge. Burgin began to think "there was something up. They were fighting with different tactics altogether."

The next day, the third day of the "three-day campaign," as someone surely noted, King moved east. The roads and buildings gave way to swamp. A small road crossed the marsh on a natural causeway of earth about a hundred yards in length. It widened into a clearing where the riflemen met some resistance. The #2 gun, along with marines from Item Company, ran across the narrow causeway and supported the assault on a small group of buildings in the larger clearing on the far side.[260] The Japanese had abandoned most of their bivouac sites there, but there was a block-house with large antenna above it.[261] King, supported by Item and elements of the 2/5, worked through the small-arms and mortar fire of the garrison and wiped out all resistance. King lost thirteen men wounded in action, its first day of double-digit loss.[262] Nearly surrounded by thick mangrove swamp, King and Item dug in facing the only avenue toward solid ground and the enemy: south.

*   *   *

THREE DAYS HAD PASSED BEFORE LIEUTENANT COLONEL SHOFNER STEPPED back ashore on Peleliu. He did not know why they had held him for so long. A small neat bandage covered the wound on his arm.[263] He set off to find the regimental head-quarters of the Fifth Marines and report to Colonel "Bucky" Harris. No one would have been in a good mood at regimental HQ, and Shofner's first impression would have been that the battle was not going well at all. Losses were high and progress slow. Harris had been wounded in the knee by a shell that had burst in his CP, kill-ing a man near him; he had refused evacuation and now walked with a painful limp. Bucky informed Shofner that he would not be returning to command 3rd Battalion. A major had been given the job and so far he was doing well. The colonel designated Lieutenant Colonel Shofner his regimental liaison officer with division HQ.

Shofner considered the liaison appointment a make-work job. As a colonel with access both to the regiment and the division, though, he was in a position to learn a lot about what was happening on the battlefield. There was a lot of bad news. The jungle canopy had obscured the terrain beneath it. The aerial reconnaissance photographs had shown a ridge north of the airfield; combat had revealed a much bigger problem.[264] The bomb blasts and the engulfing flames of napalm had exposed an expanse of roughly five ugly, wartlike coral ridges, twisted and cut into a maze of peaks and gullies. The enemy had turned each of these myriad facets into a fortress, the coral escarpments riddled with pillboxes, caves, and nasty little spider holes.

Against this fortress Chesty Puller had driven his First Marine Regiment. The First Marines had always known that their mission was the toughest. Every day since D-day, Chesty had lashed his men, exhorting them to attack, to breach the defenses. His battalions had sustained horrendous casualties. The delay in cracking open the bastion just north of the airfield had angered Chesty's boss, General Ru-pertus. Rupertus's dour disposition had become nearly insufferable.[265] He hobbled around division headquarters, pained by an ankle injury sustained a few weeks ear-lier, demanding results.[266] The plan was for the Seventh Marines, who were finishing up their conquest of the southern tip of Peleliu, to support the First Marines' attack on the ridges. The Fifth Marines would continue to receive the easiest of the three assignments.

AFTER A QUIET NIGHT, KING COMPANY SPENT SEPTEMBER 19 MOVING SOUTH across another strip of land and onto another islet on the east side of Peleliu.[267] A road ran through the open area bordered by mangrove swamps and dotted with a few buildings. On their left flank, Item got into a short firefight at a blockhouse. King

John Basilone met Lena Riggi in early 1944 at Camp Pendleton, the large Marine Corps base just north of San Diego.

Courtesy of Barbara Garner

The wedding party of Lena and John Basilone, made up entirely of marines from their respective units, stands for the formal photo. Three of the five men in Lena's wedding would be killed in action.

Courtesy of the Basilone Family

John and Lena Basilone celebrate their wedding with their friends outside a small church in Oceanside, California, on July 11, 1944.

Courtesy of the Basilone Family

The SB2C Helldiver, pictured here with a wingman, produced lots of headaches for Lieutenant Mike Micheel, both as a pilot and as his squadron's mechanical officer. *National Archives*

On the deck of USS *Hornet* during the summer of 1944, Micheel took his turn posing for a photo seated in the cockpit of his squadron's aircraft, an SB2C Helldiver. *Courtesy of Vernon Micheel*

The Helldiver aircraft in Mike's squadron had a tendency to drop their bombs on the flight deck of USS *Hornet* when landing. On the afternoon of May 28, 1944, a brave crewman came out to wrestle a hundred-pound wing bomb. *National Archives*

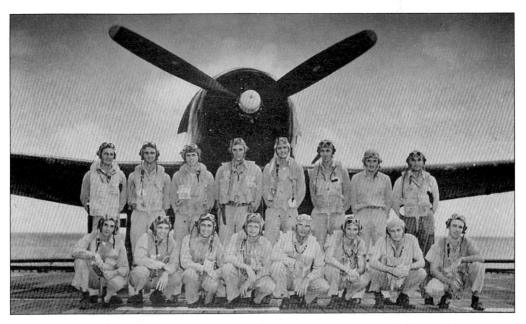

Lieutenant Vernon "Mike" Micheel, fourth from left in the front row, commanded a small experimental squadron of "fighter-bombers" in the summer of 1944. They flew the F6F Hellcat and proved the viability of the concept of combining the two missions. *Courtesy of Mike Micheel*

Lieutenant Colonel Austin Shofner, seen with his radio man (*right*), were photographed twenty-five yards in from the beach used to invade Peleliu on D-day. Shofner struggled all day to coordinate the movements of his three companies, most especially King Company.   *National Archives*

On the morning of September 15, 1944, the day of the invasion of Peleliu, a photographer snapped Shofner's command post in this ditch, two hundred yards inland from the beach.   *National Archives*

Each pillbox on Peleliu—and there were several hundred—exacted a price from the First Marine Division.

National Archives

Signs like this one on Peleliu did not keep out all the gawkers, many of whom lived less than a mile from the hard fighting on Bloody Ridge. Marines like Eugene Sledge, who were in the ridge, needed no such warning.

National Archives

Sid (*top row, center*) escaped the boredom of Boca Chica Naval Air Station, in Key West, Florida, in November 1944.

Courtesy of Dr. Sidney Phillips

The Battle of Iwo Jima came to symbolize the savagery of the Pacific War.
National Archives

The savagery of the fighting increased with every step toward Tokyo.

National Archives

Lieutenant Colonel Austin Shofner, seen here with a map, briefs the men of his military police unit two days before the invasion of Okinawa on April 1, 1945. Shofner hated the job of provost marshal, but he saw it as his route back to a combat command. *National Archives*

A former POW, Shofner took care of the people of Okinawa displaced from their homes while the war's greatest battle was fought across their homeland. *National Archives*

A type 89 Japanese artillery piece stands near its cave on Okinawa. In this battle, the artillery of both sides earned their nickname: the God of War. *National Archives*

A snapshot of combat on Okinawa, where the explosions outnumbered the marines. *National Archives*

When the monsoon came to Okinawa in late May, it created conditions that pushed Eugene Sledge to the brink of his sanity. *National Archives*

The surviving members of King Company's mortar section on August 10, 1945, following the battle of Okinawa. R. V. Burgin is second from left in the back row. Eugene Sledge is second from left in the bottom row.

Courtesy of R. V. Burgin

General and Mrs. Douglas MacArthur, their personal B-17, and the name of the defeat that forever hung over his head, in 1943. *Courtesy of the MacArthur Memorial, Norfolk, Virginia*

Sledge developed a deep respect for China and a love for its people while serving there.

Courtesy of Jeanne Sledge

Few equaled and none surpassed Lieutenant Colonel Austin Shofner's length of service overseas in the Pacific War. He is seen here returning from China in 1946.

Courtesy of the Shofner Family

Eugene Sledge and Mary Houston, taken soon after the war.

Courtesy of Dr. Sidney Phillips

Lena (*second from right*) stood with John's mother and sisters underneath the statue erected in his honor in Raritan, New Jersey.

Courtesy of Barbara Garner

In December 1945, Lena Basilone dedicated USS *Basilone*, a new destroyer, in
Beaumont, Texas.   *Courtesy of the USMC*

Lena Basilone, John's widow, accepted his Navy Cross on his behalf in 1947. She never remarried.

National Records Center, St. Louis

Sledgehammer (*right*) and Snafu meet at a reunion of K/3/5 decades later. For Eugene, it was like coming home. *Courtesy of Auburn University Archives*

Robert "Scotty" MacKenzie (*left*); his trusted sergeant, R. V. Burgin (*center*); and their comrade "Bucky" Pierson at a reunion. *Courtesy of the MacKenzie Family*

faced almost no resistance.[268] Behind them, the enemy's heavy artillery fire began to slacken. It also became harassing fire because it was obviously not targeted.[269]

The job of patrolling this confusing checkerboard of soil and swamp was not completed by the end of the day. The temperature relented, though, dropping into the high eighties.[270] The next morning most of King Company walked out to still another islet, this one with a coastline on the Pacific, and set up camp on Purple Beach. Captain Haldane ordered a reinforced patrol; he joined Burgin's #2 gun, the war dog and his handler, and a machine-gunner squad to the riflemen of the First Platoon, their mission to search the southern tip of the larger islet behind Purple Beach.[271] They moved out. Eugene eyed the war dog curiously because he loved dogs, but he had learned back on Pavuvu never to attempt to pet one.

The patrol went well during the day. They dug in near a lagoon in the late afternoon, the dense mangrove trees cutting visibility to a few feet. Another peninsula could be glimpsed on the far side of the cove. No one knew exactly how all of these pieces of land fit together. The word was there were fifteen hundred enemy troops over there. "We were there," as the #2 gun squad understood it, "to see that they didn't cross that lagoon while the tide was out." When someone reported hearing voices over there, the men began to wonder just when the tide went out. The vegetation rendered the 60mm mortar all but useless. Burgin took one last look before dark and concluded, "If the japs came across in mass swarms, they'd have killed every one of us."[272] He had been with King Company during the Battle of Cape Gloucester, when it had held off a series of banzai attacks, but it had taken a lot more men and a lot more firepower to do it. They sat in the darkness waiting for the shit to hit the fan.

"It wasn't too long after dark this guy began to scream and holler." It horrified everyone. Even in the pitch-black darkness Burgin could tell the yelling came from the war dog handler because he was "within arm's reach." Orders to shut his mouth failed to stop his growing insanity. A medic found his way over and administered morphine. One shot made no effect. Burgin watched as "he gave him enough morphine to kill a horse. And it didn't affect him any more than if it had been water in the needle that he was using. And he went completely berserk, and he was hollering and screaming and he was giving our position away and, you know, that couldn't happen. And, uh, so he was killed with an entrenching tool that night, to shut him up." From the sound of it the crazed marine did not die immediately.

In the light of the next morning, it had to be faced. "One of their own" had been killed by one of their own. Most men concluded that it had had to happen. Burgin was grateful that he had not had to do it himself. Sergeant Hank Boyes called it "a terrifying night."[273] No one spoke the name of the man who had wielded the entrenching tool.

The lieutenant, a rifle platoon leader nicknamed Hillbilly, called Captain Haldane and "told him that he was bringing the troops in—he wasn't staying another night there." His small force could not hold off a force of that size. "And so the company commander told him, 'Okay, bring them back.' So we come back and joined the company."[274]

King Company had set itself up on the northern tip of the islet called Purple Beach because it fronted the ocean, far from the battle but not far from infiltrating Japanese. Gunshots could be heard on an islet across the canebrake from them. The shots came from marines in Item Company, who cleared it out and came over to say they had killed "about 25 japs."[275] That day, September 21, ended without any casualties in King. Its men had survived six days on Peleliu. Their thoughts might have been with their friends in Love Company, still attacking the ridges near the airfield, and also with the thirty-four wounded and four marines killed thus far.[276] These figures did not include the war dog handler, since he had not been on King's muster roll, but they represented a hefty toll on the 240 men who were.

JUST AFTER FIVE A.M. ON SEPTEMBER 21 THE PHONES RANG IN THE STATEROOMS OF the wolves aboard the flattop USS *Hornet*. They assembled in the ready room to get their preflight briefing on their target: the city known as the Pearl of the Orient, Manila. The wolves were here to start the process by which the Filipinos and the American POWs would be liberated. With the city of Manila bearing 250 degrees and 142 miles away, the skipper led the first deckload of SB2Cs off the deck at seven fifty-nine a.m.[277] Mike walked out to the flight deck at about eight thirty. The clouds and squalls of rain surrounding *Hornet* would add another challenge to the day's mission. No rear seat gunner met him. The Hellcat, clad in a dark navy blue with white roundels, had clean, angular lines, which contrasted sharply with the rounded forms of the Helldivers spotted on the stern. For the carrier's second strike of the day, twelve fighters took off first, then Lieutenant Micheel's six fighter-bombers, followed by twelve SB2Cs.

The sky cleared of mist as they arrived over Manila Bay. Campbell's earlier strike had left a fleet oiler of the IJN smoking badly and listing hard. It was just one of about fifteen ships out in the center of the vast natural harbor. Mike could see another ten ships inside the breakwater of Manila's port.* Most of them looked

---

*Micheel's briefing did not include any warning about the fact that Japan was shipping thousands of U.S. POWs back to its home islands in unmarked ships. The navy brass may not have apprehended the situation in September 1944. Even if they had, they could not have ordered their pilots to stop destroying all Japanese shipping.

small enough to qualify as interisland steamers, sampans, or boats. He focused on the most important ship, the destroyer. His fighter-bombers went first, the echelon rolling over into steep dives to avoid the canopy of flak with which the destroyer covered itself. The F6F could handle a steep dive. The destroyer turned too fast, though, and all six five-hundred-pound bombs missed. The SB2Cs made the second pass and also missed the "tin can." After their runs, the Helldivers joined up to return home, their gas tanks reading half empty.

Unlike the Beasts, though, the F6Fs had plenty of gasoline. They also had rockets under their wings. Mike set his men free to hunt for "targets of opportunity." Downtown Manila was off-limits and they ignored the island of Corregidor. Some of them went looking for airfields. Most followed Mike, racing along the shore of Manila. Japan's three-inch and five-inch AA guns emplaced along Dewey Boulevard threw up lots of flak, but they failed to so much as dent the fighter-bombers. With their rockets, Mike's wing of Hellcats set the small ships at the piers on fire. At the outskirts of the city, he triggered the six .50-caliber machine guns on "anything that looked like Army vehicles running down the road." He noted with satisfaction, as the others joined up on his wing, that "there wasn't much left."

Micheel landed back aboard in time for lunch. Two more strikes on Manila and its environs were launched off his flattop later that day. His friend Hal Buell took a turn.

The next morning began with bogeys flying toward their task group. Two raiders appeared on the radar screens just after five a.m. These faded from the screens after the CAP was routed out to meet them, and the first strikes against Manila took off. The bogeys kept coming, though, dancing in and out of the radar's range. *Hornet* began to lead her group in a series of course and speed changes as more enemy aircraft popped onto her radar screens. The Hellcats of the CAP reported "splashing" a few bogeys, but just before seven a.m. "two bomb explosions in the water on port bow, 225°, 2700 yards," made everyone jumpy. Had the two bombs been jettisoned by a U.S. plane? No one could say for sure. Mike's flattop continued her evasive maneuvers, signaling its task group "to form cruising disposition 5V." Changing direction away from one bogey, though, sent it toward another, and she came about again. Fifteen minutes later, a bogey attacked *Monterey*, off *Hornet*'s starboard quarter, dropping two bombs that landed a few hundred yards from her port-side bow.

Hornet signaled "for emergency speed 25, turn right to 300°." The carrier came out of its left-hand turn and swung right (starboard) as she sped up. The port battery of AA opened up on a Zeke, or an enemy fighter, "diving from clouds 190° relative, approximate range 4500'." The aft battery also fired as the bogey made a strafing run on the aft flight deck, the pilot matching his plane's 7.7 machine guns and 20mm cannon against *Hornet*'s five-inch, 40mm, and 20mm guns. "The plane then made a sharp left turn and pulled up and away on port quarter." Its bullets had hit one of the carrier's gun tubes and left the wooden planking of the flight deck smoldering. The screening vessels continued to fire at the Zeke and the CAP vectored out after it. With her guns blazing at a second bogey, Mike's carrier continued her sharp turn until she almost collided with *Wasp*. As the captains evaded one another, *Hornet*'s gunners opened fire "on Zeke on [the] port quarter bow outside of screen."[278] Firing at an enemy plane off the far side of their destroyer screen meant they were jumpy. The bogey got away again. In the break, a lot of talk between the ships of the task group concerned AA guns firing too close to other ships of the group. The sky cleared enough for strike waves to be launched and recovered. Another wave of bogeys arrived around eleven a.m., though, and the flattop remained on high alert for the rest of the day, as the ship's gunners and her combat air patrol protected their carrier.

The task group steamed south that evening, away from the hive of bogeys it had encountered. The reaction to this retreat by Jocko Clark, who was on board as an advisor to the new task group commander but not empowered to make decisions, was to tell the new admiral he needed a better fighter director. The morning of the twenty-third began with preparations for more incoming bogeys. When the air remained clear, *Hornet* held funeral services for two crew members who had been killed by the strafing attack. The task group steamed south along the Philippine Islands. Micheel and the wolves flew a few more missions, and the fighter-bombers got credit for one clear hit and several near misses on a troop transport before the task group set course for the fleet anchorage. The anchorage had moved to a new harbor in the Admiralty Islands.

FOR FOUR DAYS, KING COMPANY LIVED ON PURPLE BEACH, SENDING OUT PATROLS to look for snipers and awaiting orders. It sustained no casualties. The division HQ, knowing how important mail call was to morale, began sending forward bags of mail to the line companies.[279] The marines ate both C and K rations, supplemented by issues of canned fruit and fruit juice. The weather remained cool. The notes Gene kept about his experiences in battle included none of these facts. His mind was still reeling with all he had seen. The keen observer, he knew already that the battle for Peleliu was far worse than anything the 1st Marine Division had yet encountered.

From his pack he took his copy of Rudyard Kipling's poems. The sprawling, bawdy antics of "Gunga Din" no longer captivated him though. A different Kipling verse, entitled "Prelude," grabbed him.[280] In it, the poet admitted that the verses he had written about war were a bad joke to anybody who knew better. Until September 15, 1944, Sledge had been one of the "sheltered people" who had laughed at the antics of "Gunga Din" because the ballad danced past the truth he now knew. Many of the men Gene had come to love were going to die in extreme pain. His mind recoiled at the thought. Gene had sacrificed a lot to become a United States Marine. He was so fiercely proud of having bonded with the men of King Company. Kipling's question to the "dear hearts across the seas," he now apprehended, put into words the grief and bitterness in the soul of any veteran whose friends lay buried on some foreign battlefield. Private First Class Eugene Sledge was not at all sure that the death of Robert Oswalt could ever be justified. It felt like a colossal waste.

Beyond the prospect of death (his own or that of his friends), Gene saw plainly that this battle might cost him his soul. Combat reduced men to savages. Sledge respected order. He prided himself on his cleanliness of habits and mind. He did not doubt that the marines would win through to victory. In his heart he knew the stains created by what his marines were being forced to do—to kill a brother with an entrenching tool—were permanent and, perhaps, overwhelming. They had been forced to kill the war dog handler because of Japanese fanaticism and it made him hate the enemy all the more.

Gene sought solace from these thoughts by wading along the shore. He found some tiny shells he thought beautiful and decided to take a few for his mother, so she would know he had always been thinking of her.

On the morning of September 25 the remains of the First Marine Regiment began to arrive on Purple Beach.[281] Puller's marines had sustained 54 percent casualties, a rate seldom reached in warfare. As the First Marines took over Item and King's positions, Sledge heard plenty about what had happened on "Bloody Nose Ridge." All of the navy's ordnance had not destroyed the enemy's positions. To assault one pillbox meant putting the squad under fire from a myriad of other positions. The riflemen could not see the openings from which all the bullets had come. Colonel Puller had kept the pressure up, had kept ordering his marines to race into the enemy's interlocking streams of machine-gun bullets, even after his battalions had broken, his companies had shattered, his squads had disintegrated. One man said Puller "was trying to get us all killed."[282] Looking at the few exhausted, dirty men who survived, Sledge found Chesty's conduct of the battle "inexcusable."[283]

In the few hours the men of King Company had with the First, the veterans of the battle for the ridge would have tried to communicate other, more specific truths. Men from the 2/1 reported that the Japanese had tried to use the 2/1's passwords and countersigns to approach their line. The 1/1 reported that "the bodies of jap officers"—the ones carrying the coveted Samurai swords—had been booby-trapped.[284] They also had determined that the rifle grenades were all defective and should be thrown away.[285] Wishing the First well, King Company walked across the narrow causeway of solid ground that led to the larger islet. The Fifth Marines' regimental HQ had been set up there.[286] Field kitchens, equipment, and the staffs of both the regiment and of the 3/5 had taken up residence there. Item Company joined them. Love Company was still in combat near the ridges.

The word was the Fifth Marines had been ordered to secure the northern end of Peleliu. Marines in combat were running short on ammunition, officers said, "so take everything you had with you."[287] At one p.m., trucks began hauling away the 1st Battalion, followed by Eugene's 3rd, with the 2nd Battalion coming later.[288] They drove back across the causeway to Peleliu, swinging southwest through the ruins of the buildings around the airfield. The division artillery was shelling the ridges to their right. The Seventh Marines were fighting into that high, broken country. To his left, service troops had set up supply depots. Gene noticed some of the Seabees looking at him. "They wore neat caps and dungarees, were clean-shaven, and seemed relaxed. They eyed us curiously, as though we were wild animals in a circus parade."[289] E. B. Sledge described himself as "unshaven, filthy, tired, and haggard." The grizzled veteran of three days in combat and four days on Purple Beach found "the sight of clean comfortable noncombatants [the Seabees] . . . depressing."

IN LATE SEPTEMBER GUNNERY SERGEANT JOHN BASILONE AND THE OTHER senior NCOs in Hawaii heard that their 5th Division had been placed on "alert status." It had to be prepared to reinforce the 1st Marine Division on Peleliu quickly, if the call came.[290] The officers of John's division held daily briefings on the Peleliu operation. Not a lot of details would have trickled out of those meetings, but the alert clearly signaled that the battle, code-named "Operation Stalemate," was not going well.

In light of the Battle of Peleliu, the focus of the men's training in the 5th Division changed.[291] Instruction in jungle warfare disappeared. The fire teams of each rifle squad hereafter honed the application of their different weapons (M1 rifles, grenades, and Browning automatic rifles), and their smooth coordination with supporting weapons (flamethrowers, bazookas, and machine guns), in the assault on hardened enemy positions. It had become clear the demolition men completed the process by hurling a satchel of C-2 explosives into it and collapsing the pillbox's firing port. Peleliu and other recent battles had also seen a high number of casualties among the junior officers (lieutenants and captains) and NCOs. The revised training schedule emphasized the need for every man to assume any role of the fire team or use any of its weapons.[292] Enlisted men in the 1/27 took a turn firing a .30-caliber machine gun and watched as someone demonstrated the flamethrower.

Despite the casualties, Bucky Harris refused to give Shofner another command. Perhaps Shifty had already guessed that his new position had to do with his performance on September 15. The companies in his battalion had been confused throughout D-day; nightfall had found two of them dangerously isolated. Shofner, when he confronted this talk, would have pointed out that some of the confusion resulted from having two 3rd Battalions (his and the Seventh's) land next to one another. When the landing craft dumped them in the wrong spot, as they often did, chaos had ensued because there were two King Companies, two Love Companies, and so on. More important, the destruction of his CP and communications equipment had severely hampered his efforts. The radios were not reliable. Such arguments, however, did not explain why Shofner had not, once he understood the situation, hiked out to King and Item companies and set it straight.

Whispers around the HQ questioned why Shofner had located his CP in an antitank trench. Everyone knew the enemy had these trenches preregistered with artillery. Poor judgment, the gossip went, had helped that mortar shell hit him. Worst of all, though, was the story that when he was hit, Lieutenant Colonel Shofner had tried to turn over his command to the battalion doctor. Word had it that, at a critical moment, Shifty had "gone bananas."[293] Had he heard the whispers, Shifty Shofner would have demanded to know how a man could be held responsible for what he said after being hit by the blast of a mortar shell. His bell had been rung. More likely, though, he knew only that before he again fought the Japanese, he would have to fight for the job.

After passing Bloody Nose Ridge on Sledge's right, his truck took a right turn and drove north, on a flat coral road running between the ridge and the ocean on their left. The 3/5 passed through an abandoned Japanese bivouac site on the shoreline, now held by the U.S. Army as it waited in reserve. A "Zippo" accompanied King's trucks farther north.[294] Named for a popular brand of cigarette lighter, the Zippo LVT had a big tank of napalm and a pump powerful enough to blow its sticky flame 150 yards. Farther along, the ridge on their right began to drop in height and back away from the road until the trucks stopped near a dense forest. They had gotten as close to the front line as a truck would take them. A few men had already been hit by sniper fire. The Fifth Marines' 1st Battalion had the task of continuing north along the road to secure a radio station area. While the 2/5 remained in reserve, the 3/5 struck off to the east to secure a conical-shaped hill that dominated the terrain. Item and King, rejoined by Love Company, broke into their skirmish lines and moved warily eastward, into the jungle. Love stayed in contact with the 1/5 to the north, where the enemy concentrated his artillery fire. King took the center and Item the right flank. They encountered a thick jungle and sporadic mortar fire.[295]

It was growing dark as the rifle squads approached the sharp coral hill. In the sky above them, giant star shells opened. The navy ships were hanging five-inchers up there and all of a sudden the way ahead was visible. The enemy shrank from the light, contesting the marines' drive to the top of the hill with occasional streams of their distinctive whitish blue tracers. Another half hour of star shells allowed the men to get their barbed wire strung, because they knew a counterattack would come.[296] Creating a defensible line on the jagged landscape took time. The light made the mission so much easier; the officers who had called the navy for this help decided to call the conical hill Starlight Hill.[297] Star shells, while helpful, also created the problem of "flare blindness." As soon as the light died, the men's eyes had to refocus. Smart NCOs, therefore, learned to order one of every two men in a foxhole to shut his eyes, and thus be unaffected and ready to fire.[298]

Just as expected, the Japanese attacked the front line that night. Back near the road, the 60mm mortar squads either did not have mass clearance to fire or lacked an FO, or forward observer, to aim their rounds. Artillery shells from the big howitzers in the rear began exploding in front of the 3/5's lines, effectively pulverizing the enemy. The attack broke, although one never knew for how long. Infiltrators came at the mortar section dug in near the road. Sledge saw two dark figures.[299] Burgin saw three men dive into the foxholes near him.[300] A few shots were fired and there were sounds of a struggle. When one of the figures emerged from the foxhole, he was killed. Everyone else sat tight, ready to fire.

In the morning, one marine lay dead. Sledge spoke to a number of men and arrived at a definite conclusion as to what had happened. Burgin and others disagreed, but while Sledge noted every grisly aspect of it, they knew they had to pass it off.[301] Burgin had seen the same thing on Cape Gloucester. The word came to move out. King and Love companies secured the craggy mass of Starlight Hill that morning. That night proved to be quieter and easier.

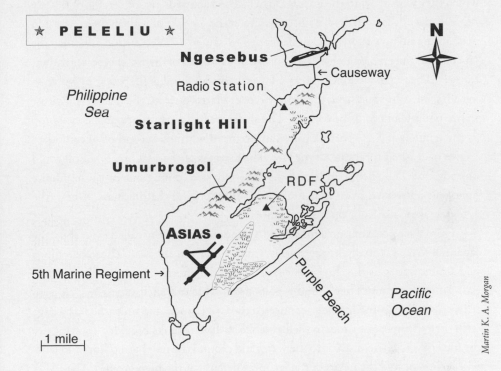

On the morning of September 27, King Company left Love and Item to hold Starlight Hill. Sledge's company marched north to support the 1/5's attack on a hill mass up there.[302] On the way up, the whole company was laughing at a story making the rounds. The previous night a scout in one of the rifle platoons, Bill Leyden, had eaten a can of Japanese food he had found in a cave on Starlight Hill. The tin of food had created an "intestinal fury" inside Bill that had led quickly to "the runs like I was going to explode."[303] On the front line and unable to move from his foxhole, Bill had had to relieve himself in empty C ration containers. He then dropped the full containers off the side of the hill. The way the story went, shouts of disgust and protest could be heard coming from the enemy below; other marines thought the voices signaled an attack, and everybody started shooting. Leyden himself enjoyed mimicking the unintelligible outrage he had heard after he bestowed his gifts before he concluded: ". . . and you know, my God, you can only imagine what he was saying. He was definitely cursing in Japanese." Everyone could relate to the story because by this time everyone had had to relieve themselves in a C ration can.

The laughter would have faded as they passed the junction of the West Road, which they were on, with the East Road, which led south on the other side of Bloody Nose Ridge.[304] They halted with orders to stand by. Up ahead of them, the 1/5 massed the firepower of tanks and Zippos to savage a collection of hills that the Japanese engineers apparently had turned into hunks of Swiss cheese with their tunnels. The regimental CO, Bucky Harris, had added to his firepower by borrowing a huge 155mm gun from the army. Colonel Harris ordered the massive howitzer to fire point-blank into the caves.[305] The shells created a painful double concussion as the ignition and the shells' explosions occurred within a second of one another. Waves of crushed coral slid off the face. The marines of the 1/5, however, still could not advance. The enemy's rifle and machine-gun fire coming out of those infinite holes was buttressed by mortar fire coming from behind the hill mass. Worse, the 1/5 was taking fire from the opposite direction.

From their positions on a tiny island a hundred yards away called Ngesebus, the Japanese were essentially hitting the 1/5 and the 2/5 in the rear. Those battalions had a difficult day as the shit hit the fan. Late in the afternoon, nine tanks churned past King Company. They found a point from which to shell Ngesebus, close to where a small man-made bridge connected the two islands, and unleashed a barrage with their 75mms, every fourth shell a smoke shell. The tanks provided covering fire for four LVTs. These drove into the water and around the northern point of Peleliu, where they located the nexus of the Japanese defense of the high ground. The LVTs fired point-blank into a large blockhouse. The enemy resistance on the near side began to crumble without its heavy mortar support. Tank dozers drove up the north road and pushed coral and earth into the lower pillboxes.[306]

Although the area to their north was far from secure, the 3/5 would not be needed. Late in the day, army units relieved the 3/5 at the crossroads. King, Item, and Love moved south to an assembly point near the regimental HQ. To shield their movement, the artillery provided another screen with its smoke shells. A short round landed near the regimental HQ and, to everyone's horror, "squarely in the midst of the war dogs." The dogs had been brought up to help protect the marines from night infiltration. The white phosphorus used to produce "smoke" covered them and burned through their flesh. The dogs shrieked and yelped at the merciless pain. Bucky Harris saw no other way. He ordered the war dog handlers to shoot them, which they did, "all of them with eyes brimming with tears."[307]

At dusk on September 27, word came that the 3/5 would invade the small island they could see a hundred yards away called Ngesebus.[308] The Japanese over there had not only been firing at the marines on Peleliu; they had been sending over barges filled with reinforcements at night. Sledge's stomach churned at the thought of another amphibious assault. During the past few days, King had suffered only one or two casualties a day.[309] An amphibious assault on another island would likely increase that ratio. Dug in near an army unit, Sledge had a chance to speak with them. The soldiers of the 321st Regimental Combat Team had already secured the small island of Angaur a few dozen miles away. They had come to Peleliu to reinforce the 1st Division, and E. B. Sledge welcomed them as comrades in arms and respected them as equals.[310] The Eugene Sledge who once had laughed at the "damn doggies" for being sloppy and pathetic had disappeared.

USS *HORNET* SAILED AWAY FROM THE PHILIPPINES TO THE RHYTHMS OF GENERAL quarters, flight ops, and gunnery practice for the AA batteries—all of the ceaseless preparations that had brought her to a high state of combat effectiveness—even though she had earned a break. On September 27, Rear Admiral Joseph "Jocko" Clark assembled the crew, both black shoe and brown shoe, on the flight deck to present decorations for jobs well done. The following day the carrier docked in Berth 16 of Seeadler Harbor, Manus Island, Admiralty Group. Air Group Two had completed its mission and began to disembark. Reporting aboard the following day would be its replacement, Air Group Eleven. Jocko Clark held a farewell dinner for his pilots. The host thanked his naval aviators for their efforts while the guests tucked into their steaks, potatoes, fruit and vegetables, topped off with a cigar. In a few days Lieutenant Vernon Micheel and the wolves would board a troopship for the ride home. In the six and a half months of their squadron's combat tour, thirteen of the forty-six pilots of Bombing Two had given their lives in the service of their country, as had fifteen rear seat gunners.[311] Micheel hated to distinguish between the deaths classified as "operational" as opposed to "combat related."

Lieutenant Micheel knew the navy would assign him to a naval air station somewhere in the States. The younger men could only guess what would happen next. They all knew they had been one small part of the team that had decisively defeated the enemy's carrier fleet. When its enemy fled the battlefield, the U.S. Navy's fast carrier task forces had denied the enemy the use of "the Jimas" as well as the port of Manila, albeit for short periods. The once vast Empire of Japan had withered. To the extent Mike and his friends considered the future course of the Pacific War, they "worried about what was going to happen with the ground fighters when they make their landing in Japan. How were we going to handle some big country like that? We had a lot of carriers and a lot of ships, but they're pretty small when you put them against a whole country and area and people."

*   *   *

NAVY CRUISERS AND DESTROYERS BEGAN FIRING AT NGESEBUS AT SIX A.M. THE Fifth Regiment's artillery ranged in as well. The firestorm had come again, so close that the 3/5 had a ringside seat. Amid the swelling tempo of destruction, forty amtracs, forty of the assault amtracs with the snub-nosed 75mm, and fifteen swimming tanks lined up on the beach on the northwestern corner of Peleliu.[312] The preinvasion bombardment lasted three hours. Navy and Marine Corps planes made passes over the target, strafing and bombing. One of King Company's riflemen, Bill Leyden, noted that the USMC pilots, flying in their distinctive Corsairs, "always seemed to come in lower, to try harder to knock out jap positions, and the marines loved them for it." The Corsairs' last pass came with the lead tanks thirty yards offshore.[313] After an eleven-minute run, the first wave of twenty of the assault amtracs landed on Ngesebus at nine eleven a.m. An enemy soldier attacked one of the LVTs with a Bangalore torpedo.[314] The amtrac threw a track and the lone assailant was killed. A few minutes later, King Company landed on the left flank of the beach, Item on the right. Riding in a new amtrac with a rear ramp, Sledge did not have to clamber over the side. As the troops disembarked and charged forward, the assault amtracs aimed their cannons and fired at the defensive bunkers from close range.[315] Behind them the Sherman tanks swam ashore. The whole battalion assault team had landed by nine thirty a.m.

Securing the beachhead went quickly and the rifle squads led the way inland. The enemy's return fire increased rapidly as the marines raced across the small airfield to the buildings and taxiways at nine forty-two a.m. In the scrub beyond, they encountered a stiff resistance that stopped forward momentum. A series of caves, bunkers, and pillboxes had to be "reduced," as the officers liked to put it. The terrain within King's area became rugged and more difficult for the tanks to support.

Burgin's #2 gun squad halted as they saw the riflemen take cover ahead. Using a bunker as cover, Snafu and Sledge set up the 60mm to be prepared to fire. Burgin needed to figure out how best to support the assault teams. Sledge said, "Burgin, there's some Japs in that thing." Burgin glanced at the oddly shaped little building half buried in the sand. It stood about five feet tall, was about sixteen feet in length, and four feet wide. His sergeant had told him "there wasn't any japs in there," so he replied, "Oh, Sledgehammer, do you know what you're talking about?"[316]

"Yeah, I can hear them jabbering." Burgin saw a small ventilation port near him. "I crawled up on the side of that bunker and looked into there, and that jap had his face right up against the hole. . . . Well, I pumped about four or five shots on him before he could get his head down." Even after he emptied his clip, "they kept jabbering and a machine gun came out and fired a few rounds." They threw grenades out of the ports as well.

"Sledge," Burgin ordered, "look up and see what you can see." Sledgehammer ran over and peeked over the side of the door. He fell to the ground just as fast. A machine gun fired. "Well, him being a rookie," Burgin concluded, "I shouldn't have never sent him up there to begin with." The #2 gun squad leader also began to wonder "how many japs is in that thing, you know, I need to do something here. Uh, if we don't, we might all get killed." The enemy's grenades went off, and fragments hit two of his squad. Burgin sized up the bunker. The thick concrete would stop anything he had; they had a machine gun in there, grenades—who knew what else. He "decided that we weren't doing a very damn good job, you know, and I knew that if we kept messing around there, there's somebody going to get killed." R. V. Burgin ran back to get some firepower.

Seventy-five yards back toward the beach, he found a Sherman tank and Womack, one of the men in King who carried a flamethrower. Burgin told Womack he needed his help and started to guide the tank from behind, using the phone. The return trip took just a few anxious minutes. The Sherman fired three or four rounds at close range until one shell penetrated the concrete and exploded inside. Womack stepped forward and loosed a great gush of flame into the breach. The violence of it made Burgin think the enemy must have been killed, but they came running out the side doors, some holding up their pants with one hand, some with splotches of burning napalm on their bodies. Most of them carried rifles.

Snafu and Sledgehammer and the others shot the enemy as they emerged. A short pause after the first rush of men ended when another Japanese soldier emerged. Sledge "lined up my sights on his chest and began squeezing off shots. As the first bullet hit him, his face contorted in agony . . . the grenade slipped from his hand."[317] The moment became seared into Gene's heart as his sharp eyes noted every detail of the first time he killed another human being. "The expression on that man's face filled me with shame and then disgust for the war. . . ." Another thought struck him hard: the foolishness of "feeling ashamed because I shot a damned foe before he could throw a grenade at me!"

Burgin waited a moment before walking around to the narrow passage leading inside. Stooping his six-foot frame, he entered the room to find out how they could have absorbed such punishment. "There was a jap laying there that I didn't think looked dead to me, and, uh, I stuck my foot in his—in his, uh, rib cage and— and, uh, attempted to roll him over. And he wasn't dead, so I plugged that one." He counted seventeen bodies on the floor as he moved through the different rooms.

They had been heavily armed. Burgin realized "we was damn lucky that nobody didn't get killed." The two wounded men in his squad did not require evacuation, so he gave himself a pat for "a pretty good job well done."

A number of similar successes along the line allowed the 3/5 to cross the enemy's main defensive line at twelve fifty p.m.[318] The Japanese never gave up, though, and the ships of the navy had finished their work as artillery batteries and ceased firing.[319] King and Item had advanced only 350 yards by five p.m. when they dug in for the night. A few platoons of reinforcements came up an hour later. The infiltrators would creep toward them hours later causing brief, vicious exchanges. All over Peleliu and Ngesebus, mortar teams fired their illumination rounds, sometimes keeping a few floating in the air above them at one time.[320]

The next morning the attack jumped off at six thirty a.m. and at eight a.m. the first marines began to reach the far shore of Ngesebus.[321] Before they could relax, "a large jap 77mm gun fired point-blank at the rifle companies."[322] King Company did not take part in the firefight, which eliminated the enemy's gun crew. It had already sustained the highest casualties of any company in the battle for Ngesebus (three killed and nine wounded) and the worst losses since the invasion.[323] Most of the day was spent "mopping up," which meant carefully making sure no enemy concentrations had been overlooked. It also gave the marines time to find souvenirs. Stripping enemy bodies was, so far as Corporal Burgin was concerned, "common practice."

The vulgarity of his friends stripping dead bodies combined with the aftershock of the sudden devastation wreaked by the enemy's 77mm gun filled Gene's eyes with tears. "I was so terribly tired and emotionally wrung out from being afraid for ten days on end that I seemed to have no reserve strength left."[324] E. B. Sledge would take note of the words of encouragement he received at that moment from the mortar platoon lieutenant, Charles Ellington. Nicknamed "Duke" because he shared a last name with the famous black jazz musician Duke Ellington, the lieutenant had seen him struggle and said, "I feel the same way." The gesture helped Eugene. He looked up to Duke, just as he revered all of the officers of King Company. He saw them as strong, brave, and true of heart. His opinion reflected his innate love of order and his deference to authority. He needed to believe now more than ever in the courage and righteousness of his commanders. E. B. Sledge's perception, however, overlooked the growing anger within Corporal Burgin, who doubted Lieutenant Ellington's bravery in battle. Duke never seemed to be where the action was.[325]

When the word came, they walked back to the invasion beach to the sound of artillery on Peleliu. An army unit relieved the 3/5 at six p.m. The amtracs carried King to Peleliu, and trucks ran them south, around Bloody Nose Ridge, then east across the first causeway to the regimental HQ on the first islet. Being so near Purple Beach, the new port area, brought the hope that they were going there in preparation to ship out.[326] After a decent night's sleep, King Company had a long rainy day off to clean their weapons, get some hot chow from the mess hall, and wonder if the scuttlebutt was true.[327]

PRIVATE FIRST CLASS SIDNEY PHILLIPS WAS NOT CRAZY ABOUT LIFE AT BOCA Chica Naval Air Station, even though it turned out to be only seven miles to the north of Key West, Florida. Most of the marine unit stationed there were, like him, recently arrived veterans of the 1st Division. They all disliked being stationed out in the boonies or, more correctly, on one of the little islands sticking out into the Gulf of Mexico. A marine could only get to Miami if he had a long weekend liberty. The jobs of guarding the front gate, the gasoline storage tanks, and other important government property seemed almost pointless.

Most of the navy pilots stationed there had just graduated from flight school and received their wings of gold. The first taste of the glamour of being a pilot as well as the pay and the respect accorded an officer often went to their heads. Ensigns were likely to look down on a lowly marine at the gate and might decide to thank him for "guarding our airplanes." The senior officers sometimes knew better than to treat a salty marine that way, but one afternoon a car with four captains drove up to the main gate. Sid noticed the four stripes on their uniforms. He also noticed one of them lacked an ID card. He did not wave them through. The salty veteran with the big "1" on his shoulder patch had started to ask about the missing ID when the car started to move forward. Sid "placed my hand on my revolver, and told them to stop, made them all get out and go into the guard house for clearance. This was all done with firm politeness, and snappy salutes."

Sid and the other veterans enjoyed playing games with the swabbies. Other navy officers coming to the front gate might be asked to get out and open their trunks for inspection. Sailors ducking through an illegal hole in the fence around the base might hear a gunshot. They assumed it had been aimed at them and it got them to stop their unauthorized egress. These kinds of stunts also earned Sid and his friends a reputation as the "mean and bad Pacific veterans."

He did venture into Key West a few times. One bar sat next to another bar, next to another. Sid visited too many of them on one trip and woke up in a strip club, drunk. He observed his friends explaining to the MPs why they did not need to bother with him. By his right elbow he soon noticed a girl "bumping and grinding . . .

to the tune of the Hawaiian War Chant." She was lathered in sweat and had long stringy hair. "My thought was up close she isn't very attractive and then I slid to the floor. Deacon would have given me several of his long lectures."

AT EIGHT A.M. ON OCTOBER 1, IT BECAME THE 3/5'S TURN. THE OTHER TWO battalions of the Fifth remained in relative safety while Sledgehammer and his comrades walked toward Bloody Nose Ridge.[328] The 3rd Battalion had been attached to the Seventh Marines, whose CO announced his unit would "make an all out drive to erase the remaining jap garrison."[329] The Seventh would continue the push north begun by Chesty Puller's First. The walk to the front line for King, Item, and Love was not very far. The ridge came into view. The ceaseless battering by every weapon in the corps' vast arsenal upon the high ground had burned and blasted away the jungle, exposing several dreadful columns of Bloody Nose Ridge.

The 3/5 relieved the 2/7 on the eastern side of the main ridge complex. Some company-sized units of the 2/7 came down from the heights that had already been taken. The men being relieved had not eaten hot food or enjoyed a safe place to sleep since September 17. Just getting ammo and medical supplies and the wounded out had been difficult, their officers reported, since snipers were everywhere and the terrain was crazy.[330] A few of them led the men of Item Company back up the steep paths into the coral walls to show them their positions. King and Love remained on the valley floor, back from the point of furthest penetration. The air over the forbidding terrain shimmered with heat and malevolence. The sound of gunfire at all times attested to the fact that somewhere nearby, someone was getting hurt. As the platoons of King found their places that afternoon, snipers killed two men and wounded two others.

The attack northward did not jump off the next day. The 2/7 shifted to the right in order to face a solitary ridge along the island's eastern shore. The plan worked out for October 3 involved the Seventh Marines seizing the ridge in front of it. To the left of the Seventh's ridge, across a flat open valley, stood the coral redoubt known as the Five Sisters, the object of the 3/5.[331]

The #2 mortar squad joined the chorus of mortars that began firing at six thirty a.m. Fifteen minutes later, the heavy artillery opened up, trying to force the Japanese back from their firing positions and therefore allow the riflemen to close with their targets. The high-explosive shells gave way to smoke shells at six fifty-five. The riflemen of Item and King took the point, moving forward along the flat and open ground, the bulk of Bloody Nose Ridge running along to their left and the Five

Sisters five hundred yards dead ahead. On the 3/5's right flank, two tanks and three half-tracks of the Seventh nosed into the long valley known as the Horseshoe. On the far right, the riflemen of the Seventh assaulted the ridge on the shoreline.[332]

The 60mm mortarmen were not leading the charge, but they still came under direct fire. "Almost every cave in the side of the ridge on the left flank was full of japs," as King's skipper, Captain Haldane, discovered. "Tanks, portable flamethrowers, grenades, bazooka, and demolition charges were used to eliminate them." To Love Company fell the task of mopping up the areas behind the advancing King and Item.[333] The seemingly endless permutations of hardened coral faces demanded the marines' attention to detail in the face of punishing small-arms fire. In the course of such work the marines learned to dislike the flamethrowing LVTs, or "Ronsons."[334] To be effective with flame, the tank had to get very close to its target, and, since troops and tanks had to work together, that meant the troops had to approach the pillbox closer than they would have had to with a standard Sherman tank. Anything the Ronson could hit with flame, the Sherman could hit with a 75mm shell from a safer distance. For all of the frightening hostility of napalm's sticky sheet of flame, it caused less damage than an HE round and King Company measured its gains in yards of violent destruction.

The lead elements of King reached the base of the Five Sisters at noon. One platoon found a sharp ravine on the left side of the sisters and took a tank in with them to investigate. Love came up on their right, Item fell back to mop up, and the riflemen began to scale sisters one, three, four, and five. The mortarmen waited, ready to lay down suppressing fire or smoke rounds. Knowing when to press the attack and when to fall back demanded a cold assessment of a combat situation the likes of which no one there had endured. It fell to Captain Haldane, the skipper, to expend his men's lives as judiciously as possible, while producing the gains his superiors demanded. Haldane made sure he made that decision from the front. At that moment there was seemingly no cover. Rifle fire from unknown locations drove King to the ground.[335] The volume of fire increased. The call for the smoke rounds came to the mortarmen. As the 60mm mortar tubes coughed, King fell back two hundred yards. Over to their right, the Seventh had also had to withdraw out of the Horseshoe because of the casualties in men and to its armored vehicles. Some of the caves held guns big enough to destroy a tank.[336]

The assault cost King Company seven killed and about thirty wounded, including Sergeant Hank Boyes.[337] The high number of casualties came as a shock.[338] The men spooned out some K rations, all too aware of what the night would bring. The mortar section had nearly used up its supply of 60mm mortar illumination rounds.[339] The enemy must have watched the marines dig in because they seemed to know which foxhole to jump in and where to throw their grenades. The infiltrators came all night long. It got so bad that when a sergeant hollered, "You guys need help up there?" he got a quick "Shut the fuck up!" for his trouble.[340] At daybreak, Sledge heard men call out, "Get down, Joe," and "Get down, Pete," as they shot the remaining infiltrators scant feet from one another.[341] Once secure, the marines counted twenty-seven dead enemy bodies within the company's small perimeter.[342] They moved out and up into the Five Sisters again. Burgin and the mortarmen made it to the base of the escarpment. Even though he had heard about the cave system it amazed Burgin to see it. "A jap could run into one entrance and reappear on the other side of the ridge." A few feet past the entrance, the tunnel usually took a ninety-degree turn to the left or the right and another a few feet farther. These twists and turns helped shield the inhabitants. "Some of the caves had a steel door on them," he noticed. "We finally got the artillery up and busted the doors down and used the flamethrowers, and weeded them out of there."

"The difficulty," Sledge noticed about the destruction of a cave, was "getting any-where near it 'cause of crossing fire from other caves."[343] As a forward observer for his team, Burgin went forward with an intelligence-gathering team. He came across a few marines who had been tied up and used for bayonet practice. The dead men had had "their testicles cut out and their throat cut, you know, and mutilated. And, any one of the bayonet deals would have killed a man. But they [the Japanese]— they didn't know when to quit. They just kept brutalizing the—the marine. And you don't have to see very much of that until you—you get a great hatred before you." Tanks pulled up at the base of the Five Sisters to evacuate the wounded just before ten a.m.[344] The riflemen ahead and above Burgin found that the caves they had cleared the day before were active again. The enemy killed in the mouth of the cave the day before might look like "frankfurters on a grill, they're sizzling and pop-ping," from the flamethrower treatment, but a bullet or a stream of bullets could issue forth at any moment.[345]

The squads of King and Love gained the ridge while other marines worked through the ravine on the left. Both were trying to get to the second sister, just out of reach to the north. Too much rifle fire from too many holes forced the marines to pull back again. The smoke rounds started falling in the early afternoon and by five p.m. the line had pulled back about seventy-five yards from the sisters.[346] A half hour later a 155mm mortar shell exploded near the 3/5 aid station.[347] The day's casualty list grew to six men killed and thirteen wounded.[348] Captain Haldane kept some men with him to hold the front line about three hundred yards south of the Five

Sisters overnight. He sent King farther south until it backed around the southern base of Bloody Nose Ridge.

Sledge's company moved into the area where the First Marine Regiment had been cut into small pieces on D-day. Many Seventh Marines had fallen here as well. Their bodies had been removed. The enemy's dead, however, had not been. Looking around, Burgin could see corpses in all directions. The bodies "would bloat up and flies would be going all through their body from their mouth on out." With so much food, these green blowflies reproduced quickly and soon there were great swarms. His movement near one corpse caused a huge number to dash noisily into the air, "so thick that they would make a shadow, just like a cloud came over between them and the—between them and the sun." The flies made it difficult for the marines to eat. They could land on a ration in that short moment from when it was opened to when it was to be inserted into the mouth. Brush one off and another took his place. So brash, "you couldn't chew them off." The stench of the decaying corpses mixed with that of the exposed excrement suffused their existence. The odor "was something that I don't think any human being ought to ever have to endure."

Exhausted after the assault on the Five Sisters, Burgin got permission to find a spot a little farther back. He lay down in a shell hole near the 81mm mortar batteries and fell asleep. The mortars fired all night long, harassing the enemy and providing illumination with star shells. "I heard about three shells and that was it" until his sergeant woke him the next morning at eight a.m.

DAYBREAK ON OCTOBER 5 FOUND THE CO OF THE 1ST DIVISION, GENERAL Rupertus, in a difficult position. One of his regiments had been shipped back to Pavuvu, broken. Another, the Seventh, had lost its combat effectiveness. The Fifth's recent foray into the ridges had produced casualties at a similarly alarming rate. Little advance on the battlefield had been made. As one senior officer described it, "a sense of gloom and futility was rife."[349] Lieutenant Colonel Shofner witnessed this because recently he had been banished permanently to Rupertus's division HQ.

Colonel Harold D. "Bucky" Harris of the Fifth Marines had sat Shofner down at the end of September and told him he thought he was a fine officer in many ways, and an excellent marine. Harris had, however, recommended Shofner "be returned to the United States for a period of one year before serving again in the field." The Fifth Marines' CO "believed that the strain caused during his imprisonment by the Japanese has left a nervous condition that makes it undesirable for this officer to remain in the field at this time." Colonel Harris knew that he was ending Shofner's career as a line officer with this fitness report. Shofner, who only wanted to fight, knew as much when he signed it.[350]

Three days later, though, a stroke of luck had come. The division's provost marshal was wounded on October 3. Shifty received the assignment, as well as command of the division's headquarters battalion, while Harris's recommendation for his removal went off to higher authorities. The irony of Shofner's new staff job, which included the supervision of the enemy POWs, was lost on no one.

As he supervised the division HQ, Shofner became aware of Rupertus's difficult situation. He may not have known, however, that the general had turned over the future operations on Peleliu to Bucky Harris. Harris not only commanded the most powerful regiment; he had warned Rupertus not to continue battering the coral fortress head-on. When the Fifth and the Seventh's "all out attack" failed to make appreciable gains, the general called Bucky into a secret meeting at which he collapsed in tears and wailed, "I'm at the end of my rope." On October 5 he gave Harris permission to look for another way into the enemy's fastness.[351]

Colonel Bucky Harris went up into a small spotter plane and flew back and forth over the small area, looking for the right place to send in the Fifth Marines. His choice would affect the course of Shofner's life almost as much as those of the #2 gun squad.

THE #2 GUN SQUAD SPENT OCTOBER 6 HARASSING THE ENEMY.[352] BURGIN CALLED in orders for searching fire to the left or right. Snafu dialed in the azimuth. Sledge removed the correct number of charges from the base of the shell, hung it, and dropped it down the barrel when ordered. Their fire and that of the other 60mms provided part of the cover for a lot of movement and reorganization on the front.

The Seventh Marines used the cover to extricate themselves from the front line. They were headed for Purple Beach and a trip to Pavuvu, leaving the battle to the Fifth. Bucky sent the 2/5 and most of his tanks around the West Road and up to the northern edge of the Japanese fortress. When ready, they would attack south. A hodgepodge of marines from artillery and support units manned a defensive line in front of the Five Sisters, the Horseshoe Valley, and the eastern ridge. Heavy artillery was brought up to help support these men. The 60mms of the 3/5 continued to fire while those men moved into position. Getting the Seventh Marines off the eastern ridge, where they had made some forward gain, required a lot of smoke and the cover

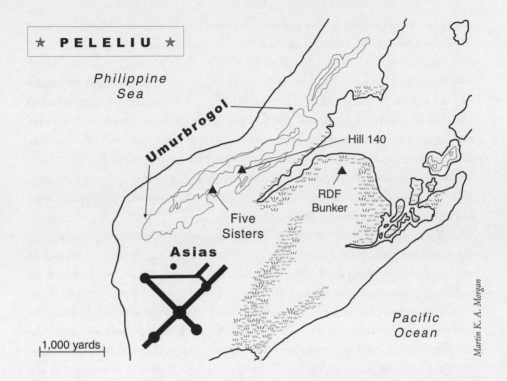

★ PELELIU ★

Philippine Sea

Umurbrogol

Hill 140

RDF Bunker

Five Sisters

Asias

Pacific Ocean

1,000 yards

Martin K. A. Morgan

of darkness. The 1st Battalion took the Seventh's position—ordered to carry a unit of fire and a day's worth of rations with them.*

On October 7 all three of Bucky's battalions attacked from three directions. King Company remained in position, though, as Love and Item attempted to crack into the Five Sisters. The 2/5 came toward it from the other direction and the 1/5 fired at it from across Horseshoe Valley.[353] The big guns of the Eleventh Marines, the artillery, supported the effort as usual. Item advanced about two hundred yards into the Horseshoe, the riflemen and their supporting tanks blasting and burning a lot of caves, before enemy bullets from three sides made their position untenable. Love had been stopped cold when it attempted to follow another ravine northward. The mortars belched smoke rounds all over the front to protect the withdrawal. Love and Item had lost eight men wounded and four killed. They rejoined King and

---

*A unit of fire is the amount of ammunition needed to sustain a marine's weapon (carbine, 60mm mortar, whatever) for one day of heavy combat.

the 3/5 spent the next two days just south of no-man's-land. The position put them in between the airport and the ridges.

Above the 3/5 flew the Corsairs of the USMC, their bombing missions of such short duration that the pilots had neither time nor necessity to pull up their wheels. On the eighth the planes dropped thousand-pound bombs into the gorges and on the cliffs as requested.[354] Harris also had the planes drop hundreds of pounds of napalm on the western and northern parts of the Japanese stronghold, burning away more of their concealment. The colonel followed that up immediately with massed artillery fire on the new targets.[355] He applied firepower at the maximum level available to him as two of his battalions, the 1/5 and 2/5, continued the fight in their respective zones of action for the next few days.

King lived amid the dead bodies, excrement, and broken buildings, eating cold C rations and waiting for their turn.[356] The fly population had decreased, thankfully, as aircraft sprayed the island with chemicals. The marines went four days without suffering a casualty, while 105mm and 155mm howitzers fired point-blank at any openings in the coral walls.[357] The mission Sledge's company received on the tenth and continued the next day was to find the sources of the sniper and mortar fire that continued to issue from the southernmost ridges—ridges that had been overrun by the First Marines weeks previously. The patrols along the edge of the ridges became a grim business for those on them—they found no clear evidence, much less a clear shot at the enemy—and suffered one killed and seven wounded.

The mortarmen rarely went on such patrols. Seeing his friends in the rifle platoons cut down by an unseen hand, though, made Corporal Burgin livid. This was not warfare as he knew it. Snipers shooting individuals could not halt the U.S. victory. It was just naked evil. The Texan choked on his frustration. The enemy "were in those damn caves and you just, and you didn't know who, what you, you didn't . . . you couldn't see what you was fighting. And they wouldn't come out and fight you. . . ." The Japanese stayed in their caves, silently keeping watch. When the Americans were looking the other way, "they'd shoot one or two rounds and then they'd disappear"; the patrols "had a hell of a time finding which cave they were shooting out of or where the cave was. . . ."[358]

No antisniper patrols went forth on October 11. King's skipper, Haldane, and the other captains of the 3/5 went to meet the officers of the 2nd Battalion and be briefed on their position on the north side of the ridges. Another push into the coral chaos was on the horizon. Their officers were at least trying to find another way in. When such attempts were made, Sledge invariably heard marines exclaim, "Thank God 'Bucky' is our CO, and not Chesty." The delay increased the boredom that had crept into the marines of King Company, who had lived on the outer edge of the combat zone for nearly a week. Guys wanted to get souvenirs from the nearby caves. Although ordered not to hunt for Japanese Samurai swords and the like, some of the "hard heads," as Sledge called them, would "enter for souvenirs and never return."

THE 1ST DIVISION HQ HAD GROWN INTO AN IMPRESSIVE COMPLEX ON THE AIR-field. Thousands of men operated the airport and supported the combat troops. The foxholes of the combat troops situated on the southern end of the ridges were not too far from the men who lived in tents and went about their daily work.[359] Thus the commander of the division's headquarters battalion, Lieutenant Colonel Shofner, lived in close proximity to combat troops as he endured his mundane chores. Some of his marines kept the division HQ neat and tidy. In typical Shofner fashion, he made sure they did their job.[360]

In his other job as provost marshal, Shofner commanded the division's unit of military police, or MPs. The MPs guarded key storage dumps and kept the traffic flowing. His men also picked up any stragglers and brought them back to their as-signed units. While the stragglers included marines from line companies who could not explain why they were so far from their foxholes, stragglers also included men from service units who could not explain to the MPs why they were on the front line. The problem of "marines from supporting units making their way into the hills . . . to find souvenirs to trade with sailors" became big enough for a number of officers to arrive at the same solution at about the same time. Shofner ordered "marines near the front without their weapons" to be "issued new ones and assigned to a rifle com-pany in the assault, where they remained until their own officers came to retrieve them. All Marines leaving the front line were required to haul stretchers of wounded down the steep hills to awaiting ambulances."[361] With other officers having issued similar orders, the tourist and salvage trips ended abruptly.

Shofner, the man who wanted to return to combat, was punishing wayward ma-rines by sending them to the front while he served as a staff officer, or, as expressed in marine parlance, served "in the rear with the gear." Only one thing could have been worse for Shifty Shofner—being sent home.

His assignment as provost marshal had one interesting aspect: being in charge of the POWs. No one expected Imperial Japanese soldiers to surrender, although an attempt had been made. Two weeks earlier the garrison in the ridges had been given the opportunity from noon to four p.m.[362] Six men had come out. More recently, a rumor had gone around that marines had discovered a cave of seventy-five female

Japanese. The women had also refused to come out, so the cave had been sealed. Nonetheless the provost marshal had internees for whom to care. The POWs spoke freely, providing valuable intelligence. One man said his recently formed unit had been instructed to "enter the water naked" at the time of an invasion, and "swim out as far as possible and then attempt to knock out landing craft with explosives."[363]

In all, a few hundred men from the enemy garrison had been captured thus far. A lot of those were Koreans who had been conscripted as workers.[364] At least seventeen of the POWs incarcerated in the stockade were Okinawans.[365] They had been brought in to build the airport. When food had run short, the Japanese had allowed the Okinawans, clad only in breechcloths, to surrender.* The few captured enemy combatants, which included members of Japan's navy as well as its army, had either been wounded or were so weak from malnutrition and thirst they had not been able to resist. The U.S. stockade provided them cots, blankets, and water. Twice a day they walked to the supply depot to draw rations. Colonel Shofner made sure that angry marines did not shoot the prisoners "like fish in a barrel." So far as the provost marshal could tell, however, the recovery of their health elicited disdain, not gratitude, from the Japanese prisoners. With the help of the USMC's language officers, Shifty made sure the captives understood that he had seen how the Japanese treated their POWs in China. In some detail he described his own experience as a POW in the Philippines. He ordered the translator to emphasize that "compared to the conditions that he had endured, they were living like kings."[366] The point Shifty most wanted to make—his hatred of them—he drove home himself, uttering it in the "prison camp Japanese" he had learned the hard way.

On October 12, the 3/5 departed early. They went up the West Road. Before reaching the junction with the East Road and Starlight Hill, they turned off to the right. At seven a.m., the 3/5 began to relieve the 2/5 on the northern side of the Japanese final defensive stronghold deep inside the ridges.[367] The mad jumble of terrain features had been given nicknames by the units that had been there previously. The army had held a blocking position in the area weeks ago. The Seventh had begun an assault there that eventually had been taken up by the 2/5. The problem with nicknames, however, was that men could disagree upon their application—particularly in

---

*The chain of islands that includes Okinawa was a recognized part of Japan long before World War II. The episode described here attests to the complicated relationship between the "Japanese" from Okinawa and the Japanese of the "home islands."

the wilds of Peleliu.[368] Relieving the 2/5 in their positions—the terrain forbade anything resembling a front line—took great care. Love Company had to make its way the farthest east, to the tip of Hill 140, before turning to face south. Love's left flank was secured by the hill's vertical cliff face. King moved on to Hill 140 to secure Love's right flank, with Item on King's right flank as the 3/5 prepared to push southward.

In order to orientate himself that morning, King Company's skipper, "Ack-Ack" Haldane, crept forward to review his sector. Japanese machine guns had pinned down the unit that his company was there to relieve. The substitution would be tricky. He needed to know where the enemy was. A sniper spotted him and shot him in the head. Up until that moment, Captain Andrew A. Haldane had been big enough to keep the men in his company believing they could accomplish this mission because, while other officers told their men, "You will do this," he had said, "We'll do this."[369] Word spread that the skipper had been killed. Haldane's runner, Dick Higgins, went berserk at the news and had to be held down by four men and carried to the rear. The loss touched everyone. It engulfed Gene Sledge in grief at the waste of such a talented, charismatic man.[370] Captain Haldane had embodied everything E. B. Sledge loved about the United States Marine Corps. The skipper had quietly expected his King Company to give only as much as he did: 100 percent. In shock and under fire, King Company found it difficult to get into position.

The company's executive officer, Lieutenant Thomas J. "Stumpy" Stanley, became the new skipper. The relief of the 2/5 went slowly that morning and lasted into the afternoon as the skipper ordered his platoon leaders to lead their men into forward positions.[371] The area the 3/5 entered had been prepared by Sherman tanks firing point-blank and Ronsons hosing down swaths hundreds of yards in diameter with napalm.[372] The departing marines left their spare grenades and ammunition in the foxholes to help the new guys.[373] The demolition crews reported that the three large caves in the area "had 400 to 500 japs dead or unconscious from the tank shells and napalm."[374] To get tied in, communications wire needed to be run to each of the platoons and the mortars situated in a secure spot. The marines also manhandled a 75mm pack howitzer up to a high point of their forward position, Waddie Ridge, and assembled it.[375] Short of both sandbags and sand, the marines also carried up pieces of armor in an attempt to create a safe emplacement for the operators of the gun. In these processes a few of the men from 2nd Battalion who were trying to get out of there were hit by enemy gunfire, which also wounded seven and killed one man in King.[376]

Burgin happened to be next to the man who was killed. A sniper had shot into his forehead. The corpsman came to take him away. Another marine took his place on the edge of the coral face, looking out over a steep drop of sixty feet to more ugly blobs of coral beyond. As a forward observer, Burgin took a place along the line, his #2 gun squad well behind him. Each man on the line carved out a place for himself within arm's reach of the other. "And we was sitting up there on the edge of that and firing across the valley and picking off any jap that showed himself on the other side." As night came, the men practiced their usual routine. Every other man on the line slept, while the others stood their turn on watch.

After midnight, Burgin heard two men fighting two holes away. He could not see much and he could not move from his position. Were more infiltrators coming? Would a marine get jumpy and begin shooting at the shadows? Burgin gripped his rifle and felt the adrenaline rush through him. A man screamed "one of the bloodiest screams I have ever known or heard in my life." It came from a body falling over the cliff. "And he screamed all the way down 'til he hit the bottom." Everyone went on alert, waiting to find out what happened next. When dawn broke hours later Burgin asked the other man what had happened. "I knew that I was gonna die," he replied, "because I couldn't break his hold." He had started to black out. The answer had come like a flash. "I reached behind the jap's head with one hand; and clawed his eyes out . . . with the other one." When the hold on him broke, the marine grabbed his assailant "by the nape of the neck and the seat of the pants, and threw him over the cliff." His story was one of many in the company that morning. Even with flares hanging in the sky, it had been a night of "continuous activity."[377]

Burgin's mortar squad had a busy day, delivering fire on the forward areas to provide cover for the patrols seeking avenues of advance. The terrain prevented the employment of armored vehicles. Riflemen from Item Company made some progress in their sector. They closed some caves, allowing King to move along Hill 140. A pack howitzer was brought up to blast away more obstructions.[378] Before dark, they strung some concertina wire in front of them. When they heard sounds that night, the marines pitched grenades. Daylight revealed six dead infiltrators.[379] The OP of the 3/5 reported that they could see the enemy going to the pond in the canyon at night. That sounded promising. The artillery had a new mission. It would bracket the pond with a barrage occasionally each night. The first night he tried it, Bucky Harris reported his artillery "netted 24 nips, and the second night a round dozen."[380]

King was not there to see the second night's tally. On October 15, guides brought up soldiers from the army's 81st Division, the Wildcats. Enemy machine-gun and sniper fire did not interrupt the relief of the marines' positions, a mark of the progress the 3/5 had made.[381] The 3rd Battalion, the next-to-last marine unit still in combat, walked out to the West Road, then north to the tip where they had once fought. While the rest of their regiment enjoyed the hot showers and screened mess halls near Purple Beach, the companies of the 3/5 took turns watching the northern ridge. More infiltrators were up there. Harris did send around a "generous beer ration" to them.

They had a day to relax. Once again, Sledge had a chance to speak with some soldiers. The army "seemed to regard us as rugged and doers of great things. It really amused me too, for we are no more rugged than they or any others. We are just American boys like they are." The 3/5 received word the following morning that they were going back into action. The army's assault team on Hill 140 had advanced too quickly and found itself under fire from positions on its flanks. The word was for the 3/5 to clean their weapons, top off their canteens, and wait. The trucks arrived. A few hours later, at eleven a.m., Colonel Harris told them to stand down. Since "he knew how grief stricken they would be at missing a last chance upon the hot coral ridges," Bucky issued another two cans of beer per man.[382]

In the days that followed, cots, hot food, showers, and movies became available.[383] The decompression required for some marines to enjoy these staples of civilian life could take time.[384] King Company was reorganized into two platoons. The only officers the company had left were Stumpy Stanley and Duke Ellington. Gene estimated that it had suffered 64 percent casualties. As bad as it was, the men of the 3/5 knew that their regimental commander had stuck his neck out for them. Bucky Harris had demanded that a new route into the objective be tried, rather than continuing to batter the regiment northward against the Five Sisters. They were very grateful for it.[385]

Although the daily mail call resumed, three days passed before Eugene could write his parents. The letters he received from them became more frantic with each advancing postmark. Their growing alarm at the gap in letters had been stoked by news from Europe of their oldest son. Edward had been wounded in action for the second time. On October 18 Eugene sent a brief note special delivery to let them know he was all right. The Red Cross distributed some stationery and he composed a longer letter. He apologized for the delay, for he knew how concerned they were, "but we were always in action except for a little while here or there and there was no mail service." He assured them that his weekly letters would resume. Thoughts of his parents let his mind wander to the woods and fields around Georgia Cottage, where "fall is just breaking," and out of the tropics, where "it's always stifling and smelly." His father would soon be out in all those beautiful fall colors, with his new dogs, hunting. "Just realize how much I'd love to be with you," he wrote. He hoped

Sid might get to join his father and asked that, if so, they take some photos. Gene also requested a picture of their new puppy. His parents had named their new dog Grunt.

On October 20 a brief ceremony took place at the U.S. Armed Forces Cemetery Peleliu Number One; 1,058 men from all service branches had been laid to rest about fifty yards inland from Orange Beach Two.[386] Captain Haldane was buried just about exactly where he had led King Company ashore on D-day. If he attended, Gene would have dwelt once again on "Prelude," the Kipling poem that had been festering inside of him for four weeks:

> I have eaten your bread and salt.
> I have drunk your water and wine.
> The deaths ye died I have watched beside,
> And the lives ye led were mine.
> Was there aught that I did not share
> In vigil or toil or ease,—
> One joy or woe that I did not know,
> Dear hearts across the seas?
> I have written the tale of our life
> For a sheltered people's mirth,
> In jesting guise—but ye are wise,
> And ye know what the jest is worth.[387]

The enemy dead numbered approximately 10,685. The corpses not sealed inside their caves were dumped into mass graves at convenient locations by working parties from service units.[388]

On October 20 General MacArthur waded ashore on the island of Leyte in the Philippines. In what was hailed as a daring move, MacArthur had bypassed the most southern island of the chain, Mindanao. His return received worldwide news coverage. The world considered it a dramatic step toward the end of the war. To Shifty Shofner, the man he reviled had chosen to invade a smaller and less important island. Skipping Mindanao meant that the hour of liberation for his friends in the Davao Penal Colony had been postponed. Their suffering would continue.

*   *   *

ALL THE INK DEVOTED TO THE ACCOUNTS OF MACARTHUR IN THE PHILIPPINES seemed to drive the Battle of Peleliu from the front pages of the newspapers. The reason for taking Peleliu, to protect MacArthur's flank while he invaded Mindanao, had obviously been rendered moot. As the men of King Company rested and read their mail and listened to the news, these two facts were clear to all who paid attention. Gene Sledge paid attention and the thought of all that sacrifice having been in vain engendered within him a profound bitterness. "It was all for nothing."[389]

Gene and his friends would have also noted unhappily that the units around the airfield and the rest of the Fifth Marines at Purple Beach enjoyed a higher standard of living than the 3/5 up on the northern tip of Peleliu. Where they were, enemy stragglers came down out of the hills occasionally. It never occurred to the enlisted men to try to get the Japanese to surrender. The marines shot them immediately.[390] Burgin watched his friend Jim Burke casually borrow a rifle from a bystander, shoot a Japanese wading in the sea, and say thank you as he handed the weapon back. Watching Jim shoot to kill, Burgin was struck by "how damn calm he was."[391]

Ten days of rest made barely a dent in their exhaustion. On October 27, trucks drove them out to Purple Beach. The 3/5 rejoined the rest of its regiment. A fleet of DUKWs began driving the regiment out to the troopship bit by bit.[392] King Company assembled on the beach and Sledge watched as "some joker broke out an old box camera from somewhere and took a posed picture of the survivors of K Co."[393] More than a few managed to smile.

The Fifth Regiment had come to Peleliu in three troop transports and six LSTs. The "survivors," as Sledge called them, fit aboard one ship, USS *Sea Runner*.[394] They struggled to climb the net from the DUKW up to the deck. The men of the 3/5 reported to compartment A2 of the ship, put their gear on their bunks and stood by until all men were loaded and the regulations were issued. The hours for chow were announced and each man would get in line with his mess kit and his new mess card. Marines from 3rd Battalion would stand guard duty on days five and six. All troops would stand inspection daily at ten thirty a.m. A security inspection would be held at ten p.m. At least servings of cold milk and fresh bread followed the regimentation. High seas slowed the loading of their gear and two days of regimented life aboard *Sea Runner* passed before she finally weighed anchor.[395] Scuttlebutt had it that they were headed for Australia.

The crew of *Sea Runner* kept the ship's clocks accurate as they crossed time zones, which meant waking the marines up an hour earlier on some mornings, a requirement sure to make the troops unhappy. The ship steamed into Pavuvu's Macquitti Bay on November 7. The 3/5 unloaded before noon to find large quantities of mail, beer, Coke, and rotation lists waiting for them.[396] Most of the men who had joined up after the attack on Pearl Harbor and who had fought on Guadalcanal found their names on the rotation lists. With a few exceptions, they were going home. The first shipment of replacements had already arrived.[397]

As Gene disembarked, he saw a Red Cross woman serving the men a cold drink. The sight shocked him. He had seen American women on Pavuvu and at the big base on Guadalcanal. His world of anguish, however, could not admit the beauty and civilization she represented. "She's got no more business here than some damn politician," he thought. A lieutenant saw Sledge hesitate and said, "OK, sonny, move out." Sledge turned to see the untanned skin and crisp uniform of "a brand-spanking new boot-lieutenant."[398] The new officer looked into the veteran's eyes and saw nothingness. The sight made the lieutenant uncomfortable and he quickly found something else to do. The moment represented part of what Eugene Sledge had wanted to gain by being a marine: the self-confidence of the combat veteran. As it turned out, though, the blank stare came not from the easy calmness of one who had been tested and knew his own courage. Scenes of naked atrocity clouded his vision, producing an inability to care.

LIEUTENANT MICHEEL ARRIVED BACK IN ALAMEDA, CALIFORNIA, ON NOVEMber 1, 1944, much as he had in December of 1942. This time, however, he was prepared for the quick sorting job the navy was going to give the veterans of Bombing Two. He made some phone calls: to his girlfriend, Jean Miller, in Philadelphia and to his old skipper, Ray Davis, still flying a desk at a base near Norfolk. On November 2, Lieutenant Micheel was ordered to report to NAS Jacksonville, Florida. Mike was going to be an instructor after he enjoyed a one-month furlough. He asked for and received permission to travel by personal transportation, but he took a train home to Davenport. He saw his parents and he paid another visit to John Lough's parents.

Trading in the '36 Dodge coupe he had stored in a shed for a newer Dodge sedan required only a little cash. Getting gasoline was the trick, since it was still rationed, much to everyone's disgust. The navy had given him some coupons, but not enough to drive to Jacksonville, Florida, by way of Pennsylvania. Waiting for him when he arrived in Davenport, though, was an envelope of gas cards supplied by Jean's father. Jean's enclosed note had a funny story about how her dad had finagled the extra coupons. The cards gave Micheel enough gas to get to Philadelphia, where he spent a long weekend with Jean and her family. He drove to

Norfolk to spend a night catching up with Ray, who gave him enough cards for the drive to Jacksonville.

ON NOVEMBER 2, 1944, MAJOR GENERAL WILLIAM RUPERTUS REPORTED ON THE fitness of Lieutenant Colonel Austin Shofner, who was on the division staff. In many ways, Shofner had improved. Most of the categories were now marked "Excellent," including training of troops, handling of men and handling of officers, and he earned a mark of "Outstanding" in loyalty. The provost marshal fell down to "Very Good" in cooperation, in intelligence, judgment, presence of mind, and leadership. For all that he liked about Shofner, Rupertus believed that "as previously reported, his experience as a POW has made this individual highly excitable." While Shofner's incarceration had "not affected his courage or devotion to duty," the general recommended more recuperation for Shofner before he again saw combat. General Rupertus wrote the fitness report on the day he himself was relieved of his command and summarily shipped stateside for his own failure on Peleliu.

Soon after his return to Pavuvu, Shofner also received a letter from the office of the Commandant of the Marine Corps regarding his claim for reimbursement of the personal property he had been forced to abandon in Olongapo on Christmas Day 1941. While his personal clothing, including a number of exotic items, such as a white sharkskin suit, fell within the corps' guidelines, a lot of items did not appear on the "approved schedule of allowances," including the selection of women's lace negligees, the collection of women's handbags, and the elegant household items like the carved ivory elephants. The director of personnel had decided not to factor in the "depreciation" that Shofner had included in his claim, however, and awarded him every last cent of the claim, $2,621.90.

Lieutenant Colonel Shofner had a visit from one of his former sergeants, Hank Boyes of K/3/5. Hank had recovered from his wounds and had come to ask for help. Sergeant Boyes told Shifty a story about D-day, when he had used a tank to clear out some key enemy emplacements. "I got up on the tank," Boyes reported, "and told him [the tank commander] we were K-3rd but I didn't say 5th [regiment] and he was still with us till 2pm and out of ammo before he found out we were not the 7th Marines."[399] Put another way, Hank had used a little trickery to keep the tank around to help King in combat. When the tank commander, a Sergeant Meyers, found out the truth, he had raced back toward his assigned regiment, but not before Meyers's superior officer had noticed his absence. Meyers now faced a court-martial.

Shifty enjoyed Hank's story and was happy to tell Meyers's CO that his tanker had not been derelict in his duty. The charges against Meyers were thrown out.

PAVUVU DID NOT LOOK SO BAD TO EUGENE SLEDGE NOW. NO INFILTRATORS IN-terrupted his sleep. In a rather amazing display of devotion, his parents had sent him eighteen packages while he was in combat. He did not reply immediately, however. He slept, munched on snacks, took two to three showers per day, and began reading some of the new magazines and letters. The *Mobile Press* had Peleliu as a front-page story.[400] It stressed "the most crushing aerial bombardment" that had preceded the invasion. Gene would have noticed a critical fact that probably escaped most readers: the nine-day preinvasion bombardment had been focused not on Peleliu, but "on Babelthuap, largest of the Palaus." The newspaper assured its readers that the Marine Corps had "coordinated" its offensive against the enemy stronghold "with General MacArthur."

The Mobile newspapers carried a lot of stories about the U.S. Army's march across France, where his older brother Edward served. Among the many letters Eugene opened from his parents, one informed him that Edward had been promoted to captain. A letter from Sidney Phillips described how he had almost been killed by a hurricane at his base in Boca Chica. All of the personnel of the naval air station and all of their airplanes had been evacuated in advance of the powerful storm— all except for the marines, who had been left there to guard whatever survived. Sid wrote his story as if it was a hilarious joke.

Eugene did not feel much like writing. The Marine Corps' birthday on November 10, an anniversary that had merited an effusive letter a year ago, passed without mention. He went to see Sid's friends in H/2/1. He had to find out how Sid's friends had fared. Among the men he said hello to would have been Deacon, who had survived Peleliu and was waiting for a trip home. The 1st Division had never suffered casualties like it had on Peleliu and a lot of marines felt a similar need. All over the island, men were showing up at other companies to check on a buddy. Bill Leyden, one of King Company's riflemen, went around asking after friends. Some were in the hospital on the island of Banika nearby. Others had been wounded so bad they were on a ship bound for the States. Often, though, he asked about a good friend and "his buddies would—in the tent—would tell you how it happened to him and then you'd stare . . . and they'd say, sit down and they'd offer you a beer if they had a beer . . . because they knew just how you felt. And then you'd leave and go back to your outfit." Gene already had heard a fair amount about the fate of the First Marines. Deacon's 2/1 had suffered higher casualties in five days on Peleliu than the 3/5 had in thirty. As a veteran, Deacon had been shocked by the enemy's fortifications that had withstood the relentless pounding. Peleliu, he concluded, had been "Japan's Corregidor."

The first time Sledge put pen to paper would have been to capture some of the specifics of the battles of Peleliu and Ngesebus.[401] The memories he could not forget, but the details would be lost if not recorded, and E. B. Sledge understood the importance of the details. After a few weeks, he began to write his parents regularly again. The belated birthday wishes from his parents began to arrive in late November and their love moved him. He responded in kind. The seashells he had collected on Peleliu had survived and he had them strung into a necklace for his mother. "I carried them through that operation & Ngesebus," he told her. "I hope because those dainty little seashells came from such a dreadful place that you won't fail to see their beauty and know . . . you were in my mind continually." As he was writing a letter to his parents, the mail call came. As usual, he was handed a package. It contained a Colt .45 automatic pistol—just the thing for nights in combat. While he shared the goodies with his tent mates, the .45 became "the apple of my eye. I care for it like a baby." The pistol represented the deep connection between them and their shared love of hunting. "Pop, I know I'm closer to you than many boys dream of being with their fathers."

November 29 saw another ship full of replacements arrive at the steel dock. A large number of the veterans found themselves turning in their weapons and preparing to ship out. Sergeant St. Elmo Murray Haney shipped out. After only a few days on Peleliu, "Pop" Haney had decided combat "was a young man's game" and taken himself out; no one thought ill of the forty-six-year-old man who had volunteered for combat duty. Haney transferred stateside after being promoted to gunnery sergeant.[402] Richard Higgins, Captain Haldane's former runner, also received a ticket home after three battles. King's new skipper, Stumpy Stanley, gave Higgins their late captain's personal effects: a pocketbook, and flag, and a few other mementos. On behalf of the company, Stumpy ordered Higgins to go see Andy Haldane's parents. A lot of King Company gathered at the pier as the veterans of Guadalcanal walked up the gangway. "The Rubber Lipped Division Band did its damnedest," Stumpy noted approvingly, to give them "a proper send off."[403] The band played the song they had learned to love in Melbourne, "Waltzing Matilda." It had become their anthem. Like the Old Breed before them, the "Canal Men" sailed for home, entrusting their 1st Division to the next generation.

The draft of replacements meant reorganization. Sergeant Hank Boyes became gunnery sergeant of King Company.[404] Lieutenant George Loveday, who had served with the 3/5's weapons company on Peleliu, became the company's executive officer. R. V. Burgin was promoted to sergeant and oversaw the mortar section, which expanded from two guns to three. The mortar section lost Duke Ellington to a transfer and gained Lieutenant Robert MacKenzie, fresh from Officer Candidate School (OCS). A number of other new lieutenants joined the company, especially in the rifle platoons. Hank Boyes took the new officers aside one by one and said, "Lieutenant, I'm going to introduce you to your NCOs. They are good, proven men. You can learn a lot by observing and being with them and asking them questions."[405]

Eugene had not been promoted. He had, however, earned what he had long coveted: the reputation, as the saying went, of being "a good man in the field." The respect of his peers meant everything to him. Being a good marine on Peleliu was the bar to which all the replacements would have to measure up, regardless of rank. The new arrivals could not mistake the angry "1,000 yard stare" that some of the vets had, or their ennui.[406] The replacements would learn who the heroes of K/3/5 were in the same manner in which the Old Breed had once greeted the Canal marines: by telling them they were unlikely to ever measure up. While every veteran of King Company had stories of courage to share, one name stood out.

In early December, the working parties finished carving out a new baseball diamond from the coconut trees on Pavuvu. They hung a large painted plaque on a wooden stand bearing the inscription "Haldane Field."[407] Thirty marines joined the honor guard and fired a three-volley rifle salute. These thirty marines had been led by Captain Andrew Haldane during the "Battle of Suicide Creek" on Cape Gloucester, and had followed him across the wastelands of Peleliu and Ngesebus. Of all the dear friends they had lost, he was the one they had to honor together. Andrew Haldane had seen himself as a man fulfilling his duty rather than a career officer.[408] He had joined the Marine Corps reserve while attending Bowdoin College, completing OCS in time to serve on Guadalcanal, where he had proven himself. He had fallen forty-eight hours short of his trip home. At the dedication of the field one of the majors from battalion HQ tried to say what Sergeant Hank Boyes later wrote. "Haldane was a very outstanding leader with calmness, consideration of all possibilities and the courage to carry out his decision. He certainly set the example and had the respect of every man in K Co."[409] After the ceremony, the guys took off their shirts, put on their shorts, and the regimental officers played a team from the 3/5 on a beautiful sunny afternoon. The home opener at Haldane Field went scoreless until late in the game, when the enlisted men drove in two runs.

*   *   *

Lieutenant Colonel Shofner looked at the rotation lists hoping not to see his name. He wanted more than anything to lead again in combat, in part because he was a professional marine and in part because he had to expunge the blotch on his record. Two things worked in his favor. General Rupertus's disappearance was one. The other was the looming possibility that some veterans of Guadalcanal would be required to fight a fourth campaign. It posed, as all senior officers well knew, a "serious morale problem."[410] This problem was averted by a plan to rotate home almost six thousand enlisted men and officers. The plan, begun in early November, would take several months to complete because a man was released only when another arrived to take his place. When the process was completed, the division expected its ranks to be divided roughly into thirds. One-third of the men would be veterans of two battles (Cape Gloucester and Peleliu); one-third of one invasion; and one-third would have no combat experience. An experienced officer who wanted to stay, therefore, might be needed.

The transfer orders that came to him at three thirty p.m. on December 15 could not have been more of a surprise. The new commanding general of the 1st Division, General Pedro del Valle, found Lieutenant Colonel Shofner in the officers' mess and tossed him an envelope, saying, "Read it and weep."[411] The orders notified Shofner that he would be transported "to such place as the 14th Army Corps may be located . . . you will report to the Commanding General, Fourteenth Army Corps for temporary duty as an observer or to perform such duties as may be assigned to you by the commanding general of the Corps or other competent authority." Put another way, Shifty Shofner had been assigned as a Marine Corps liaison and advisor on guerrilla affairs to the command of Douglas MacArthur for the invasion of Luzon. Shifty hustled off to get his bags packed. He and MacArthur were returning to the island where their wars had begun.

In December the pace of training for the 5th Division on the big island of Hawaii slowed. More weekend passes were handed out, although the only destination was the small, rather quiet town of Hilo. Their base on the Parker Ranch had a USO club and a PX, but these did not get a man very far from his routine. The marines played a lot of sports. Of all the games, getting out on the gridiron was the most dangerous. The rigorous training had them in top shape. They knew the pause meant they would ship out soon. It tended to make a man do anything—playing poker, drinking, playing football, or fighting—with abandon. Gunnery Sergeant John Basilone stuck to softball.

The process of packing up their gear had begun when the sergeants of the Twenty-seventh Regiment threw a Christmas party. Few officers were invited.[412] It was the kind of evening when the marines provided some of their own entertainment. Some doggerel written by the 1st Marine Division in Australia had become a favorite.

Bless 'em all, Bless 'em all
The long and the short and the tall
There will be no promotion
This side of the ocean
So cheer up, me lads, bless 'em all.
They sent for MacArthur to come to Tulagi
But General MacArthur said, No.
He gave for the reason it wasn't the season,
And besides, they had no U.S.O.

Taken from an English drinking song, it was the kind of ditty that had new verses added every time it was sung. A few days after Christmas, the Twenty-seventh Regimental Combat Team began departing the camp. Another two weeks and the New Year's Eve celebration, however, passed before John's battalion got on the trucks to ride to the dock. They boarded USS *Hansford* and steamed around the Hawaiian Islands for a few days, watching while naval officers practiced maneuvering the big fleet.

The days of boredom ended with their ship pulling into Pearl Harbor. After being in Hawaii for six months, the 1st Battalion would at last get its chance to go ashore in the big city. Standing on the ship's deck, they could see that ships of every kind jammed the harbor, including the transports holding about twenty thousand marines of the 4th Division. John had to tell his men that liberty would be granted to only a quarter of his men each day. *Hansford* and the ships weighed anchor two days later, much to the disgust of half the men. The fleet stood out from Pearl Harbor on January 21, prepared to take on the Japanese.

The next morning, though, found them drilling again, this time as a division. The careful landing plans disintegrated into a snafu.[413] Ships as big as LCIs missed their marks; smaller boats swamped. The marines raced out of their LVTs and toward their objectives. The soft volcanic ash made movement difficult for men and machines. The ash pooled around their feet; it rose in great clouds of fine dust.[414] They were told that this island closely resembled Island X, their target.[415] After a cold dinner of K rations, they spent an even colder night on the island. *Hansford* and the rest of the fleet returned the division to Pearl, where half the men could debark each day. Free beer and sporting equipment were made available near the docks. Honolulu was eight miles away and every mode of transportation was strained to capacity. Lots of marines chose to buck the crowds, feeling the need to pull a liberty in the big city.

Gunnery sergeants had a lot easier time having fun in Hawaii than the average enlisted man. John and his friend Watters managed to look up John's brother George.[416] They passed a few pleasant hours and took another photo for their parents. It was not like John to get serious about what awaited them. As they were leaving, he said, "See you on the beach."[417] Before he shipped out, John wrote his mom to tell her he was okay. He apologized for not writing sooner, "for we were a little busy," and let her know George "sure is looking good mom." He had gotten a letter from Mary and Delores just the other day. "Tell Delores everybody liked her picture she sure came out beautiful in it." He sent "love and kisses to all. Love always, Johnny."[418]

SID PHILLIPS SAW A NOTICE FOR THE V-12 PROGRAM ON THE BULLETIN BOARD OF NAS Boca Chica. It offered the chance to become an officer, a prospect for which Sid had no enthusiasm, and the chance to earn college credits, about which he was "extremely anxious." The first stop was his unit's top sergeant, who checked the private first class's folder and exclaimed that he had never seen a higher score on the general aptitude test. Sid had the qualifications. An officer had to sign the application, though, and they both knew their major was a mean and vindictive man who might step in Sid's way. The sergeant said he had a way around the major if Sid could be patient.

At the end of the year, a colonel from Washington, D.C., came to inspect the marine detachment. Colonel Hill wore the 1st Division patch, so Sid knew he was "one of us." The colonel finished his inspection with a short talk to the marines standing before him on the parade ground. He offered them the chance to come see him in the office if they needed something. "As he said this the top sergeant looked right at me and nodded his head ever so slightly."

Sid stowed his gear and raced over to the office. The top sergeant appeared as well, making sure Colonel Hill understood. Hill looked over the application and put it in his briefcase. He turned to Sid "and told me to pack my seabag, that the papers would be on the Commandant's desk Monday morning." Hill asked Sid if he had ever met General Vandegrift. Sid told him a story about bathing in the Lunga River on Guadalcanal with a lot of others. A bar of soap had floated down to him.

Sid looked upstream to see his commanding general with his hand out, asking for it back. Hill laughed and promised to remind Vandegrift of it, at which point Sid "saluted and floated out of the office. I wanted to hug the top sergeant."

On Wednesday morning, Sid was told to report to the office. "The top said, 'Here are your papers. You catch the bus at the main gate in one hour.' My cobbers carried my seabag out to the main gate and bid me goodbye." The bus off the Florida Keys and on to Miami had plenty of seats. "It seemed the pattern in the service," he observed, was "to constantly alternate between mountain tops of joy and deep valleys of misery."

Colonel Shofner met up with the U.S. Army's Fourteenth Corps in Port Moresby, New Guinea—not a long trip from Pavuvu. Shifty "had no love for the Army and no interest in serving with them. He had heard that all of the men who served with MacArthur were chosen for their loyalty to MacArthur and not for their ability on the battlefield."[419] He reported to the corps headquarters and was assigned to its 37th Division as an observer. Without any official duties, he stepped aboard USS *Mount McKinley* on December 31 for the trip from New Guinea to Luzon. His ship sailed past Mindanao, still in enemy hands. A week later, as the convoy of ships neared the northern tip of the Philippines, Japanese planes flew out to attack them. These planes did not attempt to drop their bombs on the ships. These planes were bombs. Their pilots attempted to crash themselves into the largest, nearest ship they could find, preferably an aircraft carrier.

Shofner watched the air attacks, which the Japanese government had referred to in the Tokyo newspaper as its Kamikaze Special Attack Force; they had been expected. The enemy suicide planes did not hit *McKinley*. They struck other ships in the convoy, however, by the dozen. The navy pilots aboard the escort carriers lived on full alert, as did the ships' AA gunners. The numbers of kamikaze involved in this effort and the praise of the special attack force found in the Japanese media betrayed the rapid growth of a serious problem. The eagerness of the enemy to commit mass suicide in order to raise the cost of the U.S. victory came as no surprise to a veteran of Peleliu.

The invasion day bombardment was also something Shofner had seen before, although not to this scale. One thousand ships filled Lingayen Gulf on January 9 as the opening salvos from the battlewagons cleared away all life-forms in the soldiers' paths. The 37th landed that day and so did Shifty at the same location the Japanese had invaded in 1941. He watched the companies and battalion perform. General MacArthur had 131,000 combat troops and another 80,000 in support. Very quickly Shofner became highly critical of the army leadership at the corps level and above. The assault, he felt, took too long to drive inland.* His disgust came partly from interservice rivalry; it resulted also from his intense desire to free the Americans locked inside Cabanatuan POW Camp Number One.

His attitude won him few friends on the Fourteenth Corps staff. Shifty also believed that the army commanders "brushed aside" the guerrillas, refusing to use them for anything more than scouts and intelligence. Although he had no direct contact with General MacArthur, Shofner came to believe that the general refused to involve the Filipinos because they had continued to fight the enemy long after he had fled. The attitude, one Shofner considered prevalent among army officers, angered him because he believed the Filipino guerrillas were "heroes" who had "committed their lives and fortunes and their sacred honor to fight the Japanese and care for their people."

The officers of the 37th Division would have questioned the logic of Shofner's insistence that one of the most powerful invasion forces ever assembled should coordinate its advance with the large and well-intentioned, but fractious and ill-equipped, guerrilla movements on Luzon. To the soldiers, the visiting marine colonel's assessment also overlooked the decades of service in the Philippines by General MacArthur and some of his top generals. Moreover, MacArthur's staff had been in constant communication with the guerrillas for years. Shifty had firsthand knowledge of MacArthur's relationship with the guerrillas, however, just as he had with the general's leadership of the battle of Bataan, and it led him to a different conclusion.

In a meeting on January 23 Shifty Shofner insisted that the 37th Division needed to focus on helping the POWs. Thousands of Americans had died slow deaths and had been buried in unmarked graves. To rescue the surviving POWs, the soldiers would need the help of the Filipino guerrillas. The army officers brought in a stenographer to type up his comments.[420] Shifty gave a description of Cabanatuan and Camp O'Donnell and Bilibid Prison. Having been a prisoner, though, meant that his geography was a little fuzzy. He believed, however, that this memo was exactly the reason he had been brought to Luzon.[421] That same day, he found himself detached from further duty and sent to the airport to await transport. On the twenty-seventh he boarded a flight to Guadalcanal and from there winged his way to Pavuvu.

* * *

---

*Although not made public at the time, General MacArthur agreed with Shofner that General Krueger's assault lacked speed and aggressiveness.

A LOT OF THE MARINES SPENT THEIR IDLE HOURS ON PAVUVU FIGURING OUT WAYS to ferment raisins or anything handy into moonshine known as "raisin jack." The beer bottles issued a few times a month did not contain enough to wash down the boredom and not all marines were interested in the stacks of books in the recreation hall. After one beer ration was issued, Eugene "sat on my bunk and watched the drunks beat each other. Finally after tearing up their bunks they were quieted by the O.D. [Officer of the Day]. The whole thing was certainly disgusting to me but to them was more fun. So I continue to sell my beer to the suckers and let them show their caveman instincts for bashing each other." At least the poker games—which Eugene noticed tended to end with guys "at each others throats"—were usually held in the tent next door.

Gene liked to hang out at his tent with the men in his squad. Drill or an inspection usually took up the morning, but in the afternoon they had time to shoot the breeze. Aside from an occasional steak or scoop of ice cream, the chow they were served was, like the training, part of the hardship they endured together. They shared the goodies their families sent. No family sent as much as Dr. and Mrs. Sledge, but Snafu got a big can of fried chicken for Christmas, which he shared. Gene smoked one of the pipes his father had sent him and showed off some of the Confederate money from his "good old Rebel country." The marines who had been in Australia told so many stories, the new guys assumed "the Battle of Melbourne may have been the biggest battle the Marine Corps ever fought."[422] Snafu might have had something to do with enhancing that reputation, but not R. V. Burgin. His time in Melbourne had been devoted to one Miss Florence Riseley and Burgin had promised to make it back to her. Gene read a bit from one of his mother's recent letters out loud. She declared that "Peleliu was spoken of with awe." His buddy George jumped in with, "Yeah, with aw hell!" The joke got a good laugh. It was just a little moment, one of many that Gene treasured. He belonged.

In the New Year the 1st Division began to train its men in "street fighting," which encouraged the enlisted men to guess about the location of their next assignment. Formosa, mainland China, and Japan itself were mentioned.[423] Gene's mother always wanted to know about what was going on in her son's life. She asked questions. She wondered how his experience compared with his brother's war in Europe. "Ed's outfit," Gene replied, "certainly is good to get so many commendations. I hear we got the Prez citation for Peleliu. I don't know if it's true or not."* When Mrs. Sledge began to wonder about his next assignment, he wrote: "Don't try and figure out the things

---

*Sledge was referring to the Presidential Unit Citation. The 1st Marine Division had indeed been awarded this distinction for Peleliu, as it had for the Battle of Guadalcanal.

the higher-ups do—I long ago learned its useless figuring. Realize we are in God's hands, and he will unite us all at Georgia Cottage before long."

AUSTIN SHOFNER RETURNED TO PAVUVU AFTER A BITTER BATTLE WITH THE U.S. Army on Luzon. He did not arrive to find a new battalion awaiting his command. The one bright spot for him was that he had "found both a friend and an inspiring leader in General Pedro del Valle," CO of the 1st Division. Del Valle had problems because "the departure of the experienced men was not well timed with the arrival of the new men."[424] Since some of his senior officers were not eligible for stateside duty, the general had begun sending them to Australia for a long furlough. It made the training schedule difficult to keep. It was a problem with which Shofner was familiar and he did his best to help his new CO.

A SERIES OF BUSES AND TRAINS TOOK SID PHILLIPS AND HIS SEABAG BACK TO NEW River, North Carolina. He arrived on a cold January day in his dress greens and was given a ride to his barracks. The base he had known as New River had become a sprawling complex of buildings now called Camp Lejeune. He threw his bag on a cot. The others there said hello and someone asked, "What state are you from?"

"Alabama," he replied in a loud voice. A big guy asked, "What city?"

"Mobile."

"Me, too," said the big guy, and just like that Sid had a new cobber. Marion Sims, nicknamed "Bunk," had seen action at Saipan and Tinian. They had time to get to know one another because the V-12 program had not officially started its semester. "We were told the Marine Corps was experimenting with the idea of putting combat veterans into the V-12 program because so many V-12 students had been intentionally flunking out of the program so they could get into a combat unit." Before they attended classes, though, the two hundred or so marines in Sid's class first had to endure several weeks of harsh discipline. Sid found it to be "every bit as bad as Parris Island." The program stripped them of their ranks and also demanded they remain single until they completed it, at which point they would be commissioned as second lieutenants. A number of men disliked the loss in pay suffered from being busted in rank and the attendant abuse. They were allowed to return to their former ranks and stations. Sid "took it gladly" because he "had had enough of the mud and troopships and C rations."

*   *   *

THE 1ST BATTALION OF THE TWENTY-SEVENTH MARINES BOARDED USS *Hans-ford* and shipped out on January 27. The battalion's commanding officer, Colonel Butler, waited two days before announcing their destination on the ship's public address system.[425] He confirmed what some of John Basilone's men had heard already: they were sailing for an island called Iwo Jima. The 5th Marine Division and the 4th Marine Division were going to invade an island closer to Japan than any marine had yet been. Detailed briefings would follow.

All the briefings involved maps. Maps of the Pacific showed Iwo Jima in relation to the airfields on Saipan, from which the air corps' B-29s flew to bomb Japan. Other maps focused solely on the target island, or showed the different sectors into which "Iwo" had been divided. Each navy ship would bombard one sector. A lot of ships meant the sectors were small. Big, 3-D maps made of plaster indicated heights and features. For the next few weeks, the marines spent a part of every day in front of at least one map or aerial photo, being briefed by some officer. Each man was told in some detail why Iwo Jima had to be taken. Each man came to know the terrain and the location of the enemy's emplacements. The men of 1st Battalion were told why the Battle of Iwo Jima would last three days, five at the outside.[426]

That the Japanese would fight fanatically until death was a given. U.S. intelligence estimated that the Imperial High Command had committed some fourteen thousand troops to hold it.* The island's complement of forces was also suspected of including a number of prostitutes.[427] To soften up this force, the army's bombers had begun dropping bombs on it every day for three months. Even a cursory look at the aerial photos showed that the buildings that had once dotted the island had disappeared. The navy ships would begin shelling the island three days in advance of the landing. Counting all of the reinforcing units (including the 3rd Marine Division), the "expeditionary force" topped 111,000 men in 500 ships. In less than forty-five minutes, 482 amtracs and an array of other amphibious craft would deliver 9,000 marines from the 5th Division and the 4th Division on Iwo's shore.

John Basilone had never cared much for lectures. Iwo Jima, like Guadalcanal, had an airfield that the Japanese held and the United States needed. The marines had to go ashore and seize it. The strategic logic probably made little impression on John. Certainly he understood the basics. Taking the airfield would make it easier for the B-29s to ignite the paper and wood structures in Tokyo. The bigger the fire, the sooner they all went home.

---

*The intelligence estimates given to the marines aboard ship were wrong. The Japanese had reinforced Iwo Jima with roughly twenty-two thousand men.

Briefings concerning his battalion's specific mission captured more of John's interest. The 1st and 2nd Battalions would land in the center of the long invasion beach. Futatsu Rock, the lone rock feature jutting out of the water just off the vast length of beach, divided their landing. John's 1st Battalion would land on the right side of Futatsu at Red Beach Two; Baker Company on the left. The colonel placed Able Company in reserve. John's C/1/27 added to B/1/27 meant about five hundred marines crossing Red Beach Two at H hour. In concert with the companies of 2nd Battalion, they would seize the southern end of the airfield, known as Motoyama Number One, about six hundred yards inland. An advance of another fifteen hundred yards would bring them to the opposite shore. Once on the far side they would swing right and head north and work with the 4th Division to seize the wider part of the island.

At a minimum, the marines were told, they must establish a solid beachhead by day's end because the Japanese were going to mount an all-out banzai attack either the first evening or early the next morning.[428] The enemy only had enough fortifications to house four of their nine infantry battalions. The remaining five battalions and their tanks were, according to the intelligence officers, going to charge the ma-

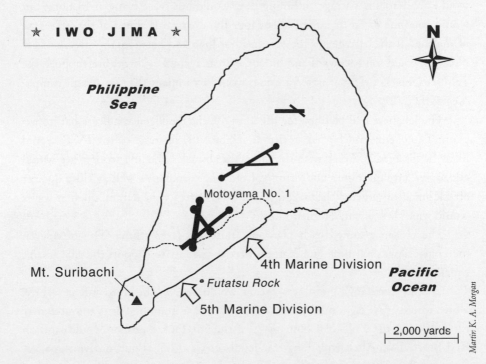

★ **I W O J I M A** ★

Philippine Sea

N

Motoyama No. 1

Mt. Suribachi

° *Futatsu Rock*

4th Marine Division

5th Marine Division

Pacific Ocean

2,000 yards

Martin: K. A. Morgan

rine lines.[429] Once this banzai charge had been destroyed, the advance was expected to roll forward quickly.

Charlie Company's first challenge, as photographs of Red Beach Two showed, were the steep gradients in the sand created by the ocean's waves. To assist the scaling of these so-called terraces, the first wave of 1st Battalion would bring scaling ladders. Once across the several terraces on the wide beach, though, Charlie Company would encounter a relatively flat area all the way across the island, intersected by Motoyama's runways and taxiways. Bomb craters were everywhere.

After studying the terrain, the intelligence section rolled clear overlays over the maps. The overlays marked the Japanese pillboxes and bunkers in red. There was a lot of red. Enough enemy positions of various sizes had been marked in red to cause a man's gut to wrench, or even make it seem pointless trying to memorize where they all were.[430] Officers explained that the navy's preinvasion bombardment would last three days. On D-day, the battleship *New York* would handle Charlie Company's landing sector. Once they got off the beach and onto the airfield, they would be in the zone of the heavy cruiser *Salt Lake City*. The end of the airfield also marked the start of the zone of the battleship *Arkansas*. The massive batteries on these ships would fire a "rolling barrage," meaning they would not cease firing at H hour, but would continue to fire at targets about four hundred yards ahead of the first wave of marines. If the barrage got too far ahead of John and his men, the stream of explosions would roll backward and hit some areas again. For direct fire support, the 75mm cannons of eight armored amtracs would accompany the two assault companies of the 1/27.

The Japanese had planned for the amtracs, the intelligence officers had to explain. The enemy had buried steel rails in the surf, so some of the LVTs would likely be disabled.[431] Along with the undersea obstacles, the first troop wave would encounter antitank mines and drums of burning gasoline, as well as "close quarter attack units," or targeted banzai charges.[432] To counteract the flames, the first waves would wipe "flash cream" on their faces.

The officers planned each platoon's route across Iwo Jima. The fifty-seven men of Basilone's machine-gun platoon were divided up to support the rifle assault squads.[433]

Charlie Company's gunnery sergeant would land in the third infantry wave, which would arrive eight minutes after the armored amtracs.[434] Thirty minutes after the first wave, the tanks of Company A of the 5th Tank Battalion would land on Red Beach Two. After explaining the details of C/1/27's assault on Iwo Jima, officers gave instructions on handling POWs, identifying enemy aircraft, and combat first aid. Since the Japanese often yelled "Corpsman!" in order to shoot them, 1st Battalion was told to yell "Tallulah!" if they needed medical attention. Most of the marines would have recognized that the code word with all the *l*s was the first name of a popular actress, Ms. Tallulah Bankhead.[435] Single-dose dispensers of morphine, called syrettes, were also distributed. In between lectures, the seasoned NCOs insisted on the daily cleaning of weapons; not to relieve boredom, but because the salty air corrupted metal at an alarming rate.[436]

The convoy arrived at Saipan on February 11, where the 3rd Division waited to join the 5th and the 4th divisions. Basilone's Charlie Company disembarked *Hansford* and stepped aboard LST 929.[437] It was one of the three LSTs carrying the 1/27's assault waves and their amtracs.[438] The marines would have considered the discomfort they experienced aboard their "Large Slow Target" as the quintessential experience of being a marine; the swabbies, however, told them these particular ships had just come from launching the army's invasion of Luzon.[439] Around them, five hundred ships took their places. The Fifth Amphibious Corps, created for this mission, had been joined.

As always, a few days of inexplicable boredom had to pass. Another full-scale landing exercise on a nearby island had to follow. Basilone ended up spending a lot of time on a ship in Saipan's harbor. On clear days the gleaming silver bodies of giant four-engine B-29 bombers took off from Saipan and Guam and flew north, over his head. John's LST lifted anchor on February 15 and steamed north. The trip to Iwo Jima would last four days.

THE NEWS BROKE ON JANUARY 31 AND IN THE NEXT FEW DAYS BECAME A SENSA-tion that eventually reached Lieutenant Colonel Austin Shofner on Pavuvu. A unit of General MacArthur's Rangers had gone deep into enemy territory to rescue the Allied prisoners held at a POW camp called Cabanatuan. The story of the daring rescue and of MacArthur's meeting with "ninety friends of Bataan and Corregidor" on February 1 made for newspaper and radio stories powerful enough to stir the heart. Here was redemption—not just for MacArthur, but for America. Shofner did not know what role, if any, his memo had played.* He had done what he could. If the

---

*Shofner's memo traveled beyond the commander of the 37th Division and above the Fourteenth Corps' commander to the intelligence staff of General Walter Krueger's Sixth Army. These were the men who planned the raid. His memo arrived on their desks two days before local guerrilla leaders told them that the Japanese camp guards were likely to murder all of the POWs before the camps were overrun. Shifty's memo, therefore, helped to inspire the mission that has come to be known as the Great Raid.

world thought the rescue of 531 POWs sounded like a lot, though, to Shifty it must have sounded like the extreme hunger and thirst and punishment inflicted at Cabanatuan had slowly and painfully destroyed a thousand men he had known. Austin was, though, a man who said his prayers and this was a moment to give thanks and praise. The long horrible nightmare was over.

On February 1, he took up his position as the provost marshal again. Later that month, he received a Purple Heart "for injuries received as a result of enemy action at Palau."

EUGENE'S PARENTS HAD COMPLAINED THAT HE DID NOT WRITE AS OFTEN AS HE once had. This had been true in late 1944, but by February 1945 he wrote them more frequently. He usually had something to thank his parents for, like his dad signing him up as a member of the National Rifle Association. Censorship was still strict enough, though, to narrow the range of topics. Complaining about the heat on Pavuvu, which he found to be worse than the heat of Alabama, failed to fill a page. "Jay P. de Leau of Los Angeles is one of my very best friends. We were together on the late campaign, and I might say he is the nearest thing to Sid I've met." Speaking of Sid, Eugene had just received a letter from his friend, who had described all the ways Eugene's parents had been kind to him. Eugene thanked his parents and, in case they had not heard, passed on the news that said Sid "got the first step toward V-12. I hope he isn't headed for an unavoidable mishap like that which befell me. I wrote him today and congratulated him."

Among the many magazines Sledge's mother sent him in February he found a month-old copy of *Life*. It featured a story on the Battle of Peleliu written and illustrated by a USMC combat artist who had landed on D-day, Tom Lea. Lea offered a vivid and unforgiving look at the brutality. The carrier planes had wiped out "visible targets" three days before the marines arrived, so "the 12,000 Japs on Peleliu" had moved into their bunkers and waited, as Lea observed, "with plugs in their ears and hatred in their hearts."[440] In a large portrait he entitled "The Last Step," Lea caught a marine in the final seconds of his life, at the moment when he realized he could not move because the last explosion had torn away large parts of his flesh, muscle, and bone. The artist had seen that man in that moment and knew "he never saw a Jap, never fired a shot." Lea quoted Colonel Herman Hanneken, who like Colonel Chesty Puller had fought in many wars in his thirty-one years of duty: "This is the bitterest, fiercest conflict I've ever seen."

At one point in the narrative, the author asked, "How much can a human being endure?" Eugene sent the clipping of Lea's article home to be saved. The question posed by the author was one he was struggling to answer himself.

The nineteenth of February dawned clear and warm, too breezy to be hot. John Basilone and his men went through their routine and their amtrac dropped off the tongue of the LST about ten thousand yards from shore. The panorama of violence and power stormed above them, around them, ahead of them, magnificently. They churned slowly to four thousand yards from shore. The island's volcano rose gradually on the left. The shelling stopped at eight a.m. A wave of bombers made a run on the island, followed quickly by dozens and dozens of carrier planes, which swarmed over Iwo Jima for twenty minutes. At eight twenty-five, the planes disappeared and the navy's ship bombardment resumed. Five minutes later, the first wave of amtracs uncoiled from its circle, moved into line abreast, and crossed the line of departure. The second wave followed. Then the third caught John's attention. Then his own wave straightened out and motored toward shore about three hundred yards behind the wave in front.

The amtracs churned through the line of battlewagons, close enough to feel a heat flash each time a salvo crashed forth, the guns firing faster and faster in the final minutes until it stopped just before nine a.m. The carrier planes made another pass, sweeping up from the south past the volcano at 150 knots, flying low and strafing the ground, putting on a show. An amber parachute flare burst over the beach. The first wave had landed. John's amtrac was a few hundred yards from shore, Futatsu Rock just off to his left.

His LVT crawled out of the water at 0912. Coming down the back ramp, he would have noticed that most of the LVT (A)s, the first wave, were milling around near the water's edge; they were supposed to have gone inland to engage targets with their 75mm guns. Empty amtracs were grinding back toward the ships. John felt his feet sinking into the black sand. Carrying his carbine, he slogged to the foot of the black dune, its crest fifteen to twenty feet above his head. There were no ladders in sight. It took both hands digging and both legs pumping furiously to gain the top of the height, as the loose black sand offered little purchase. A fair number of men lay at or near the crest.[441] As his head popped over the edge, he looked across an open swath of beach to another, smaller terrace of black sand. Some marines had crossed to the next terrace; some were making their way between enemy mortar explosions, but about 70 percent had not. The expanse of black beach offered no cover from the enemy mortar shells.

They were also confused. Baker Company had landed on Charlie's beach. Officers and NCOs of both companies were shouting and struggling mightily to get their platoons organized while huge navy shells shrieked overhead. Japanese mortars exploded on the open ground. There were wounded men. On the next terrace above him, he would have just discerned the impatient staccato of machine guns firing.

As gunnery sergeant of Charlie Company, John's job was to make sure his men got organized properly into squads and fire teams at their rendezvous area. The riflemen needed supporting arms. Machine gunners needed ammo carriers. They all expected to fight next to men they knew and trusted. John needed to help get the fire teams organized and moving forward. He would have tried.

The intensity of the enemy mortars exploding on Red Beach Two dramatically increased at nine thirty-five a.m.[442] Every marine started digging a hole. With every handful of ash scooped out, another slid back in. There was no other cover. The noise made it impossible to hear a shout from a few feet away. The officers of Charlie Company, like John, could see that a crisis had come.[443] John shouted, "Come on, you guys, we gotta get these guns off the beach!"[444] He stood up, signaled the men near him to "follow me" and started his legs churning forward.[445] A few marines followed. Picking his way through the men lying in the black sand, he crossed to the next terrace. Another stretch of open black sand lay ahead. The marines there were ducking under enemy machine-gun fire. John could tell he had joined the men of the first wave because they wore a heavy white cream on their faces to prevent being burned by gasoline fires. The flash cream gave them a ghoulish appearance. The fury of mortars made yelling at the men pointless. John got up and ran across the terrace to the next lip. A machine-gun team lay there.

Basilone thumped the gunner's helmet to get his attention, then pointed at the aperture of a blockhouse.[446] The marine turned to him. It was Chuck Tatum, the young man from Baker Company he had met a year ago on his first day back. Tatum was unsure. John had him look right down his arm and that did it. The snout of a large-caliber cannon emerged from a large concrete blockhouse in the face of a small ridge. The cannon was firing at the beach to their right. Into his ear, John yelled, "Get into action on that target!" Tatum slapped down the tripod and his assistant put the pintle into the slot. They loaded it; Tatum cocked it and pulled the trigger. Nothing. Opening the breach, the young marine saw it was clogged with black sand. Tatum rolled a bit and left his assistant to get the cleaning gear from his pack. He began cleaning the firing mechanism with a toothbrush. Basilone waited. Tatum snapped the cover shut, pulled the bolt and started firing. John took one look at where the tracers were hitting and realized the angle was bad. The firing port faced to their right. He signaled Tatum to shift to his right. Tatum and his buddy picked up the gun and moved about thirty yards along the terrace.

When they opened fire, their bursts found the mark. Pinned down, the Japanese inside quit firing. John had already spied the next move. He sent Pegg, a demolitions expert, forward. Moving alongside Tatum's bullets, Pegg got near the pillbox. Basilone ran over and whacked Tatum's helmet. The machine gun stopped firing. Pegg threw the satchel full of C-2 explosives into the aperture and ran like hell. Everybody ducked. After it exploded, it was the flamethrower's turn. Tatum fired a few rounds to cover his approach. The flamethrower stuck the barrel into the mouth of the pillbox and gave it a couple of long squirts.

John handed Tatum his carbine, unlocked the Browning from its tripod, grabbed the bail with his left hand and the handle over the trigger with his right, and sprang forward. Gaining the ridge, he fired at the soldiers who were escaping out the back of the burning pillbox. Holding the machine gun at his hip, he fired full trigger at eight or nine Japanese, most of whom were covered in burning napalm. It was a textbook approach. Tatum, his assistant gunner, and other riflemen joined him. They fired at the bodies. Basilone exchanged the machine gun for his carbine and waved them to follow.[447]

They left the black ash behind and moved into a nightmarish landscape. The stunted trees and bushes had been burnt into blackened stumps. The coarse grass and twisted limbs still burned with napalm. The bombs had cratered the earth and demolished the network of low rock walls that had once divided the area. They paused frequently, looking for pillboxes and timing explosions. John led them through the few hundred yards from the last terrace to the edge of the airfield, Motoyama Number One. A steep embankment off to their right revealed where the main runway ended, its grade well above their heads. They ran around the southern end of the runway. They clambered up the embankment as explosions went off near them, so they jumped into holes. Basilone landed in one with Tatum, the assistant gunner, and two riflemen. They caught their breath. In one direction lay the wrecked planes and equipment with the shell-pocked airstrip just beyond. The volcano, about fifteen hundred yards away in the opposite direction, towered over them. Looking back, they saw the way they had come. No one was there. Tatum looked at his watch. "It's 10:33. We landed at 0900. We have been on Iwo for one hour and thirty minutes."[448] The barrage grew intense. It sounded like some of it was coming from Suribachi, above them, and some from the other side of the airfield. Then the navy started shelling them—the rolling barrage was rolling back. It was like sitting in the bull's-eye. Two marines began moving back to the beach.

John stopped them. "We took this ground and now it's up to us to hold it! Dig in! I am going back for more men! Stay here come hell or high water!"[449] With that, he ran back for the beach. Racing down two terraces, John found three tanks struggling to get out of the terraces and minefields. Tanks drew fire like magnets. He had been trained to get behind the tanks and get on the phone and direct them. Instead, he stood up in front of the lead tank, so they could see him. Exposing himself gained the trust of the skittish tankers, who had already lost four of their comrades. John was calm as he walked them to solid ground.[450] With the tanks headed into the brush, John ran for the beach. Hundreds of marines watched him from the safety of shell holes, aghast.

The enemy barrage on Red Beach Two had become a torrent.[451] Large-caliber artillery shells exploded at regular intervals moving in one direction parallel with the beach. At a certain point, the explosions shifted a hundred feet toward the beach or away from it, and came walking back. Heavy mortars also came swishing down in great numbers. The violence of it all overwhelmed the senses. Every marine knew he had to run forward. The knowledge made his heart pound. Yet to run forward without expecting to get hit was like expecting to run in a rainstorm without getting wet. The soft black sand, which made walking difficult, also sucked their bodies into ground level, and that felt wonderful. The amtracs, now aided by Higgins boats and LCMs, had succeeded in getting the regiment ashore.[452] The entire regiment was pinned down.* The enemy's guns had turned enough landing craft into geysers of water, wood, and metal that landing operations had been shut down. The numbers of wounded and dead were climbing fast.

John gathered up some more men and set off for the airfield, running from shell hole to shell hole.[453] Clearing the last terrace, he happened upon Clinton Watters and some of his squad. John jumped in a shell hole with his buddy. Watters had lost a lot of men just crossing the beach. Some had been hit; others were still endeavoring to heft their machine guns up the terraces. The area in front of them, so quiet on John's first trip, had come alive with small-arms fire.

Watters had been stopped by a couple of Japanese throwing grenades from a trench system ahead. John yelled, "Let's you and I go in. You go that way and I'll go this way. We'll go in."[454] An explosion caused Watters to duck. John did not wait. By the time Watters caught up to him, John had jumped into the enemy's trench and was shooting them with his carbine. Once they killed the soldiers, Watters heard

---

*At ten forty-two a.m. the Twenty-seventh Regiment HQ radioed this message: "All units pinned down by artillery and mortars. Casualties heavy. Need tank support fast to move anywhere."

John yell something about "let's do this . . ." and set off. For the next twenty minutes, every rock seemed to have become a pillbox. Before Watters understood either the target or the plan, John surged forward to go do it. Not every gunnery sergeant would have chosen to lead the attack rather than direct it, but Basilone did not even look back to see if they were following him. Watters chased Basilone. The rest of the squad followed.

As they crossed the plateau of burnt scrub brush and shell holes on the way to the airfield, the artillery fire grew intense. The Japanese were plastering the area to halt the advance. The navy guns were preparing the airfield for the advance of the marines. Carrier planes roared overhead, dropping canisters of napalm. Small-arms fire was coming from every direction. Watters and Basilone and their rump squad got separated.

John still had four NCOs behind him as he approached the end of the runway. They jumped into some foxholes. A mortar round exploded in the hole with the four NCOs. Charlie Company lost more of its leadership.[455] John stood up to run. Bullets hit him in the right groin, the neck, and just about blew off his left arm completely.[456] John Basilone died a painful death in the dirt near Motoyama Airfield Number One. In the rain of fire the men nearby could not reach him, nor was it their job to do so. The dead were left for the graves registration unit. The word went out, though. "John got it."[457] Watters heard those words when he reached the hospital ship a bit later. The sailor who said them did not know Clint or his relationship with Basilone. Everybody knew John.

ON THE OTHER SIDE OF THE INTERNATIONAL DATE LINE, LENA BASILONE happened to see a newspaper headline on February 19 as she was cooking in the mess hall. It announced that ten thousand marines had landed on Iwo Jima. Though she had never heard of the island, it startled her and she spilled the pan of hot grease she was holding. The grease burned her badly on her lower leg and foot. She was taken to sick bay.

"I HAVE A LOT OF SYMPATHY FOR THE BOYS ON IWO," EUGENE WROTE HIS PARENTS on February 24, "for I have a pretty clear idea of what they are facing." He did not elaborate. Gene as always did his best to avoid writing anything that might add to their concern, without pretending that he was entirely safe. His difficulty was that the battle of Peleliu had changed him in ways that he was only beginning to understand. The expectation of going into another battle before too long, and the laws of censorship, prevented him from exploring the dominating aspect of his consciousness with the two people he trusted most. On bits of paper that he kept with his pocket Bible, he set down the basic facts of his experience—small markers to help define the wild demons of horror loose within him.

He had seen on Peleliu the bodies of marines carved into grotesque figures by enemy knives. The sight had engendered within him a consuming hatred. He became a marine with pity only for his own kind. "My comrades would fieldstrip their packs . . . and take their gold teeth," E.B. wrote, "but I never saw a Marine commit the kind of barbaric mutilation the Japanese committed if they had access to our dead."[458] For now, though, his attempts to define morality in combat had to stay inside him.

Sledge's parents, careful readers, would have discerned some of their son's turmoil. A mention of having finally gained back the weight he had lost must have made them wonder what had caused him to drop it. When he wrote of the fun he had playing volleyball, which was all the rage on Pavuvu, he added, "It certainly was fun to get out and play like a bunch of kids again." When his mother told him one of his chums at home was preparing to enlist, Gene cautioned: "Tell Billy, I always thought a lot of him and that he had plenty of sense and if he has [good sense], not to join this outfit." Although some marines got easy jobs stateside, Gene predicted that "it would be just Billy's luck to get into some bulldog outfit like this." His mother must have wondered at his reply, which came even as he requested her to have seven copies printed of a photo of him with Snafu, Burgin, and the other men of the #2 gun squad.

By the middle of February 1945, the signs of an imminent departure for another battle were all there. The new men had had a few months in which to train. Gene found peace in worship. He found meaning in poetry, particularly the wrenching nihilism of the English poets who had survived the trenches of World War I. He found joy in classical music, although there was very little of it on Pavuvu and for good reason. Professional musicians had come to Pavuvu a few weeks after the division's return from Peleliu and attempted to put on a concert down at the steel pier. The marines had booed the musicians off the stage.[459] A USO show came to Pavuvu soon after and wowed a packed house with pop songs and bawdy humor. Eugene Sledge knew he was different from the average "Leatherneck." When he needed to get away, he read his *Muzzleloader* magazines and admired the photos of his family, his home, and his pets.

A letter from Sid Phillips could always cheer Eugene up. In late February, Sid wrote to share good news. He had gotten through the first part of the course, at Lejeune. Eugene let his parents know that Sid "is going to get a furlough and then going to the U. of North Carolina. I sure hope he makes out alright. He will be out to the house when he gets his furlough. I really appreciate the swell way you and pop treated him on his other furlough." Gene's conversation with his parents about his future plans led him to write the polytechnic institute in northern Alabama, for a list of its course offerings, and to ask his parents what they thought of a major in forestry as a start to his career.

With orders to report to the University of North Carolina at Chapel Hill in his pocket, Sid Phillips went home to Mobile for ten days feeling like he was the king of the world. He borrowed Dr. Sledge's extra car again and drove directly to the Merchant's Bank, downtown, "to see if that gorgeous teller was still there and not married. She was there with no ring on her finger," so he came up with a pretense to go speak with her. He introduced himself. "Oh yes," she said, "I remember." They spoke for a bit and made a date. Sid came back to the bank a few minutes before closing "and spent the time talking to the old bank guard in his fancy uniform at the door telling him war stories, some of which might have been true. Then out the door came Mary Victoria Houston, dressed in a navy blue polka dot dress and high heels with her brown curly hair bouncing." The sight of her made his head spin. They walked across the street and up the block before he realized he had no idea where he had parked the car. Panic set in. Sid mumbled his way through a fib about having moved it so many times that day and needing to look for it. Mary "cooed not to worry, that she knew where I would park and we went to the parking lot by the old jail and there the car was. When I asked her how she knew, she replied that her family always parked there when they came to town." The rest of his furlough passed quickly.

The smell of a naval air station—that distinctive blend of sea spray and high-octane gasoline—bathed NAS Melbourne, Florida, just as it had NAS Wildwood, NAS North Island, and all the other stations where Lieutenant Vernon Micheel had lived and worked for months at a time, perfecting his craft. Late February 1945 found him pleased to be the operational instructor for fighter pilots at NAS Melbourne. The missions of a naval aviator had continued to evolve. Micheel taught classes in the use of rockets for ground support and the technique of glide bombing of targets, as well as "Advanced Combat."

Mike enjoyed his job. He flew about thirty hours a month in a Hellcat and gave some classroom instruction. The small town of Melbourne, which faced the Atlantic Ocean, was a short drive. His girlfriend, Jean Miller, continued to write him twice a week and he answered her as he could. He would not think about getting serious until the war ended. Part of this stemmed from a desire to protect Jean and himself. Part of it had to do with the navy's continued preference for "unmarried pilots" in its assignments. At twenty-seven years old, Mike wanted to advance. His prospects looked good. His commanding officer gave him an outstanding fitness report, lauding Lieutenant Micheel's leadership, abilities, and "quiet, agreeable personality." Asked for his preference, Mike requested carrier duty in the Pacific. There was still a job to do. He had heard "that the marines moved a foot at a time" when they landed on Iwo Jima and thought "we didn't knock out very many of the guns we were aiming at."

ON MARCH 7, LENA BASILONE CELEBRATED HER THIRTY-SECOND BIRTHDAY IN her bed at the base hospital. She was recovering from the bad burn on her leg suffered on February 19. Her birthday found her ready for discharge.[460] Her lieutenant came up to her ward carrying a slip of paper and spoke to the doctor. The doctor walked over to her bed and told her that he wanted her to move to a private room. "You told me I could go back to the barracks today," Lena said.

"Well, just for now because I need this room." They wheeled her into another room and her lieutenant handed her the telegram. It informed her of Johnny's death and asked her not to divulge any information to the press. She screamed. The doctor gave her a shot that knocked her out. When she awoke, she had been given a ten-day furlough. The news of her husband's death, though, seemed inescapable.

THE 1ST DIVISION SAILED TO GUADALCANAL FOR FULL-SCALE PRACTICE MAN-euvers at the end of February. Practicing on the Canal felt like the start of Peleliu all over again, although this time Lieutenant Colonel Shofner commanded a company of military police instead of an assault battalion.[461] His division's next target, the island of Okinawa, required it to coordinate with other divisions for the first time in the war. The Tenth Army, including several army divisions as well as two other marine divisions, would wrest from Japan's grip a large island not far from Tokyo. The several hundred thousand Okinawans living there presented new problems. These people needed to be separated—the harmless from the dangerous—and housed in safe areas and fed. For this large mission, Shofner's small MP unit was attached to the military government unit of the Tenth Army.

The military government unit (MG), as he quickly became aware, was a conglomeration of units like his from all of the participating divisions, with a small nucleus of staff trained in international law. When he met with them on Pavuvu, it became clear the MG staff had been given a mission and that they knew a lot about the "obligation of the occupying forces under international law."[462] The military government specialists had not been informed where their equipment and supplies were, or how this cargo would be delivered to Okinawa. The MG unit had received supplies of placards covered in Japanese writing. The creators of these posters had cleverly left empty spaces to be filled in as needed, but for weeks the MG staff had no idea what the posters said, much less how they should be used. When the division began its practice assaults on Guadalcanal in late February, the MG staff at last found the six Japanese-language speakers it had been promised. These Nisei (Nee-say) translators were Americans whose parents had been born in Japan. The Nisei had been raised to speak Japanese. Their ability to speak to the Okinawans made the mission of governing the civilians, as opposed to simply incarcerating them, possible.[463]

A few of these translators, who looked Japanese but spoke like Americans, were assigned to help Shofner. Shofner also received a company of MPs from the army, which he quickly absorbed into his company. His MP unit, designed as an "A Detachment," would stay with his division as it moved across the island, establishing civilian collection points as well as collecting and interning POWs (enemy combatants). The plan called for him to turn both captured groups over to "B Detachments" for long-term care as his 1st Division displaced forward. The military government men gave the MPs a series of lectures "covering principles of military government, public safety, the law of belligerent occupation, treatment of the enemy property, and the practical problems they were likely to face."[464] Any experienced officer could see, however, that the lack of a clear logistics plan jeopardized the whole military government strategy. Each U.S. infantry division had been ordered to supply the MG units with thousands of tents and hundreds of thousands of rations, while simultaneously defeating the Imperial Japanese Army.

The ships of the 1st Marine Division sailed in early March of 1945 out of the Solomon Islands. They sailed to Ulithi Atoll, the navy's new forward base, arriving on March 21. Colonel Shofner's view of the grand navy fleet changed hour by hour as hundreds of ships swung on their anchors. The most impressive sight, a line of Essex-class carriers like *Hornet* towering over the assemblage, appeared soon thereafter; it was nicknamed "Murderers Row." As Shofner contemplated his mission, he received some good news. Major General Pedro del Valle, commander of the 1st Marine Division, handed him his fitness report to sign. He had rated Shofner excellent in all categories except for "loyalty," which was "outstanding." The general described him as "young, energetic, does a good job." Shifty was on his way back.

At Ulithi, Eugene Sledge and his comrades went ashore to escape the confines of their troopship for a little bit and "enjoy some not so cold cokes and beer."[465] On March 24, the carrier *Franklin* came to Ulithi. R. V. Burgin came "within thirty yards of the Franklin." It had been heavily damaged by enemy suicide planes a week earlier, when the carriers had steamed close to Japan and attacked its air bases. The condition reds that sounded most nights in the great bay of Ulithi warned the marines that enemy spy planes were keeping an eye on them.

The briefings on the battle of Okinawa were already in full swing with endless numbers of maps and photographs. King Company CO Stumpy Stanley told them about deadly snakes and warned all men not to "drink, wash or bathe in any water other than that issued by the purification outfits."[466] Having had the hardest assignment on Peleliu, the First Marines would be in reserve; the Seventh and the Fifth would lead the assault. With all of the invasions taking place in the Pacific, the planning staffs had designated the invasion day as Love Day, instead of D-day, to avoid confusion. Everyone knew the beaches of Okinawa would be "heavily defended" on Love Day.[467] Along with all of their talk of the preinvasion bombardment clearing their path, the briefers acknowledged that the Fifth Marines "were going to have to hit the beach here and go up ladders"; their landing zone "was supposed to be right at the base of the cliff at the base of the beach."[468] Climbing a ladder meant extreme vulnerability. The job of being first up the ladder, though, fell to other companies. King Company would land in the fifth wave. It stayed aboard a troopship while those companies in the assault transferred to LSTs for the last leg of the trip.

In the several weeks since he had left Pavuvu, Eugene Sledge wrote a handful of letters. They sounded as though he had written them while lying on his bunk in a hot tent amid the coconut plantation. His insistence that war news not be sent to him from the States became rather strident. No matter what he or anyone he knew thought or said about the war, it "will end just as quickly." He requested his mother not to "ask me why they don't use certain weapons and tactics—I'm just one of the Americans fighting it & if I did know I couldn't tell you." Eugene Sledge's remarkable powers of observation had come, however, from his parents, so they might read his request for a "knitted cap" to be sent "via first class mail, if possible," as a signal of his departure from the heat of the tropics.

Mail call also found the #2 mortar squad aboard their troopship. Sergeant R. V. Burgin received "a letter from my dad, telling me that my brother . . . had been killed in France. He was killed in February, and here it was the latter part of March before I got word that he was killed." Burgin's family knew a little about Joseph's death because "the captain of the company wrote my mother and dad and told them that he was killed by artillery and died instantly." Burgin spoke to Sledge and his friends in the squad about his younger brother Joseph, just eighteen, and confessed, "I don't even know what company he was in—he had just got there, you know, he'd just been there a day or two when he got killed." It angered R.V. to think about his brother in combat as "a raw recruit" because Burgin knew that being the new guy meant Joseph "didn't have anybody."

Eugene received a letter about his brother Edward before the troopships weighed anchor at Ulithi. His older brother had added a Bronze Star to his Silver Star and two Purple Hearts. His mother wondered why Gene never found time to write him, so he promised he would congratulate Edward, "a brother to be proud of," as soon as he could. In the meantime, he begged his parents to get his dog, Deacon, "the best of treatments" for the heart trouble of which they had informed him. The troopships and the carriers and the support ships departed on different days, but by March 27, all were under way.

On the morning of April 1 the great cacophony opened up. It exceeded the invasion of Peleliu in all aspects: the amount of shelling, the number of aircraft overhead, the number of ships—the word was there were more ships here than had been in the Normandy invasion—but the veterans of King Company watched from their troopship APA 198 unmoved.[469] They knew none of this mattered. The enemy was underground, waiting for the marines to arrive. When they climbed down the cargo nets and into Higgins boats, they once more left the protective custody of the great ships and soon the only protection they would have from flying metal would be their cotton dungarees. Sledge thought, "we all hated the idea of the invasion being on Sunday, much less Easter. General Stonewall Jackson [the Confederate general] never initiated battle on Sunday and said something like this, 'he who presses battle on the Sabbath Day invites God's wrath.'" Sergeant Burgin, however, thought of the way the Japanese had butchered marines—had hacked off hands, heads, and genitals—and resolved "to kill every last one of them." As for his own fate he gave himself over to his Maker. "God, take care of me, I'm yours."

By nine thirty a.m., the 3/5's boats were at the reef about four thousand yards from the beach. The Higgins boats they were in could not cross it, necessitating their transfer into amtracs. The amtracs had come from the beach. Somebody asked a crewman, "What's it like?" He said, "You guys are walking in, no problem."[470]

The veterans of Peleliu arrived on the beach at about ten thirty a.m. and were astonished. Everyone was standing up. No shells rained down. No great wall had to be scaled. Men and tanks and 75mm howitzers were coming ashore as if borne by a giant conveyor. The navy's big guns had certainly cleaned out the beachhead. No one knew what the Japanese were up to, but the fact that it was April Fools' Day drew many a comment. With the mouth of the Bishi Gawa River off to their right, they were where they were supposed to be. Companies of the 1st Battalion could be seen on the high ground in the distance, pushing methodically forward through a patchwork of tiny farms. Gene could only conclude, "God must be with us, for he has certainly treated us well and looked after us here."

They formed up. The 3/5 followed four hundred yards behind the 1/5, which would hold the right flank of the entire division. K Company had the right side of their battalion's line. Thousands of marines marched forward into a strange, unexpected world, along tiny little dirt roads, or across farmland and pastures. Progress was at a plodding pace, though much faster than expected. The shelling faded away quickly. The skeletons of houses and villages dotted the landscape, 90 percent of the buildings destroyed.[471] The inhabitants had seemingly fled, but a few civilians had to be rounded up and delivered to the regimental HQ.[472] As the day wore on, word came of marines getting attacked by small groups of enemy soldiers. The battalion HQ had been attacked by a handful of diehards, apparently bypassed by 1st Battalion, and the 3/5's CO had been wounded and was evacuated. Major John Gustafson had taken them all the way across Peleliu and he disappeared on a clear, breezy day when everything seemed to be going well.

Looking westward toward the setting sun, the #2 gun squad saw the ocean below them, a great navy riding the swells. Overhead, an airplane streaked westward toward the ships in the distance. Burgin and Sledge watched it. It was Japanese. The ships began firing, their antiaircraft guns pumping faster and faster. They waited for the plane to be hit by one of the puffs of black flak, but it kept boring in. A moment later, the kamikaze flew into what looked like a troop transport. Smoke and flame roiled up. Burgin let out a quiet, "Oh hell."[473]

They dug their mortar positions in a barley field. Sledge donned several layers of wool under his field jacket to ward off the chill. As darkness brought Love Day to a close, the anticipation of a banzai attack began to make everyone jumpy. Even the vets got nervous in the service. Marines in the rifle platoons threw grenades at any noise in the darkness.[474]

In the morning, Love Day plus 1, the strange noises turned out to be sheep and goats bleating.[475] Orders from above placed 3rd Battalion on the right flank of the division, moving abreast of the other two battalions. K Company would assume the right of the battalion, making it responsible for guarding the division's right flank.[476] They launched their attack at seven forty a.m., but it turned into a long walk. The weather was pleasant, even chilly at times. They walked through farm country, with livestock and gardens and occasional civilians. The Japanese had erected lots of dummy gun emplacements in the area through which they passed. Snipers and holdouts were expected behind every wall and on every hill. The enemy had tens of thousands of men on the island. The war had to break out at any moment.

LIEUTENANT COLONEL SHOFNER, HIS MPS, AND THE MILITARY GOVERNMENT team landed on Love Day plus 1, among the last of the division's units to land. The HQ had been established amid the ruins of the town of Sobe.[477] Shofner found about five hundred civilians had been rounded up already. The Okinawans were older people and mothers with young children. They had spent the night on the beach without cover. What food they had received had been proffered by passing marines. The medical teams of the division complained that these conditions were unsatisfactory. The lawyers of the MG staff agreed. Although the people his men guarded looked harmless, the provost marshal had to assume the locals were hostile. The older Okinawans spoke a dialect of Okinawan, not Japanese, so the Nisei translators had trouble. Shifty's A Detachment and the army's B Detachment worked together and moved the civilians into the remains of the buildings in the town of Sobe.

The lack of resistance from regular Japanese military units created a great deal of confusion. The rapid advance of the U.S. military across the island had also begun to stretch the logistical network. The trucks of supplies created traffic jams that needed MPs to unsnarl them.[478] Amid a sea of trucks, the MPs could not locate any transportation to move the elderly and the wounded. For a few days, the MPs and MGs had difficulty locating food and could serve their captives only one meal per day. The MPs lacked wire with which to create an enclosure. Just as the MGs' supply problems eased, the rifle companies moved beyond the supporting range of the artillery, which now had to be moved forward. No one could spare a truck to move civilians. In order to function at a basic level, Shifty's MPs "commandeered" a

DUKW. They used it to move civilians, leaving the MG units to conduct scouting and liaison work with field units on foot.

In the next few days, some ten thousand civilian refugees became Shifty's problem. The 1st Division, meantime, had displaced its HQ far to the east, as its rifle companies approached Okinawa's far shore. The support and supply teams on the beaches and in Sobe were working at breakneck speed to support the advance. Many of the "roads" on the island turned out to be "paths." The MPs were hard-pressed to guide the flow of trucks.

Shofner left Sobe in care of the B Detachment, as per the plan, and took his men forward and established a new camp at Ishimiwe Kutoku, nearer the "front line." He found more traffic jams and "a sizable number of marines who had become separated from their units." The MPs gathered in more and more civilians, most of them elderly and fragile. Only a few of them looked like potential POWs. Their numbers and their needs overwhelmed the MPs, even as Shofner felt a duty to stay with his division. By Love Day plus 10, the MPs and the military government teams supervised fourteen thousand civilians at two camps: one in Sobe, the other at Gushikawa, near the 1st Division's HQ on the east coast, a quiet, pastoral area with few roads.

The 1st Marine Division had accomplished its objective easily, within a few days. In the meantime the other U.S. divisions of the Tenth Army had located and engaged the IJA in the northern part of the island and also in the southern half of it. While others fought the battle, the 1st Division secured the center of the island and waited. It seemed like the perfect time for Shofner to turn over control of the prisoners to C Detachments, from the amphibious corps headquarters, as the plan ordered. The challenges presented by the massive numbers exceeded his unit's capacity to care for them, much less to evaluate each individual. The Nisei language officers Shifty had on his team could communicate with the Okinawans with some difficulty. The Nisei had not, however, been trained in the art of translation, the procedures of intelligence gathering, or the practice of interrogation, making it difficult for the MPs to secure the rear areas from saboteurs.[479]

The Okinawans eagerly cooperated to the best of their ability. Moreover, the U.S. intelligence officers had also learned that the Japanese military on Okinawa had conscripted all male Okinawans between the ages of seventeen and forty-five. These facts, however, did not liberate Shifty from his duty. As he put it, "a large, potentially pro-Japanese population could not be allowed to roam freely between the invasion beaches and the front lines." He wanted to turn over his charges to a competent authority. However, the staff of the amphibious corps, as well as the staff of the Island Command, made up reasons why the C Detachments were not able to assume responsibility. Worse, their replies indicated that they were not likely to do so in the near future.[480]

THE 3/5 HAD REACHED THE EASTERN COAST OF OKINAWA, MUCH TO ITS COLLEC-tive amazement, in four days.[481] The entire Fifth Regiment had killed twenty-one en-emy and captured four POWs.[482] The Fifth had lost four marines and twenty-seven wounded, most of those to accidents. The numbers of refugees coming through their lines went from a trickle to a flood on the fourth day. On the dirt paths and small roadways, the marines came upon groups as large as seventy-five people, made up of the very old, the very young, and the wounded. The adults carried a few belong-ings in knapsacks or baskets. Many walked barefoot. The officers grew nervous with thoughts of what would happen if the Japanese attacked and the shooting started while their marines sifted through a throng of villagers.

Since he saw only the very old and the very young, R. V. Burgin wondered if all the younger, able-bodied civilians were aiding the enemy. He had also heard, though, that the Japanese had raped and tortured the Okinawans, killing any that offended them. From what he could see, the Okinawans "were happy that we were there. They wanted us to liberate them from the Japs. They were sick of the Japs. They didn't like them." E. B. Sledge found the Okinawans "pathetic." He saw "fear, dismay, and confusion on their faces."[483]

The land the marines had hiked across reminded Sledge of North Carolina, with streams running through the valleys and pines growing along the ridges. Cart paths connected small villages to the farms. They had heard of skirmishes, but had not seen any. During a march on April 6, a fragmentation grenade exploded acciden-tally. A corporal in one of the rifle platoons had hooked it to his belt.[484] "After that you didn't have to tell anyone about 5-pace interval," one marine noticed. "Everybody was about 15 paces between men. It shook us up."[485] That evening, 3rd Battalion set up a perimeter around the village of Inubi to protect the regimental headquar-ters located in the town.[486] Delighted not to be in combat, Eugene noticed that the buildings in the village tended to have tiled roofs, while in the countryside the farm-ers' houses had thatched roofs resting upon rock walls. The farms grew crops with which he was familiar, like barley, as well as the terraced paddies for rice.

For the next ten days, they stayed in one bivouac, and this allowed them to set up their pup tents. As the days passed, the marines began to raid the farms. At first they checked for eggs in the henhouses, dug up potatoes, and cut lengths of sugarcane, but this quickly gave way to helping themselves to the Okinawans' cows and pigs. The mortar squad eventually gathered six horses for carrying their gear, which they thought was terrific. They also provided for a bit of fun, as Sledge and the others went riding. On horseback, he continued to survey the new terrain. The pine trees seldom grew more than twenty feet tall, and he noticed that the doves in the fields were "very similar to those in Alabama although these here have lighter speckle backs and sail quite a bit while in flight."

Reveling in the peaceful countryside, Sledge revised his opinion of the Okinawans. He sought out opportunities to meet them. Their black hair framed faces of olive skin and dark eyes. Most of them were shorter than Eugene, who thought they looked like Indians, except they wore kimonos tied with sashes and clad their feet in shoes made of wood. The Okinawans welcomed his kind attention. One young girl tried to teach him how to count to ten, but he could not get beyond three. All of the women seemed to have a baby on their back, to the point where he suspected "farming and children are the island's main products." Quaint customs, like washing their feet before entering their homes, endeared them to him. He obtained one of their kimonos and its silk sash, rolling them up and putting them in the pouch that formerly had held his gas mask. He had another gift for his mother.

These easy days of living in a pup tent and accompanying the occasional patrol had a somewhat unreal quality to them, since none of the veterans ever doubted that the Japanese were going to fight for their homeland. Word of the fighting down south—the army divisions down there had run into stiff opposition—reached the mortar squad. They could hear the distant thunder and flash of artillery, see the planes going over, or look offshore and see spotlights searching the sky. Not everyone took the hint. It seemed to the veterans that every night, "all the new kids said, 'Come on, you guys keep telling us about the war. This is a picnic.'" To which the vets replied, "Yea, wait, wait, wait, wait!"[487]

News of the death of President Roosevelt arrived in King's camp at Inubi on April 13. Sledge, who had never cared for him, hoped that Vice President Truman could be installed "without a lot of political bickering." Mail also began making it through, now that some of the logjams had been worked out with regard to supplies. Eugene's parents sent him the clipping of his brother Edward's Bronze Star and the news that Ed had been wounded a third time. Sid sent a letter and some photos. Eugene went to a Red Cross station to get some stationery and had begun some letters when, on April 15, the military dropped its censorship of mail. The enlisted men were free to write what they chose, since it no longer mattered. The next stop after Okinawa was Honshu and the other islands of Japan.

Freed from restrictions, Sledge still avoided topics in his letters that might upset his family. He described the Okinawans and their customs and asked for a "cheap box camera" so that he could capture some of what he saw. He wrote about listening to the radio broadcast by Tokyo Rose, who played popular music to get the marines' attention, and intercut it with propaganda. On April 17 Tokyo Rose made wild claims as to the number of casualties the United States had sustained thus far and launched into a denunciation of "American Imperialism." The charge made Gene laugh.

Duties were so light that his friend Jay de l'Eau came to visit him. Jay had been with King on Peleliu and had been moved to the special weapons platoon of Headquarters Company, commanded by Lieutenant Duke Ellington. Jay now carried a bazooka. He and Gene had similar tastes in music and books. Unlike Eugene, Jay and his squad did not think much of Lieutenant Ellington. The visit was a rare treat for the two friends, even though companies of 3rd Battalion camped close to one another. Jay had to help out around the battalion CP, while Gene went on patrols.

The patrols through the countryside yielded little. One afternoon, Gene's squad saw an elderly Okinawan man walking toward them, a hoe balanced on one shoulder. "Sledgehammer," someone said, "you know these people's language. Ask this old man where a geisha house is." Gene liked the idea of showing the guys how he was "mastering this language." He addressed the Okinawan and attempted to ask him. "No," the old man replied in perfect English, "I don't know of any geisha house now. There was one in Naha but I'm sure that it's been bombed."* While shock registered on Sledge's face, "everybody was cartwheeling all over the ground, laughing at Sledgehammer for speaking Okinawan to this old fella who spoke perfect English."[488] Gene being Gene, he had to ask the man how he had learned English.

"I went to California one time and was down in the agricultural fields on a passport for about two years."

"Why didn't you go to Japan to work?"

"Well, the Japanese are so cruel to Okinawans it was better to go to the States."

Rumors that the islands just off Okinawa's eastern shore needed to be checked became a mission for King and Item companies in late April. Amtracs would land them on the northern beach of Takabanare. Preparing for this shore-to-shore amphibious assault quickly became another case of "hurry up and wait," as everybody just stood around, until Burgin heard the spoon fly off of a hand grenade. He'd heard it too many times to mistake that sound, which meant a grenade had been armed. His body instinctively reacted, his pulse jumping madly, but instead of an explosion,

---

*Naha was Okinawa's largest city.

"it just went pop." Someone had removed the explosive charge so only the detonator fired. It was a joke. Burgin hollered, "Who's the stupid son of a bitch that pulled that . . . ?" In front of his mortar platoon, Lieutenant Robert MacKenzie admitted, "I did. It didn't have any powder in it." Burgin let out a "How damn stupid can you get for crying out loud?!"[489] The outburst shocked E. B. Sledge, who would not dream of speaking to a superior officer in that manner.[490]

The ride to Takabanare took almost three hours. The two companies rolled through the center of the island and its main village by day's end. Patrolling the island turned out to be more of the same, only it seemed to Burgin that there were more civilians. After a long day of searching houses, he and Lieutenant MacKenzie, who had been given the nickname "Scotty," pulled some rugs out into a secluded spot and lay down for the night. Burgin happened to notice his lieutenant's .45.

"Scotty, your safety is off on that pistol."

"What?"

"Your safety is not on. It's off," Burgin repeated. Scotty looked at it and said, "Well I'll be damned." Scotty explained that he had taken the safety off that morning, when they had searched the first house, and so it had probably been off all day. "Oh shit," Burgin thought, "you're going to get somebody killed or kill yourself." For behavior like that, some of the guys started referring to Lieutenant MacKenzie behind his back as "Mad Mack."[491]

Even the veteran sergeant, however, struggled a bit with this strange world of war without combat. One afternoon, Burgin became so intent on his search that he forgot about where he was. After checking the house, he went out to search the barn by himself. Inside in the dim light he walked around hoping to find perhaps a chicken and was rooting around with both arms engaged when a man stepped out from his hiding place. A rush of adrenaline coursed through Burgin. His right hand reached for his pistol and he felt safer when he had it up and aimed. Another moment passed. This man had only been hiding. There was no danger. Had there been, Burgin knew he would have been killed by his mistakes: he had been alone, unarmed, and inattentive.

After four days on Takabanare, K Company moved back to the regimental base around Inubi. A few quiet days passed; then they were called into formation and told, "Get ready. We're leaving tomorrow, we're going south."[492]

While some of his friends went hunting for a cow to get some fresh meat, Eugene sat down to write on April 30, a "cool clear day with high wind," as King prepared to march to the sound of the guns. He sounded hopeful. The war might end soon, he had had a chance to send his mother the kimono, and the knitted wool cap he had requested had arrived and was proving "just the thing for the nights." Mrs. Phillips, Sid's mom, had sent lilies to his mother, a connection that delighted him. Even without the censorship, Eugene knew better than to betray the awful fear churning inside of him. In the one paragraph of sadness, he reacted to the recent news of his dog Deacon's death by recalling the day he had gotten him as a puppy, the details of that day still fresh in his mind. Deacon, he concluded, "is in dog heaven."

BY MID-APRIL, LIEUTENANT COLONEL SHOFNER AND THE OTHER OFFICIALS OF the military government had a firm grasp of the situation. The number of civilians greatly exceeded the amount anticipated.[493] The vast majority of refugees, it was clear, posed no threat. In a few instances, Japanese soldiers dressed in civilian clothing, armed civilians, or civilians forced to be human shields for soldiers—the distinctions were not at all clear—clashed with U.S. forces. The Okinawans also had an unfortunate penchant for moving at night. They might move toward the camps for refuge or they might try to get back to their homes and farms. This could not continue because marines fired at anything that moved at night. The refugees needed to be collected in one spot in order to facilitate medical care and food distribution. Virtually every civilian had become a refugee because the war completely dislocated life on the island.

The MG staff, however, had no manpower with which to handle these difficult problems. They had asserted the right to give orders to Provost Marshal Austin Shofner's MPs and continued to attempt to do so. The MGs needed the MPs to bring order. Shifty would have none of it. His men answered to him and him alone.

The commander of the 3/5, Shifty's former battalion, came to see him. Colonel Miller complained that Okinawans were "destroying their passes and . . . roaming about freely." Miller assumed that these people were in contact with the enemy.[494]

Faced with shortages of everything and the needs of tens of thousands of refugees, Shofner made a decision without consulting any of the military government specialists. The long peninsula extending east into the ocean would make a perfect camp. All it needed was a fence where it connected to Okinawa. Shifty chose some of the most able-bodied Okinawans and had them build a wire fence across the narrow neck of the Katchin Peninsula. He had his MPs, assisted by some riflemen from his division, move the civilians into the area, over the protests of the other MG staff.[495] In short order, more than twenty-five thousand Okinawans were on the peninsula. The military government men had to admit his solution "did cause the night incidences practically to cease."[496]

Needing more help to care for all of these people, Shofner personally met with all of the able-bodied male Okinawans. The translators had an easier time with some younger men, who had been forced to learn to speak Japanese. Those men Shofner judged problematic he sent to the POW camps, as ordered. He identified 204 men, though, whom he considered healthy enough and cooperative. These he dubbed the "Okinawan Seabees" and he put them to work. They erected tents, filled sandbags, and built air raid shelters. The lawyers of the MG staff "urged the provost marshal to discontinue this method because it raised questions as to the treatment of civilians and represented usurpation of military government function." The Okinawan Seabees were, however, "so useful and the method of handling was so efficient" that the 1st Division HQ authorized Shifty to continue.

The briefings Shofner received at division HQ would have made it clear that Okinawa had become the battle everyone feared. The 6th Marine Division had borrowed some battalions from the 1st Division to help it clear out the northern end. The area to the south, though, contained the bulk of the IJA. Advancing south, several divisions of the U.S. Army faced a system of ridges and hills all connected to the ancient Okinawan seat of power known as Shuri Castle. The IJA had fortified

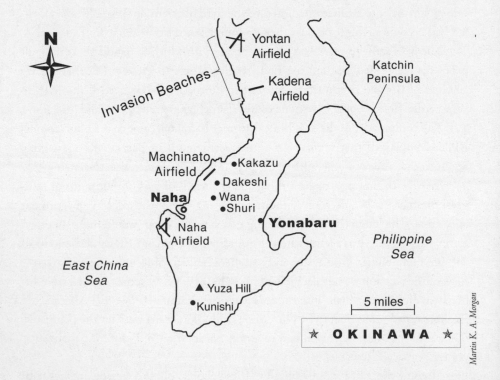

Martin K. A. Morgan

its network with more heavy artillery than the U.S. military had ever faced and the toll it was taking was astounding. Shofner's commanding officer, General Pedro del Valle, had a lot to worry about and was pleased that his provost marshal had taken one of those problems off his hands. When the general praised him, Shofner made sure to remind his CO that he was "an infantryman, if he needed anyone with that talent."

The process of creating a rudimentary government in Shofner's camp on the peninsula moved forward toward the end of April, with the MG officers' oversight. Headmen were selected and native police appointed. The headmen were put in charge of overseeing the distribution and rationing of food. Work parties of civilians went out with guards to search for clothing and to carry back provisions. The challenges continued as the numbers in the eight main camps on the island swelled past a hundred thousand. The crisis, however, had passed. On April 27 the Tenth Army HQ alerted the 1st Division to prepare to head south and into combat. One of the army divisions that had been in combat arrived and began to assume the MP duties. In due course, the Civil Affairs officers in the military government credited Lieutenant Colonel Austin Shofner. "The provost marshal during the first phase was an active, aggressive officer, who was eager to do at least his full share, if not more, with respect to the civilian problem. He did an extraordinarily effective job of collecting and moving civilians in large numbers to segregation areas, to a degree to which any military government unit would be hard put to it to equal."[497] As Shofner put it himself, he "did not like the Japanese," nor did he wish to be the provost marshal. He had, though, "understood the necessity to care for the prisoners and the refugees."

K/3/5 DEPARTED THE VILLAGE OF INUBI BY TRUCK AT SIX THIRTY A.M. ON MAY 1.[498] Aside from the streams of Okinawans going in the opposite direction, the ride south resembled going ashore in a Higgins boat: they rode slowly toward the sound of the guns. The temperature had dropped and the occasional rain shower passed over. As King Company neared their destination, they would have passed battery after battery of big artillery—105s and 155s. Hearing their great eruptions, feeling those concussions, made stomachs tighten; some new marines discovered an unpleasant, metallic taste in their mouths. By the time they climbed down from the trucks off Highway 5 and heard the enemy shells coming in, they all knew they were scared.[499]

The Fifth Marines moved into positions being vacated by the 105th and the 106th Infantry Regiments of the army's 27th Division. The 3/5 occupied the positions on the right of the line, the 2/5 took the left, and the 1/5 dug in behind them in reserve. Word passed through King Company that the Japanese had pinned these soldiers here for more than a week, which a few interpreted to mean that the doggies weren't trying hard enough.[500]

Smoke rounds were fired to obscure the movement, but even as King Company rushed for the foxholes, incoming artillery and mortars began to cause casualties. Under fire and in a cold drizzle, the marines probably could not see that the army regiment they were replacing had been whittled down to the size of their 3rd Battalion.[501] As his unit relieved one of the army units, R. V. Burgin heard one of the army sergeants give orders to one of his men. The soldier responded, "Go to hell. Do it yourself." That shocked him. Sergeant R. V. Burgin just could not believe his ears, or imagine a marine in #2 gun squad saying such a thing to him. It didn't matter. It was raining. The Japanese were dropping mortar rounds on them and word passed to the riflemen that tomorrow morning "we're going over this ridge. Keep running until you come to an embankment."[502]

As the forward observer for his mortar platoon, Burgin got up where he could assess the situation. It was just like old times. "The japs had dug themselves into the high ground." They had perfect firing positions on the marines and they seemed to fire at any movement. The valley between the enemies had the familiar, ugly appearance of a no-man's-land. By the time they went to sleep under their ponchos, the men of the 3/5 had sustained fifteen casualties. The shelling, like the rain, continued intermittently that night.

The next morning a full barrage of U.S. artillery and naval gunfire hit the ridges in front of the Fifth Regiment. The battalions of artillery to the rear fired at the same time at the same spot, creating a new level of ferocity. While the other companies of 3rd Battalion spent the day consolidating their front lines, King Company's rifle platoons prepared to cross the field to the embankment on the far side. A patrol went forward to reconnoiter. It found a large "nip mortar" and its crew on the company's flank; Stumpy radioed back to his artillery, "Will you take care of them?"[503] The patrol soon had to run for it. Burgin's mortar squad began firing smoke rounds to cover their return. The task of the three 60mm mortars the next day would be similar: to support the assault platoons, first by obscuring the advance with some smoke, then by hitting the enemy's positions—if not to kill the defenders, then at least to get their heads down long enough for the riflemen to get close.

Another night passed for the marines dug into the dark earth of Okinawa. A ship offshore provided illumination for them. Once again they awoke to the cataclysmic violence of dozens of 105s and 155s destroying the ridges in front of them. At eight thirty a.m. that Wednesday morning, May 3, King's riflemen started across the field; Love Company failed to join them on time. Farther left, though, marines from the 2/5 were also charging. The riflemen had not taken many steps before enemy artillery shells and mortars began exploding around them. Much of the machine-gun fire came at them from a bluff to their left, in front of the 2/5. From shell hole to shell hole they went. The forward elements made it to the embankment, which offered some protection from the direct fire weapons. Artillery and naval gunfire were requested. Two rocket trucks came up, prepared to unleash volleys of scream-ing fury.[504]

Beyond the embankment, the riflemen started up the ridge. They had the most dangerous job, as in small fire teams they fought their way to the mouth of each cave by using bazookas, small arms, and machine guns. They had to get a flamethrower in a cave to clean it out, had to throw a satchel charge into it to seal the entrance. It was the old "blast, burn and bury" treatment they had perfected on Peleliu.

The mortar squads displaced forward in support of the advance. Burgin noticed a large earthen barrier, maybe thirty feet wide, had been built up in front of what he assumed was a cave. Every time a marine tried to move around this barrier, a ma-chine gun opened up on him. The position was preventing them from moving for-ward. "I looked and I looked and I could not spot where that Japanese machine gun was coming from. I could hear it. I knew the general vicinity, but on the pinpointing, I couldn't pinpoint him." Burgin tried moving around to the right, thinking he might find defilade there and be able to spot the machine gun without being hit. As he came around the right side of the knob, the machine gunner "put two bullet holes in my dungarees in my left leg, and he put one bullet hole in my [dungarees'] right leg, between my knee and ankles." Burgin had not been hit, however, and he had seen the muzzle flash of the machine gun. So had Hank Boyes, who signaled Burgin with a new set of coordinates. The 60mm fired one round and Boyes called in an adjust-ment. The second round "must've hit directly between the jap and the machine gun, 'cause the jap went one way and the machine gun went the other way . . . so that took care of that one."

By early afternoon, the companies had advanced some three hundred yards and gained the high ground. It was an important step, allowing the battalions on the flanks also to advance. The enemy, however, unleashed a furious barrage. The flank-ing fire and the mortars soon made their position untenable. A small enemy "knee" mortar had gotten behind King's forward position and was firing at their backs. King Company men started to fall in rapid succession.[505] The shit had hit the fan. Marines retreated off the ridge. Love Company, to the left, fired a barrage of 81mm mortars and moved to retake the key point of it. King tried to support it, but fierce shelling stopped them. From somewhere behind them, Stumpy radioed Hank Boyes, the gunnery sergeant, to pull the company back. The 2/5 could not hold on either, and both units made a run for it as Burgin's men started dropping smoke bombs. Sergeant Hank Boyes could be seen on the top of the hundred-foot promontory, wearing a hat instead of a helmet, throwing smoke grenades to protect the stretcher bearers as they got the wounded out. They carried eighteen casualties with them, the bulk of the twenty casualties the 3/5 suffered that day.

Boyes was the last of the company to return.[506] He had a bullet hole in his cap and some shrapnel in his leg.[507] His company had lost another rifle platoon leader, a platoon sergeant, and nine riflemen. So far as Gene Sledge could tell, the whole attack had been "a disaster."[508] From the rear, marines brought up more ammo for his 60mm mortar. Among the men carrying the boxes was a captain who was a staff officer with the division HQ. Paul Douglas did not have to be running through a rice paddy to bring Sledge ammo. Some of the young marines thought he was a crazy old coot. Despite Douglas's gray hair and captain's bars, he carried more ammo and made more trips than the others.[509] No one was surprised. He had done the same on Peleliu.

King needed to reorganize its units. The next day it remained near the battalion aid station while Love and Item pushed forward, gaining the redoubt they had taken to calling Knob Hill in a ferocious firefight. Tanks were able to support their advance on the far side of the ridge. An air strike came in. Some of its rockets hit Item men. Toward the end of the day, King moved up to the rear of Item's position. Love and Item fought off a counterattack at about nine p.m. that evening, which seemed to break the resistance, because in the following two days they gained six hundred yards. King still took casualties, including two more second lieutenants who were hit a few yards from their foxholes. Hank Boyes happened to be nearby and tackled one of the wounded men, who was trying to run on his one leg, so that they could get some morphine into him and get him treated.

On the afternoon of May 5, King advanced to clean out the area on the battalion's left flank. On moves such as these, Burgin would go back to his mortar squads to make sure he was tied in properly. Positioning the mortars, under fire, could be difficult work. Burgin often found, when he came back to the mortar squad, it had set itself up in a bad spot. "For God sakes," he'd yell. "I want to show you something. Look at the terrain. Look where you're at." Bad positioning could "get your ass killed." Burgin ordered them to move. Moving the guns meant breaking them down, hauling them through the mud, and digging new foxholes and gun pits. Invariably, someone would grumble that "Scotty" (Lieutenant MacKenzie) had told them to set them up in that spot. Burgin said, "'Scotty, we need to move this over here.' He never did argue with me." Scotty knew enough to listen. The rifle platoon called for a lot of smoke rounds that day.

The 3/5 spent three days mopping up their area. Flamethrowing tanks arrived to spread napalm on problem spots. Ahead of them, the USMC Corsairs dropped tons of napalm and the battalions of artillery battered the ridges. The shelling on May 8 featured one gigantic salvo by all available guns from artillery battalions and the navy ships, to honor the victory in Europe. "I can't see how the beasts stand the terrific pounding we give them day and night," Sledge pondered. "They can't be human and are probably doped up to the fullest."[510] In the meantime the marines used tanks and the M-7, a self-propelled 155mm howitzer, to clean out caves by firing point-blank into them. Riflemen had to accompany the vehicles to protect them from suicide squads armed with mines. The battalion lost thirty men in the process. Among the losses were men suffering from concussions caused by the endless explosions.[511]

On the afternoon of May 9, after the big guns had done all they could do, King and Item moved forward into Awacha Draw. Burgin watched the riflemen move forward. Even after all of those fusillades, the enemy popped up and started returning fire. The IJA's mortars could not, Burgin reasoned, be in the cliff face. They had to be in some kind of declivity up on top, which might explain why ordnance expended against the faces of the ridges was not completely effective. He had an idea. "I made up my mind that I was gonna saturate that thing with 60 millimeter mortar shells."[512]

He got on the phone back to his mortar platoon and laid out his plan. The #1 gun would fire at a position on the left, then walk its barrage to the right. Snafu's #2 squad would aim fifteen yards farther at a position on the right and walk it to the left. The #3 would fire another fifteen yards farther south, and move left to right. When Burgin said he wanted each gun to fire twenty rounds, he heard his lieutenant, Scotty, get on the phone.

"Hell no, we're not gonna fire no twenty rounds—we don't have that much ammunition, you know, that could put us completely out of ammunition."

"Uh, yeah," Burgin said, "we are gonna fire that." Scotty, who was back with the mortars, began to bluster and Burgin would have none of it. "I finally told him if, uh, he was gonna do the damn observing, get his ass up there on the front line and not a hundred yards back, or let me do the observing."

"Well, Burgin, we just don't have the ammunition. I mean, we'll be completely out of ammunition," Scotty said.

Whereupon Burgin asked the switchboard to connect the call to the command post. When he heard someone pick up, he asked, "CP?"

"Yup."

"This is Burgin. Can you get me a hundred rounds of HE up here pronto?"

"It's on the way." Burgin addressed his mortar platoon, which was still on the line: "Fire at my command." The gun crews got their mortars' sights adjusted, gave their forward observer the prompt, and he unleashed the first salvo. Just after four p.m. King Company and Item Company moved out. They seized the crest of a ridge at the mouth of the Awacha Draw by seven p.m. They had their objective. Fire from the next ridge farther south halted them. It was time to dig in before it got dark.

Burgin could not wait to see what he had hit. Behind the ridge the ground sloped sharply down to a road that ran parallel with it. Behind the road, the ground rose back up another fifteen to twenty feet. The roadway, then, had complete defilade. The Japanese had set their mortars inside this deep cut, while their observers and riflemen manned positions on the ridge. The marines' artillery and the navy's shelling had been either hitting the front face of the ridge, where it did little good, or the shells went over and landed in the field behind the second fold of ridge. Burgin's 60mm rounds, however, had come straight down. More than fifty bodies lay on the road. He counted them.

The next morning the Fifth Marine Regiment began the assault on Dakeshi Ridge with the help of the Seventh Marines. The aircraft providing ground support dropped their bombs forty to fifty yards ahead of the 3/5's lines. King Company made a small advance; by doing so, they established the connection between the two regiments. The units that had closed with Dakeshi Ridge at midday found themselves pushed back that evening. Another twenty-nine men of the 3/5 had fallen, with little to show for it.

It was on a night like this that Burgin, Scotty MacKenzie, and a few others happened to share a foxhole. Burgin listened as Scotty and the others discussed the wounded and the dead. It was a common conversation. MacKenzie observed that a lot of the casualties were officers. Burgin said, "Yeah, the second lieutenants are worth about a dime a dozen when it comes to combat," because they get killed or wounded quickly. Junior officers weren't the only ones disappearing. King Company's first sergeant, W. R. Saunders, turned in sick without telling anyone. Gunnery Sergeant Boyes took on the task of going from foxhole to foxhole, "to get the muster and find out what happened to each missing man for the morning report."[513]

The Seventh Regiment pressed on to assault the heights of Dakeshi on May

11. The Fifth stayed where it was, giving its men some rest. The noise diminished and three days passed without observing the enemy. Everybody knew that bypassed Japanese could come out at night to attack unwary marines or that artillery could find them. It was still better than being on the front. The following day Boyes sent Snafu back to the hospital to recover from a bad infection in his lungs.

THE MOPPING UP OF DIE-HARD ENEMY SOLDIERS ON IWO JIMA WAS STILL CON-tinuing when the 5th Marine Division dedicated its cemetery. A chaplain stood before them and confessed that he was struggling to find words. "Some of us have buried our closest friends here. . . . Indeed, some of us are alive and breathing at this very moment because men who lie here beneath us had the courage and strength to give their lives for ours." Some of the men buried here had served their country just as their forefathers had in the Revolutionary War. Others "loved her with equal passion because they themselves or their own fathers escaped from oppression to her blessed shores." Rich and poor, black and white, enlisted men and officers, these marines lay here in "the highest and purest democracy." The chaplain asked all to make sure their sacrifice had not been in vain. From the suffering must come "the birth of a new freedom for the sons of men everywhere."[514]

One of the marines listening to the chaplain was John's brother George Basilone. In mid-May, George wrote Lena a letter from Iwo Jima to let her know that John had had a proper burial. One day he would tell her all about it.[515]

Lena had heard enough about John. The news of his death had been well reported. It revived interest in his service on Guadalcanal and on the Third War Loan Drive. The kicker to the story was what reporters called "Manila John's choice."[516] As a star and a hero "he could have stayed safe in the United States." In the coming months she would receive a kind note from Johnny's commanding officer on Iwo Jima, who referred to himself as John's "friend and fellow worker," along with his personal effects.[517] It was not much, consisting primarily of a locket of hair, a rosary, his wedding band, and a few photos.

"CHAPEL HILL," SO FAR AS SIDNEY PHILLIPS COULD TELL, "WAS HEAVEN ON EARTH to a Marine private."* Discipline was lax. The living quarters, though Spartan, were

---

*In his memoirs, Sidney Phillips capitalized the word "Marine," as many proud marines do. It is not a convention observed by historians.

comfortable. The laundry service delighted him and the navy mess hall served great chow. Classes ran six days a week from eight a.m. to five p.m. in an accelerated semester program. He kept his nose in his books, delighted to be earning college course credits. Every two months the semester ended. Sid spent his two weeks in Mobile with Mary Houston. He "was a hopeless basket case of adoration for her." Impressing her parents seemed to go well, but he was concerned about her six older brothers, "four of them in the Navy and three of them officers. I knew they would not care for their beautiful sister to be dating a common disgusting Marine private. I therefore tried to pretend to have good sense."

THE SIEGE IN WHICH THE 1ST DIVISION FOUND ITSELF, REMINISCENT OF THE trenches of World War I, made the job of the provost marshal a bit easier. Few civilians dared show their faces in the maelstrom and therefore collection dropped to near zero in the first few weeks of May.[518] Shofner and his team maintained the mobile collection units, trying to alleviate one concern from the battalion commanders' shoulders. His hard work paid off. When one of the division's battalion commanders fell, the commanding general called for Shifty.

Lieutenant Colonel Shofner turned over his duties "as quickly as he could" and reported to headquarters on May 10. He spent several days as the executive officer of the First Regiment in order to get up to speed. The battalion commander he was replacing had been wounded during the attack on Hill 60. His new battalion, the 1st Battalion of the First Marines, had suffered heavy casualties. It had swept over the top of Hill 60 in spite of the losses, however, in an amazing display of courage and teamwork. On May 13, 1945, Austin Shofner received what he had been fighting for since September 1944. He went forward to take command of the 1/1.

The First Regiment assigned Shofner a radioman and the two set off for the 1/1's headquarters, about seven hundred yards away. They had hiked about three hundred yards when a sniper's bullet felled his radioman. The man was dead. Shofner yelled to some engineers nearby and ordered them to take care of the body. He strapped on the radio, picked up the codebooks, and pressed on. As he approached the front line, Shofner spied a large hole and slid into it. He found himself eyeball to eyeball with a marine rifleman.

"Who are you?" asked Shofner.

"I'm Pfc. Roberts, Charlie Company, 1st Battalion, First Marines, and who are you?"

"My name is Shifty Shofner, and I'm your new battalion commander, and you are my new radioman." Shofner led him to the battalion HQ, where he met his XO and his operations officer. He was told the 1/1 was in reserve. The big news of the day was that a code book had been found that identified the enemy unit facing the 1/1 as the Twelfth Independent Infantry Battalion.[519] Shofner went to find his company commanders and scout the terrain. The other battalions of the First Marines had destroyed a Japanese counterattack that morning. The chance to see the enemy in large numbers in the open and kill them had given all hands a grim satisfaction. In the afternoon, just before Shofner's arrival, the 2/1 and 3/1 had attacked Wana Ridge, in support of the Seventh Marines' assault on Dakeshi. They had not advanced very close to the mouth of Wana Draw. It was after dark when Shofner made it back to his HQ. He sent his new radioman, Private First Class Roberts, back to his squad. The radio operators of the 1/1 were Navajo Indians, Shifty would have learned that day, "who spoke their own language openly on the radio, confident that it was completely unintelligible to the enemy."[520]

The scouting work was a part of Shifty's determination "to use every trick in the book to continue the advance and yet save as many American lives as possible." He wanted to avoid the mistake of Colonel Chesty Puller, who Shofner felt had relied exclusively "on the frontal assault" on Peleliu. The ridges of high ground he confronted, however, stretched beyond his zone of action into the areas of other divisions, thus offering few opportunities for flanking maneuvers. The enemy seemed to have every avenue covered. The advance of the Tenth Army relied on massed firepower to break open a path for the riflemen.

The 1/1 led the attack on May 14 and it went well. The 1st Battalion reached its objective, the western tip of Wana Ridge. One of Shofner's companies, Charlie, had made the most progress. It began digging in to defend the gain. He sent Charlie their mail as a reward. Charlie could not, however, tie in to the Seventh Marines on the left. The gap left the company dangerously exposed. The first sign of danger came when four Sherman tanks tried to drive around the western tip of the ridge and were knocked out by a gun buried somewhere on the southern side of it.[521] Just after seven p.m. the Japanese launched a rare daylight counterattack, swarming down the ridge to cut Charlie Company off and destroy it. Mortars crashed in Shofner's CP. The skipper called Shifty and asked for permission to pull back. The colonel assented, mostly because he could not get reinforcements up to help, and called for smoke rounds.[522] The skipper of Charlie Company was wounded while getting his men and their wounded off Wana Ridge. The First Marines came out of the line on May 15, allowing the Fifth Marines to take the lead.

Moving into regimental reserve put the First back far enough for its men to take a hot shower, get hot chow, and be issued clean uniforms.[523] For the moment, though, the men were happy to collapse wherever they were.[524]

THE FIFTH MARINES' ASSAULT ON WANA RIDGE AND WANA DRAW INVOLVED vast amounts of gunfire and napalm. Flamethrowing tanks, no longer the old Ronson but a more powerful version called a Satan, supported the infantry. The riflemen also enjoyed the support of the rocket platoon—one twelve-ton truck carrying the M7 rocket launcher firing the navy's 4.5-inch rocket. Eugene Sledge and the rest of the 3/5 were in reserve, though. The 3rd Battalion received replacements and waited as the other two battalions fought on one of the dominating features of the defensive system around Wana, Hill 55. On the afternoon of May 14, the enemy counterattacked toward King Company's position.

Scotty could see that the mortar squads needed ammo badly. He formed a working party with some of the replacements. The enemy's 90mm mortars and 105mm howitzers began to fire at the mortar section in support of the assault. In his foxhole, Gene heard the 105 shells approach and felt like he was "being called to Jesus right there."[525] The working party had picked up the boxes of mortar shells and was returning when the rounds started landing close. Scotty yelled, "We're all gonna be killed. Throw that stuff down and hit the deck." The men responded. Sledge noticed Snafu running out to the working party. Snafu's return was good news. Snafu was short, and because he had almost no neck, "when he had his helmet on he looked like a turtle but he was the meanest son of a gun" Sledge had ever known. Snafu pulled the clip out of his tommy gun and stuck it in his jacket. As he approached Scotty, he held his gun by its barrel. Sledge could not hear what he said, but Scotty got the men under way. The ammo came up and the 60mm mortars played their role in beating off the enemy. Later, Sledge asked Snafu what he had told Scotty. "I told him, 'God damn your soul, if you don't get your ass on the ball and get them people to move this ammo up to the front, I'm gonna bust your brains out with this tommy gun.'" Sledge considered the incident more proof about Mad Mack. Sergeant Burgin, however, had come to respect Scotty. Unlike his predecessor, Duke Ellington, Scotty spent his time on the front line. Although he had made the wrong choice at that moment, he was learning.

On May 17 Sledge put pen to paper to send a letter to his parents and thereby avoid the heartache they had all endured during Peleliu. After a "pretty tough" period, he admitted, the last few days had been okay and the good weather had held. He had been getting mail pretty frequently—surprising enough given the situation—and kept waiting to get the letter that said his brother Edward was on his way home. Gene sought to allay Dr. and Mrs. Sledge's worry that Ed would be sent "over here" by telling them that Ed's three Purple Hearts and Silver and Bronze stars meant a ticket home. As for himself, Gene was succinct: "I couldn't ask for a better name or finer heritage, and I know my parents are the two most lovable Christians in the world . . . when we are together at Georgia Cottage again, God will have filled my prayers."

The 3/5 would have heard that the other battalions of the Fifth Marines had nearly cracked Hill 55 and Wana Ridge "after intense hand-to-hand fighting," and that marines had begun to peer up the road to Shuri Castle when the rains came on May 21.[526] It began as a light rain that chilled the bones. Rather than pass, the rain clouds settled in. Gene's unit got the word that it would be moving up to relieve a battalion of the Fourth Marines. The rain slowed everything, as did the enemy's shelling.

The shelling began as it normally did. The heavy artillery, what men called the God of War, began to fire. R. V. Burgin was manning the forward observation post with his friend Jimmy. As the rounds started to get close, they threw themselves into a shell hole. They only just made it. Burgin landed on his stomach at the bottom and felt the concussion of the explosion, then the weight of the earth falling on top of him. He had been buried. Jimmy dug him out. Things got a little hazy after that. "They were shelling the hell out of us . . . it was one hell of a deal."

The U.S. approach to Shuri Castle had touched off a maniacal fury of artillery.[527] Apparently the enemy's concerns about keeping his guns hidden or managing his dwindling supply of shells no longer mattered. To the men of the 3/5, "it seemed to some that the japs were no longer aiming at the marines' artillery, as one might expect. They were trying to destroy the very morale of the marines on the front line, and they were doing a pretty good job of it, because you just can't stand to be actually shelled like this day-in-and-day-out."[528] The constant explosions disassociated the cause from the effect: trees disappeared in flashes of fire and smoke but the ear could not discern any Doppler effect, any directional sense, or even the sound of the shell destroying the tree. The pounding robbed the senses, disorienting the mind. "The artillery was going most directions and men was getting hit . . . and shrapnel was flying everywhere," when a brief pause came. Burgin heard Katz "just praying up a storm, out loud you know." Burgin yelled, "Katz! Shut the hell up. If you're going to pray, pray . . . silently. Don't be praying out loud like that . . . it unnerves my troops."

Not unnerved so much as deadened by the concussions, R.V. "sat down on my helmet and was eating a can of ham and lima beans, and a piece of shrapnel about three and a half inches long hit me in the neck." He touched the jagged metal and burned his fingers. So he picked up something to knock it out of his flesh and put the piece in his pocket. "Katz put some sulfur and a bandage on the wound and I walked back to an army field hospital, about a half mile back." An ambulance then took him back to a larger hospital.

ALONG WITH THE NEW CLOTHES, THE MARINES IN SHOFNER'S UNIT RECEIVED replacements. The replacements were actually an extra 10 percent of men that the 1st Division HQ had trained on Pavuvu and stuck into various "work parties" unloading ships until needed. The replacements had two days to get assigned and trained. "Intensive training of these men began immediately," as the division commander decreed. "Use of weapons, as well as squad and platoon tactics were emphasized."[529] On May 18 Shofner went with the regimental commander to scout the positions of the Seventh Marines because the next day they would relieve the Seventh. Shofner's 1/1 took the place of the 1/7, which was in "static situation." The 3/1 pulled the difficult duty of going directly on to Wana Ridge. Within twenty-four hours, though, all three battalions of the First Marines began seizing Hill 55 and Wana Ridge yard by yard, exchanging gunfire and grenades with the enemy at close range.

Shofner's Charlie Company again captured part of Wana Ridge, a point his men called "Snag-tooth."[530] Just because it held the ridgeline, however, did not mean that the Japanese in holes on the far side of the ridge would retreat. The enemy used its cover effectively and counterattacked that night. One hundred marines fought hand to hand with one hundred to two hundred Japanese. The Japanese battled their way back to the top until the early hours of May 22; Charlie Company reorganized itself and drove them down. The problem had become clear. The heavy artillery, and even the mobile tanks and self-propelled 105mms, could not fire at the reverse side of slopes. The engineers threw a hose over Wana Ridge and pumped napalm by the hundreds of gallons through it. When ready, they ignited the pools of jellied gasoline with white phosphorus grenades. The flood of burning napalm also failed to silence the defenders.

DURING THE DAY ON THE TWENTY-FIRST, THE RAINS CONTINUED, AND THEY WERE gaining strength on May 22 when word passed that King Company was moving out the next day.[531] Battalion HQ also warned its marines to "be on the alert for Nips with American uniforms." More rain made the slog forward more difficult. They began to relieve the 2/4 at 1400. The 3/5 found out that as bad as the shelling had been in the previous days where they had been, just behind the lines, its effects had been far worse here, on the front line. Gene saw a "cratered, corpse strewn morass with its muddy, shell blasted ridges" and it repulsed him.[532] The mortar squads found watery holes occupied by dead marines or dead Japanese. The mud and the shelling prevented men from moving or burying the corpses. The guys took to calling the area "Maggot Ridge."[533]

The next day's patrols were not sent out by Stumpy Stanley. Overcome by malaria, he was led away. Sledge watched him being taken away, aghast. Not only had he lost another member of what he considered the Old Breed, but he knew that the company's XO would take his place. Sledge disliked Lieutenant George Loveday, nicknamed "Shadow." Loveday lacked neatness in his appearance, E. B. Sledge noted, and was cold to his men. E.B. hated the fact that Shadow had been entrusted with "our individual and collective destinies."[534] Sergeant Burgin and Gunnery Sergeant Hank Boyes, however, noticed that Shadow had uncommon courage. Lieutenant Loveday led from the front. While he did so, Hank Boyes remained at the company CP, seeing to the logistical needs of King. When Shadow had to return to battalion HQ for briefings, Boyes came forward to check on things. Unnoticed by Sledge, King's gunnery sergeant and the new skipper worked as a team to handle the load. This cooperative arrangement in part recognized Boyes's experience and in part stemmed from the loss or disappearance of other key company personnel, like the first sergeant.[535]

The patrols Shadow ordered on May 24 made almost no headway in the sticky mud and under fire from weapons of all calibers. The third patrol left at five p.m. It forced its way to the village of Asato, where it reported "encountering 50 japs" and killing twelve of them before being driven off. Shadow had some of his men blowing caves on the ridge when the enemy began laying a lot of smoke. It might mean a counterattack. He called his men back. Nothing developed. Dusk brought an end to the day's work.

Patrols the following morning also made it past Maggot Ridge, also known as Half Moon Hill, and into the village of Asato, just before noon. The enemy snipers fired from all directions and King Company beat a hasty retreat and the Japanese reoccupied the positions. Gene stood a watch on the OP, up with the riflemen on the front line. The Japanese managed to position a 70mm to his extreme left and they "fired that sucker straight down our line."[536] They knocked out tanks with their first round. They also fired it at the foxholes of King Company. Gene watched the third shell hit two foxholes away from him. One of the three men in it went flying in the air. The two men in the foxhole next to Sledge jumped out and began running around; one yelled, "Jesus Christ, I'm hit!" The other said, "Christ, let me die it hurts so bad." The latter marine toppled over soon thereafter. Eugene yelled for a corpsman as he and others began to get out of their foxholes. A sergeant yanked Gene from the chaos, yelling, "Sledgehammer, get back to your mortar. You may need to give fire on that jap gun."

King Company soon fired everything it had at the 70mm artillery piece. Working in his gun pit, Gene saw the stretchers taking away some of his friends. One marine asked as he was carried by, "Sledgehammer, do you think I'll lose my leg?" He had already lost his lower leg. Gene lied and said, "Buddy, you'll be alright." As he said the words, he saw the man die. Gene called out to the other marine on a stretcher, Bill Leyden, but he was unconscious and possibly dead.

In the days that followed, patrols from King "could get but two to three yards in front of the front lines."[537] Battalion HQ warned them to "conserve all ammunition. Prepare for an all out counterattack."[538] How the enemy could attack was information not given. The enemy's big field pieces reigned supreme in daylight, the largest an eight-inch cannon said to have been brought in from Singapore.[539] The rain continued, filling each hole with water, flooding the roads into soup. In the deepening quagmire, the wounded went out by amtrac.[540] With the road network mostly washed out, navy pilots came over in Avengers and dropped supplies. The marines' morale plummeted as the situation, dominated by the God of War, came to seem hopeless and intractable. The men in King Company "just kept scratching at the ground, trying to get in deeper into the mud."[541] Fatalism grew within them, the feeling that "the only way you're going to get out of there is to get killed."

Snafu and Eugene shared "a deep foxhole and our ponchos as a roof. It didn't leak, but one of us stayed up constantly to bail out the water that seeped in through the ground. We had a wooden floor and it allowed the water to run under it into a special hole and then we bailed out with a can."[542] They hunkered down, trying to keep themselves and their weapons ready for action. In the foxholes around them, men broke—especially the new men.

Shadow brought up some replacements one morning. Gene counted about twenty-five new men being hustled into position. By the end of the day, only six of them remained. Most of them, who had come almost directly from boot camp stateside, "went absolutely bananas. The place was so horrible they couldn't even stand the physical appearance of the battlefield."[543] The guys said they had "combat fatigue"; Hank Boyes recorded them on the muster roll as "non-battle casualties" and had them sent to the rear. Their numbers exceeded the number of men killed. Gene often thought he would "just fold up" as his own dread smothered him and his senses filled with the decay and filth around him. He began to hallucinate; he caught himself watching dead bodies rising up like wraiths.[544] He watched Hank Boyes make the rounds of the foxholes "giving encouragement," or "doing something brave as hell," and it set an example for him.[545] Giving up meant giving his share of the burden to Snafu, Hank and the others; he wasn't there quite yet.

BETWEEN MAY 24 AND MAY 27, THE MEN OF THE 1/1 HUNKERED DOWN AND awaited better weather and more ammunition and food. The storm grounded the airplanes. Their supplies arrived on the backs of other marines. Shofner would have heard from division GQ that there had been a lot of enemy movement seen in the area of Shuri Castle.[546] After the initial report came a spotter reporting large numbers of enemy soldiers walking south. They were falling back to the next line of prepared positions. Thirteen minutes after the call went in, the first shells of artillery and naval gunfire arrived at the coordinates. Aircraft soon followed, even in awful weather. The prize was too big. The effort paid off handsomely. As General Pedro del Valle put it, the "nips were caught on the road with kimonos down."[547] The clouds broke on May 28. The roads were still impassable, but division HQ believed the Japanese had abandoned Shuri for another line. Battalion commanders like Lieutenant Colonel Shofner received a lot of pressure to make sure the enemy was pursued. He, like others, demanded more replacements to fuel the attack.

A light rain welcomed the twenty-ninth. Good news arrived at nine thirty a.m. Elements of the Fifth Marines had entered Shuri Castle against "little or no opposition."[548] They hung a Confederate flag on the former command center of the Imperial Japanese Army. The First Marines were ordered to support them. The 3/1 led the way and made it up the steep hill and the massive rock walls of Shuri by four p.m. Shofner's 1/1 was ordered to attack Shuri from the west. His rifle companies, whittled down to less than half their original strength, slogged around Hill 55 and ran into a nasty firefight. Rather than clean out the positions firing on them, though, Shifty spoke to his regimental commander about a new plan. Covered by a barrage of artillery, the 1/1 swung a bit farther south in single file and entered Shuri near its barracks and tied in with the 3/1. They had gotten behind a group of Japanese still holding the northern face of the castle. The two marine battalions moved quickly to create a unified defense, facing north and south, before dark. They did not have enough water, though, and thirsty men drank water from shell holes. The Japanese rifle fire did increase in the darkness, and one of his machine gunners killed thirty-five enemy in one of the stone alleyways, but no major push evolved.[549]

Navy planes dropped bags tied to parachutes loaded with supplies the following day as Shifty's 1/1 held the great bastion with the 3/1. The two battalions were in the southern end of Shuri. Patrols sent northward through the complex, back toward the U.S. lines, ran into enemy troops armed with a 47mm cannon and machine guns. The marines backed away, needing more support. That night the Japanese abandoned the ancient fortification entirely. Shofner's patrols the following morning quickly revealed a lack of organized resistance. The process of mopping up the holdouts in and around Shuri Castle began.[550]

THE BREAK BY THE 1/5 INTO SHURI CASTLE HAD BEEN A MORALE BUILDER IN King Company and in all of the 3/5. The day the 1/5 entered the bastion, Sledge and his comrades were pinned down after advancing six hundred yards past Maggot Ridge. They took heart in the knowledge that the locus of the enemy's resistance had been destroyed, although the Japanese troops in front of them betrayed no change in their doggedness. The marines entered a horseshoe-shaped area with, they counted, fifty-eight caves, each one manned with snipers and machine guns. Boyes radioed battalion HQ they would not be able to move forward until the caves were cleaned and/or sealed.

More rain showers fell as King Company worked on the horseshoe the next day, May 30. At least the enemy artillery had fallen off to a sporadic level. At two thirty p.m. the Avengers flew over to resupply them with water and the six types of ammunition they needed.[551] The problem with the bundles dropped from airplanes was that they were a contrived response to a problem, not a solution. The men who packed the bundles and the pilots who dropped them had no preparation or training.[552] The marines used colored panels or colored smoke to mark the drop zone to the best of their ability. The Japanese set off the same color of smoke to confuse the situation. The pilots flew at 250 feet and were traveling a little faster than the plane's stall speed, or about ninety-five knots, into the canopy of arching shells fired from both sides of the line.[553] King Company as a rule received minimal amounts of necessities, and often opened the packages to find items that were not needed.[554] Combat efficiency suffered.

More bundles of rations came floating down under parachutes the following day, May 31, arriving about fifteen minutes before the riflemen of the 3/5 poured from their foxholes and pushed south. The fall of Shuri had broken the enemy's defenses and for the next few days King spearheaded advances of fifteen hundred to eighteen hundred yards a day in their sector. Enemy artillery was light to nonexistent. They crossed a key highway and later seized a bridge over the Kokuba River intact. Occasionally a skirmish broke out, as it did on the far side of the bridge, on any high ground like Hills 42 and 30, or in important villages like Gisushi. Night infiltration was rarely a problem until the night of June 2, when the Japanese made a concerted effort all along the line. The marines had long since developed a range of countermeasures—some technological, some training-based—that prevented the enemy from inflicting much damage. The marines liked planting the M-49 trip flare around their positions, when they had them, and shooting anything that moved.

Trucks with supplies did not accompany the move south because the roads were still impassable. Supplies came on the backs of marines or in the bellies of navy Avengers. Keeping their marines supplied demanded a lot from Shadow and Sergeant Boyes. On June 5 their job became a little easier when the first trucks arrived at the town of Gisushi.[555] The following day King Company sent some patrols up to the summit of Hill 107. These met with no resistance. Companies from the First Marines arrived to take over. Having taken no casualties in three days, the 3/5 went into reserve.

THE RIFLE COMPANIES OF THE FIRST MARINES RECEIVED REPLACEMENTS WHILE mopping up Shuri Castle. All the marines joining them had been humping supplies forward to them except for one, the regimental chaplain, who had cheerfully volunteered to lug forty-pound ration boxes with the privates.[556] The new men took their first steps as combat troops while exploring vast caverns underneath the castle, well constructed and undamaged by the salvos from battleships or 155mms.[557] The replacements' indoctrination period lasted until June 4, when the 1/1 hustled south and passed through the lines of the 2/5 and 3/5 on Hill 107. Shofner's orders were to continue the offensive from Hill 107 and seize the high ground north of two villages called Iwa and Shindawaku. As he prepared to carry out the mission, orders came to wait until the supply problems were worked out. A half hour later, the orders reversed again because the Seventh Marines on his right flank had advanced and the Seventh's left flank could not be left exposed. At four thirty p.m. Shofner's riflemen pushed forward, leaving the Fifth Marines in their foxholes on the hill. The 1/1 advanced about eight hundred yards without a shot being fired. A stream, raging with all the recent rains, halted progress. Shifty received word that no bridges existed along the division's entire front line—except the one footbridge his scouts had found in his sector. The intact bridge represented a key tactical objective. He immediately ordered his men across.[558]

Two platoons from Charlie Company crossed the bridge. Machine guns in the high ground fired down upon them. Mortar shells began to explode. Charlie Company was pinned down. The mud, rain, and cloud cover impeded support from the battalions of artillery and the ships onshore. Shofner had his men dig in and provide what covering fire they could. After sunset the process of pulling his men and their wounded back across the river began. Marines wanted to be safe in their holes on a rainy night, not moving around, but they needed the cover of darkness to shield them from the machine gunners. When everyone had crossed the bridge, Shofner ordered the 1/1 to fall back to the line of departure for the night of June 4.

The regimental commander did not order the 1/1 to try the footbridge again. Instead, Shofner was allowed to lead his men sideways, into the army's zone of action, then south, in order to flank the high ground that had stopped him. It meant a lot of hiking through the mud, which began to suck the soles of their boots off. The weeks of living in watery holes had loosened the binding and it became another problem.[559] During the forced march fifty men from the 1/1 dropped out of ranks from exhaustion.[560] Shofner lost contact with regimental HQ and with some of his companies. Resupply that day, as reported by the regimental HQ, "was almost nonexistent."

Having flanked the high ground, the 1/1 moved westward at dawn, then turned north to attack the enemy positions around Iwa from the rear. Shofner spread his companies out in a long skirmish line and they advanced northward, passing another marine unit moving in the opposite direction. They found some abandoned machine-gun nests and captured some prisoners. His men caught a few soldiers in the act of changing into civilian clothes, much to everyone's alarm. With very little gunfire the 1/1 had cleaned out its zone by two p.m., including the ridge overlooking the footbridge. Soon thereafter Shofner got the word that his battalion had earned a rest.

ALTHOUGH KING COMPANY FOUND ITSELF IN "CORPS RESERVE" AND THUS WELL behind the front line, few comforts awaited them. The rain abated on June 5 but it had prevented the division's rear echelon from following them south at the same speed. New clothes and hot showers were not readily available, although chow and ammo were. R. V. Burgin walked into the company bivouac just as Sledge, Snafu, and the others began to dry out. Burgin had recovered from the wound on his neck and had hitched a ride back to King. Sledge and the others tried to tell him how he had missed all the rain and the mud and the lack of supplies. Burgin "only smiled" at such talk. He had endured Cape Gloucester.

On June 9, the 3/5 hiked south in a column to keep close to the advancing front line. King sent out some patrols. What they found were not enemy, but Okinawans seeking safety. After a few weeks of not seeing a single Okinawan, the marines received a thousand a day on the eleventh and twelfth.[561] When a few days without one battle casualty passed, it began to feel like the Battle of Okinawa was coming to a close. King received forty-nine enlisted replacements and one officer, a lieutenant; whereas this number of new men once would have amounted to one platoon, it now effectively doubled the size of the entire company.[562] Fresh from boot camp in the States, these men were attached to units in reserve in order to give them at least some time—hours or days—to get some instruction. Sergeant Hank Boyes quietly informed the new lieutenant that he would not be a platoon leader. An experienced private first class would continue to lead Third Platoon. His decision was "no reflection on the officer," as Hank saw it, "but we could not disrupt our continuity of command at such a critical point." Along with the replacements came mail, with a few letters for Eugene.

He had time to reply. "That was about the worst 12 days I've ever seen," Gene began, his candor perhaps unavoidable, although he could also report good news. He had heard that "Nimitz says this campaign is nearly over." The thought that "it won't be too long" before he was on his way home encouraged him to admit "we were under almost constant mortar and artillery fire, and it rained so hard you couldn't hardly see at times." In a follow-up that he began writing on June 14, Gene declared, "I'm sick of this foreign duty. I want to be a civilian again. But I hope it won't be long before I am once more." He thanked his father for including in one of the envelopes the paper target he had used during a recent round of rifle practice on the shooting range. It reminded Eugene of their shared love of guns and the sport of hunting. He showed it to his friends, who were suitably impressed and declared that Dr. Sledge "must be a crack shot."

On June 8 Shofner's men went back into the line, relieving the 3/1 in a village called Yuza at four p.m. The bad news they received was that the Japanese resistance seemed to be stiffening and U.S. planes "had bombed, strafed, and rocketed the area near the 3rd Battalion causing two casualties."[563] That day, though, supplies came forward in greater quantity as the roads dried out and the airplanes became more proficient at dropping packages. Shofner had a day to prepare for his next mission. The regimental HQ ordered Lieutenant Colonel Shofner's 1/1 to cross the Mukue River and seize Yuza Hill, "the high ground approximately 700 yards west of Yuza," on June 10.[564] The 2nd Battalion had already seized the high ground on the right flank, so it would support Shofner's assault by firing at targets of opportunity. To his left, elements of the U.S. Army's 96th Division would assault an escarpment called the Yuza Dake, which was connected to his target. The combined attack would be important enough to merit the maximum support of the artillery battalions and ships' cannons offshore. The day before the attack, bulldozers cleared the roads and pushed enough dirt into the Mukue River to create a ford for tanks to cross. The time devoted to preparation and the arrival of armored support meant one thing. "This time," Shofner admitted to his company commanders, "they had to do it the hard way."

A rolling barrage began the day, sweeping forward across the bottomland and up the sides of Yuza Hill. Shofner's Charlie Company jumped off at nine fifteen a.m. On the far side of the Mukue River the riflemen crossed an open flat area. The enemy's machine guns and artillery waited for the right moment and caught them. Of the 175 men in the company, 75 fell before the lead squad reached the foot of Yuza Hill. Shofner kept waiting for the army units on his left flank to engage and relieve some of the pressure on Charlie Company. The 96th Division, however, was pinned down. Shofner's Baker Company attempted to swing through the army's sector and come at Yuza Hill, but the enemy positions in the Yuka Dake poured fire on them. Charlie Company reached the crest with the help of its tanks. The enemy still occupied many fortifications around them, still fired mortars from unseen positions on the reverse slope of the hill and from the Yuza Dake. Charlie was exposed and in danger. Late in the afternoon Shofner ordered Baker Company to fall back, move to their right, and follow Charlie's path up the hill. The two companies dug in to hold their gain. The disaster continued, though, as mortar and heavy artillery shells dropped on them and the enemy machine gunners sent bullets grazing over the landscape.

Shofner had watched his men charge that day in the face of raging machine-gun fire and seize Yuza Hill "in the tradition," he believed, "of the Halls of Montezuma," referring to one of the Marine Corps' early battles that had become its touchstone. He called in as much artillery support as he could. He went over to confront the commander of the regiment from the army's 96th Division. Shifty walked into the CP and demanded to know why his "flank had been left wide open." The army colonel complimented Shofner's 1st Battalion and explained what had happened with his soldiers on the Yuza Dake. Unsatisfied, Lieutenant Colonel Shofner told the colonel, "You and your men are responsible for the death and maiming of many of my marines. You will understand why I will not trust you again" and walked out in disgust.[565]

The "constant deluge" of high explosives on the 1/1 continued through the evening until four a.m., when the enemy came out of their holes and charged. Charlie and Baker held, although all of Charlie Company's officers "were either dead or wounded" and the total casualties of both depleted companies exceeded 120 men.[566] The next two days demanded more hard fighting and courage to clear Yuza Hill, endure the shelling, and await the 96th Division's destruction of the attached headwall called Yuza Dake. On June 15, Shofner's 1st Battalion was relieved by his former command, the 3/5. Whatever discomfort he may have felt at the memory of Peleliu, Shifty believed he had proven himself to the 1/1 in the past few weeks; his leadership, particularly his leadership at Shuri Castle, had earned their trust. At the regimental HQ, Shofner was given the good news: the regiment was being pulled back into division reserve; and the bad news: it had lost twenty officers and 471 enlisted personnel in twelve days.[567] For their part the men of the First Marines were "praying we don't have to go back up on the lines."[568]

KING COMPANY ESTABLISHED A GUARD ON THE BAILEY BRIDGE, ERECTED BY THE engineers, over the Mukue River on June 15. The other companies of the 3/5 crossed the bridge and walked up to the summit of Yuza Hill to relieve the 1/1. One look at the 1/1's position on Yuza Hill confirmed that it had been taken in a nasty fight with lots of casualties. Worse, the Seventh Marines were being badly mauled in their attempt to take the next ridge to the south, called Kunishi, and the 2/5 had gone to help them.

Enough Japanese soldiers had surrendered, however, to encourage Tenth Army HQ to attempt to reach out. U.S. aircraft and the 105mm howitzers of the artillery dropped a lot of leaflets on enemy positions around southern Okinawa, encouraging the enemy to surrender and explaining how best to do so. The so-called war of paper also included an edition of the weekly newspaper *Ryukyu Shuho*, to offer the recipients a glimpse of an alternative future.[569] To veterans of Peleliu, though, it could only be a matter of time before Sledge and his comrades got called back into combat. An explosion of paper would never defeat the IJA. The call came on the afternoon of June 17.

As night fell, the 2/5 had claimed "approximately three-fourths of the 1,200 yards of Kunishi Ridge in the regimental zone."[570] The 2nd Battalion's hold, however, was weak. Rockets, tanks, self-propelled 105s, ships, and aircraft had all punished Kunishi Ridge for days, but the countering fire came so thick and fast, wounded marines had to be evacuated by tanks. An armed bulldozer had begun to cut a road up the ridge. King Company made the run to the base of the ridge and began sliding into contact with the 2/5. The new lieutenant, Brockington, ordered a fire team out to "see if you draw a fire."[571] One of the men observed, "That was probably the shortest mission by a K Co. fire team during the campaign." The marines dug in as the volume and intensity picked up after four p.m. About 250 Japanese came out of the caves and launched a counterattack that night, coming over the ridge and down on the 2/5, but also hitting King. The war so often dominated by huge cannons had come to a fight with small arms at close quarters. It lasted well into the following morning.[572]

The 1/5 swung around the western end of Kunishi during the day of the eighteenth to attack another section of it. The 3/5 moved out in support of the 1/5 later that day, waiting for darkness to cross a field and climb back into the ridge, certain only that they were fighting for another hill, or ridge, or Japanese holdout position that had no significance in the war, only to the soldiers, civilians, and marines involved. Tanks brought up their water, chow, and ammunition.[573] The night's firefight ended the fierce resistance on Kunishi Ridge. The slow, dangerous process of destroying the caves and the snipers and the infiltrators had only begun. King came down off Kunishi late in the day, having lost fifty enlisted men and Lieutenant Brockington.[574] Not all the men had been killed but a lot of the dead had been shot at close range in the head.[575] Sergeant Hank Boyes drew less than sixty rations from the quartermaster to feed all of his men.

The morning of June 19 began with a bang, as nine 47mm shells detonated in the 3/5 area, causing casualties and damage.[576] The cave from whence the shots came was not immediately identified. Hank and Shadow got the men of King organized and they set off in the rear of the other two companies of 3rd Battalion, which were following in the footsteps of the Eighth Marine Regiment. The Eighth Marines had become the spearhead. The 3/5 passed through a village; Item Company stopped and secured it. King Company took the high ground, called Komesu Ridge, and Love walked all the way to the beach. The 1st Division had reached the southern tip of the island of Okinawa. Still the final shot had not been heard. The Eighth Marines and other units were engaged on various hills. Hundreds of civilians needed to be processed. That night, King killed thirty-five infiltrators. The enemy's refusal to surrender, even when "there was no where they could go," and their desire to kill more marines, despite being beaten, built a fury inside Eugene. "What's the matter with these crazy damn people?"[577] Tanks drove up the next day and the work of blast, burn, and bury continued for days. The 3rd Battalion estimated it killed 175 more enemies at a cost of five marines.

The long, difficult battle had not ended. It had tapered off into a difficult world. The men were exhausted and heartily sick of always being on edge and of living in the bottom of a foxhole. They had no choice. One afternoon while the company walked in single file a few paces apart, "a bullet came through that queue within half an inch" of R. V. Burgin's ear. "Oh man, what a wicked sound." A lot of thoughts went through his mind: "I guess he picked me out 'cause I was as tall as any of them"; and that snipers "fired and then they'd wait awhile . . . so we couldn't pick up their position." The divisions of the Tenth Army controlled all of Okinawa. The U.S. Navy controlled the Pacific Ocean. The remaining Japanese soldiers, however, chose annihilation in the hopes of killing a few more marines. "In most cases the enemy was armed only with grenades and sabers and did not put up much resistance," the 3/5's commander concluded.[578] Their fanaticism seemed meaningless and inexplicable to the marines, a font of pain, sorrow, and hatred. According to Eugene, every man in King Company knew they had to "kill every one of them to get off that damn island."[579] Safety for the men of K/3/5 came slowly.

Eugene found a spot on a little knoll covered in pine trees where he could sit. He and his friend Jay enjoyed the view, the breeze, and caught up. "The scene on the southern tip of the island is the one scene we all wanted to see," Eugene thought, for "it means the fight is won." Now that the fighting had ended, the losses had begun to be totaled. The Fifth Regiment had lost about two-thirds of its men. The 3/5 had lost eight company commanders, but this total was not the highest in the regiment.[580] Looking around, they could see that King Company numbered less than a hundred, the majority of them replacements. The standard strength of an infantry company was 235. King had received 250 replacements during the course of the battle.

The statistic that fascinated Eugene was the number of men who had survived both Peleliu and Okinawa. He referred to these men as "the originals" and, after checking with Sergeant Hank Boyes, Gene calculated that of the sixty-seven men who had fought in both battles, twenty-six of them were in King's camp at the end of June.[581] Half of the twenty-six originals, he figured, had not left the unit for a day due to illness or wounds. Both R. V. Burgin and Snafu had fallen out for short periods. Sledge's use of the word "original," a curious term for someone who had joined the Raggedy-Assed Marines in the summer of 1944, conveyed his fierce pride at having stuck it out. The Imperial Japanese Army had thrown everything it had at him. He had done everything he had been asked to do.

* * *

THE MEN OF THE 1/1 HAD WATCHED THE FIFTH MARINES MAKE THE FINAL assault on Kunishi Ridge "like it was a movie."[582] In the following few days the rear echelon arrived, bringing showers and hot chow.[583] The commanding general of the Tenth Army announced that Okinawa would be transformed into a massive army, navy, air corps, and marine base for the coming invasion of Japan. On June 22, Lieutenant Colonel Austin Shofner led his battalion north a few miles. They took up blocking positions along the cross-island highway, facing south. Other units in the south marched northward toward them, clearing caves, salvaging discarded equipment and supplies, and flushing out the diehards. Shifty's men had the easy job as the Eighth Marines and others went about the job of killing an additional eighty-nine hundred enemy troops, while managing to accept the surrender of almost three thousand Japanese military personnel.

With the battle over, the men of the 1st Division expected to be sent to Hawaii to recuperate. It seemed only fair, since the Raggedy-Assed Marines had lived in the boonies since it left Melbourne two years previously. No other marine division had been away from civilization that long. General del Valle had promised his men a trip to Hawaii and some of the division's rear-echelon men left on Pavuvu had been sent to Pearl Harbor to prepare the way. The rumor went around, however, that when the last marine stepped off the island of Pavuvu and aboard ship "millions and millions of rats and land crabs came down to the dock and made obscene gestures to let it be known that Pavuvu was the only Pacific island the First Marine Division could not conquer."

EUGENE SLEDGE AND THE OTHER PRIVATES OF KING COMPANY HAD BEEN PICKING up the large brass shell casings left by the artillery at the direction of their sergeants, like Burgin. They hated it and looked forward to getting back to civilization. On June 30, 1945, it was announced that the 1st Marine Division would remain on Okinawa.[584] It would have to build its own camp. Morale plummeted. A few days later the division traveled north, crossing the length of the long skinny island. The Okinawa they saw had changed. Squadrons of B-29s and fighter aircraft filled the airfields in the center of the island. New airfields, bigger roads, depots, hospitals, HQs, and administration buildings had been or were being built. Reaching the Motobu Peninsula, the division found a thousand men already setting up their tents in a quiet area along the west coast.

Eugene Sledge found it "the most beautiful area on the entire island." They set up tents near a stream and started to catch up on their sleep. At mail call Eugene received an entire mailbag of letters, boxes of goodies, and magazines from his folks. A few weeks previously his parents had obtained a new cocker spaniel because Gene had taken the loss of Deacon so hard. When he learned of their desire to name the dog Semper Fidelis, he objected. "I don't want anything connected with the service when I get out." With little else to write, he thought of home. Hunting with his father and attending church with his family topped his list, although news that one of his parents' friends had given him some more "Confederate relics" delighted him and he made sure to say thanks. "I'll always remember how Mrs. Dole Parco used to let me explore her old slave quarters and barn." Lying on his cot, Gene and a friend whiled away hours talking about the Civil War and making plans to see some of its more important sites.

THE MONTH STARTED OUT ON A GOOD NOTE FOR LIEUTENANT COLONEL Austin Shofner. On July 4, 1945, General del Valle sent him a letter of commendation for his services as provost marshal. "Although the Military Police available were considerably inadequate, you utilized the force available most efficiently. Your methods in directing traffic control and in assisting with the collection of over thirty thousand civilians greatly reduced congestion in the forward areas." The letter of commendation would not be something Shifty hung on his wall or mentioned to friends. It went into his file, though, where it counted as another step forward in his career.

Plans for the next step in the defeat of Japan had already been developed and Shofner would have received briefings about Operation Downfall, to be commanded by General MacArthur. The projections as to the enemy's intentions and abilities came, of course, from the recent experiences on Iwo Jima, Luzon, and Okinawa. The experience of the Tenth Army also furnished a picture of what awaited the U.S. troops. Leaving out the navy's significant losses off Okinawa's shores, more than seven thousand Americans had been killed in action; more than thirty-one thousand had been wounded; and more than twenty-six thousand had been "non-battle casualties," or lost due to combat fatigue. Estimating the casualties of the next campaign by extrapolating from the Tenth Army experience produced frightful results because so many more divisions would participate in the Battle of Japan.

While contemplating a dreadful future, Shofner found himself in charge of the mundane. He spent the month of July serving as the president of the court-martial. A rise in the number of infractions being reported signaled the tightening of discipline on veterans and replacements alike. The veterans in the 1/1 and across the division grumbled that the "chicken shit" was starting up again.[585] The spit-and-polish formality would have been expected in Hawaii, had they been rotated there. Officers knew that the men's morale was very low and that this stemmed in part from the missed liberty in Honolulu.[586] Something more important, however, was at work under the surface. After surviving the biggest and longest battle of the Pacific, the marines found themselves at a dead end. The fact was self-evident. The next time they went into combat, they would be landing on the shore of Tokyo Bay. As a man in Shofner's battalion put it, "No one was going to survive. No marines. No japs."[587]

THE MEN OF KING COMPANY WERE ALSO GETTING BRIEFED. THE 1ST MARINE Division would not participate in the first invasion of Japan, scheduled for November. Rather, it would land on the isthmus that creates Tokyo Bay in March of 1946, along with twenty-four other divisions in the largest amphibious assault of all time. Amid descriptions of how this operation would more than double the size of D-day in Normandy came also the news that the first men off the boats and up the bluffs were not expected to survive. Junior officers, like Lieutenant Scotty MacKenzie, were told, "You are expendable."[588]

Eugene Sledge knew that he would serve in the next campaign because a "point system" for rotation stateside had been posted. General del Valle had established the system to prevent the onset of a serious morale problem. The system allowed the general to ship out the eight hundred men in the division who had been overseas for thirty months, as well as begin to rotate the more than three thousand who had been with the division for two years. After reviewing the "point system" in light of his one year with the division, Sledge knew that guys like him "won't be released until the war is over." His buddy Snafu had eighty-seven points and shipped out one morning in mid-July.[589]

Attempts to make life more enjoyable for the remaining men—by installing lights in the tents, bringing in a USO show, and building the mess hall on a bluff overlooking the South China Sea—could do little to assuage Gene's fear of the approaching apocalypse. His fear fueled an angry hatred of all things Japanese. His fear also found another, more surprising target. He included in one of his letters a check for $225, representing his pay for the Battle of Okinawa and a few of the months preceding it. "A ship worker," he asserted, "makes that much for loafing in two weeks time." The caustic observation followed his decision to cancel his subscription to

Leatherneck magazine because he found it to be "too much of a boot-ish, flag-waving affair."* His comments revealed a growing cynicism toward those Americans who seemed happy to dress up the nasty, vicious experience he had just endured with platitudes about glory and courageous sacrifice, while they themselves made little, if any, sacrifice. "I'm just praying that the terrible mess will soon be over because I don't want any more good American blood lost."

On August 9, Gene heard on the radio "that Russia had declared on Nippon. I surely hope its true—it would really shorten the war." The radio had also announced the second use of a new weapon, an atomic bomb, and "everybody is laying bets on what is going to happen." For his part Gene began to think of his future. "I'll soon be 22, and I'm no closer to getting set for postwar than I was a year ago. So I'm hoping that I can get back to civilian life very soon. Maybe I'm too impatient, but I'm anxious to get started back to college." A lot of marines, particularly his officers in King Company, celebrated the news by getting drunk. Gene got a record player and for once the popular music he disliked (jazz in general and Frank Sinatra in particular) gave way to Tchaikovsky's *Nutcracker Suite*.

"We hear so much scuttlebutt and dope," Eugene admitted, that he was not sure what was going on during the next few days. Daring to hope Japan would surrender could seem by turns possible and ludicrous. On August 13 he heard that Japan had surrendered. "No doubt, the new bomb made up the minds of the yellow men that they are finally beaten." Still, the idea of the Japanese surrendering was not easy to accept with finality. Admiral Nimitz had warned to "beware treachery," because the enemy had long used surrender as a means of killing a few more marines. While a friend of his had Frank Sinatra "crooning through one of his numbers on the record player," Gene and his friends discussed the big question: "if the war does end now . . . how soon will we be home . . . ?"

THE DAY PRESIDENT TRUMAN ANNOUNCED AMERICA'S VICTORY OVER JAPAN, August 14, Sidney Phillips and his friends "built a gigantic bonfire in the middle of the main street of Chapel Hill." The blaze "set the asphalt pavement on fire and burned up the traffic light hanging in the middle of the intersection."

*   *   *

---

*Leatherneck magazine was created within the Marine Corps in 1917, which made it semiautonomous in 1943. Its mission is to celebrate the United States Marine Corps.

LIEUTENANT MICHEEL CELEBRATED THE END OF THE WAR WITH THE OTHER officers at the Naval Auxiliary Air Station in Kingsville, Texas, where he had been transferred a few months previously. He had joined a night fighter training group, the most dangerous specialty a navy pilot could have, given the rudimentary electronics available. The war's end prompted the navy to disband the night fighter group. The immediate needs had ended and the age of the jet engine had dawned. Once again in his navy career, Mike would be "thrown to the winds."

LEGACIES

JAPAN'S LEADERS HAD BET THAT IF THEY MADE THE COST OF THE WAR HIGH enough, the United States would relent on its goal of unconditional surrender. The kamikaze represented the logical extension of that policy. The second atomic blast convinced Emperor Hirohito to overrule the other members of the junta and surrender his country. An alternative future became possible. A U.S. invasion of Japan would have had all the savagery of Okinawa or Iwo Jima at five times the scale. The absence of this apocalypse allowed the United States of America to be magnanimous to her defeated foe. Her combat veterans reacted differently, of course, to the peace and prosperity that followed. A man's capacity to let go of his pain, or to recognize the advancement of human civilization that America's victory enabled, was not solely a function of his personality, but also of where, when, and how he had served.

ON THE SAME DAY ADMIRAL NIMITZ ORDERED OFFENSIVE ACTIONS AGAINST the Japanese to cease, August 14, 1945, Lieutenant Colonel Shofner and other senior officers learned that the 1st Marine Division would sail for China at the end of September. The marines had to accept the surrender of the Japanese forces in China; secure the cities controlled by the Japanese and the stockpiles of Japanese weapons and equipment; and turn it all over to the nationalist forces. The communists in China would be denied these key locations and essential equipment. Shofner's enlisted men could be expected to hate this assignment; many of them had already begun to assert that the 1st Marine Division—as the first in and the last out—merited a ticker-tape parade in New York City. Others said Tokyo. A lot of the division's officers could also be expected to covet a quick ticket stateside. They certainly had the points for rotation.

It would have been impossible for any marine or soldier on Okinawa to have served in combat for a longer period than Austin "Shifty" Shofner. He had been there the day it all began. He did not wish, however, to go home. Commanding the 1st Battalion, First Marines, had given him enormous satisfaction. He was a professional marine and he had a black mark on his record. Serving in China would bring him back to where he started and give him another chance to excel. His record changed markedly, however, a few days later. General del Valle awarded Lieutenant Colonel Austin Shofner the Legion of Merit for "exceptionally meritorious conduct." The citation read, in part:

Assuming command of his battalion in the midst of a critical battle, Lieutenant Colonel Shofner, by his tactical skill, untiring determination and outstanding personal courage, directed the activities of his unit to the successful completion of numerous assigned tasks. Although his battalion was reduced in efficiency by severe casualties, his continued personal leadership and supervision in the face of fierce enemy resistance . . . was an inspiration to his men in his command.

His regimental commander, Colonel Mason, followed up the medal with an excellent fitness report. Although in a few areas, like "cooperation with others," Shofner's performance dipped to the "very good" category, Mason described him in the comments section as "a particularly aggressive officer of the go-getter type." Shifty was back because he had never given up.

EUGENE SLEDGE REPRESENTED THE MAJORITY OF ENLISTED MARINES WHEN HE wrote in late August, "I got in the Corps to help win the war—it's won and I can't get out any too fast to suit me." The point system for rotation had been changed recently to fit the army's system. Gene received 1 point for each month of service, 1 point for each month of being overseas, 5 points for each decoration, and 5 points for each campaign in which a battle star was issued. A few other factors, like dependent children, added points. The magic number was 85. Gene informed his parents that he had 60 points. "Small compared to Ed, eh?" His older brother was already on his way back home. His buddy R. V. Burgin would depart soon. Gene faced the prospect of being overseas awhile. Remaining on Okinawa would have been acceptable—Gene liked it there and thought so highly of its people he was known to bow to elderly Okinawans.[1] He had fought the IJA too long, though, to forgive the Japanese, whom he called "blackhearted." He fervently hoped he would not be sent to Tokyo. On September 1, he submitted his request for a discharge from the USMC, just in case.

The news of late August and early September—on radio, in newsprint, and in the newsreels—often featured the name of Douglas MacArthur. In a daring move, the general landed at an airfield outside Tokyo in his personal airplane, the word "Bataan" stenciled on its nose, on August 30.[2] Millions of Japanese soldiers in the vicinity had not yet officially surrendered. He had stepped down onto the tarmac in a khaki uniform, without a jacket, tie, or medals. He wore aviator glasses and carried a corncob pipe. His cap, famous around the world, was that of the field marshal of the

Philippines National Army. Standing on Japanese soil, he said simply, "Melbourne to Tokyo was a long road, but this looks like the payoff."[3] A few days later, MacArthur presided over the ceremony in which the representatives of Japan's military government signed the instrument of unconditional surrender. The legal documents that they and the leaders of the Allied powers signed had been printed on a rare parchment found amid the wreckage of Manila. The ceremony took place on the deck of the battleship USS *Missouri*, lying at anchor in Tokyo Bay and surrounded by the vast U.S. fleet. MacArthur's statements affixed no blame; instead he offered a prayer that "peace be now restored to the world." He expressed the hope that "out of the blood and carnage of the past" a better world would emerge. "Nor is it for us here to meet . . . in a spirit of distrust, malice or hatred. But rather it is for us, both victors and vanquished, to rise to that higher dignity which alone befits the sacred purpose we are about to serve."[4]

"Well, now that the war is won," Eugene exclaimed, "who has completely taken over? MacArthur. Nimitz, Halsey, and the Marine generals won the war. Now it's all an army show and the Navy & Corps sit back and smirk while all the Army brass hats eat up the credit." Like many marines, Eugene believed the Central Pacific Campaign, led by Admiral Nimitz, had been more important than the South Pacific Campaign, led by MacArthur.* The newsreels of MacArthur wading through the surf to return to the Philippines or presiding over the surrender were therefore interpreted as grandstanding by many marines in the field. "I think the Corps has gotten its share of the credit and so has the Air Force, but not the Navy. We sure have a good Navy too. We all hate to see Nimitz left out in the cold after the fine job he and the Navy have done."

The armed services of the United States, with the enemy defeated, prepared to maintain a military presence in countries across the Pacific, most especially Japan itself. The men of King Company began to receive daily instruction in occupational duties. Eugene not only wondered where he might be sent, but what areas needed to be occupied. "America will keep Okinawa," he hoped, "for it's a good base to watch the nips with. . . . They will behave perfectly and humbly and when they think no one is watching—bingo—they pull some sort of treachery." When each marine in the 3/5 received three new blankets, an overcoat, long underwear, and wool clothing, Gene guessed they would be leaving Okinawa. Soon thereafter he and the other enlisted men learned they were shipping out for duty in China.

R. V. Burgin, who had long figured he would ship out for Texas any day, got

---

*Historians have since debated the wisdom and the necessity of America's two-prong drive to Japan.

the word on September 15, 1945. He was being transferred stateside. "I almost volunteered to go to China with the 1st Division, and I got to thinking about it and I thought, well hell, I've already been through three battles and I go to China and get run over by a damn rickshaw or something, and get killed . . . that doesn't make sense to me, so I'm going home." He said his good-byes and caught a truck south, to the port area. Two weeks later, his company made its own journey to the port.

The First Marines departed for China after the Seventh Marines, who had landed ashore as assault troops, and before the Fifth Marines. Lieutenant Colonel Austin Shofner's 1/1 boarded USS *Attala* and sailed west. They disembarked on October 1 at the port of Taku, on the Hai Ho River. Trucks, many of them formerly the property of the Imperial Japanese Army, took them seven miles upriver to the city of Tangku, which they had been told had a population of a hundred thousand, "and they all must have come out to greet us when we marched into the city. We started marching 4 abreast, but were squeezed single file as all those people pressed in, hugging and kissing us."[5] The people knew the sacrifices made to defeat Japan and were grateful. Trains took the 1/1 on to Tientsin, a city of more than a million people. The battalion moved along broad, paved streets to an area of the city that had a distinctly Western look. Their quarters had been built by the English and until recently had been used by the Japanese Army as their barracks.

While the Chinese people showered the marines with gratitude and affection, the ancient civilization fascinated them. The fears of U.S. commanders like Shofner that the fifty thousand Japanese troops stationed in his area might choose to fight proved unfounded. The occupation of China began with a few weeks of problems of logistics and supply, which meant that one of Shofner's first concerns was making sure his troops got fed. With the arrival of the Fifth Marine Regiment, the units of the 1st Division spread out in order to protect a few key cities, their ports, and the railways that connected them. The division HQ and the Fifth Regiment took up residence in Peiping, China's ancient capital city. The First Marines remained in Tientsin, and the Seventh guarded Chingwangtao.*

In front of the French Municipal Building, the First Marines accepted the surrender of the enemy's military forces stationed in and around Tientsin on October 6. The ceremony took place before a great crowd of Chinese, who filled the streets, the windows, and the rooftops. The officers of the Imperial Army offered their swords

---

*Peiping is now known as Beijing, Tientsin is Tianjin, and Chingwangtao is now spelled Qinhuangdao.

to their counterparts and filed off to their camps "to the strains of The Marine's Hymn."[6] With the formalities completed, the marines began to inspect the bases and barracks of the Japanese. Without any foot-dragging, the Japanese complied with all instructions, surrendering all material not needed for subsistence. Their prompt cooperation earned them the right to continue to administer themselves in their camps. Each tenth soldier was allowed to keep his rifle and five bullets. The United States had determined that the Japanese needed a few rifles to protect themselves from angry mobs of Chinese.

The animosity of the Chinese to the defeated foe grew into an attack on October 13 in Tientsin. The First Marines shoved their way in and separated the two sides. In this and other actions, the United States enforced its policy. The Japanese were going to be repatriated as quickly as possible. In the meantime, retribution for their crimes against the people of China would not be exacted by angry civilians. One afternoon, two well-dressed Japanese gentlemen appeared before Shofner at his headquarters. They had asked to speak with the marine commander and were brought before his desk. They introduced themselves to him, explaining that they had been officials of the Japanese consulate before the surrender. The two men had come to say, "Thank you very, very much for protecting our people."

"This incident shows the difference in honor between my country and yours," Shofner replied. He let that assertion sink in for a moment before he told them about Bataan, Bilibid, Cabanatuan, and Davao. The two diplomats became uncomfortable and eventually declared that they had known nothing of these places. When Shifty decided he had enlightened them sufficiently, he said, "Your thanks are not wanted. You are free to go."[7]

As strange as protecting Japanese soldiers and civilians seemed, the other mission of the marines surpassed it. The protection they extended over the cities, rails, and ports denied these assets to the Chinese communists. The Chinese nationalist government, which had been at war with the communists for many years, was too weak to garrison these important locations with its own troops. The marines guarded as many key sites as they could. Since there weren't enough marines, though, the nationalists left units of Japanese forces in place. The U.S. stance angered the communists, who threatened war but could only afford to engage in the occasional skirmish. Austin Shofner's 1/1 was not only expected to protect the enemy, but to fight alongside them. The world the 1st Marine Division encountered in China had proven to be far stranger than they ever imagined.

*   *   *

THE BRICK BUNGALOW WHERE KING'S MORTAR SECTION TOOK UP RESIDENCE HAD hot and cold running water, electric lights, sofas, and two sunporches. It reminded Eugene Sledge of a college campus, although it had served so long as quarters for servicemen it was, he thought, "haunted by the spirit of Rudyard Kipling."[8] The warmth of the welcome from the Chinese he described as "a rosy dream and I just can't believe it. Four months ago I was sitting in a foxhole on Okinawa—last night I was sitting in the dining hall of the Wagon Light Hotel eating a five course dinner and listening to Strauss waltzes by a Russian pianist and a violinist. The [dinner] was free and given us by the Chinese government."

The section of Peiping in which he lived boasted the ancient city's best restaurants and theaters. Every other day, he received liberty from two p.m. to ten p.m. A ride in a rickshaw cost him a nickel, so he set off to visit the Forbidden City, to drink his first glass of milk in nineteen months, and to make the most of this great opportunity to experience an ancient and beautiful culture. A lot of his comrades, in the meantime, "spend their time in one of the three cheap imitations of stateside beer joints and know nothing more of Peiping than I do of London." In the Forbidden City, Gene saw a solid gold statue of Buddha standing five feet tall, every inch of its generous girth covered in precious stones. He quickly learned to love Chinese cuisine, started to eat with chopsticks, and escaped "the mess hall with its dehydrated chow." He befriended the owner of one restaurant who spoke English and enjoyed teaching Gene about his culture and language.

Some of the officers of the 3/5 attempted to bar enlisted men from a few choice restaurants. Sledge called them "the Semper Fidelis officers (hooray for me & to hell with you)" and was delighted when their effort failed.* "Of course the days on the lines that we all lived together, ate with the same spoon, and used nicknames are now forgotten by the gentlemen and they are once again bathing in the glory the rifleman made on Peleliu and Okinawa." As he related it to his parents, "the Army may have officers like Ed, who did things themselves which brought decorations, but [in] this outfit—the men did the deeds and the officers got the credit." Gene may have been referring to Lieutenant George Loveday, "Shadow," who received the Bronze Star in late October for his actions on June 1 on Okinawa.[9] Shadow rotated home soon thereafter. In a book about his experiences, E. B. Sledge later recounted a series of problems with the new officers and NCOs

---

*Translated from the Latin, Semper Fidelis means "Always Faithful." It is the motto of the United States Marine Corps. In World War II the shortened version "Semper Fi" was often used by marines who were not of a mind to grant a request made by a fellow marine, or as Sledge used it above.

who arrived to replace the vets. He resented taking orders from men who had not served in combat.[10]

Gene's duties inside the city were light and he never failed to note something of interest, like the locals' attempts to entice marines with signs that read, "Please come upstairs and drink and cakes." He went into the shops, looking for special presents for his family. "As the nips carried most of the real silk articles to Nippon with them finer things are pretty scarce." He also became friends with a Chinese family and spent much of his free time enjoying their company. The Soong family "opened their hearts to me" and their friendship deepened his respect for the Chinese people. Their friendship helped him start to heal the wounds in his heart.[11] As winter came on, he found he could distinguish between someone speaking in Chinese and Japanese. The former had a delightful singsong quality, the latter "is snappy & sounds like chattering with the mouth barely open." The Japanese still living in Peiping, however, tried to stay quiet and off the streets. When the former enemy saw Sledge, they saluted him, regardless of their rank. Whenever Sledge saw "a Nip on the streets," he watched "the Chinese point to them and make a motion of throat cutting."

In late October, Eugene pulled duty in an area between Peiping and Tientsin where the communists were active. Not only was the duty cold and uncomfortable, it was dangerous. On at least one occasion, shots were fired. Although he did not write home about the incident, his letters changed dramatically. The fond wishes of a quick return to Mobile so he could go hunting with his father and horseback riding and so forth gave way to a pointed criticism of U.S. foreign policy.

"In my opinion, the statement that we are staying here till all Japanese have returned home is a farce. As long as we remain here the Communists are afraid to enter Peiping & as the National government is too weak to stop them we are here. There is no reason in the world for us being involved in a Chinese civil war, and every U.S. Marine in this area resents being here and having their lives in danger." The marines had also noticed that the average Chinese civilian found the communist government more appealing than the nationalist.[12] U.S. military officers had explained that a lack of shipping had slowed the process of rotating men stateside. Gene had no patience for such rhetoric. "About 10 days ago 21 American transports took about 20,000 japs home." These shipments had been going on for months. The navy had also aided the nationalist government by ferrying their forces from one area to another. When he missed his brother Edward's wedding, Eugene's patience at this "outrage" ran out. In letter after letter, he began to press his mother to join with other "Marine Mothers" and "put up a squawk to get us point men home." Eugene now had more points toward rotation than anyone in King Company. "If anyone asks you why I'm still in China," he advised his parents, "say I'm looking out for the future of American big business in China."

IN LATE 1945 AUSTIN SHOFNER RECEIVED A LETTER FROM THE WHITE HOUSE. It had been sent to all Americans who were repatriated prisoners of war.* The president of the United States wanted "to welcome you back to your native shores and to express, on behalf of the people of the United States, the joy we feel at your deliverance from the hands of the enemy. It is a source of profound satisfaction that our efforts to accomplish your return have been successful." This letter reached Shofner not at home in Shelbyville, Tennessee, but in Tientsin, China. It indicated that someone other than Lieutenant Colonel Shofner had liberated him. The person credited in the U.S. media for liberating the POWs was General Douglas MacArthur.

Austin Shofner may have wondered when MacArthur was going to put Emperor Hirohito, Japan's absolute ruler, on trial. Shifty "longed to see the Emperor of Japan hang for the atrocities he allowed his troops to visit on their POWs and their occupied nations." Many Americans felt as he did. The first trials of war criminals, begun in December in Tokyo, had not included Hirohito. General MacArthur had decided the emperor was "a complete Charlie McCarthy."† MacArthur quietly began to convince Washington that Hirohito should not stand trial for war crimes. He also remade Japan.¹³

"From the moment of my appointment as supreme commander," General Douglas MacArthur later wrote, "I had formulated the policies I intended to follow, implementing them through the Emperor and the machinery of the Imperial Government . . . the reforms I contemplated were those which would bring Japan abreast of modern progressive thought and action. First destroy the military power. Punish war criminals. Build the structure of representative government. Modernize the constitution. Hold free elections. Enfranchise the women. Release the political prisoners. Liberate the farmers. Establish a free labor movement. Encourage a free economy. Abolish police oppression. Develop a free and responsible press. Liberalize

---

*Of the 1,343 marines who surrendered on Corregidor and Bataan, 490 did not live to see their freedom won, according to the USMC's official history of its operations in World War II. When included in with all of the POWs taken by the Japanese (the largest group being from the U.S. Army), the fatality rate dropped significantly. The chances of survival, however, were much lower than that of the U.S. POWs in Germany.

†Charlie McCarthy was a wooden puppet. The ventriloquist who operated him had a world-famous comedy routine at this time.

education. Decentralize political power. Separate church from state."[14] The unprecedented changes MacArthur wrought went beyond what he had been authorized to do. At its core, though, his program represented the will of his people: revenge cost more than humanity could pay.

Sidney Phillips's semester ended in late December 1945. The V-12 program had been canceled. He returned to Mobile with two years of college credits and the opportunity to finish his degree because passage of the GI Bill meant that Uncle Sam would pick up the tab. Feeling a little flush, he "spent every penny I had to buy Mary a watch, and she pouted, and said she wanted a ring." After Christmas, he took a quick trip back to North Carolina for December 31, when his enlistment expired. Sid Phillips received an Honorable Discharge from the United States Marine Corps for four years of faithful service.

The end of 1945 found Mike Micheel serving at NAS Miami. The navy, like all of the service branches, had begun to scale back its manpower dramatically to fit a postwar world. It knew the ones to keep, though, and had promoted Micheel to lieutenant commander. He settled into a routine as the head of the ground school. His CO described him as "aggressive in a friendly fashion that encourages friendship with his associates and facilitates working with others." Early in 1946 he got a phone call from his girlfriend, Jean Miller. She had been in a car accident. With plenty of rest, she would make a full recovery. Her doctor had suggested she escape the icy winter in Philadelphia and go someplace warm to recuperate. She thought Miami would be just the place and asked him if he thought that was a good idea. "Oh, sure," he said. Jean came down to Miami and stayed at a hotel on the beach.

The 5th Marine Division returned to Camp Pendleton in December 1945 and was disbanded. Lena Basilone was still stationed there, so she would have heard from the marines of her late husband's unit that the navy had known prior to the invasion of Iwo Jima that the seventy-two days of bombing by the B-24s had produced "negligible results" and that the number of hardened enemy positions had continued to increase in the months leading up to D-day.[15] The navy had still cut the length of the preinvasion bombardment. There were angry men in the 5th Division. Of the fifty-seven men in her late husband's machine-gun section, twenty-nine had been wounded and thirteen had been killed. The fate of the five smiling men in her wedding party could hardly have been worse. Johnny had been buried near his friends Edward Johnston and Jack Wheeler. Rinaldo Martini and Clinton Watters had both been seriously wounded. Clinton's leg healed fine. Rinaldo lost an arm on Iwo Jima.

The duty her Johnny had once fled now fell to her. At the invitation of the secretary of the navy, she traveled to Beaumont, Texas, on December 21. She christened a new destroyer, USS *Basilone*, and gave an interview on the radio.[16]

THE FLOOD OF REPLACEMENT MARINES ARRIVING IN CHINA REACHED ELEVEN thousand by mid-January 1946, enabling the remaining "60 point men," like Eugene Sledge, to ship out at the same time as the "50 point men." It took three weeks to cross the Pacific. His discharge at Camp Lejeune in mid-February caught him in the midst of an automatic promotion to corporal. He did not care. The USMC checked his belongings to ensure he had the clothing and uniforms to which he was entitled, but nothing more. He had to turn in his cartridge belt, canteen, haversack, fork, knife, spoon, knapsack, and "1 can meat with cover." Gene had served for one year, eleven months, and three days. The corps paid him the amount remaining in his account, added an extra $100 for mustering out, and handed him an Honorable Service Lapel Button. Asked for his future plans, Eugene said he planned to go to college, but remained undecided as to job preference. The course of study that most interested him was history.

ON FEBRUARY 5, 1946, LIEUTENANT COLONEL AUSTIN SHOFNER FLEW HOME FROM China by way of India. As a senior officer, he was allowed to bring home one hundred pounds of baggage free of charge. The baggage allowance and the earlier reimbursement for his personal items had not settled the score, according to Shifty, however, and one of his first orders of business was to submit another claim for the items he had had to abandon on the dock on Olongapo in December 1941. He figured the USMC owed him another $600. The corps reviewed the paperwork, disallowed the ivory statues of Chinese women, and eventually paid Shifty another $410.

Home on leave before departing for his next duty station, Shifty went to Knoxville to visit his alma mater, the University of Tennessee.[17] He had to go see his old football coach, Bob Neyland. Neyland had returned to coach the Volunteers after serving as a brigadier general in the army during the war. Shofner had been a starter on the team in 1936 and 1937, during some disappointing seasons.[18] They sat together in the coach's office with some of the current players and Shofner told him about his long war. Any expressions of disgust at MacArthur would not have found a receptive ear with the coach, who had served under MacArthur years earlier as an assistant football coach at West Point. General MacArthur, though, did not define the story of Shifty Shofner, who had gone from one end of the war to the other. Neyland wondered how he had survived all of it. "General," Shifty said, "I just did like you said we should do." Neyland looked astonished at this. Shifty continued. "You always told us to make our breaks on the field and when we forced a break, to score ... your words kept me alive."

MARY HOUSTON WANTED TO GET MARRIED ON HER TWENTY-FIRST BIRTHDAY, April 15, 1946. Sidney Phillips said, "Yes, dear." On the appointed day the Trinity Episcopal Chapel in Mobile was bedecked with Easter lilies. Mary wore "a bolero suit of periwinkle blue."[19] Sid asked Eugene Sledge to be his best man. The ceremony began at five p.m. "Thank goodness the Japs bombed Pearl Harbor," Sidney thought. "It kept the boys away from Mary until I could grow up." Sid went on to medical school and became an MD in 1952. As a general practitioner, he spent a career serving a small community outside the city of Mobile until he retired in 1991. Mary and he had three children. He lost Mary in 2000, four days before their fifty-fourth wedding anniversary. "I will be OK and get over her death in about 25 more years." These days he works outside, tending his property. On Fridays he meets with the "lunch bunch," all of them veterans, "and we tell lies." Listening to him recount his tales, one could easily assume that his service in the war was a lark. He has always believed "the Marine Corps had been really good to me."

IN THE SPRING OF 1946, LIEUTENANT COMMANDER VERNON MICHEEL TRAVELED home to Iowa. He went to see his uncle, who ran the family's dairy operation, and asked, "What happens if I come back? Can I implement some of my ideas?"

"Not unless you got more money in it than me," said his uncle. That was not encouraging. Mike had also sounded out Jean about returning to Iowa. She had "decided Mike and I would be pen pals if he moved there." Mike returned to Miami and eventually applied for a transfer out of the naval reserves and into the regular navy, which was approved. Vernon Micheel and Jean Miller married in August 1946 in her hometown, Philadelphia. He served his country for another thirty-one years, rising to the rank of captain, and in a variety of capacities, including as the commander of air wings of jet fighters. Over the years, he received more medals for his service in World War II, including four Air Medals, a Distinguished Flying Cross for his leadership in the attack on Manila Bay, and a Gold Star in lieu of a second DFC for landing his SB2C aboard *Hornet* with a big hole in her wing from an AA gunner on Peleliu. All of the men with whom he served aboard USS *Enterprise* and USS *Hornet*—black shoe and brown shoe—received the Presidential Unit Citations. Unknown to Mike, his old skipper, Ray Davis, had recommended him for a second Navy Cross for his service on Guadalcanal. "With utter disregard for his own safety," Ray wrote, "he carried out all assigned missions unflinchingly." The dairyman from Iowa has had a distinguished career in the United States Navy.

For more than sixty years, Jean Miller has watched her husband get quiet whenever the talk came to the war. "He could not say 'I did this,' or 'we did that.' He would just sit and listen to others." Still, his job has required him to put on his dress uniform on certain occasions and it comes with a lot of ribbons. Captain Micheel's ribbons tend to elicit questions from men who knew their significance. Whenever navy pilots hear a little of his background, they have to ask, You flew at Midway? Yes, he replies. Follow-up questions, Jean knows, "get a yes or no." Avid students of the Battle of Midway press further, knowing that several bomb hits from Scouting Six's first sortie on June 4 remain unattributed. His friend Hal Buell calls Mike's refusal to say that his bomb hit the Japanese carrier *Kaga* modesty. Mike calls it fair.

AUSTIN SHOFNER FOUND HIS FUTURE SOMEWHAT IN DOUBT IN THE IMMEDIATE postwar years because of the uncertainty over the future of his beloved Marine Corps. While he served at the marine base in Quantico, Virginia, the United States Congress debated the idea of the "unification" of the armed services. In general, the army supported the idea of creating a single Defense Department, while the navy opposed it. General Archer Vandegrift, the commandant, believed the bill would result in the marines'"subjugation to the status of uselessness and servility." The great hero of the Battle of Guadalcanal told Congress, "The bended knee is not a tradition of our Corps."[20] He preferred to have it disbanded than to see it subsumed.

Vandegrift won his key point in July 1947, when President Truman signed the National Security Act, which established the Marine Corps' special amphibious function. Only two divisions of the six that fought the war survived. The 1st Marine Division, the last marine division to return from overseas duty, returned in 1947 and made its home at Camp Pendleton.

That same year, Austin Shofner married his college sweetheart, the former Miss

Kathleen King of Knoxville, Tennessee. During the next twelve years, Shifty would hold a variety of positions, including as the naval attaché at the American embassy in Peru and as a member of the staff of the chief of naval operations in Washington. More awards came to him as the years passed, including a Bronze Oak Leaf Cluster in lieu of a second Silver Star for gallantry in action on Corregidor in April of 1942, and the "Special Breast Order of the Cloud and Banner" from the National Government of the Republic of China. He also wore the Presidential Unit Citation due all men who served with the 1st Marine Division on Okinawa.

Shofner received a promotion to the rank of brigadier general upon his retirement in 1959. He and his wife and their five sons returned to Shelbyville, Tennessee, where he became active in numerous businesses. They would lose one son in a tragedy and watch the other four become men of great achievements. Most of the men with whom Shofner escaped wrote accounts of their time as guerrillas on Mindanao. Shifty, who had his daily diary, never published an account.

After the Korean War, Shifty received a phone call from Private First Class Arthur Jones, who had served as his message runner on Corregidor in 1942. They arranged to meet. Jones said he still had the plaque of the Fourth Marines that Captain Shofner had entrusted to him on the day Corregidor surrendered. Jones had been sent back to a camp in Japan to work and had been liberated in August of 1945. He had been close to death many times. Keeping the plaque safe had been part of what sustained him. Arthur Jones wanted to give it to Austin to complete his mission. Shofner loved the story and the gesture, but he said the plaque did not belong to him. It belonged to the Marine Corps. They arranged to give it to the marines' museum. At the small ceremony, Jones said, "The plaque has a story which tells about the discipline, loyalty, spirit and stamina and fortitude of Marines. . . ."[21] Shifty declared, "Once a Marine, always a Marine."

Brigadier General Austin "Shifty" Shofner passed away in 1999, a few years after his beloved "Koky." At his funeral, the pastor concluded with a fact about him that his neighbors all knew. In his conversations with them, he liked to ask, "Is there anything I can do for you?" Following his death, the people of Shelbyville erected a memorial marker to him at 615 N. Main Street.[22] The large metal sign with small letters only just manages to outline the military career of Shifty Shofner.

EUGENE SLEDGE'S MEMORIES OF COMBAT DISTURBED AND PAINED HIM. THE gratitude of the Chinese people for their liberation and the love of the Soong family had helped wash away some of his anguish and grief. Being reunited with his family meant everything to him. Attending Government Street Presbyterian Church with his family, that long-awaited moment, however, did not mark his return to an easy and joyful life. When at last he went hunting with his father, he realized he had no interest in it. "The war," E. B. Sledge would later write, "had changed me more than I realized."[23] He labored under what he called a "severe depression."[24] He spent much of 1946 writing a detailed account of his war, using the notes he had kept in combat and the longer pieces he had recorded while on Pavuvu and in China.[25]

Adding to the psychic trauma he had suffered in Peleliu and Okinawa, Eugene found himself "totally unprepared for how rapidly most Americans who did not experience combat would forget about the war."[26] As for a career, he considered following in his father's footsteps. He learned that the failing grades he had incurred in the V-12 program in order to serve his country now prevented him from attending medical school.[27] It was a bitter irony, since only by enduring combat had he returned to his interest in science. He studied business administration at Alabama Polytechnic Institute (now Auburn University) and tried his hand as an insurance salesman. His brother Edward, on the other hand, made a good start in a career upon his return. It seemed Ed was, as he had always been, one step ahead of Eugene.

Most every man Gene met in the late 1940s described himself as a veteran. He noticed that "even those who had been mail clerks in Noumea" had a lot to say about their war. Their complaints, and civilians' inability to distinguish between "rear echelon troops" and "combat troops," galled him. The sheltered people had no idea. "It has always seemed a bit strange to me," he wrote a friend, "that the guy who got a million-dollar wound and was evacuated was considered a decorated hero, whereas his buddy who never got hit but stayed in it until his mind broke from stress is listed as a non-battle casualty." The nightmares would not abate. Working in insurance brought him no joy, either.

At a friend's wedding, he met Jeanne Arceneaux, also a native of Mobile. Their relationship grew quickly and they married in March of 1952, less than a year later. Although he did not describe his war to her, Gene's aunt warned her never to wake her husband by touching him—he would instantly leap to her throat. Jeanne learned to put her lips close to his ear and whisper, "Sledgehammer." His eyes would snap open.[28] She also noticed that he always carried a canteen of water with him on outings. "Why do you do that?" she asked.

"Well, we got so terribly thirsty the first day on Peleliu that it just seared into my brain that I would never be without water within reach the rest of my life."[29]

He eventually went back to school to study science, earning a PhD in biology from the University of Florida. Mastering the data of his new career, he found, allowed him to escape the nightmares. As the years passed, Gene noticed many combat veterans, including his older brother, struggle with their memories in ways that made their lives and their families' lives more difficult. E.B. became a professor of biology at the University of Montevallo in northern Alabama. In his spare time he collected books about World War II and the Marine Corps. He continued to fill pages with his recollections of combat.

In 1968, Sledge almost gave up writing. He had recently received the muster rolls for K/3/5, and reading those names and seeing the entries of when and where his friends were wounded or killed hurt him. Although it felt like he had "finally reached the end of my tether," he could not stop. As he later explained to R. V. Burgin, "My feeling of obligation to our buddies to tell it like it was wrote me on—often against my will."[30] The books he read failed to convey the horror of war because they too often relied upon official records and quoted men who had not served in a rifle company.[31]

In the next decade, the 1970s, Japan emerged as a powerful economy, a stable democracy, and a staunch U.S. ally. Americans tended not to celebrate the wonderful transformation they had done so much to create, nor to recognize the tremendous perseverance and hard work of the Japanese to raise their nation from the ashes. Americans regarded Japan as an economic rival. In 1972, the United States gave the island of Okinawa back to Japan. Japan considered the return of Okinawa the final act of the war. Two years later, the former commanding officer of Second Lieutenant Hiroo Onoda of the Imperial Japanese Army flew back to the Philippines to assure Onoda that Japan had indeed capitulated (not surrendered) and to order him to lay down his weapon. Lieutenant Onoda walked out of the jungle in 1974 in his uniform. He was armed with several hand grenades, his rifle, and five hundred rounds of ammunition. In the twenty-nine years since the war ended he had exchanged fire with local Filipinos on several occasions and killed about thirty people. He returned to Japan a hero and wrote a book.[32]

In December of 1980 E. B. Sledge completed his manuscript. He described it as "not a history, but a personal narrative of combat."[33] His narrative candidly revealed the riot of fear and the wrenching dehumanization he had endured. Both he and Jeanne, who turned his handwriting into a typed draft, hoped it would encourage leaders not to use war as a means of resolving conflicts.[34] An editor helped cut the draft down from the more than eight hundred typed pages. E.B. wanted to entitle it *Band of Brothers*, but it was changed to *With the Old Breed at Peleliu and Okinawa*. As it went off to press, he wrote his friends R. V. Burgin and Stumpy Stanley to say:"Now I'm ready to lay down the pen. Now, I think I've earned the privilege of trying to forget. I fulfilled an obligation I felt to write it all down in memory of buddies living and dead. Now, I want to enjoy the happiness of those wonderful K/3/5 friendships at the reunions, and forget what I tried to remember for so long."[35] That same year he attended the annual reunion of the 1st Marine Division for the first time. He saw R. V. Burgin, Snafu, and so many comrades dear to his heart. They told stories of the war, used nicknames not heard in decades, and caught up on one another's lives. Burgin had made a career with the U.S. Postal Service in Texas; Snafu, with a lumber company in Louisiana.

On the plane ride home from the reunion, Gene cried. He loved his wife, his two sons, and his life, but saying good-bye to King Company "felt like I was leaving home." He was fiercely proud of having served with K/3/5 even as he hated the war. Riven by that contradiction and propelled by a pervasive honesty, Sledge's memoir has become the most important personal account of the Pacific War ever written. The success of the book made it difficult for him to continue to attend reunions. He remained in touch with his friends and enjoyed rehashing the war with Bill Leyden. Seeking to help them both come to terms with their experience, Leyden wrote, "Our comrades that lost their lives were loved by their Creator just as much as the survivors. . . ." Eugene Bondurant Sledge passed away March 3, 2001. A year later, Jeanne Sledge published another section of the original manuscript entitled *China Marine*.

THE LEGEND OF MANILA JOHN BASILONE GREW IMMEASURABLY ON AUGUST 12, 1946, when the secretary of the navy awarded him the Navy Cross posthumously. Awarded for his service on Iwo Jima, the citation began, "In the forefront of the assault at all times, he pushed forward with dauntless courage and iron determination . . . [and] contributed materially to the advance of his company during the early critical period of the assault." The recommendation had been written soon after the battle by a lieutenant in Charlie Company who had landed with John on Red Beach Two.[36] The medal placed him in an elite pantheon of American military heroes. Lena accepted it in a ceremony in December of that year, wearing the dark clothes of a woman in mourning. She was always careful "never to say or do anything that would tarnish her husband's name."[37]

Lena was discharged from the corps the following January. She went back home to Oregon for a time and later worked as a secretary. As a woman of limited means, she was unable to attend the second burial of John's body at Arlington National Cemetery in March 1948, although she had chosen it for him.[38] Nor could she witness the parade that the city of Raritan staged in memory of John in June. Scores of civic and community groups marched past a crowd of ten thousand. As the highlight of the celebration, John's mother, Dora, unveiled a statue of him at the American Legion Triangle, where three of the city's important streets intersected.[39]

Lena came east in 1949. She met John's parents and his sister Mary in Boston for the commissioning ceremony of USS *Basilone* in July.[40] John's widow served as the ship's sponsor but she did not speak. The captain pronounced USS *Basilone* "ready for any service demanded by our country in peace or war." Lena next paid a visit to her husband's hometown and his family. Dora and her daughters showed her the statue of him. She brought them a few pictures of the wedding. Their meeting was strained, though, as the earlier meeting had been. They did not know her or trust her. She had married him after he had become famous and, as Sal and Dora saw it, at a time when John should have been closer to home. The Basilones had heard the news of their son's death from a reporter, who had arrived at their house before the telegram. The reporter had been looking for a quote. A radio announcement followed the telegram's arrival by a few minutes. The first visitors and more reporters began showing up soon thereafter. The family's grief had been played out in the media and in front of most of Raritan. The challenge of sharing their Johnny came again on the day of Lena's visit. To commemorate their meeting, the local newspaper took a photo of them all admiring John's portrait.[41]

Making the most of her trip, Lena met a friend and they went south to Washington and visited John's grave in Arlington National Cemetery. After lunch, she and her friend Lauretta hailed a cab. Taking a chance, Lauretta asked the cabdriver "if he knew of an American Legion Post in Arlington named after John Basilone?"[42] The cabbie smiled knowingly. "Yes," he said, "there was such a post."

"We've been trying to find it," said Lauretta, "but it isn't in the phone book and we haven't been able to trace it."

"That's easy," the cabbie said and laughed. "I'm a member of it myself."

"Well," said Lauretta, "this is Mrs. Basilone." The words snapped his head around. Vance, the cabbie, introduced himself to the two ladies and then set about creating a warm welcome. That night, the John Basilone American Legion Post put together a reception for Lena at their temporary headquarters in Arlington's Jefferson Firehouse. She met marines who had fought at Iwo Jima and elsewhere. Of all the friends they had lost, of all the brave marines they had known, they had dedicated their post to him. They also had contributed money to pay for the statue of him in Raritan, a picture of which hung on the wall. She was their guest of honor. Lena, who "had come in search of a memory," had found it. It was the last time Lena traveled east.

In the years that followed, John's legacy continued to touch her, as it did the Basilone family.[43] It became clear to one and all that America would never forget Gunnery Sergeant John Basilone. Memorials to him have been created every few years. For his family and to his widow, these tributes were just and fitting. In John's case, though, while the legacy endured, the legend grew.

In late 1962 John's sister Phyllis Basilone Cutter published a multi-installment history of his life in the local newspaper, the Somerset *Messenger-Gazette*. Her heart was in the right place. The Cold War had prompted her to remind Americans "that no matter . . . how desperate our situation is, somehow, somewhere, in this great melting pot, there arises a great American to give life and hope to a tired and weary people, and to inspire and lead them from the bitter depths of despair to the heights of victory by his shining example of raw courage and dedicated devotion to his country."

Based upon her memory, her talks with some of his friends, and a loose interpretation of the newspaper articles in her family's scrapbook, Phyllis created a bigger and better John Basilone. Her brother had been the U.S. Army's undefeated boxing champion in Manila. He had run around Guadalcanal for two days barefoot, singlehandedly winning the battle. He had been such a star on the bond tour that the Marine Corps had wanted to keep him on it indefinitely. John had had to fight to get off it. He had returned to a combat unit knowing full well that he was going to die in combat, but went anyway. For the most part, Phyllis's brothers and sisters agreed with this portrait of him.[44] Written about a man who once joked about being "a bull thrower," her article opened the floodgates.

Every few years since Phyllis Cutter's series of articles in the Somerset *Messenger-Gazette*, a writer of military history has found John's story as told by Phyllis Cutter. The articles bear such titles as "The Perfect Marine Who Begged to Die" and "Medal of Honor Winner Rejected a Hero's Life for a Hero's Death."[45] The legend of Manila John Basilone has grown beyond all proportions. A newer and as yet unproven claim holds that General Douglas MacArthur called John Basilone "a one-man army."

In 1981, the students of the Raritan-Bridgewater Elementary School Band wrote a letter to the borough council, asking why there was no longer a parade in honor of John Basilone. The members of the council thought the parade was a good idea and formed a parade committee.[46] The first parade, somewhat modest, formed up at the railroad tracks, took a little jog around La Grange Street, marched all the way down Somerset, and ended at the statue of Manila John. The members of the Raritan-Bridgewater Elementary School Band proudly marched. The John Basilone Memorial Parade has grown ever since.

By the time the parade became an annual tradition, Lena Basilone had stopped attending public memorials to her husband. She also refused to speak with most of the authors who wrote about him. She made her career as a secretary. After she retired, she remained active in her church in Lakewood, California, and with a veterans' support group. She never remarried. When, late in life, Lena was asked why she had remained a widow, she said, "Once I had the best, I couldn't settle for second best."[47] Lena Basilone passed away in June of 1999 and was buried wearing her wedding ring.

ENDNOTES

ACT I

1 The story of Brig. Gen. Austin C. Shofner relies upon the following sources: interview with Col. Elmer Davies of the USMC Historical Division, 1978, USMC Oral History Collection; "The WWII Memories of BGen. Austin Shofner, USMC," unpublished MS, January 18, 2000, by Austin C. Shofner, author's copy courtesy of Shofner Family; "The End of the Beginning," unpublished MS by Austin C. Shofner, date unknown, author's copy courtesy of Shofner Family; "The Diary of Austin C. Shofner, 1941–1943," unpublished MS, typed transcript by Tennessee State Library and Archives, Nashville; Colonel Hawkins interview with author, author's collection; the USMC Official Personnel File of Austin C. Shofner, National Records Center, St. Louis, Missouri (hereafter referred to as NRC); Report of Captain A. C. Shofner, USMC, 3 December 1943, Box 7, RG 127, National Archives and Records Administration (hereafter referred to as NARA).

2 "Life in Olongapo," *Leatherneck*, January 1939, vol. 22, #1, pp. 5, 6.

3 Kenneth W. Condit and Edwin T. Turnbladh, *Hold High the Torch: A History of the 4th Marines* (Washington, D.C.: USMC Historical Division, 1960), p. 190.

4 Tom Bartlett, "Against All Odds," *Leatherneck*, June 1976, vol. 59, #6, p. 38.

5 Hanson W. Baldwin, "The Fourth Marines at Corregidor: Part I," *Marine Corps Gazette*, November 1946, vol. 30, #11, p. 15.

6 The story of Vernon "Mike" Micheel relies upon the extensive interviews and correspondence between Micheel and the author; the Playtone Collection of interviews with Micheel, supervised by the author; the Official US Navy Personnel File of Vernon Micheel; the Flight Log of Vernon Micheel and other personal papers and orders related to his service; the Deck Log of the USS *Saratoga*, December 7, 1941; the Deck Logs of the USS *Enterprise* of 1942 (inclusive), NARA; the After Action Reports of VS-6, NARA.

7 Deck Log of the USS *Saratoga*, December 7, 1941.

8 The story of Dr. Sidney C. Phillips relies upon the Playtone Collection of interviews with Dr. Phillips, supervised by the author; Dr. Phillips's WWII memoir entitled "You'll Be Sor-ree," unpub-

lished MS, author's copy courtesy of Dr. Phillips and which the author obtained written permission to quote; the daily diary of John Wesley "Deacon" Tatum, unpublished MS, furnished by the Tatum Family; extensive correspondence and interviews by the author with Dr. Phillips; interviews with a dozen veterans of H/2/1 (Dr. Phillips's company); After Action Reports of the First Marines; Muster Rolls of 2nd Battalion, First Marines, NARA.

9 Richard Greer (D-1-7) interview with Bruce McKenna, Playtone Collection; "The Life and Death of Manila John," *Time*, March 19, 1945.

10 Richard Greer interview with author, author's collection; Phyllis Basilone Cutter, "The Basilone Story," *Somerset Messenger-Gazette*, series beginning November 15, 1962 (hereafter PBC Articles).

11 Ed Sullivan, "Little Old New York," undated column in unidentified newspaper, Raritan Public Library Collection, Raritan, New Jersey (hereafter referred to as RPL); PBC Articles.

12 Keith Sharon, "Shooting Star: The Story of John Basilone," Part 1, *The Orange County Register* online (www.ocregister.com), October 2004.

13 PBC Articles.

14 Keith Sharon, "Shooting Star: The Story of John Basilone," Part 1, *The Orange County Register* online (www.ocregister.com), October 2004.

15 Richard Greer interview with Bruce McKenna, Playtone Collection.

16 Official USMC Personnel File of John Basilone, NRC.

17 "Brother: Johnny Went Back to 'Those Kids' at War," undated clipping from unidentified newspaper, RPL.

18 Baldwin, "The Fourth Marines at Corregidor: Part I," p. 15.

19 Ibid.

20 Condit and Turnbladh, *Hold High the Torch*, p. 202.

21 William Milhoun, "Awn Up Reep!" *Leatherneck*, April 1946, vol. 29, #4, p. 19.

22 Condit and Turnbladh, *Hold High the Torch*, p. 219.

23 Baldwin, "The Fourth Marines at Corregidor: Part I," p. 52.

24 Ibid.

25 John Costello, *The Pacific War* (New York: Quill, 1982), p. 196.

26 USMC Personnel File, John Basilone, author's collection.

27 "Some Find Glory, Some Find Death, Some Find Trouble," *Newsweek*, 1945.

28 Clinton Watters (D-1-7) interviews with author; Albert Masco (D [C?]-1-7) interview with author; Richard Greer (D-1-7) interviews with author.

29 Fitness Reports of John Basilone January–April 1942, Basilone USMC Personnel File, author's collection.

30 USMC Personnel File, James P. Morgan, NRC.

31 Ed Sullivan, "Little Old New York," undated column in unidentified newspaper, RPL.

32 Col. Jon T. Hoffman USMCR, *Chesty: The Story of Lieutenant General Lewis B. Puller, USMC* (New York: Random House, 2002), p. 138.

33 Marshall Moore (former CO of C-1-7) letter to Gary Cozzens, author's copy courtesy of Gary Cozzens.

34 Baldwin, "The Fourth Marines at Corregidor: Part I," p. 54.

35 Table of Transportation, Annex A to Embarkation Plan Number 1-42, 1 January 1942, RG 127, NARA.

36 "War Strikes Japan! Planes Raid 4 Industrial Areas," *Honolulu Star Bulletin*, April 18, 1942, p. 1.

37   Ibid. p. 4.

38   "Japanese Solve Mystery of Raids," *Honolulu Star Bulletin*, April 20, 1942, p. 1.

39   Commanding Officer Scouting Squadron Six, Report of Action, June 4–6, 1942, dated June 20, 1942, NARA.

40   www.cv6.org.

41   Clarence E. Dickinson, *The Flying Guns* (New York: Charles Scribner's Sons, 1942), p. 41. Dickinson was Micheel's division leader.

42   Edwin P. Hoyt, *The Carrier War* (New York: Lancer Books, 1972), p. 37.

43   Condit and Turnbladh, *Hold High the Torch*, p. 232.

44   Baldwin, "The Fourth Marines at Corregidor: Part II," *Marine Corps Gazette*, December 1946, vol. 30, #12, p. 31.

45   Ibid. p. 28.

46   Baldwin, "The Fourth Marines at Corregidor: Part IV," *Marine Corps Gazette*, February 1947, p. 40.

47   Report of Capt. A. C. Shofner USMC, 3 December 1943, General Subject File 1940 to 1953, Box 7, 38-2 HQ USMC, RG 127, NARA.

48   Cmdr. Melvyn McCoy USN and Lt. Col. S. M. Mellnik USA, as told to Lt. Welbourn Kelley USNR, "Prisoners of Japan," *Life*, February 7, 1944, vol. 16, #6, p. 27.

49   Dickinson, *The Flying Guns*, p. vii.

50   Robert J. Casey, *Torpedo Junction: With the Pacific Fleet from Pearl Harbor to Midway* (New York: Bobbs-Merrill Co., 1942), p. 290. This book, by an experienced military journalist, is an excellent source of information about "what did they know and when did they know it."

51   Dickinson, *The Flying Guns*, p. vi.

52   Edward P. Stafford, *The Big E: The Story of the USS Enterprise* (Annapolis, Maryland: Naval Institute Press, 2002), p. 84.

53   Casey, *Torpedo Junction*, p. 337.

54   Dickinson, *The Flying Guns*, p. 135.

55   Casey, *Torpedo Junction*, p. 423.

56   Ibid. p. 340.

57   Unit Report, 3d Marine Brigade, FMF, 10 June 1942, NARA.

58   Basilone Service Record Book, Pay Book entries May–August 1942, John Basilone Official USMC File, NRC.

59   Richard Greer interview with author.

Act II

1   Casey, *Torpedo Junction*, p. 361. As do many other sources, Casey makes it clear that a lot of people in Hawaii, particularly within the navy, knew in some fashion about the coming battle.

2   Dickinson, *The Flying Guns*, p. 137.

3   Casey, *Torpedo Junction*, p. 374.

4   Commanding Officer USS *Enterprise*, Battle of Midway Island, June 4–6, 1942—Report of, Commander in Chief, Pacific Fleet Report, Serial 01849 of 28 June 1942, World War II Action Reports, NARA.

5   Dickinson, *The Flying Guns*, p. 73.

6   In the *Enterprise*'s report on the battle, "Air Battle of the Pacific, June 4–6, 1942, report of," by Admiral Spruance, the Japanese fleet was said to be "maneuvering radically." Neither Micheel nor his division leader, Lt. Clarence Dickinson, recalled it that way.

7   Dickinson, *The Flying Guns*, p. 172.

8   Ibid. p. 153.

9   Commanding Officer Scouting Squadron Six, Report of Action, June 4–6, 1942, dated June 20, 1942, NARA.

10   Capt. N. J. "Dusty" Kleiss e-mail to Battle of Midway Roundtable, 5 January 2008, Issue No. 2008-02.

11   Commanding Officer Scouting Squadron Six, Report of Action, June 4–6, 1942, dated June 20, 1942, NARA.

12   In the VS-6 Action Report, June 4–6, Gallaher stated that (a) the entire Third Division failed to return and (b) William Pittman flew in the Third Division. Pittman, however, landed aboard *Enterprise*. The same report listed his participation in later sorties.

13   Dickinson, *The Flying Guns*, p. 140.

14   Robert J. Cressman et al., *A Glorious Page in Our History* (Missoula, Montana: Pictorial Histories Publishing Co., Inc., 1990), p. 108.

15   Commanding Officer Scouting Squadron Six, Report of Action, June 4–6, 1942, dated June 20, 1942, NARA.

16   Cressman et al., *A Glorious Page in Our History*, p. 140.

17   "Jap Communiqué: 'We Beat the U.S. at Midway—Our Troops Are on the Aleutians,' " AP story, *San Francisco Chronicle*, June 11, 1942; Stafford, *The Big E*, p. 117.

18   Casey, *Torpedo Junction*, p. 396.

19   Ibid. pp. 393, 408.

20   Deck Log of USS *Enterprise*, June 1, 1942–Sept. 23, 1942, General Records, Logs of Ships and Stations, 1801–1946, RG 24, Records of Bureau of Naval Personnel, NARA.

21   Dickinson, *The Flying Guns*, p. 110.

22   "Jap Battleship, Plane Carrier Hit," *San Francisco Chronicle*, June 5, 1942 (based upon a June 4 AP story from Honolulu), p. 1.

23   "Huge Jap Invasion Fleet Smashed at Midway—Fleeing!" *San Francisco Chronicle*, June 6, 1942, p. 1.

24   "Jap Disaster," *San Francisco Chronicle*, June 7, 1942, p. 1; "Knew Jap Task Force Was Coming—and Were Ready," *San Francisco Chronicle*, June 7, 1942, p. 3.

25   Robert Turnbull, "Eyewitness of Victory: Col. Sweeney Tells How His Squadron Smashed Japan's Invasion Attempt" (dateline: With the United States Army Air Force in the Pacific, June 11), *San Francisco Chronicle*, June 12, 1942, p. 1.

26   Dickinson, *The Flying Guns*, p. vi.

27   Stafford, *The Big E*, p. 121.

28   Robert Leckie, *Helmet for My Pillow* (New York: Random House, 1957; ibooks, 2001), p. 52.

29   "MacArthur Day: Army Plans Big Show with P-38s in Spectacular Maneuvers," *San Francisco Chronicle*, June 10, 1942, p. 1; "MacArthur Day: Kezar Stadium Becomes a Battleground, a Warning to All of America's Enemies," *San Francisco Chronicle*, June 14, 1942, p. 1.

30   Stafford, *The Big E*, p. 119.

31   Much of the story of Shofner's life as a POW rests upon his daily diary and upon a report he wrote in Australia and submitted to MacArthur's headquarters. The latter was dated December 3, 1943.

32   "Prisoners of Japan," *Life*, p. 29.

33 *The Bataan Death March*, documentary, Executive Producer Charlie Mayday, The History Channel.

34 "Prisoners of Japan," *Life*, p. 29.

35 Capt. A. C. Davis's Narrative Report of Operations in Support of Guadalcanal—Tulagi Landings, Action Report, USS *Enterprise*, 24 August 1942, NARA; Official Flight Log of Vernon Micheel.

36 Deck Logs of USS *Enterprise*, June–August 1942, RG 24, Box 3, NARA.

37 Col. Clifton Cates, "Now It Can Be Told," July 30, 1942; author's copy courtesy of Dr. Sidney Phillips.

38 "Plan of the Day," August 6, 1942, USS *Enterprise*, www.cv6.org.

39 Capt. A. C. Davis's Narrative Report of Operations in Support of Guadalcanal—Tulagi Landings, Action Report, USS *Enterprise*, 24 August 1942, NARA.

40 Stafford, *The Big E*, p. 125.

41 "Plan of the Day," August 6, 1942, USS *Enterprise*, www.cv6.org.

42 Ibid.

43 Capt. A. C. Davis's Narrative Report of Operations in Support of Guadalcanal—Tulagi Landings, Action Report, USS *Enterprise*, 24 August 1942, NARA.

44 Report of Action 7 and 8 August 1942, August 22, 1942, *Enterprise* Air Group, Enclosure A, by CO of VB-6, RG 38, Box 351, NARA.

45 Capt. A. C. Davis's Narrative Report of Operations in Support of Guadalcanal—Tulagi Landings, Action Report, USS *Enterprise*, 24 August 1942, NARA.

46 Report of Action 7 and 8 August 1942, August 22, 1942, *Enterprise* Air Group, Enclosure A, by CO of VB-6, RG 38, Box 351, NARA.

47 Commander, *Enterprise* Air Group, "The Tulagi-Guadalcanal Air Action and Landing Force Operation of 7–8 August, 1942—Narrative and Comments Concerning," 10 August 1942, NARA.

48 Ibid.

49 "Plan of the Day," August 11, 1942, USS *Enterprise*, www.cv6.org.

50 A. A. Vandegrift as told to Robert B. Asprey, *Once a Marine: The Memoirs of General A. A. Vandegrift, USMC* (New York: W. W. Norton & Company, Inc., 1964), p. 126.

51 Capt. A. C. Davis's Narrative Report of Operations in Support of Guadalcanal—Tulagi Landings, Action Report, USS *Enterprise*, 24 August 1942, NARA.

52 Report of Action 7 and 8 August 1942, August 22, 1942, *Enterprise* Air Group, Enclosure A, by CO of VB-6, RG 38, Box 351, NARA.

53 Lt. Ray Davis Recommendation for a DFC, Micheel Navy File, NRC.

54 Capt. A. C. Davis's Narrative Report of Operations in Support of Guadalcanal—Tulagi Landings, Action Report, USS *Enterprise*, 24 August 1942, NARA.

55 Ibid.

56 "Action Report, Anti-Submarine Action by Aircraft, Report of," CO VB-6, 12 August 1942.

57 "History of the First Marine Regiment" Phase II (H Hour 7 August–Evening 9 August) 1st Marines Guadalcanal After Action Report, RG 127, Box 42, NARA.

58 Ibid.

59 Leckie, *Helmet for My Pillow*, p. 77.

60 "History of the First Marine Regiment" Phase II (H Hour 7 August–Evening 9 August) 1st Marines Guadalcanal After Action Report, RG 127, Box 42, NARA. This document specifically states that the captured POWs reported coming from "Guam, Japan, and Truk."

61 Commander of the *Enterprise* Air Group, "Report of Action in the Solomon Islands Area Aug. 22–25, 1942, Narrative," September 2, 1942, RG 38, NARA.

62 Commanding Officer of *Enterprise*, "Action of August 24, 1942, Including Air Attack on USS *Enterprise*, Report of," September 5, 1942, RG 38, NARA.

63 "Report of Action August 24, 1942," Bombing Squadron Six, August 31, 1942, RG 38, NARA.

64 USS *Enterprise* War Diary, August 24, 1942, www.cv6.org.

65 "Report of Action August 24, 1942," Bombing Squadron Six, August 31, 1942, RG 38, NARA.

66 Deck Logs of USS *Enterprise*, June–August 1942, RG 24, Box 3, NARA.

67 Henry I. Shaw Jr. and Douglas T. Kane, *History of the U.S. Marine Corps Operations in WWII: Isolation of Rabaul, Volume II* (Washington, D.C.: USMC Historical Division, 1963), Appendix E; see also p. 34.

68 John Basilone USMC Service Record, NRC.

69 PBC Articles.

70 Ibid.

71 Richard Greer (D-1-7) interviews with author.

72 Gilbert Lozier (C-1-7) interview with Gary W. Cozzens, Gary Cozzens Papers, USMC Archives, Special Collections, Quantico, Virginia. The author would like to express his appreciation to Gary Cozzens, who sent me his manuscript about C-1-7 entitled "Suicide Charlie," tracing the company's history up through Operation Desert Storm (copyright 1994). This manuscript alerted the author to the interviews of 1/7 men conducted by Mr. Cozzens as well as by the author Eric Hammel. The donations of this research by Messrs. Cozzens, himself a former CO of Charlie Company, and Hammel, a renowned author of WWII books, has allowed this author and future scholars to continue their work.

73 Hoffman, *Chesty*, p. 153.

74 Col. Charles Kelly correspondence with Eric Hammel, Eric Hammel Papers, USMC Archives, Special Collections, Quantico, Virginia. The author's thanks to Mr. Hammel are above in entry 72.

75 Gilbert Lozier interview with Gary W. Cozzens, USMC Archives.

76 "Platoon Sergeant John Basilone," undated MS, author unknown (John Basilone is presumed to have dictated this MS), RPL; Basilone Personnel File, USMC, NRC; Summary of Operations of the 1st Battalion, 30 September 1942, RG 127, Box 44, NARA.

77 Thomas Boyle (D-1-7) interview with author, March 10, 2004.

78 Summary of Operations of the 1st Battalion, 7th Marines, 18 September 1942, RG 127, Box 43, NARA; Summary of Operations of the 1st Battalion, 30 September 1942, RG 127, Box 43, NARA (hereafter Puller 1/7 Reports).

79 Albert Masco (D-1-7) interview with Bruce McKenna, Playtone Collection.

80 Puller 1/7 Reports.

81 Hoffman, *Chesty*, p. 157.

82 "Report on Period of Captivity," for the Commandant of the USMC, by Capt. M. H. McCoy USN, March 1946; Shofner USMC Personnel File, NRC.

83 Marshall Moore to Capt. Gary W. Cozzens, May 7, 1986, author's copy courtesy of Gary W. Cozzens.

84 "The Life and Death of Manila John," *Time*, March 19, 1945. There is reason to believe this letter made it past the censors, or was sent before an effective process of enforcing censorship was in place.

85 Richard Greer (D-1-7) interview with author, March 30, 2004, file #2.

86 Puller 1/7 Reports.

87 Lester W. Clark, *An Unlikely Arena* (New York: Vantage Press, Inc., 1989), pp. 94–95.

88 Gilbert Lozier interview with Gary W. Cozzens, USMC Archives.

89 Muster Roll, D-1-7, October 31, 1942, NARA.

90 PBC Articles.

91 John Basilone Personnel File, NRC. The Muster Roll of Company D, 1st Battalion, 7th Marines recorded that John Basilone did not participate in the actions of October 7–9. The records in his personnel file, however, indicate he did.

92 Richard Greer (D-1-7) interview with author, author's collection.

93 Capt. Marshall Moore correspondence with Eric Hammel, USMC Archives.

94 Charles Kelly correspondence with Eric Hammel, USMC Archives.

95 Hoffman, Chesty, p. 175.

96 Charles Kelly correspondence with Eric Hammel, USMC Archives.

97 Muster Rolls for C-1-7 and D-1-7, October; Charles Kelly correspondence with Eric Hammel, USMC Archives.

98 Puller 1/7 Reports.

99 Charles Kelly correspondence with Eric Hammel, USMC Archives.

100 PBC Articles.

101 Marshall Moore correspondence with Eric Hammel, USMC Archives; PBC Articles.

102 Lt. Col. Frank Hough et al., History of USMC Operations in WWII, Volume I (Washington, D.C.: USMC Historical Divison, 1989), p. 320.

103 Muster Roll of Officers and Enlisted Men of the U.S. Marine Corps., Company "D," 1 Battalion, Seventh Marines, First Marine Division, Fleet Marine Force, in the field, October 1–31, 1942, USMC, NARA.

104 Marshall Moore correspondence with Eric Hammel, USMC Archives.

105 Charles Kelly correspondence with Eric Hammel, USMC Archives.

106 Charles Kelly and Marshall Moore correspondence with Eric Hammel, USMC Archives.

107 Puller 1/7 Reports; Dog Company and Charlie Company 1/7 Muster Rolls, October 1–31, 1942, NARA.

108 Richard Greer interviews with author, author's collection. Jockstrap was also mentioned in a letter from Richard Greer to John Basilone dated 1943, Basilone Family Collection.

109 PBC Articles.

110 Ibid.

111 Dog Company 1/7 Muster Roll, October 1–31, 1942, NARA.

112 Thomas G. Miller Jr., The Cactus Air Force (New York: Bantam Books, 1987), p. 126.

113 MAG23 War Diaries, August 20–November 16, 1942, Cactus Air Force, Box 14, 1054, RG 127, NARA.

114 Ibid.

115 Clark, Unlikely Arena, p. 97.

116 Miller, The Cactus Air Force, p. 73.

117 Ibid. p. 129.

118 Arvil Jones and Lulu Jones, Forgotten Warriors: Challenge at Guadalcanal (Paducah, Kentucky: Turner Publishing Co., 1994), p. 46.

119 Miller, The Cactus Air Force, p. 132.

120 Ibid. p. 130.

121 Guido Colamarino, "Marine Earned Navy Cross Despite Faulty Machine Gun," Marine Corps Times, October 8, 2007, courtesy of Dorsorgna Family.

122 Ed Sullivan, "Little Old New York," undated column in unidentified newspaper, RPL.

123 Hoffman, *Chesty*, p. 181.

124 "Sergeant Basilone Tells Story of Exploit That Made Him a Hero, Gives Buddies Credit," *Somerset Messenger-Gazette*, September 9, 1943, p. 1, Basilone Family Collection (hereafter "Basilone Tells Story").

125 Dog Company 1/7 Muster Roll, October 1–31, 1942, USMC, NARA.

126 "Basilone Tells Story."

127 "Platoon Sergeant John Basilone," undated MS, RPL.

128 Puller 1/7 Reports; Marshall Moore letter to Gary W. Cozzens, USMC Archives.

129 Marshall Moore letter to Gary W. Cozzens, USMC Archives.

130 "Basilone Tells Story." See also "Recap of October 24–25 '42," unpublished MS by John Basilone, RPL (hereafter JB MS); this document seems authentic to the author based upon its content and its style.

131 Puller 1/7 Reports.

132 "The Hero on the Cover," *Collier's*, June 24, 1944 (hereafter *Collier's* "The Hero").

133 The account of this action is drawn from an assembly of all the interviews John Basilone gave to reporters, principally an interview with a USMC reporter on Guadalcanal, as quoted in *The Old Breed: A History of the First Marine Division in World War II* by George MacMillan (Washington, D.C.: Infantry Journal Press, 1949), p. 107; see also "Basilone Tells Story" and JB MS. Discrepancies between these accounts exist. Other sources will be cited as necessary.

134 Map of 1/7 Lines, October 23–25, by George McGillivray, author's collection.

135 The information given by Marshall Moore in a letter to Eric Hammel dated 1963 differs slightly on this point from his statements in his letter to Gary Cozzens dated 1986, USMC Archives.

136 MacMillan, *The Old Breed*, p. 107. MacMillan is quoting a USMC reporter who interviewed John Basilone soon after the battle.

137 PBC Articles.

138 JB MS; PBC Articles; "Marine Hero Visits Buddies at Manville," undated Johns-Manville Corporate Publication, Basilone Family Collection.

139 JB MS; "Basilone Tells Story."

140 JB MS.

141 Citation letter for John Basilone by Col. Lewis Puller.

142 "Appreciates a Hero," undated clipping from unidentified newspaper, RPL.

143 Navy Cross Citation for Pvt. Billie Joe Crumpton, SPOT AWARD, Serial 777, signed by the Secretary of the Navy on August 17, 1943.

144 *Collier's* "The Hero." This was written while Basilone was still in Camp Pendleton, California; it is therefore likely the reporter spoke to him.

145 Ibid.

146 *TM 9-1005-212-25 (Machine Gun, Caliber .30: Browning, M1919A4)*, Department of the Army Technical Manual, by James Jones, June 1969.

147 *Collier's* "The Hero."

148 JB MS; "Hero Praises His Buddies," September 4, 1943, *Somerset Messenger-Gazette*, Basilone Family Collection.

149 "Basilone Tells Story."

150 Navy Cross Citation for Pvt. Billie Joe Crumpton; Muster Roll of D-1-7, 1 October to 31 October 1942, NARA.

151 *Collier's* "The Hero."

152 MacMillan, *The Old Breed*, p. 107.

153 Charles Kelly correspondence with Eric Hammel, USMC Archives.

154 Ed Sullivan, "Little Old New York," undated column in unidentified newspaper, RPL.

155 JB MS.

156 Lewis Puller letter of October 31, 1942, to the Commanding Officer, First Marine Division, Basilone Personnel File, author's collection.

157 "Basilone Tells Story."

158 Lewis Puller letter of October 31, 1942, to the Commanding Officer, First Marine Division, Basilone Personnel File, NRC.

159 Ed Sullivan, "Little Old New York," undated column in unidentified newspaper, RPL.

160 "Marine Hero to Appear Here" and "Welcoming Committee," undated clippings from unidentified newspapers, Basilone Family Collection.

161 *Collier's* "The Hero."

162 James Golden, Boot Staff Writer, "Platoon Sergeant Basilone Held His Ground," undated article [circa October 1943] in unidentified publication, USMC Historical Division File (hereafter Golden Article). It is known that Golden wrote for *Parade* magazine and conducted his interview with John for, in his own words, "a popular syndicate."

163 Golden Article.

164 Puller 1/7 Reports; Marshall Moore to Gary W. Cozzens, USMC Archives.

165 JB MS.

166 JB MS; "Basilone Tells Story." In his interviews, Basilone's numbers changed somewhat. Colonel Puller's report cites different figures; Basilone's recollection is used here.

167 Lewis Puller Medal of Honor letter, 31 October 1942; Puller 1/7 Reports; Muster Roll C-1-7, 1 October 1942 to 31 October 1942, NARA.

168 MacMillan, *The Old Breed*, p. 107.

169 Manuel Berkowitz interview, Playtone Collection.

170 Marshall Moore to Gary W. Cozzens, courtesy of Gary W. Cozzens.

171 Navy Commendation Citation Medal; Cozzens, "Suicide Charlie," unpublished MS, p. 4.

172 D-1-7 Muster Roll October 31, 1942, NARA.

173 Colamarino, "Marine Earned Navy Cross Despite Faulty Machine Gun," *Marine Corps Times*.

174 Micheel Navy Personnel File; Ray Davis Recommendation for Micheel Navy Cross, February 1943.

175 Miller, *The Cactus Air Force*, p. 179.

176 MAG23 War Diaries, August 20–November 16, 1942, Cactus Air Force, Box 14, 1054, RG 127, NARA.

177 Charles Kelly letter to Gary W. Cozzens, courtesy of Gary W. Cozzens.

178 Summary of Operations of the First Battalion, Seventh Marines, period 3–8 November, 1942, RG 127, Box 43, NARA (hereafter included in subsequent citations for Puller 1/7 Reports).

179 Marshall Moore letter to Gary W. Cozzens, courtesy of Gary W. Cozzens; Charles Kelly correspondence with Eric Hammel, USMC Archives.

180 "Basilone Tells Story."

181 Ibid.

182 Richard Greer letter to John Basilone, November 27, 1943, Basilone Family Collection.

183 "Basilone Tells Story"; Clarence Angevine interview, Playtone Collection.

184 Albert Masco interview, author's collection.

185 "Prisoners of Japan," *Life*, p. 99.

186 John Basilone USMC Personnel Record.

187 Unless otherwise noted, the descriptions of Eugene Sledge's life story are based upon the lengthy letters he wrote his parents every few days from 1942 to 1946; interviews with him (courtesy of Lou Reda Productions, Kenwood Productions, and the USMC Archives); interviews with the men with whom he served; and his USMC Personnel File, NRC. The letters of Eugene Sledge are a part of the Eugene B. Sledge Collection, Auburn University Special Collections and Archives (hereafter SCAU), and are used here by permission.

188 Cressman et al., *A Glorious Page in Our History*, p. 108.

189 Reinforced Regimental General Order Number 1-42 "Possession of Army Clothing," 28 December 1942, NARA.

190 "Prisoners of Japan," *Life*, p. 99.

Act III

1   USMC Personnel File of James Pierpont Morgan.

2   Micheel Navy Cross Citation, Micheel US Navy Personnel File.

3   Capt. M. H. McCoy USN, "Report on Period of Captivity," for the Commandant of the USMC, March 1946, Shofner USMC Personnel File, NRC.

4   "Prisoners of Japan," *Life*, p. 105.

5   Richard Greer (D-1-7) interview with author, March 30, 2004, author's collection.

6   Richard Greer interview, Playtone Collection.

7   "Prisoners of Japan," *Life*, p. 106.

8   Ibid.

9   Leckie, *Helmet for My Pillow*, p. 161.

10 Capt. M. H. McCoy USN, "Report on Period of Captivity," for the Commandant of the USMC, March 1946, Personnel File of Austin Shofner, NRC.

11 Michael Dobervich to Dear Shof and Family, December 4, 1995, SCAU. Mellnik gave a different version in the three published accounts he either wrote or to which he contributed. (All three of these accounts are cited elsewhere in this volume.) The account by Dobervich and Shofner was supported by Grashio in his book (cited elsewhere); by Hawkins in interviews with the author; and by McCoy, in the letter he wrote during the war that is in Shofner's official USMC file (cited elsewhere).

12 In *On the Warpath in the Pacific: Admiral Jocko Clark and the Fast Carriers*, Clark Reynolds stated that the air group came aboard on May 6 (p. 191); I prefer to rely upon Micheel's flight log.

13 Richard Greer to John Basilone, November 27, 1943, Basilone Family Collection.

14 USMC Personnel File of James P. Morgan, NRC.

15 Mitchell Paige, *A Marine Named Mitch* (Palo Alto, California: Content Management Corporation, 1975), p. 175.

16 "Appreciates a Hero," undated clipping from unidentified newspaper, RPL.

17 Col. Mitchell Paige, a marine of great character and achievement, was bothered by the moniker hung on John Basilone—the first enlisted marine to win the Medal of Honor. Paige believed he had been the first. For more on this see *Leatherneck* magazine, "Mitchell Paige: Forgotten Hero," by

Tom Bartlett, October 1992. The action for which Basilone earned the Medal of Honor, however, occurred the night before Paige's action. Furthermore, at the moment he received the decoration in May 1943, Paige was an officer, not an NCO. Paige based his claim upon the date on which his paperwork went through; this seems like an unfortunate bit of hairsplitting to the author. The truth is neither Paige nor Basilone was the first enlisted man in WWII to receive the Medal of Honor, as will be seen.

18   PBC Articles.

19   Official USMC photographs and captions (#56749, 56785, 56971, 56974, 56786, 56588, 56987), Still Pictures Branch, NARA.

20   "Appreciates a Hero," undated clipping from unidentified newspaper, RPL.

21   "Basilone's Company 'Most Decorated' Marine Unit," undated clipping from unidentified newspaper, Basilone Family Collection.

22   USMC Photograph #56532, RPL.

23   Clinton Watters letter to author, November 22 , 2007.

24   Clark G. Reynolds, *On the Warpath in the Pacific: Admiral Jocko Clark and the Fast Carriers* (Annapolis, Maryland: Naval Institute Press, 2005), p. 192.

25   *The Fighting Lady*, a documentary filmed aboard the ship in 1943–1944, by 20th Century Fox, as cited in Reynolds, *On the Warpath*, p. 196.

26   Reynolds, *On the Warpath*, p. 197.

27   "USS *Hornet* (CV-12), Report of Shakedown Cruise in Chesapeake Bay, Bermuda Area and enroute 28 December 1943 to 1 February 1944," Box 1038, RG 38, NARA.

28   "Raritan Marine Gets Top Medal Killed 38 Japs on Guadalcanal," undated clipping from unidentified newspaper, Basilone Family Collection; "Raritan Remembers Sgt. John Basilone," *Somerset Messenger-Gazette*, September 25, 1986, Basilone Family Collection.

29   "Congressional Medal Given Basilone for Heroism as Guadalcanal Marine," June 24, 1943, clipping from unidentified newspaper, Basilone Family Collection.

30   " 'Just Did Duty'—Basilone," undated clipping from unidentified newspaper, RPL.

31   "Many Letters," undated clipping from unidentified newspaper, RPL.

32   "Marine Held Off Entire Jap Regiment for 3 Days," AP story, June 24, 1943, clipping from unidentified newspaper, Basilone Family Collection.

33   "Sidelights," undated clipping from *Raritan Valley News*, RPL.

34   Richard Greer interview with author; Sgt. Thomas J. McAllister to Mary G. Basilone, May 25, 1985, Basilone Family Collection. While Mitchell Paige, in his book *A Marine Named Mitch*, recalled that Basilone was pleased by the prospect of going home, I have deferred to the memory of the men who knew him best.

35   " 'Just Did Duty'—Basilone," undated clipping from unidentified newspaper, RPL.

36   USMC Personnel File, John Basilone.

37   Report of Action 7 and 8 August 1942, August 22, 1942, *Enterprise* Air Group, Enclosure A, by CO of VB-6, RG 38, Box 351, NARA; see also Harold L. Buell, *Dauntless Helldivers* (New York: Orion Books, 1991), p. 100.

38   Harold L. Buell interview with author.

39   Buell, *Dauntless Helldivers*, p. 205.

40   William "Billy" Bush, "Memories: Bombing Squadron Two," unpublished MS, March 2002 (hereafter Bush Memoir), not paginated, author's copy courtesy of Vernon Micheel.

41   Edwin Wenzel et al., "Chock to Chock . . . Being a Chronicle of Bombing Two from June 1, 1943, to

November 1, 1944" (privately published MS, limited edition of 200 copies, not paginated), courtesy of Vernon Micheel (hereafter "Chock to Chock").

42 Dickinson, *The Flying Guns*, p. 147.

43 USMC Personnel File, Eugene Sledge.

44 *Georgia Tech Alumnus*, May/June 1943, p. 87, courtesy of the Georgia Institute of Technology Archives.

45 Map of Campus and Environs of Georgia School of Technology, 1940–41, published by Alpha Phi Omega, courtesy of Georgia Tech Historical Center.

46 USMC Personnel File, John Basilone.

47 Photographic Collection of Richard Greer; interviews with Richard Greer.

48 "Visits Buddy," undated clipping from unidentified newspaper, Basilone Scrapbook, RPL.

49 This story comes entirely from Sid Phillips's unpublished memoir "You'll Be Sor-ree!" (p. 78). It is used by permission.

50 "Chock to Chock."

51 Ibid.

52 *The Seahorse*, a publication of the Roosevelt Base, August 28, 1943, Basilone Family Collection.

53 "Basilone Tells Story."

54 John Basilone Western Union Telegram to Mrs. Dora Basilone, August 25, 1943, Basilone Family Collection.

55 Dorothy Zimmer letter to John Basilone, November 10, 1943, Basilone Family Collection.

56 Basilone USMC Personnel File.

57 Ibid.

58 "Brother of Manila John Prefers Air Corps to Army, Marines," undated [September 1943] clipping from unidentified newspaper, Basilone Family Collection.

59 "Basilone Day," *Raritan Valley News*, July 1, 1943, RPL.

60 George Basilone letter to John Basilone, July 22, 1943, Basilone Family Collection. This letter, given its date, could not have reached John in Australia. It shows that George knew details of the event in Raritan, and he was excited to tell his brother.

61 "Basilone Day," *Raritan Valley News*, July 1, 1943, RPL.

62 USMC Official Orders, Basilone Family Collection; Basilone Personnel File.

63 Dorothy Zimmer letter to John Basilone, November 10, 1943, Basilone Family Collection.

64 Samuel C. Grashio and Bernard Norling, *Return to Freedom* (Spokane, Washington: University Press, 1982), p. 29.

65 Maj. Austin Shofner to the Commandant of the Marine Corps, March 16, 1944, Personnel File of BGen. Austin Shofner, NRC; Grashio and Norling, *Return to Freedom*, pp. 154–155.

66 Report: Motion Picture Industry in 3rd War Loan Campaign, War Activities Committee of the Motion Picture Industry, undated, Basilone Family Collection.

67 Lawrence R. Samuel, *Pledging Allegiance* (Washington, D.C.: Smithsonian Institute Press, 1998), p. 58.

68 Samuel, *Pledging Allegiance*, p. 5.

69 "Jersey Marine Cited: Killed 38 at Guadalcanal, Wins Congressional Medal for 3-day Machine-gun Rampage Without Let-up," *New York Herald Tribune*, June 23, 1943, Basilone Family Collection.

70 "Basilone Family Busy with Mail," undated clipping from unidentified newspaper, RPL.

71 "Marine Held Off Entire Jap Regiment for 3 Days," June 24, 1943, clipping from unidentified newspaper, Basilone Family Collection.

72 "Basilone to Make Bond Tour, Harry Hirshfield Accepts MC Job," undated [June or July 1943] clipping from unidentified newspaper, Basilone Family Collection.

73 "Poohs Japs' Brains," undated AP clipping and wire photo, Basilone Family Collection.

74 "Marine Calls Japs Gorillas," AP story, New York Journal-American, September 4, 1943, Basilone Family Collection; see also "Congress Medal for Killing 38," New York Journal-American, September 3, 1943, courtesy of the Dorsorgna Family.

75 "Marine Hero to Appear Here," undated [before bond tour] clipping from unidentified newspaper, Basilone Family Collection.

76 Undated photo of John Basilone in dress blue uniform with one stripe (Pfc.), Basilone Family Collection.

77 Interview with W. Burns Lee, in the documentary The Saga of Manila John, undated, Chuck Tatum Productions.

78 "For Propaganda Use," undated, unknown source, Basilone Family Collection.

79 "Dimout Gives Way to New Brownout; Effective Monday," The New York Times, October 27, 1943.

80 "Basilone Starts War Bond Tour Today," undated [September 9, 1943] clipping from unidentified newspaper, Basilone Family Collection.

81 July 23, 1945, clipping from unidentified newspaper, Basilone Family Collection.

82 Giovanni Basilone, Certificate of Birth, New York State Department of Health, City of Buffalo (registered 11393), date of certificate November 6, 1919 [date of birth November 4, 1916], Basilone Family Collection.

83 Report to the Congress of the United States: A Review of the Restrictions on Persons of Italian Ancestry During WWII, United States Department of Justice, www.usdoj.gov/crt/Italian_Report.pdf.

84 Ibid.

85 Ibid.

86 "Listen, Benito: We're Proud of Buffalo-born Basilone," UPI story, June 24, 1943, Basilone Family Collection.

87 "N.J. Marine Wrecks Jap Attack," New York Post, June 24, 1943, Basilone Family Collection.

88 "Marine Hero Comes Here," undated clipping from unidentified newspaper, Basilone Family Collection; see also "Jersey War Hero His Gun Slew So Many He Had to Move," UPI story, Newark Star-Ledger, undated, RPL.

89 Donald Basilone interview with author.

90 "Hero Praises His Buddies," Somerset Messenger-Gazette, September 4, 1943, Basilone Family Collection; "Basilone Tells Story."

91 "Meeting Mayor LaGuardia," a film file found on www.youtube.com.

92 Sunday Mirror, September 5, 1943, Basilone Family Collection.

93 "Guadalcanal Hero Welcomed by City," The New York Times, September 5, 1943.

94 "Hero Praises His Buddies," Somerset Messenger-Gazette.

95 Fitzpatrick, "Basilone Tour Biography," undated MS, Basilone Family Collection.

96 Ed Sullivan, "Little Old New York," undated column in unidentified newspaper, RPL.

97 Report: Motion Picture Industry in 3rd War Loan Campaign, War Activities Committee of the Motion Picture Industry, undated, Basilone Family Collection.

98 "Basilone Starts War Bond Tour Today," September 8, 1943, clipping from unidentified newspaper, Basilone Family Collection.

99 "Airmada" advertisement, unidentified newspaper, undated, Basilone Family Collection.

100 Bond Tour Photo Collection, Basilone Family Collection.

101 "Film Stars to Launch 3rd Bond Drive," undated clipping from unidentified newspaper, Basilone Family Collection.

102 Fitzpatrick, "Basilone Tour Biography," undated MS, Basilone Family Collection.

103 "War Heroes Help Sell $2,000,000 in Bonds," undated clipping from unidentified newspaper, Basilone Family Collection.

104 Samuel, *Pledging Allegiance*, p. xix.

105 "War Heroes Help Sell $2,000,000 in Bonds," undated newspaper clipping.

106 "Albany Ready to Welcome Hero Caravan," undated clipping from unidentified newspaper, Basilone Family Collection; "Heroes, Stars Set for Evening Rally Program," undated clipping from unidentified newspaper, Basilone Family Collection.

107 "Jap Killer Waves Greeting," undated clipping from unidentified newspaper, Basilone Family Collection.

108 "Corp. Schoenecker's Mother Plans Talk With Son's Pal," undated clipping from unidentified newspaper, Basilone Family Collection; untitled and undated clipping, Plainfield newspaper, Basilone Family Collection.

109 "I'm Glad to Get Overseas Duty," by GySgt. John Basilone, USMC Archives.

110 Bond Tour Photo Collection, Basilone Family Collection.

111 George Walker letter, September 20, 1943; Mrs. Lloyd T. Schenker letter, September 10, 1943, Basilone Family Collection.

112 "Corp. Schoenecker's Mother Plans Talk With Son's Pal," undated clipping from unidentified newspaper, Basilone Family Collection.

113 Sgt. Thomas J. McAllister to Mary G. Basilone, May 25, 1985, Basilone Family Collection.

114 "I'm Glad to Get Overseas Duty," by GySgt. John Basilone, USMC Archives.

115 Mrs. C. B. Butts to John Basilone, October 13, 1943, Basilone Family Collection.

116 "Record Crowd, Celebrities Hail Basilone at War Bond Rally," *Raritan Valley News*, September 23, 1943.

117 "Screen Stars, Military Units, 12 Bands in 2-Mile Parade," *Raritan Valley News*, September 16, 1943, Basilone Family Collection.

118 "*Life* Goes to a Hero's Homecoming," *Life*, October 11, 1943 (hereafter *Life* Article).

119 "Record Crowd, Celebrities Hail Basilone at War Bond Rally," *Raritan Valley News*, September 23, 1943.

120 Golden Article.

121 "Brother of Manila John Prefers Air Corps to Army, Marines," undated clipping [September 1943] from unidentified newspaper, Basilone Family Collection.

122 Film footage of the John Basilone Day Parade, author's collection.

123 "Sidelights," *Raritan Valley News*, September 16, 1943, Basilone Family Collection.

124 *Life* Article.

125 "Record Crowd, Celebrities Hail Basilone at War Bond Rally," *Raritan Valley News*, September 23, 1943.

126 "General Bowers Warns Basilone Day Crowd Against Rosy Dreams," undated clipping from unidentified newspaper, Basilone Family Collection.

127 "Fearless Sgt. Basilone Awed by Actress's Kiss," "20,000 Honor Raritan Hero of Guadalcanal," "Rally Nets $1,300,000 Bonds," all from *New York Herald Tribune*, September 20, 1943.

128 Movietone News Report, "Marine Sergeant John Basilone Comes Home," in author's possession, as well as a longer, unedited version of the same film footage.

129 John Basilone Speech, handwritten notecards, undated, Basilone Family Collection.

130 "General Bowers Warns Basilone Day Crowd Against Rosy Dreams," undated newspaper clipping.

131 "Manila John," lyrics by W. A. Jack and music by Joseph Memoli, MS, Basilone Family Collection.

132 "Basilone Day," undated clipping from *Raritan Valley News*, RPL.

133 "Marine Hero Visits Buddies at Manville," Johns-Manville Corporate Publication, undated, Basilone Family Collection.

134 "I'm Glad to Get Overseas Duty," by GySgt. John Basilone, USMC Archives.

135 Sledge to Dear Mom, September 28, 1943, SCAU.

136 "Raritan Recalls Its Hero Marine as a Brave Kid," undated clipping from *New York Journal-American*, RPL.

137 "Welcoming Committee," undated clipping from unidentified newspaper, Basilone Family Collection.

138 Ibid.

139 "Raritan Hero Got Action He Sought in Marines," June 24, 1943, clipping from unidentified newspaper, Basilone Family Collection; see also *New York Herald Tribune*, June 23, 1943.

140 "Welcoming Committee," undated clipping from unidentified newspaper, Basilone Family Collection. The story of John's prowess at boxing has been included in most every account of his life. Along with this interview, the author cites John's official USMC file, which asked for his preferences in sports. He checked "softball" and "golf" [twice], but not boxing.

141 Golden Article.

142 "Welcoming Committee," undated newspaper clipping.

143 Golden Article.

144 Ibid.

145 Sgt. James J. Nicholl letter to John Basilone, November 15, 1943, Basilone Family Collection. Nicholl writes that he received John's letter "about a month ago." Adding the time it took John's letter to reach him, that puts the date of John's letter in late September.

146 Albert Masco (D-1-7) interview, author's collection.

147 Virginia Greer to Mary Basilone, October 11, 1943, Basilone Family Collection.

148 Julia McCarthy, "He Got Ammunition—And Medal of Honor," unidentified newspaper, "Brooklyn Section," October 15, 1943, Basilone Family Collection.

149 Ibid.

150 John Basilone Personnel File; interviews and e-mails with Donald Basilone, author's collection.

151 Donald Basilone interview with author, author's collection.

152 Sylvia Spears to John Basilone, October 14, 1943, Basilone Family Collection.

153 Lt. Pat Heles, Co A, 29th Bn, Ft. McClellan, Alabama, October 14, 1943, Basilone Family Collection.

154 Report: Motion Picture Industry in 3rd War Loan Campaign, War Activities Committee of the Motion Picture Industry, undated, Basilone Family Collection.

155 "Visits Buddy," undated clipping from unidentified newspaper, Basilone Scrapbook, RPL.

156 Undated clipping from unidentified newspaper, Basilone Family Collection; see also letter from Richard Greer to John Basilone, November 1943, Basilone Family Collection.

157 Family Photos, Basilone Family Collection.

158 John Basilone Western Union Telegram, November 2, 1943, Basilone Family Collection. John sent

a telegram to Mary, asking about having someone meet him at the Raritan train station at ten p.m.; he was on his way back from Pennsylvania.

159 Thomas J. "Stumpy" Stanley, "To All Hands," 1982, SCAU.

160 "Chock to Chock."

161 Jean Micheel interview with author.

162 John, Carlo, and Angelo Basilone, November 9, 1943, LWO 5833, GR11, 6B3, Library of Congress.

163 Dorothy Zimmer letter to John Basilone, November 10, 1943, Basilone Family Collection.

164 Cpl. Carolyn M. Orchovic letters to John Basilone, October 23, November 1, and December 14, 1943, Basilone Family Collection.

165 Thomas Gallaher, "The Marine Who Had to Go Back," undated article from unidentified magazine, USMC Archives.

166 Don Basilone interviews and e-mails with author, November 2008, author's collection.

167 Interview with Mary Basilone, in the documentary *The Saga of Manila John*, undated, Chuck Tatum Productions.

168 Sgt. James J. Nicholl to John Basilone, November 15, 1943, Basilone Family Collection.

169 Since the war, other escapees have written books about their experience. All sorts of differences exist, of course, in the details. Shofner's memo to MacArthur's HQ, dated 3 December 1943, was used here in combination with his memoir and his diary because this is Shofner's story. See also: Stephen Mellnik, *Philippine War Diary*; Jack Hawkins, *Never Say Die*; Sam Grashio and Bernard Norling, *Return to Freedom*; Ed Dyess's serialized account in the *Chicago Daily Tribune* (beginning January 30, 1944); Melvyn McCoy and Stephen Mellnik, *Ten Escaped Tojo*; and Michael Dobervich's letter dated December 4, 1995, to Dear Shof and Family, SCAU.

170 Martin Shofner e-mail to author, author's collection.

171 Flyer and photos of this event are available at www.cimorelli.com/pie/heroes/basilone.

172 "Invest in America," undated photo, *New York Journal-American*, Basilone Family Collection.

173 Ibid. A lot of Basilone's biographers assert that Basilone spoke to Vandegrift at this event, asking to be reassigned. A close reading of the documents, however, reveals that no definitive date on which Basilone made this request can be ascertained. The underlying assumption, that Basilone would have needed help from Vandegrift to get reassigned, has not been proven and remains suspect. It seems clear that if Basilone did speak to Vandegrift here, he had to repeat his request later. For the author, the date inscribed upon the base of John Basilone's statue in Raritan, combined with the recollection of his sister Mary Basilone, is instructive. The base lists his return date as December 27, 1943. This date does not correlate with John's transfer orders or with any of the official paperwork related to his transfer. It is the date when he departed Raritan to return to active duty in D.C. This date, when combined with the Mary Basilone quote as well as the tiny news item "Guadalcanal Hero Tires of Talk, Wants Action" in the Basilone Family Collection, points to John telling his parents before he left for D.C. that he was going to request reassignment. He did not return home, and therefore December 27 became the date his mother gave the sculptor. The first request for John's transfer made by the commandant's office was dated December 29, 1943, but it does not name the commandant. Given the date, the commandant referred to would have been Gen. Thomas Holcomb, Vandegrift's predecessor.

174 "Service Men Honored," December 11, 1943, clipping from unidentified newspaper, Basilone Family Collection.

175 Richard Greer to John Basilone, November 27, 1943, Basilone Family Collection.

176 "Chock to Chock."

177 The story of meeting his girlfriend, as related on p. 70 of Shofner's "WWII Memories," was confirmed by the author's interview with Col. Jack Hawkins. Much of the rest of Shofner's description
in his memoir of his visit to D.C. is, however, at odds with the official records in his personnel file,
with the reports he wrote, and with his diary.

178 Col. Jack Hawkins interview, author's collection. This film was never made because, according to
Colonel Hawkins, the censors rejected the screenplays. Hawkins returned to active duty and served
in the Battle of Okinawa.

179 The diary of John W. Tatum provided the date on which his company was briefed on the details of
the invasion. The details themselves are found in "Phase II, Part II, Green Beach Landings," Special
Action Report of the First Marines, Box 232, RG 127, NARA.

180 "A Family Look at John Basilone," *Observer*, February 11, 1988, p. 9, RPL; see also interviews
with his family members in *The Saga of Manila John*, a documentary produced by Chuck Tatum
Productions.

181 John Basilone USMC Service Record Book, Personnel Records, NRC.

182 Interview with Mary Basilone, in the documentary *The Saga of Manila John*, undated, Chuck Tatum
Productions.

183 Interviews with Angelo and Carlo Basilone, in the documentary *The Saga of Manila John*, undated,
Chuck Tatum Productions.

184 "Guadalcanal Hero Tires of Talk, Wants Action," undated clipping from unidentified newspaper,
Basilone Family Collection. This brief news item appeared after John had departed for California.

185 "Sergeant John Basilone, Hero of Marines Killed on Iwo Jima," undated clipping from unidentified
newspaper, RPL.

186 "Guadalcanal Hero Tires of Talk, Wants Action," undated newspaper clipping.

187 "Basilone Killed While Leading Platoon on Iwo," *Courier News*, March 8, 1945.

ACT IV

1   "Phase II, Part II, Green Beach Landings," Special Action Report of the First Marines, Box 232, RG
127, NARA.

2   The Special Action Report of the First Marines states that the enemy hit G Company. However,
Tatum's diary and Phillips's memoir make clear that How Company sustained the majority of the
casualties.

3   This figure comes from Tatum's diary. The actual figure of enemy dead, according to Masters's
report, was 83. The enemy wounded had been dragged away.

4   "Chock to Chock."

5   John McCarthy, in his memoir "Scouting Six at Midway," available at www.cv6.org, discusses these
fuel-saving procedures.

6   "Chock to Chock."

7   Ibid.

8   "Phase II, Part II, Green Beach Landings," Special Action Report of the First Marines, Box 232, RG
127, NARA.

9   Robert Witty, *Marines of the Margarita: The Story of Camp Pendleton*, 1970, p. 10. A veteran made some
of this book available to the author, but the publishing information was not included.

10   Charles W. Tatum, *Iwo Jima: Red Blood Black Sand Pacific Apocalypse* (Stockton, California: Chuck Tatum Productions, 2002), p. 36.

11   Howard M. Conner, *The Spearhead: The WWII History of the Fifth Marine Division* (Nashville, Tennessee: The Battery Press, 1950), p. 2.

12   Walter Bandyk interview, Headquarters Company, 27 Regiment, author's collection.

13   Interview with Lt. Col. Justin Duryea, in the documentary *The Saga of Manila John*, Chuck Tatum Productions.

14   Tatum, *Red Blood Black Sand*, p. 41; Chuck Tatum interviews, author's collection. Basilone's Service Book does not show he ever served in B Company, 1/27, but he was assigned to the battalion HQ for a period before being assigned to C/1/27.

15   "I'm Glad to Get Overseas Duty," by GySgt. John Basilone, USMC Archives.

16   Tatum, *Red Blood Black Sand*, p. 33.

17   Lt. John Keith Wells, *Give Me Fifty Marines Not Afraid to Die* (privately published, 1995), p. 89.

18   Tatum, *Red Blood Black Sand*, p. 38.

19   Charles Tatum interview, Playtone Collection, 07B.

20   Tatum, *Red Blood Black Sand*, p. 39.

21   John Basilone to Dear Mom and Pop, undated, Basilone Family Collection.

22   Letter to John Basilone, signature illegible, dated Tuesday 25th [January] 1944, Basilone Family Collection.

23   Proceedings and Debates of the 78th Congress, 2nd Session, Appendix, Vol. 90, Part 11, "General MacArthur's Role in the War Against Japan, Remarks by Hon. Carl Hatch," pp. A3943–A4906. Hatch quotes Governor Thomas Dewey of New York, who delivered the remarks cited here.

24   www.imdb.com.

25   Senate of the United States, "Exchange and Treatment of Prisoners of War: Remarks of Hon. Elbert D. Thomas," 78th Congress, 1st Session, November 18, 1943, p. 1. Senator Thomas of Utah stated that "the office of practically every Senator is calling my office and asking questions regarding war prisoners held in the Far East."

26   "Promotion of Certain American Prisoners of War," Hearings Before the Committee of Military Affairs, United States Senate, 78th Congress, First and Second Sessions (October 15–December 1, 1943), pp. 1, 29.

27   Ibid. p. 11.

28   Lt. Col. W. E. Dyess, "Dyess—One Man Scourge of Jap Supply Fleet Off Bataan," *Chicago Daily Tribune*, February 2, 1944, p. 1.

29   "The Beasts of the Pacific," *Chicago Daily Tribune*, January 29, 1944, p. 10.

30   John H. Criders, "Ruin Japan!" *The New York Times*, January 29, 1944, p. 1; see also "War Bond Sales Soar Here in Reaction to Atrocities," *The New York Times*, January 29, 1944, p. 1.

31   "Promotion of Certain American Prisoners of War," Hearings Before the Committee of Military Affairs, p. 23.

32   Condit and Turnbladh, *Hold High the Torch*, p. 195.

33   "Chock to Chock."

34   After Action Report, VB-2, author's copy courtesy of the National Naval Aviation Museum, Pensacola, Florida.

35   Charles Tatum interview, Playtone Collection; Tatum, *Red Blood Black Sand*, pp. 45–46.

36   Wells, *Give Me Fifty Marines*, p. 97; Tatum, *Red Blood Black Sand*, p. 33.

37   Conner, *The Spearhead*, p. 1.

38   Wells, *Give Me Fifty Marines*, pp. 95–96.

39   Charles Tatum interview, Playtone Collection.

40   William Douglas Lansford, "The Life and Death of 'Manila John,'" *Leatherneck*, October 2002, vol. 85, #10.

41   Charles Tatum interview, Playtone Collection.

42   Interview with Roy Elsner, Lucille Otis, and Clinton Watters, author's collection.

43   "Brother: Johnny Went Back to 'Those Kids' at War," undated clipping from unidentified newspaper, RPL.

44   Tatum, *Red Blood Black Sand*, p. 67.

45   Charles Tatum interview with author, author's collection.

46   Charles Tatum interview, Playtone Collection; Tatum, *Red Blood Black Sand*, p. 67. The line promotion is dated February 11 in Service Record Book, Medical Records, Basilone USMC Personnel File, NRC.

47   "Public Voucher for 6 Months Death Gratuity Pay," John Basilone Personnel File, NRC.

48   Sledge's letter announcing his arrival was dated February 17, 1943; the date of arrival listed in his USMC Personnel File is April 16, 1943.

49   Jack Hawkins interviews, author's collection; Grashio and Norling, *Return to Freedom*.

50   "I'm Glad to Get Overseas Duty," by GySgt. John Basilone, USMC Archives. The polished writing and use of obscure words make it obvious that Basilone did not write this article himself. The piece was not picked up immediately by any newspapers so it likely was a proactive effort on the part of the USMC, possibly at Basilone's instigation. The mention of the "girl back East" means it was written before he met Lena and after his promotion to gunnery sergeant.

51   John Basilone to Dearest Mother and Dad, undated letter, Basilone Family Collection. John begins it with a reference to his brother George's survival of the 4th Division's invasion of the Marshall Islands.

52   Clinton Watters interview, author's collection; C-1-27 Muster Roll, January 31, 1945.

53   Clinton Watters letter to author, July 5, 2007.

54   Ibid.; Watters letter to author, November 22, 2007.

55   "Basilone Legacy Lives On in Heart of WWII Veteran," undated news item in the *Scout*, the newspaper of the USMC base at Camp Pendleton (hereafter Lena Basilone interview, *Scout* Article); Lucille Otis interview with Dustin Spence, author's collection. All of the participants disagree as to the exact date of their meeting. Lena herself gave different statements. Her most powerful memory—of going on leave the day after she met him—has been tracked to her USMC Personnel File, which lists the date of that leave.

56   Lena Basilone interview, Traditions Military Video, www.militaryvideo.com.

57   Ibid.

58   *Scout* Article.

59   Cmdr. Harold L. Buell USNR, "Death of a Captain," *Proceedings*, February 1986, p. 92.

60   USS *Hornet* (CV-12) War Diary, Box 953, RG 38, NARA.

61   Ibid.

62   Bush Memoir.

63   Ibid.

64   Reynolds, *On the Warpath*, p. 327.

65   USS *Hornet* (CV-12) War Diary, Box 953, RG 38, NARA.

66   *Scout* Article.

67   Barbara Garner interview with Dustin Spence, author's collection.

68   Lena Basilone interview, Traditions Military Video, www.militaryvideo.com.

69   Lena Riggi Basilone Service File, NRC.

70   Witty, *Marines of the Margarita*.

71   "Reply to NPRC Inquiry," 24 July 1999, Lena Riggi Basilone Service File.

72   USMC Personnel Files of John Basilone and Lena Riggi Basilone.

73   Tatum, *Red Blood Black Sand*, quoting Lena Basilone.

74   Barbara Garner interview with Dustin Spence, author's collection.

75   Photograph of John with Lena and her friends, March 8, 1944, Lucille Stacy Otis Collection.

76   "Chock to Chock."

77   Ibid.

78   After Action Report, VB-2, entry of March 30, 1944, National Museum of Naval Aviation.

79   The After Action Reports of Bombing Two (VB-2) are difficult to decipher, since the times and dates of strikes do not coincide with the dates in Micheel's log book nor those of *Hornet*'s War Diary, nor do they make sense (e.g., most strikes are listed as having occurred at midnight). The author concluded that this discrepancy was due to the VB-2 AAR practice of using GMT time, not the local time. The *Hornet* War Diary, which put times and dates in local time, and Micheel's log book, both of which the author considers reliable documents, were used.

80   After Action Report, VB-2.

81   Micheel USN Personnel File, NRC.

82   After Action Report, VB-2.

83   Bush Memoir; After Action Report, VB-2, entry of April 1, 1944.

84   Bush Memoir.

85   Reynolds, *On the Warpath*, p. 331.

86   Ibid. p. 332.

87   Cmdr. Harold L. Buell USNR, "Death of a Captain," *Proceedings*, February 1986, p. 94.

88   Ibid.

89   Reynolds, *On the Warpath*, p. 335.

90   Bush Memoir.

91   After Action Report, VB-2, NARA.

92   Buell, *Dauntless Helldivers*, p. 230.

93   Bush Memoir.

94   After Action Report, VB-2, NARA.

95   John Basilone to Dear Mother and All, April 22, 1944, Basilone Family Collection.

96   John Basilone letter, undated, Basilone Family Collection.

97   Conner, *The Spearhead*, p. 3.

98   Clinton Watters letters to author, July 5 and 10, 2007, author's collection; Calvin Anderson interview with author, May 2004.

99   William Douglas Lansford, "The Life and Death of 'Manila John,'" *Leatherneck*, October 2002, vol. 85, #10, p. 25.

100 Clinton Watters letter to author, May 22, 2007.

101 William "Bill" Lansford (HQ-1-27) interview, Playtone Collection; Jim Turner (A-1-27) interview with author, March 22, 2004; Calvin Anderson (C-1-27) interview with author; Charles Tatum (B-1-27) interview, Playtone Collection.

102 Bush Memoir.

103 USS *Hornet* (CV-12) War Diary, 1–30 April, 1944, Box 953, RG 38, NARA.

104 "Annex A and Annex B to ACA 1 Report 20-44," After Action Report, VB-2.

105 The *Hornet* War Diary for May 1–28, 1944, notes the explosion of the 100-pound bomb, but not the loose 500-pound bomb. This latter incident comes from the author's interview with Vernon Micheel and from the VB-2 memoir of William "Billy" Bush.

106 Bush Memoir.

107 Hoffman's great biography of Colonel Puller, *Chesty*, stated that he held his first inspection after the replacements came in (see p. 261). John "Deacon" Tatum's diary on the date of Chesty's first inspection, however, was clear. Puller would not come through again for another five days.

108 Cmdr. Harold L. Buell USNR, "Death of a Captain," *Proceedings*, February 1986, p. 95.

109 Reynolds, *On the Warpath*, p. 339.

110 Cressman et al., *A Glorious Page in Our History*, pp. 214–216. Written by a group of leading historians of naval aviation in WWII, this book argues that Miles Browning was a master of tactics who had played an essential role at Midway, despite his personality problems. For an opposing view of Browning's abilities, see Buell's "Death of a Captain" article in *Proceedings* (February 1986). Buell repeats Clark's story about Browning almost running *Hornet* aground the first time he took it into that atoll. Clark Reynolds's biography of Jocko Clark, *On the Warpath in the Pacific: Admiral Jocko Clark and the Fast Carriers*, though, asserts that this was the admiral's misapprehension, not the captain's oversight.

111 Conner, *The Spearhead*, pp. 1, 5.

112 Lena Basilone interview, Traditions Military Video, www.militaryvideo.com.

113 *Scout* Article.

114 Ibid.

115 Romus Valton Burgin interviews with the author, 2003–2009, author's collection.

116 Merriell Allen Shelton USMC Personnel File, NRC.

117 Mike Jernigan, "Through Memories, Sledge Reveals the Horrors of Warfare," *Auburn Alumnews*, May 1990, pp. 9–10; Dr. Sidney Phillips interview with author, May 19, 2009.

118 Daily Diary of John Wesley "Deacon" Tatum, entry of June 6, 1944, author's collection.

119 USS *Hornet* (CV-12) War Diary, 1–30 June, 1944, Box 953, RG 38, NARA. In his fine biography of Admiral Clark, *On the Warpath in the Pacific: Admiral Jocko Clark and the Fast Carriers*, Clark Reynolds stated on p. 342 that USS *Hornet* sortied from Kwajalein, but on this point the carrier's War Diary was clear.

120 Reynolds, *On the Warpath*, p. 335.

121 Bush Memoir.

122 After Action Report, VB-2, author's copy courtesy of The National Museum of Naval Aviation.

123 Buell, *Dauntless Helldivers*, p. 212.

124 After Action Report, VB-2.

125 USS *Hornet* War Diary, 1–30 June, 1944, NARA.

126 Reynolds, *On the Warpath*, p. 347. *Hornet's* War Diary makes it clear Clark returned at 1518, not 1600 as Reynolds has it.

127 USS *Hornet* War Diary, 1–30 June, 1944, NARA.

128 John Basilone to Dearest Mother, undated, Basilone Family Collection.

129 Lee W. Merideth, *Grey Ghost: The Story of the Aircraft Carrier* Hornet (Sunnyvale, California: Rocklin Press, 2001), p. 43.

130 Bush Memoir; After Action Report, VB-2.

131 After Action Report, VB-2.

132 Ibid.

133 DFC Commendation of July 1947, Micheel Personnel File, NRC; After Action Report, VB-2 (see map for strike location).

134 USS *Hornet* (CV-12) War Diary, June 1–30, 1944; After Action Report, VB-2, NARA.

135 In *On the Warpath* (pp. 352–353) Reynolds made it clear that at least one pilot recalled hearing the admiral's idea. Although neither Micheel, nor Bush, nor Buell could recall fifty to sixty years later having heard of this idea, the author included it as a supposition because (a) pilots loved to gossip about such an important idea and so if one of them heard it, it likely passed quickly, (b) the idea itself would have been almost self-evident to veteran pilots, and (c) as difficult as it is for a man to recall details half a century after they occurred, it is even more difficult for him to recall events that did not occur.

136 USS *Hornet* (CV-12) War Diary, June 1–30, 1944; After Action Report, VB-2, NARA.

137 "Chock to Chock."

138 USS *Hornet* (CV-12) War Diary, June 1–30, 1944; After Action Report, VB-2, NARA.

139 Ibid.

140 Ibid.

141 The *Hornet* War Diary and the VB-2 After Action Report have some minor discrepancies as to numbers.

142 After Action Report, VB-2.

143 Official USN Flight Log Book of Vernon Micheel.

144 Buell, *Dauntless Helldivers*, p. 264.

145 Ibid. p. 261.

146 Ibid. pp. 263–264.

147 After Action Report, VB-2.

148 Ibid.

149 In his book *On the Warpath*, Reynolds states that these hits on *Zuikakau* were scored by *Yorktown* planes. He may be referring to information received later or it may have been a typographical error. The author is concerned with what Bombing Two knew at the time. The hits were entered into the After Action Report of VB-2.

150 USS *Hornet* (CV-12) War Diary, June 1–30, 1944; After Action Report, VB-2, NARA.

151 Interview with Lena Basilone, in the documentary *The Saga of Manila John*, undated, Chuck Tatum Productions.

152 Interview with Monsignor Paul Bradley, in the documentary *The Saga of Manila John*, undated, Chuck Tatum Productions; see also "Father Paul's Quiet Heroism," by Judy Peet, *Newark Star-Ledger*, July 8, 2005, RPL; and "Retired Navy Chaplain Recalls Raising of Flag at Iwo Jima," *AMS News*, Summer 2002, RPL. Father Paul Bradley earned a Bronze Star and a Purple Heart for his service with the 28th Marines on Iwo Jima.

153 Lena Basilone Interview, *Scout* Article.

154 John Basilone USMC Personnel File.

155 Lena Basilone interview; *Scout* Article.

156 "Guadalcanal Hero to Wed," AP story, July 8, 1944, USMC Historical Division file on John Basilone.

157 George W. Garand and Truman R. Strobridge, *History of the U.S. Marine Corps Operations in World War II: Western Pacific Operations, Volume IV* (Washington, D.C.: USMC Historical Division, 1971), p. 89.

158 Ibid. p. 52.

159 "Third Battalion," in the file "Headquarters, 1st Marine Division FMF in the field/station lists (25 Aug 1944)," Box 305, RG 127, NARA.

160 Ibid.

161 Garand and Strobridge, *USMC Operations in WWII, Vol. IV*, p. 90.

162 Machine Gun Platoon Co. "C" Roster, 1945, copy courtesy of Clinton Watters; photographs of the Riggi-Basilone wedding ceremony courtesy of Lucille Stacy Otis, Barbara Garner, and Basilone Family Collection.

163 Wedding ceremony photographs, Basilone Family Collection and Barbara Garner Collection; Basilone marriage certificate, Lena Basilone USMC Personnel File, NRC; Lucille Otis interview, author's collection.

164 USMC Official Press Release, July 12, 1944, Official of Assistant Director of Public Relations (West Coast Area), USMC Official John Basilone File. This press release incorrectly listed Edward Johnston as a corporal. His rank on the Company C roster was sergeant.

165 Interview with Lena Basilone, in the documentary *The Saga of Manila John*, undated, Chuck Tatum Productions.

166 Interview with Monsignor Paul Bradley, in the documentary *The Saga of Manila John*, undated, Chuck Tatum Productions.

167 Lucille Stacy Otis interview with Dustin Spence, author's collection; USMC Official Press Release, July 12, 1944, Official of Assistant Director of Public Relations (West Coast Area), USMC Official John Basilone File. While sources gave different lengths of their furlough—Lena herself has given several different accounts—the author used the information in the USMC Official Press Release printed the day after their marriage.

168 After Action Report, VB-2; USS *Hornet* War Diary, July 1–31, 1944; Vernon Micheel interview with author.

169 After Action Report, VB-2.

170 Merriell Allen Shelton USMC Personnel File.

171 Romus Valton Burgin interview, author's collection; USMC Personnel File courtesy of R. V. Burgin.

172 Gen. Gordon Gayle interview with author. General Gayle commanded 2/5 during the Battle of Peleliu and later wrote a monograph on it.

173 Garand and Strobridge, *USMC Operations in WWII, Vol. IV*, p. 91.

174 General Gayle interview, August 1, 2005, author's collection; Thomas Stanley to Eugene Sledge, "Thoughts on Bucky's Notes," August 17, 1981, SCAU.

175 Henry "Hank" Boyes to Eugene Sledge, December 16, 1979, SCAU; Eugene Sledge, *With the Old Breed at Peleliu and Okinawa* (Novato, California: Presidio Press, 1981), p. 70 footnote.

176 Garand and Strobridge, *USMC Operations in WWII, Vol. IV*, p. 103.

177 Eugene Sledge to Henry "Hank" Boyes, January 14, 1980, SCAU; Thomas Stanley, "Canal Men Who Made Peleliu," unpublished MS, September 15, 1980, SCAU.

178 Boyes to Sledge, January 28, 1980; R. V. Burgin interview, Playtone Collection; William "Bill" Leyden interview, Playtone Collection.

179 Reynolds, *On the Warpath*, p. 383.

180 Interview with Lena Basilone, in the documentary *The Saga of Manila John*, undated, Chuck Tatum Productions.

181 Lena Basilone interview, Traditions Military Video, www.militaryvideo.com.

182 Adolf Bursa interview, author's collection; William Lansford interview, author's collection.

183 Interview with Lena Basilone, in the documentary *The Saga of Manila John*, undated, Chuck Tatum Productions.

184 Lena Basilone interview, Traditions Military Video, www.militaryvideo.com.

185 Wells, *Give Me Fifty Marines*, p. 110.

186 Conner, *The Spearhead*, p. 13.

187 Ibid. p. 15.

188 Wells, *Give Me Fifty Marines*, pp. 112–113.

189 Appendix #1 Annex E to Operation Plan 1-[?], CT-5, Cont'd p. 3, file: B13-1 5th Marine Regiment, administrative order 1–44 (11 August 1944), NARA.

190 Garand and Strobridge, *USMC Operations in WWII, Vol. IV*, p. 95.

191 Report on Fitness of Officers of the USMC, Lt. Col. Austin Shofner USMC File, August 18, 1944, to September 20, 1944, signed by Colonel Harris.

192 "Operations of the Fighter-Bomber Group," Annex A, After Action Report, VB-2, NARA.

193 *F6F Hellcat*, documentary, produced by Teleteam, Inc.

194 Captain Flagg, War Diary: Peleliu, RG 127, Box 299, NARA.

195 USMC Photo #57862, Still Pictures Branch, NARA.

196 Boyes letter to Sledge, January 28, 1980, SCAU.

197 Conner, *The Spearhead*, pp. 15–16.

198 Tatum, *Red Blood Black Sand*, p. 82.

199 Clinton Watters photographs and interviews with author.

200 Basilone letter, undated, Basilone Family Collection. This letter was written before September 15, since Lena's photo of George and John together in Hawaii was dated September 17, 1944.

201 USS *Hornet* (CV-12) War Diary, September 1–30, 1944, NARA.

202 After Action Report, VB-2, NARA.

203 Sid Phillips letter to Mrs. Sledge, October 1, 1944, SCAU.

204 Sterling Mace (K-3-5) interview, author's collection.

205 This meeting is based on an entry in John Basilone's Service Record Book, stipulating his 20-minute flight on September 14; on the photograph of him and George that Lena had dated September 17; and on the undated clipping "Basilones Meet in the Pacific," from an unidentified newspaper, which described the meeting, in the Basilone Family Collection.

206 Pfc. George W. Basilone to Sgt. Lena Basilone, May 8, 1945, Basilone USMC Personnel File.

207 Sterling Mace interview, author's collection.

208 Appendix #1 Annex E to Operation Plan 1-[?], CT-5, Cont'd p. 3, file: B13-1 5th Marine Regiment, administrative order 1–44 (11 August 1944), NARA.

209 Sterling Mace interview, author's collection.

210 R. V. Burgin interview with author.

211 Record of Operations of the Third Battalion, Fifth Marines, FMD, During the Period 26 August 1944 to 7 November 1944, SCAU, original in NARA (hereafter 3/5 Record).

212 Eugene B. Sledge interview in "Combat Leadership," USMC training film, courtesy of the USMC.

213 Sledge, *With the Old Breed*, p. 57. Sledge wrote that his LVT stalled after a near-miss from an enemy shell. In his recorded interviews, and in the memories of R. V. Burgin, it was the coral reef that stalled their craft.

214 Dr. Eugene B. Sledge interview, in the documentary *Peleliu 1944: Horror in the Pacific*, Kenwood Pro-

ductions, Minneapolis, Minnesota, 1991 (hereafter KPI). The unedited version of this interview was provided to the author by R. V. Burgin.

215 Dr. Eugene B. Sledge interview, Lou Reda Productions, used by permission (hereafter LRP).

216 3/5 Record; Captain Flagg War Diary: Peleliu, RG 127, Box 299, NARA.

217 Air Intelligence Group Excerpts from Narratives of Action—Palau, US Army Report, NARA.

218 LRP.

219 Thomas Stanley to Sledge, February 18, 1980, SCAU.

220 Henry "Hank" Boyes to Sledge, May 5, 1980, SCAU.

221 R. V. Burgin interview, author's collection.

222 Sterling Mace interview, author's collection.

223 Photograph of 3/5 HQ on the morning of September 15, 1944, USMC Photo #95503, 127-GW-713, Still Pictures Branch, NARA.

224 Thomas Stanley to Sledge, December 17, 1981, SCAU.

225 D-2 Journal, 1st Marine Div., Peleliu, RG 127, Box 299, NARA.

226 Sterling Mace interview, author's collection.

227 Henry "Hank" Boyes to Sledge, May 5, 1980, SCAU. Reconciling the many interviews and the official sources became easier when a distinction was drawn between the airfield and the airstrip.

228 Ibid

229 Ibid. Boyes earned a Silver Star for this action, and a copy of his citation (typed by Hank) is in the Sledge Collection. Sledge, however, wrote on p. 70 of With the Old Breed at Peleliu and Okinawa that the marine who performed this act was "tragically . . . killed by a sniper." He may have been referring to the first individual who approached the tank.

230 D-2 Journal, 1st Marine Div., Peleliu, RG 129, Box 299, NARA.

231 Garand and Strobridge, USMC Operations in WWII, Vol. IV, p. 118.

232 3/5 Record, p. 3. The grid maps "Special Map—Oct. 4, Central Section," which were used by 3/5, were used by the author to chart the daily course of 3/5 during the battle for Peleliu. The Special Map was found in folder B12-3 1st Marine Div. Field Orders—Peleliu, Box 305, "Geographic Files, Peleliu," RG 127, NARA (hereafter Special Map).

233 3/5 Record; Boyes to Sledge, January 28, 1980, SCAU.

234 R. V. Burgin interview, author's collection.

235 Lieutenant Colonel Shofner to Commandant of the Marine Corps, 9 March 1950, RG 127, Box 6, NARA.

236 LRP.

237 KPI. There are a number of differences between the events he recounts in the Kenwood Productions documentary Peleliu 1944: Horror in the Pacific as opposed to his book With the Old Breed at Peleliu and Okinawa and in his LFP interviews.

238 LRP. Dr. Sledge says this incident took place after his unit had been pulled back from its farthest point of penetration, but this could not be so. All other accounts have King being pulled back after nightfall.

239 Thomas Stanley to Lt. Col. James Rogers, August 21, 1980, SCAU.

240 Sledge, With the Old Breed, p. 69.

241 Thomas Stanley to Lt. Col. James Rogers, August 21, 1980, SCAU; Hank Boyes to Sledge, January 28, 1980, SCAU; 3/5 Record.

242 Comments of Col. Harold Harris, p. 130, Box 2 of 5, RG 96, SCAU (hereafter Harris Comments); 3/5 Record.

243 Hank Boyes to Sledge, January 28, 1980, SCAU; Naval Gunfire Report, Palaus [sic] Operation, p. 4, October 14, 1944, A4-8, Box 298, RG 127, NARA.

244 R. V. Burgin interview, author's collection.

245 3/5 Record, p. 3.

246 Hank Boyes to Sledge, May 5, 1980, SCAU.

247 KPI.

248 R. V. Burgin interview, Playtone Collection; Richard Higgins interview, author's collection.

249 Harris Comments; 3/5 Record, p. 3.

250 KPI.

251 Sledge mentioned this decision in several letters he wrote during the completion of his manuscript, including his letter to Walter McIlhenny dated May 31, 1977 (SCAU).

252 Sledge, *With the Old Breed*, p. 80.

253 R. V. Burgin interview, Playtone Collection. Bucky Harris also describes a "friendly fire" incident at this location in Harris Comments.

254 D-2 Journal, 1st Marine Div., Peleliu, RG 127, Box 299, NARA.

255 Boyes to Sledge, May 5, 1980, SCAU.

256 G-2 Report No. 5, September 19, 1944, III Amphibious Corps, A4-16, Box 298, NARA.

257 Harris Comments, p. 132.

258 3/5 Record, p. 4; Special Map.

259 KPI.

260 Harris Comments.

261 Army Report of Japanese Defenses, Box 305, NARA; 3/5 Report, p. 4.

262 Thomas J. "Stumpy" Stanley, "To the Men of K-3-5," unpublished MS, October 17, 1980, SCAU.

263 Photograph of Lt. Col. Austin Shofner on Peleliu, Peleliu Collection, Still Pictures Branch, NARA.

264 In *USMC Operations in WWII, Vol. IV*, p. 58, Garand and Strobridge say the jungle "cloaked the contours beneath and defied all attempts of pre-invasion aerial reconnaissance." See also General Harris to Stumpy Stanley, July 17, 1981, SCAU.

265 Harris Comments; Stanley to Sledge, "Thoughts on Bucky's Notes," August 17, 1981, SCAU.

266 Garand and Strobridge, *USMC Operations in WWII, Vol. IV*, p. 94.

267 D-2 Journal, 1st Marine Div., Peleliu, RG 127, Box 299, NARA.

268 Harris Comments; 3/5 Record.

269 G-2 Report No. 5, September 19, 1944, III Amphibious Corps, A4-16, Box 298, NARA.

270 Ibid.

271 3/5 Record, p. 5; R. V. Burgin interviews, author's collection.

272 R. V. Burgin interview, author's collection.

273 Boyes to Sledge, May 5, 1980, SCAU.

274 R. V. Burgin interview, author's collection. Sledge wrote on p. 102 of *With the Old Breed at Peleliu and Okinawa* that the lieutenant (Hillbilly Jones) called battalion HQ and spoke to Major Gustafson. It's possible, but it is outside the normal chain of command. This is what R. V. Burgin, who used a telephone regularly, recalled.

275 3/5 Record.

276 Thomas J. "Stumpy" Stanley, "To the Men of K-3-5," unpublished MS, October 17, 1980, SCAU. Stanley and Sledge were both sharply critical of the USMC's casualty figures and went to great time and expense to come up with their own, based upon official records and buttressed by interviews with their comrades.

277 USS *Hornet* (CV-12) War Diary, 1–30 September, 1944, NARA; After Action Report, VB-2, The National Museum of Naval Aviation.

278 USS *Hornet* (CV-12) War Diary, 1–30 September, 1944, NARA.

279 Annex G—Phase II—Special Action Report—Palau Operation, p. 1, Box 298, RG 127, USMC Geographic Files, Peleliu.

280 Sledge to Walter McIlhenny, May 31, 1977, SCAU: "As a young Marine P.F.C., a 60mm mortarman in K-3-5, during World War II, I carried a book of Kipling's poems, which included his 'Prelude.' The theme of the poem was constantly in my mind [on Peleliu]."

281 3/5 Record, p. 6.

282 LRP.

283 Sledge to Stanley, January 16, 1984, SCAU.

284 G-2 Report No. 5, September 19, 1944, p. 3, III Amphibious Corps, Box 298, NARA.

285 Commanding General, III Amphibious Corps to CMC, 18 October 1944, "Defective Ammunition," Box 298, RG 127, USMC Geographic Files, Peleliu, NARA.

286 3/5 Record; Harris Comments, pp. 132–133.

287 Harris Comments, p. 134.

288 Unit Report, 26 September 1944, No. 11-44 0800 25 September to 0800 26 September, CT-5, file A6-3.

289 Sledge, *With the Old Breed*, p. 103.

290 Conner, *The Spearhead*, p. 19.

291 Ibid.

292 Ibid. p. 23; Charles Tatum interview, Playtone Collection.

293 Gen. Gordon Gayle interview, November 22, 2006, author's collection; Thomas Stanley, "Peleliu Veterans—A Roll of Honor with K-3-5 at the End of Okinawa," unpublished MS, undated, SCAU.

294 Stanley to Sledge, August 17, 1981, SCAU.

295 3/5 Record, p. 6; Harris Comments, p. 134. Both of these accounts are clear about the battle. Sledge recalled it differently, but it's obvious he did so without consulting the 3/5 Record—and he also almost certainly received the Harris record too late in his writing process to include it.

296 Harris Comments, p. 134. Harris Comments disagree slightly with 3/5 Record; the author chose Harris's account, since the night obviously meant so much to him.

297 Harris Comments, pp. 134–135, 136.

298 Commanding General, III Amphibious Corps to CMC, 26 May 1945, p. 2, Army Intelligence Report, Box 306, NARA.

299 Sledge, *With the Old Breed*, p. 106.

300 R. V. Burgin interview, author's collection.

301 Ibid.; Sterling Mace interview, author's collection.

302 Unit Report, 26 September 1944, No. 11-44 0800 26 September to 0800 27 September, CT-5, file A6-3.

303 William "Bill" Leyden interview, Playtone Collection. Bill Leyden could not say for sure when this

event occurred. However, it had taken place on a hilltop or ridge. Since Starlight Hill was the only hill Bill encountered before he was wounded on Ngesebus, the correlation was strong enough to merit inclusion of the story here.

304 3/5 Record, p. 6.

305 Harris Comments, p. 135.

306 Unit Report, 28 September 1944, No. 11-44 0800 27 September to 0800 28 September, CT-5, file A6-3.

307 Harris Comments, p. 136.

308 3/5 Record, p. 6.

309 Thomas J. "Stumpy" Stanley, "To the Men of K-3-5," unpublished MS, October 17, 1980, SCAU.

310 Sledge, *With the Old Breed*, p. 104.

311 While not an official tally, this statistic comes from the manuscript "Chock to Chock." Written by the veterans of VB-2, it includes a list of the members and those who were killed in action.

312 3/5 Record.

313 Comments of 1st Division Monograph (Peleliu) by Lt. Col. L. W. Walt, USMC, RG 127, Box 6, NARA.

314 Ibid.

315 Unit Report, 29 September 1944, No. 11-44 0800 28 September to 0800 29 September, CT-5, file A6-3.

316 R. V. Burgin interview, author's collection.

317 Sledge, *With the Old Breed*, pp. 116–117.

318 Unit Report, 29 September 1944, No. 11-44 0800 28 September to 0800 29 September, CT-5, file A6-3.

319 Naval Gunfire Report, Palaus [sic] Operation, pp. 5, 6, October 14, 1944, A4-8, Box 298.

320 Ordnance Report, Palau Operation, by Corps Ordnance Officer, p. 5, 24 October 1944, Box 298, NARA.

321 Unit Report, 29 September 1944, No. 11-44 0800 28 September to 0800 29 September, CT-5, file A6-3.

322 3/5 Record, p. 9, Special Map.

323 Eugene Sledge was highly critical of the USMC's casualty figures. He and Thomas Stanley labored mightily to develop their own. In this case, Stanley came out with the numbers cited here. Sledge used the figure of eight KIA and twenty-four WIA for the company.

324 Sledge, *With the Old Breed*, p. 125.

325 R. V. Burgin interview, author's collection; Stanley to Sledge, March 1980 (day unknown), SCAU.

326 Sterling Mace interview, author's collection.

327 Harris Comments, p. 136.

328 Unit Report, 2 October 1944, No. 16-44 0800 1 October to 0800 2 October, CT-5, file A6-3.

329 Harris Comments, p. 137.

330 1-7 Marines War Diary, p. 16.

331 Unit Report, 3 October 1944, No. 17-44 0800 2 October to 0800 3 October, CT-5, file A6-3; 1-7 Marines War Diary, p. 16; 3/5 Record, p. 11.

332 1-7 Marines War Diary, p. 18.

333 3/5 Record, p. 11.

334 Ordnance Report, Palau Operation, by Corps Ordinance Officer, p. 9, 24 October 1944, Box 298, NARA.

335 Special Map; 3/5 Record, p. 11.

336 1-7 Marines War Diary, p. 18.

337 Henry "Hank" Boyes to Sledge, December 16, 1979, SCAU.

338 Thomas J. "Stumpy" Stanley, "To the Men of K-3-5," unpublished MS, October 17, 1980, SCAU.

339 D-2 Journal, 1st Marine Div., Peleliu, RG 127, Box 299, NARA.

340 Sterling Mace interview, author's collection.

341 E. B. Sledge, "Lecture to the Squadron Officer School," 1993, SCAU.

342 3/5 Record, p. 11.

343 Eugene Sledge to Dear Mother and Father, February 5, 1945, SCAU.

344 1-7 Marines War Diary, pp. 19–20.

345 Sterling Mace (K-3-5) interview, author's collection.

346 Unit Report, 5 October 1944, No. 17-44 0800 4 October to 0800 5 October, CT-5, file A6-3.

347 1-7 Marines War Diary, pp. 19–20.

348 3/5 Record; Thomas "Stumpy" Stanley, "To the Men of K-3-5," unpublished MS, October 17, 1980, SCAU. Stanley compiled a different total for this day, as is often the case. His figures are seven WIA and one KIA.

349 Harris Comments, p. 137.

350 Report on Fitness, 18 August 1944 to 30 September 1944, signed by Colonel Harris, Shofner USMC File, NRC.

351 Harris Comments, p. 137; General Bucky to Stumpy Stanley, July 17, 1981, SCAU.

352 Field Order No. 1-44, CT-5, In the Field, 5 October 1944, Box 305, Peleliu, USMC Geographic Files, RG 127.

353 3/5 Record, p. 13; Unit Report, 8 October 1944, No. 20-44 0800 7 October to 0800 8 October, CT-5, file A6-3.

354 Unit Report, 9 October 1944, No. 21-44 0800 8 October to 0800 9 October, CT-5, file A6-3.

355 Harris Comments, p. 138.

356 Stanley to Sledge, "Thoughts on Bucky's Notes," August 17, 1981, SCAU.

357 Thomas J. "Stumpy" Stanley, "To the Men of K-3-5," unpublished MS, October 17, 1980, SCAU; Captain Flagg War Diary: Peleliu, RG 126, Box 299, NARA.

358 R. V. Burgin interview, Playtone Collection; Stanley to Sledge, "Thoughts on Bucky's Notes," August 17, 1981, SCAU.

359 Frank O. Hough, *The Assault on Peleliu* (Washington, D.C.: USMC Historical Branch, 1950), p. 162. This book states that 3/5 was near the division CP.

360 Gen. Gordon Gayle interview, author's collection.

361 Shofner, "WWII Memories," pp. 83–84. Shofner claimed that he developed this response. His claim is hard to prove, since it is obvious from the available testimony that many officers came up with the same solution. It is likely that the practice began with line company officers, who noticed the tourists in their zone of action.

362 Daily Diary of John Wesley "Deacon" Tatum, author's copy courtesy of Tatum Family.

363 G-2 Report No. 5, September 19, 1944, p. 3, III Amphibious Corps, A4-16, Box 298, NARA.

364 Derrick Wright, *The Battle for Iwo Jima* (Phoenix Mill, UK: Sutton Publishing Limited, 1999), p. vii.

365 Harris Comments, p. 141.

366 Shofner, "WWII Memories," pp. 82–83. Shofner's descriptions of this incident include a lot of rich detail. The author, having examined the memoir composed late in Shofner's life against the written record, concluded that some of his descriptions had become embroidered a bit.

367 Unit Report, 12 October 1944, No. 25-44 0800 11 October to 0800 12 October, CT-5, file A6-3.

368 The unit diary of 3/5 lists their location on October 12 as Wattie Ridge. The same location was listed in the USMC Historical Division's *The Assault on Peleliu*, p. 137, as "Waddie Ridge." This example, while not the most consequential, is apt for explaining the many small discrepancies found in the unit reports of 3/5.

369 Richard Higgins interview, author's collection.

370 Sledge to Walter McIlhenny, May 31, 1977, SCAU.

371 The representation of Lt. Thomas J. "Stumpy" Stanley's combat leadership, at odds with the way he is portrayed in Sledge's book, comes from the author's interviews with R. V. Burgin, Ray Wilson, Sterling Mace, and other veterans of K/3/5.

372 Unit Report, 12 October 1944, No. 25-44 0800 11 October to 0800 12 October, CT-5, file A6-3. See also Harris Comments, pp. 138–139; the Fifth Regiment CO describes this process at some length.

373 Commanding General, III Amphibious Corps to CMC, 26 May 1945, RE: Army Intel Report: Peleliu, RG 127, Box 306, NARA.

374 Harris Comments, p. 140.

375 Unit Report, 13 October 1944, No. 26-44 0800 12 October to 0800 13 October, CT-5, file A6-3, NARA. The unit report incorrectly names the ridge—its actual name was Wattie Ridge. The incorrect name is used here because that's what 3/5 called it on the day. *The Assault on Peleliu* by the USMC Historical Division, a fine reference work, reported that the 75-mm gun was established on Hill 140. The author chose to use Harris's report. The evidence indicates that as many as three 75-mm howitzers were placed on the ridges in this area, but distinguishing exact times and locations is impossible.

376 The casualty figure comes from the 3/5 record. It is just one of the many instances where it provided a different figure from from the one created by Thomas J. Stanley; see "To the Men of K-3-5," unpublished MS, October 17, 1980, SCAU.

377 D-2 Journal, 1st Marine Div., Peleliu, RG 127, Box 299, NARA.

378 Sledge to Henry "Hank" Boyes, July 25, 1970, SCAU; see also note 375 above.

379 3/5 Record; Unit Report, 15 October 1944, No. 28-44 0800 24 October to 0800 25 October, CT-5, file A6-3.

380 General Harris to Stumpy Stanley, July 17, 1981, SCAU.

381 Harris Comments, p. 141.

382 Harris to Stanley, July 17, 1981, SCAU; Harris Comments, pp. 141, 143.

383 Annex G—Phase II—Special Action Report—Palau Operation, p. 1, Box 298, USMC Geographic Files, Peleliu, RG 127.

384 3/5 Record, p. 16; Harvey Lund (K/3/5 corpsman) interview, author's collection.

385 Stanley to Harris, December 30, 1983, SCAU; Sledge to Stanley, January 16, 1984, SCAU.

386 Annex G—Phase II—Special Action Report—Palau Operation, p. 3, Box 298, USMC Geographic Files, Peleliu, RG 127.

387 Rudyard Kipling, "Prelude," *Departmental Ditties*, 1886.

388 Annex G—Phase II—Special Action Report—Palau Operation, p. 1, Box 298, USMC Geographic Files, Peleliu, RG 127.

389 KPI. In this interview, Sledge asserted that he and his friends knew that taking the ridges was unnecessary even as they were taking them. Given the date of MacArthur's landing, however, his assertion seems a trick of memory.

390 3/5 Record.

391 3/5 Record, p. 16, mentions the stragglers; R. V. Burgin interview, author's collection. In his book *With the Old Breed at Peleliu and Okinawa* (p. 138), Sledge tells the story a bit differently.

392 Stanley to Sledge, October 7, 1980, SCAU.

393 Sledge to Henry "Hank" Boyes, July 25, 1970, SCAU.

394 5th Marine Regiment—Movement Order—Peleliu, No. 1-44 October 24, 1944, p. 1, B13-3, Box 305, RG 127, NARA.

395 3/5 Record.

396 Ibid.

397 Daily Diary of John Wesley "Deacon" Tatum, author's collection; Stanley to Sledge, December 10, 1982, SCAU.

398 Sledge, *With the Old Breed*, p. 164.

399 Henry "Hank" Boyes to Sledge, May 5, 1980, SCAU; Boyes to Sledge, December 16, 1979, SCAU.

400 "Americans Invade 2 Major Jap Island Bases," *The Mobile Register*, September 14, 1944, #133, p. 1.

401 Sledge to Walter McIlhenny, May 31, 1977, SCAU: " . . . right after we came off Peleliu I began writing notes on what my comrades and I experienced there."

402 St. Elmo Haney USMC File; Stanley to Sledge, November 30, 1983, SCAU. Hank Boyes said Haney left after two days. Sledge recalled him being on the ill-fated "war-dog patrol" a few days later.

403 Thomas J. "Stumpy" Stanley, "To All Hands," 1982, SCAU.

404 Henry A. "Hank" Boyes to Sledge, January 28, 1980, SCAU.

405 Sam Menzelos (2d Lt. K/3/5) interview, author's collection.

406 Harry Bender (K/3/5) interview, author's collection.

407 USMC Photographs #106562, 106564, and 106565 and their captions (in the Still Pictures Branch of the National Archives) tell this story.

408 Correspondence of Andrew A. Haldane, Special Collections and Archives, Bowdoin College. The author thanks Steve Moore, Haldane's nephew, for providing him with copies of these documents.

409 Henry "Hank" Boyes to Sledge, December 16, 1979, SCAU.

410 Garand and Strobridge, *USMC Operations in WWII, Vol. IV*, p. 87.

411 Brig. Gen. Austin C. Shofner, USMC Personnel File, NRC. This file contains copies of his transfer orders. The description of his time with the US Army comes from Shofner's "WWII Memories," p. 82. A note about his memoirs is necessary. Written in 2000, the memoirs reflect the memories of a man who may have had too long a time to burnish them or, as has been suggested by others who knew him, of a man who had a failing memory. In either case, there are overstatements and misrepresentations that can be proven as such. Other assertions found in his memoirs can neither be proved nor disproved at this date. The author has included only those aspects that were independently verified.

412 Wells, *Give Me Fifty Marines*, p. 118.

413 Ibid. p. 134.

414 Conner, *The Spearhead*, p. 25; Garand and Strobridge, *USMC Operations in WWII, Vol. IV*, p. 483.

415 Tatum, *Red Blood Black Sand*, p. 112.

416 Clinton Watters interview, author's collection.

417 PBC Articles.

418 John Basilone letter to parents, undated, Basilone Family Collection.

419 Shofner, "WWII Memories," p. 85.

420 "Memo to 6th Army G-2," dictated by Austin Shofner, January 23, 1945, RG 338, Entry 44469, Box 24, Folder 383.6, and attached routing slip signed by Col. Horton White and others, NARA.

421 Austin Shofner wrote in his "WWII Memories" (p. 85) that Admiral Nimitz had requested Shofner's presence and that he served alongside General Krueger on that assignment. The orders found in Shofner's USMC service file, however, show that this assignment came from the 1st Division staff. The memo Shofner dictated was completed by the staff of the 37th Division, who forwarded it up to Krueger's HQ. Shofner also insisted that he was there to greet the POWs freed from Cabanatuan on January 31, 1945. His orders, as well as the account he wrote in 1945, make clear that he departed Luzon on January 23, before the "Great Raid" began.

422 Harry Bender interview, author's collection.

423 Thomas J. "Stumpy" Stanley, "To All Hands," 1982, SCAU.

424 Garand and Strobridge, USMC Operations in WWII, Vol. IV, p. 87.

425 Charles "Chuck" Tatum interview, Playtone Collection.

426 J. R. Kerin, unpublished memoir and interview with author; Calvin Anderson and Adolf Brusa interviews with author.

427 Wells, Give Me Fifty Marines, p. 146.

428 Garand and Strobridge, USMC Operations in WWII, Vol. IV, pp. 474, 523.

429 Conner, The Spearhead, p. 35.

430 Wells, Give Me Fifty Marines, p. 137.

431 Tatum, Red Blood Black Sand, p. xi.

432 Garand and Strobridge, USMC Operations in WWII, Vol. IV, p. 473; Adolf Brusa interview, author's collection.

433 C/1/27 Machine Gun Platoon Roster, courtesy of Clinton Watters.

434 Clinton Watters interview with author; Charles "Chuck" Tatum interview with author.

435 Charles "Chuck" Tatum e-mail to author, author's collection; Tatum, Red Blood Black Sand, p. 123.

436 Lynn Kessler, Never in Doubt (Annapolis, Maryland: Naval Institute Press, 1999), p. 53.

437 John Basilone USMC Service File.

438 Conner, The Spearhead, p. 40.

439 Kessler, Never in Doubt, p. 53; Tatum, Red Blood Black Sand, p. 134.

440 Tom Lea, "Peleliu," Life, January 1945, p. 61.

441 J-O-U-R-N-A-L, UNIT Headquarters, 1st Bn, 27th Mar, 5th MarDiv, 0800 19 Feb 1945 to 1600 19 Feb 1945, NARA.

442 Ibid.

443 Report by CO of C-1-27, April 24, 1945; Navy Cross Citation for John Basilone, Basilone USMC Personnel File, NRC.

444 Bob Gallo article, undated and unidentified newspaper, RPL. An article in Newsweek from 1945 has a similar quote from Basilone at this moment.

445 Roy Elsner interview; Joe Rawlinger interview, May 3, 2004; William Weber e-mail to author; all in author's collection.

446 Charles "Chuck" Tatum, "The Death of Manila John Basilone," unpublished MS; Charles "Chuck" Tatum interviews, author's collection.

447 Chuck Tatum's account, written in "The Death of Manila John Basilone" as well as delivered in an interview (Playtone Collection), differed somewhat from that found in the Navy Cross Citation, which has John destroying the pillbox "single-handedly."

448 Tatum, "The Death of Manila John Basilone."

449 Tatum, "The Death of Manila John Basilone"; Charles "Chuck" Tatum interview, Playtone Collection.

450 Company C. Report, 24 April, 1945, Basilone USMC Personnel File, NRC; Statement of Witness George Migyanko (C-1-27) 24 April 1945 for Basilone's Navy Cross Citation; Adolf Brusa interview, author's collection.

451 J-O-U-R-N-A-L, UNIT Headquarters, 1st Bn, 27th Mar, 5th MarDiv, 0800 19 Feb 1945 to 1600 19 Feb 1945, NARA.

452 TransDiv 47 1st Trip of Boats, RG 127, NARA.

453 Roy Elsner interview; Tatum, "The Death of Manila John Basilone"; Charles "Chuck" Tatum interview; Joe Rawlinger interview; Calvin Anderson interview; Jim Turner (A-1-27) interview; William Weber (C-1-27) e-mail; all from author's collection.

454 Clinton Watters interview and e-mail, author's collection. In fairness to Mr. Watters, his doubts about the account by Mr. Tatum concerning his action with Basilone should be mentioned here.

455 Roy Elsner interview; Tatum, "The Death of Manila John Basilone"; Charles "Chuck" Tatum interview; Joe Rawlinger interview; Calvin Anderson interview; Jim Turner interview; William Weber (C-1-27) e-mail; all from author's collection. In *The Spearhead*, p. 48, Howard Conner stated that four men were hit with him.

456 Basilone Medical File, "Abstract of Medical History," February 19, 1945, Basilone USMC Personnel File. A fair number of veterans interviewed for this project claimed to have been nearby when John Basilone was killed. All of them give different versions, but they agree that a mortar round killed John, which is the version found in written accounts. With all marines dressed alike, and with all the witnesses in extremis at that moment, it is possible that their memories have been clouded by the fog of war. In the case of the written accounts, these were not informed by the medical file cited here. Since the men of Graves Registration had to examine the body and take the dog tags and keep records and bury the body, their account is definitive.

457 Col. J. Shelton Scales USMCR to author, September 10, 2007, author's collection; Adolf Brusa interview, Charles "Chuck" Tatum interview, and Clinton Watters interview, all from author's collection; Kessler, *Never in Doubt*, p. 123.

458 Sledge, *With the Old Breed*, p. 148.

459 Daily Diary of John Wesley "Deacon" Tatum, entry of November 24, 1944, author's copy courtesy of Tatum Family.

460 *Scout* Article; Barbara Gardiner interview and Lucille Otis interview, both from author's collection; Lena Basilone interview, Traditions Military Video, www.militaryvideo.com.

461 "Marine Company get final arms inspection by officers of Co under Lt. Col. Shofner," March 29, 1945, is the USMC Photograph #116686 caption in the Still Pictures Branch, NARA. The 10th Army MG Plan cited below appears to differ on the number of men Shofner commanded.

462 HQ 10th Army, Tentative Operations Plan 1-45: Military Government, HQ Tenth Army, Folder B-16, Box 278, RG 127, NARA.

463 Capt. H. Prudhomme USMCR (Asst. Civil Affairs Officer), "Enclosure K: Comments on Military Government Operations, Okinawa, 1st Marine Division, April 1–June 26 1945," June 6, 1945, Box 278, RG 127, NARA (hereafter Enclosure K).

464 Ibid.

465 Benis M. Frank and Henry I. Shaw Jr., *History of the U.S. Marine Corps Operations in World War II: Victory and Occupation, Volume V* (Washington, D.C.: USMC Historical Division, 1968), p. 94.

466 Thomas J. Stanley to William "Bill" Leyden, June 20, 1980, SCAU.

467 R. V. Burgin interview, author's collection.

468 Sterling Mace (K/3/5) interview, author's collection.

469 Pfc. A. R. Fournier USMC, "Diary of King Company, 3rd Battalion, 1st Marines," Box 260, RG 127, NARA (hereafter Fournier Diary).

470 Sterling Mace interview, author's collection.

471 Report of Military Government Activities, July 1, 1945, Box 278, RG 127, NARA.

472 3rd Battalion Special Action Report, RG 127, Box 260, NARA (hereafter 3rd Bn SAR).

473 R. V. Burgin interview, author's collection; Fournier Diary.

474 Harry Bender oral history, author's collection.

475 Sterling Mace interview, author's collection.

476 3rd Bn SAR; 5th Regiment Special Action Report, RG 127, Box 260, NARA (hereafter 5th Regiment SAR).

477 HQ—Bn, 1st Marine Div.—Journal—Okinawa, NARA.

478 First Marine Division, SAR II Okinawa, RG 127, NARA.

479 Enclosure K.

480 Ibid.

481 3rd Bn SAR.

482 5th Regiment SAR.

483 Sledge, *With the Old Breed*, p. 192.

484 Thomas J. "Stumpy" Stanley to William "Bill" Leyden, June 20, 1980, SCAU.

485 Harry Bender (K/3/5) interview, author's collection.

486 3rd Bn SAR.

487 Sterling Mace interview, author's collection.

488 E. B. Sledge, "Lecture to the Squadron Officer School," 1993, SCAU.

489 Romus V. Burgin interview, Playtone Collection.

490 Sledge, *With the Old Breed*, p. 203.

491 Boyes to Stanley, March 14, 1981, SCAU.

492 Sterling Mace interview, author's collection.

493 First Marine Division, SAR II Okinawa, RG 127, NARA.

494 Frank and Shaw, *Marine Corps Operations in World War II: Vol. V*, p. 172.

495 Fournier Diary.

496 Enclosure K.

497 Ibid.

498 3rd Bn SAR.

499 5th Regiment SAR.

500 Sterling Mace interview, author's collection.

501 Frank and Shaw, *Marine Corps Operations in World War II: Vol. V*, p. 199.

502 Sterling Mace interview, author's collection.

503 3/5 Radio Log, May 1–July 14, 1945, RG 127, Box 258, NARA.

504 Ibid.

505 Sam Menzelos interview, author's collection; Sterling Mace interview, author's collection; 3rd Bn SAR. The 3rd Battalion Special Action Report and the 3/5 Radio Log offer different accounts of which companies led the assault on this day.

506 USMC Press Release, undated. Written by a USMC correspondent in the field shortly after the incident, the document was included in a letter from Boyes to Sledge, May 5, 1980, SCAU.

507 Boyes to Sledge, May 5, 1980, SCAU.

508 Sledge to Boyes, March 31, 1980, SCAU; Boyes to Sledge, May 5, 1980, SCAU.

509 Boyes to Sledge, May 5, 1980, SCAU.

510 Sledge to Dear Mom and Pop, April 17 [May 17], 1945, SCAU. The letter is obviously misdated; given the contents of the letter, it could not have been written on April 17.

511 Stanley to Sledge, June 9 Tuesday (year unknown), SCAU.

512 Romus V. Burgin interview, author's collection. Burgin told this story as if it occurred on May 1, but the only day when King made a rapid advance on a hill and held it (the whole point of the story) was May 9.

513 Boyes to Sledge, January 28, 1980, SCAU.

514 Conner, The Spearhead, pp. 123–124.

515 Pfc. George W. Basilone to Sgt. Lena Basilone, May 8, 1945, Basilone Personnel File.

516 The date of the Treasury Salute given by the Library of Congress sound recording archives is 00/00/194, narrated by Hally Hull, LWO 5757 r28A4. See also "Some Find Glory, Some Find Death, Some Find Trouble," Newsweek, 1945, p. 25; "Sergeant John Basilone, Hero of Marines Killed on Iwo Jima," undated clipping from unidentified newspaper; and "Hero of Guadalcanal Killed in First Wave of Iwo Attack," UPI story by Lisle Shoemaker, dated February 21 "delayed"; all in the RPL.

517 Edward Kasky to Lena Mae Basilone, May 10, 1945, Basilone Personnel File.

518 First Marine Division, SAR II Okinawa, RG 127, NARA.

519 D-2 Reports (Liaison) 1st Marine Regiment, Okinawa, NARA.

520 Ted Reuther (1/1, Communications) personal history, Northwood Institute, Midland, Michigan.

521 "Notes on Interview with Lt. Col. Austin C. Shofner, USMC," by Capt. James R. Stockman by request of Headquarters, U.S. Marine Corps, 19 March 1947, NARA.

522 1st Marines Special Action Report, Box 258, RG 127, NARA (hereafter 1st Marines SAR); Frank and Shaw, Marine Corps Operations in World War II: Vol. V, p. 239; 3/5 Radio Log, May 1–July 14, 1945, RG 127, Box 258, NARA.

523 1st Marines SAR.

524 Fournier Diary.

525 E. B. Sledge, "Lecture to the Squadron Officer School," 1993, SCAU. The date of this incident comes from the Muster Roll of Officers and Men of the U.S. Marine Corps, Third Battalion, Fifth Marines, First Marine Division, 1 May to 31 May 1945, which listed the dates of Snafu's hospital stay.

526 Ronald J. Brown, A Few Good Men: A History of the Fighting Fifth Marines (New York: Ballantine Publishing Group, 2001), p. 185.

527 3rd Bn SAR.

528 William "Bill" Leyden interview, Playtone Collection.

529 1st Marines SAR.

530 "Notes on Interview with Lt. Col. Austin C. Shofner, USMC," by Capt. James R. Stockman by request of Headquarters, U.S. Marine Corps, 19 March 1947, NARA.

531 3rd Bn SAR.

532 Sledge to Stumpy, March 20, 1980, SCAU.

533 Carlisle L. Tiller to Stumpy, April 28, 1985, SCAU. Tiller said he learned the ridge's actual name only when he read Sledge's book.

534 Sledge to Stanley, February 6, 1980, SCAU.

535 Boyes to Sledge, May 5, 1980, SCAU. The biggest criticism the men of K/3/5 had of Sledge's book was his portrayal of George Loveday. Sgt. Johnny Marmet, GySgt. Hank Boyes, and Sgt. R. V. Burgin all thought Sledge had done him an injustice. Some of Sledge's disgust undoubtedly stemmed from an incident that took place between him and Loveday in China. See Sledge's *China Marine* (Tuscaloosa, Alabama: The University of Alabama Press, 2002).

536 E. B. Sledge, "Lecture to the Squadron Officer School," 1993, SCAU; Sledge letter "To Whom It May Concern" [Leyden medical claim], October 26, 1982, SCAU.

537 3rd Bn SAR.

538 3/5 Radio Log, May 1–July 14, 1945, RG 127, Box 258, NARA.

539 Sterling Mace interview, author's collection.

540 Hank to Sledge, March 31, 1980, SCAU.

541 William "Bill" Leyden interview, Playtone Collection.

542 Sledge to Dearest Mom and Pop, June 12, 1945, SCAU.

543 E. B. Sledge, "Lecture to the Squadron Officer School," 1993, SCAU.

544 Sledge, *With the Old Breed*, p. 269.

545 Sledge to Boyes, March 31, 1980, SCAU.

546 G-2 Periodic Report, 25 May 2400–26 May 2400 1945 #50, 1st Marine Regiment, Okinawa, NARA.

547 Frank and Shaw, *Marine Corps Operations in World War II: Vol. V*, pp. 277–278 footnote.

548 1st Marines SAR.

549 "Notes on Interview with Lt. Col. Austin C. Shofner, USMC," by Capt. James R. Stockman by request of Headquarters, U.S. Marine Corps, 19 March 1947, NARA.

550 1st Marines SAR; G-2 Periodic Report, 28 May 2400–29 May 2400 1945 #53, 1st Marine Regiment, Okinawa, NARA.

551 3rd Bn SAR.

552 First Marine Division, SAR II Okinawa, RG 127, NARA.

553 Frank and Shaw, *Marine Corps Operations in World War II: Vol. V*, p. 374.

554 Hank to Sledge, March 31, 1980, SCAU.

555 3rd Bn SAR.

556 "Notes on Interview with Lt. Col. Austin C. Shofner, USMC," by Capt. James R. Stockman by request of Headquarters, U.S. Marine Corps, 19 March 1947, NARA.

557 G-2 Periodic Report, 30 May 2400–31 May 2400 1945 #55, 1st Marine Regiment, Okinawa, NARA.

558 1st Marines SAR.

559 Ibid.

560 Frank and Shaw, *Marine Corps Operations in World War II: Vol. V*, p. 327.

561 3rd Bn SAR.

562 Sledge to Boyes, March 31, 1980, SCAU; Boyes to Sledge, May 5, 1980, SCAU.

563 1st Marines SAR.

564 Frank and Shaw, *Marine Corps Operations in World War II: Vol. V*, p. 333.

565 Shofner, "WWII Memories," p. 96. It must be noted that Shofner's version of this particular action, written late in his life, contains some overstatements and/or misrepresentations that have been omitted. The story is included because he described the casus belli in "Notes on Interview with Lt. Col. Austin C. Shofner, USMC," by Capt. James R. Stockman by request of Headquarters, U.S. Marine Corps, 19 March 1947, NARA.

566 1st Marines SAR.

567   Ibid.

568   Fournier Diary.

569   First Marine Division, SAR II Okinawa, RG 127, NARA.

570   Frank and Shaw, *Marine Corps Operations in World War II: Vol. V*, p. 345.

571   Carlisle L. Tiller to Stumpy, April 28, 1985, SCAU.

572   3rd Bn SAR contradicts Sledge's *With the Old Breed at Peleliu and Okinawa* slightly as to the chronology of events on Kunishi Ridge (see p. 294).

573   Sledge to Dearest Mom and Pop, June 24, 1945, SCAU.

574   Boyes to Sledge, May 5, 1980, SCAU; Sledge to Boyes, March 31, 1980, SCAU. The 3rd Bn SAR totaled only thirty-one casualties for this action, but Sledge and Boyes make a compelling case for the higher figure.

575   Stanley to Sledge, June 9 Tuesday (year unknown), SCAU.

576   3rd Bn SAR.

577   KPI.

578   3rd Bn SAR.

579   KPI.

580   Brown, *A Few Good Men: A History of the Fighting Fifth Marines*, p. 191.

581   Sledge to Stanley, August 26, 1980, SCAU; see also Stanley, "Peleliu Veterans—A Roll of Honor with K-3-5 at the End of Okinawa," undated MS, SCAU; Boyes to Sledge, January 28, 1980, and May 8, 1980, SCAU; Sledge to Boyes, March 31, 1980, SCAU.

582   Sgt. Joe Frangona (1/1) interview with Dr. Dave Thompson, March 3, 2004, author's collection.

583   Fournier Diary.

584   Brown, *A Few Good Men: A History of the Fighting Fifth Marines*, p. 191.

585   William Phillips (1/1) interview, author's collection.

586   First Marine Division, SAR II Okinawa, RG 127, NARA.

587   Ted Reuther (1/1, Communications) personal history, Northwood Institute, Midland, Michigan.

588   Sam Menzelos (K/3/5) interview, author's collection.

589   Merriell Allen Shelton USMC Personnel File, NRC.

Act V

1   Jeanne Sledge interview, Playtone Collection.

2   Frank L. Kluckhohn, "Atsugi 'Parade' On," *The New York Times*, August 30, 1945, p. 1.

3   Richard B. Finn, *Winners in Peace: MacArthur, Yoshida, and Postwar Japan* (Berkeley, California: University of California Press, 1992), p. 8.

4   Ibid. p. 10.

5   Ted Reuther (1/1, Communications) personal history, Northwood Institute, Midland, Michigan.

6   Frank and Shaw, *Marine Corps Operations in World War II: Vol. V*, p. 557.

7   Cpl. Bill Farrell, "Hot Irony," *Leatherneck*, April 1946, vol. 29, #4, p. 19.

8   E. B. Sledge, *China Marine* (Tuscaloosa, Alabama: The University of Alabama Press, 2002), p. 24.

9   Thomas Stanley to Sledge, December 10, 1981, SCAU.

10   Sledge, *China Marine*, p. 102.

11   The healing love provided by the Soong Family, although touched on by Sledge in his letters home, was most fully described by him in his second book, *China Marine*.

12 Frank and Shaw, *Marine Corps Operations in World War II: Vol. V*, p. 532.

13 Finn, *Winners in Peace*.

14 Douglas MacArthur, *Reminiscences* (New York: McGraw-Hill, 1964), pp. 282–283.

15 Frank and Shaw, *Marine Corps Operations in World War II: Vol. V*, p. 492.

16 *Scout* Article; USS *Basilone* Commissioning Ceremony Program, RPL; Lena Basilone Service File, NRC.

17 Shofner, "WWII Memories," p. 73, stated that this meeting took place in 1943. Coach Neyland, however, served overseas during the war and thus this important meeting could have taken place only in 1946.

18 Bob Gilbert, *Neyland: The Gridiron General* (Savannah, Georgia: Golden Coast Publishing Co., 1990).

19 "Houston-Phillips Wedding of Interest," undated clipping from unidentified newspaper, Sidney Phillips Collection.

20 J. Robert Moskin, *The U.S. Marine Corps Story* (New York: McGraw-Hill, 1977).

21 Tom Bartlett, "Against All Odds," *Leatherneck*, June 1976, vol. 59, #6, pp. 39–41.

22 Kay Rose, "New Plaque Honors Shofner," *Shelbyville Times-Gazette*, May 5, 2003, p. 1, courtesy of Col. Otto Melsa.

23 Sledge, *China Marine*, p. 154.

24 Sledge to Stumpy and Valton, December 3, 1980, SCAU.

25 Sledge to Stanley, February 6, 1980, SCAU; Sledge to Hank Boyes, July 25, 1979, SCAU; Sledge to Walter McIlhenny, May 31, 1977, SCAU.

26 Sledge, *China Marine*, p. 135.

27 Dr. Sidney Phillips interview, author's collection.

28 Jeanne Sledge e-mail to author, 2008, author's collection.

29 KPI.

30 Sledge to Stumpy and Valton, December 3, 1980, SCAU.

31 Sledge to Stanley, January 16, 1984, SCAU. It is clear that Sledge did not have access to the 3/5 Record or the 3rd Bn SAR cited frequently here. When he saw the former document years later, it disgusted him.

32 The story of Hiroo Onoda was taken from an entry of www.wikipedia.com.

33 Sledge to Stanley, January 16, 1984, SCAU.

34 Jeanne Sledge interview, May 2004, Playtone Collection.

35 Sledge to Stumpy and Valton, December 3, 1980, SCAU.

36 Lieutenant Kasky (CO of C-1-27), April 24, 1945, Basilone USMC Service File, NRC.

37 *Scout* Article.

38 Carlo Basilone to Gen. A. A. Vandegrift, April 12, 1946, Basilone Personnel File; A. A. Vandegrift to Mrs. John Basilone, September 29, 1947, Basilone USMC Personnel File; "World War II Hero's Sister Dies in Somerville Car Accident," *Newark Star-Ledger*, November 15, 2003, RPL; photograph of the funeral at Arlington, Basilone Family Collection; Ed Sullivan, "Little Old New York," undated column in unidentified newspaper, RPL.

39 "Raritan to Unveil Statue of Basilone; Parade Set," *Courier News*, June 4, 1948; "Dedicate Statue of Basilone," June 7, 1948, clipping from unidentified Newark, New Jersey, newspaper, RPL.

40 USS *Basilone* Commissioning Ceremony Program, RPL.

41 "Meets His Family," undated clipping from unidentified newspaper, Basilone Family Collection.

42 Herbert Lansner, "Chance Call for Taxi Reunites Widow, Hero Husband's Pals," undated clipping from unidentified newspaper, Basilone Family Collection.

43   "Her Hero Husband Didn't Come Back," *Newark Star-Ledger*, May 28, 1950, Basilone Family
     Collection.
44   "A Family Look at Hero John Basilone," *South Plainfield Observer*, February 11, 1988, p. 9, RPL.
45   Jim G. Lucas, "Medal of Honor Winner Rejected a Hero's Life for a Hero's Death," *New York World-
     Telegram*, 1962, Basilone Family Collection; Robert Leckie, "The Perfect Marine Who Begged to
     Die," *Saga Magazine*, 1964, courtesy of Robert Leckie Family.
46   "How School Kids Started Parade in '81," Forbes Newspaper Supplement, September 19, 1990,
     RPL.
47   Lena Basilone interview, *Scout* Article.

INDEX

Hugh Ambrose is a noted historian and was a consultant on the documentary *Price for Peace*, for which Steven Spielberg and Stephen Ambrose were the Executive Producers, as well as on *Beyond All Boundaries*, a 4-D WWII experience Executive Produced by Tom Hanks. He was a consultant to his father on his books, and also served as the historical consultant on HBO's *The Pacific* miniseries. Ambrose is also the former vice president of the National WWII Museum and has led battlefield tours through Europe and along the Pacific Rim. He lives in Helena, Montana. Visit the author's Web site at www.HughAmbrose.com.

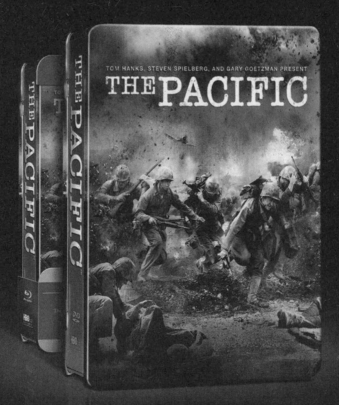